DEVIANT
BEHAVIOR

SEVENTH EDITION

DEVIANT
BEHAVIOR

ERICH GOODE
University of Maryland

PEARSON
Prentice
Hall

Upper Saddle River, New Jersey 07458

Library of Congress Cataloging-in-Publication Data

GOODE, ERICH.
    Deviant behavior/Erich Goode.—7th ed.
      p. cm.
    Includes bibliographical references and index.
    ISBN 0–13–185052–0 (alk. paper)
    1. Deviant behavior. 2. Criminal behavior. I. Title.

HM811.G66 2005   2004040121
302.5′42—dc22

Publisher: Nancy Roberts
Executive Editor: Chris DeJohn
Editorial Liaison: Sharon Chambliss
Director of Production and Manufacturing: Barbara Kittle
**Editorial/Production Supervision
  and Interior Design:** Rob DeGeorge
Copyeditor: Virginia Rubens
Manufacturing Manager: Nick Sklitsis
Prepress and Manufacturing Buyer: Mary Ann Gloriande
Cover Design: Bruce Kenselaar
Director of Marketing: Beth Mejia
Marketing Manager: Marissa Feliberty
Editorial Assistant: Kristen Haegele

Photo Researcher: Beaura Kathy Ringrose
Image Permission Coordinator: Debbie Hewitson
**Manager, Cover Visual Research and
  Permissions:** Karen Sanatar
Manager, Visual Research: Beth Brenzel
Manager, Rights and Permissions: Zina Arabia
Director, Image Resource Center: Melinda Reo
Cover Art: Larry Moore/Stock Illustration Source
Composition: Integra
Printer/Binder: Phoenix/Book Tech
Cover Printer: Phoenix Color Corp.
Text: 10/11 Times

Credits and acknowledgments borrowed from other sources and reproduced, with permission,
in this textbook appear on appropriate page within text or, in the case of photographs,
on p. 433.

Pearson Education LTD.
Pearson Education Singapore, Pte. Ltd
Pearson Education, Canada, Ltd
Pearson Education—Japan
Pearson Education Australia PTY, Limited

Pearson Education North Asia Ltd
Pearson Educación de Mexico, S.A. de C.V.
Pearson Education Malaysia, Pte. Ltd
Pearson Education, Upper Saddle River,
  New Jersey

10 9 8 7 6 5 4 3 2 1
ISBN 0-13-185052-0

Brief Contents

Contents

Preface

Humans are rule-making and rule-enforcing creatures. Our society, all of the social categories and groups to which we belong, and all of the persons with whom we interact, tell us what to do, how to think, and even how to look. Not all of us are able, or willing, to conform to these rules, however. In other words, in addition to making and enforcing rules, humans are also rule-*violating* creatures: We are naturally rebellious and irrepressible. There is virtually no set of rules that all of us follow. No system of social control is completely successful. All of us violate some of the rules we are told to follow, and some of us violate many of them. This means that some of us are more likely to be on the receiving end of rule making and rule enforcement, while others are more likely to be at the making and enforcement end. Moreover, many social categories and groups in every society compete for dominance; that is, they try to get everyone in the society to follow their set of rules. As a result, all of us are subject to certain kinds of sanctions or punishments, whether formal or informal. In addition, some of us are accused of things we didn't do or don't believe. In other words, *deviance and social control are fundamental fixtures of all human existence*. These processes of rule making, rule violation, and rule enforcement are very likely the core of human life everywhere. The study of deviance is not an inquiry into marginal, exotic, subterranean activities and people, but an investigation into the human condition.

Given the importance of the sociology of deviance, the fact that this field of study has come under attack should be puzzling. Some sociologists don't *like* the fact that others study deviance in the first place, and proclaim its study out of existence. To address the charge that the field is defunct, I located the contemporary curricula and enrollments in institutions of higher learning around the country (Goode, 2003) and discovered that the charge is completely bogus. The field of the sociology of deviance is flourishing; in most respects, it is as vibrant and vital as it was in its glory days. It is clear that attacks on the field have a political agenda. Advocates of the left-wing perspective (Sumner, 1994) seem to believe that the field disrupts the radical agenda, while the ideological right wing (Hendershott, 2002) seems to feel that the field disrupts the conservative agenda. One might be tempted to conclude that, with enemies like these—each side arguing that the field is "dead," but with exactly opposite motives—the field must be doing something right. What these critics object to is the field's foundation stone: relativity. When a political ideology is based on convincing the public that its way of looking at things is the only legitimate way, then any field that argues that reality can legitimately be looked at in a variety of ways is certain to represent a threat.

I have made substantial changes in this, the seventh, edition of *Deviant Behavior*. Former Chapters 1 and 2 in the sixth edition have been streamlined and merged into the current Chapter 1. Chapter 5, on the methods of studying deviance, is completely new. I have recast Chapter 6 into a discussion of violent crime and have reconceptualized white-collar and corporate crime as a form of organizational deviance, in Chapter 13. Reflecting the declining deviant status of homosexuality, I no longer devote an entire chapter to the subject; instead, it is discussed in a section in Chapter 9, on sexual deviance. Chapter 13, on organizational deviance, is new, as I said, and in fact presents a different way of conceptualizing a variety of seemingly diverse behaviors under a coherent umbrella. (See McCaghy, Capron, and Jameson, 2003, Chapter 7, for a similar conceptualization; those authors do not, however, explain their rationale for the subject's conceptual coherence.) It adds a fourth type of deviance to Erving Goffman's classic three-part division of stigmas (1963) and offers a schema by which white-collar and corporate crime can be integrated into the field of the sociology of deviance. The appendix, presenting student projects, is new. And all the personal accounts in the book are new.

Each new revision of this book has taken more and more of my time. Indeed, this revision required more effort than it took for me to write the first edition from scratch. But each revision is a learning experience for me; the fact is, I enjoy rewriting this book and bringing it into focus with new developments.

I would like to thank the contributors of the personal accounts that appear at the end of each chapter. Those who have given me their own accounts must, quite obviously, remain anonymous. However, those who have interviewed others and wish to be named deserve a special thanks; they are: Shelley Shupp, Shawna Stoltenberg, Danielle Fritze, Gretchen Kowalick, and Chris Berry. In addition, I would like to thank the students who gave me permission to print their papers in this book: Steven Clayton, Cara Delguidice, Rhonda Hurston, Jennifer Webb, Andrea Kearns, Krista Gawkowski, Alexis M. R. Mitchell, Mary Doherty, Berenice Juarez, Sachin Vaidya, Ariel Prager, Megan Scribner, Marie Quigley, and Matthew Slade. In addition, I'd like to thank the students who have taken my deviance course at the University of Maryland and at SUNY Stony Brook. I've learned a great deal from their challenging questions and points of view. I have also profited from discussions with Nachman Ben-Yehuda, Barbara Weinstein, and my dad, William J. Goode, who tragically died in May 2003. In addition, Thor Bjarnason shared his and his students' insights with me concerning the conceptual and methodological chapters of this book. Geraldine Foudy, at the McKeldin Library, University of Maryland, and Clare Imholtz, at the Center for Substance Abuse Research, were helpful in locating references. I'd also like to thank the reviewers of the earlier editions for their extremely helpful suggestions for its improvement, as well as the reviewers of the seventh edition: Thoroddur Bjarnason, SUNY at Albany; William Kelly, Auburn University; Myron Orleans, California State University–Fullerton; and Michael Perez, California State University–Fullerton. And lastly, as always, I'd like to thank the researchers and authors who investigate and write about the lively and fascinating topic of deviance.

A few paragraphs in this book, and in one case, a chapter, were borrowed or adapted from my previous publications: *Drugs in American Society* (sixth edition), McGraw-Hill, 2005; *Paranormal Beliefs: A Sociological Introduction*, Waveland Press, 2000; *Deviance in Everyday Life*, Waveland Press, 2002; and "The MacGuffin That Refuses to Die: An Investigation into the Condition of the Sociology of Deviance," *Deviant Behavior*, vol. 24, November–December 2003, pp. 507–533. Permission to reprint this material is gratefully acknowledged.

Erich Goode

DEVIANT
BEHAVIOR

CHAPTER 1

Introduction

Adam sells Ecstasy and marijuana to his classmates. Elizabeth weighs nearly 300 pounds. Steve describes himself as a former "computer pirate" who once illegally downloaded, copied, and sent millions of dollars' worth of movies, files, computer programs, and software to customers who ordered them. Victor masturbates in front of consenting females he does not date. Sally wears a metal tongue ring, which her employer has asked her to remove while she is on the job. Jan is a "transitioning transsexual." Omar is an ex-convict who served two years for motor vehicle theft and armed robbery. Jackie is a bisexual who engages in sadomasochistic practices with her partner. Robert is a manic-depressive who takes four different medications for his disorder. Annette, a "God-fearing conservative Christian," is having an affair with a married man. Samantha, a 20-year-old fundamentalist Christian, refuses to have sex before she gets married. Mark drinks himself into a stupor three or four nights a week; he lost his driver's license because of drunk driving convictions, and will probably flunk out of college at the end of the current semester. Helga works as a stripper to put herself through college. William strongly believes in paranormal powers.[1]

Are these activities, beliefs—or expressions of belief—and physical conditions, as well as the people who engage in them, hold them, or possess them, *deviant*? If they are, what *makes* them examples of deviance? On what *basis* are judgments of deviance made? What other instances of deviance could we think of? What is "deviance" in the first place? *Who* is a "deviant"? Who *decides* what's deviant? What makes the subject of deviance sociologically interesting and worthwhile? And what is *your*—the reader's—reaction; that is, which of the actions, beliefs, or conditions do you feel *should* be condemned—and which ones shouldn't?

If asked, almost anyone can come up with a number of examples of what he or she regards as "deviant." From time to time, on the first day of class, I ask the students in my deviance course to

---

[1]These cases were described to me in papers by the students in my course on deviant behavior at the University of Maryland; in each instance, permission to use them was granted by the author who narrated them to me. All names have been changed.

define and come up with some examples of deviance. The last time I did this, the students who were enrolled in this course were able to name an average of six examples each; well over 100 separate activities or conditions were named. Drug use (59 percent of the students named it), murder (54 percent), and rape (40 percent) were the most commonly mentioned examples of deviant acts, followed by stealing or theft (37 percent), homosexuality (35 percent), alcoholism (34 percent), crime generally (22 percent), obesity (16 percent), robbery (15 percent), child abuse (13 percent), and mental illness (12 percent). However, it was much harder for these students to define deviance *generally*; in fact, many of them did not answer this question. Although most of us can think of many *specific* examples of deviance, it is a bit more difficult to locate the *general property or characteristic* that defines an act, a belief, or a condition *as* deviance.

What comes to mind when you encounter the terms "deviance" and "deviant"? To many students, and to the hypothetical man and woman in the street, the terms sound distinctly evil, vile, degraded, and degenerate—perhaps even perverted. Some observers equate the terms' stereotypical or popular understanding with "nuts, sluts, and deviated preverts" (Liazos, 1972; Sumner, 1994, pp. 259–261). To many people, they conjure up images of wicked deeds, degenerate practices, activities of an abysmally corrupt nature. "Deviants," the popular image would hold, are perverts, junkies, murderers, child molesters, skid-row alcoholics, pimps, drag queens, sadomasochistic sex maniacs, bearded 50-year-old 300-pound tattooed Hell's Angels bikers, prostitutes, rapists, lust-killers, perhaps inmates of insane asylums—in short, all manner of sick, twisted, dangerous, corrupt, decadent people.

The first and most fundamental axiom that anyone observing, thinking about, or describing a social scene or aspect of reality must accept is: Things are often not what they seem (Berger, 1963, p. 23), a theme echoed by the recent "Matrix" movies, *The Matrix* (1999), *The Matrix Reloaded* (2003), and *The Matrix Revolutions* (2003). The public image or stereotype of deviance may bear an extremely loose relationship to what we would find if we were to take a closer look at it. It is the job of the sociologist of deviance to take as close a look at deviance and deviants as possible. In doing this, we can assemble a richer, more accurate, and more meaningful picture if we adopt a *subterranean* view of it. In other words, we cannot rely on popular notions of deviance—ideas we might hold before learning much about it. Though popular myths and stereotypes about deviance and deviants may have an impact on the behavior and the people they incorrectly describe, they are not the very phenomenon they pretend to describe. We want to look *behind* publicly approved versions of reality, see *through* official smoke screens portraying the way things are supposed to be, to understand *why* and *how* popular myths and misconceptions arise and are sustained. We need, in other words, to understand deviance itself. In the sense of being true to the phenomenon under study, our approach can be called *naturalism* (Matza, 1969, pp. 3ff.).

DEVIANCE IN EVERYDAY LIFE

Just about everyone has done *something* that someone else disapproves of. Perhaps we've stolen something, or told a lie, or gossiped about another person in an especially nasty manner. Maybe more than once we've gotten drunk, or high, or driven too fast or recklessly, or gone through a red light without bothering to stop. Have we ever worn clothes someone else thought were out of style, offensive, or ugly? Have we ever belched at the dinner table, broken wind, or picked our nose in public? Have we ever cut class or failed to read an assignment? Do we like a television program someone else finds stupid and boring? Didn't we once date someone our parents and friends didn't like? Maybe our religious beliefs and practices don't agree with those of some other members of the society.

Humans are evaluative creatures. We continually make judgments about the behavior, the beliefs, or the appearance of others. And each one of us does exactly the same thing—evaluate others. Societies everywhere have rules or *norms* governing what we may and may not do, how we should think, what we should believe, even how we should look; and those norms are so detailed

and complex, and so dependent on the views of different evaluators, that what *everyone* does, believes, and is, is looked on negatively by *someone*—indeed, in all likelihood, by *lots* of other people. Believers in God look down on atheists; atheists think believers in God are misguided and mistaken. Fundamentalist Christians oppose the beliefs of fundamentalist Muslims, and vice versa. Liberals dislike the views of conservatives; to conservatives, the feeling is mutual. Tall people quite literally look down on persons who are shorter; persons of average stature make disparaging comments about seven-footers. Many college campuses are divided into mutually exclusive ethnic and racial enclaves; in student unions, the whites sit together in their own area and African Americans in theirs. Jocks and druggies, brains and preppies, Greeks, geeks, hippies—the number of possible ways that what we believe, or do, or are, could be judged negatively by others is almost infinite.

There are four necessary ingredients for deviance to take place or exist: one, a rule or *norm*; two, someone who violates (or is thought to violate) that norm; three, an "audience," someone who judges the normative violation to be wrong; and four, a measurable likelihood of a negative reaction by that audience—criticism, condemnation, censure, stigma, disapproval, and so on. To violate a norm and engage in deviance, it isn't even necessary to violate one that is serious, such as the Ten Commandments. Norms are everywhere, and they vary in seriousness, and different people have different norms. "I've never done anything seriously wrong," we might tell ourselves. "There's nothing deviant about me!" we add. But "wrong" according to *whose* standards? And "deviant" in what *sense*? We might feel our belief in God is a good thing, but, as we saw, an atheist is likely to disagree. Chances are, we think our political position is reasonable; many of our fellow citizens will disagree, finding our politics foolish and wrong-headed. Our friends are probably in sync with us with respect to lifestyle and taste in clothing; but unbeknownst to us, behind our backs, there may be others who make fun of us because of our way of dressing and acting. The point is, nearly everything about every one of us—the reader and the author of this book included—is a potential source of criticism, condemnation, or censure in *some* social circles, from the point of view of *some* observers.

We think eating dogs is improper. In the Western world, there is a prohibition or *norm* against eating dogs. In contrast, in certain regions of China, eating dogs is perfectly acceptable; there, no such norm exists. Most Americans consider pork a desirable item on their menu; Orthodox Jews and the majority of Muslims do not. Even within the same society, among mainstream segments of the population, different groups and social circles vary with respect to the judgments they pass regarding acceptable and unacceptable behavior. Vegetarians consider eating meat disgusting; meat-eaters consider vegetarianism a bit silly and irksome. Since the dawn of humanity, rules that dictate right and wrong behavior, beliefs, and social characteristics have been laid down; but not everyone is able or willing to abide by these rules. Variation in behavior, beliefs, and appearance exists in every society, and along with this variation come multiple sources of evaluation.

The point is, deviance is not a simple quality resting with a given action, belief, or trait and inherent in, intrinsic to, or indwelling within it. A given act, for example, is not regarded as deviant everywhere and at all times. (Though some acts are *more widely* condemned than others are.) What makes a given act deviant is the way it is seen, regarded, judged, and evaluated and the way that others—audiences—treat the person who engages in that act. Deviance is that which is reacted to negatively, in a socially rejecting fashion. Acts, beliefs, and traits are deviant *to* certain persons or audiences or *in* certain social circles. What *defines* deviance are the actual or potential *reactions* that acts, beliefs, and traits generate or are likely to generate in audiences. It is this negative reaction that defines or constitutes a given act, belief, or trait *as* deviant. Without that reaction, actual or potential, we do not have a case of deviance on our hands. When that reaction takes place, or is "stored up" in someone, we do.

Humans are not only evaluative, in the sense that they create and enforce rules; nearly all of us also *violate* society's rules. We park in "no parking" zones; we make fun of bosses, parents, and professors behind their backs; we smoke where we're not supposed to; shoplift when we don't have enough money or don't feel like waiting in line; speed to get where we're going a little faster; or have sex with the wrong partner. Not one of us is a passive creature, obeying all rules like a robot, programmed to follow society's commands. The human animal is active, creative, and irrepressible. Even though all societies generate a multitude of rules, their violations, likewise, are multitudinous. In fact, the more numerous and detailed the rules, the more opportunities there are for normative violations.

Hardly anyone abides by *all* rules *all* the time. Indeed, that is a literal impossibility, since some rules contradict one another. No rules are considered valid by everyone in any society. As we saw, there is in every society on earth—in some far more than in others—a certain degree of variation in notions of right and wrong from one person to another, one group or category to another, one subculture to another. Especially in a large, complex, urban, multicultural, multiethnic, multinational society such as the United States, the variation is considerable—indeed, immense. This means that almost any action, belief, or characteristic we could think of is approved in some social circles and condemned in others. Almost inevitably, we deviate from *someone's* rules simply by acting, believing, or being, since it is impossible to conform to all the rules that prevail.

But remember, deviance is a matter of degree, not an either-or proposition. At the same time, in every society, as well as in all social contexts, there is a set of central "core" or "master" principles, rules, or norms just about everyone is expected to follow. They spell out behavior, beliefs, or conditions that if violated bring *serious* punishment to the violator. Murder is regarded as a serious—a heinous—act by the vast majority of the population of all societies on earth. Treason against one's own country results in execution—or at the very least a long prison sentence—in just about every nation around the globe. Blaspheming Allah is likely to result in ostracism and harsh punishment in all predominantly Muslim societies. Nowhere is being ugly or malformed regarded as desirable; ugly people face ostracism—in varying degrees, of course—everywhere. Using heroin and crack cocaine is likely to result in arrest in Chicago; engaging in homosexual acts is likely to result in ostracism in a small village in Mexico; being obese is likely to result in being socially shunned in Paris; molesting a child is likely to result in both legal and social difficulty everywhere. (As we'll see throughout this book, judging how specific acts *belong* to these categories is another, and important, issue.) While there is a great deal of variation from one society to another in what's regarded as wrong or illegal, the fact is, there is some *patterning* to the picture. Certain acts are considered wrong almost everywhere; others, while acceptable in some societies, are *strongly* condemned or punished in others. In other words, the variation in what's defined and reacted to as deviant is not infinite.

SO, WHAT *IS* DEVIANCE?

While the sociology of deviance has been, since its birth, and remains to this day, a controversial subject, it is nonetheless possible to define its subject matter in a fairly straightforward fashion. To sum up: Sociologically, deviance exists when we have (1) something that violates a social norm or rule; (2) a person or persons to whom that violation is attached; (3) an audience or group of persons who judge and evaluate the normative violation; and (4) the likelihood that negative social reactions will follow the discovery of that violation.

Once again, in every human collectivity that has ever existed, rules for proper behavior are laid down; and again, all people violate the rules of one or another group, or of the society at large; likewise, again, in every human collectivity, reactions of some members of these collectivities express disapproval of such violations. There has never existed in any society or social circle a condition under which every member—or, indeed, *any* member—has perfectly conformed to every rule or norm and hence has escaped ridicule, censure, or punishment from everyone. The very diversity of humanity, the variation in definitions of right and wrong and of true and false, and the very fallibility of humans—their inability or unwillingness to conform to the many rules of society, or subcategories of society—set the stage both for normative violations and for the negative reactions they touch off. Although *what is regarded as deviant* varies considerably—but not randomly—from society to society and from one social category to another, the punishment of enactors, holders, and possessors of unacceptable behavior, beliefs, and traits is universal.

Does saying that something is deviant in a certain social circle or a society mean that we *agree* that it should be condemned? Of course not! We have our own views, and they may agree or disagree with the audiences whose reactions we are looking at. Does this mean that when we use the term "deviant" we seek to denigrate, put down, or humiliate anyone to whom the term applies? Absolutely not! Again, we may *agree* or *disagree* with the judgment, but if we observe it, and it hits us like a pie in the face, we would be foolish and ignorant to pretend that it doesn't exist. If we say that a president's approval rating is high, or low, this does not mean that we approve, or disapprove, of that president. What it means is that we take note of public opinion. When we say that in American society generally, prostitutes, homosexuals, and atheists tend to be looked down on and regarded as deviants, this does not mean that we necessarily agree with that judgment. It means that, as sociologists, we recognize that certain negative consequences are likely to result from announcing to a cross-section of American society that one is a prostitute, a homosexual, or an atheist. In other words, the terms "deviance" and "deviant" are absolutely *nonpejorative*. This means that they are descriptive terms that apply to what others think and how they are likely to react. You may hate a particular movie, but if it is number one at the box office, you can still say it is a "popular" movie—because it *is*. You could be an atheist and still say that atheism is deviant. *Even if you don't agree with that judgment*, it is real and must be acknowledged.

Consider the list of examples of deviance in Table 1.1 as well as the list of examples of negative reactions to these examples.[2] Members of all societies express their disapproval of the

---

[2]In the next chapter, I'll explain a crucial but missing element in this table—the *social construction* of the categories listed. That is, *who is regarded as or judged to be* a "creep," a juvenile delinquent, an alcoholic, a racist, is not a simple matter of fact, but is variable from one observer or setting to another. In other words, what is missing from Table 1.1 is *who* makes the judgment that a given act, belief, or trait belongs in a given deviant category. Indeed, many of the negative reactions are also socially constructed. Exactly what sort of behavior *constitutes* being snubbed, attacked, censured, denounced, and so on, again, is not an undisputed fact but varies according to the observer.

TABLE 1.1 EXAMPLES OF SOCIAL DEVIANCE AND NEGATIVE REACTIONS

BELIEFS, BEHAVIOR, OR CHARACTERISTICS	NEGATIVE SOCIAL REACTIONS
being a "creep"	keep one's distance from
being obese	stigmatize
homosexual behavior	socially isolate
prostitution	censure
murder	denounce
illicit drug selling	arrest
blasphemy	slap
drug addiction	fire from a job
being an albino	gossip maliciously about
being extremely ugly	ridicule
being an alcoholic	express hostility toward
being autistic	pity
having a bipolar disorder	express anger toward
being blind	become indignant about
being a dwarf	expel
sexual promiscuity	disapprove of
adultery	discredit
corporate crime	imprison
being a political radical (among conservatives)	withdraw affection
being a political conservative (among radicals)	socially avoid
being an atheist	snub
being schizophrenic	express contempt toward
holding creationist beliefs (among scientists)	reject
holding a belief in evolution (among fundamentalists)	disdain
believing that UFOs are real	repudiate
holding Muslim beliefs (among fundamentalist Christians)	renounce
holding Christian beliefs (among fundamentalist Muslims)	spurn
being a racist	scorn
heresy	institutionalize
being poor	disown
being illiterate	be irate about
rape	express rage toward
wife-beating	infuriate
being a juvenile delinquent	be offended by
robbery	take revenge against
joining a "cult"	feel sorry for
being Black (among racist whites)	attack
being white (among Black nationalists)	lynch
being an Israeli (among Palestinians)	resent
being a Palestinian (among Israelis)	bear a grudge against
being heavily tattooed	punish
treason	distrust
betrayal	stereotype
being an eccentric	discriminate against
being a "weirdo"	exclude

behavior, beliefs, and characteristics of other members in varying ways, as indicated by the many examples of negative social reactions listed. Of course, the specific *way* someone expresses disapproval varies. As a general rule, persons who hold power over others are able to express a wider repertory of negative reactions than are persons who are powerless. Moreover, the disapproval of more powerful persons tends to have a more substantial impact on the lives of the powerless than the other way around; indeed, this is one way we define the concept of power. At the same time, the relatively powerless have many social resources at their disposal. In *Weapons of the Weak*, historian James Scott describes "everyday forms of peasant resistance" through which powerless people struggle against the actions of their oppressors through a variety of reactions, including "evasion and resistance" (1985). People everywhere, as well as up and down the social class ladder, have resorted to the many negative social reactions spelled out in Table 1.1. Such reactions, whether expressed or latent, *constitute* or *define* what sociologists *mean* by deviance. Whenever they are present in human interaction, sociologists are confident they have a case of deviance on their hands.

In short, deviance is an analytic category. This means that it applies in all spheres and areas of human life. Indeed, deviance is a trans-historical, cross-cultural concept. The dynamics of deviance have taken place throughout recorded history and in every known society. Deviance takes place in the classroom, the dorm room, the living room, the boardroom of General Motors, and the Game Room of the Pentagon. Everywhere, people are evaluated on the basis of what they do, what they believe, and who they are—and they are reacted to accordingly. Deviance takes place during a basketball game; during your professor's office hours; during "happy hour" in the local bar; during final exams; in department stores; on the street; in the church, synagogue, and mosque; and within the bosom of the family. Deviance is everywhere and anywhere people engage in behavior, hold and express beliefs, and possess traits that others regard as unacceptable. Normative violations, and reactions to normative violations, occur everywhere. They exist and have existed in all societies

everywhere and for all time. They are central to who we are as human beings.

To go back to the examples that opened this book, Adam's drug selling is a violation of a certain kind of norm, a formal norm that is referred to as a law, that is likely to result in arrest if one is apprehended by an agent of law enforcement. In addition, Adam's parents disapprove of his dealing activities and are likely to use whatever powers they have at their disposal to get him to stop. Elizabeth, the obese woman, faces ridicule from people on the street, while trundling a cart through a supermarket, and on line everywhere. One of Steve's computer "pirate" colleagues was arrested, and Steve himself received a "cease and desist" order from a motion picture studio, both of which are quite obviously negative reactions from parties who judged that he was violating the law. They were effective in convincing him to stop stealing copyrighted computer material, to destroy his hard drive, and to put an end to his piracy. Victor, the exhibitionist masturbator, is gossiped about among his classmates, who giggle when his name is mentioned; however, so far, his unusual sexual practices have not resulted in serious punishment of any kind. Sally, the wearer of the tongue ring, divides her life between her on-the-job hours working as a waitress, when she takes the ring out, and her off-the-job hours, when she wears it. But she is fully aware of the fact that if she were to wear that tongue ring *on* the job, she'd be fired. In each of these cases, we have the violation of a norm, people making the judgment that a norm has been violated, and a person who elicits the negative reactions that the violation is likely to bring forth. In short, in each of these instances, we have a case of *deviance* on our hands.

To summarize, deviance is that which violates a social norm or rule; is considered bad, wrong, unacceptable, undesirable, or offensive to the members of one or more specific groups, social circles or categories, or societies; and is likely to elicit negative reactions if that violation is discovered. To repeat, for deviance to exist, we need, *first*, a normative violation (or a perceived normative violation); *second*, one or more persons to whom judgments of wrongdoing are attached and who therefore become targets of the negative social reactions that normative violations elicit; and *third*, persons making the judgment that a normative violation has occurred and who react to the violator accordingly.

SOCIETAL AND SITUATIONAL DEVIANCE

So far, it seems that I've been arguing that *anything* can be deviant; that if a collectivity of people—a group, a social circle, a segment of the population, any assemblage of people, really—regards something as unacceptable, by our definition, it is deviant. This is only half true. I would argue that at this point, it is necessary to make the distinction, formulated by Kenneth Plummer (1979, pp. 97–99), between *societal* and *situational* deviance.

"Societal" deviance is composed of those actions and conditions that are widely recognized, in advance and in general, to be deviant. There is a high degree of consensus on the identification of certain categories of deviance. In this sense, rape, robbery, corporate theft, terrorism, and transvestism are deviant because they are regarded as reprehensible to the majority of the members of this society. Even though specific individuals enacting or representing specific instances of these general categories may not be punished in specific situations, *in general*, the members of this society see them as serious normative violations. Certain acts, beliefs, and traits are deviant *society-wide* because they are condemned, both in practice and in principle, by the majority.

On the other hand, "situational" deviance does not exist as a general or society-wide quality, but in actual, concrete social gatherings, circles, or settings. A given individual may not have been regarded as a deviant situationally—for instance, in his or her specific community or group—but may enact a category of behavior or possess a condition that is so widely condemned that it is *societally* deviant. Thus, in this culture, "homosexuality must be regarded as societal deviance. All members of [the] society must acknowledge (even if they strongly disagree) that homosexuality is commonly regarded as deviant. . . . Yet to acknowledge that homosexuality is societal deviance is not to acknowledge that it is situational deviance," since, in many cases, actual, concrete condemnation is lacking (Plummer, 1979, pp. 98, 99). For

instance, in certain cities or communities in the United States (Greenwich Village in New York, for instance, or San Francisco generally), homosexuality is accepted by the majority; hence, *in* such cities or communities, homosexuality *is not deviant*. But in the country *as a whole*—though this is, as we'll see in Chapter 9, quickly changing—the majority still condemns it.

Our distinction also recognizes the fact that certain acts, beliefs, and conditions may be *situationally but not societally* deviant. For instance, among ultra-Orthodox or *haredi* Jews, heterosexual dancing is not permitted. If a couple were to engage in it at a social gathering such as a wedding or a bar mitzvah, they would be chastised by the *haredi* community and, if they persisted, ejected from the gathering. In other words, situationally, *among the haredi*, heterosexual dancing is deviant. But in the United States, societally, as everyone knows, heterosexual dancing is not only not deviant, it is accepted as conventional; indeed, to *refuse* to dance with a person of the opposite sex is likely to be regarded as deviant.

The distinction between "societal" deviance (acts, beliefs, and traits that are considered bad or wrong in a society generally) and "situational" deviance (acts, beliefs, and traits that are considered bad or wrong specifically *within* a particular group, social circle, setting, or context) frees us from having to make the silly, meaningless, and indefensible statement that "everything is deviant." It is true that "everything is deviant" to *someone*, but that is not a very useful statement, since, societally, certain things (murdering an infant in its crib) stand a *much* higher likelihood of being condemned than others (chewing bubble gum). Understanding the dynamics of deviance *demands* that we make the distinction between societal and situational deviance.

The concepts of "societal" deviance looks at normative violations and potential negative reactions in *vertical* terms. Such a conception defines deviance as how the majority or the most powerful segments of the society judge wrongdoing, that is, vertically or *hierarchically*. Large and/or powerful social categories define what's deviant for the society as a whole; small, relatively powerless social categories do not. In contrast, "situational" deviance looks at normative violations and negative reactions in *horizontal* terms. This means that in judgments of what's deviant, what counts is not what the majority or the most powerful think or do, but the norms and reactions from one group to another—"across" society, so to speak, or horizontally.

Looking at deviance from a vertical (or hierarchical) perspective raises the question of the *dominance* of one category or society over another. That is, even though different groups, categories, social circles, and societies hold different views of what's deviant, some of them are more powerful, influential, and numerous than others. In addition to looking at variation from one setting to another, we also have to look at which categories or groups have the power to influence definitions of right and wrong in other categories, or in general. Social scientists say that a dominant belief or institution is *hegemonic*: It holds sway over other social groupings in the society. The "vertical" conception of deviance is obviously compatible with the "societal" definition of deviance; it defines the *hegemonic* view of what's deviant *as* deviant, that is, what the majority or the most influential segments of the society regard as deviant. Acts, beliefs, and conditions that are societally deviant are those that are regarded as wrong nearly everywhere in a given society. They may be regarded as *high consensus* deviance in that there is widespread agreement as to their deviant character (Thio, 2004, pp. 13–14).

In contrast, the "horizontal" property of deviance refers to the fact that a given act, belief, or trait can be a normative violation in *one* group, category, or society but conformist in *another*. The "horizontal" quality of deviance allows us to see society, or different societies, as a kind of "mosaic" or a loose assemblage of separate and independent collectivities of people who do not influence one another. In the "horizontal" view of deviance, we have a jumble of side-by-side audiences evaluating behavior, beliefs, and traits only within their own category, independent of what's going on in other categories. Enacting certain behavior, holding a certain belief, possessing a certain characteristic makes someone a conformist in one setting and a deviant in another. Such a view does not examine the impact of these settings, groups, or societies on one another. Clearly, the "horizontal" approach to deviance is compatible with the "situational" definition of deviance. Acts, beliefs, and

conditions that are situationally but not societally deviant may be regarded as *low consensus* deviance, in that public opinion is *divided* about their deviant status (Thio, 2004, pp. 13–14). What fetches condemnation in one social circle produces indifference or even praise in another.

For certain purposes, the vertical or hierarchical side of deviance is more crucial than the horizontal or mosaic side. Ask yourself: Is someone more likely to get into trouble as a result of violating the norms of powerless groups or of more powerful ones? Clearly, the violation of the norms of more powerful groups results in punishment more often. And just as clearly, it's more than a simple matter of belonging to one group or another. Much of the time, one must move in social circles other than one's own. Even within one's own group, the definitions of right and wrong intrude into the life of the group. The more power a category or a society has to enforce its rules—that is, the more hegemonic it is—the greater the likelihood that someone who violates those rules will get into trouble for doing so.

At the same time, the norms of the more powerful categories are not always in operation. It is possible for people to *isolate* or *insulate* themselves from the more dominant views of right and wrong by confining most of their interactions to their own social circles. For certain purposes, the vertical (or societal) view of deviance is the more fruitful; for other purposes, the horizontal (or situational) view is. We must keep both in mind when contemplating the phenomenon of deviance.

THE ABCs OF DEVIANCE

As we can see, norms or rules are *about* lots of different things. In other words, norms may be violated in a variety of different ways; that is, there may be different *reasons* why some people react negatively to the behavior, belief, and characteristics of others. Elizabeth violates a norm that states that women should not weigh more than a stipulated amount—let's say, less than 90 and more than 140 pounds. To be obese in our society is to have violated a weight norm, a rule about our physical appearance. Annette has violated a norm about behavior—indeed, a norm that is one of the Ten Commandments, "Thou shalt not commit adultery." It is a norm, moreover, in which she herself believes very strongly, and the violation of which has caused her considerable guilt. William, our paranormal believer, has violated a norm that prevails in much of educated society, which says that ghosts, extrasensory perception, communication with the dead, and other such extraordinary spiritual powers or phenomena do not and, given what we know about how nature works, *cannot* exist. In other words, William has violated a social norm that centers around acceptable and unacceptable beliefs. Clearly, then, there are distinctly different *types* of deviance.

To recapitulate: Sociologists refer to behavior, beliefs, or characteristics that violate or depart or "deviate" from a basic norm and that are likely to generate negative reactions in persons who observe or hear about that norm-violation as *social deviance* or simply "deviance." Many courses and books on the subject (including the book you are reading at this very moment), as well as the major academic journal in the field, bear the title "deviant *behavior.*" This isn't exactly accurate. "Deviant behavior" is a handy term that sociologists of deviance use to refer to the field. The field might better be referred to as "social deviance," but unfortunately, we are stuck with the handy term because it's easily recalled. But the field isn't *only* about deviant behavior. It's about deviant behavior—and a great deal more. It's also about deviant attitudes or beliefs, and about deviant traits or characteristics—in short, anything and everything that results in interpersonal or institutional rejection or punishment. Adler and Adler (2003, pp. 8–9) refer to the "ABCs of deviance—*Attitudes, Behavior,* and *Conditions.*" "Attitudes" refers to unpopular, unconventional beliefs that may or may not manifest themselves in overt actions. "Behavior" is made up of any overt action (which includes the failure to act) that is likely to attract condemnation, hostility, or punishment. And "conditions" include physical characteristics or traits that, likewise, make someone a target of an audience's disapproval, avoidance, derision, or other type of negative social reaction. In short, to the sociologist, deviance encompasses all three of the "ABCs"—attitudes, behavior, and

conditions. Let's look at each one, starting with behavior.

Deviant Behavior

Most people who encounter the study of social deviance imagine that the field is entirely and exclusively about *behavior* that is regarded as unacceptable and likely to generate negative reactions. It is true that *most* forms of deviance that we're likely to think of, as well as most of those that tend to be punished, are behavioral in nature. As I said above, over the years, on the first day of class, I've asked the students in my deviance courses to list examples of deviance that they can think of. The vast majority that are offered are types of behavior. In addition, a perusal of deviance textbooks and anthologies verifies that most of the forms of deviance that are discussed are, again, behavioral. In short, nonnormative *behavior* is an element of most people's stereotype of what's deviant.

And it is true that *much* of our evaluation of one another is based on what we *do.* "Actions speak louder than words," we say—and most of the time, to most of us, they do. A man says he loves his wife—and he may in fact love her very much—but if he is out every night, having affairs with other women, it is his behavior that is likely to weigh most heavily in his wife's assessment of him as a decent husband—not his protestations of love. A woman says she believes that cocaine is a harmful drug—that no one should or can play around with it—but if she uses it regularly, no one is likely to take her professed beliefs very seriously. In other words, *even if we actually do believe something,* our behavior is weighed more heavily than our beliefs. We'll come back to the ideas of sociologist Erving Goffman (1922–1982) again and again, because some of his ideas remain important, relevant, and insightful for students and researchers in the field of deviance. His book *Stigma* (1963) is a classic. The fact is, as Goffman says, most of us see behavior we regard as deviant as indicating "blemishes of individual character" (1963, p. 4). A dishonest character is revealed or manifested mainly by dishonest *behavior*; a weak will and an inability to resist temptation are revealed by drug abuse, alco-holism, adultery, gambling, and so on.

To repeat, while deviant behavior is a major type of social deviance, it is not the only type. In this book, we intend to look at several others as well.

DEVIANT ATTITUDES AND BELIEFS

Is simply expressing an unpopular belief a form of deviance? Of course! As Patricia and Peter Adler argue, behavior is not solely or exclusively a set of physical or mechanical motions. When someone expresses a point of view, it is not the physical act of talking or writing that counts but the content of *what* that person says, the *worldview* that those words express, and what that worldview *means* to the people listening to or reading those words. Holding unconventional, unorthodox, unpopular—or deviant—beliefs may be regarded as *cognitive deviance*. This category includes religious, political, and scientific beliefs that are regarded as unacceptable. The negative reactions toward people who hold such beliefs are very similar to those that would be touched off by the discovery of participation in behavior that is regarded as unacceptable.

Indeed, it is possible that, in the history of the world, holders of unacceptable beliefs have been attacked, criticized, condemned, arrested, even persecuted almost as often and almost as severely as enactors of unacceptable behavior. Consider, for example, the Spanish Inquisition (1480–1834), during which thousands of "heretics" were executed for their real or supposed beliefs; the Crusades, the attempt by Christians during the eleventh to the fourteenth centuries to wrest Jerusalem from "unbelievers," that is, Muslims; the current Islamic *jihad*, which, according to its architect, Osama bin Laden, targets "Crusaders," that is, Christians, as well as Jews; the death sentence pronounced on Salman Rushdie follow-ing the publication of his *The Satanic Verses* (1988), considered blasphemous by many ortho-dox Muslims; and, in ancient times, the execution of Christians who refused to worship the Roman emperor as a god.

Could a self-proclaimed atheist be elected pres-ident of the United States? It is extremely unlikely;

a majority of Americans would vote against such a candidate, simply because of his or her atheistic views. Hence, to much of the population, not believing in God is deviant in American society. In a department of biology, would a graduate student who believes in creationism be looked on or treated in the same way as one who accepts the evolution of species as fact? Of course not! Indeed, some faculty members believe that there is no place for creationists in biology departments (Madigan, 2003; Brulliard, 2003). Hence, *in* biol-ogy departments in the United States, believing in creationism is *deviant*. In universities throughout the Western world, expressing what are regarded as blatantly racist views results in ostracism and social and academic isolation (Schneider, 1999)—in short, it is deviant. Peter Duesberg, a cancer researcher, has become an academic pariah because he believes, and has written, that HIV does not cause AIDS. He has lost all his grants; research assistants have abandoned him; graduate students no longer want to work with him; and he "hasn't been invited to an academic party in five years" (Schneider, 1999, p. A12). Because of his belief that HIV does not cause AIDS, Peter Duesberg has become a deviant among his colleagues and in his university. Holding or expressing unconven-tional beliefs is such a crucial form of deviance that it would be a mistake to ignore it. We'll look at cognitive deviance—holding unconventional beliefs—in detail in Chapter 10.

One absolutely crucial point in any examina-tion of cognitive deviance: Beliefs are *not* deviant simply because they are wrong. They are deviant because they violate the norms of a given society, or of an institution or social circle within a society, and, as a result, are likely to elicit negative reactions. When we see these neg-ative reactions, we know we have a case of deviance on our hands.

You, the reader, believe that racism is bad; so do I. But to the sociologist, racism is not deviant *because* it is bad, immoral, or wrong in some abstract sense. The expression of racist views is deviant in certain sectors of this society because it offends many, most, or certain members of this society. Before the Civil War, if a white south-erner were to argue in the South, among slave-owners and other whites, for the abolition of slavery, that view, and the person who expressed it, would have been regarded as deviant. Again, not because it was wrong—indeed, everyone today agrees that it was the correct position—but because it was considered deviant *to* southern whites generally, and *to* slaveowners specifically. Once again, "deviant" does not mean "wrong," it means "offensive *in* certain social circles."

Nearly all biologists and geologists believe that creationism is scientifically and factually wrong. But to the sociologist, creationism is not deviant because it is scientifically wrong. Indeed, belief in *evolution* is deviant as well—to fundamentalist Christians and Muslims, and to Orthodox Jews. The reason we know that certain beliefs are deviant is that their expression violates prevailing norms in certain social groups and generates negative reactions among the members of those groups.

Likewise, it is not clear that atheism is "wrong" or "right" in some abstract sense. Indeed, most scientists and philosophers believe that the factual matter of theism or atheism can't be tested factually. What *makes* atheism deviant is that it violates a norm of theism, or a belief in God, held by 90 to 95 percent of the American public. The fact is that, in many social contexts, atheists are not treated the same way that believers are; they are, in those contexts, looked down on, vilified, and condemned. As we have stated, most Americans would not vote for an atheist candidate for president of the United States. Moreover, a majority of the American public (in a recent poll, 58 percent) believe that "it is necessary to believe in God to be moral" (Kristof, 2003)—a clear statement that atheism is not only deviant but immoral as well.

What *makes* Duesberg's belief that HIV does not cause AIDS deviant is that it contradicts what medical scientists *believe* to be true, and it is this sort of belief that causes scientists to punish the believer. After all, many beliefs once thought to be false have turned out to be true (Ben-Yehuda, 1985, pp. 106–167), and the scientists who held them then were ostracized just as much as those scientists who hold beliefs we now regard as false. In the 1850s, the physician Ignaz Semmelweis (1818–1865) discovered that the patients of doctors who delivered babies after washing their hands had lower rates of maternal mortality than the patients of doctors whose hands were dirty.

He was ridiculed for his theory and hounded out of the medical profession, eventually being driven to insanity and suicide. Semmelweis's discovery was not accepted until the 1890s, but, although scientifically *true*, for nearly half a century his belief was *deviant*.

PHYSICAL CONDITIONS

What about physical traits, characteristics, or conditions? Can someone be regarded as deviant as a result of possessing certain undesirable, involuntarily acquired physical characteristics—such as being extremely ugly, short, obese, disabled, or deformed? Ask yourself: Is a disabled person treated the same way as the rest of us? Do many "abled" persons socially avoid or shun the disabled? Do some of them tease, humiliate, joke about, or make fun of the handicapped? Do they pity or scorn them? Stereotype them? Is a great deal of the social interaction between those with a "normal" appearance and one who is disfigured strained, awkward, distant, and difficult? Haven't obese children often become objects of taunts, ridicule, harassment, and condemnation? Aren't the possessors of certain undesirable physical characteristics excluded from full social participation? Hence, if we mean by "deviant" the fact that persons with certain physical traits are often treated in a condescending, pitying, scornful, and rejecting fashion, the answer is, *of course* possessing unconventional, unacceptable physical traits is deviant! To the extent that the disabled experience negative social reactions from the abled, they are deviant.

Is this fair? Of course not! Most people with an undesirable physical trait have not done anything wrong to acquire it. Hence, it is unfair for others to reject or otherwise treat them negatively. But notice: It is not the *sociologist* who is being unfair here or who is rejecting the possessors of these traits. Rather, it is the social *audience*—that is, the majority—that rejects them and, hence, treats them unfairly. Sociologists of deviance aren't rejecting the disabled; they are merely noticing that many abled members of the society do so. It doesn't matter whether behavior, beliefs, or physical characteristics are freely chosen or thrust upon us. Again, if they result in social rejection of some kind, they are deviant, and may qualify their enactors, believers, or possessors as deviants. The fairness or justice of this rejection is a separate matter. We'll be looking at physical characteristics as deviant in Chapter 12.

The fact that physical characteristics represent a major form of deviance points up a distinction that has been a fixture in the field of sociology for practically its entire existence: the distinction between *achieved* and *ascribed* statuses (Adler and Adler, 2003, p. 9). Some social statuses are "achieved" (although they may have been *assisted* by certain inborn characteristics). Being a college graduate is something that has to be accomplished: One has to *do* something—have a high school record good enough to be admitted, enroll in courses, study to pass the courses one takes, complete all the graduation requirements—to graduate from college. But being born into a rich family or a poor one; a Black, white, Asian, or Hispanic one; or one in which one's parents are themselves college graduates or high school dropouts—these are *ascribed* statuses. They are not achieved, but are thrust upon the infant at birth. There is nothing a child can do to achieve or choose his or her family or parents.

As with statuses in general, so it is with deviant statuses: They may be achieved or ascribed. Being a drug addict is a result of making certain choices in life: to use drugs or not, to use them to the point that one's life becomes consumed by them or not. Clearly, being a drug addict is an *achieved* status. In contrast, being a dwarf or an albino is ascribed. One is born with certain characteristics or traits that are *evaluated* in a certain fashion by the society in which one lives. It is these evaluations, and the reactions that embody them, that determine whether or not a given ascribed characteristic is deviant. To the extent that these evaluations and reactions are negative, derisive, rejecting, or hostile, we have an instance of deviance on our hands. Is this fair? Once again, of course not. But the sociologist would be foolish to pretend that these negative evaluations and reactions *do not exist* and *do not have an important impact on people's lives*. In fact, it is *only* when we understand them—their basis, their dynamics, and their consequences— that we can face and deal with society's many injustices.

TRIBE, RACE, RELIGION, AND NATION

Consider the following quote, from a speech delivered almost 40 years ago by Dr. Martin Luther King, Jr.: " . . . when you are humiliated day in and day out by nagging signs reading 'white' and 'colored,' when your first name becomes 'nigger' and your middle name becomes 'boy' (however old you are) and your last name becomes 'John,' when your wife and mother are never given the respected title 'Mrs.'; when you are harried by day and humiliated by night by the fact that you are a Negro, living constantly at tiptoe stance, never quite knowing what to expect next, and plagued with inner fears and outer resentments; when you are forever fighting a degenerating sense of 'nobodyness'—then you will understand why we find it difficult to wait." These eloquent, saddening words capture the essence of racism. And they also point to what Erving Goffman termed the "tribal stigma of race, religion, and nation." I refer to this phenomenon as *collective deviance*.

In February 2002, an angry mob of Muslims set fire to a train holding Hindu militants who, some observers said, were shouting anti-Muslim slogans; at least 57 were killed (Lakshmi, 2002a). A day later, a mob of Hindus looted and burned shops, offices, and homes in a Muslim neighborhood; at least 76 died (Lakshmi, 2002b). For years, Osama bin Laden, a militant Muslim who is hostile to anything American, Western, Christian, or Jewish, has taught his followers, "Kill the Jew and the American, wherever you find them." On September 11, 2001, 19 of his acolytes followed through on bin Laden's teachings by hijacking airliners and crashing them into the World Trade Center towers and the Pentagon, killing close to 3,000 people. In the year after the attacks of September 11, the number of hate crimes committed against persons of Middle Eastern descent, Muslims, and South Asian Sikhs—who are frequently mistaken for Muslims—increased 1,500 percent from the year before, from 28 to 481. A caller threatened to kill members of the family of James Zogby, director of the Arab American Institute (Fears, 2002). These incidents, too, point to the phenomenon of collective deviance. They refer to the fact that the members of some categories of humanity stigmatize *all* the members of another category—simply on the basis of that membership alone.

Superficially considered, it seems shocking to look at racial, ethnic, national, and religious membership as a form of deviance. Indeed, some would say, such an exercise taints, stigmatizes, and labels categories of humanity who are themselves victims of racism, discrimination, and intolerance. Why victimize the powerless? a critic might argue. Doesn't such a discussion *justify* the very behavior it presumably investigates? My position is that the questions and the position they imply are mistaken.

So far, we've looked at "blemishes of individual character" and "abominations of the body" (Goffman, 1963, p. 4). Sociologists of deviance *almost never* look at Goffman's third type of stigma, tribal stigma—what I am referring to here as "collective deviance"—as a form of deviance. The question is, why? One possible explanation is that it would court charges of prejudice, as I indicated above, producing the kinds of questions an instructor who does teach the course in this way might hear. It is not "politically correct" to appear to accuse minorities of being "deviants." Hence, most instructors of deviance, especially those who work and live largely in liberal, humanistic communities, avoid such an accusation by not discussing minorities in their courses. It's even possible that such instructors accept the logic of these questions—that they themselves feel minorities to be tainted by the term *deviant*.

But the fact is, if the term *deviant* taints racial, national, and religious minorities, it also taints enactors of unconventional behavior and possessors of undesirable physical characteristics. If deviance is, by definition, that which violates society's norms and attracts condemnation, then the term applies to conditions as well as behavior. And it works for race, nation, and religion as well. The logic is the same; there is no conceptual or theoretical difference between them. The only difference is that most of us are more politically and interpersonally sensitive about tribal characteristics—those that apply to race, nationality, and religion—than to behavioral labels. In other words, there is no *sociological* reason to avoid the topic, only an ideological one. In this chapter, I intend to explain why even the ideological argument doesn't make sense.

Goffman argued that stigma "can be transmitted through lineages and equally contaminate all members of a family" (1963, p. 4). These are the "tribal stigma of race, nation, and religion." Goffman includes religion not simply in the sense of religious beliefs, but in the sense of belonging to a religious category as a *status group*, such as being Jewish, Episcopal, Muslim, or Catholic—*irrespective* of one's religious beliefs. In other words, the "religion" part of Goffman's "tribal stigma" is the categorical thinking that some outsiders use to typify *any and all* persons to whom the label is applied. Here, deviance is a quality not of an individual but of an entire collectivity. One is deviant because, in certain social circles, it is stigmatizing to belong to a particular category of humanity. With all stigmas, "the same sociological features are found: an individual who might have been received easily into ordinary social intercourse possesses a trait that can obtrude itself upon attention and turn those of us whom he meets away from him [or her], breaking the claim that his [or her] other attributes have on us. He [or she] possesses a stigma, an undesired differentness from what we had anticipated" (p. 5). The person with a stigma is regarded as "not quite human." On this assumption, "we exercise varieties of discrimination, through which we effectively, if often unthinkingly, reduce his [or her] life chances. We construct . . . an ideology to explain his [or her] inferiority and account for the danger he [or she] represents, sometimes rationalizing an animosity based on other differences, such as those of social class. . . . We tend to impute a wide range of imperfections on the basis of the original one" (p. 5).

The fact is, this description of Goffman's three-part stigma is also a perfect description of racism.

There's another reason why the tribal stigmas of race, nationality, and religion are an appropriate and fitting subject to discuss in a course on deviance—a reason Goffman did not anticipate. This is the phenomenon of "mutual deviantization" (Aho, 1994, p. 64), in which members of opposing "tribal" groups regard members of *the other* one as deviant. Among militant Muslims, especially militant Palestinians, it is anathema to be an Israeli; among militant Israelis, it is anathema to be a Muslim and an Arab, especially a Palestinian. Among militant, nationalist Indian Hindus, Muslims are considered undesirables; among militant Indian Muslims, Hindus are considered undesirables. During periods of violent conflict in Northern Ireland, Catholics and Protestants have demonized one another; during and after the 1990s, many Bosnian Serbs, who are Catholic, and Bosnian Muslims, have regarded one another as the enemy. Throughout much of recorded time, conflict has been the rule. Much of this conflict has taken place between the members of different ethnic and religious groups, and it has produced attitudes and behavior on the part of the members of each group that have turned those of the other category into deviants. Collective deviance has been a significant fact of life in many regions of the world during a major swath of human history.

Of course, many, perhaps most instances of collective deviance take place within a setting in which the dominant ethnic group holds so much power that mutual deviantization does not take place. The Jews in Nazi Germany—and, during World War II, in most of Europe—were stigmatized, demonized, verminized, persecuted, and murdered; they did not stigmatize or persecute non-Jewish Germans. In this case, the deviance process was entirely one-sided. During the second half of the nineteenth and the first quarter of the twentieth century, white Americans discriminated against, stigmatized, and excluded the Chinese. While the Chinese did not embrace members of non-Chinese ethnic groups with open arms, the fact is that the deviantization process here worked pretty much in only one direction. Mutual deviantization works only when competing ethnic groups are a bit more equal in power than in these two examples.

Throughout recorded history, then, members of one ethnic group have stigmatized, "deviantized," or demonized members of another group simply because of the category to which they belonged. Any exploration of deviance must take a look at Goffman's "tribal stigma of race, nation, and religion"—in short, *collective*

deviance. "Collective" deviance simply means that one is *automatically* discredited as a result of belonging to a racial, national, ethnic, and religious category of humanity. It is every bit as important as deviance that is determined by behavior or beliefs.

A FOURTH TYPE OF DEVIANCE

I'd like to add one more type of deviance to Goffman's trilogy of "blemishes of individual character" (such as homosexuality, insanity, alcoholism, and prostitution), "abominations of the body" (like being disabled, blind, obese, an albino, a dwarf, or being elaborately tattooed), and "tribal stigma of race, nation, and religion." This type of deviance still depends on behavior, so in a sense it falls under Goffman's "blemishes of individual character," but it is such a distinctive type of deviance that it deserves a separate discussion. This is *organizational deviance*.

What is distinctive about Goffman's examples of blemishes of individual character is that *anyone* (or practically anyone) could be marked by them. These "blemishes" are relevant to just about *every member of every society on earth*. Societies do not regard such characterological signs in the same way, of course—for instance, in some societies, it is not stigmatizing to engage in homosexuality—but, in principle, nearly *all* members of *all* societies could be put down for being marked by them. Theoretically, under certain circumstances, every single member of the society (everyone, let's say, above a certain age) *could* engage in homosexual behavior, become mentally ill, drink himself or herself into a stupor every night of the week, and engage in sex for pay. In any case, in Western society in general, and in American society specifically, everyone *could be* sized up with respect to where they stand on the dimensions of homosexuality-heterosexuality, mental health or illness, consumption of alcohol, and sexual virtue or the absence of it. Even if we don't agree with the judgments that others make, we are forced to be aware of those judgments.

Possessing "abominations of the body," likewise, is a dimension that everyone could get sized up on. *All* of us are evaluated with respect to weight, what is taken to be physical "normalcy," our capacity to perform important physical tasks (seeing, walking, hearing), height, and so on. Again, even if we don't agree that certain physical characteristics are relevant or stigmatizing, *no one* escapes this evaluation process. It is relevant to everyone in the society.

In a racially, tribally, and religiously charged society, likewise, no one is outside the sizing-up process. One is Black, white, or Asian; Catholic, Protestant, Jewish, Muslim, atheist; Swedish, French, Indonesian, Brazilian; and so on. Everyone gets put into a pigeonhole. (The increase in multiracial, multiethnic members of the society makes this a bit complicated, but the principle is the same.) When people are asked, in the United States at least, "What are you?," what is being asked about is ethnicity, national background, and/or religion. *Some* members of the society evaluate everyone on the basis of this pigeonholing, that is, where they "belong" in this elaborate collective categorization process. For some, it is "good" to belong to certain categories and "bad" to belong to others. No matter that this characterization process is largely fictional (that is, socially constructed), no matter that the qualities attributed to the members of those categories are largely likewise fictional. The fact is, it takes place and it influences all of our lives.

Organizational deviance is very different from Goffman's classic three-part typology of stigmata. This is because, given the way society is organizationally and institutionally structured, certain types of behavior *cannot* be performed by everyone. These types of behavior, by their very nature, can *only* be performed by the incumbents of certain positions or formal roles, positions that have relevance for and exist *only* within a given organizational structure. Corporate crime can only be performed by an executive in a corporation; only police officers can be guilty of police corruption and brutality; only students or candidates for certain professions or jobs can cheat on exams; only professors can demand sex for good grades; only psychiatrists can be guilty of breaching the therapeutic relationship by having sex with their patients. Everyone can shoplift; not everyone can engage in employee theft. This is what makes organizational deviance different

from our classic three-part classification of deviance: *It is not relevant* to the vast majority of the members of the society. Of course, some nonorganizational forms of deviance can be performed only by the occupants of certain social statuses: adultery (only by married persons); child molestation (only by adults); underage drinking (only by a minor); and so on. But the institutional quality of organizational deviance lends to it special sociological significance. As we'll see in Chapter 13, it makes for an entirely different causal dynamic and an entirely different stigmatization process.

WHAT DEVIANCE IS NOT

Sociologically, deviance is a normative violation that is likely to elicit negative reactions from observers and audiences. Now, let's be clear about what deviance is *not*.

First of all, deviance is *not* an absolute judgment of right or wrong. When sociologists say that in the United States, engaging in homosexual relations is deviant, they do not mean that it is wrong in some absolute or eternal sense. They mean that the majority of Americans condemn the practice and are likely to react negatively to a known homosexual. The absolute wrongness of a particular act, belief, or condition is not a meaningful sociological issue. Sociologists recognize that certain groups, categories, and social circles make such judgments, but they themselves do not. Fundamentalist Christians (Falwell, Dobson, and Hindson, 1996) proclaim that homosexuality, abortion, and the consumption of pornography are intrinsically, absolutely, abstractly, for all time and in all places, wrong, sinful—and hence, in our vocabulary, *deviant*. The sociologist notices this judgment and agrees that this is the view of fundamentalist Christians, but this does not decide the issue for all observers or audiences. Likewise, when conservatives argue that the sociological concept of deviance ought to be redefined as behavior that is *absolutely* and *abstractly* wrong (Hendershott, 2002), again, the sociologist takes note of this view but does not agree with it. To us, since views of right and wrong vary so much, absolute wrongness cannot be a criterion of deviance.

Second, deviance has nothing to do with mental disorder or illness. Most persons judged as deviants are just as sane as you or I. Mental disorder or illness are *not* definitional criteria or elements of deviance. Psychologists and psychiatrists make judgments of mental disorder; sociologists do not. It is true that most mentally disordered persons are likely to be regarded as deviants, but deviance is a far broader category, and the vast majority of persons engaged in deviant behavior, persons who hold deviant beliefs, and persons who possess physically deviant characteristics are as mentally and psychologically normal as the population at large. The notion of mental disorder should be flushed from the mind of every student enrolled in a deviance course. Mental disorder does not *define* deviance, although mental disorder may itself *attract* censure, punishment, and scorn.

Third, deviance is not dependent on unusualness or statistical difference from the population at large. Being in the minority is not necessarily being a deviant. Indeed, many minority practices, beliefs, or conditions are not deviant at all—that is, they do not violate a norm and they do not attract condemnation. Do you drive a Mercedes? Play tennis? Collect stamps? Live in Kansas? Wear a straw hat? Well, in each case, this is true of only a minority of the population of this country. But does that mean that each of these activities—or any of them—is deviant? Of course not! We *cannot* equate "deviant" with "different." Indeed, many activities that are extremely common—indeed, that are participated in or believed by the majority—are nonnormative, considered wrongful, and likely to attract punishment if discovered. Lying? Most of us have lied at one time or another in our lives. Do our friends like being lied to? Nope. Are they likely to react negatively if they discover that we've lied to them? Yes, they are. Is it a nonnormative activity? Of course it is. Is it deviant? Yes, it is. It is a common, even majority, activity—but it is still deviant. It is true that deviant activities, beliefs, and conditions *tend to be* statistically different from those of the majority. But differentness is *not* a definitional criterion of deviance. Lots of things that are different are conventional, and lots of activities that are engaged in by the majority are deviant.

And lastly, deviance is not defined by harm. The two dimensions, deviance and harm, are separate and independent of one another. Many harmless activities are deviant, and many harmful activities are conventional—indeed, we would be deviant if we did *not* participate in them. Engage in the following experiment. The next time you order steak at a restaurant, grab it and tear it apart with your teeth. Observe how others react to your strange manner of eating. Are you hurting anyone? Of course not! Is your behavior "deviant"? Obviously; by observing the reactions of others to your behavior, you can determine the act's deviant status. Shave your head bald and paint your face blue. What's the harm in that? None, but you are going to find that a lot of people react to your condition in ways that can only be described as disapproval. Having tattoos over one's entire body cannot, by any stretch of the imagination, be regarded as harmful, but it is likely to cast the possessor into a category most of us would have to regard as deviant (Sanders, 1989). Is wearing black lipstick harmful to anyone? It's difficult to imagine how. Yet Carla Chapman, a 13-year-old Kentucky girl, was suspended from school specifically for wearing black lipstick (Curra, 2000, p. 30). Clearly then, deviance cannot be *defined* by harm, since it is a simple matter to think of many examples of behavior that are harmless but nonetheless deviant.

Contrarily, wars have been fought since humans have existed on this planet, and most have been supported by the majority of the societies that waged them. Indeed, the *refusal* to fight these wars has been regarded as an act of cowardice—and, consequently, a form of deviance. Corporate crime steals far more money from the pockets of the general public than ordinary street crime does, yet the big-time crooks almost always manage to avoid the inside of a prison cell and usually emerge from their underhanded activity, if not heroes, then at least not villains. Juries often refuse to convict or, if they do convict, refuse to sentence corporate crooks to long prison terms because, well, after all, they are respectable folk (Friedrichs, 2004). Cigarettes kill vastly more Americans—440,000 of them each year—than do illicit drugs, maybe 20,000 (Horgan, Skwara, and Strickler, 2001), but we don't lock up or stigmatize their manufacturers. Indeed, even today, with very effective antismoking drives, most Americans don't condemn tobacco executives. Deviance and harm? They are very, very loosely related. Deviance is not *defined by* harm.

RELATIVITY

Another absolutely crucial point: The sociology of deviance is *relativistic*. The concept of relativity has been grossly misunderstood. Some people think that accepting relativity means that we have no right to make our own moral judgments (Hendershott, 2002). This is completely false. Accepting relativity as a fact does not take away our right to make moral judgments. Relativity says: Judgments of what is good and bad vary, and these judgments play a role in actors' and audiences' lives, depending on where they are located. We have the right to our own judgments about good and bad, but if we are studying deviance, we have to pay attention to how such judgments vary through time and space. How *we*—how I, the author; how you, the reader; how *any* observer—feels about or reacts to an act, a belief, or a condition is a completely separate issue from how members of a given society feel and act toward it. We may *despise* the injustice that we feel an act inflicts on its victims, or the injustice that punishing or condoning an act entails, but as sociologists of deviance we cannot permit ourselves to be so ignorant that we fail to recognize that the act *is* enacted, punished, or tolerated in certain places or at certain times.

For instance, the practice of female genital mutilation is common in parts of Africa and the Middle East—a fact amply documented by African-American novelist Alice Walker and filmmaker Pratibha Parmar, both in print (1993) and in the film *Warrior Marks*. The existence, practice, and acceptance of this brutal practice in some societies constitute a fact—one that Walker and Parmar wish to change. In my view, accepting relativism poses no ethical "dilemma," as some have argued (Henshel, 1990, p. 14). It does not advocate a "hands off" policy toward practices we consider evil. It simply says that what we consider evil may be seen as good to others—that is a fact we have to face—and that before we attack that evil, we have to understand how others come to view it as good and come to practice it.

Relativism simply says that our personal view of things may be irrelevant to how beliefs are actually put into practice and what their reception is in a given context. Hang on to your own moral precepts, relativity says, but make sure you realize that others may not share them, and that *their* moral precepts may guide them to do things *you* consider immoral.

A man, naked from the waist down, walks down the aisle of a meeting room, his penis fully erect. He invites members of the audience to touch his erection. Is this a deviant act? Before relativists answer this question, they would need to know more about the situational *context* of this act. The time is 1983, and the context is a meeting at which a physician, Giles Brindley, is showing off the results of his research—a drug-induced erection. The man with the erection was a medical scientist who developed a drug that was a precursor to Viagra, a pill that treats male sexual inadequacy. Brindley was simply dramatically demonstrating that his research produced a product that worked. In response to the distress people might feel at hearing about Dr. Brindley's seemingly exhibitionistic behavior, sex researcher Irwin Goldstein shrugged and commented to a reporter: "It was a bunch of urologists" (Hitt, 2000, p. 36). In other words, he was saying to us, touching an erect penis is no big deal. In the context of that scientific meeting, was Dr. Brindley's act deviant? Goldstein's statement says it all: of course not.

The most important characteristic of an act, relativists say, is how a society, or major segements of it, view it, and how people react to it and to someone who enacts it. Behavior is not deviant in itself; it only becomes deviant when it is seen and reacted to in a society or in a particular social context. Is adultery deviant? Not in some societies, such as the Lepcha of Sikkim, a tiny state in northern India. The Lepcha tolerate and even encourage adultery (Gorer, 1967). In other societies, such as Saudi Arabia, adultery is most decidedly deviant; the female partner, if caught engaging in it, is likely to be severely punished, and, in principle, in some areas, could even be put to death (Minai, 1981, p. 115). What about at an orgy? Is adultery deviant in that particular social context? No; in fact, at an orgy, to *refuse* to engage in sex with a partner not your own spouse would be deemed deviant. What is crucial here is not the nature of the act itself, which represents the same outward action in the various locales in which it takes place, but the *meaning* of the action to those who evaluate it, and the actual or potential reactions by others to the act and its perpetrators.

It might seem that this is a noncontroversial and universally accepted notion—that every sociologist agrees that definitions of right and wrong are relative, that they vary from one society to another (Merton, 1971, p. 827). This is not entirely true. Some approaches are more likely to emphasize the *universals* in deviance than the *relativity*. Functionalism, for instance, has argued that some actions are more likely to be punished—that is, regarded as deviant—more or less universally, in societies and cultures around the world, because they are *dysfunctional*, because tolerating them would lead to their widespread enactment and hence, to a weaker, less cohesive, less viable society. Incest is just such an act: Cultures almost everywhere prohibit incest because it undermines the foundation of the society, the family (Davis, 1949, pp. 401–404; 1976, p. 226). Likewise, certain actions are highly likely to be regarded as crimes in nearly all societies with a penal code because they are inherently harmful; any society that did not discourage them by outlawing and penalizing them would be seriously jeopardized (Newman, 1976).

Moreover, even though some types of acts (such as the unprovoked killing of a member of the society or group) are condemned everywhere and at all times, exactly which *specific* acts fall into a deviant category and hence, qualify as worthy of condemnation, varies a great deal. In the Middle East, the murder of Arabs by Jews may be seen as heroic—not deviant—among some Jews (but not others), while the murder of Jews by Arabs, likewise, may be praised, not condemned, among some Arabs (Cowell, 1994; Greenberg, 1995). The recognition of this fact varies considerably among sociological perspectives. Hence, though most other perspectives are, at most, only *moderately* relativistic in that they are more likely to stress the universals in deviance and crime— that is, the similarities from one moral code to another—the constructionist approach may be referred to as much more *radically* relativistic in

that it is more likely to emphasize differences, that is, the variation or relativity in moral and legal codes from one society to another.

In addition, the relativist approach emphasizes variations in judgments of deviance from one group, subculture, social circle, or individual to another *within the same society*. For instance, some social circles approve of marijuana use, while others condemn it (Johnston, O'Malley, and Bachman, 2003a, pp. 8, 9, 52–54). Some individuals condemn homosexuality while, increasingly, others do not (Minton, 2002). Heroin addicts see themselves, in many important respects, as superior to the members of conventional, middle-class society (Pearson, 1987; Carnwath and Smith, 2002). We will *almost always* be able to locate certain circles of individuals who tolerate or accept forms of behavior that are widely or more typically condemned within a given society. Some of these circles are, of course, practitioners of deviance themselves. But others are made up of individuals who, although they do not practice the behavior in question, do not condemn those who do.

Variations in definitions of deviance over *historical time* are at least as important as variations from one society to another. In 1993, the then-senator from New York State, Daniel Patrick Moynihan, argued that deviance has been redefined over time to the point where a great deal of crime and other harmful behavior that once generated stigma, condemnation, even arrest, is now tolerated and normalized, its enactors exempt from punishment. The mentally ill have been released onto the street, no longer held behind the walls of mental institutions. Unwed mothers, whose lack of a stable relationship with a man produces conditions conducive to their children failing in the essential performances considered necessary to a functioning society, no longer bear the burden of social stigma. And levels of crime once considered alarming are now regarded as acceptable, tolerable—business as usual. Defenders of the old standards of decency are powerless to halt this process of "defining deviancy down," Moynihan argued.

In response, social and political commentator Charles Krauthammer asserted that, true, some forms of deviance have been defined "down," but a parallel and equally important process is taking place as well: "Defining deviancy up" (1993).

Behaviors that once were tolerated have become targets of harsh condemnation. Just as the deviant has become normal, "once innocent behavior now stands condemned as deviant" (p. 20). Entirely new areas of deviance, such as date rape and politically incorrect speech, have been discovered. And old areas, such as child abuse, have been "amplified," often to the point where groundless accusations are assumed to be true. While two out of three instances of ordinary street crime are never reported, "two out of three reported cases of child abuse are never shown to have occurred" (p. 21). Overreporting of child abuse, Krauthammer claims, results from "a massive search to find cases." Where they cannot be found, they must be invented (p. 22). Date rape, Krauthammer claims, is so broadly defined as to encompass any and all sexual intercourse. In some social circles, he argues, the distinction between violence and consensual sex has been erased (p. 24). And the right to hold notions that differ from the mainstream has been taken away, Krauthammer claims. "Thought crimes" and "speech codes" have replaced differences of opinion and their expression.

It is possible that both Moynihan and Krauthammer have overstated their cases, but their point should be clear: Definitions of right and wrong vary over time. What is defined as wrong at one time may be tolerated at another; what is accepted during one era may be condemned in another.

In sum, relativity applies across societies and cultures and up and down through the corridors of time. In order to understand deviance, just as we must be relativistic from one society and social circle to another, we must also be relativistic from one historical time period to another. While for some behaviors consensus in judgments of wrongdoing may be widespread, as students of deviance, we find the variation at least as significant. The concept of relativity will continue to make its appearance throughout this book. It is one of the basic building blocks of the sociology of deviance.

ARE WE ALL DEVIANTS?

In a similar vein, given that nearly every act, belief, or physical characteristic is "deviant" to someone or to the members of some group or social category, should we conclude that we are all deviants? Does having engaged in one or more actions, holding one or more beliefs, possessing one or more characteristics, make us deviants? Of course not! There are at least four reasons why *violating a norm* is not the same thing as *being a deviant*.

First, we have to consider the matter of *degree*. Some actions are so *seriously* deviant, so *strongly* condemned that, if one were widely known to have engaged in them, one would indeed be regarded as a deviant; committing a brutal murder is an obvious example. Being convicted of murder pretty much automatically catapults one into the status of being *a* deviant. But the fact is, most of the acts, beliefs, or characteristics that are disapproved of by others attract only a *slightly* negative reaction from others. Clearly, then, deviance is *a matter of degree*. The condemnation we may have experienced, or could face, for telling a small lie is not the same thing as the punishment that is likely to be inflicted on us for having committed murder, the armed robbery of a bank, or the molestation of a small child. Put another way, some actions are strongly *discrediting*; others are only mildly so. The same applies to beliefs and physical characteristics: *Minor* departures from the norm rarely call forth such a strong negative reaction that they become the basis for casting us into the role of a deviant. Some actions, beliefs, and characteristics are regarded as mildly deviant; others are savagely condemned and are seen as seriously deviant. These two categories cannot be equated. Engaging in *mildly* unacceptable behavior does not make us a deviant; engaging in *savagely* condemned behavior often does. There seems to be something of a threshold here: Committing a small sin does not a sinner make, but committing a serious one most decidedly does.

Second, we also have to consider the matter of *numbers*. Some actions, beliefs, or traits are condemned by small, scattered numbers of people, while others are condemned by nearly everyone. If only a small circle of a few dozen people feel a given action or belief should be the basis of condemnation, a particular person in the society who violates that norm is unlikely to be subject to it—unless he or she is a member of that same social circle. Satanists may condemn Christians and Christians may condemn Satanists, but as we saw, these are not parallel judgments. Christians rarely run afoul of satanic norms because Christians are in the majority and Satanists are in a very tiny minority. It makes no sense to refer to Christians as deviants, at least in the abstract, since they so rarely suffer from condemnation as a result of their beliefs and practices. In other words, in considering who is a deviant, the sociologist pays close attention to the *number* of people who hold a given normative standard. The number of people likely to condemn a given action or belief is a major factor in determining whether the sociologist refers to the actor or believer as *a* deviant. This point obviously dovetails with our point about "societal" and "situational" deviance.

Third, sociologists must consider the matter of *power*. The reason why someone who may have violated a particular norm may not be regarded as a deviant is that, even when their numbers are the same, certain categories of people have more power to enforce their will on others. One aspect of the dimension of power is the capacity to enforce a particular interpretation of right and wrong on the relatively powerless. For instance, the power of the police, backed up by the legitimacy of the state, is greater than the power of persons who violate the law, even though the latter category may be numerically greater. The police have the power to arrest criminals; criminals do not have the power to arrest or otherwise legally punish the police. (Criminals may "punish" a cop *informally*, but such behavior is judged by the law as especially heinous, and if they are caught, it is they, not the police, who stand a high likelihood of being incarcerated for their act.) Parents who define eating cookies before dinner as wrong have more power to enforce that norm than small children, who may feel that such behavior is perfectly acceptable. Even if there are four children in a family and only two parents, it is the parents' definition of right and wrong that tends to hold sway, and this is because they have more power. Hence, once again, the mere infraction of a rule is not enough to make someone *a* deviant. Before we decide who is a deviant—and what constitutes deviance—we have to understand the *distribution of power* in a given social setting, group, or society.

And fourth, the transformation of someone who has simply done something wrong, or who holds an unconventional belief, or who possesses an unacceptable characteristic, into someone who is regarded as a deviant is a *sociologically patterned process*. The simple violation of a rule does not automatically transform someone into a new species of humanity. Sociologically, being *a* deviant means something quite specific. This is such an important process that I will devote a portion of a later chapter to the process of going "from deviance to deviant."

At this point, suffice it to say that there are two ways someone can *become* a deviant: first, by being personally stigmatized by others; and second, by being associated with a category or collectivity that attracts widespread stigma or public scorn. In other words, no, we are not all deviants, but yes, all of us have engaged in behavior, held beliefs, or possessed traits that some others don't approve of, to some degree. (Does violating a law *once* automatically turn us into a "criminal"? In most cases, no.) But the "some" others and the "to some degree" are absolutely crucial here. They spell out the difference between behavior, beliefs, and traits we can refer to in the abstract as deviant (to some people, somewhere on the planet) and persons who possess a deviant *identity*. When sociologists refer to someone as *a* deviant, they mean that someone possesses a deviant *identity*. And that means much more than the simple violation of a norm or a rule.

DEVIANCE AND CRIME: A ROUGH DIVISION OF LABOR

In the study of deviance and crime, most American and Canadian sociologists have followed a rough division of labor. In most of the college and university curricula, courses that focus on deviance tend to examine a distinctly different subject matter from those that deal with crime. In contrast, for British sociologists the two subjects overlap much more heavily; there, not infrequently, both "crime" (or criminology) and "deviance" can appear together in a book's title (Taylor, Walton, and Young, 1973; Downes and Rock, 2003).

If we were to look at the study of deviance and crime, taken as a whole, we'd notice three more-or-less distinctive emphases.

First, there are the criminologists. The field of criminology tends to focus on "hard" or "high consensus" deviance, that is, those activities whose enactment is likely to result in arrest and imprisonment—for instance, robbery, rape, murder, and burglary. In the United States, criminology has been dubbed the "Eastern" school of deviance (Ben-Yehuda, 1985, pp. 3–4) because many of its practitioners received their training, or much of its research has been conducted, or many of its researchers have been located, on the East Coast of the United States—places such as the University of Pennsylvania, the State University of New York at Albany, the University of Maryland, and the University of Delaware. Most practitioners of this school are positivists; they generally adopt a natural science model and study criminal behavior by means of official police statistics, formal interviews, questionnaire studies of crime victims, and self-report crime surveys. (Research methods will be explained in Chapter 5.) The central issue in the natural science model adopted by criminology is *etiology*, or the cause or causes of criminal behavior. "Why do they do it?" is the central concern of its practitioners. In part because the study of criminology can lead to a career in criminal justice; this field is very large. For instance, there are over 4,000 subscribers to the field's flagship journal, *Criminology*.

A second emphasis of researchers of deviance and crime is that adopted by Marxists, radicals, and "critical" theorists. They are not so much interested in criminal behavior as in the processes adopted by the ruling elite to control persons and behavior its members regard as troublesome. This perspective is a "top down" approach: Rules and laws issue from the most powerful strata of the society, they say, because their representatives aim to protect their own interests. In this view, national alcohol prohibition (1920–1933) was instituted because the capitalist elite wanted to maintain an efficient, hard-working labor force; prohibition failed because the capitalist elite was fearful that widespread violations of the liquor laws would create a disrespect for the law generally and hence, threaten its interests (Rumbarger, 1989). The vagrancy laws passed in England in the 1300s and the 1500s were designed, in the earlier era, to protect the interests of the landowning class by keeping peasants on the land, and in the latter era, to protect the merchant class by keeping rogues and idlers who might rob carriers off the highways (Chambliss, 1964). Even academic *theories* of crime and deviance are designed to protect the interests of the rich and the powerful (Quinney, 1979; Pfohl, 1994; Sumner, 1994). Or so these radical criminologists argued. Today, this school of deviance and crime studies has very nearly died out; most of its advocates from 30 years ago have given up their previous approach and adopted a very different perspective.

A third emphasis in research on deviance and crime is adopted by sociologists who see themselves as studying deviance *as opposed to crime*. This emphasis has sometimes been referred to as the "Western" (Ben-Yehuda, 1985, pp. 3–4) or the "Chicago/California" school (Petrunik, 1980). Its researchers usually focus on "soft" or "low consensus" deviance—that is, behavior that may (or may not) be technically against the law but is unlikely to lead to arrest and is punished mainly informally, unofficially, interpersonally. Examples of such behavior include alcoholism, marijuana use, homosexuality, nudism, being tattooed, nude dancing, and prostitution. In addition to deviant *behavior*, members of this school have also examined unconventional beliefs (Lofland and Stark, 1965; Lofland, 1966, and Chapter 10 in this book), mental disorder (Sampson et al., 1964, and Chapter 11 in this book; Mercer, 1965) and undesirable physical characteristics (Davis, 1964; Freidson, 1966; Miall, 1986; Sanders, 1989; and Chapter 12 in this book). Even when its practitioners do look at criminal behavior, they do so not from the perspective of what causes it but from the perspective of its social definitions, meanings, and interpretations (Schwartz and Skolnick, 1964; Scully and Marolla, 1984, 1985; Katz, 1988). More generally, regardless of what generates it, practitioners of this, the "Western" or "Chicago/California" school, tend to look at the creation of deviant categories; deviant stereotypes; deviant identities; being socialized into deviant subcultures; deviant "careers"; deviants' justifications, explanations, or accounts of their behavior, beliefs, or conditions; and the adjustment to labeling and stigma. And they tend to conduct their research by means of participant observation (an ethnographic or anthropological research method) and/or focused, qualitative interviews. The anthologies by Adler and

Adler, *Constructions of Deviance* (2003) and Rubington and Weinberg, *Deviance: The Interactionist Perspective* (2002) exemplify this approach, as does the journal *Deviant Behavior*.

In this book, I have observed this division of labor by focusing mainly on deviance and only secondarily on crime. In the study of deviance, we are more interested in the exercise of *informal* sanctions than in formal ones: How deviant categories are created, how persons are classified and reacted to as deviants, how they cope and deal with those social reactions, how they experience what they do. To the extent that the study of crime focuses on the etiology of crime and the machinery of the criminal justice system, the fact is, there is another field that studies these matters—criminology—and dozens of textbooks that discuss them. As Plummer says (1979), the sociology of deviance is not coterminous with the field of criminology. The two fields study different although overlapping phenomena. Hence, the approach I adopt in this book and the topics I cover will look a great deal more like the landscape laid out by the "Western" or "Chicago/California" school of deviance than by the "Eastern" school of criminology.

Some critics claim that the topics covered by deviance texts (including a previous edition of this text) overlap too much with the topics that are covered in criminology texts (Bader, Becker, and Desmond, 1996). Approximately half the behavioral topics discussed in these texts, these critics say, deal with criminal acts. The instructor of deviance should ensure that students do not receive "the same information" in both courses (p. 319). They suggest that a discussion of the usual crimes be dropped, and they propose that a wider range of noncriminal but deviant phenomena be substituted, including unconventional political and religious beliefs; a variety of conditions, both psychic (mental illness) and physical (obesity, physical disability, AIDS); nudism, homelessness, suicide, and so on.

I agree with this criticism—up to a point. To begin with, in some jurisdictions, certain behaviors are technically illegal (and hence, formally a "crime") but the laws against them are rarely enforced. Homosexuality is usually given either very scant, or no, coverage in a criminology course. Is it a crime? Technically, in some states,

it is, but for all practical purposes it is not. It is interesting mainly because it tends to be interpersonally stigmatizing—not because of its legal status. Criminologists refer to the deviant and illegal behavior discussed in this book as "public order" or "moral" crimes—prostitution, drug possession and sale, gambling, public intoxication. These types of activities tend to receive short shrift in criminology textbooks.

In addition, certain concepts that center around defining deviance, deviant labeling, stigma, acquiring an unconventional identity, the neutralization of deviant definitions, deviant "careers," and exiting from deviance, are as relevant for legal violations (that is, "crimes") as for the violation of informal rules or norms. Hence, in making a point about a *concept*, it may be necessary to refer to its relevance to certain types of criminal behavior. For instance, Benson's "Denying the Guilty Mind" (1985) discusses how white-collar criminals explain or justify their involvement in the behavior for which they were convicted and imprisoned. Hence, what that article is primarily about is *deviance neutralization,* and only secondarily white-collar crime. The same applies to Scully and Marolla's "Convicted Rapists' Vocabulary of Motive" (1984); the *subject* is rape—a criminal act—but the relevant analytic *concept* is deviance neutralization. In other words, separating the deviance curriculum from the criminology curriculum should not be achieved at the expense of sacrificing conceptual and theoretical issues (Kunkel, 1999). In short, the subjects "deviance" and "crime" only superficially discuss the same topics. They discuss the "same" topics *from a different point of view.* Crime can be discussed *as a form of* deviance, which is different from discussing it *as crime.* The etiology of, and criminal justice adjudication of cases of, rape are topics that belong to the field of criminology; the social construction of rape and the stigma that attaches to the rapist—and to the rape victim—are more likely to be investigated by sociologists of deviance.

An examination of the behavior under investigation is not an end in itself. What counts is what that behavior tells us about the human condition—about social life in general. As a result, while discussions of crime can be reduced to reduce overlap between deviance and criminology courses, they cannot be eliminated altogether. Nonetheless, in this book, I have ensured that chapters on criminal behavior be kept to an irreducible minimum. At the same time, since it generates condemnation and punishment, crime is a form of deviance—albeit a specific *type* of deviance. Crime usually elicits both formal and informal condemnation. As such, it deserves at least some discussion in any deviance text.

SUMMARY

Humans evaluate one another according to a number of criteria, including beliefs, behavior, and physical traits. That is, if, according to the judgment of a given audience doing the evaluation, someone holds the "wrong" attitudes, engages in the "wrong" behavior, or possesses the "wrong" traits or characteristics, he or she will be looked down upon by others and will be treated in a negative fashion. Sociologists refer to beliefs, behavior, or traits that violate, depart, or deviate from a basic norm held by a collectivity of people, and that are likely to generate negative reactions among the members of that collectivity who observe or hear about that norm-violation, as *social deviance* or simply *deviance*.

There are four necessary ingredients for deviance to take place: one, a rule or a norm; two, someone who violates or is thought to violate that norm; three, an "audience" that judges the normative violation; and four, the likelihood of negative reactions from this audience. What defines or constitutes deviance is the actual or potential negative reactions that certain acts, beliefs, or traits are likely to elicit.

Defining deviance is not a mere matter of departing from just *anyone's* norms, however. The sociologist is interested in the likelihood that a given normative departure will result in punishment, condemnation, and stigma. Hence, we must focus on the *number* and the *power* of the people who define a given act, belief, or trait as "wrong." The greater the number and power of the people who regard something as wrong, the greater the likelihood that its believers, enactors,

and possessors will be punished, condemned, or stigmatized—and hence, the more deviant that something is.

The distinction between "societal" and "situational" deviance is crucial here for understanding the *likelihood* of attracting condemnation, censure, punishment, scorn, and stigma. "Societal" deviance includes acts, beliefs, and conditions that are widely condemned pretty much throughout the society—in a phrase, "high consensus" deviance. Looking at deviance as a societal or society-wide phenomenon adopts a "vertical" perspective—that is, it sees judgments of right and wrong as being hierarchical in nature: Some judgments have more influence than others. In contrast, "situational" deviance is whatever attracts condemnation, censure, punishment, scorn, and stigma specifically in *particular* groups or social circles. This view of deviance looks "horizontally" or "across" the society and accepts the idea that different groups, circles, and categories have different judgments of right and wrong and hence, different notions of deviance. "Situational" deviance is usually "low consensus" deviance since there is a low level of agreement that such acts, beliefs, and traits are deviant.

Contrary to the stereotype, deviance includes more than behavior. Sociologists refer to the "ABCs" of deviance—attitudes, behavior, and conditions. True, behavior constitutes a major form of deviance, but so do beliefs and physical traits or conditions. Throughout history, people are judged to be normative violators for their beliefs almost as often, and almost as severely, as for their behavior. And judgments of physical appearance, likewise, are sharply judgmental, pervasive, and deeply determinative of society's rewards and punishments. In addition, racial, ethnic, religious, and "tribal" distinctions play a major role in judgments of deviance; Goffman analyzes such distinctions in his delineation of sources of stigma. I refer to tribal stigma as collective deviance. Some members of certain ethnic groups stigmatize *every* member of one or more other groups, regardless of what any given individual has done to deserve it.

I've added a fourth type of stigma to Goffman's classic three: *organizational* deviance. It shares some qualities in common with abominations of individual character, in that engaging in certain forms of unacceptable behavior *taints* the actor's character and leads to certain kinds of negative reactions. But it is different in at least one other respect: One can engage in the behavior *only* if one has a specific position within a given organization. Only cops can engage in police brutality; only professors (or teaching assistants) can demand sex for grades; only executives can engage in corporate crime; and so on. In a sense, it is the setting that generates the deviant behavior.

Deviance is a coat of many colors; it assumes myriad forms, varieties, and shapes. Deviance is a conceptual category that cuts through a diversity of acts, beliefs, and traits. Hence, it might seem that, on the surface, the phenomena that sociologists refer to as deviant share very little in common. But the very fact that the concept points to such diversity is what gives it its power. The concept of deviance highlights or illuminates features of social life that we might not otherwise have noticed. In the struggle to attain respectability, members of one category may resent being categorized with a less respectable category. For instance, self-avowed homosexual spokespersons have written to me, criticizing earlier editions of this book for referring to homosexuality as a form of deviance along with murder, rape, and robbery. They feel that the term "taints" them and their behavior. This is an example of what philosophers called the "fallacy of reification," that is, identifying the part with the whole. "Deviance" represents only one dimension, and *in some ways*, homosexuals and murderers *do* share important characteristics—that is, their behavior and their identity are discredited in the eyes of much of the public. When I ask these spokespersons, "Are homosexuals discriminated against and looked down upon by most Americans?" their answer is an immediate, "Of course!" My reply is, "That's exactly what I'm taking about!" In a similar vein, adultery, using cocaine, prostitution, being an atheist, and being autistic are also deviant.

Several criteria are used by the naïve, uninformed student to define deviance: absolute criteria, mental disorder, statistical departures from the norm, and harm to individuals and to the society. But as we've seen, these are false criteria,

naïve definitions of deviance. Sociologically, deviance is not defined by absolute criteria, mental disorder, unusualness, or harm. Indeed, many absolute definitions of wrongness or deviance have been proposed, but everyone has his or her own such definition, and none of them have anything to do with how the majority reacts to certain behavior, beliefs, or conditions. Most "deviants" are mentally normal, so clearly, mental disorder is separate and independent from deviance. Unusual behavior, beliefs, and conditions are not always deviant, and common ones are not always conventional. And lots of harmless acts are deviant, while many harmful ones are conventional. Clearly, these four definitions of deviance are misleading and naïve; sociologically, they are dead-ends.

The sociology of deviance accepts the precept of relativity. Relativity does not mean that we are forced to give up our own views of right and wrong. Indeed, when we study deviance, we have a right to our own moral judgments; but we have to recognize that others may not share our own sense of morality. Even though we may regard the behavior of others as unacceptable or immoral, their morality, however different it is from ours, is an undisputed fact that has important sociological causes and consequences.

A substantial proportion of instructors of the sociology of deviance courses have followed a "division of labor" between deviance and crime. Deviance is the violation of society's norms, whether formal or informal. By the lights of this definition, crime is a form of deviance. At the same time, there exists an academic discipline that explores the violation of formal norms—referred to as laws—and that field is criminology. Hence, to examine crimes, or the violation of formal norms, in a course on deviance would repeat material that is covered in a criminology course. As a consequence, these instructors have minimized the part that a discussion of crimes plays in their deviance courses. This demarcation tends to focus on "soft" or "low consensus" deviance and leaves the discussion of "hard" or "high consensus" deviance to the criminologist. Such a decision tends to focus on an ethnographic approach to studying the field rather than a more quantitative approach.

PERSONAL ACCOUNT: A Computer Pirate Tells His Story

The contributor of the following account, Steve, is a 21-year-old college senior. His story illustrates a number of interesting principles about deviance, one of which is that behavior that may be tolerated—even revered—among one category of people may be considered not only deviance but a crime among another. It also shows that committing deviance is not necessarily generalizable; someone who is fairly conventional in one sphere of life may engage in wrongdoing in another. And third, Steve's account illustrates the fact that there may be many rewards for engaging in deviance, some of them intrinsic (that is, those that come from the fun of the activity itself) and some secondary (the respect that the behavior generates from others).

I had heard all the speeches from my parents about staying away from drugs, alcohol, loose women, and fraternities, but the speeches had always been half-assed. In high school, I had always been a pretty good kid and I don't think my parents were all that worried about me. I graduated with honors and a 3.8 GPA, and I was the second leading tackler on the football team. I dated a cheerleader and hung out with what could be considered the preppy kids. For the most part, we stayed out of trouble, aside from the occasional party that got raided by the police. I spent most of my free time in the gym, and enjoyed playing computer games online. . . . I was an Eagle Scout. My parents knew they had raised a physically and mentally strong son. When they helped me move to college, I could tell they were proud of me. My Mom cried and my Dad smiled. Once again, I heard all those speeches I had heard over and over. "Stay away from drugs." "Don't drink." "For every hour you are in class, you should study for two hours." I had heard them so many times I stopped listening long ago. As much as they nagged and worried, I think my parents knew I would be OK. After all, I was your All-American average child.

I applied and was accepted into the University's Scholars Program. . . . We were assigned in one of thirteen programs. I was in the Science, Technology, and Society Program. All of us in that program lived together in the same dorm and took a special seminar. Many of us shared the same majors—I was in computer science—and thus shared many of the same courses. Through classes, our similar interests, and the fact that we all lived together, it was really easy to make friends. The more people I met, the more I realized I was surrounded by nerds. However, it didn't take me long to adapt.

I began playing several computer games. . . . The university has an extremely fast connection to the Internet, which gave me an advantage over my opponents. It didn't take me long to find out I could also download music from the Internet. The idea of not having to purchase CDs absolutely delighted me. There I was, a few weeks into my first semester of college. I went to all my classes, sat in the front of the class, did all my homework, did all the reading for my courses, visiting my professors during their office hours, and got good grades. In my free time, I went to the gym, played football, and played on my computer. I spent most of my time on the computer playing games, downloading music, or chatting on Instant Messenger. For a month or so, my life pretty much followed this pattern. But before long, everything changed.

Her name was Jen. She was in one of my computer courses. She was cute and really funny. We usually sat together in class and even studied for our first exam together. At some point, I asked if she'd like to hang out during the coming weekend. She said she'd love to and there was a movie she really wanted to see but she didn't have any money to pay for it. Normally, I'd jump at the opportunity to pay but I didn't have any money either. I left that conversation feeling more than a little annoyed.

Later that night, I told a friend what had happened and he told me he had the movie on his computer. It was too good to be true. Not only could I watch the movie with Tess, we could lie down on my bed instead of sitting in those awful movie theater chairs. I had my friend send me

PERSONAL ACCOUNT: A Computer Pirate Tells His Story (cont.)

the file right away. That weekend Jen came to my room and we watched the movie. The night was fantastic. I knew I had found something great. The next day I nagged my friend until he told me how he had gotten the movie. He introduced me to IRC, Instant Relay Chat, which is a program that allows you to meet people in chat rooms to talk and exchange files. To use IRC, you just need to choose a nickname and connect to a server. I chose the nickname "Bear" and I was off. I joined the chat room and tried to absorb everything that was going on. The chat room was run by a group of people called "Chimera." To download movies, you connect to people who are running servers, request the files you want, wait in line, then they send them to you. It was easy. It was awesome.

I became intrigued by this system of distributing movies. There were three types of people on the system—ops, the voiced, and peons. The "ops" (for "operators") ran and had total control of the chat room. If they didn't like you, they could kick you out or permanently ban you from the room. In the case of this particular chat room, the ops were the members of Chimera. Each one of them contributed to the process of distributing these movies. Below the ops were the "voiced people." They were either friends of the ops or people who ran the servers. The voiced had no actual power but when their nicknames were displayed, a plus sign appeared. I guess it's a little like the Queen of England—she doesn't have real power but people look up to her. Finally there are the "peons." These are the people who wander in to download movies for their own use. (Ops and voiced people call them "leeches.") Everyone starts as a peon. You stay there unless you do something special. This is where I began my journey, as a leech, just downloading and collecting movies.

My everyday life didn't change much. I still went to nearly all my classes and was on top of my work. Other people on my floor began finding out that I had newly released movies. Friday nights, students in my dorm began gathering in my room to watch whatever hot new movie

I had. They'd comment on how cool it was I could download these movies and save everyone eight dollars. Pretty soon people I didn't know dropped by my room and said they heard from a friend I had a particular movie and asked if I could send it to them. I became a kind of mini-celebrity in my dorm. I was the man to go to for movies. I loved making new friends but more important, I loved the attention. I loved controlling access to what they all wanted. I was hooked.

So I sent a message to one of the ops asking how I could become more involved. He gave me instructions on how to serve. So I set up a little file server and let three people at a time download movies off me. Since my Internet connection was so fast, I quickly became one of the more popular servers. The ops took notice of my server, and they made me one of the voiced. It felt great. Peons said "Hi!" to me and asked about my day. People sent me messages begging me to let them skip to the front of the line for my sends. It felt great. People liked me, respected me, even looked up to me. It didn't matter that I would never meet most of them face-to-face, the feeling of power was addictive. I couldn't get enough of it. I wanted more. I began sending out more files and trading files with other voiced people to increase my collection. I had built up my reputation to the point where I believed I should join Chimera and become an op. Internal conflicts caused some members of Chimera to leave and form their own movie release group, and I went with them. We formed The Ghost Dimension, and I was made an op in that group.

Founding a new movie release group proved to be much more work than I could have imagined. In Chimera, ops simply sent me movies and I stored them and sent them to others. But now that I was an op, I had no new movies to send. The other founders of Ghost Dimension and I spent the next few weeks calling in favors and tracking down sources and contacts. Sources are people who get the movies straight from theaters or in prerelease and supply us with them. We were able to acquire several bootleggers in

Singapore, the movie piracy capital of the world. What they did was they brought a digital camcorder into a theater and taped the movie off the screen. So, after about two weeks, we had enough sources to go public. The quality was pretty bad, but the movies were new and free so not too many people complained. We also acquired the cooperation of a theater manager local to one of our guys who let us set up a stationary camera to capture the video from the screen, and we recorded and mixed in the audio later. This method produced relatively good quality movies. Our real prize arrived when one of the founders of Ghost Dimension managed to convince a critic working for a TV station to join our group. He was able to supply us with screener tapes, which are movies sent by studios to critics before they are released to the public. The files we created from these tapes were nearly theater quality. We also got them ahead of time, so getting the critic was a huge break for us. It was the reason why we gained notoriety so quickly. Also, someone associated with our group was able to modify the way we created our files . . . [which] opened our products to a whole host of users who did not have broadband Internet.

The new demands of being an op began to significantly impact on my everyday life. Most nights I wouldn't get to sleep until four or five in the morning. I survived on naps and caffeine. My class attendance began to fade and my homework became second priority, which was reflected in my grades. My trips to the gym became less frequent, and the time I used to spend with my friends I spent napping so I could stay up all night and get the newest release out. I never felt lonely, though. I found all the friends I needed online. I was an op in a channel that had over 500 people in it at any given time. They all looked up to me. They all wanted what I had. They all wanted to be like me. The power went straight to my head. It was great. It was unbelievable what people would do to get the new release. Girls sent us naked pictures and videos of themselves. Guys sent us all kinds of software. We literally had access to whatever we wanted.

It was through one of these transactions that I furthered my online piracy career. A user offered to trade some software for the newest movie release. When he saw how fast my connection was, he told me he was a member of a group called "Russian Roulette," perhaps the most notorious software piracy group ever to exist. They were founded by Russian hackers in the mid–1990s, and since then spread all over the world. When my user told me Russian Roulette was looking for an East Coast dumpsite, I readily agreed to join. As a dumpsite, I would archive the releases and distribute them back to the other members of the group and a few select VIPs. Distributing pirated software turned out to be a lot riskier than stealing movies, though. At the time, movie piracy was relatively new, but software piracy had been around for a while and had proved to be a huge problem for software companies. They were already aggressively hunting down pirates.

A week after I joined Russian Roulette, a competing piracy group was busted and several members were charged with criminal offenses. So Russian Roulette recruited help from Snafu, one of the more elite group of hackers. Snafu provided us with a number of security programs to help us operate without detection by providing us with what's called a tracer. . . . So there I sat, on top of the online world. I obtained movies before they came out, I had any software I could possibly want, and I was an op in The Ghost Dimension and Russian Roulette, with power over 1,100 people every day. It was an incredible feeling, having all those people hang on my every word. This must be what people feel like when they get high on some really fabulous drug. I was insane and I was addicted. At this point, I had pretty much stopped going to nearly all of my classes. I did manage to make it to a few afternoon classes and my exams, but that was about it. My grades were horrible; I ended up with a 1.4 for that semester. My face-to-face interactions with my friends were becoming rare. I spent almost all of my time in front of a computer. Yet I was still on

PERSONAL ACCOUNT: A Computer Pirate Tells His Story (cont.)

top of the world. I was a god to these people, and I loved it. . . .

In November of the following year, I received an email from Universal Studios ordering me to cease and desist from my pirating activities immediately. The message was accompanied by some evidence that I was distributing copyrighted materials. Upon a careful analysis of their evidence, I know it was not sufficient to hold up in a court of law, but the point was made. I was no longer invincible. In the face of a criminal lawsuit, I decided to retire from the piracy scene. . . . I destroyed the hard drive on which I stored the movies and files. When I destroyed it, my 80-gigabyte hard drive was nearly totally full, with over 400 different programs and movies on it. Just recently, Russian Roulette made the headlines as the target of an international police sting operation. The FBI executed 100 search warrants against Russian Roulette in the United States. It claimed that at the time of the raids, Russian Roulette was responsible for 95 percent of all pirated software that was available online. . . .

To give you an idea of how active I was in the online piracy world, over the period of just one year, my server sent out over 15 terabytes of data. (A terabyte is 1,000 gigabytes, and one gigabytes is 1,000 megabytes.) On average, a movie runs about 200 megabytes and a full program is about the same. During my career as a computer pirate, I served around 75,000 programs and movies. The most downloaded file I had was Adobe Workshop, a graphic arts program, which cost then about $400. If all the files I sent out had been Adobe Workshop, I would have sent out roughly $30 million in illegal programs. Of course, nothing else I sent out was nearly this expensive. I probably sent out no more than between one and two million dollars worth of software, if it had been purchased legally.

Did I engage in deviance? Of course. I was engaged in an illegal operation that smuggled stolen merchandise across the world. How could that not be deviant? I kept my online activities from my family and friends because I was afraid of how they would react if they found out. I don't think I should be treated like a common thief who steals merchandise off the shelves of a store, but what I did was a crime nonetheless. . . . Stealing from the Internet is very impersonal. You never see whom you take stuff from and you never see how it affects them. . . . Still, the value of what I pushed greatly exceeded the value of anything I could have taken off a shelf. During the time I was actively pirating, I probably would have told you my behavior wasn't deviant at all. To the subculture of computer piracy with whom I interacted daily, this behavior was common and strongly encouraged. At that time, that subculture was basically my world, my reality, so I would have said no way was it deviant. Still, during nights when we created a new file, we sent out two or three gigabytes overnight, more than the average college user sends out over an entire semester. When I came back to my dorm room, before I entered the hallway, I always checked to see if there were police officers standing outside my door.

Yes, at that time, there was something different about my lifestyle, and I guess it might be seen as deviant, but I didn't think of it that way. I have no regrets about what I did. I'm still friends with some of the people I met online, I had a lot of fun, and in the end I think I learned a valuable lesson or two. The recent sentencing of a Russian Roulette member to 10 years in a federal prison helped hammer home the point to me that what I did was illegal. In the last analysis, I knew what I did was wrong. After that sentencing, the FBI announced it would be executing more warrants in the Russian Roulette case; I had to admit I didn't sleep at all for a few nights after that. Yet sometimes I miss the feeling of absolute power I had. Piracy isn't about money, it's about power and respect. Believe me, they're the most addicting things I know.

QUESTIONS

In your estimation, was Steve committing a deviant act when he engaged in computer piracy? Do you regard what he did as stealing? If so, is it stealing in the same way that shoplifting is? If not, how is it different? Who is the victim here? And if it is not wrong, what is the motive of the FBI in prosecuting cases such as his? Do the creators, producers, manufacturers, and distributors of CDs, DVDs, and files lose money by having their copyrighted materials pirated? Should there be copyright laws protecting their intellectual property from piracy? Or should it all be free? If so, shouldn't supermarkets distribute free food, doctors dispense free medical care, and teachers work for free? What was Steve's motive in engaging in computer piracy? Do you picture Steve engaging in a life of crime? Or do you figure he has reformed and is highly likely to lead a more-or-less conventional life?

CHAPTER
2

Approaches to Deviance

So far, we've learned that "deviance" is that which violates the norms of a society, or of a segment of the society, and calls forth punishment, condemnation, or censure of the norm violator. In this chapter, I'd like to take a step further and suggest that the study of deviance is really two independent but interlocking enterprises. When sociologists look at normative violations and censure of the violator, they think along two tracks and investigate two separate types of questions. In other words, they are engaged in two entirely different endeavors.

When we think deviance, the question we should ask ourselves is this: *What is to be explained?* The precise *way* that deviance is approached by the lens of two very different perspectives toward reality is the subject of this chapter. These two perspectives are referred to as *positivism* and *constructionism*. Let's look at a few recent news stories that will help illuminate these two perspectives.

- In Washington, an FBI agent betrays his country by selling government secrets to Russian agents.
- In Boston, a Catholic priest sexually abuses a 12-year-old choirboy. The boy tells his mother, who complains to the priest's superior, and the priest is referred to a therapist and transferred to another parish. The mother and the boy hear nothing more from the church about the incident, and the police are not informed of the priest's crime.
- In Switzerland, a 74-year-old wheelchair-bound paraplegic suffering from an incurable disease commits suicide by taking a lethal dose of a barbiturate prescribed by his physician.
- In Afghanistan, two journalists are arrested for publishing "sacrilegious" articles, and all of the copies of their newspaper are confiscated by the government.
- In Colorado Springs, a female cadet of the Air Force Academy is raped by a classmate; when she informs the Academy's administration, she is told to keep quiet about the incident.
- In New York, a professor embezzles money from a research grant and spends it on CDs, a vacation to the Caribbean, and heroin for his own use.
- In New Jersey, a poet accuses the Israeli government of knowing about the attack on the World Trade Center in advance and informing

all Israelis working there not to show up for work on September 11, 2001.
- In Buffalo, a fundamentalist Christian affiliated with The Army of God, an extreme right-wing antiabortion organization, shoots and kills a physician who performs abortions.
- In Nigeria, after being convicted of theft, a man receives ten lashes across his back with a whip.
- In Clinton, Mississippi, an accountant tells an auditing committee that the corporation she works for had inflated its profits by almost $4 billion—later revealed to be as much as $9 billion. It is the largest accounting fraud in history. Within months, the executives responsible for the fraud are led away in handcuffs, investors lose over $3 billion, and more than 17,000 of the firm's employees lose their jobs.

What is interesting and important about these events and developments? Our two perspectives have very different answers to this question. These two approaches can be regarded as "master visions." They seem contradictory, but in fact they complement one another; they are two halves of the same coin.

Positivism's answer to the "What is to be explained?" question is that it is the *deviant behavior, beliefs, or conditions themselves* that must be explained. What causes these things to happen or exist? is their guiding concern. The ruling questions that the positivist is likely to ask are: What kind of person would do such things? And: What social arrangements or factors encourage such behavior? Why is the crime rate so much higher in some societies or countries than in others? What *kinds of people* violate the norms of their society? For instance, why are men so much more likely to engage in most forms of deviance than women? The young more than the old? Urban dwellers more than people living in small towns? Which categories in the population are more likely to engage in violence? Among industrialized societies, why is the rate of criminal homicide in the United States so high? Why is it so much lower in Western Europe? Who uses and abuses psychoactive substances, and why? Is homosexuality caused by genetic or environmental factors? What conditions cause obesity? What causes some young people to engage in sex at an early age? What factors or variables encourage, cause, or influence white-collar crime? These are the sorts of questions asked by positivists who study deviance and crime.

For instance, among our examples of deviance, what interests the positivist would be the "Why?" of the actions described. Why would a priest engage in the sexual abuse of a child entrusted to his care? Why would anyone betray his country for money? Why would people in a trusted position sell government secrets to agents of another country? What was it in the life or background of this and other such traitors that led them to betray their country? What is it in the condition of the times, the society, and the historical circumstances of the day that leads people to betray their country? What would cause an Air Force cadet to rape a female cadet? Why do people commit suicide? What could cause an academic researcher to appropriate funds for private use and take an illegal drug—actions which, if discovered, would certainly lead to the termination of his grant and being fired from his university position? Why would a well-known poet—a former college professor, political activist, and self-proclaimed seeker of truth—make declarations that, quite literally, *cannot possibly* be true? What would lead someone to kill for what he perceives to be a religious cause? Why do some corporate executives commit fraud and other such criminal acts, risking a prison sentence and often driving the companies they work for into bankruptcy, losing billions for shareholders, and forcing employees onto the unemployment line? How are they different from executives who do *not* engage in corporate crime? Do corporations vary with respect to the likelihood that their executives will engage in fraud and other such criminal endeavors? What leads some people to criticize their politicians, their government, their religion, their society? And what general, societal, or structural factors would tend to encourage such behavior? How do we explain these behaviors? In each case, the positivist's question is: *What kind of person would do such a thing?* Or: *What kinds of social conditions or circumstances encourage or generate such behavior?*

In contrast, the approach we call *constructionism* or "social constructionism" answers this question by saying that it is *thinking about* and *reacting to* these developments that is crucial.

This approach argues that it is the *rules*, the *norms*, the *reactions to*, the *representations of* certain behavior, beliefs, or conditions that need to be looked at and illuminated. In other words, constructionism is curious about how and why something comes to be *regarded as* or *judged to be* deviant in the first place, what is *thought, made of, said about*, and *done about* it. How are phenomena generally, and deviant phenomena specifically, *conceptualized, defined, represented, reacted to*, and *dealt with*? How do certain actions *come to be regarded* as "crime," "homosexuality," "prostitution," "treachery," or "incest"? How are certain beliefs conceptualized *as* "heresy," "blasphemy," "godlessness," "disloyalty," "ignorance"? Why are certain physical characteristics even *noticed* in the first place? Are the disabled stigmatized? Are they integrated into the mainstream or "abled" society—or are they, in some ways, excluded? Why is a specific behavior, belief, or trait condemned in one society but not in another? Why does atheism cause the nonbeliever to be burned at the stake in one place, at one historical era, and ignored or tolerated elsewhere, at another time? Do the members of a society think of corporate crime as "real" crime? Are jurors willing to sentence convicted white-collar criminals to long prison sentences? What does the treatment of the mentally disordered tell us about how they are viewed by the society at large? How do the media report news about drug abuse? What do the members of a society *do* to someone who engages in a given behavior, holds a particular belief, bears a specific trait? In turn, how does the person who is designated as a deviant *react to, handle*, and *deal with* the deviant designation, the label, the stigma?

The constructionist is more interested in issues that have to do with thinking, talking, writing about, narrating, or reacting to such actions. How is it that the sexual abuse of children by priests became a major issue only in the past few years? Why was it kept secret by the Catholic Church for so long? What makes assisted suicide accepted in some countries but condemned—indeed, interpreted as a crime—in others? How has it come to pass that religious crimes still exist in Muslim societies, but disappeared from Western societies a century or more ago? What is the reaction of the antiabortion movement to the murder of abortion doctors, who, its members believe, are *in fact* committing murder? Why does theft generate the punishment of a beating in one society but a prison sentence in another? How do the media deal with white-collar and corporate crime? With crime in general? Who gets locked up for which crimes and who doesn't? Why do drug offenders get sent to prison in much larger numbers today than was true 20 or 30 years ago? Why are some activities, beliefs, and traits on a society's radar screen while others are ignored? Why do we care about certain things and not others? How are certain activities and actors described or narrated in a society's depictions of them?

POSITIVISM: AN INTRODUCTION

What is positivism in the social sciences? *It is the application of the scientific method to the study of human behavior.* The practitioners of positivism maintain that sociology and criminology are not so radically different from the natural sciences that explaining human behavior is impossible. They believe that deviance and crime can be studied in much the same way that natural phenomena, like stars, chemicals, and ocean tides can be studied—naturally making the necessary adjustments in research methods for the subject matter under study.

Positivism is based on three fundamental assumptions: one, *empiricism*; two, *objectivism*; and three, *determinism*.

Empiricism

Positivism assumes that the material world is real and that the scientist can know the world through the five senses; in other words, the positivist is an *empiricist*. Empiricism is the belief that seeing, feeling, hearing, tasting, and smelling are capable of conveying meaningful information—information that gives the observer sense impressions of the way things are. Of course, often these senses must be aided by instruments (such as a microscope, a telescope, or an oscilloscope). In addition, there are many things can never be directly observed, such as biological, historical, astronomical, and geological events that happened in the distant past; hence, reasoning about them

entails making inferences from the data that is available to the scientist. Moreover, the data of the senses must be integrated into extant or preexisting concepts, theories, frameworks, and perspectives that help to make observed data meaningful. But the guiding principle of the empiricist is: "I trust my senses to tell me what's true." And it is the guiding principle of all positivists. Most positivists believe that if phenomena are not observable directly or indirectly through the information provided by the five senses and cannot be integrated into existing or conceivable theoretical and conceptual perspectives, questions asked about them are not scientifically meaningful. Not wrong, just nonscientific—outside the scientific framework. Hence, the question of whether a given work of art, poetry, form of behavior, belief, or political regime is "good" or "bad," or whether or not a painting or a musical composition is "beautiful," or whether or not God exists, are considered *nonempirical*, and hence, nonscientific, questions.

The fact that certain things cannot be directly observed by the scientist is especially crucial for the sociologist and the criminologist because *most* human behavior cannot be seen at the moment it is enacted. Instead, social scientists must infer what happened through a variety of indirect indicators, including the answers to questions *about* the behavior of subjects provided by informants and interviewees. Researchers have developed a variety of methods to determine the validity of answers to questions about behavior, and some of them get very close to the reality they are attempting to describe. Indeed, some research methods *do* entail direct observation—participant observation as well as field and laboratory experiments, for instance. But most research methods rely on indirect indicators, and here, the researcher must be skeptical, clever, and resourceful. I'll have a great deal more to say about research methods in Chapter 5.

Objectivism

The second assumption of positivism—objectivism—means that phenomena in the material world are *objectively real*, that they possess certain objective or internally consistent characteristics that distinguish them from other phenomena.

In line with our interests, the social scientist can distinguish deviant behavior from conventional, conforming behavior. In other words, the many forms of deviant behavior share a *common thread*, a *differentiating trait* that distinguishes them from conventional, conforming, legal behavior. Travis Hirschi expresses this thought when he says: "The person may not have committed a 'deviant' act, but he did (in many cases) do *something*. . . . And it is just possible that . . . if he were left alone he would *do it again*" (1973, p. 169). It is this "something" that the positivists argue is the object of the social scientist's scrutiny. In other words, positivists *reject* the notion that definitions of right or wrong are really as relative as constructionist sociologists of deviance argue (Curra, 2000). Public perceptions of right and wrong do not vary much across societal lines; there *is* a "common core" from society to society to what's regarded as deviant (Newman, 1976).

The same thing applies to crime. While positivistic criminologists will warn that there is no "essence," no common core, to criminal behavior (Nettler, 1984, p. 16), most will nonetheless regard correlations between this phenomenon, this entity, this phenomenon or *thing* and key sociological characteristics as extremely important. If crime were not a real "thing" in the world, then how could it possibly manifest statistical relationships with key variables such as race, socioeconomic status, gender, and residence? Crime is not a simple product of the process of social construction, they say. There *is* a material reality to crime above and beyond social and legal definitions. Crime is much more than a mere social construction; there is an identifiable behavior core (or "essence") to criminal behavior.

At the very least, the specific types of deviance or crime (such as homosexuality, robbery, drug use, adultery, mental illness, alcoholism, and homicide) share key characteristics in common. It is the scientist who determines what deviance is, and what each specific type is, by observing the behavior in question and classifying it appropriately according to its objective characteristics. The characteristics of deviant behavior *are contained within the actions themselves*. It is their possession of certain observable properties that makes them deviant in nature. All positivists

know that deviance is defined by norms, and that norms are relative to time and place. Still, they feel that there is enough internal consistency within and among deviant categories that an explanation for their existence is possible; there must be *something* about them that leads the scientist to examine them together as a category. If labels were not at least minimally internally consistent, there would be no point in studying them as an analytic category—they would have no coherence; they would possess nothing in common except their label.

All positivists who attempt to explain deviance and crime know that norms and laws are socially constructed. They all realize that what is considered wrongdoing varies from society to society and from one historical era to another. In other words, all positivists are aware of the *relativity* of definitions of right and wrong. Nonetheless, positivists tend to stress the *common thread* or *common core* in deviance and crime. They emphasize the fact that what is regarded as wrong is *not* completely arbitrary and does *not* vary randomly across societal and time boundaries. In other words, there are limits to relativity (Newman, 1976). There is likely to be an identifiable phenomenon or syndrome hidden in most of the behaviors and beliefs that are identified as deviant or criminal, say the positivists. Definitions of deviance and crime are not constructions alone; there *is* a "there there." They have, in other words, certain objective properties that can be located and explained.

For instance, are definitions of mental illness arbitrary? Could a person who is labeled mentally ill in one society be considered sane in another? Is there a common thread in mental disorder? Is the term *nothing but* a label applied by psychiatrists, or by the general public? Does the principle of relativity apply to conditions that are commonly referred to as mental disorder, as some claim (Curra, 2000, pp. 169–185)? Is the enterprise of psychiatry little more than an updated version of "witchcraft," as some observers have argued (Turner and Edgley, 1983)? Positivists say no. Mental disorder is an identifiable "thing" or condition in the world and not the mere imposition of a socially constructed definition (Spitzer, 1975, 1976). Says Gwynn Nettler, an outspoken advocate of the positivistic position in the study of deviance and crime: "Some people are more crazy than others; we can tell the difference and calling lunacy a name does not cause it" (Nettler, 1974, p. 894).

Does homosexuality have a common thread? Is it an identifiable condition with clear-cut properties and characteristics that do not vary from society to society and that is, in all likelihood, caused by genetic factors? Says Frederick Whitam, advocate of the latter position: "Homosexuality is . . . a sexual orientation and no useful purpose can be served by regarding it as anything else" (1977, p. 2). Homosexuality, he adds, is not culturally variable, is not a product of a social construction, and is not relative to time and place. Instead, it is a universal condition that manifests itself in more or less the same way everywhere and throughout recorded history (Whitam and Mathy, 1986).

Is beauty "in the eye of the beholder"? Is what is considered beautiful—and ugly—variable across cultural lines? Do different societies and different eras have varying interpretations of what's attractive and unattractive? Would some of the same people who are considered homely in one society be regarded as beautiful in another, and vice versa? Is the evaluation of attractiveness nothing more than a social construction? Would the obese, who are condemned and reviled—and considered deviants—in the modern industrial West, be admired and revered in other places, at other times? No, say many observers. Standards of beauty and attractiveness are "hardwired" into our brains. It is our genes that tell us what's attractive and unattractive, and these messages are standard, uniform, and universal everywhere and throughout historical time. The key to beauty is not society's construction of it but the impulse to pass on one's genes to later generations (Buss, 1994; Etcoff, 1999).

Determinism

The third assumption positivists make is determinism—that is, what *causes* the deviant behavior, beliefs, or conditions? For centuries, the question *Why do they do it?* has been asked about persons who stray beyond society's moral or legal boundaries. What is it that influences some people to violate society's norms—the Ten Commandments, for

example—while most of us do not? Or, taking the question to a higher or broader level, what is it about certain societies or categories of people that leads to so much higher rates of deviance among their ranks than in other societies or other categories? Do specific social *conditions* encourage deviance? Do other conditions inhibit it? These sorts of questions ask for an explanation of deviance as a certain type of action or behavior.

In other words, positivism looks for cause-and-effect *explanations* for the acts, beliefs, and conditions that are regarded as deviant. The belief that the world happens in a cause-and-effect fashion is referred to as *determinism*. And an explanation for a general class of phenomena or events is called a *theory*. The positivist assumes that the phenomena and events of the world do not take place at random, by accident. In other words, there is a *reason* for their patterning. A theory addresses the question: Why are things the way they are? This means that the reasons for the patterns and regularities we observe must be sought. When we discover that men are more likely to violate society's norms than women, we want to find out *why* this is so. Knowing that the rate of criminal homicide is so much higher in the United States than it is in Western Europe, we must understand why this comes to be the way it is. Urbanization increases rates of drug abuse; strong ties to conventional others decrease rates of deviance; anonymity increases the likelihood that nonconformity will take place. Conditions or factors such as these *cause* or *influence* specific forms of behavior, deviance. It is the scientist's job to locate the dynamics of the cause-and-effect sequences that exist in the world.

Some positivistic approaches are *individualistic* (or "micro") in that they focus on the characteristics of categories of individuals who violate norms or break the law. They argue that deviants share a trait or characteristic in common—which nondeviants lack—that can be isolated, which will help provide an explanation for deviance. Other positivistic approaches are more *structural* and *sociological* (or "macro"). They look at the "big picture" and argue that certain *deviance-inducing conditions* share a common thread or trait or characteristic that can be discovered, which will lead to an explanation of deviance—such as urbanism, anomie, society-wide income distributions, and so on. Either way, whether individual or structural, deviance is produced by these traits or conditions or factors in a cause-and-effect fashion, which can be discovered and explicated by the scientifically inclined sociologist of deviance and crime.

Notice that we cannot equate the positivistic sociology of deviance with explanations that focus on biological factors alone. *All* positivistic theories seek an explanation; all ask the question "Why?" This means that *any* theory that attempts to explain or account for deviance in general, or types of deviance specifically, is positivistic. Theories that focus on social or sociological causes are positivistic, as are those that focus on psychological causes, as are those that focus on biological causes. The relevant distinction is not between biological and social explanations but between those that seek cause-and-effect explanations and those that do not.

Positivists seek general explanations for why things are the way they are. Scientists are not satisfied with explanations of specific, particular, or unique events. The goal of every scientist is to explain as many events, phenomena, or observations in the material world as possible. This means that they all look for *patterns* or *regularities* in the material world. When criminologists study criminal violence in one delinquent gang, they are really looking for patterns of criminal violence in delinquent gangs *in general*. To the positivist, a case study of one prostitute is meaningful only insofar as it sheds light on *all* prostitutes, or on the institution of prostitution *as a whole*. A detailed examination of a case of corporate crime that takes place in *one* company is not enough; what we need to know is what the picture of corporate crime *generally* looks like. Positivists are not interested in particulars or specifics for their own sake. They want to know how and to what extent these particulars fall into recognizable *patterns* that will enable them to make generalizations about how the world as a whole works.

In the field of medicine, the study of these patterns is referred to as *epidemiology*, the study of how diseases are distributed in the population. Age, sex, race, and place of residence are some of the epidemiological factors that are examined in the search for patterns and generalizations. The study of deviance does not use the term "epidemiology," but research in crime, drug abuse, and

mental disorder does. Is armed robbery more likely to take place in cities or in rural areas? And how *much* more likely? Is the Black-white difference in rates of criminal homicide real or an artifact of differences in arrest patterns? Are males or females more likely to suffer from mental disorder? And *which* disorders are more characteristic of males? Of females? Are married men and women more or less likely to suffer from mental disorder? How is drug abuse distributed by age? Are teenagers or adults more likely to abuse illicit drugs? Does alcoholism vary by age? These are the sorts of epidemiological questions that positivists who study crime, mental disorder, and drug abuse are likely to ask.

CONSTRUCTIONIST APPROACHES TO DEVIANCE: AN INTRODUCTION

A very different sort of approach from that of positivism is adopted by constructionism. This approach focuses on the creation of social categories, the imputation of deviance to those categories, and questions of why certain rules exist, how they work, what their consequences are, and what the dynamics of enforcement are. The constructionist does not ask the "Why do they do it?" question. The issue of the causes for deviant behavior, beliefs, and conditions is very much in the background for the constructionist. How do members of the society picture, talk about, and react to the behavior, beliefs, and conditions becomes the sociologist's central focus. As we saw, to the constructionist, the fact that the administration of the Air Force Academy told a rape victim to keep quiet about the incident is more interesting than the reasons why the classmate raped her; the way the Catholic Church dealt with cases of child abuse by priests is more interesting than the causes of the abuse itself; the fact that in some societies, whipping is a form of punishment for theft is more interesting than the whys and wherefores of theft; the fact that assisted suicide is condoned in some societies but not in others is more interesting than the reasons why some patients end their lives and some doctors help them; the fact that, in certain societies, a category of deviance that is referred to as "sacrilege" exists and calls for punishment by the state is more interesting than why some people engage in it. In short, the constructionist looks at *how deviance is defined and represented* and *what is made of it.*

The constructionist enterprise is made up of four steps.

• One, how do the members of a society assemble a classification scheme out of the total universe of behavior, beliefs, and conditions? How is human behavior assembled into identifiable *categories*, each with its own name and mental pigeonhole: incest, dwarfism, murder, sodomy, heresy, blasphemy, obesity, homosexuality? These categories do not drop from the skies. Why do they exist in the first place? How does homosexuality come to be seen as a form of behavior distinct from heterosexuality? How does it come to pass that some behaviors are regarded as so noteworthy and internally consistent as forming a *type* or *category* of behavior? Some categories of human behavior have existed—*as categories*—since the dawn of humanity. In contrast, the emergence of others is a much more recent development. Before the feminist movement emerged in the 1970s, no such category of behavior existed as sexual harassment. (The *behavior* existed; the *social categorization* of the behavior did not.) Since that time, it has become fixed into law and in the public mind as a distinct and identifiable kind of behavior.

• Two, how does a given general category come to be judged as *wrong*, as a normative violation, as worthy of social or societal condemnation—as a type of deviance? What is the process by which a moral valuation is placed on an entire category of behavior, belief, or conditions? What makes homosexual behavior an abomination in one society—a possible cause for execution—but acceptable, indeed, expected in another? Why are first cousins prohibited from marrying in one society but expected to do so in another (Ford and Beach, 1951)? Are there variations in this respect within the same society? Why?

• Three, given the creation of general categories and their moral valuation, how do certain *specific*, concrete acts, beliefs, or conditions come to be regarded as *instances of a given general category*? What concrete instances in the material world are put *into* these categories?

For instance, all societies have a category that is referred to as incest, and everywhere, incest is condemned. But the rules that *determine* what constitutes incest vary from one society to another. Why? What determines this classification scheme? How does it come to pass that a certain *type* of killing is classified as an act of heroism and another as an instance of cowardice?

• And four, how does a specific person—the actor, the believer, or the possessor—come to be stigmatized, regarded as a person who is considered shameful—in short, become *a* deviant? Is there variation in this process? Is punishment or stigma mitigated by factors unrelated to the behavior? Why in one instance is the killer of his brother protected by the community in which he lives (Bogdan, 1992), while practically everywhere else, killers are arrested and subject to long prison sentences? What are the conditions under which a rejected homosexual "pass" at a heterosexual results in no stigmatization whatsoever (Kitsuse, 1962)? Why do the members of one circle of juvenile lawbreakers receive no social rejection whatsoever while those in another are arrested, expelled from school, and regarded as troublemakers (Chambliss, 1973)?

Permit me to restate these steps in a slightly more detailed discussion.

Conceptualization

Here, the relevant issue is not why some people "do it" but why and under what conditions "it"—whatever it is—tends to be *conceptualized* and *condemned*. In this approach, its "wrongness" is not assumed. Indeed, its wrongness is the central intellectual puzzle; that is what needs to be explained. Indeed, as we see in step one, above, even the very categorical *reality* of the behavior, belief, and condition needs to be explained. Thus, the very first step in the construction process is how certain actions, beliefs, or characteristics come to be focused on as a category. Out of all the things in the world, why do members of a society select these as real and worthy of attention—and, simultaneously, ignore others that are equally real but, seemingly, unworthy of serious attention? To the constructionist, then, the first step in the deviance process is *the creation or construction of a category*. Categories do not assemble themselves out of thin air; they have to be noticed and made a part of a society's cultural lore.

For instance, Pfohl argues (1977) that child abuse was "discovered" in the 1960s. He is not saying that, before that time, parents did not beat or torture their children. They did, and, chances are, in much more substantial proportions than is true today. What Pfohl is saying is that "child abuse" did not exist as a publicly recognized or acted-upon *conceptual category of behavior*. Other categories fall out of the public classification scheme; over time, certain types of behavior fail to elicit pigeonholing. Most of us do not think of "blaspheming" as a type of behavior. Unless one is a fundamentalist Christian, Jew, or Muslim, blaspheming simply fails to register on most Americans' mental radar screen as a type of behavior; it is irrelevant to the way we divide up the universe of things people do. But for most of us, the distinction between engaging in homosexual versus heterosexual sex is extremely important, as is being mentally retarded versus having an average intelligence; being three feet tall versus six feet tall; selling one's body for money versus engaging in sex exclusively with one's spouse; engaging in behavior or having the mannerisms most of us would refer to as eccentricity versus not being eccentric; being homeless versus living in a stable residence with one's family; holding a theory about a United Nations conspiracy, headed by the Jews, to take away all the guns of American citizens and herd them all into concentration camps versus regarding that theory as nothing more than a paranoid fantasy. In other words, certain behaviors, beliefs, and traits are thought of as significant *phenomena*, as categories that become the basis for dividing the human world into types of people.

Condemnation

The second step in the constructionist enterprise entails an investigation of *condemnation*. Constructionists ask why homosexuality is a condemned category in one society but not in another; why obesity is despised more now than in the past; how theft came to enter the legal code

as a crime; why accusations of rape by a woman bring suspicion and condemnation on the accuser and why men so often escape criminal prosecution for this crime; why wife-beating and sexual harassment have been tolerated—even encouraged—for so long; why alcoholism is regarded as a sin at one time, a disease at another time; why the possession and sale of certain drugs was legal in 1905 but is illegal in 2005; what led to the huge upsurge in incarceration in the United States during the 1980s, 1990s, and into the twenty-first century; how, over time, smoking came to be an abomination in certain social circles; why members of one group consider tattoos a sign of moral degeneracy, while those in another are encouraged and expected to tattoo their bodies; why atheists were put to death at one time but tolerated and ignored in another; what led to institutionalizing national alcohol prohibition in the United States in 1920 and why it had failed by 1933.

Clearly, questions asking for an explanation of condemnation are very different from questions asking for an explanation of behavior that *only happens to be condemned*; they are entirely different enterprises. Asking why behavior of a certain sort takes place regards that behavior as a particular type of *action*, an action with more or less clearly discernible features. There must be something *about* that action that makes a coherent explanation possible. In contrast, asking why behavior (or a belief, or a condition) is condemned sees it as an *infraction*—as a violation. Instead of looking for the cause in the *actor* who engaged in the behavior, we have to look for the cause in the *condemners*. What is it about them that generated this sort of reaction? What is it about certain types of societies that generates—or does not generate—condemnation of specific categories of behavior, belief, or conditions? We cannot assume that these categories will be regarded as wrong everywhere and at all times.

Assigning Particulars to Categories

Third, even after we take note of the conceptual creation of categories of behavior, belief, and physical condition, and even after we acknowledge their moral evaluation, we have to understand the social rules by which a specific, concrete act, belief, or condition is regarded as belonging to a larger and more-or-less homogeneous category of acts, beliefs, and conditions. Lines are drawn through phenomena in the concrete world at different places, and drawing these lines follows a certain social and cultural logic. How is it that *the very same behavior* that was once referred to as "strict parental discipline" is now classified as child abuse? Why is behavior that in one society is seen as "enjoying a touch of the grape from time to time" in another is labeled as alcoholism? The category "making an unwanted sexual pass" existed in the past, and then, as now, it was considered unacceptable behavior; but today, the *line* at which such behavior is drawn includes a much wider set of acts than was true previously. Where was that line drawn for what was regarded as pornography in the 1950? Is that line drawn at a different place today, over 50 years later?

Along these lines, then, we would ask why acts that are defined as homosexuality in one context or society are not so regarded in another. In prison, for example, just as in the world outside, there is a category of homosexual behavior, and, just as on the outside, that category is negatively morally weighted. But in prison, what specific acts are seen or regarded *as* homosexual behavior follows an entirely different set of rules from those observed outside of prison. The aggressor or male "insertor" in the sex act is not regarded as engaging in homosexual behavior at all, while the "insertee" is. In some societies, marrying or having sex with one's second or third cousin is regarded as incest. In our own society, this is not the case; such marriages are tolerated and are legal. Both societies condemn incest, but they define it differently. What is included in a given deviant category, what is excluded? Categories are not hard-and-fast entities, with outlines that stay the same in all cultures, subcultures, and social situations, at all times, now and forever. Exactly how a specific *incident* of concrete behavior becomes regarded as an *instance* of a more general category is intellectually problematic. This process can't be assumed; it has to be investigated and understood.

From Deviance to Deviant

And fourth, the constructionist is curious about the process that transforms someone from an enactor of a certain type of behavior, holder of a certain belief, possessor of a certain trait, to the category of *a deviant*. The step *from deviance to deviant* is not simple or straightforward, as we saw in the first chapter. It is dependent on other factors, other processes—each of which needs to be examined. Why is one heavy drinker seen as an alcoholic, while another who consumes the same quantity is seen simply as a heavy drinker? What goes into this categorizing or labeling process? Why is a particular person who enacts a certain type of behavior, holds certain beliefs, and possesses a certain condition condemned, socially isolated, stigmatized, and punished, while another person who engages in the same behavior, holds the same belief, or possesses the same condition is tolerated, accepted, indulged in his or her difference from the mainstream? What factors lead to mental hospitalization, *given the same degree of seriousness of mental condition*? When is someone who is "different" accepted and regarded merely as a harmless eccentric? What are the conditions under which another person, equally different, is rejected as an outcast? Are there periods of time when the assignment of certain people to the deviant category is especially swift, especially certain, and made on the basis of relatively little evidence? These are the sorts of questions a social constructionist asks. They see the transition "from deviance to deviant" not as automatic but as in need of an explanation. It is their intention to supply that explanation.

What Constructionism Can Do That Positivism Can't

The social constructionist approach opens a line of inquiry that cannot be pursued by the positivist or "Why do they do it?" researchers: It permits inquiry into *false accusations*. The central issue is not "Why do they do it?" but "Why are there rules, why are they enforced, and who is accused of wrongdoing?" As a consequence, it becomes secondary (although far from irrelevant) that the accused person didn't "do it." Why were hundreds of thousands of women persecuted for witchcraft in Renaissance Europe? The positivist sociologist is powerless even to ask the question because, in all likelihood, the women accused of witchcraft *didn't* engage in the crimes of which they were accused. In contrast, the constructionist is very comfortable about asking why the witch-craze arose (Ben-Yehuda, 1980) and why particular women (and men) were accused and punished for a nonexistent crime. The fact that the crime was nonexistent is crucial for the positivist, because how can you explain something that someone didn't do? In fact, to the sociologists looking exclusively at the causes of behavior, the witches weren't deviant at all because they didn't *do* anything to attract the condemnation. To the constructionist, the enterprise of persecution is *independent* of the enactment of the behavior of which deviants are accused.

To the social constructionist, the distinctions between voluntary behavior, beliefs, and involuntary conditions are irrelevant. What counts is how people who are seen as violating the law are *thought of* and *treated* in a particular society. Are blind people more likely to be socially accepted by the sighted today as compared with centuries past? Does acceptance or rejection of blind people vary from one society to another? Does acceptance or rejection vary in the same society at the same time by social category or group? How do blind people regard their condition? How do they relate to the sighted? Do they interact mainly with one another or do they integrate into the world of the sighted? We can ask much the same questions about a variety of social conditions, including obesity, dwarfism, albinism, physical disfigurement or disability, extreme ugliness, and so on. That the conditions are not voluntary is not the issue; the fact that persons in such categories are treated in a certain fashion *is* the issue. For instance, the Greeks and other ancient peoples abandoned deformed children to the elements to die, believing that a stigma adhered to such imperfect creatures; in some societies, adulterers have been stoned to death, so serious is the stigma of the sin of adultery. Both the condition—physical deformation—and the voluntary behavior—adultery—are deviant in that they generate serious stigma and the ultimate punishment.

Regardless of what caused them, from a constructionist perspective, both are deviant.

Please note that these two intellectual enterprises are not contradictory but complementary. On the one hand, there are reasons why some people violate society's rules and why some societies experience more deviance than others, and these reasons can be discovered and explained. The violation of a society's norms is not randomly distributed from person to person or society to society.

On the other hand, these norms are created and enforced as a result of systematic, identifiable sociological processes. While the sociological positivist takes the norms and their enforcement *as if* they were a given, the fact is, they are not; they are every bit a social product, and every bit as needful of an explanation as deviant behavior.

DEVIANCE AND SOCIAL CONTROL: AN INTRODUCTION

The methods that members of a society use to ensure conformity to norms are referred to as *social control.* Sociologists define social control as *efforts to ensure conformity to a norm.* Every time we do something to induce someone to engage in behavior we believe is right, we are engaged in social control. Every time others do something to induce us to engage in behavior they believe is right, they are engaged in social control. When a mother yanks her child's hand out of the cookie jar, she is exercising social control. When a police officer arrests a burglar for breaking and entering an apartment, that officer is engaging in social control. When a professor gives a student caught cheating on an exam a grade of zero, she is practicing social control. When someone avoids or shuns a friend for getting drunk and boisterous at a party, he or she is engaged in social control. Social control includes "all of the processes by which people define and respond to deviant behavior" (Black, 1984, p. xi). Social control can be formal or informal, governmental or interpersonal, blatant or subtle, and internal as well as external.

To the constructionist who studies deviance, social control is a central—perhaps *the* central—

concept. Now and throughout human history, all societies everywhere in the world have set and enforced norms—rules about what their members should and should not do. Norms are found everywhere, from the dinner table to the Oval Office, from the marital bed to the Vatican. As we cast our gaze backward through time and across the world's many nations and societies, from the Sahara to the Amazon, from the teeming streets of Hong Kong, Cairo, and New York to the McMurdo Station near the South Pole, we notice that, though rules and norms differ, along with the nature and severity of the punishments for violating them, nonetheless, *rules and norms themselves are universal*. All societies have them and the members of all societies enforce them. There is not and never has been any ongoing country, society, or collectivity where "anything goes." If any such existed, it could not long survive, for rules are the very cornerstone of human survival. Even in societies that experience extreme brutality, violence, and upheaval, there are rules: It's acceptable to kill the enemy but not one another.

A "norm" is simply a rule that calls for proper behavior, a kind of blueprint for action. Implied in a norm is that violators are punished or sanctioned when they violate it. Some norms apply in specific contexts, settings, or situations. For instance, one must *not* laugh at a funeral, but one is *expected* to laugh at a comedy routine. The injunction against laughing is specific to certain settings, and the expectation of laughter, likewise, applies only to specific settings.

Other norms apply to the behavior of members of certain groups or collectivities but not others. Members of a tough street gang are expected to meet the challenge of an insult, a taunt, or a shove with verbal and physical aggression. The failure to do so would result in sanctions or punishment from other members of the gang. However, if the members of the faculty at a university or the medical staff of a hospital were to respond as aggressively to a perceived insult, it is their behavior that would be sanctioned. Such a response would be regarded as undignified, unprofessional, unacceptable—in a word, deviant.

Still other norms apply across the board, that is, to everyone in a given society. For instance, no one is permitted to kill a tiny baby in its crib simply because its crying is annoying. There is

no person in the society who is exempt from that norm, and there exists practically no situation or context when such behavior is allowed.

Regardless of whether a given norm applies to all situations or only to some, to certain people or to all of them, the fact is, *everyone, everywhere* is subject to *certain* norms. Being human means being subject to the norms of the groups to which one belongs and of the society in which one lives.

As we saw, some minimal level of punishment for wrongdoing is necessary to ensure a minimal level of social order. At some point, the lack of norms in a given society would result in a state of collapse—a "war of all against all," in which life would be, in the words of seventeenth-century English philosopher Thomas Hobbes, "poor, solitary, nasty, brutish, and short." The central question for the functionalist sociologists, whose theories will be discussed in Chapter 4, is, given the natural human tendency to be selfish: *How is social order possible?* If there were no rules and we were permitted to obtain anything we wanted in any way that was effective—rape, murder, robbery, assault—then how is it possible for societies to survive and even prosper? Why *don't* we collapse into a state of chaos, disorder, and disintegration? For the functionalists, a partial answer to this question is that *social control*, through both learning the acceptable norms and punishing unacceptable and rewarding acceptable behavior, operates to ensure a society's survival. The Sixth Commandment, "Thou shalt not murder" (*not* "kill," since the ancient Hebrews *did* kill a substantial number of their enemies—for instance, in warfare), is an obvious example of such a norm.

Actually, it is surprising how *few* norms are designed to condemn, punish, or protect a society or its members from injurious or predatory actions, such as murder, rape, robbery, or serious assault. Most norms attempt to discourage behavior that neither directly harms anyone nor threatens the society with chaos and disintegration. Most norms are intended to make a statement about what is considered—by some, many, or most members of a society—to be right, good, and proper. They embody certain principles of moral correctness—separate and independent of what they do for the society's physical survival. Norms such as "Thou shalt not murder" are in fact in the minority of all the rules that members of a society learn and, for the most part, abide by. No one would be injured, nor would society be threatened with disintegration, if some of us were to wear our clothes backwards, speak every word twice, or (as in a previous example) eat steak by grabbing it with our hands and tearing at it with our teeth. But if any of us were to engage in these acts, others would greet us with disapproval, condemnation, and derision. Clearly, protecting the society from actions that are so harmful as to threaten our, and hence the society's, survival is not the only purpose for the norms or the punishment of their violators. There is implicit in norms and their enforcement a version of moral correctness, an ethos, a way of life that is *an end in itself*. We are expected to do certain things because, well, because they are *right*, because *that's the way things are done*.

Ensuring conformity to society's norms constitutes social control. There are several distinctly different varieties of social control. *Internal* social control operates through the process of *socialization*, that is, by learning and adopting the norms of the society or a particular group or collectivity within the society. All people are socialized by identifiable *agents*. The family is, of course, the earliest agent of socialization, one of whose primary functions is attempting to internalize into children the norms of the society in which they live. To the extent that the family fails to do so, children are likely to engage in behavior that is regarded as deviant by the society. Later on, schools, peers, and the mass media represent other, also powerful, agents of socialization. Much of their socialization represents efforts at internal social control.

When the norms of the society are accepted as valid, they can be said to be *internalized*. To the extent that internalization is successful, persons would feel guilty if they were to engage in the behavior the society or their collectivity considers wrong. When they refuse to do so, it is in part as a consequence of the fact that the relevant norm was successfully internalized. We do not kill or assault people who make us angry not merely because we will be punished for doing so but in large part because we feel that murder and assault are wrong.

Socialization is only one weapon in society's arsenal of social control. In one way or another, society is almost always unsuccessful in instilling its version of the norms into us. There are always some people—for the most important norms, usually a minority—who don't accept the legitimacy of the norms. Moreover, even people who are usually conformist and law-abiding will find situations that call for exceptions to any rule or norm. (If we are faced with an especially tempting reward, many of us reevaluate our complete adherence to the norm.) The fact is, most of us are incompletely and to some degree partly *unsuccessfully* socialized. As a consequence, another form of social control is necessary; society moves to *external* social control. A great deal of social control is coercive and repressive; it relies on punishment and force. Often, many of us want to move "outside the lines." When we do, and certain agents of social control detect our behavior, they will use some sort of punishment, coercion, or *external* social control to bring us back into line. Of course, rewards also make up a form of external social control, although, usually, we are not rewarded for things we are expected to do; we are simply not punished.

Most sociologists of deviance focus on external social control rather than internal. External social control is made up of the system of rewards and punishments that persons, parties, agents use to induce others to conform to a norm. Rewards and punishments are referred to as *sanctions*. Obviously, a positive sanction is a reward and a negative sanction is a punishment. Slapping, screaming at, damning, ignoring, shunning, snubbing, ridiculing, insulting, taunting, gossiping about, firing, divorcing, giving a failing grade to, humiliating, frowning at, disparaging, denouncing, reprimanding, admonishing, berating, criticizing, nagging, arresting, "dissing" (not demonstrating sufficient respect), mocking, stigmatizing, showing contempt toward, acting in a condescending fashion toward, laughing at, booing, hooting at, jeering, hissing—these and a host of others are negative reactions to someone whose behavior, beliefs, and physical traits, in the estimation of a particular audience, fail to measure up. (In most cases, we can't change our involuntarily acquired ascribed characteristics, which means that these reactions cannot bring us into line. But they do serve as a reminder to us all of what an audience's standards are.) They are all *negative* and *external* forms of social control. And social control is the very foundation stone of the sociologist's definition of deviance. *Deviance is that which calls forth efforts at social control.*

FORMAL AND INFORMAL SOCIAL CONTROL

Sociologists distinguish between *formal* and *informal* social control. In between, we find what might be referred to as "semiformal" social control.

"Informal" social control takes place in interpersonal interaction between and among people who are acting on their own, in an unofficial capacity. As we saw, reactions such as a frown or a smile, criticism or praise, shunning or being warm toward someone are ways we have of exercising *informal* social control. They act to remind someone that their behavior annoys or pleases us. Since most people seek the approval of others whom they care about, they tend to adjust their behavior to avoid the disapproval of significant others by discontinuing the offensive behavior or hiding it from public view.

However, in large, complex societies, especially with a substantial volume of contact between and among strangers, informal social control is no longer sufficient to bring about conformity to the norms. In such societies, it becomes easy to ignore the disapproval of others if you do not care enough about them to be concerned about how they feel about you. So, *formal* social control becomes necessary. "Formal social control" is defined as "an effort to bring about conformity to the law by agents of the criminal justice system such as the police, the courts, and correctional institutions" (Conklin, 1998, p. 560). In principle, agents of formal social control act not as individuals with their own personal feelings about whether behavior is wrong or right, but as occupants of specific statuses in a specific bureaucratic organization, that is, the criminal justice system. The sanctions they apply to wrongdoers flow from their offices or positions, not from their personal relationship with the rule-violator. It is the job or function of such agents to act, when transgressions occur, to bring about conformity to the formal code, that is, the law.

Of course, it should be said that both formal and informal social control may operate at the same time. A drug dealer may simultaneously be arrested by the police *and* shunned by his neighbors. A child molester may serve a ten-year sentence and be exposed and humiliated by the members of the community in which he lives after he is released.

Somewhere in between informal social control, which is based on personal and interpersonal reactions between and among interacting parties, and the formal social control of the criminal justice system—the police, the courts, and the correctional institutions—we find "semiformal" social control. Here we have a huge territory of noncriminal, nonpenal bureaucratic social control, administered by the government, that attempts to deal with the troublesome behavior of persons under their authority. If a person's behavior becomes extremely troublesome to others, an array of agencies, bureaucracies, and organizations may step in to handle or control that person, to punish or bring him or her into line with the rules. In other words, persons deemed difficult or problematic by members of a community come under "the purview of professional controllers" (Hawkins and Tiedeman, 1975, p. 111). These "professional controllers" do not have the power of arrest or incarceration, but they can make recommendations to agents of the criminal justice system that may have bearing on arrest and incarceration. Such agents include social workers, psychiatrists, truant officers, and representatives, functionaries, and officers of mental hospitals, civil courts, the Internal Revenue Service and other official tax agencies, social welfare offices, unemployment offices, departments of motor vehicles, and public schools.

Some sociologists of deviance equate "social control" with formal and semiformal social control. They ignore the private, informal, interpersonal reactions to behavior and beliefs by individuals as a means of keeping people in line with the rules and norms of the society (Cohen, 1985a; Horwitz, 1990, p. 4). The reason is that such a focus is consistent with the theory that social control is highly centralized and repressive (Meier, 1982, p. 47). On the other hand, if you broaden your conception of social control to include informal social control as well, you have to recognize the fact that interpersonal relations are messy, untidy, less likely to conform to a pattern, far less centralized, and far less subject to elite control. These "social control" thinkers (Foucault, 1979; Cohen, 1985a; Lowman, Menzies, and Palys, 1987; Scull, 1988) equate state or state-like control with all social control, making the assumption that state control, much like an octopus, reaches out and grabs agencies and organizations spread throughout the society.

But the fact is, contrary to these "social control" theorists, *most of the time* that social control is exercised, it is informal. Most of the time deviance is sanctioned, the actor is punished or condemned by individuals, not by representatives of a bureaucratic organization. Informal social control is the "meat and potatoes," the "nuts and bolts" of the labeling process. Relatively speaking, formal social control tends to be much less common and more fitfully applied. In point of fact, the vast majority of rule-breaking behavior—from making unwanted sexual passes at parties to being an eccentric, from breaking wind at the dinner table to insulting one's peers—is *ignored* by the apparatus of formal and semiformal social control. The fact is that informal social control is the foundation of social life. In other words, ironically, an entire school of deviance studies whose advocates pride themselves on focusing on social control ignore the most basic and fundamental ingredient of social control: *informal* social control.

SUMMARY

There are those among us who argue that dividing the human world into categories of people toward whom we ought to behave in a certain fashion is useful. We do it, they would say, to predict how others are likely to treat us. After all, who wants to climb into a car when an alcoholic is behind the wheel? Who is willing to entrust his or her seven-year-old to the care of a compulsive pedophile? Why should we become friendly with a paranoid schizophrenic when he or she may include us in a long list of imaginary persecutors and enemies?

But as we shall see throughout this book, the matter is not quite so simple. We are led to draw lines around certain behavior, beliefs, conditions, and people for far more than practical reasons of self-protection. Prior notions of who certain people are lead us to *believe* that they are likely to be a threat to our well-being. It is almost certainly true that *some* categories of people are more likely to be threats to us than others are, but our fear and avoidance of some of them, but not others, is often independent of their concrete, measurable threat to us. There is clearly a great deal more to the picture of deviance than the objective or concrete threat of danger.

All the perspectives, theories, or schools that follow in Chapter 3—social disorganization, anomie or strain theory, learning theory, control theory, and what is referred to as a "general" theory of crime—are positivistic in nature. That is, all apply the natural science method to social phenomena. All believe that theories should be testable or falsifiable by using empirical evidence, that is, the data of our five senses. All argue that deviance—or crime—possesses a common thread, or one or more identifiable "objective" properties. All seek a general explanation of deviant behavior. And all stress deterministic cause-and-effect mechanisms in generating deviant behavior. Even if they are skeptical about generic theories of deviance, all believe that the social scientist can explain or account for certain *forms* of deviance, such as mental illness, homosexuality, crime, prostitution, corporate crime, suicide, drug abuse, and alcoholism. Moreover, none is especially interested in the social construction of deviance—that is, the social and cultural creation of the norms, how the criminal law came into being, the contingencies or accidents of the labeling process, or how and why specific types of deviance are thought about and talked about in certain ways. For the positivist, those issues are taken for granted, assumed—put on the "back burner." All the points made about positivism discussed in this chapter apply to all of the theories that are discussed in the next chapter. If there are two halves to the phenomenon of deviance—on one half, how is it *defined*, and on the other, what *causes* it—positivist theories are concerned more or less exclusively with the second of these two halves. *Why do they do it?* positivists ask; *what causes deviance?*

In contrast, Chapter 4, on constructionist theories, discusses the first half of the equation—*how is deviance defined?* Constructionism seeks to understand (1) how distinctive social *categories* are created; (2) how those categories are infused with valuative meaning—that is, how they are assigned the qualities of being good or evil, true or false, desirable or undesirable, positive or negative, discrediting or affirming; (3) how these qualities are attached to specific persons; and (4) how appropriate reactions to those persons are indicated and carried out.

In *Gulliver's Travels*, a fanciful novel by Jonathan Swift (1667–1745), we come upon a people who waged war against another people on the basis of whether they cracked open their eggs at the top or the bottom. While it seems difficult to imagine a distinction being made on such a trivial basis, people have been persecuted and stigmatized for practices that seem to the outsider to be equally trivial—if not how people crack open their eggs, then what food they eat; what clothing they wear; to what god or gods they pray; how they say their prayers; if they are Christians, how they cross themselves; how literally they stick to sacred scriptures; who they want their rulers to be; how they engage in sex; what books they should or should not read; and which of their fellow human beings should be included in a society's civil community. These distinctions *have* generated stigma, a denial of human rights, and mass violence; they are the very nature of what the study of deviance is all about.

Even acts that, and actors who, threaten the very existence of a society, or the institutions within a society, are reacted to differently from one society to another. In other words, it is true that all societies, everywhere and throughout history, punish murder. But what *defines* murder? What acts are *categorized* as murder? The Sixth Commandment of the Bible supposedly says, "Thou shalt not kill." But as any biblical scholar will tell you, this is a mistranslation. The Hebrew word for "kill" is *laharog*, but that is not the word that is used in the Sixth Commandment. Instead, the injunction reads: "*Lo tirtzach*"—Thou shalt not *murder*. Murder is a specifically *deviant* form of killing. After all, David killed Goliath, but that was an authorized or *righteous* killing; the Bible most emphatically did *not* enjoin David from killing Goliath. Murder may be a universally condemned act, but that is only because it is *predefined* as wrong. In fact, in all societies at all times, some killings have been acceptable while others have not. It is glib and misleading to assume that certain universally condemned acts are not socially constructed. What every social constructionist wants to know is how certain acts, beliefs, and conditions—*even if they seem to threaten the well-being of a society*—come to be defined and dealt with in societies everywhere. Even acts that are regarded as murder, universally punished though they be, are handled differently in different societies around the world. For instance, some societies have the death penalty and others do not; some societies apply the maximum penalty to certain offenders but not to others; and so on. While *definitions* of deviance are not universal, the relativity of reactions to—in other words, the *social construction* of—deviance is everywhere a reality. This applies to violence no less than sexual diversity, suicide no less than theft, and drug use no less than mental disorder (Curra, 2000).

PERSONAL ACCOUNT: A Stripper Mom Tells Her Story

What follows is an interview with "Candee," a "stripper mom"—a 24-year-old woman who is the mother of a five-year-old son. The interview was conducted by Shelley Shupp, who was then a student at the University of Maryland.

To quote from Shelley's paper: "Mainstream society characterizes exotic dancing as deviant, and those who engage in this behavior ... fall outside the spectrum of conventionality.... Social constructionists would say that there is

PERSONAL ACCOUNT: A Stripper Mom Tells Her Story (cont.)

nothing wrong within the behavior itself that is wrong, but it is the label that society has given the behavior that makes it deviant."

A positivist would look for factors in Candee's background that caused her behavior. Here is Shelley's summary of Candee's background: Her parents married right out of high school and had a brief marriage. "Her father raised her until the age of 13, when he remarried. . . . When her father remarried, she acquired a stepsister, with whom she felt she was in 'constant competition.' Candee was a mediocre student [but] graduated in four years without difficulty. After high school, she met Jason and ran away from home, due to conflicts with her stepmother, to live with him. Soon after, she [became pregnant and] decided to keep the baby; she had had two abortions during her summer after high school graduation. . . . Soon after [her son] Keith's birth, however, problems arose between her and Jason and they broke up. Candee was not allowed to move back in with her father and stepmother and went to live with her mother for a while. Since then, she had a falling out with her mother and they no longer talk. Candee got a job as a bank teller and moved into a modest apartment, where she and Keith shared a bedroom. She admits that there was a steady flow of men in and out of her life, none of whom stayed for very long. . . . Two years and three abortions later, Candee quit her job as a bank teller and became a waitress. She barely made enough money to support herself and Keith. She soon decided to start stripping. Exotic dancers notoriously make good money and Candee thought this would be an easy way to get on top of things in her life."

Shelley has known Candee since childhood; she explains that Candee "had a rather sexual way of thinking. Even playing dress-up, she would often suggest, 'Why don't we pretend to be strippers?' " For a long period of time, Candee did not tell her family about her profession. (Secrecy is a clue that an activity is deviant.) Instead, she said she was a "waitress at a fancy restaurant near Baltimore." When her father,

mother, and stepmother discovered what her profession was, an argument ensued, along with mutual estrangement.

The interview was conducted at Candee's place of employment, a strip club. Shelley observed a "set," during which Candee performed her dance. These are her comments: "It is clear that she is working hard for tips. She singles out a few guys and dances for them erotically. . . . Exotic dancing establishes a false intimacy between the dancers and the customers. This is apparent in watching Candee perform. Especially during a lap dance, the men can be seen leaning their heads back, biting their lip, rubbing their erect penis through their pants with their hands, or maybe the dancer is doing it for them. A dance comes dangerously close to sex, which is what makes it so appealing for most" of the men who frequent the club.

Shelley speculates on whether Candee's stigmatizing profession will follow her and her son after she retires from stripping. She believes that Candee is fooling herself that her job is not deviant or stigmatizing, arguing that she has managed to convince herself that it is not only because she has "lost the bond with her parents and other family, she has detached herself from most social bonds outside of the club"; "her feelings are untrue," Shelley concludes. And lastly, Shelley believes that Candee has managed to convince herself of a patently untrue belief because she is in a setting in which "deviant socialization" takes place, one in which the strippers and their customers "establish a subculture within the club," convincing one another that they are engaging in conventional, acceptable behavior.

From a constructionist point of view, Candee's belief that stripping is not deviant is neither wrong nor right; it is—if it actually is—her belief, and to the constructionist, it is that *belief* that defines the reality and validity of a phenomenon. But to the constructionist, the beliefs and reactions of audiences *also* define a phenomenon. In other words, to the constructionist, two contradictory beliefs can be "true" simultaneously. The

PERSONAL ACCOUNT: A Stripper Mom Tells Her Story (cont.)

fact that audiences regard Candee's profession as deviant is *constituted*—or defined—by their reactions. Think of the many ways that Candee's audiences (her parents, friends, customers, employers, the general society, as well as her son's teachers) react, and how those reactions define her job's deviant status.

SHELLEY: So, Candee, is it kind of awkward having me talk to you like this, considering we grew up together?

CANDEE: No, not at all. I'm so proud of what I do. I mean, I invite my friends to come watch me all the time or vote for me on the club website. Have you voted for me yet?

SHELLEY: No [laughs]. I don't want anything to go to your head.

CANDEE: We actually get benefits, cash bonuses actually, if we are voted the best stripper on any given month. They also will increase our hours if votes show that we are one of the guys' favorites.

SHELLEY: Are the same few dancers the favorites every month?

CANDEE: No, it depends on what kind of shows they did that week. Sometimes we have themed performances with costumes and stuff. Usually the girl who has done a really raunchy performance wins. We are rated on different categories, though, so Lara, Gilly, and I usually get [voted as] the best overall dancer every month. Which is nice because that means an extra $200 in our paycheck, and so we get "overtime," so to speak. It's all based on how the men rate us. Really, we are working to gain votes from the men. If we become favorites, we earn more money.

SHELLEY: How long have you been working here at the Waterfront Club?

CANDEE: Less than a year. I think about seven months.

SHELLEY: Is this your first job as an exotic dancer?

CANDEE: Uh huh.

SHELLEY: How did you get started here?

CANDEE: My ex-boyfriend is the bartender here. You remember Russell, the guy I lived with after I left Jason? He got me a job as a hostess. After like a month [laughs] I decided I wanted to dance.

SHELLEY: What's up with you and Jason?

CANDEE: He couldn't stand that I was a dancer, so we broke up.

SHELLEY: Oh, so you're single right now?

CANDEE: Yep. So anyway, I talked to Sam [the club owner] and he told me my boobs were too small [laughs], so I went out and got a boob job so I could start dancing.

SHELLEY: So you had to get breast implants to get the job?

CANDEE: Yes, it was one of the conditions of employment, or so they said, to be at least a B-cup.

SHELLEY: Interesting. Did they pay for it or at least part of it?

CANDEE: *No!* I had to fork out all the money, and it is *not* cheap. We have to pay for all our own outfits, too. But I have totally made back the amount plus in the past couple of months. Plus, having bigger breasts has lots of benefits.

SHELLEY: Does it? Like what?

CANDEE: You get so much more attention from men. Not always positive attention, but attention. I love it. I mean, sometimes they aren't even looking at your face when they talk to you. It's crazy. Free drinks, better tips, getting into other clubs for free. I've even had guys just come up and grab them. Or you tell someone they are fake. I'm really open about it. And [so] they want to touch them and squeeze them to feel the difference [laughs]. Some people are unreal [both laugh].

SHELLEY: Is this your only job?

CANDEE: Yeah, I used to work as a bank teller about a year ago. I quit that job because I wanted a job where I could meet people. Then I was a waitress at Su Casa, but they tried to get me to

PERSONAL ACCOUNT: A Stripper Mom Tells Her Story (cont.)

work these insane hours all the time and I can't do that because of Keith. I go to school though. . . . I am almost done now. I graduate next semester with a degree in nursing.

SHELLEY: So what made you decide go to into this line of work?

CANDEE: Nothing really. I mean it's better money, that's for sure. It is quick, easy money. I get paid to let guys eye me up [and down]. I just get up there and dance around for a few minutes. It's quick and easy! I don't have to work much to earn the money I do. That's good for school too. I can study more.

SHELLEY: Do you think you will continue to strip after you get your degree?

CANDEE: Oh, definitely. I love it. I probably won't even look for a nursing job until I'm too old and falling apart to be an exotic dancer [laughs]. This is such a fun job and it's the sort of job that you keep until you literally can't do it any more. Which means the customers aren't into you any more. They just fired a girl because the men said she was starting to look "too sloppy" and they weren't interested in seeing her dance.

SHELLEY: Getting back to why you dance, it seems you do it both because of the money and because you enjoy it.

CANDEE: Well, yes, I love the money. But it's really important that you enjoy what you are doing. If you don't, the customers will notice and you won't appear as attractive. You have to present this certain degree of sexuality and it is hard to do it if you aren't having a good time up on stage. It is really obvious when we hire new girls and they are very uncomfortable or shy up on stage. They just won't go for it. Or nights that are amateur night. Basically, anyone can come in here and hop up on stage. Some girls are having a good time. The men are cheering them and whatnot. However, there are some girls, most likely ones who had their boyfriends talk them into it, and [they are so bad that] the guys practically boo them off the stage. Confidence is everything in this business.

SHELLEY: So you have amateur night?

CANDEE: Oh, yeah, twice a month. Anyone can come in here and do a number. Well, only females.

SHELLEY: Does that usually draw a big crowd?

CANDEE: *Yes!* Men love to see girls who barely know what they are doing up there, shaking their ass around [and] flashing their breasts. Some girls will go up there in groups. The guys always get into that. They all want to see girls dancing all over each other. I remember this one time there were these two younger girls up there [on stage] and they were, well, let's say we had to end it because they broke the rules. They were about two seconds from having hard-core sex on stage. Of course the guys loved it, but that is against the rules.

SHELLEY: Does the club have a lot of rules?

CANDEE: As far as amateur nights go, the girls have to be at least 18, with some kind of identification to prove that, and they are not allowed to remove all of their clothes. The managers generally persuade them to dance only topless [that is, not to remove their panties] simply because once they leave the club, they have no protection or anything. Some of the guys in here are real weirdoes. [She imitates gagging herself with one finger down her throat and she rolls her eyes. Shelley laughs.] Apparently a few years back there were stalker incidents. So now the club makes all amateur dancers sign a waiver [to the effect] that the club will not be held responsible for any repercussions as a result of their routine.

SHELLEY: What are some of the rules for the regular strippers?

CANDEE: Just the typical rules for any strip club.

SHELLEY: And those are? You'll have to pardon my ignorance. I've never really been to an adult entertainment club before.

CANDEE: [Laughs almost hysterically.] An adult entertainment club! Wow! We call it a strip club just like anyone else. That's like all these people who refer to us as exotic dancers. I'm a

PERSONAL ACCOUNT: A Stripper Mom Tells Her Story (cont.)

damn stripper and I'm fine with that! Don't make it out to be more than it is. You know, spice it up to sound more decent. Stripping is a dirty job. We might as well admit it.

SHELLEY: [Laughs to herself.] So, like I said, what are the rules for regular dancers?

CANDEE: OK, for one, we are not allowed to have any kind of intimate skin-to-skin contact with the men. I can run my hand down his chest or something like that outside his shirt, but I couldn't reach down his pants or something like that. They [the men] are in no way allowed to touch or fondle us. They know that. We have to keep everything shaved, including our, um, equipment [pubic area].

SHELLEY: Interesting.

CANDEE: Yeah, well, that's what the men like.

SHELLEY: As far as the touching, as I look around, it is obvious this club allows personal lap dancing.

CANDEE: Oh, yes, we get a lot of these. We have a room in the back. [It costs] a hundred bucks just to get in there for a private dance. You can have more than one stripper at a time in there, but you have to pay more for each girl. Some guys come in here and request the same stripper every time. I have a few guys like that. They come in here and always request me. They are great. It's nice to have regulars. They are real good tippers, plus they know the rules.

SHELLEY: Are the rules always followed?

CANDEE: No. The customers and the dancers break the rules all the time. That's how we make the good money. You know, you get some guy who buys a private lap dance and you let him feel your tits or [you] play with his dick for a few minutes and you get a huge tip. Usually these guys are total losers or married and their wives aren't sexual. So they come in here and we make them feel special, real special. Some bending of the rules is expected, I guess. . . . Occasionally, we will get some pervert in here who wants a cheap thrill and completely mauls a dancer. But the bouncers here jump right in and kick them

out. They [the club managers and the bouncers] generally don't tolerate that kind of thing. As far as table dances [are concerned], we have to be more discreet. If the bouncers see us getting too friendly with a guy, they will end it. A lot of times, the guy will jerk off while we freak in their lap to disguise what they are doing. These guys generally tip big and we don't even have to touch them, so that's always nice.

SHELLEY: Wow, so a lot goes on sort of undercover?

CANDEE: Oh, yeah, definitely.

SHELLEY: So how much do you make on average a night?

CANDEE: Hmmm, if I am doing straight sets, which means I'm not available for table dances or private dances, I make about $500 a night. But if I am doing table and private dances, I can double that easy.

SHELLEY: How often do you go beyond the call of duty or bend the rules to make a little extra?

CANDEE: Shit, all the time!

SHELLEY: I've heard that Waterfront is kind of a rough club? What are your thoughts on that?

CANDEE: Like I said, we occasionally get some jackass in here. Or we get the younger college-aged guys who are total jerks and are looking for a piece of ass. But in general, it's not too bad. I've never had any huge problems.

SHELLEY?   Not any huge problems, huh? Any minor problems?

CANDEE: Well, of course, I've had my share of stalkers who follow me home and want my number and want to date me. We all have those.

SHELLEY: What are some of the other problems with this line of work?

CANDEE: Well, the simple fact that you are a stripper sort of stigmatizes you, especially when you have a child. You know, you tell someone, "Hey, I'm a stripper," and they think, "Oh my God, I better call child welfare services" and whatnot. Please! I don't think my job affects my personal life.

PERSONAL ACCOUNT: A Stripper Mom Tells Her Story (cont.)

SHELLEY: Would you say the benefits outweigh the problems?

CANDEE: Oh, yeah, for sure.

SHELLEY: So let's go back to the fact that you are a working mother.

CANDEE: Don't think because I am a stripper that I am not a good mother. I take care of my son.

SHELLEY: I wasn't going to go that route, Candee. I was actually going to ask how this job has affected him, if at all.

CANDEE: How do you mean?

SHELLEY: Well, OK, does he even know what you do at work?

CANDEE: Well, he is only five so I don't think he fully understands what mommy does at work. He's been here [at the club] a few times. You know, I sometimes stop by to pick up a paycheck or something, and he has come in. Sure, there is a half-naked woman on stage, shaking her stuff, but he is too little to understand. It's funny because at school, they did drawings of their parents, and he attempted to draw me naked like he's seen on stage. I thought it was cute, but I got called to school and they totally chewed me out about being irresponsible.

SHELLEY: Where is Keith while you are working?

CANDEE: Well, on weekends, he is with Jason [his father]. Other times, I find him babysitters.

SHELLEY: Does he go to a lot of different babysitters?

CANDEE: Well, not really. There are a few guys I've met at the club who come to my apartment and watch him for me.

SHELLEY: Are these guys former customers?

CANDEE: Former and current. They are nice guys, though. I trust them.

SHELLEY: So you're saying you let your customers get involved in your personal life?

CANDEE: To be honest, they are guys I've either dated or just slept with. Sometimes after they

babysit for me, they spend the night, sometimes they don't. It all depends on whether they are going to be paid in cash or, well, to be blunt, sexual favors. If I don't feel like paying them, they will stay the night. Other times I am not in the mood and I've got to pay them. It's a win-win situation. [Laughs slyly.]

SHELLEY: Uh, don't you have a one-bedroom apartment?

CANDEE: Yes.

SHELLEY: Well, where is Keith when these guys are spending the night?

CANDEE: He's in the [bed]room.

SHELLEY: And where are you having sex with these men?

CANDEE: Here's there, but he doesn't know what's going on. Well, maybe he does a little [laughs]. I took him to his grandparents and got a call that he was playing with a massager and moaning, saying things like, "Oh, yeah, ohhh, yeahhh, baby!" But these are little things.

SHELLEY: So how does your family react to your being a stripper?

CANDEE: They didn't know I was stripping for a long time until my dad came across my pictures on the web. Just shows that he can't hate me for it. I mean, he was the one looking at it on the Internet. Of course, I got a lecture from my stepmom. I don't really talk to my mother though. Judy [her stepmother] hates me for it. She has called social services a few times on me. But then again, so have neighbors and [representatives of her son's] school. Everyone else who knows really doesn't want to discuss it. They hide it from the rest of the family. Not a lot of my family knows about it. It doesn't really bother me that they hate it that I strip. I am happy doing it and I can better support my kid.

SHELLEY: So, to wrap things up, how would you say stripping has impacted your life?

CANDEE: Well, I definitely have more money, I have an endless supply of men who want me,

PERSONAL ACCOUNT: A Stripper Mom Tells Her Story (cont.)

I have a nicer car and apartment, I live in a nice area, Keith has clothes and shoes he likes. Materially, it has improved. I am so much less stressed out now that I don't have to constantly try to make ends meet. Life just seems easier.

SHELLEY: So, overall, things have worked out for the better [as a result of] choosing to be a stripper?

CANDEE: Definitely.

SHELLEY: Even with the stigma and problems with customers?

CANDEE: Yep.

SHELLEY: Would you consider your behavior deviant? Because most of society would agree that being a stripper, especially while being a mother, is deviant.

CANDEE: I wouldn't say it is deviant. Maybe a little unconventional. How many working mothers do you know are strippers? Probably not many, if any. The point is, the only true relevance is how I feel about myself being a stripper. It doesn't matter what society thinks. As long as I can go home to my kid at the end of the night and feel good about what I've just done, then screw society.

QUESTIONS

Do you think that Candee's belief that stripping is not deviant is realistic? What indicators would you use to determine whether a given activity is deviant or conventional? Is how the actor feels about an act the only "true relevance" of an act's deviant status? Is it always possible to say, "screw society"? How does the general society see or "construct" stripping and strippers? Is Candee's justification for stripping—that she is a single mom and has to take care of her son—convincing? Why or why not? If you had to guess, would you think that her lifestyle is harmful to her son—or not? Realistically speaking, when Candee completes her education in nursing, do you believe she will stop stripping? What might be some possible explanations for stripping? Who does it and why? In what sorts of societies does stripping flourish? In what sorts of societies is it rare or nonexistent? Which is more interesting to you—the constructionist's approach to stripping or the positivist's? Is either one the only correct explanation or approach? Does one being correct mean the other is wrong?

CHAPTER 3

Explaining Deviant Behavior: Positivist Theories

The earliest theories of wrongdoing—what sociologists now call deviant behavior—typically concentrated on the question: *Why do they do it?* Why adultery, witchcraft, thievery, disobedience to authority, insanity?

In addition to deviant behavior, since religious dogma was much more important in the past than it is today, members of societies hundreds or even thousands of years ago also wondered about deviant *beliefs* and their expression: Why heresy? Why blasphemy? Why unbelief? Why godlessness?

And third, since undesirable *physical characteristics* were thought to be a consequence or product of evil deeds or thoughts, people in the past asked questions such as: Why are some of us afflicted with the curse of leprosy? What causes birth defects? Why are some women "barren," or childless? What causes blindness, albinism, curvature of the spine, dwarfism, extreme ugliness, and any manner of undesirable traits?

In short, members of societies in the past attempted to account for the deviant "ABCs" I mentioned in Chapter 1—attitudes, behavior, and conditions (Adler and Adler, 2003, p. 8).

Although the explanations that were devised in earlier times were inadequate or fallacious from today's vantage point, they all centered around an effort to account for anomalous and inexplicable phenomena—undesirable differentness that needed explaining. They cannot be referred to as "positivistic" theories because they lacked the essential ingredients of scientific theories: They were not empirical—that is, they could not be falsified by observable evidence of any kind. And they were not theoretical; they did not offer a satisfying, materialistic or scientific cause-and-effect account of how certain behavior, beliefs, or traits came to be. But the important point is that, however crude from today's vantage point, past theories of wrongdoing *did* ask "*Why do they do it?*" This sort of question has ancient roots.

Current positivistic theories of deviance have this same quality; they attempt to *explain* or *account for* deviance. In this chapter, I will discuss causal, explanatory, or positivistic theories that ask "Why do they do it?" (or, in one case, "Why *don't* they do it?"). In contrast, the constructionist concerns, those that focus on the issue of why rules and laws are made and what accounts for reactions to breaking rules and laws, are much more recent.

I will save a discussion of perspectives that examine *reactions* to rule-breaking for the next chapter. As I said earlier, contemporary sociological theories that attempt to explain deviance nearly always focus on behavior, only occasionally deal with belief, and, by their very nature, *almost never* address involuntarily acquired characteristics, such as shortness, extreme ugliness, and blindness.

Everywhere and at all times, rules have existed. Wherever there are rules, wherever there are laws, they will be broken, even if only occasionally. Everywhere, virtuous, law-abiding, conventional members of a society wonder what leads some people to engage in acts of wrongdoing—as we saw, aberrant behavior or beliefs such as adultery, blasphemy, theft, witchcraft, heresy, murder, incest, cowardice, treason, suicide, mentally deranged behavior, lying, and so on. Throughout history, speculation as to the cause or causes of wrongdoing has been a major concern of the members of cultures all over the globe. And just about everywhere, explanations and theories as to why some members of society break its rules have been advanced.

Historically, the oldest explanation for deviant behavior has been *demonic possession*. For many thousands of years, evil spirits, including the devil, were thought to cause men and women to engage in socially unacceptable behavior. A half-million years ago, Stone Age humans drilled holes into the skulls of individuals who engaged in wrongdoing of some kind—who, today, would be recognized as being mentally ill—so that evil spirits could escape; indeed, this procedure was still practiced as late as the 1600s. The ancient Hebrews, Egyptians, Greeks, and Romans performed rites of exorcism to cast out demonic beings dwelling in the body and soul of transgressors. During the Renaissance in Europe (roughly, the early 1400s to the early 1600s), hundreds of thousands of women and men were burned at the stake for "consorting" with the devil and engaging in wicked deeds. Thus, among both the fairly well educated and much of the mass of society, the theory of demonic possession was a dominant explanation for wrongdoing in Europe almost half a millennium ago, and in the Salem colony in Massachusetts in the 1600s. Among intellectuals, by the 1700s in Western Europe and North America, this explanation had almost completely died out.

Of course, demonic possession has always been accepted among some segments of the public as a plausible explanation of evil deeds and beliefs, and it still is today. Frank Schmalleger taught at a small university in the South's Bible Belt. On the last day of class in a criminology course, after covering the usual explanations of crime, he asked his class how many students thought that biological theories best explained the causes of crime. Only one or two students raised a hand. Psychological theories? Roughly the same number. Sociological theories? A few more, but not many. Finally, in exasperation, he asked: "How many of you believe that 'the devil made him do it' is the best explanation for crime that we can offer?" In response, almost all the students in the class raised their hands (1996, p. 88). Although very few if any academics or researchers support the theory of demonology, it seems to be alive and well among some segments of the general public. As I said above, demonological theories are not scientific, and hence, they cannot be regarded as examples of positivism.

The term "positivism" is used by different observers and commentators in different ways. I refer to positivism as any approach that is *empirical*, that is, that takes the data of the senses (aided by instruments and theoretical coherence) as the only valid source of scientific information; that is *objectivistic*, that believes that categories have an independent existence in the world as concrete realities; that attempts to go beyond specifics and particulars and seeks *generalizations*; and that is *deterministic*, that is, believes that the job of the scientist is to explain material cause-and-effect relations between and among variables. According to this definition, *all* the approaches discussed in this chapter are positivistic in that they share the four assumptions of empiricism, objectivism, generality, and cause-and-effect determinism.

FREE WILL, RATIONAL CALCULATION, AND ROUTINE ACTIVITIES THEORY

The first sophisticated and academically respectable perspective or theory of criminal or deviant behavior is the "free will" or classical school of criminology (Vold, Bernard, and

Snipes, 2002, pp. 14–20); it is associated with the names of Cesare Beccaria (1738–1794), an Italian scholar, and Jeremy Bentham (1748–1832), an English jurist and philosopher. The period of the eighteenth century in Europe is generally referred to as the Age of Enlightenment or the Age of Reason. (However, in spite of its impressive title, much of what eighteenth-century leaders did or thought does not seem very "enlightened" or "reasonable" to us today!)

By the 1700s, then, philosophers and other intellectuals had abandoned the idea of the intervention of the devil and other evil, diabolical spirits to explain worldly phenomena and, instead, concentrated on material or worldly forces. Rather than being seen as a result of seduction by demons, the violations of rules, norms, and laws were thought to be caused by *free will*—a rational calculation of pleasure versus pain. Individuals choose among a number of alternative courses of action according to benefits they believe will accrue to them. They tend to avoid activities they believe will bring them more pain than pleasure. This model, then, sees people, criminals included, as free, rational, and hedonistic. Actions that bring pleasure to a person will be enacted and continued; those that are painful will be abandoned. Or so eighteenth-century rationalists believed. The way to ensure conformity to society's norms and laws, therefore, is to apprehend and punish offenders with celerity (or certainty), swiftness, and just enough severity to make the pain following a violation greater than the pleasure the actor derived from it. The celerity, swiftness, and severity of punishment will deter crime, these theorists argued.

The classical school made a number of assumptions that are now recognized as false. It ignored obvious disparities in wealth and power, and thereby failed to recognize forces that make certain kinds of crimes more likely among the poor and less likely among the rich. In addition, we now see that people are not completely rational in their behavior; they engage in deviance and crime for a number of reasons aside from pursuing pleasure and avoiding pain. In addition, what is pleasurable to one person may be painful to another, and vice versa. Homosexuality and heterosexuality provide relevant examples here: To someone who enjoys intercourse solely with members of the same sex, intercourse with a member of the opposite sex would not be pleasurable. Hence, to apply across-the-board penalties for offenses is likely to deter some potential offenders but not others. Moreover, most of the time when a rule or a law is violated, the offender is not caught, thereby nullifying one of the theory's major factors, certainty or celerity, making the offender's calculation of pleasure and pain far more complicated than these early thinkers imagined. In addition, detection of crimes and enforcement of laws are quite often erratic, thus muddying the cost-benefit analysis the potential criminal must make. Overall, as it was originally formulated, the classical school of criminology held a faulty model of human behavior.

The free-will perspective has made something of a comeback in recent years in more sophisticated forms than its original version. The rationality school and the strictly economic model (Becker, 1968; Cohen, Felson, and Land, 1980; Clarke and Felson, 1993) are based on some of the classical school's basic assumptions. Unlike the classical school, these contemporary models do not encompass all crimes within their scope; they tend, instead, to focus specifically on *economic* crimes.

The most often cited and discussed of all the contemporary free-will or rationality theories is referred to as *routine activities theory*. Routine activities theory argues that criminal behavior will take place when and where there is a conjunction of three elements or factors: the *motivated offender*, a *suitable target*, and the *absence of a capable guardian*. The most remarkable feature of this theory is that it makes a radical break with nearly all the other rationality theories in that it dispenses with criminal motivation. The "motivated offender" is very much in the background, a given—simply *assumed* by the theory. There will always be plenty of people who are motivated to break the law if that is profitable to them. Criminal behavior, the theory argues, is a *purposive* and *rational* means of attaining an end—that is, acquiring money more efficiently than by any other method. People tend to act according to the *utility* that the outcome of their actions has for them. Other things being equal, if homeowners leave a house unoccupied and a door unlocked, their house is more likely to be burglarized than if

they stayed in the house, locked the doors, installed burglar alarms, and kept a large guard dog. Many, no doubt most, people would not burglarize the house in the latter case because their utility is not maximized by the burglary. But for this theory to work, there's no need to conjecture about the presence of "motivated offenders," since *enough* of them will be around to make predictions about a higher likelihood of burglary under specified circumstances correct.

The theory focuses mainly on *opportunities* for committing crime—and by extension, a great deal of deviant behavior as well. (In contrast, the theory does not address deviant beliefs or conditions at all.) A "suitable target" could be money, property, even the opportunity to engage in a certain activity that might be deemed desirable by a motivated offender. And the "absence of a capable guardian" would refer to the fact that formal or informal agents of social control are not operative in a particular situation. Hence, for instance, if a potential rapist encounters a woman alone, in a physical setting in which she can be threatened or overpowered, the likelihood that a rape will take place is greater than if she were accompanied. To the extent that corporate behavior is not monitored by or accountable to government or any other social control agencies, then corporate crime is more likely to take place than if these control systems are operative. Married couples are more likely to engage in adultery when they are in private situations with desirable partners away from the gaze of their spouses or other parties who would report their behavior to their spouses. The theory would predict that unfettered access to illicit drugs would translate into vastly higher rates of use than is currently the case; that in the absence of video cameras, store guards, and the prying eyes of salesclerks, shoplifting would be much more common than it is now; and that cheating on exams would be more likely in the absence of watchful professors, observant teaching assistants, and honest fellow students. In other words, many more of us would engage in nonnormative— or *deviant*—behavior if "capable guardians" were not watching over us and able to sanction our potential wrongdoing than if they were.

The model is useful for predicting deviant and criminal behavior in a fairly crude, gross, or global fashion, but it is not as useful for a more fine-grained or close-up look at the causes of deviance and crime. In fact, rationalistic theories do not so much attempt to explain deviance and crime as take the "motivated offender" for granted and focus on the conditions that bring him or her out of the woodwork. Although rationality certainly enters into the crime and deviance equation, the fact that jails, prisons, and reform schools are full of young and not-so-young men (and women) who committed crimes impulsively, without planning, and got caught as a consequence, indicates that at the very least their calculation of whether one or more capable guardians were in the picture is faulty. Clearly, the free-will factor alone is not a totally viable explanation. The fact is, *most* individuals who commit crimes to make money could have earned more, in the long run, by working at a low-paying drudge job. Clearly, some other explanation is necessary; apparently, the thrill, excitement, and self-righteousness that much criminal behavior entails is at least as powerfully motivating as the rational acquisition of money or engaging in self-evidently satisfying acts (Katz, 1988). At the same time—even for "irrational" actors who seek more than a concrete goal such as money—opportunity is related to the enactment of deviance. For *all* actors and for *all* activities, the greater the perceived payoff and the lower the likelihood of apprehension and punishment, the greater the likelihood that deviance will be enacted. (For an argument that asserts that rationality theories such as routine activities theory are not positivistic, see Gottfredson and Hirschi, 1990, pp. 22ff.).

SOCIAL DISORGANIZATION AND THE CHICAGO SCHOOL

Prior to the 1920s, the dominant approach to the study of normative violations was *social pathology*. Its central assumption is that some individuals caused problems for the society because they refused to or were incapable of abiding by conventional norms. The social disorganization school represented a striking advance beyond this simplistic view.

Just after World War I, a school of thought emerged out of research that was conducted in the city of Chicago by professors and graduate students at the University of Chicago. Chicago sociology, in fact, came to be the sociology of Chicago (Downes and Rock, 2003, pp. 53ff.). This school came to view the factors that explained deviance and crime as being located not in the person or individual, as nineteenth-century thinkers believed, but in the social structure. In other words, it *rejected* the nineteenth-century positive school's argument that the cause of criminality lay in the biologically defective individual. The Chicago School argued that *entire neighborhoods* become so disorganized that adapting to them entailed engaging in certain forms of deviant behavior. And it was urbanization that set the stage for social disorganization. As cities grew, their residents increasingly came into contact with strangers. This encouraged impersonality, social distance, and a decline in social harmony. People no longer shared the same values or cared about how others felt about them and what they did. As a city grows, its sense of community breaks down. And as social disorganization in a given neighborhood or community increases, deviant behavior increases along with it (Park, 1926; Traub and Little, 1999, pp. 63–67).

Not all neighborhoods are equally disorganized, however; therefore, rates of deviance and crime vary from one area, neighborhood, and community to another. Certain neighborhoods of a city "give licence to nonconforming behavior" (Suchar, 1978, p. 74). Why? What is it about certain neighborhoods that makes them hospitable to delinquency, crime, and deviant behavior? Social disorganization theorists locate the mechanism influencing nonconforming behavior in *land values*. Dwelling units in neighborhoods with low rental and property value are regarded as undesirable and unattractive to live in. Hence, such dwelling units tend to attract residents with two characteristics.

First, they are geographically unstable. Proponents of the Chicago School referred to such neighborhoods as *zones of transition*. Residents of these areas invest little emotionally in the neighborhood, and move out as soon as they can.

And second, such residents are socially, racially, and ethnically heterogeneous; hence, they do not cohere into a unified and organized community. Residents who do not sink roots into the community in which they live do not care about its fate or what happens in them. Residents who are very different from one another do not care about the evaluations that others make of their behavior.

Socially disorganized neighborhoods are unable to develop "strong formal and informal linkages" among their residents; hence, residents find it difficult to "regulate the behavior of their fellow neighbors" and exercise the kind of social control that would discourage delinquency, crime, and deviant behavior (Bursik and Grasmick, 1993, pp. x, 7). In short, Chicago sociologists insisted that deviance varies systematically by physical and geographical *location*. Where somebody is located residentially determines the likelihood of that person committing deviant and criminal acts. The structural characteristics of a neighborhood—that is, whether it possesses the properties mentioned above—determine its crime rate. Deviance is relatively absent in certain neighborhoods and extremely frequent, even routine, in others. The Chicago School placed a heavy emphasis on *social ecology*—the view that physical spacing and social interdependence determine, or at least heavily influence, human behavior.

The most important factor in the social disorganization school is, interestingly enough, very closely related to one of routine activity's key explanatory variables: the absence of a capable guardian. Social disorganization is the "macro" equivalent of the many "micro" factors that do or do not guard a "suitable target." It is *entire neighborhoods* that have lost the ability, the will, or the power to monitor and sanction behavior their residents consider untoward and nonnormative. When drug dealers move into an abandoned building, the community does not root them out—or lacks the clout with the police department to have them displaced. Prostitutes are permitted to patrol the streets, harass residents, and engage in sex in cars without local interference. Junkies shoot up on front stoops, homeless men urinate in hallways, burglars routinely rip off apartments and clean out their contents—and little or nothing is done to stop them. For the criminal and the deviant, a socially disorganized neighborhood is their playground. Clearly, such a community is the "absence of a capable guardian" writ large.

The Chicago School was charged with what came to be regarded as a middle-class bias; that is, it assumed that behavior that departed from that of comfortable, respectable, small-town folk was "disorganized." Its researchers failed to see that many socially disapproved activities are frequently committed as much by the affluent, middle-class members of society as by representatives of the lower and working classes. The Chicago sociologists made the erroneous assumption that deviance was almost exclusively an underclass phenomenon. They examined street prostitution without considering the middle-class call girl, the skid row alcoholic but not the affluent drunk, the street narcotic addict but not the middle-class recreational drug user.

It must be emphasized that the school's generalizations apply almost exclusively to delinquency and to the more traditional common-law or "primal" crimes. Their applicability to many of the forms of deviance we'll be examining is far more tenuous. For instance, do they explain homosexuality? Of course not; in fact, with homosexuality, in many ways, the causal process works in a fashion that is precisely the *opposite* of that which social disorganization theory would predict. That is, in many large cities of the world, a substantial number of homosexuals gravitate *to* certain neighborhoods whose residents are less likely to harass them than those in the neighborhoods they left. Thus, here, in a sense, the dependent and independent variables are reversed. (It's even possible that in low-rent districts, where crime can often gain a foothold, homosexuality would be even *less* acceptable than in more affluent communities!) And, while the concomitants of social disorganization in a given community may contribute to alcoholism, just as likely, the streets of a disorganized community become a kind of magnet for homeless alcoholics.

White-collar and corporate crime receive no illumination whatsoever from social disorganization theory, of course. In fact, it is in the more affluent and *least* disorganized communities that the corporate offender is most likely to live! And while the most virulent forms of drug abuse and addiction can almost certainly be accounted for by a revamped version of social disorganization theory—that is, one that takes into account power and external political and economic factors—the more casual, recreational forms of drug use that were so common from the 1970s on remain unexplained by the Chicago School's approach. Are any of the forms of deviance that fall under the umbrella of "cognitive" deviance explained by social disorganization? It seems unlikely.

The Chicago School of deviance, with its emphasis on social disorganization, had its heyday between the two world wars, roughly from 1920 to 1940. By the end of World War II, it was widely regarded as obsolete. In 1987, a sociologist claimed that the social disorganization school "has been soundly dismissed" (Unnever, 1987, p. 845).

However, in the late 1980s and early 1990s, the social disorganization school made a comeback; a substantial volume of research and writing on deviance is making use of the Chicago School's approach, concepts, and theories. Although it will never regain its former dominant status in the field, social disorganization theory is experiencing a renaissance. However, to reenergize this approach, some theoretical reformulations were necessary.

What the early social disorganization theorists did not entirely grasp was the dimension of power and its relevance for their analysis. They never figured out how important decisions made at the top of the power structure were for the life of the community. A municipality can build a highway that cuts a community in two, destroying contact between residents in the two halves. Bridges, highways, commercial buildings, housing projects, parks, and beaches are often built in these neighborhoods, and serve to disrupt and destroy the foundation of once-viable communities. Factories can be moved from one community to another, siphoning jobs away from the first into the second. Tax breaks and "sweetheart" deals can be extended to builders who tear down small houses inhabited by families with modest incomes to build big buildings that can be afforded only by residents who are rich. Zoning ordinances and variances are designed and implemented to favor certain interests over others. They reflect the exercise of power, and they influence the lives of residents of certain neighborhoods and communities. The fact is, the fate of communities and the behavior of their residents is tied to political and economic realities. A community's

ties to the municipal, state, and federal power structure was not considered by the early social disorganization theorists. Contemporary theorists are looking at deviance, crime, and other phenomena in part through the lens of the social disorganization perspective; social disorganization is being revived, but with a sharper, tougher, power-oriented edge. The idea of community control of deviance is being given a political thrust, which it did not have in the 1930s (Feagin and Parker, 1990; Currie, 1993).

Thus, the classic or original social disorganization perspective did not take a number of factors or developments into consideration that current research indicates are crucial in the neighborhood-crime equation. Rather than seeing these deficiencies as fatal, however, some sociologists argue that the neglected factors or developments can be *grafted onto* the social disorganization perspective to produce a still-viable approach to the study of crime, delinquency, and deviance. The first of these is the recognition that a *reciprocal* relationship between crime and disorganization may exist. That is, a high level of crime in a community may act as an independent variable, leading to an increase in a neighborhood's lack of desirability, disorder, and economic decline, thereby acting back on disorganization, which, in turn, increases its crime rate (Skogan, 1986, 1990). The original Chicago School theorists did not consider the possibility that there could be a two-way street between disorganization and crime; considering that possibility strengthens the perspective.

Second, the social disorganization school of the 1920s and 1930s pictured areas of a city as stable, their crime rate being a function of their desirability, which, in turn, was a function of their land values. Waves of succeeding ethnic groups move into and out of them, but their socioeconomic composition results from the range of economic choices available to their residents. But recent research in urban sociology has shown that areas of cities are not necessarily stable—that many experience huge swings in fortune over time; some become "gentrified," with affluent residents moving in and less affluent ones moving out, while in others, there is a decline in economic fortune (Bursik and Grasmick, 1993, pp. 49–51).

In addition, many observers saw something of the same middle-class bias in social disorganization's view of deviance and crime as the earlier social pathology perspective displayed. Single-parent families are bad for children, illegitimacy is bad, drugs are bad, prostitution is bad, immigrants have to be socialized to mainstream, middle-class American values, and so on. Much of the field reacted against these biases. Today, progressives are rethinking their views on how some forms of deviance and crime impact on the life of the community. Much of what the social disorganization theorists said so long ago seems to be making sense.

One has only to listen to the voices of African-American politicians to appreciate what crime does to a community's viability. When the police have become corrupt and cynical, when drug dealing is blatant, incursive, and voracious, when criminal homicide becomes the leading cause of death among young, urban Black males, when children are gunned down on the street in a crossfire between rival gangs, when middle- and working-class people with jobs leave the community for more peaceful neighborhoods and the children who remain have few employed adult role models—it is difficult to invoke the argument that we are resorting to preachy middle-class moralism when we examine the impact of deviance and crime. These are life-and-death issues; it has become necessary to consider how crime can be kept from victimizing and destroying the community. In short, the sense of communalism, which was once regarded as a conservative value, is being revived, brushed up, and given a progressive slant. Some observers now feel the Chicago School's "bias" may have been right all along.

A major contribution of the social disorganization or Chicago School was *empathy*: It asked readers to imagine that deviants, delinquents, and criminals were people much like themselves (Pfohl, 1994, p. 209). Since it located the cause of deviance not in biological defect but in neighborhood dislocation, the social disorganization school forced us all to realize that, in the shifting tide and fortune of an evolving society, we, too, could have been caught up in the process of ecological transition. Deviants are the way they are as a result of the fact that they are "disproportionately exposed to the disruptive forces of rapid social change"

(p. 209). If the rest of us had been exposed to the same forces, we might very well have ended up doing or being the same thing.

Anomie or Strain Theory

Anomie theory was born in 1938 with the publication of Robert Merton's article "Social Structure and Anomie" (1938). Influenced by the nineteenth-century study *Suicide* by French sociologist Emile Durkheim (1858–1917), Merton was struck by the insight that deviant behavior could be caused by a disturbance in the social order, which Durkheim called *anomie*. When a society's stock market crashes and its citizens suddenly experience economic depression, its suicide rate increases; however, when a society suddenly experiences economic prosperity, its suicide rate also increases. Societies undergoing rapid industrialization experience significant increases in their rates of suicide. After Italy unified in 1870 and Germany in 1871, their suicide rates increased. These changes illustrate *disruptions in the traditional social order*, resulting in a state of anomie, followed by a form of deviance—suicide.

After reading Durkheim, Merton was convinced that states of anomie influenced the frequency of deviant behavior. He argued that anomie must vary from one society to another and from one group or category in the same society; consequently, their rates of deviant behavior must also vary correspondingly. He reasoned that *"social structures exert a definite pressure upon certain persons in the society to engage in nonconforming rather than conforming conduct"* (Merton, 1957, p. 132). Certain pressures, Merton concluded, could produce very *unconventional* behavior from very *conventional* origins and motives. Anomie theory is also referred to as *strain* theory, because it hypothesizes that a certain kind of strain, or pressure, produces deviant behavior.

In fashioning his argument, Merton completely reconceptualized anomie. In fact, in many ways, his theory was almost precisely the *opposite* of Durkheim's. To Durkheim, anomie was a disruption of the social order. It was characterized by a state of normlessness, where norms no longer gripped the populace or held them in check. It is the social order that restrains our behavior and our desires and keeps us from engaging in deviant behavior. To Durkheim, the norms keep deviance in check, and an *absence* of the norms—anomie—results in deviance. When periods of anomie prevailed, the populace was no longer guided by culturally approved appetites. Unlimited greed was the rule; human desires ran rampant. People no longer had any guidelines as to what was permissible and what was not, what was possible and what was not. Their lust for anything imaginable was unleashed.

Merton's conception of anomie was entirely different. In his view, deviance resulted not from a *too-weak* hold of society's norms on actors, as Durkheim's did, but, in a sense, a *too-strong* hold—that is, from actors *following* society's norms. In addition, Merton's conception of anomie was far more specific than Durkheim's. To Merton, anomie was conceptualized as a disjunction between *culturally defined goals* and *structurally available opportunities*. Culturally defined goals are "held out as legitimate objectives for all or for diversely located members of the society" (1957, p. 132). These goals, Merton claims, are widely shared; more or less everyone in the society wishes to attain them. Merton shared Durkheim's view that anomie was instrumental in unleashing greedy behavior—behavior that is directed at attaining goals which, under different circumstances, would not be sought. Behind both Durkheim's and Merton's conceptions of anomie was a loud and vehement voice clamoring, "I want! I want!" However, for Durkheim, what unleashed this voice was a *disruption* of the social order. For Merton, *it was the social order itself* that released this voice. Our greedy and lustful desires are actually *created* by our culture. And it is the gap or *lack of congruence* between the cultural order (that says we must become materially successful) and the social and economic order (which won't give us what we have been socialized to want and expect) that causes deviant behavior.

What are Merton's culturally defined goals? In Western society, including the United States, they are, of course, primarily monetary and material success. "Making it," within the scope of the American Dream, involves being affluent—rich,

if possible. Everyone in this society is bombarded on all sides by messages to achieve, to succeed. And success, for the most part, means only one thing: being able to buy the best that money can buy. This is an almost universal American value, a basic goal toward which nearly everyone aspires and by which nearly everyone is evaluated. A crucial point is that not all societies are so materialistic; some place an emphasis on entirely different goals, such as spirituality, wisdom, or learning.

Every society places certain limitations on how to achieve culturally defined goals. While everyone, or nearly everyone, in our society may value wealth, it is a separate question as to how we are permitted to acquire that wealth. Groups, institutions, and societies differ in their capacity to generate material goals, and in their restrictions as to how members may reach them. For instance, beating up, bribing, or having sexual intercourse with a professor are not considered legitimate means of achieving the goal of receiving an "A" in a course. Although any one of these methods may work from time to time, the social system of higher education in America frowns on them. They are not "acceptable modes" of reaching out for the goal of a high grade in this setting.

In contrast, in another social setting, the importance of the specific means to attain a certain goal may not matter very much; they may be of little or no consequence; the condemnation of certain modes may be mild or nonexistent. Some societies place an extremely heavy emphasis on attaining a given goal, but remain fairly tolerant about just *how* one goes about attaining it. Here we have a case of "winning at any cost." Merton maintains that we have just such a situation in contemporary America. Contemporary culture "continues to be characterized by a heavy emphasis on wealth as a basic symbol of success, without a corresponding emphasis on the legitimate avenues on which to march toward this goal" (1957, p. 139). We have an acquisitive society, in which "considerations of technical expediency" rule supreme. The basic question becomes: "Which of the available procedures is most efficient in netting the culturally approved value?" (1957, p. 135). In other words, it is less important just how one makes it; the important thing, above all, is *making it*.

In contemporary America, we have a conflict between the *culture* (what people are taught to aspire to) and the *social and economic structure* (the opportunities they have to succeed). We have, in other words, a *malintegrated* society. Aspirations cannot possibly be met by the available material resources. While the aspirations of the population are unlimited, their actual chances of success are quite limited. This creates pressure to commit deviance. "It is only when a system of cultural values extols, virtually above all else, certain *common* success-goals *for the population at large* while the social structure rigorously restricts or completely closes access to approved modes of reaching these goals *for a considerable part of that same population*, that deviant behavior ensues on a large scale" (Merton, 1957, p. 134). "It is . . . my central hypothesis," Merton wrote, "that aberrant behavior may be regarded sociologically as a symptom of disassociation between culturally prescribed aspirations and socially structured avenues for realizing these aspirations" (1957, p. 134). By itself, an ambitious monetary goal for the population will not produce a high rate of crime; by itself, the lack of opportunities to achieve that goal, likewise, does not produce a great deal of crime. It is their *combination* or *conjunction* that embues American society with an almost uniquely, almost devastatingly, high predatory crime rate among Western societies.

It should be noted that anomie theory is based on very nearly the *opposite* explanatory factor from that offered by the routine activities and social disorganization theories. Anomie theory tries to explain the motives for nonnormative behavior. It is based on the notion that the desire for material success must be *socialized into us* for deviance to take place. In other words, we need to be given a "push" to deviate. Without the desire to become—and the expectation of becoming—materially successful, our failure to succeed would not produce the necessary deviant "adaptations." In contrast, routine activities and social disorganization theories do not assume that we need to be "pushed" to deviate from society's norms. Instead, they assume that offenders will be in sufficient supply to take advantage of the absence of social control by deviating from the rules or the laws in substantial numbers. In short, anomie theory assumes that it is *deviant behavior* that needs to be explained, while routine activities and social disorganization theories assume it is the *monitoring and sanctioning of illicit behavior* that needs to be explained. But notice: The latter theories are *not* constructionist in their orientation because they *also* explain deviant behavior, but indirectly—through the *absence* of social control. For them, the absence of social control explains deviant behavior.

Another important point: Merton's theory is "macro" in scope, that is, it looks at differences between and among *large social units* such as entire societies in explaining and predicting deviant behavior. The theory does *not* focus on individual or "micro" differences in levels of anomie, and hence, deviant behavior. Merton's theory, for instance, would argue that American society is more anomic than, for example, Portuguese society, since expectations of high levels of material success tend to be much more the rule in the United States. Because of this, the theory would predict that America's rates of deviant behavior would be correspondingly higher. The individualistic version of anomie theory is usually referred to as "strain" theory, and is associated with the researcher Robert Agnew (1992). Here, I focus on Merton's more macro anomie theory rather than Agnew's more micro strain theory.

How do people who are subject to these conflicting pressures adapt to or react to them? What styles of conflict resolution should we expect from people who live within this type of social structure? Just what types of deviance should we predict for success-hungry Americans? Merton drew up a typology of different responses to goal attainment and legitimate versus illegitimate means of attaining these goals.

Conformity, or the *conformist* mode of adaptation, accepts both cultural values of success and the institutionalized, legitimate, or conventional means for reaching these goals. The conformist both strives for material success and chooses law-abiding ways of achieving success. This mode of adaptation is not of interest to the student of deviance except as a negative case. It is in the typology simply for the purpose of comparing it with various forms of deviance. Becoming an accountant, a physician, a lawyer, and striving for material success by becoming successful in one's profession—becoming affluent through a legal, legitimate profession, performed in a law-abiding, respectable fashion—is an example of the most common mode of adaptation: *conformity*. In fact, given the strength of the success values in this society, and given the relatively limited opportunities for genuine success for the population at large—indeed, given that most Americans *fail* to achieve their own standards of material success—it is surprising that so many Americans are conformists when it comes to enacting serious deviance. Conformity is not, in any case, deviance.

The mode of adaptation Merton called *innovation* involves accepting the goal of success but choosing to achieve it in an illegal, illegitimate, or deviant fashion. This adaptation is clearly the most interesting of all modes to Merton; he devoted more space to describing it than to all the other modes combined. The innovative mode of adaptation occurs when someone has "assimilated the cultural emphasis upon the goal without internalizing the institutionalized norms governing ways and means for its attainment" (1957, p. 141). An innovative mode of adaptation to the pressures of American culture and society would encompass most types of money-making criminal activities—for example, white-collar crime, embezzlement, pickpocketing, running a confidence game, bank robbery, burglary, prostitution, and pimping.

In contrast, *ritualism* entails "the abandoning or scaling down of the lofty cultural goals of great pecuniary success and rapid social mobility," but abiding "almost compulsively by institutionalized norms" (1957, pp. 149–150). The ritualist plays it safe, plays by the book, doesn't take chances. The mode of ritualism as an adaptation to American society's heavy emphasis on success is a kind of *partial* withdrawal—an abandonment of the goal of success, but a *retention* of the *form* of doing things properly, following all the rules to the letter. In many ways, ritualism is a kind of *overconformity*. "It is, in short, the mode of adaptation of individually seeking a *private* escape from the dangers and frustrations which seem to them inherent in the competition for major goals and clinging all the more closely to the safe routines and the institutionalized norms" (p. 151). A petty bureaucrat, who insists that all rules and regulations be followed in every detail, would exemplify this

mode of adaptation. In this case, the rules are adhered to, but their purpose—presumably, serving the public—has been forgotten, in fact, *subverted* by a rigid adherence to the rules.

Retreatism is a rejection of both goals and institutionalized means. It is a total cop-out, a "retreat" from the things that the society values most. Retreatists are "true aliens." "Not sharing the common frame of values, they can be included as members of the *society* (in distinction from the *population*) only in a fictional sense." In this category Merton places "some of the adaptive activities of psychotics, autists, pariahs, outcasts, vagrants, vagabonds, tramps, chronic drunkards, and drug addicts" (1957, p. 153). This mode occurs, with most who adopt it, because the individual adopts the success value but fails to attain it—being unwilling or unable to use illegitimate means, or is a failure even after attempting to achieve success by using illegitimate means. Retreatism, in short, is brought on by repeated failure, such failure causing severe personal conflict. "The conflict is resolved by abandoning *both* precipitating elements—the goals and the means. The escape is complete, the conflict is eliminated, and the individual is asocialized" (pp. 153–154). Merton feels that this mode of adaptation is the least frequently resorted to of those discussed so far.

Rebellion "involves a genuine transvaluation." It is an attempt to deal with the dominant goals and means by overthrowing them altogether. While the retreatist merely rejects them and puts nothing in their place, the rebel renounces prevailing values and introduces an alternative social, political, and economic structure, one in which the current stresses and strains presumably would not exist. The act of launching a revolution would be a clear-cut case of rebellion. Merton devotes the least attention to this mode.

The anomie theory of Robert K. Merton exerted an enormous impact on the field of the sociology of deviance for decades after its initial publication in 1938; Cole and Zuckerman (1964) list more than 80 studies published prior to 1964 that made use of the concept of anomie. (Merton's original article was expanded and reprinted as a chapter in Merton's classic *Social Theory and Social Structure* in 1949, 1957, and 1968.) In fact, it is measurably the most cited work ever written by a sociologist. At the same time, the perspective has attracted considerable criticism.

Middle-Class Bias

Anomie theory, some critics say, suffers from the same middle-class bias that distorted all earlier theories of deviance: It made the assumption that lower and working-class people commit acts of crime and deviance *in general* significantly more frequently than is true of the members of the middle class. Today, most observers readily admit that "street" crime is committed more often by individuals at or toward the bottom of the class structure than is true of those at or near the top. Yet—and here is where the problem enters—there are many criminal and deviant actions that are equally likely, or even more likely, to be engaged in by the more affluent, prestigious, well-educated, and powerful members of society. Although official police statistics on who commits crimes show that crime is a predominantly lower-class phenomenon, it is now clear that the specific crimes that middle and upper-middle-class people commit are those that are far less likely to result in police attention and action than are the ones that lower- and working-class individuals commit. This is especially the case for white-collar and corporate crimes—the crimes of the rich and the powerful. How can we explain the multimillion-dollar swindles perpetrated by extremely wealthy and successful traders on the stock market, for example, by the anomie scheme? Homosexuality is technically illegal in nearly half the states of the United States; it very rarely results in arrest and yet is most decidedly deviant in most social circles. It is a form of deviance that does not vary much by social class; hence, it contradicts Merton's theory that deviance is primarily a product of status frustration.

Irrelevance of Anomie for Most Forms of Deviance

At one point, Merton claims that anomie theory "is designed to account for some, not all, forms of deviant behavior, customarily described as criminal or delinquent" (1957, p. 178). Yet in other places, he makes a case for anomie being

the major cause of deviance in general. Deviance, he says, "is a symptom of disassociation between culturally prescribed aspirations and socially structured avenues for realizing these aspirations" (p. 134). Again, Merton writes, "It is *only* when" goals and means are disjunctive that "*deviant behavior ensues on a large scale*" (p. 146; my emphasis). Though Merton "is vague as to which behavior is covered by this explanation and which is not" (Clinard, 1964b, p. 19), he clearly believes that *rates* of deviance vary by degree of anomie. Consequently, though some forms of deviance may be exempt from the theory (Merton never explains which ones are, however), deviance *in general* is supposedly explained by it.

Although the malintegration between means and goals that characterizes contemporary American society will typically put pressure on many members to engage in certain forms of deviance, *most forms of deviant behavior will not be produced by the pressure of such malintegration.* Merton's theory is not an explanation of deviant behavior in general, as he claims, but a delineation of some of the possible outcomes of a certain kind of strain presumably indicated by specific social and economic factors. The anomie approach turns out to be largely *irrelevant* to *most* forms of deviant behavior. Activities such as nonaddicting recreational drug use, assault, criminal homicide, petty gambling, adultery, child molestation, the consumption of pornography, holding unconventional beliefs, and, once again, homosexuality *are completely unexplained by the anomie theory.* In 1964, a team of experts argued that anomie failed to adequately account for gang delinquency (Short, 1964), mental disorder (Dunham, 1964), drug addiction (Lindesmith and Gagnon, 1964), and alcoholism (Snyder, 1964)—indeed, for deviance in general (Lemert, 1964a). There are serious problems with all the forms of deviance claimed by Merton to fit into the anomie paradigm—*with the exception of innovation.* It seems almost intuitively obvious that when a culture places a heavy emphasis on a goal but far less stress on how one achieves that goal, a lot of people are going to figure out a not-quite-approved way of achieving it rather than stubbornly continuing to follow a thoroughly approved method that doesn't work.

Deviance: Normative Violation or Social Disapproval?

Closely related to the point made about most varieties of deviant behavior is the problem that much behavior that is classified by the anomie scheme *is not really deviant at all*. If only a minor stress is placed on how one reaches the major goals in a society, then one will not be condemned for employing supposedly illegitimate means. To the extent that one's choice of the means to attain a given goal is irrelevant or morally neutral, employing those means is not a form of deviance. To the extent that choosing certain means to attain a given goal (for instance, cheating on an exam to receive an "A" in a course) is mildly disapproved of, it is an act representing only a mild form of deviance. To the extent that a technical violation of the rules generates no punishing reaction from others at all, again, are we really discussing a form of deviance (Erikson, 1964)? Merton defines deviance as the violation of institutionalized expectations. But he is really discussing a situation where formally enunciated rules exist ("don't cheat on exams"), the institutionalization of which has partly or completely broken down at the personal level. If cheating does not bring down punishment or condemnation upon the head of the cheater, then it is no longer a form of deviant behavior—regardless of what the formal rules state.

ANOMIE THEORY INTO THE 1990s AND BEYOND

In the 1950s and 1960s, anomie theory was the most frequently used theoretical tradition in the study of deviance and crime (Cole and Zuckerman, 1964; Cole, 1975; Gibbons, 1992, p. 110). In 1955 (Cohen, 1955) and 1960 (Cloward and Ohlin, 1960), major theoretical reformulations were advanced and were widely cited. One deviance anthology was organized entirely around the anomie perspective (Palmer and Linsky, 1972). But by the early 1970s, the anomie perspective underwent a sharp decline in influence, and from the mid–1970s through the mid–1980s, it seemed as if it would disappear from the field altogether, tossed onto the "dustbin of history." In 1978, in a detailed appraisal of theories of deviance, crime,

and delinquency, Ruth Kornhauser stated: "Strain models are disconfirmed" (p. 253). She advised that sociologists seeking an explanation of delinquency, crime, and deviance forget anomie theory and turn their attention elsewhere (p. 180).

But, as with social disorganization theory, sometime in the late 1980s to the early 1990s, anomie theory underwent a renaissance. Some of the most potent of the theory's criticisms have been answered (to the satisfaction of some observers, although not of others), while other, less serious ones, have been ignored; and still other observers have prompted a revamping or reformulation of anomie theory. As with the social disorganization framework, anomie or strain theory will never recapture its former glory as the field's preeminent approach to the study of deviance. However, judging by a recent rebirth in research and writing adopting the theory as a lens through which to examine deviant phenomena, it remains as vital as ever (Messner and Rosenfeld, 1997). In 1995, a substantial volume of papers, each in its own way praising the anomie approach, was published bearing the title *The Legacy of Anomie Theory* (Adler and Laufer, 1995). While it has its detractors, anomie theory has experienced a renaissance.

The *Social Science Citation Index* lists articles that refer to or cite a particular work. (Unfortunately, this index is limited to a single publication venue, academic journal articles; for instance, it does not tally citations in books.) Most articles don't get cited at all. In contrast, Merton's article 1938 article "Social Structure and Anomie" has not only been cited hundreds, possibly thousands, of times; citations of it have grown rather than declined. Between 1990 and mid–2003, there were 229 published articles in the social sciences literature that cited Merton's article. In other words, this article, which appeared nearly seven decades ago, is still influential and is still referred to in the current literature. In fact, the number of article citations of this classic grew substantially from the 1970–1979 decade (86) to the 1980s (141), and grew once again during the 1990s (156). Clearly, Merton's theory is even more influential today than it was two or three decades ago. It has helped researchers illuminate violent adolescent behavior (Vowell and May, 2000); purging by adolescent girls (Sharp et al., 2001);

juvenile firearms homicide (Ousey and Augustine, 2001); "antisocial behavior" among Filipino youth (Maxwell, 2001); vindictiveness and terrorism (Young, 2003); "situational anger" (Mazerolle and Piquero, 2001); "deviant coping" among African Americans (Jang and Johnson, 2003); female deviance (Eitle, 2002); delinquent behavior (Aseltine, Gore, and Gordon, 2000; Piquero and Sealock, 2000; Mazerolle and Maahs, 2000; Wright et al., 2001)—as well as dozens of other deviant, delinquent, and criminal activities.

One of the lines of recent development of anomie theory is in the realm of white-collar and corporate crime. This is a type of deviance that might seem to represent an exception to Merton's framework. After all, why would the corporate actor work out an illicit adaptation to achieve or compensate for a goal—material success—that has *already* been achieved? If executives have become rich, why should they violate the law and risk imprisonment for further riches? Merton's answer, elaborated on by later researchers, was that one of the peculiar characteristics of contemporary industrial society is that no matter how much one earns, it is never enough. For instance, America's nineteenth-century "robber barons," Merton argued, were guilty of resorting to unethical, criminal, or illicit means to achieve the culturally acceptable goal of economic success—in a nutshell, the "innovative" mode of adaptation (1957, p. 144). Rich to begin with, corporate executives innovate because they want to become richer still, and in order to do so, they must resort to "institutionally dubious innovation" (1957, p. 141). Success in America, Merton wrote, has no "final stopping point." No matter how much they earn, Americans want to earn about 25 percent more than they do. But of course, when they achieve that goal, they want that much more again—and on and on, seemingly without end (1957, p. 136). In short, in the United States, the deviant mode of adaptation Merton referred to as innovation is "a very common phenomenon" in all social classes (p. 144). Hence, in contemporary criminology, the impact of anomie on white-collar crime has become a major research enterprise.

Anomie plays a special role in corporate life. Some observers have argued that the very goal-seeking behavior of corporations makes them "inherently criminogenic" because they operate "in an uncertain and unpredictable environment" such that "legitimate opportunities for goal achievement are sometimes limited and constrained" (Box, 1983, p. 35). In other words, to be successful, corporation executives *have* to break the law. This way of looking at anomie shifts the level of analysis away from the individual actor to the *corporate* actor. While the corporation executive may be successful with respect to earning a high salary, success in running a corporation is dependent on an entirely different set of factors, and here, in an uncertain economy, cutting corners, bending and even breaking the law, practicing "creative bookkeeping," shading the truth, even lying, and twisting arms and exercising corporate muscle are practically inevitable. This insight, I might add, is straight out of Robert K. Merton's anomie theory.

For instance, Weisburd and his associates (Weisburd et al., 1991; Weisburd and Waring, 2001) write that they have found that "extending the Mertonian typology is a useful way to understand the nature of the criminal career" of white-collar offenders (Waring, Weisburd, and Chayet, 1995, p. 213). White-collar criminals tend to be motivated by two Mertonian factors—one, economic difficulty ("need") and two, unlimited aspirations ("greed"). Small-time business ventures tend to operate at the margins of the economy. Precarious and undercapitalized, they tend to wade into economic waters that are ignored by more well-funded enterprises. Hence, the entrepreneurs who run such marginal ventures are likely to feel the hot breath of failure at their backs, and hence, the need to violate the law just to stay afloat, taking risks that more secure operations would not feel are necessary. Weisburd and his colleagues found that most white-collar crime consists of petty, low-level violations, including securities fraud, antitrust violations, and bank embezzlement, as well as postal, tax, and credit fraud. Their sample of white-collar criminals was made up of low-level Mertonian innovators who took risks because they faced poverty, failure, or financial ruin. Not being able to succeed through conventional or law-abiding routes, they chose violations of the law to achieve some small measure of success.

Another recent research endeavor that has made use of anomie theory is the study of drug dealing. Bourgeois (1995, p. 326) argues that drug dealers should be accorded "their rightful place within the mainstream of U.S. society." These deviant actors are, he states, "made in America." "Highly motivated, ambitious inner-city youths have been attracted to the rapidly expanding, multi-billion-dollar drug economy during the 1980s and 1990s precisely because they believe in Horatio Alger's version of the American Dream."

Duneier (1999, pp. 60–62, 364) describes Merton's retreatism adaptation, which he refers as "The 'Fuck It!' Mentality." This takes place when a homeless person has given up on both goals and means. It is, he explains, a pervasive state of resignation that affects "most major aspects of his life," when he "becomes indifferent to behavior that he once thought of as basic, such as sleeping in a bed or defecating in a toilet" (p. 61). It is, in Merton's "brilliant scheme" (Duneier's term, not mine), "an extreme form of retreatism" (p. 61), the end point along a continuum of an "I don't care" attitude.

Clearly, in the sociology of deviance and crime, Merton's anomie theory remains influential. It is not likely to go away any time soon.

DIFFERENTIAL ASSOCIATION AND LEARNING THEORY

In 1939, in the third edition of a criminology textbook written by sociologist Edwin Sutherland (1883–1950), a major theory of deviance was propounded for the first time (Sutherland, 1939). It was called the theory of *differential association*, and it has become one of a small number of important perspectives in the field. Sutherland set for himself two somewhat different but overlapping tasks. The first was to explain what he referred to as *differential group organization*: why crime rates vary among different groups of people; why a criminal tradition was endemic in certain social circles. The second task was to explain why some *individuals* engage in crime more than other individuals. Unfortunately, Sutherland did not develop his ideas on differential group organization in much detail. In contrast, he did spell out the individual processes behind

criminality fully and in detail, and this is his theory of differential association.

The first and most fundamental proposition of the theory of differential association states that criminal behavior, and by extension, deviance as well, is *learned*. This proposition was directed against biological theories, which assert that crime is caused by genetic, metabolic, or anatomical defects, and against the view that criminal behavior is hit upon accidentally or through independent invention. Hardly anyone, Sutherland asserted, stumbles upon or dreams up a way to break the law; this must be passed on from one person to another in a genuine learning process. The theory of differential association also opposed the view that mental illness or an abnormal, pathological personality is a major causal factor in the commission of criminal behavior. Rather, Sutherland argued, crime is learned in a straightforward, essentially normal fashion, no differently from the way in which members of American society learn to speak English or brush their teeth.

A second proposition of the theory of differential association is that criminal behavior, and, again, by extension, deviance as well, must be learned through face-to-face interaction between people who are close or intimate with one another. People are not persuaded to engage in criminal behavior as a result of reading a book or a newspaper, seeing a movie, or (today, as opposed to 1939) watching television. Criminal knowledge, skills, sentiments, values, traditions, and motives are all passed down as a result of *interpersonal*—not impersonal—means. Two major factors that intensify this process are *priority* and *intensity*. The earlier in one's life one is exposed to attitudes and values (which Sutherland called "definitions") favorable to committing crimes, the greater the likelihood that one will in fact commit crime. And the closer and more intimate the friends, relatives, and acquaintances that endorse committing crime, likewise, the more swayed one will be to break the law.

Sutherland's theory, then, argued that people who embark on engaging in criminal behavior *differentially associate* with individuals who endorse violations of the law. Notice that the theory does not say that one needs to associate with actual criminals to end up breaking the law oneself—only that one needs to be more heavily exposed to *definitions* favorable to criminal actions. One can be exposed to law-abiding definitions emanating from criminals and to criminal definitions emanating from law-abiding individuals (though, of course, it usually works the other way around). Still, as most of us know, "actions speak louder than words," and one wonders how much more of an impact the example of criminal actions has than criminal words.

In sum, Sutherland's theory of differential association holds that a person becomes delinquent or criminal because of an excess of definitions favorable to the violation of the law over definitions unfavorable to the violation of the law. The key to this process is the *ratio* between definitions favorable to the violation of the law to definitions that are unfavorable. When favorable definitions exceed unfavorable ones, an individual will turn to crime.

The theory of differential association has been criticized for being vague and untestable (Sutherland and Cressey, 1978, p. 91; Conklin, 1998, pp. 288–289). Later efforts to refine and operationalize the theory (Burgess and Akers, 1966; DeFleur and Quinney, 1966) have not been entirely successful in rescuing it from imprecision. Exactly how would a researcher measure this ratio of favorable to unfavorable definitions of violations of the law? And exactly how could "favorable" and "unfavorable" be indicated or measured? Even one of the theory's staunchest defenders admits that Sutherland's formulation of the differential association process "is not precise enough to stimulate rigorous empirical test" (Cressey, 1960, p. 57). Some conceptualizations of learning theory attempt to address these and other objections by incorporating additional factors and variables into their framework (for instance, Akers, 1998). In so doing, however, they depart so radically from Sutherland's original formulation that they become more eclectic than instances of learning theory.

A great deal of research and anecdotal evidence demonstrates that much crime is, indeed, learned in intimate social settings. However, it seems at least as overly ambitious to assume that all criminal behavior is learned in a straightforward fashion as it is to assume that all noncriminal behavior is learned. Many actions, criminal and noncriminal alike, are invented anew by individuals in similar situations. For instance, adolescents need not learn how to masturbate from other adolescents (although many, possibly most, do); many discover the activity as a result of exploring their own bodies. All behavior is not learned, at least not directly. Much of it, deviant or otherwise, may be devised in relative isolation. There is a great deal of independent invention of certain forms of deviance, delinquency, and crime. The human mind is, after all, almost infinitely creative. The idea to do something, and its eventual enactment, almost always have a cultural or learning *foundation*, but it was not necessarily learned in detail. One can, either by oneself or in the company of an equally untutored individual, "put the pieces together."

One can enact certain behaviors *in the absence of learning or learning about those behaviors themselves*; learning may take one to a certain point, after which creativity and imagination take over. Any learning theory that requires that one learn positive values *about the precise behavior itself* must therefore be incomplete and deficient. Any learning theory that includes all the other factors that go into human behavior, such as biological drives, the pleasure principle, and so on, is likely to be so vague as to be a tautology—true by definition.

Many criminal activities do not fit the differential association model at all: check forgery (Lemert, 1953, 1958, 1972, pp. 150–182), embezzlement (Cressey, 1953), child molestation (McCaghy, 1967, 1968), wartime black-market violations (Clinard, 1952), as well as certain crimes of passion (Katz, 1988), and crimes involving psychiatric compulsion (such as kleptomania). While, for many deviant and criminal activities, learning may assist their enactment, it does not cause them. Some observers (Gottfredson and Hirschi, 1990) have gone so far as to argue that one does not have to learn anything to enact deviant or criminal behavior; it is simply "doing what comes naturally." In addition, many forms of deviance and crime are not even approved of by a majority of the people who engage in them—such as mental illness, alcoholism, and child molestation. Consequently, they could not be learned in anything like the fashion that Sutherland suggests. That is, one may learn *about*, say, mental illness or alcoholism, but one hardly ever learns that they are activities or states one should emulate. In short, while it is true that much criminal and deviant behavior is learned, much of it is not. As a partial theory, differential association is valuable. As a complete or general theory, it is overly ambitious. Rather than a theory that explains all crime, delinquency, and deviance, differential association should instead be regarded as a concept that helps us to understand a particular *process* that some rule-breakers go through and some do not.

Learning is not necessarily a *cause* of much deviant behavior, although learning is *involved* in the process of becoming deviant. That is, in the process of becoming absorbed in certain deviant roles, one learns *about* that role, just as one does in more conventional roles. One learns what is expected of one if one is to be a prostitute, say, or a homosexual; one learns the prostitute or homosexual role. This is not, however, to say that the learning process causes one to *become* a prostitute or a homosexual. Rather, *in becoming* a prostitute or a homosexual, one is involved in a learning process—quite a different matter. At times, Sutherland's theory seems to confuse a *process* for a *mechanism*.

The idea that crime, delinquency, and deviant behavior is learned in a direct, straightforward fashion within certain social circles has been explored and elaborated by a number of researchers. One extension of Sutherland's theory of differential association is the "culture transmission" paradigm set forth by Walter Miller, an anthropologist (1958). Sutherland's version of learning theory locates the mechanism of acquiring deviant norms, values, and practices primarily with one's closest peers, mainly in youth, adolescence, and even adulthood. In contrast, Miller locates that mechanism as beginning with birth, in the family. In effect, Miller argues, a major sector of the society learns to become delinquent from their parents and other relatives, from the neighborhood, from their class peers.

Miller's theory locates a site of criminogenic values specifically in the lower class, arguing that gang delinquency is a direct by-product of lower-class culture. "The lower class way of life," he writes, "is characterized by a set of focal concerns—areas or issues which command widespread and persistent attention and a high degree of emotional involvement" (1958, p. 6). These "focal concerns" are trouble, toughness, smartness,

excitement, fate, and autonomy. Each concern pressures young lower-class males into direct contact with the law and agents of law enforcement. For instance, an emphasis on toughness often leads to a desire to demonstrate one's masculinity by engaging in fights, assaultive behavior, and belligerent confrontations with the police. A desire for thrills, fast-paced excitement, and danger makes "hanging out," gambling, fighting, bar-hopping, and heavy drinking appealing. Miller argued that simply by being a participating member of the lower-class subculture, one "automatically violates certain legal norms" (1958, p. 18). One is expected to break the law in many situations (which would call for law-abiding behavior for middle-class members of society). Lower-class culture, Miller writes, "is a distinctive tradition many centuries old with an integrity of its own," and that tradition includes the routine violation of the criminal law (p. 19). Miller's argument is that lower-class adolescents get into trouble because they are faithful to cultural standards learned from their parents.

A number of critics have questioned Miller's analysis. Some researchers find that self-reported delinquent behavior does not vary significantly by social class at all; they argue that lower- and working-class adolescents are no more likely to engage in illegal and delinquent acts than are middle-class youths (Tittle, Villemez, and Smith, 1978; Tittle and Meier, 1990; Tittle, 1995, p. 275).[1]

---

[1]Tittle, 1995 (p. 275), takes me and other scholars to task because we "refuse to relinquish" the idea that deviance and conformity vary by social class location. We are accused of being blinded by ideological biases, of refusing to face the evidence, and so on. There is a much simpler explanation: We hold to our position because we are not only not convinced by Tittle's evidence, we believe that contrary evidence is vastly more compelling. Most forms of behavior are influenced by social class; what would make deviance, crime, and delinquency any different? Is Tittle arguing that *no* forms of deviance, crime, or delinquency are influenced by social class? That deviance, crime, and delinquency *generally* are not so influenced? Which forms of normative violations are *not* influenced by social class? What about robbery, rape, murder, aggravated assault? Would Tittle predict that a surgeon would be just as likely to punch a colleague in the mouth or rob a bank as an unskilled, unemployed manual laborer? In my view, Tittle's insistence that social class is unrelated to deviance and conformity casts suspicion on the validity of his "general theory of deviance."

However, the studies that show no, or very little, difference between the classes in delinquent behavior are *self-report* studies; that is, they are based on asking people if they engaged in certain kinds of behavior. And although self-report studies on deviant and criminal behavior generally are fairly valid and reliable, researchers must know how to interpret their findings. In the studies that show no differences in delinquent behavior between socioeconomic strata, the problem is that most did not distinguish among *degrees of seriousness* of delinquent acts as well as *frequency of their commission* (O'Brien, 1985, pp. 63–79). While it is possible that middle-class youths have no lower rates of *trivial* delinquent offenses, lower- and working-class adolescents certainly *do* have significantly higher rates of *more serious* delinquent acts, and they tend to engage more frequently in those acts they do commit (Elliott and Ageton, 1980). The "no difference" hypothesis does not seem to hold up after all; serious acts of delinquency and crime are far more likely to be committed by members of the lower and working classes. Thus, Miller's hypothesis that lower-class culture is a "generating milieu" for delinquent and criminal behavior probably does have some basis in fact. The argument that lower-class males are no more delinquent than those from the middle classes is clearly based on a serious methodological fallacy.

However, even if lower-class adolescent delinquent and criminal behaviors were more prevalent and frequent than were those of the middle class, this still would not explain why a fairly *low* proportion of lower- and working-class boys are involved in serious violations of the law. Miller's theory *overexplains*: If we were to follow out its implications strictly, we would predict that all lower-class adolescents are delinquent, a clearly false assertion. Moreover, some argue, the supposed "focal concerns" that Miller claims characterize lower-class culture seem to be just as much a feature of middle-class culture and values (Valentine, 1968, pp. 135–138; Hirschi, 1969, pp. 212ff.). Many observers do not find Miller's "culture transmission" theory entirely convincing. On the other hand, Miller performed a service to the field by emphasizing the crucial importance of learning and that of social class, in the commission of delinquent, criminal, and deviant behavior.

SOCIAL CONTROL THEORY

Control theory is a major explanatory paradigm in the fields of deviance behavior and criminology. Control theorists see their perspective as a critique of and a replacement for both anomie theory and the subcultural or learning approaches. For instance, one study found that youths who did poorly in school and who were least concerned about it—that is, who suffered *least* from the "strain" that anomie theory refers to—had the *highest* rates of delinquency (Hirschi, 1969, pp. 124–126). Likewise, youths who were *least* attached to peers, contrary to Cohen, Cloward and Ohlin, and the subcultural approaches, were the *most* likely to commit delinquent acts (pp. 159–161). However, one important consideration about control theory is that it has been far more often used in the study of delinquency than in the study of deviance or crime generally.

While most theories ask, Why do they do it?—that is, what processes *encourage* deviant behavior—control theory turns the question around and asks, Why *don't* they do it? In other words, control theory assumes that engaging in deviance is not problematic—that, *if left to our own devices*, all of us would deviate from the rules of society. In fact, control theorists believe that deviance is *inherently attractive*. Under most circumstances, we are encouraged to break the rules; deviance-making processes are strong and obvious and commonsensical. Why *shouldn't* we lie and steal, if they are what get us what we want? *Why not* hang out on street corners and get drunk and throw bottles through windows—it's so much fun! This approach takes for granted the allure of deviance, crime, and delinquency. What has to be explained, control theorists argue, is why most people *don't* engage in deviance, why they don't engage in delinquent behavior, why they don't break the law and engage in a life of crime. What causes deviant behavior, they say, is the *absence* of the social control that causes conformity and conventional behavior. Most of us do not engage in deviant or criminal acts because of strong bonds with or ties to conventional, mainstream social institutions. If these bonds are weak or broken, we will be released from society's rules and will be free to deviate. It is not so much deviants' ties to an unconventional group or subculture that attracts them to deviant behavior, but their *lack* of ties with the conforming, mainstream, law-abiding culture; this frees them to engage in deviance.

Control theory would predict that, to the extent that a person has a *stake in conformity*, he or she will tend not to break the law and risk losing that stake; to the extent that a person lacks that stake in conformity, he or she will be willing to violate the law. Thus, jobs, especially satisfying, high-paying jobs, may act as something of a deterrent to crime. (It should be pointed out, however, that in the most important statement spelling out control theory, *Causes of Delinquency* [1969], Travis Hirschi found few class differences in delinquency.) Attending college, likewise, represents a stake or investment that many students are not willing to risk losing. Being married and having a family, too, will discourage criminal behavior to the extent that arrest may undermine stability. Everyone knows that *some* crime is committed by the employed, by college students, by married persons with families. But control theory would predict that there are *major differences* in the crime rates of the employed versus the unemployed, college students versus their noncollege-age peers, and married parents versus the unmarried. To the extent that a society or a neighborhood is able to invest its citizens or residents with a stake worth protecting, it will have lower rates of crime; to the extent that it is unable to invest that stake in its citizens or residents, its crime rate will be correspondingly higher. Home ownership, for instance, can act as a deterrent to crime, as can organizational and community involvement. A society with many citizens who have nothing to lose is a society with a high crime rate.

Of course, delinquency, deviance, and criminal behavior are matters of degree. Nearly all of us engage in *some* deviant and criminal acts at least once in our lives. Control theory does not state that individuals with strong ties to conventional society are absolutely *insulated* from deviance, that they will *never* engage in *any* deviant or criminal action, regardless of how mildly unconventional it is. It does, however, assert that both deviance and social control are matters of degree: The more attached we are to conventional society, the lower the likelihood of engaging in behavior that violates its values and norms. A strong bond to conventionality does not absolutely insulate us from mildly deviant behavior, but it does make it less likely.

The theory works a great deal better for some behaviors than for others. Many of the activities that control theory sees as natural, recreational, and requiring no special explanation are part and parcel of relatively minor delinquencies. But more seriously aggressive and violent behavior, such as murder, robbery, and rape? Are they part of the same constellation of acts that, if left to our own devices and in the absence of simple societal controls, we all would engage in? It's difficult to envision that the same logic applies. In fact, there may be a very good reason why the vast majority of the research applying control theory has been self-report surveys of relatively minor delinquencies among youths: It works best for them. As we saw, such studies run into a serious roadblock. Hirschi's 1969 study found few class differences in rates of delinquency. There is a good reason why. The most important crimes, those that criminologists are most interested in (murder, robbery, and rape) tend to be relatively rare. The least important crimes are sufficiently common to make a self-report possible. The less common the behavior, the more difficult it is to study by means of self-report surveys, since so few of the sample will have engaged in them, especially within a recent time frame. Hence, control theorists are a bit like the drunk who is searching for his keys, not in the dark, where he lost them, but in the light, where he can see better. In spite of this restriction, control theory represents one of the more powerful approaches we have to explain crime, deviance, and especially delinquency.

A GENERAL THEORY OF CRIME: SELF-CONTROL THEORY

In 1990, Michael Gottfredson and Travis Hirschi devised what they refer to as *a general theory of crime*, "crime" being force or fraud in pursuit of self-interest (p. 15). The authors claim that their theory applies to any and all crimes, regardless of type—white-collar and corporate crime, embezzlement, murder, robbery, rape, the illegal sale of drugs, underage drinking, burglary, shoplifting, indeed, any and all illegal actions. In fact, in their view, their theory is even more general than that, since it is an explanation of actions that may not even be against the law or entail inflicting force or fraud against a victim. More properly, it is a general theory of deviance and includes, besides crime, what used to be referred to as "sin," a variety of self-indulgent actions (like smoking, getting high or drunk, and, one might suppose, even being a couch potato), and reckless behavior that has a high likelihood of resulting in accidents (such as driving dangerously fast or preferring a motorcycle to a car). (Unfortunately, although the authors are meticulous about defining crime, they never define what they mean by deviance, a serious drawback.) Their theory, they say, represents a combination or synthesis of theories that stresses the factors present in the immediate or "proximate" situation of the criminal action that determine or influence its *enactment* (which they refer to as "crime") and those background or "distant" factors that determine or influence the *tendency* to commit crime (which they term *criminality*).

The origin of crime, Gottfredson and Hirschi say, is *low self-control*, which, in turn, results from inadequate, ineffective, and inconsistent socialization by parents early in childhood. Parents who breed delinquent and criminal offspring lack affection for them, fail to monitor their behavior, fail to recognize when they are committing deviant acts, and fail to control wrongdoing. What makes crime especially attractive to people who lack self-control? Criminal acts, Gottfredson and Hirschi say, are characterized by the fact that they provide *immediate* and *easy* or *simple* gratification of desires (p. 89). "They provide money without work, sex without courtship, revenge without court delays" (p. 89). People who lack self-control "tend to lack diligence, tenacity, or persistence in a course of action" (p. 89). In addition, criminal acts are *"exciting, risky, or thrilling"*; crime provides, in the typical case, *"few or meager long-term benefits"*; it requires *"little skill or planning"*; and often results in

"pain or discomfort for the victim" (p. 89). As a result of the last of these characteristics, people with low self-control and hence, frequent enactors of criminal behavior, tend to be "self-centered, indifferent, or insensitive to the suffering and needs of others" (p. 89), although they may also "discover the immediate and easy rewards of charm and generosity" (p. 90).

Since crime entails "the pursuit of immediate pleasure," it follows that "people lacking in self-control will also tend to pursue immediate pleasures that are *not* criminal: they will tend to smoke, drink, use drugs, gamble, have children out of wedlock, and engage in illicit sex" (p. 90). Some crimes entail not so much pleasure as an attempt at relief from irritation or discomfort, such as physically abusing a crying child or beating up an annoying stranger in a bar. People with low self-control have little tolerance for frustration and little skill at dealing with difficult circumstances verbally or by applying complex, difficult-to-master solutions. "In short, people who lack self-control will tend to be impulsive, insensitive, physical (as opposed to mental), risk-taking, short-sighted, and nonverbal, and they will therefore tend to engage in criminal and analogous acts" (p. 90).

Their general theory of crime, Gottfredson and Hirschi argue, is both consistent with the facts of criminal behavior and contradicts the bulk of mainstream criminological theories. The authors are not modest, either, about the reach of their theory or about its devastating implications for competing explanations. They insist that their general theory of crime *cannot* be reconciled with other theories; instead, they insist, it must of necessity *destroy* them. In fact, even Hirschi's own control theory (discussed above), formulated more than a quarter of a century ago, is implicitly abandoned. More specifically, it is *specified* in that, in control theory, the *social* controls that Hirschi saw previously as central he now views as secondary to the *internal* controls developed in childhood. Now, life circumstances such as marriage, employment, and home ownership, so crucial to control theory, are presumably rejected as irrelevant, having little or no independent impact on crime. After all, how can someone with low self-control maintain a marriage, keep a job, or buy a house? They lack emotional and psychic wherewithal—the self-control—to do what has to be done even to be *subject* to external or social controls. It is self-control that determines social control, not the other way around, Hirschi now argues.

The problem with the theories of crime that are now dominant in criminology, Gottfredson and Hirschi argue, is that they are inconsistent with the evidence. Strain or anomie theory "predicts that offenders will have high long-term aspirations and low long-term expectations," but that turns out to be false; "people committing criminal acts tend to have lower aspirations than others," while, among offenders, "expectations for future success tend to be unrealistically high" (p. 162). In anomie theory, crime is a long-term, indirect solution to current life circumstances, whereas, in reality, Gottfredson and Hirschi say, crime is an impulsive act that provides immediate, short-term, and rather skimpy rewards. Criminals lack the skills, diligence, and persistence necessary for the deviant "adaptations" spelled out by Merton. True, some criminals do possess these qualities, and do engage in these adaptations; but strain does not explain the incidence or rate of criminal behavior as a whole, since most of it is petty, impulsive, and immediate.

Likewise, the many varieties of learning theory (such as differential association theory, subculture theory, and culture transmission and, by extension, labeling and conflict theory, to be discussed in the next chapter) should be rejected as being inconsistent with the facts, Gottfredson and Hirschi argue. All such theories make the assumption that deviants engage in deviance as a result of a positive learning experience, that is, *they learn the value* of engaging in deviance and crime. In fact, one does *not* learn to engage in crime, since no learning is required. Criminal acts are simple, commonsensical, immediate, concrete, and result in immediate gratification. Neither motivation nor skill to commit them are problematic; criminals are, in fact, simply doing what comes naturally. What causes such behavior is not the *presence* of something—learning—but the *absence* of something—self-control. Learning theories simply fail utterly and completely to explain criminal, deviant, and delinquent behavior, Gottfredson and Hirschi argue.

More generally, they reject the idea that crime is *social* behavior (in fact, it is more accurate to refer to it as *asocial* in nature), that it is *learned* behavior ("when in fact no learning is required"), that the tendency to commit it can be an *inherited* trait (when it is clearly acquired, through childhood experiences), that it is *economic* behavior (when, in fact, "it is uneconomical behavior outside the labor force"). To be plain about it, they reject all other explanations of criminal behavior except their own (p. 75); only a lack of self-control is truly consistent with the facts of crime. Gottfredson and Hirschi contemptuously reject any effort to integrate their own theory with the explanations they so roundly criticize.

With two exceptions: Not all persons who exhibit low self-control commit crime; low self-control merely *predisposes* someone to commit crime. What determines which persons who are predisposed to commit crime will actually do so? In a word, opportunity. Hence, any explanation that focuses on the *patterning* and *distribution* of criminal opportunities—although incomplete—is consistent with the facts, Gottfredson and Hirschi argue. Their approach is an attempt to revitalize classical, free-will, or rational choice theory, mentioned early in this chapter, as half the crime equation. The contemporary version of the classic approach to crime, referred to as opportunity theory, the routine activity approach, or rational choice theory (Cohen and Felson, 1979; Felson, 1987; Clarke and Felson, 1993), argues that crime can take place to the extent that a *motivated offender* has access to a "suitable target" (such as money and valuables) that lacks a "capable guardian." Routine activity theorists emphasize the factors of *proximity*, *accessibility*, and *reward* (Hough, 1987). They *assume* or *take for granted* a motivated offender—the criminal—since there will always be an abundant supply of them to go around; instead, they focus on the necessary preconditions for the commission of the crime. The assumption that crime is the most rational means to acquire property is abandoned, however, since Gottfredson and Hirschi argue that most crimes do not net the offender much in the way of goods or cash. Nonetheless, they say, opportunity is a crucial element in the crime equation. (Not in *criminality*, or the individual *propensity* to commit crime, but in crime, itself that is, in the likelihood that criminal *actions* will take place.) While incomplete, Gottfredson and Hirschi say, a theory that focuses on opportunity is consistent with self-control theory. Moreover, they say, both are necessary for a complete explanation of criminal behavior (1990, pp. 22–23; 1987).

In addition, they argue, social disorganization theory is both consistent with classical theory and consistent with the facts of crime; the inability of a community to monitor the behavior of its residents complements, and is similar to, parallel parental incompetence (1990, pp. 81–82).

As might be expected, self-control theory has met with mixed reactions. Strain theorists argue that social strain and anomie are indeed significant causal precursors to criminal behavior. For instance, the aggressiveness and anger that many criminals exhibit when committing their crimes is far more than a lack of self-restraint; only strain theory explains it, they say (Agnew, 1995, p. 125). Some learning theorists argue that a lack of self-control is a basic component or element of the deviant learning process (Akers, 1991)—hence, they say, learning theory *subsumes*, or swallows up, self-control theory. Labeling or interactionist theorists (such as myself) see in Gottfredson and Hirschi's portrayal of labeling theory a distorted caricature rather than an accurate, nuanced portrait (1990, pp. 76, 113, 147, 159). Certainly the reductionistic, mechanistic, either-or logic Gottfredson and Hirschi display in their theorizing has led some observers to believe that they may have missed crucial subtleties in characterizing and explaining human behavior (Lynch and Groves, 1995, pp. 372–378). One critic takes Gottfredson and Hirschi to task for selectively reading the data, focusing on those that seem to comfirm their theory, and ignoring those that would damage it (Polk, 1991). Gottfredson and Hirschi's theory clearly applies much more to the antisocial personality disorder (Black, 1999) than to deviance in general. It is too early to assess the validity of self-control theory in anything like a definitive fashion. Chances are, contrary to its claims, bits and pieces of it will be incorporated into mainstream criminology and deviance theory, while its global, overall—and perhaps overblown—critiques of rival theories will be taken far less seriously. The fact is, it is likely that Gottfredson and Hirschi have not offered a "general theory" of crime and deviance, but a plausible account of bits and pieces of the phenomenon they purport to explain.

SUMMARY

Whenever some members of a society engage in what others regard as wrongdoing, the latter wonder why the former do it. Explanations for violating society's rules are as ancient as human existence. Historically, the most ancient of such explanations was demonic possession—the influence of the devil or evil spirits.

By the 1700s, intellectuals and the educated sectors of Western society no longer believed that the intervention of evil spirits caused people to violate the norms or the law. The eighteenth century in Europe was referred to as the Age of Reason. Hence, it makes sense that it was in this era that an explanation for crime arose that focused on humans as reasonable and rational actors, exercising their free will and guided by the pursuit of pleasure and the avoidance of pain.

With the publication of Charles Darwin's *On the Origin of Species* in 1859, more deterministic forces were seen as being at work in the crime equation. The positive school argued that criminal behavior is caused by inborn defects or "atavisms," whose possessors are genetic throwbacks to a more primitive stage in the evolutionary process. In short, criminals are biologically inferior to law-abiding segments of society; it is the possession of inferior traits or characteristics that causes them to engage in criminal behavior. Biological determinism had its heyday in the second half of the nineteenth century and the first few years of the twentieth; by the 1920s, it had suffered a sharp decline in influence. However, in the 1960s, biological reasoning was revived in a much-qualified form. Although far less influential today than a century ago, some researchers nonetheless think that biological factors play a significant role in contributing to the etiology of criminal behavior.

During the 1920s, sociologists came to see the community rather than the individual, and social relations rather than biological factors, as the source of norm violations. This approach is called the Chicago School or social disorganization theory. Some neighborhoods are unstable by virtue of their undesirability. As a result, residents are heterogeneous (and hence, often strangers to one another) and do not sink roots into the community. In such neighborhoods, wrongdoing is common, since residents cannot or do not monitor or control normative and legal violations. In sum, deviance varies systematically by ecological location. The social disorganization school was the dominant perspective in academic sociology between the 1920s and the 1940s. After World War II, it suffered a serious decline in importance and influence. Although it never regained its former glory, roughly by 1990 the social disorganization school experienced a dramatic renaissance. Today, numerous researchers are conducting studies that are guided or inspired by the social disorganization perspective.

Anomie theory is distinctive by virtue of the fact that it had its origin (except for the work of Emile Durkheim, who had something very different in mind) in a single article by a single sociologist: Robert K. Merton's "Social Structure and Anomie," published in 1938. Merton argued that, in the United States, deviance was a product of a disjunction or contradiction between the culture, whose norms urged material and financial success for all members of the society, and the social and economic structure, which granted high levels of success only to some. This condition produces a state of stress or *anomie*. As a result of failing in the traditional sectors of the society, those who were left behind were forced into one of an array of deviant "adaptations." This theory did not receive a great deal of attention until the appearance of a book, more than a decade and a half later, by Albert K. Cohen, *Delinquent Boys*, at which point the theory began to inspire an entire generation of deviance specialists. Merton's 1938 article is the most-often-cited single article in the history of sociology, and during the late 1950s and the 1960s, the anomie perspective was the most-often-used approach in the study of deviance. But in the 1970s, the approach underwent a sharp decline in influence; in 1978, in a review of theories of deviance and delinquency, Ruth Kornhauser declared that anomie theory had been "disconfirmed." However, as with other perspectives in this field, anomie theory experienced a strong rebirth, roughly beginning in 1990.

Today, once again, it is the focus of vigorous commentary and research.

Learning theories encompass a variety of perspectives, all of which center around the idea that deviance, delinquency, and crime are learned in a fairly straightforward fashion. By being isolated from mainstream society and its definition of deviance, and integrated into unconventional groups, one learns deviant values, beliefs, and norms and thus, engages in deviant behavior. Two varieties of this approach include the theory of differential association, devised by Edwin Sutherland in 1939, and culture transmission theory, which was systematized by the anthropologist Walter Miller in 1958. As with all other perspectives in the field, learning theory has been attacked, defended, amended, and added to.

Social control theory takes strong issue with both anomie and learning theory. Deviants do not have to be stressed into committing deviance, nor does anyone have to learn to become a deviant. Indeed, what requires explaining, say the social control theorists, is conformity. Deviance is readily understandable, commonsensical, and nonproblematic. In fact, left to our own devices, everyone would deviate from the norms: It's easier, more fun, and more effective in getting the actor what is desired than is true of conformity. The important question is not, why do we commit deviance? Instead it is, why *don't* we commit deviance? The factor or variable that social control theorists have isolated as the explanation is that people engage in conventional behavior to the extent that they are involved with and attached to conventional others, activities, and beliefs. To the extent that we have an investment or stake in conventionality, we will engage in conventional behavior. To the extent that we don't, we will engage in deviance.

In 1990, the fully articulated version of a major theory of deviance made its appearance— "a general theory of crime." It is based on several tenets of control theory (as well as classic, free-will, or rationalistic theory), but it breaks with it in its lack of stress on *current* conventional attachments. People violate norms and the law because they lack self-control; they tend to be insensitive, self-centered, impulsive, relatively unintelligent; they lack a long-range perspective, can't deal with frustration, and require immediate gratification. And they lack self-control because they were subject to inadequate, inconsistent, and ineffective socialization by their parents or other caregivers. Self-control theory is one of the few perspectives whose advocates argue that all other perspectives (except for rational choice and social disorganization) are completely incompatible with the facts of crime. Its advocates set out to destroy all now-dominant approaches to deviance and crime. As might be expected, self-control theory has met with a mixed reception.

Today, no single perspective or approach is dominant in the study of deviance. As we can see, all of the approaches discussed in this chapter are concerned entirely with *an explanation of deviant behavior*. In this sense, they are all positivistic or "scientific" in their general approach. In the next chapter, we'll look at theories that address a very different task, in a sense looking at the opposite side of the deviance coin. Instead of attempting to explain why deviant behavior is enacted, for the most part, they ask about the nature and operation of *definitions* of deviance and the exercise of *social control*. Instead of asking why deviance is enacted, they wonder about why deviance is conceptualized and defined a certain way, and how and why certain behaviors, traits, and persons are caught up in the web of punishment and condemnation. Although this enterprise is less traditional, less likely to be thought about by the man and woman in the street, it is every bit as rewarding and potentially enlightening as those that ask why some of us deviate. No examination

of deviance is complete without an investigation of the nature, social roots, and exercise of social control.

Before we proceed to the next chapter, however, I must issue a most emphatic warning. The perspectives we are about to examine are largely focused on how the society or segments of the society *define* and *deal with* deviance and deviants. Theories or perspectives that focus on social control constitute the *constructionist* approach to deviance. Unfortunately, two of the theories we looked at in this chapter share names that are very similar to this social control emphasis—"social control" theory and "self-control" theory. I must emphasize that they are *not* theories of social control in the sense that I'll be using the term in Chapter 4—that is, they are not constructionist in their approach. The social control and self-control theories are etiological, causal, or positivist theories of deviance. They ask: *Why do some persons engage in deviant behavior?* Or, to be a bit more precise, they ask: Why do some people *not* engage in deviant behavior? To repeat, they attempt to account for the behavior itself, not why it is defined in a certain way or why it is condemned. Proponents of these theories do not examine social control as problematic, that is, as the subject to be investigated. They do *not* ask: *Why social control?* Don't be confused by the similarity in their names. Their approaches are completely different; they share little else with the perspectives discussed in this chapter *aside from* their names.

PERSONAL ACCOUNT: Clinical Depression

The contributor of the following account is Robert, a 26-year-old college student. "Recently," he explains, referring to himself in the third person, "he was involved in an altercation that led to five felony charges being set against him and [being] committed to a psychiatric ward for 55 hours. He has no prior [criminal] record. In most aspects of his existence, Robert leads a conventional lifestyle. Yet he has been plagued by depression since he was 16. He

has only recently sought treatment and is in the process of finding a cure to what he now knows is a physical ailment related to [a disorder of the] thyroid."

Whatever disadvantage I had as a youth in the parenting department, it did not affect me. Even if it is argued that it in fact did affect me, this was not realized until much later. I do not believe that differential association [explains my condition or my behavior] in the first phase of my life. My youth was filled with situations that, according to differential association theory, should have affected me at an early age. Here I will stress only my activities and not my parents' raising me.

I can't remember when my parents didn't fight. They had heated arguments at least once a week. This often led to my father destroying various of my mother's possessions or just things that belonged to the house. They divorced for the first time when I was 6 years old. My mother went into the Army and my father took custody of me. I spent the next 10 months living with my father as he cohabited with various girlfriends while I stayed at my grandmother's house. When we were together, he took me to parties or friends' houses. There, I looked at pornographic magazines and hung out with my father's friends while they drank and smoked marijuana. I'd gamble with them; we played a type of game with quarters where you tossed them from a distance and attempted to get your quarter closest to a wall. I also made his friends mixed drinks and poured beer from the kegs they kept iced. They thought it was really amusing to see this little kid look up at them from the bar area and ask what they wanted. They tipped me a dollar a drink. After a while, I went back to gambling. Sometimes I won and sometimes I lost. When I got bored with these activities, I went back to the pornographic magazines. Every now and then he'd come up to me and ask how I was making out. I showed him the money and he'd smile. If I had anything left, we went out and got some food and maybe I'd buy a toy.

I hardly ever talked to anyone about the activities I had with my father. I didn't know it was out of the ordinary. To me, it was just my life. One time, when I was with my grandmother, I said something about these activities to my aunt, who then told my grandmother about what I had said. My grandmother interrogated my father about what I had told my aunt and later, he told me never to mention "shit" like

that again to anyone. My aunt didn't look at me the same way for many months. I figured it was because she was a Baptist. These activities continued regularly until my parents remarried 10 months later, when my mother went AWOL from the Army.

These activities tapered off and stopped altogether when my mother became pregnant with my brother. This is when my parents had their most intense arguments and began destroying property. When I was 11, in the middle of a screaming argument with my mother, my father picked up the microwave we owned and smashed it on the floor. My mom once took a crowbar and smashed up my dad's 550 Kawasaki motorcycle. She also stuck a steak knife into the tires of his Ford pickup. He also punched holes in the wall and shattered my mom's dresser mirror. On two or three occasions, he walked out to the barn with a 30/30 lever-action rifle and threatened to shoot and eat my mom's horse. It was with this same rifle that he also almost killed himself with. In one of my parents' countless heated arguments, he said that he wanted to die and placed the gun barrel under his chin. Hysterically, my mother tried to stop him and in the struggle, the gun fired a round into the ceiling. These were the encounters at which I was present, and they would always bring me to tears. I yelled, I screamed, I begged them to stop. I told them to leave each other, to let me leave and go anywhere but where they were. Altercations like this happened frequently from the time I was 7 to the time I was 15. I believe that my parents were, and still are, mentally ill because of organic causes, just as, I believe, my own mental illness is due to an organic condition. Without the medication I'm now taking, I'd be dangerous both to others and to myself.

When I was 16, my parents finally divorced for good. It involved a bitter custody battle which left me emotionally damaged from the trauma. After my parents split up, they both left the area; my father went to the Philippines and my mother went to California. I was left to stay

PERSONAL ACCOUNT: Clinical Depression (cont.)

with my grandparents in Florida. I felt abandoned. It seems I was a remnant of the past he wanted to forget. Yet he could never erase it, he could only run away. Shortly after my dad left, I went to California to visit my mother for a two-week stay. Soon after I arrived, she told me she had plans to be with her boyfriend. She handed me $400 and told me she'd be back in nine days. So I spent the time alone in an apartment complex. I spent my time eating at restaurants, buying music, playing videogames at a local arcade, and going to a club nearby. I felt alone, strange not having anyone around to look after me. I did my best to keep preoccupied. This is when I became severely depressed. I left soon after my mother returned from her escapade with her boyfriend. When I returned to Florida, my depression continued to get worse. Within a week or so, I was at the point when I wanted to die. My great-grandmother, whom I often visited when she was alive, had died recently, and I went through her house trying to absorb the life she had lived and left behind. On one of these explorations, I found her gun, tucked in the back of a dresser drawer. It was loaded. I took it in my hand, cocked the firing hammer, put the barrel in my mouth, and thought for a moment about the world I would not miss, the world that had rejected me. I pulled the trigger.

The gun was still in my trembling hand, the barrel was still rattling against my teeth, but obviously I was still alive. I pulled the gun out of my mouth, took the bullets out of the chamber, and held the one with the firing pin perforated into it. It was a dud. I stared at it for a few minutes, then put the other bullets back in the gun and nestled the gun back into the dresser drawer. I realized I didn't really want to die. I stuck the dud into my pocket, walked out of my great-grandmother's house, threw the bullet into the creek behind the house, and went home. No one ever found out about my attempt. The event left me traumatized even more; my mental health deteriorated. Even so, in the 10 years since then, I never attempted suicide again. I somehow managed to pull myself together

enough afterwards to function and pass as "normal," but I was never the same. That's the time my rage cycles began. In my senior year of high school, halfway through the year, I stopped attending class and holed myself up in my room for two months straight. By this time, my grandfather had died and my grandmother didn't know what to do with me. She had unfaltering compassion but meager parenting skills. The resulting combination enabled me to survive, but not much else. After the two-month period, my depression receded and I managed to finish high school. I transferred to a different school in an adjacent district where no one knew me, and graduated six months later.

When I went to a different high school, I wasn't leaving any friends behind—I didn't have any friends. I wanted friends, but most people avoided me like a leper. My adolescent years were, for the most part, spent alone. My depression must have turned fellow students away from me. I didn't understand how my personality was related to my depression and to my outbursts. I guess no one else did either. Back then, I had less self-control than I do now. To help deal with my rage, in my first high school, I joined the wrestling team, but it didn't give me any friends. I later found out that the other guys on the team had nicknamed me "time bomb" because they thought that one day, I'd come to practice with a handgun and open fire on them all. I thought they were all assholes. I was just serious about practice, that's all. Actually, when I found out later about the nickname, I was glad they were all afraid of me. That just made me want to stay home even more.

After that bout of depression, my aunts and uncles on my father's side never treated me the same again. I was always the black sheep. I was considered the troubled child of a father and mother who were themselves considered of poor character.

I enrolled in a local community college. I didn't have wrestling any more, so I needed another outlet for my volatile and depressive emotions, so I turned to martial arts training.

PERSONAL ACCOUNT: Clinical Depression (cont.)

That allowed me to function without attracting attention. My grades were spotty, leaving my academic counselors confused. Yet I managed to find a girlfriend. I stayed in a relationship with her for two years, but ultimately my dysfunctional emotions got the better of me and I assaulted her. We only had one argument. She was ridiculing me for acting so depressed. It made me explode into a violent rage. I grabbed her by the shoulders and threw her off the bed she was lying on. She told me later that the look on my face was what scared her the most. She ended our relationship; that left me an emotional wreck because I thought I had become my father. I hated my father for the life I had to endure as a result of my parents' emotional state, their behavior, their violence. I was distraught because I could not stop the violent episode. Only after it was over did I realize what I had done. I was angry at myself, angry at my parents, angry at everything around me that didn't help. My outburst left my girlfriend curled up in a ball in the corner of the room, crying. I spent the next hour trying to calm her down, calm myself down. I began crying myself. I apologized for what I had done over and over again. Even though she became calm, she never forgave me for that outburst. Shortly after that, she said she could never trust me again and she didn't want to go out with me. I was also distraught because I didn't know if I could trust myself either.

After the break-up of my relationship with my girlfriend, I started to teach myself to hide my emotional dysfunction. Through weightlifting and martial arts, I could sap my body of energy and fill my brain with mind-numbing endorphins. When I felt I was in an unstable state, I avoided people I normally interacted with. I didn't return phone calls and I stood people up. I found that the more I mastered this act, the more people wanted to be around me. I found another girlfriend. The trick was to balance these two parts of my life, one, the normal, nice, upstanding, cool persona, and the other the tortured, angry, volatile, severely depressed alter ego. Ultimately, my relationship

with my girlfriend turned sour; she started to see the "Mr. Hyde" in my "Dr. Jekyll." Yet I was able to hold the friendships together because they were at a distance, I could manipulate them. I even managed to stay friends with my former girlfriend and am still friends with her to this day. My "Mr. Hyde" tormented me for over a year about the end of that intimate relationship, and my torment affected my relationships with other women I had at that time.

I decided to move to New York City. I lived in a dormitory at a school for the martial arts. It was the perfect place to remedy my emotional dysfunction. I had all the opportunities I needed to focus my aggression and anger on martial arts training under the eye of the person I called "the old Japanese guy," my martial arts teacher. Yet this training didn't fully eliminate my depression. So, with the other guys in the school, I started using marijuana heavily on weekends and occasionally on weekdays. I also began drinking heavily on weekends with them as well. "The old Japanese guy" provided us with most of the alcohol; he was an alcoholic himself, though he didn't know about the marijuana. If he had, he would have kicked us out and replaced us, even though we were "prodigy martial artists." He had two rules for his students: no sex in the dojo and no drugs. We constantly broke both rules. It was our home, so we did what we did at home, which for us included sex and drugs.

I am torn between differential association theory and social control theory to explain my use of alcohol and my sexual promiscuity at the time. In one sense, the camaraderie of my peers in the school made me want to join in. Yet at the same time, I felt alienated from conventional society due to my emotional dysfunction, therefore I didn't feel bound by society's rules.

I continued in this way for a year, at which time I moved to Washington, D.C. I had maintained a long-distance friendship with the girl I had dated in community college, and so she let me stay on her couch until I could find my own place. I wanted to have an intimate relationship

PERSONAL ACCOUNT: Clinical Depression (cont.)

with her again—I wanted her to be my girl-friend—but she rejected my advances and soon after, I moved into my own apartment and got a job at a bar-coffee house-lounge. At the time, I no longer had my martial arts to help with my emotional dysfunction, so I turned even more heavily toward alcohol and marijuana as a remedy. And once I started working at the bar, alcohol was plentiful and most of the time it didn't cost me anything.

After the place closed for the night, I sat with the shift manager, the bartender, and the other coworkers and drank whatever I wanted on the house and got high. Almost every night I left work drunk unless I had a date with a girl I had picked up across the bar the night before. We usually went to my place for some sex. The girls really liked this, they felt like VIPs. Honestly, I felt better half-numb than being sober and straight and in emotional anguish. I made a lot of friends and acquaintances at the time. No one ever saw the violent, anguished, depressed side of me. It was still there—as it always was—but

the "animal" was sedated almost all the time. I liked it that way. There were a lot of people around me and I knew that if I showed my problems, they wouldn't want to be around me. In most ways, this era of my life is an example of deviant socialization. I could have dealt with my emotional dysfunction in another way, try to find out what was causing it, but instead I just followed the crowd I was exposed to. It was a remedy to my problems, and I took it. I even began stealing from work because I saw how easily many of the other employees, who were my friends, did it. I started to feel overworked, working hard for not enough money, so that's where the thievery came in. I made drinks without paying for it or used code numbers to order food from the kitchen on the house. Eventually, I had many drinks while I was working. It helped me loosen up. I felt everybody who was stealing was in a conspiracy to screw the wealthy owner of the place for whatever we could get. Only when I returned to college did I start to deal with my dysfunction in a different way.

QUESTIONS

Positivists are interested in answering the question, "Why?" When it comes to deviant behavior, they usually set in the background the process by which societies decide that an action should be regarded as deviant, and foreground or highlight the question of the *cause* or *causes* of the behavior in question. What do you think is an adequate explanation of Robert's behavior? Was it his experiences growing up in a particular family setting? Did his parents' socialization of him cause the behavior that led to the authorities taking action against him? Or was it the experi-ences he had as a teenager and young man in unconventional social groups? Do you accept Robert's explanation that a chemical or hor-monal imbalance caused his aberrant behavior? Which of the theories discussed in this chapter best accounts for Robert's behavior? Do you feel that constructionist theories of deviance have any purchase in analyzing Robert's behavior? That is, would his behavior be regarded as deviant everywhere? Or would it be accepted and tolerated in some social circles, groups, or societies? Is there something distinct and spe-cific to our society that led to Robert's being sanctioned here for his untoward behavior?

CHAPTER 4

Constructionist Theories of Deviance

The perspectives and approaches that were discussed in Chapter 3 attempt to explain the occurrence, enactment, and/or distribution of deviant or criminal behavior. They are concerned with the factors that lead certain persons to violate the rules, or those that produce higher rates of deviance in some societies than in others, or under certain conditions more than others. These perspectives focus on the question "Why do they do it?" (Or, in the case of social control and self-control theory, "Why *don't* they do it?") All attempt to provide an explanation for *why deviant behavior is enacted*—why some people engage in it, why residents of some communities or neighborhoods are more likely to engage in it, why some societies and historical time periods generate more of it than others, how and why certain circumstances encourage it. These perspectives see deviance as a type of action that needs to be explained. It should be noted that none addresses deviant beliefs as such, and none is concerned in any way with deviant traits or conditions. And none, by their very nature, inquire about false accusations.

A very different orientation is provided by approaches that ask about *the conceptualization of behavior, beliefs, and traits; definitions of deviance; what the rules are; how are they enforced; and what the consequences of that enforcement are.* Here, rather than seeing deviance as an action, these perspectives see the violation of rules as an *infraction*. That is, the focus is on what *makes* certain actions (and beliefs and conditions) infractions: why rules are made in the first place, who makes the rules, why *certain kinds* of rules are made, why certain *persons* or *types of persons* are apprehended and punished, and what *consequences* rule-making and rule-enforcement have. This approach turns the focus of attention around. Now, instead of the spotlight being on the rule-violator, or on the conditions that make for rule violation, it is on the society and the groups in the society that *make and enforce the rules*. Of course, when the issue becomes the *consequences* of enforcing the rules, the violator once again steps into the spotlight. Some constructionist approaches contain an explanatory thrust as their "minor" mode but focus *mainly* on the creation of the rules and their enforcement, their "major" mode.

The theoretical approaches or theories that adopt this perspective include functionalism, labeling or interactionist theory, conflict theory, feminist theory, and contrology or the "new" sociology of social control. As with all perspectives toward deviance, constructionists deal mainly with behavior rather than beliefs and conditions. However, *unlike* all other perspectives, constructionists—especially the labeling and the feminist approaches—devote substantial attention to phenomena *other than* behavior exclusively.

The *functionalist* approach to deviance was an early perspective that put forth two arguments, one commonsensical and the second counterintuitive or contrary to what is regarded as common sense. First (the commonsensical argument), certain behaviors harm society and its members; hence, they must be prohibited in order for the society to survive (that is, violators must be punished and condemned). And second (the counterintuitive argument), some behaviors that are widely condemned (that is, those that are "deviant") are functional or beneficial in that they protect mainstream values or institutions and therefore, supposedly, the society as a whole.

Labeling or *interactionist* theory focuses on rule making and, especially, *reactions to* rule breaking. This school shifts its attention away from the circumstances that produced the deviant act to "the important role of social definitions and negative sanctions" as well as "what happens to people *after* they have been singled out, identified, and defined as deviants" (Traub and Little, 1999, pp. 375, 376).

Conflict theory deals with the question of making the rules, especially the criminal law. Why is certain behavior outlawed? And why is other, often even more damaging behavior, *not* outlawed? Conflict theory focuses most of its attention on the role of powerful groups and classes in the formation and enforcement of the criminal law. The powerful are able to make sure that laws and rules favorable to their own interests, and possibly detrimental to the interests of other, less powerful groups and classes, are institutionalized.

Feminist theory is a variety of conflict theory focusing specifically on the role of sex and gender in deviance and crime: How do men express and maintain their dominance by defining and enforcing certain actions as deviant and criminal? Why does patriarchy exist, whose functions does it serve, and what impact does it have on deviance and social control? (Daly and Chesney-Lind, 1988).

Controlology or the "new" sociology of social control is a perspective that grew out of the work of the French philosopher Michel Foucault. It argues that social control is the central issue not only for the sociologist of deviance but for the sociologist generally. Contemporary society has devised a system for the control of deviance that seems humane and scientific, but is far more thoroughgoing, systematic, efficient, and repressive than older forms of control that entailed torture and public execution. "Knowledge is power," it asserts, and the powerful strata use scientific knowledge to control the unruly masses.

FUNCTIONALISM

Functionalism is a general term that has been used in a variety of fields, including architecture, philosophy, psychology, and sociology. In its most general meaning, functionalism refers to the view that phenomena are to be understood by their consequences. *Intention* or *motive* is explained by *interest*, and interest, in turn, is explained by *outcome*, according to the functionalist. Answering the question *"Who profits?"* simultaneously answers *How and why did this occur?* In short, *functions indicate interests.* For instance, if the consequence of the passage of a law is beneficial to the ruling elite, that elite must have *engineered* the passage of that law. If a social custom has a beneficial effect on a society, the members of that society must have *done* something to keep that custom alive. If a custom survives for centuries, it must serve a *function* for the members of the society. When we refer to functions, we are referring to consequences that explain motives—even if those motives may not be clear to the participants. A function is an outcome in which a reason must be found for a phenomenon's existence; if it exists, it must serve a function. In sociology, a functionalist examines the consequences an institution or practice has and, from it, speculates about the part it plays in the functioning and interests of a society or segments of that society.

In sociology, the term *functionalism* (also referred to as "structural-functionalism") may be distinguished from *functionalist thinking*. The approach that is referred to as functionalism is associated with a type of reasoning that is narrower than functionist thinking in general. Functionalists typically answer the question "Who profits?" by saying "The society *as a whole* profits." In contrast, functionalist *thinking* looks for specific individuals, social segments, categories, or groups who may profit at the expense of others, who may lose. But the basic reasoning process for both is the same.

Emile Durkheim (1858–1917), the first academic sociologist, is seen as the most important precursor to twentieth-century American functionalism. Durkheim believed the members of a society possessed a "collective conscience" (or, sometimes, "collective consciousness"). His work focused on the causes and consequences of societal cohesion. In his early writing (1893/1933), Durkheim pictured crime as pathological and negative in its impact, although he saw the *punishment* of crime as having a beneficial impact. However, soon after, he quickly saw crime itself as "functional" for the society (1895/1938). An entirely crime-free society is an impossibility, Durkheim argued, because even in a society of saints, the slightest transgression will generate punishment and condemnation (1938, pp. 68–69). The punishment of crime firms up the "moral boundaries" of most societies; upstanding citizens "wax indignant" about the criminal and, in so doing, reaffirm the moral correctness of conventional norms and values. Crime, therefore, is useful; it is necessary; it has a part to play in social life. Moreover, Durkheim argued, in crime there are the seeds of social change. Too much conformity produces a society that "would too easily congeal into an immutable form" (p. 71). Crime is "an anticipation of future morality—a step toward what will be" (p. 71). Durkheim offended conventional, commonsensical thinking by arguing that *crime is good for society*!

Durkheim had a powerful impact on the thinking of Talcott Parsons (1902–1979), who is regarded as structural-functionalism's founder and most prominent spokesperson. Functionalism asks the basic question, "How is social order possible?" The answer it gives is that societies, in a more or less unintended, nonconscious fashion, have protected themselves over the years by prohibiting harmful activities (that is, those that threaten their survival) and encouraging beneficial ones (that is, those that maximize societal survival). Social customs and institutions that persist over time tend to be those that are good for society because they serve one of these two functions (Davis, 1937, 1949; Davis and Moore, 1945; Parsons, 1951). That is, the *positive consequences* of certain institutions (the fact that they have a beneficial impact) somehow cause the members of the society to preserve and maintain them.

Deviance, according to the functionalists, can be either beneficial ("functional") or harmful ("dysfunctional") to the society as a whole. Certain activities by their very nature will generate hostility, discord, and conflict among the members of a society and hence, their enactment will thereby make the society more unstable and less viable; they are *dysfunctional* in nature. Hence, they are likely to be prohibited in societies everywhere. Others will promote social stability, integration, and cohesion—and will therefore be functional. Hence, they are a kind of social "resource"; these behaviors are likely to persist over time in societies everywhere.

Certain taboos will be more or less universal around the world, because the activities they prohibit will inherently sow the seeds of conflict. Specific activities will be regarded as deviant everywhere because they threaten the social order. Incest, for example, creates competition and conflict between and among family members, pitting one against another for the affection of fellow family members. The roles of family members and lovers are in conflict with one another; hence, incest, which makes the family a less stable and less viable institution, is tabooed just about everywhere (Davis, 1949, pp. 401–404).

Note that the impact of a given practice or institution on the society is examined *as a whole*, as a unit or *total social system*. Functionalists tended to focus on functions for *total societies* rather than units, groups, or classes within societies. (Although, in principle, by following the logic of functionist thinking—as opposed to functionalism—one could theorize about the functions of certain institutions and practices *for designated segments of the society*. As we'll see, this is what

conflict theorists have done, although, for the most part, functionalists have not.) In other words, for the most part, functionalists thought in *holistic* terms—the society as a whole was the unit of analysis, not diverse social categories within the society.

However, the main contribution of the functionalists lay not in their analyses showing that certain forms of deviance are harmful, or dysfunctional, and that their prohibition is therefore beneficial, or positively functional, to society. Rather, functionalism represented an advance over previous ways of looking at deviance in large part because it stressed that certain forms of deviance have a *positive* or *integrative* impact on society. "Overwhelmingly," explains David Matza, functionalists "stressed the functions—not the dysfunctions—of deviant" behavior (1969, p. 55). Of course, often, most of the members of a society will not recognize, be aware of, or admit these effects, positive or negative; they may be hidden, unacknowledged, or, in functionalist terminology, *latent* consequences of deviance. In short, deviance, the functionalists argued, is often beneficial for society, a kind of "blessing in disguise," a kind of "cloud with a silver lining."

For example, Kingsley Davis (1937, 1971, 1976) argued that prostitution serves a positive function for society: "Enabling a small number of women to take care of the needs of a large number of men, it is the most convenient sexual outlet for armies and the legions of strangers, perverts, and physically repulsive in our midst. It performs a role which apparently no other institution fully performs" (1971, p. 351). By diverting the sexual interest and energy of a large number of men away from "respectable" women, Davis argued, the traditional family is preserved and society benefits as a consequence. Prostitution "provides males with a sexual outlet that has limited liability," it produces "no emotional interference with other roles. In this way, the contraband act presents no threat to institutionalized relations" (Davis, 1980, p. 104). Robert Merton, probably the most prominent functionalist sociologist writing today, argued that deviant institutions often serve positive functions. For instance, political bossism and the local party machine of the 1930s, although corrupt, inefficient, nepotistic, favoristic, and deeply involved in criminal activity, fulfills the crucial function "*of humanizing and personalizing all manner of assistance* to those in need" (1957, p. 74). This solidifies the neighborhood and strengthens the society as a whole. Agrees Kai Erikson, deviance "may itself be, in controlled quantities, an important condition for *preserving* stability" (1964, p. 15).

The positive contribution that the *punishment* of deviance makes to the society is at least as important as that made by deviant behavior itself. The punishment of a criminal represents a "ritual expression" of group sentiment; it upholds "the institutionalized values which the criminal has violated. This ritual expression serves to consolidate those sentiments and above all to strengthen them in that part of the population which has positive but latent motivations to the deviance being punished" (Parsons, 1951, p. 310). Punishment represents "a kind of declaration" that "you are either with us or against us." "A good deal of it therefore is not directed at the criminal himself, but at others who potentially might become criminals" (p. 310). In short, the punishment of deviance and crime provides a resource for the society, a means of affirming society's mainstream values, because, in the periodic punishment of criminals, the conventional but seducible members of society are reminded of the righteousness of law-abiding behavior and the evil of breaking the law. As Erikson says, public hangings went out of vogue with the institutionalization of the mass media. In a sense, publicizing the punishment of deviants and criminals in the news serves the same function as hanging them in the public square: Everyone can see what happens to wrongdoers. In a functionalist sense, "morality and immorality meet at the public scaffold" (Erikson, 1966, p. 12).

Functionalism made three contributions to the study of deviance (Matza, 1969, pp. 31–37, 53–62, 73–80). First, it emphasized the *complexity* of the relationship between conventionality and deviance. Second, it *purged the automatic implication of pathology* from the field. And third, it emphasized an *appreciation* for deviance.

Where earlier perspectives saw deviance as almost inevitably producing *undesirable* effects on a society, functionalists argued that the effects that nearly everyone recognized as desirable often flowed from deviance. Where earlier perspectives saw deviance as *untenable*, a phenomenon that could (and should) be gotten rid of through firm and authoritarian intervention, functionalists argued that deviance provided a tenable, viable way of life for many members of society. The *persistence* of certain forms of deviance, such as prostitution—the fact that it has existed everywhere, throughout history—indicates that it makes positive contributions for both the members of society that engage in it and for the society as a whole. Where earlier perspectives saw a *disjunction* between deviance and conventionality, a yawning chasm separating the "good guys" from the "bad guys," functionalists pictured a *continuity* between them. Deviance, the functionalists argued, *shades off into* conventional behavior. Much of what ordinary, law-abiding folk think and do borders on, but usually doesn't quite become, deviance. There is deviance *in miniature* in the most conventional of behaviors, and an *incipient* or *potential* deviant in even the most conformist of souls. We should look at deviance in *linear* terms rather than in either-or, black-or-white terms. There is an *unbroken continuum* between the respectable and the disreputable. A clear break between them simply does not exist. The relationship between vice and virtue is *devious* rather than simple, *continuous* rather than dichotomous (Matza, 1969, pp. 74, 77).

Functionalists offered insight into why rules—and therefore deviance—exist in the first place, as well as into some of the major consequences of deviant behavior. It was the first major perspective historically to argue that deviance is not necessarily a result of an undesirable or abnormal condition and that it does not always produce negative consequences. Deviance is, in fact, part and parcel of the normal functioning of any society.

At the same time, the functionalist perspective suffered sustained and, in the view of many critics, fatal criticism (Gouldner, 1970). Functionalism was accused of justifying the status quo, of falsely arguing that we live in "the best of all possible worlds," of being incapable of analyzing or predicting social change, of glossing over and ignoring conflict between groups and social classes, as well as failing to take note of, indeed even justifying, profound differences in power and wealth, and the implications these have for deviant behavior. An example of the narrowness of its approach can be seen in its analysis of prostitution (Davis, 1937). Functionalists assumed that, because prostitution was beneficial for the traditional patriarchal family, it was therefore beneficial *for the society as a whole.* As feminists came to argue, what is good for the traditional male-dominant family may very well *oppress, repress,* and *be harmful to* women.

Functionalism incorrectly assumed a unity and homogeneity of interests among different groups and categories in the society; later conflict and feminist approaches assume much more diversity and heterogeneity. A given institution may be beneficial to one group or segment of the society *at the expense of another.* While functionalists paid lip service, in principle, to the notion of functional diversity (Merton, 1957, pp. 25–30, 38–46), in their concrete analyses (for instance, Davis, 1937; Davis and Moore, 1945; Parsons, 1951, p. 310; Merton, 1957, p. 74), they focused on the impact of institutions and behavior on the society *as a whole.*

Functionalism was prominent in sociology generally from the 1940s to the early 1960s. (It never became a dominant perspective in the study of deviance.) In the field of the sociology of deviance, the functionalist argument was briefly revived with Kai Erikson's historical study *Wayward Puritans* (1966), which argued that crime was functional for colonial Puritan society. But this book, although highly regarded, could not stem the decline in the perspective's influence in sociology, and by the 1970s, functionalism went into total eclipse. Nonetheless, in the 1980s, a perspective whose practitioners refer to themselves as *neofunctionalists* emerged (Alexander, 1985), giving the field a kind of mini-revival. Functionalism is currently in disrepute in sociology. It is an almost obligatory ritual for instructors of introductory sociology to demolish functionalism (Downes and Rock, 2003, p. 79). Still, as some observers point out, even though *functionalism* has all but disappeared from the field, *functionalist thinking* is still very much alive. There is an implicit or "tacit but perfectly potent functionalism still lurking in much of the sociology of deviance" (Downes and Rock, 2003, p. 103). For instance, nearly all Marxists, radicals, conflict theorists, and feminists argue that functions indicate interests—the very foundation stone of functionalist thinking.

LABELING OR INTERACTIONIST THEORY

In the 1960s, a small group of researchers produced a small body of work that came to be looked on as a more-or-less unified perspective that is widely referred to as *labeling theory.* Two of the major labeling theorists, Becker (1973, p. 178) and Kitsuse (1972, p. 233) reject both the term "labeling" and the title "theory" as a valid description of their perspective. Both prefer the term "the interactionist approach" (Kitsuse, 1972, p. 235; Becker, 1973, pp. 181, 183). Their approach, they explain, is not, strictly speaking, a theory—that is, a general explanation for why deviance occurs in the first place—and the term "labeling," they say, implies too simple-minded a connection between stigma and its outcomes. Unfortunately, in the field of deviance, the perspective is widely known as "labeling theory." I will refer to it both as the labeling *and* the interactionist approach, and I will use the terms "theory," "approach," "model," "school," "paradigm," and "perspective" more or less interchangeably.

Labeling theory was built on the work and writings of two principal precursors—Frank Tannenbaum (1938) and Edwin Lemert (1951). Tannenbaum was not a sociologist but a historian of Latin America; he had no contact with the later labeling theorists, and he did not really work out the implications of his theory. He can be regarded as the "grandfather" of labeling theory. Some of Lemert's writing is squarely in the labeling tradition, and some criticizes it sharply. Lemert may be regarded as the "godfather" of labeling theory.

Labeling theory grew out of a more general perspective in sociology—*symbolic interactionism.* This approach is based on three simple premises. First, people act on the basis of the *meaning* that things have for them. Second, this meaning grows out of *interaction* with others, especially intimate others. And third, meaning is continually modified by *interpretation* (Blumer, 1969, p. 2). These three principles—meaning, interaction, and interpretation—form the core of symbolic interactionism and, likewise, of labeling theory as well.

People are not robots, interactionists are saying; they are active and creative in how they see and act on things in the world. People are not simple "products" of their upbringing or socialization, or of their environment, but arrive at what they think, how they feel, and what they do through a dynamic, creative process. Men are not automatically patriarchal and sexist simply because they grew up as men in a patriarchal, sexist society; they continually reinterpret what they have been taught in the light of their everyday lives. Pornography does not have the same impact on all viewers, even all male viewers; the meaning of pornography is mediated through the defining and reactive filter of each viewer in a particular interactive setting. Drug use patterns—even the use of one specific drug or drug type—are not a simple product of the inherent properties of drugs themselves. How people use drugs depends on who they are and how these drugs are woven into their lives. In short, all behavior, deviance included, is an interactional product; its properties and impact cannot be known until we understand how it is defined, conceptualized, interpreted, apprehended, and evaluated—in short, what it *means* to participants and relevant observers alike. Labeling theory is not a separate theory at all, but an application of symbolic interactionism to deviant phenomena.

The year 1938 marked the publication of a book by Frank Tannenbaum; it was entitled *Crime and the Community*. Tannenbaum argued that in a slum area, nearly all boys engage in a wide range of mischievous, sometimes technically illegal behavior—getting into fights, skipping school, stealing apples, throwing rocks at windows. These actions, perfectly normal and taken for granted by the boys themselves, are typically regarded as deviant and criminal by the authorities—by teachers, the police, and the courts. In an effort to curtail this behavior, the police apprehend and punish some of these boys. If the boys persist in this behavior, they will be sent to reform school. However, punishment does not always put an end to these activities. In fact, it often has the ironic effect of escalating the seriousness of the deeds that these boys commit. Arrest and incarceration will typically result in the community regarding a boy as not merely mischievous, but incorrigible—a budding criminal in the flesh. By being treated as a delinquent and

forced to associate with slightly older and more experienced young criminals in reform schools, the troublemaker comes to see himself as a true delinquent.

Tannenbaum was the first observer of deviance to focus more on reactions to behavior than on the behavior itself. He argued, in fact, that the key factor in escalating an individual's behavior from mildly to seriously deviant was the punishment he or she received. It is possible that Tannenbaum did not believe that punishment always and inevitably resulted in this escalation process, but he certainly wrote as if he did.

About a dozen years after the publication of Tannenbaum's *Crime and the Community*, a textbook with the inappropriate and anachronistic title *Social Pathology* appeared (1951). Written by sociologist Edwin Lemert, it pursued Tannenbaum's insights, but with considerably more sophistication, complexity, and detail. Lemert distinguished between *primary* and *secondary* deviation. Primary deviation is simply the enactment of deviant behavior itself—any form of it. Lemert argued that primary deviation is *polygenetic* (1951, pp. 75–76; 1972, pp. 62–63), that is, it is caused by a wide range of factors. For instance, someone may come to drink heavily for a variety of reasons—the death of a loved one, a business failure, belonging to a group whose members call for heavy drinking, and so on. In fact, Lemert asserted, the original cause or causes of a particular form of deviance is not especially important. What counts is the social reaction *to* the behavior from others.

Secondary deviation occurs when the individual who enacts deviant behavior deals with the problems created by social reactions to his or her primary deviations (1951, p. 76). "The secondary deviant, as opposed to his actions, is a person whose life and identity are organized around the facts of deviance" (1972, p. 63). In other words, when someone is singled out, stigmatized, condemned, or isolated for engaging in deviant behavior, it becomes necessary to *deal with* and *manage* this social reaction in certain ways. One begins to see oneself in a certain way, one defines oneself in different terms, adopts different roles, associates with different individuals. Being stigmatized forces one to become a deviant—to engage in secondary deviation.

It should be said that Lemert recognized that not all primary deviation results in punishment or condemnation. Some communities or social circles display more "tolerance" for rule-breaking behavior than others (1951, pp. 57–58). When primary deviation results in punishment, however, the individuals engaging in it tend to be stigmatized, shunned, and socially isolated. They are forced into social groups or circles of other individuals who are also stigmatized. This isolation from mainstream, conventional society reinforces the individual's commitment to these unconventional, deviant groups and circles and the individual's commitment to the deviant behavior itself.

Lemert, like Tannenbaum, emphasized the ironic consequences of condemning and punishing rule breakers; it can make further deviance more likely. However, Lemert, unlike Tannenbaum, discussed both sides of this process. One possible outcome of negative social reaction to primary deviation is to "eliminate the variant behavior" altogether. Certain radical or revolutionary groups in Europe "have at times been ruthlessly hunted down and destroyed." In the United States, the practice of polygyny, or multiple marriages, "was stamped out" (1951, p. 63). Although the repression of deviance can result in its elimination, the ironic effect of strengthening it and making it more likely has captured far more attention of the labeling theorist over the years. As with the functionalist perspective, the labeling theorists wished to be original, and one way of doing that is to attack common sense, to put forth an argument that contradicts what is commonly known or thought to be true.

In addition to Tannenbaum and Lemert, most observers regard Howard Becker (1963, 1964), John Kitsuse (1962), and Kai Erikson (1962, 1966) as labeling theory's main proponents. (Erikson's work falls in both the functionalist and the labeling tradition.) Although Becker (1973) and Kitsuse (1972, 1975, 1980) later elaborated their original formulations, for the most part, what is now known as labeling theory was spelled out in the short span of time between 1962 and 1966. It should be said that, although labeling theorists have been depicted by most commentators, particularly critics, as consistent in their views, in reality, they represent a diverse group of thinkers (Goode, 1975,

p. 570; Plummer, 1979, p. 87). Still, labeling or interactionist theory can be discussed as a more-or-less unified school or perspective in the study of deviance.

According to Becker (1973, pp. 177–208; 1981) and Kitsuse (1972, 1980), labeling theory is not so much an explanation for why certain individuals engage in deviant behavior as it is a perspective whose main insight tells us that the labeling process is crucial and cannot be ignored. Labeling "theory" is not so much a theory as it is an orientation, the discussion of a "useful set of problems" centered around the origins and consequences of labeling (Plummer, 1979, pp. 88, 90). The labeling approach shifts attention away from the traditional question of "Why do they do it?" to a focus on how and why judgments of deviance come to be made and what their consequences are. Why are certain acts condemned at one time and in one place, but tolerated at another time, in another place? Why does one person do something and get away "scot-free," while another does the same thing and is severely punished for it? What happens when someone is caught violating a rule and is stigmatized for it? What consequences does labeling have for stigmatization? What is the difference between enacting rule-breaking behavior, which does not result in getting caught, and enacting that same behavior and being publicly denounced for it? These are some of the major issues labeling theorists have been concerned with.

The labeling theorists follow in the social disorganization or "Chicago School" tradition in emphasizing up-close, detailed ethnographic studies of deviant circles, groups, and subcultures. That is, in order to understand the phenomenon of deviance, they say, it is necessary to go out into the street and talk to the individuals who break the laws and norms, to get into the natural habitat of the deviant and understand how he or she lives. It will not do, they say, to receive one's views of deviance from books, from the vantage point of one's comfortable armchair, from studies that entail one-shot interviews with thousands of respondents which are then analyzed by means of complex, arcane statistics. One must immerse oneself in the everyday lives of deviants, get as close to the phenomena under study as possible—nose-to-nose with your subject, so to speak. Anthropological ethnography is a cornerstone of the interactionist's research methods.

In many ways, labeling theory is a model, quintessential, or perfect example of the constructionist approach, discussed in Chapter 2. It addresses issues such as the creation of deviant categories, the social construction of moral meanings and definitions, social and cultural relativity, the how and why of social control, the politics of deviance, the criminalization of behavior, and the role of contingency in the labeling process. Together, these issues constitute the foundation stone of constructionism. Several issues represent the hallmark of the labeling theory's central concerns: *audiences, labeling and stigma, reflexivity, the inner world of deviance*, and *the "stickiness" of labels* and *the self-fulfilling prophecy*.

Audiences

The labeling process is generated by *audiences*. An audience is an individual or any number of individuals who observe and evaluate an act, a condition, or an individual. An audience could be one's friends, relatives, neighbors, coworkers, the police, teachers, a psychiatrist, bystanders, or observers—even oneself, for you can be an observer and an evaluator of your own behavior or condition (Becker, 1963, p. 31; Rotenberg, 1974). It is the *audience* that determines whether something or someone is deviant: no audience, no labeling, therefore no deviance. However, an audience need not *directly* view an act, condition, or person; audiences can witness behavior or conditions "indirectly," that is, they can hear or be told about someone's behavior or condition, or they can simply have a negative or condemnatory attitude toward a class or category of behavior: "The critical variable in the study of deviance . . . is the social audience rather than the individual actor, since it is the audience which eventually determines whether or not any episode of behavior *or any class of episodes* is labeled deviant" (Erikson, 1964, p. 11; my emphasis). In other words, audiences can evaluate *categories* of deviance and stand ready to condemn them, even before they have actually witnessed specific, concrete cases of these categories.

Some audiences include the following:

The first audience is society at large (Schur, 1971, p. 12). It can be said, for instance, that a majority of the American public finds adulterous sex morally unacceptable and therefore deviant. They are likely to voice condemnation of the adulterer, although, in most instances, that condemnation is likely to be fairly mild. The widespread acceptance of this view leads us to say that, in American society as a whole, adultery is regarded as a form of deviance.

A second audience is the *significant others* of the potentially labeled individual (Schur, 1971, pp. 12–13), that is, those people one interacts with most frequently and intimately, and with whom one has a close relationship and whose opinions one values. It could be, for instance, that in your social circle, sex engaged in by a married person with someone other than one's spouse is perfectly acceptable. Thus, to the audience of *your* significant others, adultery is *not* deviant; you will not be condemned by them for such an action. On the other hand, in *my* significant social circle, let's say, adultery is an abomination, a sin of the highest magnitude, one that, if known about, will stigmatize an individual who engages in it, making him or her an outcast. Thus, to the audience of my significant others, adultery is most decidedly deviant.

And a third type of possible audience is official and organizational agents of social control (Schur, 1971, p. 13). Can you get into some kind of *formal* or *official* trouble for engaging in and getting caught at the behavior? Can you be arrested for it? Can you be committed to a mental hospital? Lose certain benefits or rights? In most law enforcement agencies, at least in the United States, adultery is not a legitimate cause for arrest. Thus, to the audience of agents of formal social control, adultery is not deviant. Thus, whether an act, a belief, or a trait is deviant or not depends on the audience that does or would evaluate the act. Without specifying real-life audiences, the question of an act's, a belief's, or a trait's deviance is meaningless.

Labeling and Stigma

The key elements in "becoming" deviant are labeling and stigmatizing. The processes of labeling and stigmatizing are done by a relevant audience. The audience is relevant according to the circumstances or context. Gang members can label the behavior of a fellow member of the gang as deviant *within the gang context*; the police can label an action of a gang member as deviant, wrong, or illegal by arresting or harassing him. Each and every audience or person can label each and every action, belief, or condition of each and every person as deviant—but the weight or *consequences* of that labeling process vary according to the context.

The labeling or stigmatization process entails two steps. First, an audience labels an *activity* (or belief or condition) deviant, and second, it labels a specific *individual* as *a* deviant. In these two labeling processes, if no audience labels something or someone deviant, *no deviance exists*. An act, belief, condition, or person cannot be deviant *in the abstract*, that is, without reference to how an audience does or would label it. Something or someone must be defined as such by the members of a society or a group *as* deviant—it must be *labeled* as reprehensible or wrong. Likewise, a person cannot be regarded as a deviant until this labeling process takes place. An act, belief, or condition need not be *actually* or *concretely* labeled to be regarded as deviant, however, but it is deviant if it belongs to a category of similar actions, beliefs, or conditions. In other words, *we already know* that the public regards shooting the proprietor of a store and taking the contents of that store's cash register as deviant. Even if the robber gets away with the crime, we know that if known about, it would be regarded as deviant in the society at large—that is, it is an instance of "societal deviance."

Labeling involves attaching a *stigmatizing* definition to an activity, a belief, or a condition. Stigma is a stain, a sign of reproach or social undesirability, an indication to the world that one has been singled out as a shameful, morally discredited human being. Someone who has been stigmatized is a "marked" person; he or she has a "spoiled identity." (Although, interestingly enough, as I've already pointed out, Erving Goffman, who wrote a classic book on stigma that strongly influenced the labeling theorists, stated [1963, p. 141]: "I do not think all deviators have enough in common to warrant a special

analysis.") A stigmatized person is one who has been labeled a deviant. Once someone has been so discredited, relations with conventional, respectable others become difficult, strained, problematic. In other words, "being caught and branded as a deviant has important consequences for one's further participation and self-image. . . . Committing the improper act and being publicly caught at it places [the individual] in a new status. He [or she] has been revealed as a different kind of person from the kind he [or she] was supposed to be. He [or she] is labeled a 'fairy,' 'dope fiend,' 'nut,' or 'lunatic,' and treated accordingly" (Becker, 1963, pp. 31, 32).

So crucial is this labeling process that, in some respects, it does not much matter whether or not someone who has been stigmatized has actually engaged in the behavior of which he or she is accused. According to the logic of labeling theory, *falsely accused* deviants—if the accusation sticks—are still deviants (Becker, 1963, p. 20). In many important respects, they resemble individuals who really *do* commit acts that violate the rules. For example, women and men burned at the stake for the crime of witchcraft in the fifteenth and sixteenthth centuries were deviants in the eyes of the authorities and the community (Currie, 1968; Ben-Yehuda, 1980), even though they clearly did not engage in a pact with the devil. Two day-care workers are stigmatized in a certain community for, let's say, the sexual molestation of young children. One did it and the other didn't. Labeling theory would hold that these two individuals will share important experiences and characteristics in common, *by virtue of that labeling process alone*, even though they are poles apart with respect to having committed the behavior of which they are accused. While their lives are unlikely to be *identical* simply because both are seen by the community as deviants, the similarities they share are likely to be revealing.

Reflexivity

Reflexivity means looking at ourselves in part through the eyes of others. It is what is widely referred to, although too mechanistically, as the "looking glass self." Labeling theory is based on a seemingly simple but fundamental observation:

"We see ourselves through the eyes of others, and when others see us in a certain way, at least for long enough or sufficiently powerfully, their views are sure to have some effect" (Glassner, 1982, p. 71).

Being stigmatized by others is certainly not the only factor that influences what people do in the drama of deviance, but it is a crucial one. In addition, not everyone who enacts behavior that would be punished if it were discovered is caught—nor, for that matter, punished. Nor do all people who enact certain behavior care what the majority thinks of them or their behavior; they may be focused more or less exclusively on the views of their own circle or group. At the same time, nearly all people who violate society's major norms know that they are likely to be punished, condemned, stigmatized, and labeled as deviants if they are discovered. Thus, they interact in a social world in which they are *aware* that their identities and behavior are potentially punishable. They may be able to partially insulate themselves in circles or groups whose members would tolerate what they do or who they are, but nearly all have to navigate in the "straight" or mainstream world from time to time.

In other words, both direct *and* indirect, or concrete *and* symbolic labeling operate in the world of deviance (Warren and Johnson, 1972, pp. 76–77). "Indirect" or "symbolic" labeling is the awareness by a deviance-enactor that his or her behavior is saturated with public scorn, that his or her identity is potentially discreditable, that he or she *would be* stigmatized if discovered. People who violate norms have to deal with the probable and potential, as well as the actual and concrete, reactions of the respectable, conventional, law-abiding majority. All violators of major norms must at least ask themselves, "How would others react to me and my behavior?" If the answer is, "They would punish me," then the rule breaker must try to avoid detection, remain within deviant or minority circles, or be prepared to be punished, condemned, and stigmatized.

The Inner World of Deviance

One major endeavor of the labeling theorist is the attempt to understand the *inner world* of deviance. As I said above, interactionism stresses the ethnographic, anthropological, or participant observation research method: hanging around the individuals under study, observing them in their natural habitat, getting as close to the activity of interest as possible. This means attempting an understanding of the deviant world *as the deviant lives and understands it*. For instance, how do homosexuals see and define their behavior? What is their attitude about being gay? How do they experience being homosexual? How do they look upon the "straight" world? What is the construction of *their* moral meaning like? How do they define right and wrong with respect to sexuality? What does it feel like to be a member of a minority whose members are looked down on by the straight majority? To know how the world of homosexuality is lived, it is necessary to enter that world and listen to and observe those who actually live it.

It has sometimes been said that interactionism is focused more or less exclusively on the definers and labelers of deviance, that the deviant is secondary, a passive cipher who merely responds but does not act, who becomes a product of how he or she is defined (Gouldner, 1968). Nothing can be further from the truth. Interactionists are *fascinated* by the details of the lives of individuals and groups defined as deviant. It emphasizes how *creative* and *diverse* reactions to being so defined are, how *incapable* powerful deviance-definers are in imposing their will and conceptions on deviants, how *active* deviants are in creating their own definitions and conceptions, how truly *complex* the lives of deviants are, and how totally *ignorant* outsiders are of these lives until they enter them and take the effort to find out about them. Inspect the primary documents of the labeling school—for instance Becker's *Outsiders* (1963) and the articles making up his anthology, *The Other Side* (1964). The first volume includes detailed ethnographies of jazz musicians and marijuana smokers—their lives, their inner worlds, how they see and define things, how they carve out a meaningful social existence in the face of mainstream opposition to their way of seeing and doing things. The second is a collection of articles, again detailing the lives of a specific deviant scene, circle, or group: for instance, heroin addiction (Ray, 1964; Finestone, 1964), physician narcotic addiction (Winick, 1964), homosexual prostitution (Reiss, 1964), check forging (Lemert, 1964b), mental illness (Sampson et al., 1964), gambling (Zola, 1964). All these articles reflect an interactionist approach in that they represent *detailed descriptions of an insider's view*; they all attempt to get at "the inner world of deviance." The same can be said for the more recent second, third, or fourth-generation interactionists—the theoretical descendants of the original labeling theorists. (For a representative sampling, see Kelly, 1996; Rubington and Weinberg, 2002; Adler and Adler, 2003).

The "Stickiness" of Labels and the Self-Fulfilling Prophecy

Labeling theorists argue that stigmatizing someone as a socially and morally undesirable character has important consequences for that person's further rule breaking. Under certain circumstances, being labeled may intensify one's commitment to a deviant identity and contribute to further deviant behavior. Some conventional, law-abiding citizens believe, "once a deviant, always a deviant." Someone who has been stigmatized and labeled "is ushered into the deviant position by a decisive and often dramatic ceremony, yet is retired from it with hardly a word of public notice." As a result, the deviant is given "no proper licence to resume a normal life in the community. Nothing has happened to cancel out the stigma imposed upon him" or her. The original judgment "is still in effect." The conforming members of a society tend to be "reluctant to accept the returning deviant on an entirely equal footing" (Erikson, 1964, pp. 16, 17).

Deviant labels tend to be "sticky"; the community tends to stereotype someone as, above all and most importantly, a deviant. When someone is identified as a deviant, the community asks, "What kind of person would break such an important rule?" The answer that is given is "one who is different from the rest of us, who cannot or will not act as a moral being and therefore might break other important rules" (Becker, 1963, p. 34). Deviant labeling is widely regarded as a quality that is "in" the person, an attribute that is carried wherever he or she goes; therefore, it is permanent or at least long-lasting. Deviant behavior is said to be caused by an indwelling, essentialistic trait; it is not seen as accidental or

trivial, but a fixture of the individual. Once a deviant label has been attached, it is difficult to shake. Ex-convicts find it difficult to find legitimate employment on their release from prison (Schwartz and Skolnick, 1964); once psychiatrists make a diagnosis of mental illness, hardly any amount of contrary evidence can dislodge their faith in it (Rosenhan, 1973); ex–mental patients are carefully scrutinized for odd, eccentric, or bizarre behavior; a young woman who is seen as sexually promiscuous (the label may or may not have been earned as a result of her actual behavior) will, in all likelihood, continue to be so viewed until she leaves the community.

Such stigmatizing and stereotyping tends to deny to deviants "the ordinary means of carrying on the routines of everyday life open to most people. Because of this denial, the deviant must of necessity develop illegitimate routines" (Becker, 1963, p. 35). As a consequence, the labeling process may actually increase the deviant's further commitment to deviant behavior. It may limit conventional options and opportunities, strengthen a deviant identity, and maximize participation in a deviant group. Labeling someone, thus, may become "a self-fulfilling prophecy" (Becker, 1963, p. 34) in that *someone becomes what he or she is accused of being*—even though that original accusation may have been false (Merton, 1948, 1957, pp. 421–436; Jones, 1977; Jones, 1986).

The ex-con will be regarded or labeled as dishonest, thus will find it impossible to get a straight job, and will return to a life of crime. The ex–mental patient will be defined as "still crazy," and will buckle under the strain of having to prove he or she is normal. The sexually permissive young woman may find that the only reason boys will want to date her is for short-term sexual gratification, and so will end up satisfying their demands.

Nonetheless, contrary to the stereotype about labeling theory (Davis, 1980, p. 199), interactionists are careful to point out that negative labeling does *not* always or inevitably have this self-fulfilling outcome. "Obviously," says Becker, "everyone caught in one deviant act and labeled a deviant does not move inevitably toward greater deviance" (Becker, 1963, p. 36). Indeed, such labeling could very well "stamp out," repress, or cause a discontinuation of the deviant behavior that was punished—as is often the case with marijuana use (Becker, 1955; 1963, p. 59), political radicalism in Europe, and polygyny (a man having several wives) in Utah (Lemert, 1951, p. 63). Still, the more interesting prediction, and the one labeling theorists have focused on, is that social control will lead to an intensification of the commitment to deviance, not a discontinuation of it.

It is important to emphasize that labels, stereotypes, and definitions of deviance are always in a state of flux. It is almost certain that many of the public conceptions of deviance that were widely held when labeling theorists were writing are now quite different. For instance, in the 1950s and early 1960s, when Becker wrote about marijuana use, it was regarded as a serious form of deviance (1953; 1955; 1963, pp. 41–78), one that often disqualified the known user from normal interaction in polite company. But the seriousness of marijuana use as deviance has considerably diminished since the 1950s and early 1960s. The condemnation of the non-using public has softened and the stereotypes they hold of use and users are more realistic. As a result, the capacity of the ex-user to cast off a stigmatizing label is almost certainly far greater than was true in past generations. Likewise, ridicule and stigma of the mentally ill and ex–mentally ill has diminished since the heyday of interactionist writings on the subject (Goffman, 1961, 1963; Scheff, 1966, 1984). The label of ex–mental patient is far less "sticky" today than it was in the past; being mentally ill is certainly seen as a far less irreversible condition. Today, it seems likely that the label of mental patient does not necessarily carry over into the future of former mental patients if over time their behavior does not correspond to the label. If former mental patients can act in relatively normal ways, they probably can shed their label and live a normal life (Cockerham, 2003, pp. 271ff.). Just as conceptions of deviance are relative to time and place, so is the degree of "stickiness" of deviant labels.

Labeling theory's influence has declined sharply since its heyday roughly from the mid-1960s to the mid-1970s. At that time, it was the most influential, most frequently cited perspective in the study of deviance. This was especially so among the field's younger scholars and researchers, who yearned for a fresh, unconventional, and radically different way of looking at deviance. As I said earlier, it was widely and vigorously attacked, and many of these criticisms stuck. Eventually, much of the field recognized its inadequacies and moved on to other perspectives, or sharply modified or adapted interactionist or labeling insights (Link et al., 1989; Braithwaite, 1989; LaFree, 1989). Today, there is no single approach or paradigm that dominates the field, in the way that the Chicago School did in the 1920s or labeling theory did circa 1970. What we see today is diversity, fragmentation, and "theoretical confusion" (Scull, 1988, p. 685). While the practitioners of a variety of perspectives attacked labeling theory for its inadequacies, no single perspective has managed to succeed "in establishing an alternative orientation to the field that [has] commanded wide assent" (p. 685). In spite of the criticisms, the labeling school left an enduring legacy to the field that even its critics make use of, albeit for the most part implicitly. Today it is clear that while, as a total approach to deviance, labeling *theory* is inadequate and incomplete, labeling *processes* take place in all deviance and deserve a prominent place in its study.

CONFLICT THEORY

Social scientists can be divided according to how much *consensus* or *conflict* they see in contemporary society. Talcott Parsons, for instance, saw deviance as "a disturbance of the equilibrium of the interactive system" (1951, p. 250). In other words, harmony is the rule, and a disruption of that harmony calls for steps to reestablish peace and tranquility. The members of a society are socialized to behave properly; most of them accept the central values and norms of their society, and act accordingly; a few are improperly or inadequately socialized, or, for some reason, the components of the social system are improperly integrated; deviance ensues, disrupting the social order; forces act to restore society to its former state of equilibrium (Parsons, 1951, Chapter VII). This is a *consensus* view of society: Most people agree on the central values in a given society; disagreement causes disruption, disorder, and disequilibrium, and a societal need to repair the damage that they inflict.

Consensus thinking is based on three principles. First, the values and beliefs of the members of a society are more-or-less consistent with one another; there is a high degree of consensus about basic or core values. In sociology, this view is likely to have been influenced by the thinking of French sociologist Emile Durkheim (1858–1917), who believed that societies possessed a "collective conscience," or a shared sense of morality. In other words, most people agree with one another about the most basic and important values.

Second, consensus thinkers argue that, in advanced industrial societies, the members of the society tend to be *interdependent*—they need one another to get along; each is doing something essential to the lives of others (Durkheim, 1933, pp. 111ff.).

And third, consensus theorists tend to see social life as fairly harmonious, and societies as more or less cohesive and stable. Societies display a kind of inherent and unconscious wisdom. As we saw, many social institutions that might seem destructive and repressive actually turn out to benefit the society as a whole, such as social stratification (Davis and Moore, 1945; Davis, 1949, pp. 366–368), prostitution (Davis, 1937, 1971), deviance and crime (Hawkins and Waller, 1936; Merton, 1957, pp. 78–80; Bell, 1961, pp. 127–150), and even conflict itself (Coser, 1956). The functionalists discussed at the beginning of this chapter are a good example of consensus theorists. All consensus theorists—functionalists included—agree that conflict exists, and has a crucial impact on the society; however, for the consensus theorist, much conflict turns out to serve a broader, long-range agenda: reintegrating the society as a whole, making it more cohesive, stable, and viable (Coser, 1956).

In contrast, conflict theorists do not see a great deal of consensus, harmony, or cohesion in contemporary society. They see groups with competing and clashing interests and values. They see struggles between and among categories, sectors, groups, and classes in the society, with winners and losers resulting from the outcome of these struggles. Most social institutions, they argue, do not benefit the society as a whole. Rather, they benefit some groups *at the expense of* others. Conflict theorists envision the resources of the

society as being distributed according to a "zero-sum game," that is, they are of a fixed size, and whatever is distributed to one faction or category is taken away from another. They argue against the functionalists' analysis of stratification as benefiting the society as a whole. In contrast, the conflict theorists argue, stratification benefits only the rich and the powerful *at the expense of* the poor and the weak. Moreover, it is to the advantage of the rich and the powerful to have the disadvantaged *believe* stratification is for the good of the entire society; that way, the disadvantaged will be less likely to threaten the interests and privileges of the rich. Likewise, the conflict theorists argue, prostitution does not benefit the society as a whole; it benefits representatives of groups—mainly men—who profit from society's patriarchal institutions.

Conflict theorists stress that institutions, changes, and behavior tend to have a very different impact on the various classes, categories, and groups in a society. What helps one may very well hurt another, and vice versa. And the interests of one often clash with or contradict those of another. Some groups are helped most by keeping things the way they are, by the status quo; others have an interest in radical change. No phenomenon has the same impact on all social categories equally. On many issues, there is no common ground, no plan that would help everyone, no unified or homogeneous unit—society as a whole—that would be helped or hurt by any institution, change, or behavior. What one group profits from takes away from another, and vice versa. Even stability and cohesion may be repressive, for they may prevent change and a redistribution of resources—thereby helping the advantaged and hurting the disadvantaged. Many of the very institutions the functionalists saw as "functional" for the society as a whole repress and exploit less advantaged groups and categories, such as women, African Americans, and the working class.

Groups struggle to have their own definitions of right and wrong enacted into law. The key word here is *hegemony*, or dominance: Groups struggle to legitimate their own special interests and views and to discredit and nullify the influence of those of competing groups. For instance, pro- and antiabortionists hold rallies and demonstrations and lobby in Washington and in state capitals to get laws passed, have laws taken off the books, or keep existing laws on the books. Each side is struggling for dominance or hegemony, struggling to have its own views translated into law and public opinion. Such is the order of the day, according to the conflict theorist, who sees a constant struggle among competing groups in contemporary society.

Perhaps the most conflict-oriented of all the conflict theorists are the Marxists. Their ideas are somewhat distinct and different from those of the non-Marxist conflict theorists. Conflict theorists who do not work within the Marxist paradigm are often called *interest group theorists* (Orcutt, 1983, pp. 311, 316–322), or *pluralistic conflict theorists* (Pfohl, 1994, pp. 428–431; Sheley, 1995, pp. 46ff.). I will use the terms *conflict theory*, *interest group theory*, and *pluralistic conflict theory* more or less interchangeably, and will refer to Marxist theory as partly separate from this tradition. While the Marxists, obviously, draw their inspiration from the writings of Karl Marx (1818–1883) and his followers, the non-Marxist conflict theorists are more likely to have been influenced by the writings of Max Weber (1864–1920). Since the 1980s, Marxism has plummeted in intellectual and theoretical influence—in the study of deviance, and more broadly, among sociologists, and, even more generally, among academics and intellectuals as a whole.

The central issue for all conflict-oriented criminologists is the emergence and enforcement of norms, rules, and, especially, laws. How do laws get passed? Which groups manage to get their own special interests and views enacted into laws? Who profits by the passage of laws? Which laws are enforced, and which are passed but never enforced—and why? Why are certain activities regarded as deviant while others are regarded as conventional by the members of a given society?

The answer provided by the conflict approach is that laws, rules, and norms grow out of a power struggle between and among interest groups, factions, and social classes. The most powerful group or groups in society are the ones who are successful in having their own special views of right and wrong accepted by the society as a whole and formulated into the criminal law. Likewise, the enforcement of the law represents the application of power against the powerless by the powerful.

Conflict theorists explicitly *reject* two commonly held views concerning the law. The first is, of course, the *consensus* view that the law is a "reflection of the social consciousness of a society," that laws make up a "barometer of the moral and social thinking of a community" (Friedman, 1964, p. 143), that the law reflects "the will of the people." Instead, conflict theorists argue that public views on what is regarded as conventional or deviant, law-abiding or criminal, vary strikingly from group to group in a large, complex society. Even where consensus exists on a given issue as to what should be against the law, the conflict theorist asks *how* and *why* that consensus is achieved (Chambliss, 1976, p. 3; Turk, 1980, pp. 83–84). For most issues, there is no majority consensus—only different views held by different social groups. The point of view held by the most powerful of these groups tends to be the one that becomes law.

The second widely held view that conflict theory rejects is that laws are passed and enforced to protect the society as a whole, to protect all classes and groups more or less equally. The conflict theorist argues that laws do not protect the rights, interests, and well-being of the many, but the interests of the few. There is no such thing as "the society as a whole," the conflict theorist would argue. Societies are broken up into segments, sectors, classes, groups, or categories that have very different interests. Very few laws have an equal impact on all segments of society. For instance, the earliest laws of vagrancy in England were passed to protect the interests of the wealthiest and most powerful members of English society—the landowners in the 1300s and the merchant class in the 1500s (Chambliss, 1964). The laws of theft in England, again, were interpreted by the courts in the 1400s as a means of protecting the property of merchants, the emerging powerful class at that time, a class the Crown needed to protect and curry favor with (Hall, 1952).

Conflict theorists do not see laws as an expression of a broad consensus or as an altruistic desire to protect a large number of the members of a society from objective, clear, and present danger. Rather, they are the embodiment of the beliefs, lifestyle, and/or economic interests of certain segments of the society. Thus, the law is a means of forcing one group's beliefs and way of life onto the rest of the society. Laws are passed and enforced not because they protect society in general, or because many people believe in their moral correctness, but because they uphold the ideological or material interests of a certain sector of society. This serves to stop certain people from doing what others consider evil, undesirable, or unprofitable—or to make them do something that others consider good, desirable, or profitable. The passage of a law represents the triumph of a point of view or an ideology associated with a particular group, social category, or organization—even if that law is not enforced.

Conflict theorists also emphasize the role that power and status play in the enforcement process. That is, even for the same offense, apprehension is less likely to lead to serious punishment for the person who commands more power and a higher ranking in the socioeconomic status system; for juveniles, especially, this extends to the parents of offenders. One sociologist studied two juvenile gangs, the "Saints" and the "Roughnecks," whose members were accorded very different treatment at the hands of local law enforcement. The "Saints," whose parents had respectable, relatively powerful upper-middle-class occupational positions, were treated far more leniently by law enforcement than the "Roughnecks," whose parents were lower- and working-class. None of the "Saints" had ever been arrested, while all of the "Roughnecks" had, most of them on numerous occasions; yet their offenses, and the frequency with which they had been committed, were quite comparable (Chambliss, 1973). A tenet of the conflict perspective is that not only does the *law* define actions as illegal in conformity with the interests of the most powerful segments of the society, but the *enforcement* of the law is also unequal in that, in any society, it reflects the distribution of power.

In addition to being interested in the passage and enforcement of criminal laws, conflict theorists also examine—although to a far lesser extent—the question of the *causes* of criminal behavior. These are the etiological concerns discussed in Chapter 3. What causes criminal behavior according to the conflict perspective? To be succinct about it, conflict theorists would answer this question by pointing to the *nature of the society* we are focusing on and the classes or categories in them. Conflict theorists generally would argue that inequalities in power and income cause certain types of criminal behavior; Marxists, for instance, would say that *capitalist society* is *criminogenic*—that the exploitation of the working class by the capitalist class or ruling elite causes certain kinds of crime to take place.

The conflict theorist is careful to point out that the issue is not explaining criminal behavior as such, but explaining forms of behavior that have *a high likelihood of being defined as criminal*. What forms of behavior are these? The behavior of the poor and the powerless stands a higher likelihood of being defined as crimes, while the behavior of the rich and the powerful stands a considerably lower likelihood. Thus the violent, predatory actions that the poorer strata are more likely to commit are those actions that tend to be criminalized and enforced, while the harmful, unethical corporate actions of the wealthier strata are not as likely to be defined as crimes, and, if they are, tend not to lead to arrest, and are not as often studied by the criminologist. Thus, when someone asks "What causes criminal behavior?", he or she almost invariably means, "What causes people to engage in a particular *type* of illegal behavior—namely, street crimes such as robbery, rape, and murder?"

For a century, beginning with the writings of Karl Marx (1818–1883), many of the brightest minds in the world were focused on the question of how, why, and when capitalism would collapse. They considered the demise of capitalism to be so self-evident that hardly any of them ever wondered about the demise of socialism. The fact that socialism, not capitalism, collapsed in Europe, retreated in Latin America, and has been seriously compromised in China—all within the space of a few short years—must have been a stunning blow to Marxist thinkers everywhere. In the field of the study of deviance, these developments have discouraged traditional Marxist theorizing. Marxism's decline began at least a half-dozen years before the surprising disintegration of Marxist regimes in the late 1980s and early 1990s, but the latter development further discredited Marxism as academically respectable.

This is not to say that all or even most of the ideas of Marxist or radical criminology have been discredited. Certainly social class is central to crime and its control. Certainly some features of capitalist society encourage certain crimes.

Certainly the street crime of the poor is enforced and prosecuted more vigorously than the corporate crime of the rich and the powerful. Certainly one's ideology has *something* to do with one's approach to crime and the research one conducts, and the latter *may* have political or ideological implications or consequences. Marxist criminology certainly had a positive impact on the field. However, in the long run, as an all-embracing perspective, most researchers realized that it was of limited utility, and they turned their focus on other approaches.

FEMINISM

Until a generation or so ago, most Western intellectuals viewed the world through two related biases: *Eurocentrism* and *androcentrism*.

Eurocentrism is the view that the world revolves around European—that is, Western, including North American—society and culture, and that all other societies and cultures should be measured against the European yardstick. It is only in the past 30 years or so that serious efforts have been undertaken to incorporate African, Asian, and Native American perspectives into the social sciences, history, philosophy, literature, and art. For instance, for centuries, American and European schoolchildren were taught that "Columbus discovered America." This claim is Eurocentric, since Native Americans, or Indians, as well as the Inuit, or "Eskimos," occupied North and South America for thousands of years before Columbus and his crew happened upon several islands in the Caribbean. Throughout the United States, especially in the East, signs may be seen proclaiming that the area was "settled" at a certain date. All, or nearly all, of these signs are Eurocentric because they refer solely and exclusively to settlements by persons of European ancestry; nearly everywhere, the land was "settled" much earlier by Indians. Is the study of the sociology of deviance Eurocentric? This is entirely possible, as some African-American scholars and researchers have argued (Russell, 1992; Covington, 1995).

Androcentrism is a male-centered bias. It is the view that men are the center of the universe and women are at the periphery of the action. Women

take on relevance only insofar as they relate to men and their activities. The androcentric bias in the study of deviance and crime began to be subject to criticism only in the late 1960s, and these critiques are having an impact on the way sociologists view the phenomenon of deviance. And it was *feminism* that launched this assault on androcentrism.

There is no single universally agreed-upon definition of feminism. However, perhaps the definition that might win broadest acceptance is this one: Feminism is the perspective that stresses that "women experience subordination on the basis of their sex" (Gelsthorpe and Morris, 1988, p. 224). Social scientists refer to "sex"—as distinguished from "sexual behavior"—as a biological characteristic of men and women, consisting of hormones, genitals, and secondary sex characteristics. In contrast, "gender" refers to the psychological and cultural reality of the way men and women are treated (that is, "sex roles") and how they are shaped by that treatment. Thus, feminism argues that men and women are typically treated as *representatives* or *embodiments of sexual categories*. Men are usually dominant in this process, and women subordinate. Feminists are concerned with uncovering the origins and functions of this unequal treatment, and seek to bring about a more sexually equalitarian society. For feminists, the enemy is *patriarchy*—institutions of male dominance. It is patriarchy that is responsible for the oppression of women, and it is patriarchy that must be analyzed, critiqued, and eliminated. Feminists often begin their analysis with an examination of how a given field has studied a phenomenon in the past, because this typically serves to justify patriarchy; this usually entails uncovering the sexist biases of more traditional approaches.

In 1968, Frances Heidensohn, a young British sociologist, noted that the "deviance of women" was one area that has been "most notably ignored in [the] sociological literature." At first glance, she said, this seems understandable; after all, in comparison with men, women "have low rates of participation in deviant activities." Such a defense might seem to be a reasonable explanation for the field's concentration on men, Heidensohn writes, "but not the almost total *exclusion*" of studies on female deviance and crime (Heidensohn, 1968, pp. 160, 161, 162; see also Smart, 1976). The exceptions to this rule, she argues, show that women are not only virtually invisible in the field of criminology and deviance studies, but they hold a peculiar and skewed place in its literature as well.

Some very early work on crime argued that women criminals were "atavistic and hysterical," their criminality a product of biological abnormality (Lombroso and Ferro, 1916; Smart, 1976, pp. 31–37). A later perspective argued that women engaged in criminal behavior just as often as men; however, they weren't detected as often because of their distinctively feminine trait of deceitfulness (Pollak, 1950; Heidensohn, 1968, pp. 165–166; Smart, 1976, pp. 46–53). Finally, the deviance of females was seen as an extension of the "focal concerns" of the female role. Men are pressured into committing crimes that result from the need to succeed in the occupational and financial realms, while women are pressured into committing crimes that result from the need to succeed in the sexual and marital realms. This usually means prostitution and sexual delinquency (Cohen, 1955, pp. 44–48, 137–147; Heidensohn, 1968, pp. 166–168). All of these analyses are biased from a male perspective. Feminists argue that they should be replaced with a more balanced approach. At present, Heidensohn says, "we barely possess the basic components for an initial analysis of the deviance of women. These are lonely, uncharted seas of human behaviour." What is needed to remedy this marginal, distorted image of female deviance is a "crash programme of research" (pp. 170–171).

The neglect of women in the field of criminology and deviance studies is not only characteristic of the traditional approaches. It also marked the more contemporary perspectives, such as labeling or interactionist theory and radical or Marxist theory. In an insightful analysis of the role of women in studies on deviance, Marcia Millman (1975) argues that, in many of the writings by labeling theorists, men appear as interesting, adventurous deviants who lead exciting lives, while women are depicted as boring, conventional, nagging drudges who attempt to rein in the wilder side of the men in their lives. While deviants are depicted with understanding and empathy in interactionist research, it is almost always *men* who are engaged in the deviance that is focused on, while *women* play a marginal, passive, inhibitory role. It was not until the 1980s that the implications of labeling theory were fully spelled out for the involvement of women in deviance (Schur, 1984).

Critical, radical, or Marxist criminology was no better in its analysis of women's role in deviance and crime than the more conventional perspectives. As one feminist analysis of criminological theory pointed out, there is *not one word* about women in Taylor, Walton, and Young's treatise on the "new" criminology, and Quinney, a major self-designated Marxist of the 1970s, "is all but blind to the distinctions between conditions of males and females in capitalist society." These authors "thoroughly scrutinize and criticize theoretical criminology, yet they never notice the limited applicability of these theories to women" (Leonard, 1982, p. 176). The sexism lurking in earlier writings can be illustrated by a male-centered aside made by Alvin Gouldner, critic of traditional sociology, especially functionalism, and author of a well-known critique of the interactionist approach to deviance (1968), who, in arguing that the sexual lives of sociologists may influence their work, remarks: "For example, it is my strong but undocumented impression that when some sociologists change their work interests, problems, or styles, they also change mistresses or wives" (1970, p. 57).

Three main points can be made about the depiction of women in writings on deviance prior to the 1960s and 1970s. (These generalizations apply even today, although to a far lesser extent.) The first is, as we saw, that women represented a minor theme in these writings. They were studied less, appeared less often as subjects of attention, remained marginal, secondary, almost invisible. The study of women and deviance suffers from "a problem of omission"; women have been "largely overlooked in the literature" (Millman, 1975, p. 265).

Second, the study of deviance reflects "a male-biased view" (Millman, 1975, p. 265). Not only was the deviance of women less often studied; when it was, it was nearly always *specialized* deviance. The deviance of men was deviance *in general*; the deviance of women was *women's* deviance. In a chapter entitled "The Criminality of Women," which appeared in a textbook that was eventually published in multiple editions, Walter Reckless (1950, p. 116) argued that the criminal behavior of women should not be considered "in the same order of phenomena as crime in general"—meaning the criminal behavior of men. Unlike men, in committing crimes, women are deceitful (p. 122), kill by administering poison (p. 121), throw acid in the face of a victim, "usually an unfaithful lover" (p. 122), and are prone to "make false accusations of a sexual nature" (p. 123). In short, the *forms* of deviance and crime women engage in are said to be very different from those that men commit. The three specific forms of deviance that have attracted attention from the field are shoplifting, mental illness, and prostitution. While women do play a majority role in the first of these, at least an equal role in the second, and the overwhelmingly dominant role in the last of them, they *do* commit a far wider range of deviant actions than these; their participation in deviance *has* been stereotyped in the literature, and men's deviance is *not* deviance "in general," as some observers have claimed.

And third, the role of women *as victims* of crime and deviance was underplayed until recently. This was especially the case with respect to rape, domestic assault, and sexual harassment. Not until the 1970s, when feminist scholars began a systematic examination of the ways women are brutalized and exploited by men, did deviant and criminal actions such as rape (Brownmiller, 1975), wife battering (Martin, 1976), and sexual harassment (MacKinnon, 1979) find a significant place in the literature on deviance and crime, and the suffering inflicted on women at the hands of men receive sufficient attention. In the 1980s, a number of radicals recognized that the question of women as victims of crime created "enormous theoretical problems for the radical paradigm in criminology" (Jones, MacLean, and Young, 1986, p. 3; Gelsthorpe and Morris, 1988, p. 233). Specifically, feminist research on female victims of crime has brought home to certain radicals "the limits of the romantic conception of crime and the criminal" (Matthews and Young, 1986, p. 2; Gelsthorpe and Morris, 1988, pp. 232–233). While it is true that men are significantly more likely to be the victims of crime than women, for some crimes (such as the three I just mentioned), the sex ratio is *overwhelmingly* in the other direction. Moreover, women suffer certain crimes *specifically* because of their powerless position relative to that of men. In short, women victims of crime have been "hidden from history" (Summers, 1981).

Prior to the 1970s, then, sociology and the other disciplines have been "unable to explain adequately the phenomenon of women and crime. Theories that are frequently hailed as explanations of human behavior are, in fact, discussions of male behavior and male criminality." These theories and explanations "are biased to the core, riddled with assumptions that relate to male—not female— reality. Theoretical criminology is sexist because it unwittingly focuses on the activities, interests, and values of men, while ignoring a comparable analysis of women." Any acceptable theoretical framework must either "incorporate an understanding of both male and female behavior" or, alternatively, explain exactly *why* and *how* it applies specifically or more forcefully to either women or men (Leonard, 1982, p. 181). In the words of French philosopher and writer Simone de Beauvoir, in Western society, man is the "subject," the "absolute," while woman is "the Other" (1953).

Leonard warns that the classic approaches in the study of deviance cannot provide an adequate analysis of women and crime on their own. Since they were constructed with men in mind, any reexamination of past theories of deviance must be "approached with a solid grounding in feminist understandings of the role of women in contemporary society." Otherwise, she says, they will succumb to the "partial and distorted" portraits of the past (1982, p. 190). Such a grounding would examine differences in power relations between men and women, a thorough examination of sex roles and their historical origins and contemporary functions, the part women play in the family, and their role in the marketplace (pp. 188, 190). Although Leonard has not provided that analysis herself, she has pointed the way to such an analysis.

The position of women in deviance and crime is very different in at least one major way from that of other oppressed, relatively powerless categories, such as African Americans and members of the lower and working classes. For the most part, the tendency to engage in a variety of street crimes is negatively related to power and income: The lower the power and income of a given category, the greater the likelihood that its members will engage in acts traditionally regarded as crimes. With women, we see precisely the opposite tendency: A category that is less powerful and less affluent than men engages in street crime at a strikingly lower level than men. So different are women from the general pattern that they pose a serious challenge to radical and Marxist thinking about crime. If crime is a "rational" response to oppression in capitalist society, why are women so disinclined to commit crimes? What makes them different? If the ruling elite use the criminal law to control troublesome categories and classes, why is it so rarely applied to women? If crime can be seen as a primitive means by which the less powerful struggle against oppression, why are women so often the *victims* of these struggles? In short, a systematic analysis of women's role in deviance, crime, and the law would require a serious modification of radical criminology's assertions. Indeed, this may be precisely why radical criminologists failed to deal with the issue of women and crime for so long.

A feminist approach to deviance and crime did not exist more than a generation ago; the perspective is young and still in the process of development. Perhaps it is too early to say that *a* feminist criminology of the sociology of deviance exists as a coherent and unified approach. Perhaps it is more appropriate to refer to feminism*s*, or feminist criminolog*ies*, or feminist perspectives within criminology (Gelsthorpe and Morris, 1988, p. 227). There are, at the very least, liberal, radical, and socialist varieties of feminism. Incomplete as the perspective is, however, it shows great promise to enrich and inform the discipline. No approach that treats the behavior of less than half the population as if it were behavior in general can claim to be adequate or valid. The fields of criminology and deviance studies have a long way to go before they fully incorporate the insights of feminism into the way they look at their subject matter. It is possible that feminism may have a more revolutionary impact on the field than that of any other perspective we've examined. Feminism forces us to think about sex biases and how they distort our views of deviance, crime, the law, and the criminal justice system. These biases are deep and pervasive. Confronting and overcoming them makes us better sociologists, criminologists, and students of deviance, and, just perhaps, makes us more capable of changing society for the better.

CONTROLOLOGY OR THE NEW SOCIOLOGY OF SOCIAL CONTROL

All constructionist theorists of deviance are interested in the dynamics of social control, as spelled out in Chapter 2. The perspective that gives social control a central place and views social control as almost exclusively oppressive, centralized, and state-sponsored is referred to as "controlology" or the "new sociology of social control." Perhaps the most dramatic image of this school's perspective was captured by Stanley Cohen, one of controlology's central thinkers, in the following quote:

> Imagine that the entrance to the deviancy control system is something like a gigantic fishing net. Strange and complex in its appearance and movements, the net is cast by an army of different fishermen and fisherwomen working all day and even into the night according to more or less known rules and routines, subject to more or less authority and control from above, knowing more or less what the other is doing. Society is the ocean—vast, troubled and full of uncharted currents, rocks, and other hazards. Deviants are the fish. (Cohen, 1985a, pp. 41–42)

The spiritual father of the school of thought known as the new sociology of social control is Michel Foucault (pronounced "foo-COH"), a French philosopher and intellectual. Foucault's ideas have been extremely influential; it is possible that he is the most frequently cited intellectual in the world. In the early 1960s, Foucault published a work that was to be translated into English as *Madness and Civilization* (1967). Its central idea was that as society moved into the industrial age, the brutal repression of the prison gave way to a new, different, seemingly enlightened, and more subtly repressive institution—the mental institution. Social control need not be overly and brutally repressive to be effective. Indeed, state-sponsored social control is all the more repressive as a result of resorting to reason, persuasion, and scientific authority. Foucault's argument was that physicians, psychiatrists, and scientists employ their expertise to repress and suppress human diversity.

Even more important was the book that was translated into English in 1979 as *Discipline and Punish* (Foucault, 1979). In this later work, Foucault extended his idea of enlightened but repressive social control. The centerpiece of traditional social control was torture and execution. Its goal was the mutilation or destruction of the offender's (or supposed offender's) body. Traditional means of punishment were fitful and sporadic rather than continual and ongoing. Public confessions, torture, and execution created spectacle but, increasingly, they were ineffective. Eventually, crowds came not to be seized by the terror of the scaffold but instead to protest the injustice of harsh punishment. In the end, public executions produced disorder and mob violence, not fear and compliance.

With the growing importance of portable property in the 1700s, the merchant class needed a stable, predictable means of protecting its investments from the predatory activities of the lower classes. The traditional means of punishment had to be replaced by a system of control that was more effective, certain, and comprehensive, and that operated all the time. The traditional prison was used almost exclusively to detain suspected offenders before trial or execution. It was only in the second half of the eighteenth century that the modern prison became a location specifically for the incarceration and punishment of the offender. The new prison, Foucault believed, revealed the special character of the new age.

Jeremy Bentham (1748–1832), British philosopher, reformer, and utilitarian, came up with a plan for the modern prison. It was designed so that a small number of guards could observe a large number of inmates. He called this arrangement the *panopticon*. It was Foucault's belief that the central thrust in the history of Western society was the evolution away from traditional society where the many observe the few (as was true in spectacles such as execution) to modern society, where the few observe the many (as in the modern prison, with its panopticon). According to Foucault, Bentham's panopticon was typical, characteristic, or paradigmatic of modern society in general. The panoptic principle, Foucault believed, had become generalized and imitated throughout the entire society. We live, he said, in a society in which

state and statelike agents are bent on observing and controlling the citizens in a wide range of contexts. In a sense, then, Foucault believed, modern society had become one gigantic, monstrous panopticon.

Foucault takes *thought* and *discourse* as concretely realized reality, as indicative of the way things are—in a sense, as even more "real" than actions. In fact, modern prisons are not even remotely Bentham's panopticon. As a general rule, Foucault takes consequences, including unintended consequences, as if they were a direct outcome of the motives of the powerful actors on the scene. Foucault ignores all countervailing forces that operate to control the exercise of power. In his scheme, there is no political opposition (Garland, 1990, p. 167). He nearly always presents the control potential of the powers that be as the reality (p. 168). And, for all its claims to being a political understanding of modern society, *Discipline and Punish* presents a "strangely apolitical" analysis of the exercise of power (p. 170). There is no "motive to power"—only more power, more discipline, and more control. Why and for what purpose the power is wielded is never fully explained. Foucault writes as if a society without the exercise of power is possible; he seems to be against power per se (pp. 173–174). He never presents an alternative system, one that could operate through the humane, enlightened exercise of power. In fact, to Foucault, in the context of modern society, "humane" and "enlightened" mean only one thing: insidious attempts at greater and more effective control, that is to say, *repression*.

Foucault died in 1984, of AIDS, before the emergence of the drug "cocktails"—developed by the very oppressively enlightened, scientific, state-sponsored agencies he denounced—that could have prolonged his life. His ideas have become the inspiration for a new, later generation of "controlologists." The central points of this school are these:

First, *social control is problematic; it should not be taken for granted.* By that, controlologists mean that it does not emerge "naturally" and spontaneously by the "invisible hand" of society but is "consciously fashioned by the visible hand of definable organizations, groups, and classes" (Scull, 1988, p. 686). We cannot assume, as the functionalists seemed to have done, that society will be wise enough to preserve institutions and practices that serve the whole in the best possible way by curtailing what is harmful and encouraging what is beneficial. Social control, as it is practiced, is not a product of a broad, widely shared social "need" or the workings of basic "functional prerequisites," to use functionalist terminology. Instead, the controlologists say, social control is imposed by specific social entities, usually for their own benefit, and often at the expense of those individuals, categories, and groups that are controlled.

Second, *social control is typically coercive, repressive, far from benign.* Agents of social control typically try to make control seem benign, or at least enlightened, but this is a facade; control appears as a "velvet glove" rather than an "iron fist." Traditional criminologists have looked on social control generally, and the criminal justice system specifically, as society's natural, inevitable, and beneficial means of self-protection against harmful behavior. As viewed by controlologists, social control takes on a more sinister coloration; its purpose is to repress and contain troublesome populations. Hence, the purpose of psychiatry is not to heal but to control; the purpose of the welfare system is not to provide a safety net for the poor but to control; the purpose of education is not to teach but to control; the purpose of the mass media is not to inform or entertain but to control—or rather, the mass media entertain *in order to* control. And when segments of the population under institutional control are perceived as no longer threatening, they are dumped out of the system (Scull, 1984).

Third, *social control is coterminous with state or statelike control.* The government is made up of a virtual alphabet soup of agencies of social control, including the DEA (the Drug Enforcement Agency), the ATF (the Bureau of Alcohol, Tobacco, and Firearms), the FDA (the Food and Drug Administration), the NIDA (the National Institute on Drug Abuse), the NIMH (the National Institute of Mental Health), and the INS (the Immigration and Naturalization Service, now a division of the Department of Homeland Security), all of which have one aim—to monitor and control the behavior of troublesome populations. In addition, a number of organizations,

agencies, and institutions are performing the function of social control *on behalf of* or *in the service of* the state. These include private social welfare agencies, psychiatrists and psychiatric agencies, professional organizations such as the American Medical Association, hospitals, clinics, mental health organizations, treatment facilities, educational institutions, and so on. It is the contention of controlologists that state control is increasingly being assumed by civil society. Troublesome populations can now be controlled on a wide range of fronts by a wide range of agencies. The same clients are circulated and recirculated between and among them. Even institutions that would appear to have little or nothing to do with the control of deviance as such—such as the mass media of communications—are involved in social control through shaping public opinion about deviants (Ericson, Baranek, and Chan, 1991).

Fourth, *the social control apparatus is unified and coherent.* The subsystems "fit together" into interrelated, functionally equivalent parts. Interlocking agencies and overarching institutions that work together to control troublesome populations may be referred to as the phenomenon of *transcarceration* (Lowman, Menzies, and Palys, 1987)—institutions of incarceration and control that reach across institutional boundaries. Foucault refers to this "transcarceral" system as the "carceral archipelago" (1979, p. 298), a reference to Aleksander Solzhenitisyn's description of the Soviet prison camps, *The Gulag Archipelago* (1974). The carceral archipelago transported the punitive approach "from the penal institution to the entire social body" (Foucault, 1979, p. 298). Controlologists point to a "peno-juridical, mental health, welfare and tutelage complex" in which "power structures can be examined only by appreciating cross-institutional arrangements and dynamics" (Lowman, Menzies, and Palys, 1987, p. 9). In other words, more or less all the organized entities in society have become a massive network dedicated to the surveillance and punishment of deviance.

One must be impressed with the variety and range of people-processing institutions and agencies in modern society, many of them designed to deal with or handle the behavior of troublesome individuals and groups (Hawkins and Tiedeman,

1975). No one can doubt that some of the functionaries who work for these agencies are often uncaring and insensitive. Especially in the inner cities, these agencies are overwhelmed with the sheer volume of clients, and the community is shortchanged. But most of these problems stem not from too much control but from too few resources. Once again, modern society has no precedent in the number, variety, and near-ubiquitousness of organizations, agencies, and institutions that perform statelike functions, operating in place of and on behalf of the government. And social control is certainly one of their functions. In most cases, from the clients' perspective, that may not even be their main function. It seems almost inconceivable that such service and welfare service institutions are primarily, let alone exclusively, agencies of social control. Clients themselves are more likely to see these institutions as a shield to protect them than a net to catch them.

It is one thing to say that the state and statelike agencies have been left out of the picture in more traditional analyses of deviance and crime. For instance, Cohen (1985b, p. 717) complains that Donald Black's approach to social control (1984) is "constructed as if the modern state does not exist." However, it is an altogether different matter to pretend that the only social control worthy of the name is *formal*, that is, state-sponsored or statelike social control—that a broader perspective that includes both formal and informal social control is a "Mickey Mouse concept" (Cohen, 1985a, p. 2). In effect, this pretends that interpersonal social control does not operate and does not influence deviant behavior. A criminologist focusing exclusively on formal and ignoring informal social control is a bit like someone writing the history of architecture by focusing exclusively on buildings higher than 14 stories tall. In fact, the new sociology of social control is not interested in social control per se. It is interested in how the state and its allied organizations and institutions control, or attempt to control, deviant behavior. In fact, it is not interested in deviant behavior per se, either; it is interested more-or-less exclusively in the populations whom the elites consider troublesome and against whom the elites take action. What this perspective turns

out to be is an exaggerated caricature of labeling theory, but with social control equated with formal (or semiformal) social control. It turns out to be an extremely narrow view of both deviance and social control.

SUMMARY

The other side of the coin, the "flip side," so to speak, of the etiological quest ("Why do they do it?") is the focus on the structure and dynamics of *social control*: definitions of deviance, the rules, and their enforcement. The rules and their enforcement cannot be assumed or taken for granted. A variety of perspectives have taken this side of the equation as problematic and worthy of study. Less concerned with etiology or the causes of deviance itself, functionalism, labeling theory, conflict theory, feminism, and contrology have tried to understand why certain definitions of deviance emerge and why they are enforced. While they do not deny the validity or importance of etiological or positivistic theories of deviance, these theories do limit their scope. They insist that no study of deviance can be complete without understanding the origin and dynamics of social control. They are worthy of our attention.

The earliest perspective to undertake a serious examination of rules and their enforcement was functionalism. The approach and concerns of functionalism could be broken down into two parts: first, those that were commonsensical and second, those that violated common sense. Into the first category fell a concern with why certain behaviors (such as incest) have been widely condemned, and what part the punishment of offenders plays in the functioning of societies and groups. Into the second concern fell the question of why certain deviant practices (such as prostitution) endure, in a sense seem to be encouraged by the very institutions that seem to be designed to eliminate them. Such practices endure, functionalists argue, because they make a contribution to the viability and stability of the society. Rather than undermining the society, they represent a valuable resource; it is in the interest of the society to ensure their survival because, in fact, they help the society to survive. Functionalism was the first approach or perspective to argue that deviance was not necessarily a pathological phenomenon.

The labeling or interactionist perspective had its roots in the work of two precursors, Frank Tannenbaum and Edwin Lemert, who shifted their attention away from the etiology of deviance, crime, and delinquency to an examination of what implications punishment has on the deviators' identity and the enactment of their further deviance. The labeling theorists of the 1960s (who never approved of applying the title "labeling theory" to their approach, preferring instead the term "the interactionist perspective") stressed the relativity of deviance from one time and place to another; the social construction of moral meanings and definitions; the inner or subjective world of the deviant; the impact of labeling and stigma on the person so labeled; the role of audiences in defining deviance; the role of contingencies, such as ancillary characteristics in influencing the labeling process; the reflexive or the "looking glass" self; the "stickiness" of labels; and the self-fulfilling prophecy. Although a number of its insights have been incorporated into the mainstream of the field as a whole, the labeling approach to deviance nonetheless remains controversial.

Conflict theory overlaps with the labeling approach but contrasts with functionalism on a number of key points. Conflict theory sees struggles between and among classes and categories in society, with winners and losers resulting from the outcome of these struggles. Advocates of this perspective stress the fact that (contrary to functionalists) the interests of one faction or segment of the society often conflict with or contradict those of another; what helps one may hurt another, and vice versa. For instance, the institution of prostitution may reinforce male power and help to oppress women; social stratification may be good for the rich and harmful to the poor. Classes and categories attempt to establish dominance or hegemony over others to maintain their interests. The criminal law, for instance, may help to reinforce the rule of the ruling elite and assist in exploiting or oppressing the poorest segments of the society. Marxism may be seen as a distinct variety of conflict theory. Although its influence in intellectual circles has plummeted in the past decade or two, some Marxist sociologists of deviance and crime remain. Marxists stress the economic dimension and underplay other factors in determining crime and its control.

Feminists hold that women are subordinated as a result of their sex; it is their intention to eliminate *androcentrism* (a male-centered bias), *patriarchy* (male supremacy), and *sexism* (prejudice and discrimination against women). Feminist sociologists argue that earlier researchers displayed male biases in neglecting the deviance and crime of women; they looked at the few crimes that they did examine in a distinctly skewed, biased fashion; and they neglected the victimization of women by male-initiated acts of deviance and crime. Moreover, feminists stress, the issue of the social control of female versus male deviance and crime is a neglected topic and should be examined. Do female offenders receive harsher sentences at the hands of the criminal justice system? Is women's deviance treated more punitively in *informal* social control? Are male victimizers of women (in acts of rape, wife battering, and sexual harassment) treated leniently by formal and informal social control? These and other questions have occupied feminist students of deviance and crime since the late 1960s.

Contrology, or the "new sociology of social control," received its primary inspiration from the writings of the French philosopher Michel Foucault. This perspective is interested in how psychiatric and medical expertise has been used to control "troublesome populations" in ways that are more enlightened and sophisticated than was true in the past. "Knowledge is power," Foucault said, and power translates into more repressive means of control (the "velvet glove") than the naked brutality that characterized law enforcement in past centuries (the "iron fist"). The major social control agencies in modern society have become woven into a huge net to monitor and control deviants, contrologists claim. Some critics argue that this perspective neglects informal social control and pretends that the more benign features of modern bureaucracies do not exist.

PERSONAL ACCOUNT: Cody, the Identity-Constructing Homosexual

The following account was written by, and the following interview was conducted by, Shawna Stoltenberg, a student at the University of Maryland who was enrolled in my course on deviant behavior. It highlights some fundamental issues that are central to constructing certain categories of behavior, and categories of humanity, as deviant. As we'll see, in American culture, homosexuality is gradually but unmistakably "departing from deviance." Nonetheless, young men and women feel the stigma directed at their identity and have to struggle with it for much, if not the rest, of their lives. It is this transition that dominates the discussion of homosexuality in Chapter 9, on sexual deviance.

What makes Cody deviant? In our society—one that prides itself on accepting all walks of life, people of all backgrounds—what makes homosexuality deviant? I [recently] saw a picture in the newspaper of a man wearing a leather thong riding a bicycle. In the basket of his bicycle was a dog, and attached to the basket was a sign that read "Ass-Sniffers Anonymous." If this can be printed in the newspaper without millions of complaints, how can homosexuality be considered deviant? [What makes homosexuality deviant] is the stigma that society still places on homosexuals. It is the gay jokes and the hatred and the stereotypes. It is [caused by] the ignorance of society [toward homosexuality].

For Cody, it is a matter of situational deviance. Cody is a very intelligent, white, Jewish male who is 20 years old; he was raised in suburbia. He is of medium build, has shaggy, dirty blond hair, and wears glasses. I have known Cody since the 7th grade. We all assumed he was gay, but we never mentioned that to him. We inferred that from the stereotypical signs. His room was filled with Playbills from Broadway shows, whereas his twin brother's room was filled with covers from *Sports Illustrated*. Cody was into Sheryl Crowe and folk music. And his name was Cody, a name that was androgynous—that seemed feminine in and of itself. We just knew. It was one of those things that was understood among my friends. We were just waiting for him to come to terms with it because we all had. But the rest of our classmates [outside of our little circle of friends] were not so accepting. We attended a high school where the vast majority of the students were white, middle-class snobs who wouldn't know diversity if it smacked them in the face. The parking lot was filled with Lexuses, Mercedes-Benzes, and Acuras the students had gotten on their 16th birthdays. For the most part, the parents who gave these cars to their children did not preach diversity at home. We looked through the yearbook and counted how many Black students were in our school: thirty-three. It was an appalling number, considering that our graduating class alone was 340 students.

I can remember getting comments about Cody being gay from people since I was in the 7th grade. Kids 11 years old would ask me, "You're friends with Cody and Zeke. Isn't one of them gay?" I would respond that Cody was just effeminate. Sometimes they would be okay with it, sometimes they'd push it further. . . . Granted, Cody wore jeans that were tighter than the ones most of the girls in my school wore, but that does not warrant blatant ignorance. . . . No one in my high school ever said anything to his face. They were all cowards. We knew they talked to one another, though—they talked to us about it and we were his friends—which was reason enough not to come out.

If there was little diversity based on race, there was even less based on sexual orientation. Only in my senior year was there any semblance of a gay and lesbian organization. I went to their first meeting to take pictures for the school newspaper, at which a speaker told of his first coming out. He was a high school student who, apparently, toured the area speaking about homosexuality and his experiences with it. He. . . did not look any less "normal" than you [that is, the author of this book and the instructor of the deviance course in which Ms. Stoltenberg was enrolled] or I [that is, Ms. Stoltenberg]. He did not speak with a lisp or a stereotypical gay

PERSONAL ACCOUNT: Cody, the Identity-Constructing Homosexual (cont.)

voice. If it were not for the content of his speech, you would never know he was gay.

It is here that my account of Cody as a homosexual really begins. In the months before I heard this speaker, Cody had been hinting at his homosexuality, but he never really came out. It was more as if he had opened the closet door, but he was peering rather than stepping out. After the speaker talked, I approached him and. . . told him that I had a friend who was hesitating to come out and wondered if he could give me contact information so that my friend could ask him questions. I figured Cody would be more comfortable with someone he could relate to [on that level]. . . . Little did I know that I was opening a door to a whole different experience.

"What happened after I gave you that boy's contact information?" I asked Cody. . . .

"I emailed him and we kept in touch this way for a week or so. It was nice to finally be able to talk about my feelings with someone who could relate and who wouldn't judge. I felt more able to tell him things that I would not be able to tell you guys. It's different when someone is in the same shoes. So we kept in touch through email and decided we should meet in person. . . . We met at the house of [another speaker] at the meeting I attended. I felt some sort of intense connection to him, which, looking back, was probably just that he was the first gay man my age I had come into contact with. We began kissing. Which led to more than kissing. I'd rather not go into detail, but just know that a hot tub was involved." His voice began trailing off and he had a reminiscent look in his eye.

"This was your first sexual encounter with another man, right?" I asked.

"Yes it was," he answered. "And it was intense. It left me with so many unanswered questions. And feeling so overwhelmed. It's very hard to go from 'Maybe I'm gay' to 'I'm having oral sex with a stranger.' "

"Had you ever kissed a girl before your encounter with this man?" I asked.

"No, this was my first sexual encounter of any kind," he replied, tossing his hair, which had gotten extremely long since I last saw him. . . .

"Did you continue to keep in touch with him?" I asked.

"For a little while. He decided that he couldn't have a relationship with someone who isn't out of the closet," Cody replied, almost embarrassed.

"How did that make you feel?"

"I don't know. On the one hand, I knew he was right. Here he is, touring local high schools and speaking about how open he is with his sexuality, and at the time, I had told maybe two or three close friends. On the other hand, though, it was my first experience with rejection, which was tough."

"How many people have you come out to now?" I asked.

"All of my friends from high school and mostly everyone at [the university he attends]," he responds.

"What about your parents?" I asked.

"I haven't come out to them yet. Or Zeke," he responds.

In high school, we were also friends with Zeke, his twin brother, who was teased many times for having a gay brother, even though Cody never really came out. I changed the topic and asked, "How did your identity as a homosexual continue to develop?"

"I kept hooking up with people. It was a whole new world for me and I felt the only way to find my place in it was to keep exploring it. The problem was, though, that there were not that many people to explore it with. There was no one at school and there was really nowhere else for me to turn, so I turned to the Internet. I began going to chat rooms and meeting men online. I started off just talking to them about themselves and being gay, but that led to mutual curiosity, which led to engaging in cyber sex. I'd meet these men online and act out sexual fantasies with them. But after a while, that too

PERSONAL ACCOUNT: Cody, the Identity-Constructing Homosexual (cont.)

wasn't enough. I needed to meet them. So I did. I started to arrange face-to-face meetings with people I had been meeting online. Part of me knew it was dangerous and wrong, but the other part just didn't see any other way of exploring this new identity. I met these men and sometimes we just talked, sometimes we hooked up [had sex]. It was a matter of clicking with them."

"How did this help to develop your identity?" I asked, unclear of what his rationale was. . . .

"Once you have that 'ah-hah! I'm gay' moment, you have to learn to get used to yourself as gay. You need to build up a lifestyle based on your identity. And certain things don't change. My personality isn't any different. I still have the same sense of humor, I still love my family. But now I have a gay identity, too."

"If I may get back to your sexual escapades in forming your identity," I asked, "what happened after meeting people online?"

"That summer I worked in [a well-known retail store chain] and a man came into the store every day to flirt with me. I liked the attention, especially from a stranger I met in person. This was different from cybering with someone who had never seen you. He thought I was cute. One day he asked me to go with him on my break to the lake by our house. I went with him in his car to the lake, where we engaged in sexual acts."

"Didn't you realize how dangerous that was?" I asked, shocked at his lack of concern [for his safety].

"Yes and no. Looking back, I'm lucky I didn't get killed. But at the time I felt that my newfound sexuality made me invincible. Jess realized it was not such a good idea, and essentially told my parents on me."

[*Shawna explains*: Jess is Cody's best friend and she also happens to be one of my closest friends. Cody tells her everything, including his homosexual escapades. She saw his behavior as not only deviant but dangerous. It wasn't even that he was homosexual, or even that he was being promiscuous, but it was the fact that he

was doing both with strangers that she saw as being so dangerous. She felt that for his own safety she had no choice but to step in and tell his parents. She believed that his judgment was blurred by the whirlwind surrounding his new identity.]

"What did your parents do?" I asked, confused because he told me that he has not yet come out to them.

"They sent me to counseling. I met with a therapist once a week to discuss my feelings and whatnot. My parents did not know I was gay per se. Jess didn't exactly say, 'Cody went to the lake and went down on some guy.' She was more vague than that. She just told them that I was putting myself in dangerous situations. It was never once mentioned that I was gay."

"Why haven't you come out to your parents? Why not just come out to them?" I asked, knowing the family he comes from.

[*Shawna explains*: His family is very loving and supportive. His father is an ear, nose, and throat specialist, and his mother is a librarian. Their home is filled with unconditional love, and I am almost certain that his parents would not judge him or be upset if he came out to them. They already know. They have to. I think they have come to terms with it and are just waiting for Cody to come to terms with it himself.]

He thinks for a minute. I can see how he is trying to figure out how to explain it. "Then, the time just wasn't right. It's like for you, you're not going to just tell your parents, 'I like boys, I'm sexually active.' That would be weird. Instead you'd wait until you had a boyfriend to bring home to tell them or show them. Well, I don't want to just say, 'I'm gay.' I want there to be someone there for me to show them. Maybe that doesn't make sense to you."

[*Shawna explains*: It makes sense, but to me it's just further proof that Cody is not totally comfortable with his identity as a homosexual. The fact that he has not come out to his twin brother or his parents shows how he is still

PERSONAL ACCOUNT: Cody, the Identity-Constructing Homosexual (cont.)

constructing his identity, and does not want to present it to the people most important to him until he feels he has completed this process.]

"It makes sense," I responded. "What about when you went away to school? How did that affect your identity?"

"Wow! When I first went to school, things were crazy. It was a chance to start over and create my identity from scratch. No one knew me or who I had been in the past. I came out totally at school."

[*Shawna explains*: It is important to note that Cody attends. . . an Ivy League school, which has more diversity, and more accepting students, than most universities. These students are also affluent and posh, and interested in the same things Cody is.]

"Did you make out with people there, too?" I continued to question.

"Oh, God, yes! That's all I did when I got to school. It was sort of a re-birth for me. All new people, and so much of a selection! If you think there's not much of a selection of [heterosexual] boys in high school, try being gay. But in college, yeah, there were a ton of boys, and at first, I had to make the right friends, but eventually, I just started having random hookups. I even had a threesome with two other boys."

"How do you think most people would react to all this? The promiscuity, the randomness, the homosexuality?" I asked.

"I don't really care. I don't really know. They don't know me and they don't really know what I do. Or understand it for that matter."

"What do your friends at school think?" I asked.

"Well, first of all," he answered, "I don't tell them every detail of my sexual exploits, so it's not a huge deal. But the ones I do tell don't care. They accept me for who I am."

"Who are you friends with at school? Boys, girls, gays, lesbians?"

"I am friends mostly with gay guys and straight girls," he responds.

[*Shawna explains*: It has become obvious to me that Cody deals with stigma by avoiding it. In high school, no one ever said anything to his face about being gay. We—his friends—had to field the gay jokes and comments and defend him since the 7th grade. He knew people made comments, I'm sure, but he didn't let that bother him. He always thought he was better than everyone else. That's how he got by. He threw himself into his schoolwork and the newspaper, and just went along thinking he was smarter than everyone else. In addition, he has always surrounded himself with people who would be accepting of who he was. He sometimes takes for granted how accepting we were. When he came out, we were all very supportive. He even confronted a straight friend of mine and told him that he had a crush on him. Instead of panicking and telling Cody off, he talked it through with him and told him that he was going to be there for him. In high school, we were the smart kids, so I guess we were more accepting and tolerant than other groups. He has managed to find more accepting friends in college. His friends are accepting of him as he is, and he feels comfortable around them, so he does not have to deal with the stigma that many homosexuals attract. His tactic for dealing with stigma neutralization involves avoidance of people who would stigmatize him and concentrating on people who don't.]

"Tell me about the gay culture at school," I asked him. "Are you really involved?"

"Uh—I'm not really involved. I'm not in any of the LGBT [Lesbian-Gay-Bisexual-Transgender] clubs at school. A bunch of my friends are. Basically, the gay subculture is really into hooking up and placing these ridiculous ideals on the perfect partner. I said, 'screw it!' I've given up on finding the perfect partner right now, and I'm sick of hooking up just to hook up. I don't really hook up at school any more. I'm very concentrated on my work."

[*Shawna explains*: His resistance against the gay subculture says two things to me. One, that

PERSONAL ACCOUNT: Cody, the Identity-Constructing Homosexual (cont.)

he is becoming more comfortable with himself in that he does not feel the need to subscribe to the ideals of the subculture of the new identity. And two, he is not comfortable enough with himself as a homosexual yet to really embrace the subculture beyond the sexual aspects of it.]

"One a random note," I asked, "what do you think of the words, 'queer' and 'fag'?"

"I use them sometimes. I feel like it's an acceptance thing. Being part of the group. Like how Black people can use the 'N' word—I can use the 'Q' word. I only use it to describe really gay guys, though," he replied with a sense of pride.

[*Shawna replies*: The fact that he uses derogatory words to describe the people he is the same as is another obvious sign to me that Cody is not yet comfortable with his identity. He feels cool because he can use these words, but then he uses them to describe "really gay guys," who he is clearly uncomfortable around. This is evidence that although he has taken great strides toward creating a homosexual

identity for himself, he hasn't completed this process, and he is not yet fully comfortable with the one he has created. Like many homosexuals, Cody has found comfort in surrounding himself by other gays and accepting straight people, mainly women. He doesn't feel deviant in this situation, whereas in high school, he had no choice. Although he is not completely comfortable with himself, what 20-year-old is? He is building an identity for himself; he just got a late start. Every time I see him, he's more and more flamboyant, demonstrating that as time passes, he is becoming more comfortable with his homosexuality. He needs to come to terms with himself first, create an identity that he finds acceptable, and be comfortable with himself before he presents that identity to his parents and his brother.]

"I've really turned my life around," Cody said, "and gotten it together now. I stopped the promiscuous hooking up and I am focused on what matters now. Sooner or later, I'll have it all figured out, but anyway, who has it all figured out?"

QUESTIONS

As Shawna Stoltenberg says, to the constructionist what is most interesting about Cody's account is the "situational" aspect of his homosexuality, that is, its acceptance in certain social settings and rejection in others. In other words, homosexuality is *socially constructed* as deviance here, and as acceptable there. In addition, *Cody's* construction of his own behavior and identity as a gay man and—during a time in his life—as a "promiscuous" gay man is also crucial to this chapter. Do you feel that constructionism is a productive way

of looking at deviance? Does it lead us to make interesting observations about normative violations? Aside from acceptance and rejection and identity, what other dimensions of constructionism might be explored? What about the content of a particular deviant role—that is, in Cody's case, what it *means* to be a gay man? How is a gay man supposed to act? How is he supposed to present himself to others? With respect to Cody's behavior, is constructionism a more interesting perspective to use—or is positivism? Is the *cause* of Cody's behavior the most interesting question you'd want to raise?

5

Studying Deviance: Methods in Social Research

Studying deviance presents the researcher with special problems and challenges. At the same time, it is rewarding in ways that more conventional research is not. It's difficult to imagine a research endeavor that offers more excitement or drama.

Since deviance entails behavior, beliefs, and conditions that are widely regarded as discrediting, shameful, or stigmatizing, the researcher necessarily enters a world that is partly shrouded in secrecy and deception. Deviance is often kept secret—it's the "skeleton in the closet." In addition, a certain proportion of deviant acts are illegal, and hence, to the extent that subjects, informants, or interviewees reveal their participation in them to anyone, that person risks arrest. And whenever people who talk to researchers are punished as a consequence of talking to sociologists or journalists—for instance, by being arrested—this is "bad for business." Others will find out about the arrests and draw a lesson from this: that they are also likely to be punished for being honest about what they've done. After a while, no one who has something to lose by being honest will talk to researchers. If that comes to pass, social research on deviance will have become impossible; the only research that can be conducted will be on polite, inoffensive topics. Hence, if only to protect their own interests, social researchers, like physicians, should live by the maxim, "First, do no harm" (Humphreys, 1975, p. 169): *No one* should be harmed for revealing information to the sociologist, and that harm includes arrest. (Of course, *being offended* by what the sociologist writes could be interpreted as a form of harm, but clearly that is not what I mean here. Being offensive to someone you write about is inevitable in the study of any sensitive, controversial, or unconventional behavior.) This principle isn't as simple as it sounds; I'll discuss it in detail later on in this chapter.

There are several other special risks and dangers that studying deviance and crime entails. In addition to exposing informants to arrest, simply by being around illegal activity and criminal actors the researcher may expose himself or herself to arrest (Adler, 1985, pp. 23–24). Moreover, some deviant and criminal actors are violent, and hence, by being around them, sociologists may themselves risk becoming victims of violence (Williams et al., 1992). Lastly, researchers of deviance face what's called "courtesy stigma" (Goffman, 1963, pp. 28–31): Because they interact with "deviants," among their sociologist and academic colleagues, they are considered deviants themselves. Consider the subtitle of one critic's attack on sociologists of deviance, "Nuts, Sluts, and Preverts" (Liazos, 1972), clearly an attempt to taint with a paintbrush of shame not only deviants, but also researchers who study them (Goode, 2003). All in all, researchers of deviance face risks and obstacles that sociologists who study many other subjects never even have to think about.

For instance, while studying crack dealers, Bruce Jacobs was robbed at gunpoint by a crack dealer (1998). While studying the radical environmentalist movement—a movement whose members were often engaged in illegal activities—Rik Scarce was jailed for nearly six months for refusing to turn over his field notes to the police (1995). After studying the sexual activity of men in public urinals, Laud Humphreys (1970, 1975) was vilified in print, threatened with the loss of his doctoral degree, and assaulted by one of the faculty members of his graduate institution. While conducting research on graffiti artists, Jeff Ferrell (1998) found himself running away from a police car, then pinned against a fence by an officer of the law, arrested, and charged and convicted for "destruction of private property." While studying "edgework"—extremely dangerous recreational activities—Stephen Lyng (1998, p. 221) found himself lying in dirt and weeds, "bleeding, shattered, squashed like a bug" after "screaming through an S-curve" on a motorcycle at 120 miles per hour, "running on a mixture of heavy fuel and weed." There is no doubt about it: The perils of conducting research on deviant behavior are formidable.

Risky though research on deviance is, few areas of study have as much potential for action, thrills, adventure, and personal satisfaction. Adler and Adler (1998, p. xv) refer to deviance researchers as "intrepid, brave souls" who "are willing to reveal the trials and tribulations, the horrors and joys, that they faced as they wove their way through both the institutional morass and subcultural environments," offering "a beacon of light" to readers, giving them the "hope that we can produce useful social scientific knowledge about heretofore misunderstood or under-studied groups." Mark Hamm checked into a hotel room once occupied by terrorist, bomber, and mass murderer Timothy McVeigh, and described experiencing "the blue centerlight of evil," the "bewitching allure of beauty and disaster" (1998, p. 120). More than one researcher (Ferrell and Hamm, 1998; Miller and Tewksbury, 2001) has described the fellowship and camaraderie that is generated as a result of being part of an enterprise that is hidden from the prying eyes of authorities and the general public.

It must be said that *most* research on deviance is neither as risky nor as alluring as these examples indicate. Both risk and allure depend on how dangerous the behavior is, how close the researcher gets to the activities under study, the researcher's own willingness to take risks, and how emotionally involved he or she becomes. The fact is, the sociology of deviance relies on a variety of research methods, and some take place at a distant remove from the action. In this chapter, we'll look at a variety of methodologies and get a sense of their strengths and weaknesses. Some of them involve intimate, face-to-face, day-to-day contact with subjects and informants; others rely on official documents that may be obtained at any university library or over the Internet. Some entail directly observing the behavior that is written about, while others require asking interviewees about their behavior, experiences, or beliefs. Some are even based on reading or screening the media and determining how deviant categories are *represented* to the public. One must be impressed by the sheer diversity of research techniques available to the sociologist of deviance. Indeed, this is true of almost every area of sociology. As we'll see in a bit more detail further on, the key to validity in social research is *triangulation*—getting a fix on a phenomenon with the use of multiple sources of data.

Perhaps the broadest, crudest categorization of research techniques divides them into *quantitative* and *qualitative* methods. "Quantitative" methods are those whose data can be measured and rendered into precise *numbers* or *statistics*. In contrast, "qualitative" methods are those that do not produce information that is easily measured or expressed in numbers but is rendered in the form of relevant and revealing illustrations, sense impressions, metaphors, observations, and descriptions of

behavior. Among quantitative methods, the survey method is the most popular for the majority of sociologists; reports that are based on it tend to dominate the pages of the most prestigious journals, and sociologists who conduct it usually get the best jobs in the field and receive the most money from foundations and agencies that fund research. Other quantitative research methods include laboratory and field experiments, and the use of official data. *Qualitative* research encompasses what is known as participant observation, field methods, or ethnography, as well as unstructured interviews and the use of personal accounts. Content analysis, a research method for analyzing written or pictorial material, generates data that is both quantitative and qualitative, depending on how it is done.

THE USE OF OFFICIAL DATA

One quantitative method of social research is the use of official data. Governments everywhere record, gather, and publish official information. (This category is separate and distinct from surveys that are also sponsored or conducted by the government.) Births and deaths, marriages and divorces, the sale of every officially recorded purchase—these and thousands of other facts are of interest to the government. Some of these records entail activities or characteristics that are of interest to the sociologist of deviance. Arrest figures and crimes reported to the police are recorded by the government. Each year the Federal Bureau of Investigation collects reports from nearly every police jurisdiction in the country on these two phenomena. Drug overdoses, likewise, are recorded by government agencies and reported to and tabulated by a federal agency, the Substance Abuse and Mental Health Services Administration (SAMHSA), a division of Health and Human Services. And the Department of Justice not only records the arrests that take place in the United States each year, but conducts drug tests on arrestees and publishes these data annually.

The Uniform Crime Reports (UCR)

Each year, the Federal Bureau of Investigation (FBI) gathers data on arrests and crimes known to the police from the jurisdictions containing nearly the entire population of the United States. And each year, a report is issued publishing findings of these tabulations. The FBI focuses on seven Index Crimes, that is, those offenses it considers emblematic or characteristic of street crime in general. These are murder (or criminal homicide), robbery, forcible rape, aggravated (or serious) assault, burglary, motor vehicle theft, and a grab-bag category that is referred to as larceny theft.

Two points are relevant here about the FBI's Uniform Crime Reports. The first is apparent from its list of Index Crimes: for the most part, the UCR records *street crimes.* This means that most of the types of deviance in which we are interested are not crimes, at least, not crimes that are even remotely likely to be reported to the police. Hence, most of our subject matter is not addressed by the UCR. Second, the UCR records crimes "known to the police," that is, that are reported, mostly by citizens, *to* the police. In addition, a later section records arrests for a variety of offenses, including some in which a researcher of deviance is likely to be interested: drug and alcohol offenses, prostitution, and so on. However, it is clear that neither crimes reported to the police nor arrests represent a valid measure of the total number of crimes committed in the United States each year. Many, indeed, more than half the crimes that are committed are not reported to the police. How do we know this? Here, we rely on our friend *triangulation,* that is, using multiple and independent measures and data sources. We can compare crimes reported to the police, as tabulated by the FBI's Uniform Reports, with the data collected by *victimization surveys,* that is, surveys asking a sample of the population if they have been victims of certain crimes within a specific time period (Hart and Rennison, 2003). Of course, whether or not a crime is reported to the police depends on its seriousness: The more serious the crime, the higher the likelihood it will be reported. But victims do not report a *remarkable* number of even very serious crimes. Hence, the FBI's UCR data are seriously—indeed, fatally—flawed with respect to the incidence of crime. And arrest figures are even more flawed as a measure of criminal behavior; the vast majority of crimes committed do *not* result in arrest.

In spite of the fact that the UCR's figures on the *absolute* number of crimes that take place—and hence, their rates—are extremely inaccurate, they are very useful for some purposes. What these figures are good for is *relative* or *comparative* rates. In other words, if we were to arrange social categories in the population (males versus females, young versus old, and so on), states or regions of the country, as well as over time, year by year, by their crime rate, as well as by their rate for each crime, their *ranking* is likely to be approximately correct.

For instance, the UCR's figures for robbery are nearly perfectly correlated with the size of the population of the community: As population increases, so does its rate of robbery. In 2001, the robbery rate for the ten American cities with a population of a million or more was 426.7 per 100,000 in the population; for the country's over 2,000 rural counties, the rate was 16.7—*one twenty-fifth* as high. Every criminologist in the country knows that robbery is a great deal more likely, on a per-population basis, to take place in large cities than in rural areas—and the UCR's data accurately reflect this disparity. In other words, *for certain purposes,* crimes reported to the police are an accurate measure, if not of the "true" crime rate, then at least of the *relative* crime rate, that is, in sorting out which categories have higher, and which have lower, rates of crime.

Another example: The crime rate rises and falls over time, revealing trends in criminal behavior. The overall crime rate in the United States registered by the UCR dropped throughout the 1990s and into the early twenty-first century. For instance, between 1992 and 2001, the country's murder rate declined by 33 percent. Pretty much the same picture prevails during this period for all the Index Crimes. This trend is so consistent that criminologists feel confident that the crime rate actually *did* decline in the United States in the past dozen or so years. (The decline reflected in the UCR is also mirrored by victimization surveys.) In short, in spite of the UCR's undercount of crimes, in many cases, its *rankings* of the crime rates of jurisdictions, years, and categories in the population is almost certainly fairly accurate.

DAWN (the Drug Abuse Warning Network)

The federal government, through a program called the Drug Abuse Warning Network (DAWN), collects information on the incidence of two crucial drug abuse indicators in the United States. These are, first, emergency department (ED) episodes and second, medical examiner (ME) reports, in which, in the estimate of the county coroner, one or more drugs caused or contributed to the death of the deceased.

Whenever someone comes or is brought to a hospital emergency room experiencing what is regarded as a drug-related reaction, it is counted as an "emergency department episode." These episodes include panic reactions, hallucinations, any other undesirable (and undesired) psychic effects, and overdose reactions requiring medical care, such as suicide attempts, unconsciousness, extreme pathological allergic reactions; emergency departments also count patients who present requesting detoxification, withdrawal, or "drying out." More than one drug can be counted in a single nonlethal emergency-department episode; each year, in roughly half of all ED episodes, more than one drug was recorded. The drugs that are recorded are those either mentioned *by the patient* or those whose use can be inferred as a result of a variety of indicators.

Another drug-related indicator tabulated by DAWN is found in medical examiner (ME) reports. Deaths in which drugs are deemed to play a significant role are tallied by the area's coroner or medical examiner, who conducts autopsies on nonroutine deaths. (Autopsies performed by areas that are included in the DAWN program make up 70 percent of *all* autopsies that are performed in the United States.) If drugs are thought by the medical examiner to have been a factor in the death, it is counted as an ME episode. Year by year, roughly two-thirds of the ME deaths recorded were classified as lethal overdoses—that is, were "drug-induced deaths"; while in a third, drugs were deemed to have played a "contributing" role in the death. Again, more than one drug can be counted in a single fatal overdose or ME report; about three-quarters of all incidents entailed more than one drug. Thus, in a given drug-related death, which is counted as a single

drug episode, six drug "mentions" can be recorded. We cannot know for certain *which* of these hypothetical six drugs "caused" the death; it may be all of them, taken together, or mainly one. All we know is that the six are "implicated" in some way. At the same time, when a drug shows up many times in DAWN's figures—especially if that one is the only one taken—it is likely to be dangerous, at least given the manner in which it is currently used. Unfortunately, the data on which DAWN's ME reports are based are not completely standardized from one jurisdiction to another; hence, they must be regarded as only extremely rough approximations to the "true" rate of lethal drug overdoses.

DAWN's data are extremely valuable to the researcher of deviance. If the methods by which its data are drawn are standardized as to the areas that contribute data and procedures by which overdose events are classified, we have a moving picture of drug abuse: in some areas versus others, over time, and among different categories in the population. In addition, the rise and decline of the abuse of specific drugs can be determined from DAWN. It is from DAWN that we learn, for instance, that between the late 1990s and the early 2000s, the use and abuse of "club" drugs (such as Ecstasy and ketamine) increased enormously; that among older drug users (those 35 and over), death by overdose is *much* more likely to occur than among younger users; that many legal prescription drugs (such as antidepressants and antipsychotics)—which are practically never used recreationally—cause far more deaths than many illicit drugs (such as PCP and LSD). These are valuable lessons for the deviance researcher because they point to possible discrepancies in which types of drug use are condemned, and hence, suggest some possible reasons as to why this might be the case. In other words, DAWN's data addresses the concerns of both positivists and constructionists.

ADAM (the Arrestee Drug Abuse Monitoring Program)

If you want to know about the relationship between drugs and crime, what better place to begin than the drug use of people who have been arrested for criminal behavior? In 1987, at the initiative of drug researcher Eric Wish, the National Institute of Justice established DUF—the Drug Use Forecasting program. In 1997, the name of the program was changed to ADAM—the Arrestee Drug Abuse Monitoring Program. During each year, a sample is drawn of persons in the counties in which most of the nation's largest cities are located who are arrested for violent, property, drug, DWI, and domestic violence crimes. These arrestees are approached and asked if they would be willing to be interviewed and supply urine samples. Responses are confidential, and neither testing positive for drugs nor giving information about illegal activities results in any legal consequences whatsoever.

In 2000, for adult males and females, roughly 85 percent of the arrestees who were approached agreed to an interview, and of these, 94 percent agreed to provide a urine specimen. Initially, 12 sites were in ADAM's program, and only adult males were included in its samples. Today, four separate samples are drawn. In 2000, the adult male sample numbered nearly 40,000 in 34 sites, and the adult female sample numbered roughly 30,000; the juvenile male sample was 2,100 in nine counties, and the juvenile female sample was 423 in eight. In future years, the size of the sample, the number of counties in the sample, and the scope of the data gathered will expand.

What is so remarkable about ADAM is that it accesses populations that are inaccessible by means of more conventional research methods, such as surveys. Most of ADAM's respondents would not be drawn in by the samples collected by the two major government-sponsored drug surveys: the National Survey on Drug Use and Health, which studies a sample of the entire population—because many of them do not live in conventional households—and Monitoring the Future, which studies schoolchildren—because practically none of them are in school. Thus, for anyone interested in the relationship between drug use and crime, ADAM is very probably the best place to start (Wish, 1995; Yacoubian, 2000).

ADAM tells us that the relationship between drug use and criminal behavior is very close indeed; that arrestees are *many* times more likely than the general populace to test positive for the presence of drugs in their system; that the use of certain drugs (methamphetamine is the best

example) is very unevenly spread around the country; that among arrestees in the last 10 or 15 years, the use of cocaine has declined while the use of marijuana has increased; and that some drugs stereotypically thought to be common among criminals—such as PCP and heroin—are in fact very rarely used by them. Among other things, the story of the extremely strong connection between illicit drug use (a type of deviance) and criminal behavior (another type of deviance) speaks to the possible validity of one or more theories of deviant behavior (for instance, Gottfredson and Hirschi, 1990).

SURVEY RESEARCH

Survey research is the methodology of choice among positivist or explanatory sociologists. It is the research method that is most likely to be employed by criminologists—as opposed to deviance specialists. A perusal of the most prestigious journal in the field of criminology, *Criminology*, will verify the first of these assertions, while leafing through the field of the sociology of deviance's premier journal, *Deviant Behavior*, will verify the second. This is not to say that in the field of deviance, researchers never make use of survey research. In fact, it is extremely useful for certain purposes, as I'll point out shortly. But the fact is, most sociologists who regard deviance as their specialty area do not conduct survey research, at least not as their main methodology. But it is important to know what it is and what its limitations and uses are for deviance researchers.

Survey research entails asking a sample of respondents formal, standardized, structured, and uniform questions about their past or future behavior, beliefs, attitudes, and/or characteristics. Ideally, surveys are based on a large number of respondents, preferably thousands of them, who were chosen in such a way that everyone in the target population (or "universe") had an equal chance of appearing in the sample. Many surveys select such a huge sample that one or two researchers cannot conduct the interviews themselves. In fact, researchers of most large surveys "farm out" or subcontract the interviews, and sometimes even the data analysis, to an organization that conducts such studies for a fee. The National Opinion Research Corporation in Chicago (known as NORC) is one of the most respected of such organizations. Public opinion polls are the surveys with which the public is most likely to be familiar. Every few months, polling organizations, such as the Roper Center or the Gallup Poll, conduct surveys on a variety of subjects; some of them include public attitudes toward controversial topics such as abortion and homosexual marriage.

Survey researchers are interested in finding out about three things. First, what's the *number* or *percentage* of people in the population who engage in certain activities, hold certain beliefs, or possess certain characteristics? For instance, what's the percentage (and therefore the total number) of people who used one or more illicit drugs during the past month? Or the percent of the population who report having been robbed during the previous year? Second, what's the *relationship* between key factors or variables and certain behaviors, beliefs, and characteristics? For instance, are men more likely to have engaged in adulterous sex than women? Which categories in the population are most likely to approve of homosexual marriage? Which ones are least likely? And third, what's the *cause* of the behavior, the beliefs, or the traits asked about, as well as their condemnation? For instance, *why* do young people engage in delinquent behavior? What causes moral crusades against certain activities and leads to the passage and enforcement of criminal legislation against them?

Representativeness

In surveys, the selection of the sample is extremely important. Except for the U.S. Census, which is conducted only once every ten years, *no* survey is based on the entire population. (In fact, even the Census is moving toward adopting samples for certain segments of the population.) It would be prohibitively expensive to do so. Instead, researchers must select a *subset* of the population—a sample—to "represent" or stand in for the entire population. For a sample to yield answers that reflect those that would be given by the population at large, it must be a *cross-section* of or *look like* the population at large (or "universe") in crucial respects. A sample can represent or be a cross-section of the population as a whole *only* if it is drawn in a random fashion—that is, if every person in the population has an equal chance of appearing in the sample. If a study over-samples specific groups or categories in the population (for instance, too many men and too few women, too many young people and too few older ones, and so on), it produces what's called a *biased* or "skewed" sample, which means that the answers we get may not reflect the total picture.

Researchers make use of extremely sophisticated and sensitive methods to ensure that their samples represent the total population. For certain purposes, a sample of only a few hundred and for others, only a few thousand, is sufficient to represent a much larger population. For other purposes, as we'll see, even samples of tens of thousands are not sufficient. A given "universe" need not be the population as a whole. (Though often, it is.) The universe is whatever population or segment of the population the researcher is interested in. It could be everyone who is eligible to vote; all residents of California; every homeowner in the country; all unemployed persons; all high school seniors; everyone over the age of 65; everyone who was arrested in a given city during a given period of time; and so on. Or it *could* be the entire population. Whatever population it is, the researcher attempts to select a sample that looks like or "represents" it in important ways.

It must be said that not all—or even most—surveys are based on representative samples. In fact, a very substantial proportion are based on "convenience" samples: the students in a particular course at a particular university; the residents of a particular city or community; the members of a particular organization or work site; or what's called a "snowball" sample, that is, a sample in which people known to a researcher supply the names of additional interviewees, who in turn supply others, and so on. (There is no shame in doing such surveys; I have conducted a few myself.) Such samples are generally small—a few dozen or two or three hundred respondents. And they do not "represent" any known universe or population except themselves. And surveys based on such samples *cannot* give us an accurate picture of the number or percentage of people in the population at large who engage in certain activities, hold certain beliefs, or possess certain traits, or who do or do not condemn people who do. What such surveys are better at doing is giving us an idea of which categories in the population share these characteristics, and why this is so. I'll have more to say about this matter in a moment.

Truthful Answers?

Surveys usually ask questions in one of three different ways: one, face-to-face interviews; two, telephone interviews; and three, self-administered questionnaires. (Some surveys have used a combination of these methods.) Which of these a given survey uses depends in part on budgetary restrictions and the nature of the questions asked. Obviously, one major problem facing researchers who conduct surveys—especially those that deal with touchy or deviant topics—is whether respondents are answering truthfully.

Surveys are based on the assumption that if the researcher asks direct questions, even about sensitive, controversial, deviant, and criminal subjects, people will give more or less truthful answers. It is something of a cliché that nobody will give truthful answers when asked about shameful or illegal behavior. This isn't entirely true. In fact, it is remarkable how honest—up to a point—people are when they are convinced that they are anonymous, that the answers they give will not be traced back to them personally, and that they will not get into trouble for revealing information about illicit behavior.

How do we know this? Through a process I referred to earlier as *triangulation*. "Triangulation" means getting a fix on something by looking at it from several different angles. If we use multiple and independent sources of data that say the same thing, we have more confidence that the respondent is telling the truth. On the other hand, if what the respondent says is *different* from what we learn from "hard" or very reliable data sources, chances are the respondent is *not* telling the truth. For instance, we can compare answers to the question, "Have you used an illicit drug in the past 24 hours?" with the results of a drug test. Or, "Have you ever been arrested?" with official arrest data. Answers to questions about deviant behavior are more truthful than the stereotype claims, but less truthful than researchers would like. I'll have more to say about this issue momentarily.

The Response Rate

The response rate is just as much of a problem as the issue of truthful answers. The response rate of a survey is important because of the issue of representativeness. A *sample* may have been drawn in a random fashion, but if there is a very high nonresponse rate, then the respondents may not represent the total *universe*. A response rate of 90 percent or higher is excellent; 75 percent is adequate; and much below 75 percent is poor. For the researcher of deviance, a key problem in drawing representative samples inheres in the fact that many segments of the population are difficult to locate and hence, do not get into samples. For instance, if we draw as our sample a national cross-section of high school seniors, and want that to represent or stand in for all 17-year-olds, we have to face the problem that many 17-year-olds have dropped out of school, while others were absent on the day the survey was held. If we want to locate a sample of the population of the country as a whole by drawing a cross-section of people who live in households, we have to face the fact that many people are homeless and hence, do not live in households. And what about members of the military? Residents of mental institutions? Convicts? They don't live in households we could contact. One practical solution is to redefine our target population—students, instead of 17-year-olds; people living in households, rather than the entire population; and so on. At some point, we have to recognize that our sample represents a huge swath of our targeted universe, but it is nonetheless limited.

Descriptive and Explanatory Statistics

Surveys seek to produce, as I said, quantitative data, that is, information that can be expressed in the form of precise numbers, either *absolute numbers* (how much or many of something) or *percentages* (what proportion of something). Most of us call these numbers *statistics*. There are two kinds of statistics: *descriptive* statistics and *explanatory* statistics. The number of people who were diagnosed with HIV in the United States during 2004 is a descriptive statistic. The murder or criminal homicide rate for that year is a descriptive statistic. The percentage of 18-year-olds who said they drank an alcoholic beverage during the previous year is a descriptive statistic. Descriptive statistics say that this is the way things are at this time—no more, no less. *Explanatory* statistics are much more ambitious, more theoretical, even a bit speculative. They argue that this is the *cause* of the way things are.

For descriptive statistics to be considered valid and reliable, it is absolutely essential that randomized samples of respondents be drawn, the number of respondents be sufficiently large, the questions be worded properly, the respondent's anonymity be assured, and the interview or questionnaire situation be conducive to honesty. These are formidable and exacting requirements. But for explanatory statistics to be considered valid by researchers, the matter is much more complicated. For the quantitative, positivist social scientist, devising a theory and getting an explanation accepted as true by a field of study is the prize, the king's ransom, the ultimate goal of all research. But persuading one's colleagues and peers that one's explanation is correct requires a great deal of rigor, imagination, and even luck. Luck because to be accepted, an explanation needs to be consistent with existing theoretical assumptions and compatible with the mood and subculture of a given field as well as the era in which the social scientist works. And rigor requires the researcher to think seriously about variables, correlations, and controls.

Variables

Reasoning rigorously, systematically, and *scientifically* in cause-and-effect terms means abandoning many of our commonsensical assumptions and thinking abstractly and impersonally. Social scientists are interested mainly in the influence of one variable on another variable. A variable is anything that varies or changes, whether from one time period to the next, from one condition to another, or from one person to another. Age is a variable. Looking from one person to another, or the same person over time, we notice variations in age, stretching from childhood to old age. Sex is a variable: Some people are male, some are female. So are race, geographical residence, household income, education, marital status, and so on. In addition, drug use, sexual identity and orientation, criminal behavior, and beliefs are variables.

When positivists reason in cause-and-effect terms, they distinguish the *independent* from the *dependent* variable. The "independent" variable is the *causal* variable, the factor that influences or causes or has an effect on the dependent variable. Age causes or has an effect on drug use: Young people are much more likely to use illicit drugs than older people. Hence, in this case, age is the *independent* and drug use is the *dependent* variable. Sex causes or has an effect on criminal behavior: Men are significantly more likely to commit serious illegal acts than women. In this case, *sex* is the independent, and *criminal behavior* is the dependent, variable. Not all cause-and-effect relationships are this easy to untangle. It is the job of the positivist social scientist who studies deviance and crime to trace out the cause-and-effect relationships between and among the many variables under study.

Does drug use cause criminal behavior or the other way around? Is homosexuality caused by inborn, genetic, hormonal, or neurological factors, or is it caused by environment, socialization, and experience? Is the higher rate of arrest among African Americans versus whites a product of a biased criminal justice system or higher rates of crime? Is white-collar crime a product of individual predilection or institutional environment? These are the sorts of questions positivists looking at deviance and crime attempt to answer.

The lion's share of these researchers' efforts involves determining which independent variables have what kind of an impact on specified dependent variables. In all (or nearly all) positivistic studies of deviance and crime, enacting deviant and criminal behavior is the *dependent* variable—the factor on which independent variables have an effect. The independent variable is *always* the "explanatory" factor—the variable that causes or influences the deviant or criminal behavior. Positivist theories always ask: What causes deviant behavior? What causes criminal behavior? *All* positivistic theories of deviance have this same basic logic: *variable X* (the factor on which the theory is based) causes *variable Y* (deviant or criminal behavior). And usually, the *name* of the theory constitutes what is variable X: social disorganization theory (social disorganization causes deviance and crime), anomie theory (anomie causes deviance and crime), self-control theory (a lack of self-control causes deviance and crime), differential association theory (differentially associating with persons who express positive "definitions" of deviance and crime causes engaging in deviance and crime), and so on.

Exceptions to the Rule

Notice that the way that social science reasoning operates, it is not necessary that a given formulation explain everything. Every generalization has exceptions to the rule. Robbery is overwhelmingly committed by males, but even though the relationship is very strong and very consistent, roughly 5 percent of robbers are female. These 5 percent are the "exceptions to the rule." As people age, they become decreasingly likely to use illicit drugs. In the 2001 national household drug use survey, only 1 percent of all people age 65 and older used one or more illegal drugs in the previous year (SAMHSA, 2002, p. 121). We could make the generalization, "among adults, the older the person, the less likely he or she is to use illicit drugs"—and that would be a completely valid statement. In fact, 18-year-olds are nearly 40 times as likely to use illicit drugs as persons over the age of 65. Still, we do have that 1 percent; the people in that 1 percent are, again, "exceptions to the rule." Exceptions do not disprove a rule—they remind us that no rule is absolute. Generalizations with exceptions are still valid. What counts to the positivist social scientist is the patterns, the generalizations—what holds true in general, not in each and every case.

Correlations

Quantitative social scientists pay close attention to what statisticians call *correlations*. A correlation is a statistical relationship between two or more variables. Some correlations can be expressed in *linear* terms—that is, as one variable increases, another also increases, or when one increases, the other decreases. For instance, the correlation between size of community of residence and the per-population robbery rate is a *positive* relationship: As we saw, as the size of the community increases, the likelihood that robberies will take place, out of every 100,000 in the population, will also increase. On a person-for-person basis, robbery increases as size of community increases. Likewise, as the size of the community increases, again, on a per-population basis, the likelihood that persons with a homosexual identity live there increases as well. On the other hand, some correlations are *negative*: As one variable goes up, the other goes down. When we say that younger people are more likely to use illicit drugs, what we mean is that there is a negative correlation between age and drug use. This means that as age goes *up*, drug use *declines*. The same thing applies to the relationship between household income and criminal homicide: As household income increases, the likelihood that a member of the household will commit homicide decreases. Not all correlations are linear, however. For instance, men are more likely to engage in homosexual behavior than women, and to have such experiences earlier in their lives. Here, for the independent variable—sex—there is no such thing as an "increase" or a "decrease," only statistical differences between men and women.

A correlation does not *demonstrate* causality—it only *suggests* it. Just because two variables are correlated with one another does not prove that one causes the other. They both could be caused by a third or common variable. We know there is an extremely strong correlation between the use of psychoactive drugs (both legal and illegal—but especially illegal) and criminal behavior. But does drug use *cause* criminal behavior? Does engaging in criminal behavior cause drug use? Or are they both the *effects of a common cause*—for example, poor parenting, leading to low self-control (Gottfredson and Hirschi, 1990)? Using marijuana in the mid-teens is *very* strongly correlated with using "hard" drugs such as cocaine, methamphetamine, and heroin in the late teenage years. This is an indisputable fact. But does the use of marijuana per se *cause* the use of more dangerous drugs, as some claim (O'Donnell and Clayton, 1982)? Or is the relationship an artifact of some third variable, such as *the kind of person* who uses marijuana or the friends and acquaintances one makes when using marijuana (Earleywine, 2002, pp. 49–65)? It is extremely important to understand that in tracing out cause-and-effect sequences, correlations are only a first, not a final step.

Here's a very important point: When sociologists and statisticians refer to correlations, they do *not* mean that all or most of the people in one category do, believe, or possess a certain thing and that no, or every few, in another category do. What they mean is that there are important *differences* between members of these categories in this respect. For instance, very, *very* few men commit murder. Nonetheless, there is an extremely strong *correlation* between sex and murder; in the United States, men are *nine times* more likely to commit murder than women are. Correlations exist even where the members of one category—vastly "more likely" to do, believe, or possess something than the members of another—*are extremely unlikely* to do, believe, or possess that something. Again, exceptions do not disprove the rule.

Controls

The way that social scientists determine cause-and-effect relationships by separating correlation from causality is by applying what they call *controls*. To apply a control is to *hold things constant*. Every generalization a scientist makes is qualified by the implicit qualification, "other things being equal." This means that when we look at the causal relationship between two variables, it is in a kind of "pure" state, with all other variables taken out of the picture. When we say one runner is faster than another, we assume that the conditions under which they run are the same. If Jane runs on a level track and Sally has to run uphill, the conditions are not the same. By "controlling" for other factors or variables, we *make* them the same, even if only theoretically or on paper. Eating ice cream is correlated with the rate of rape. This correlation is true—but is it meaningful? Does this mean eating ice cream *causes* men to rape women? Of course not! Ice cream is eaten more in the summer than in other seasons, and it is in the summer when rates of rape are the highest. If we looked at *each season separately*, there is *no* relationship between ice cream consumption and rates of rape. In this case, we have "controlled" or *held constant* the effect of the season of the year. When we apply one or more controls and a relationship that previously existed disappears, we say that our original explanation

that one variable caused the other is *spurious*, or false. If a correlation between two variables holds constant regardless of what controls are applied, social scientists feel confident that there is a cause-and-effect relationship between them.

Survey Research: Two Sex Surveys

Peter Berger (1963, p. 19) wrote that sociologists are sublimated voyeurs who are "tempted to look through keyholes, to read other people's mail, to open closed cabinets." Naturally, a major portion of that voyeurism involves the desire to know about other people's sex lives. While physicians and psychiatrists at least as far back as Krafft-Ebing (1840–1902) and Freud (1865–1939) investigated and wrote about the "abnormal" sex lives of their patients, it was not until the 1940s that researchers carried out a survey on "normal" sexual behavior in the general population. Alfred Kinsey was a biologist who studied gall wasps. As a faculty member at Indiana University, Kinsey was asked to teach the unit on sex in a course on marriage. Surprised that virtually no information was available on the subject, he decided to conduct what he referred to as a "taxonomic investigation" of human sexuality. He located respondents wherever he could find them—in classes, student groups, fraternities and sororities, parent-teacher associations, clubs, hospitals, prisons, rooming houses, circles of friends, people who just stepped forward and volunteered to be interviewed, even hitchhikers he picked up on the road. Kinsey's sample was huge—18,000, almost unheard of at the time.

The famous "Kinsey Reports," *Sexual Behavior in the Human Male* (Kinsey, Pomeroy, and Martin, 1948) and *Sexual Behavior in the Human Female* (Kinsey et al., 1953) were as boring and unerotic as books on sex can possibly be. Filled with hundreds of extremely detailed tables, charts, and graphs, and choked with the dry, antiseptic prose of, well, an expert on gall wasps, these books almost literally could not be read cover-to-cover. And yet, the Kinsey Reports were best-sellers and their findings shocked and titillated a nation. The reason is simple. Aside from the fact that Kinsey peeked into the bedrooms of Americans with the techniques of what passed at the time for social science research methods, these books were startling because they revealed that a huge proportion of the American public engaged in sexual practices that most then regarded as deviant. Kinsey believed that behavior that took place frequently was "normal" and "natural," and he and his associates found that a great deal of behavior widely felt to be abnormal and unnatural—not to mention immoral—was extremely frequent. One-third of Kinsey's male sample engaged in at least one homosexual act; half of his female sample were not virgins on their wedding night; half of all married men and a quarter of married women had had at least one adulterous sexual experience; and so on, on and on, one seemingly shocking revelation after another. Or so it seemed in the mid-twentieth century.

Many Americans found Kinsey's unwillingness to denounce the unconventional behavior he uncovered extremely distressing. Indeed, he seemed to endorse certain practices, such as adulterous sex and masturbation. He even argued that too much concern about child molestation might be more harmful than the molestation itself. The very revelation that such practices were widespread shocked many observers. Said evangelist Billy Graham of the volume on females: "It is impossible to estimate the damage this book will do to the already deteriorating morals of America" (Michael et al., 1994, pp. 20–21). In 1953, Kinsey was investigated by a congressional committee, the Reece Committee, for possible communist sympathies; his books, the members of the committee reasoned, seemed designed to corrupt American morality and make the country ripe for a communist "takeover." At least one recent biographer (Jones, 1997) argues that Kinsey reached his conclusions because he was a sexual deviant himself.

Alfred Kinsey was both lionized and vilified, but the fact is, he deserved neither unqualified praise nor savage condemnation. The plus side is that he attempted to study sexual behavior in a systematic, empirical fashion. But the negative side is that his research is an example of producing extremely faulty findings from a poor, skewed, or *biased* sample. Kinsey's sample was so badly selected that, even though his respondents may have been telling the truth about their sexual behavior and experiences, it did not represent the population as a whole, and hence, their behavior

and experiences were unrepresentative as well. People who step forward and volunteer for a sex survey tend to have had a wider range of sexual experience than people who wait until they are asked—or who refuse—to be interviewed. Prisoners are much more likely than the general population to have engaged in homosexual acts. Members of the groups and associations Kinsey approached were more liberal and sexually permissive than the public as a whole. All in all, the flaws in the Kinsey study's sampling techniques were so huge that, as a description of sexual behavior in America, the findings in its two volumes are all but worthless. As it turns out, these findings *hugely* overstated the incidence of unconventional sex in the American population.

Early in the 1990s, goaded by the AIDS crisis, four sociologists affiliated with the University of Chicago—each with expertise in a particular area—decided to conduct a survey on sexual behavior, based on a nationally representative, randomized sample. Originally, the study was to have been supported by a grant from the federal government, and the sample was to total 20,000 respondents. However, conservative and religious lobbies got wind of the study and sought out the support of North Carolina Republican Jesse Helms, who denounced it—and its researchers (including a former colleague of mine)—on the floor of the U.S. Senate. Government sponsorship of the study was canceled and the researchers were forced to resort to a much smaller level of private funding. The sample, still nationally representative, was scaled back to 3,500 respondents. Its response rate was 80 percent, which is considered adequate for a study of this sort. Respondents were assured that their answers would be held in the strictest confidence, that their privacy would be protected, and that their answers would be reported either as part of a statistical pattern or, if they were quoted, there would be no way that they could be personally identified. The findings of this survey sharply contrasted with those of the Kinsey studies. The sexual behavior of the American public, according to the survey published in 1994 by the team of Chicago sociologists, took place less frequently and was substantially less adventurous, more conservative, more conventional, less deviant, and more "vanilla," than the results of the Kinsey

Report indicated (Laumann et al., 1994; Michael et al., 1994). Ironically, unlike Kinsey's findings, conservatives would have liked the results of the survey conducted by the Chicago sociologists.

Perhaps the most consistent finding, one that ran throughout all aspects of the study, was that, whether or not marriage was the aim of the relationship, people usually have sex with partners who are *similar* to themselves—in age, race and ethnicity, socioeconomic status, and especially education. Second, in addition to the *conventionality* of the avenues through which partners met and from which they drew their "pool" of sexual candidates, there was the conventionality of the behavior itself. More than eight Americans in ten had had sex with either no partners (12 percent) or only one partner (71 percent) in the previous year; only 3 percent had had sex with five or more partners. Since the age of 18, not quite six in ten (59 percent) had had sex with four or fewer partners; only 9 percent said that they had had sex with more than 20 partners in their lifetime. Three-quarters of the married men (75 percent) and 85 percent of the women said that they had been sexually faithful to their spouse during the course of their marriage. Among married persons, 94 percent said that they had been faithful during the past year. The study's data on homosexual behavior were even more surprising, given a widespread assumption in many quarters that one out of every ten Americans is gay. Only 2.8 percent of the men in the sample, and 1.4 percent of the women, identified themselves as homosexual or bisexual. Only 2 percent of the men and the women said that they had had sex with a same-gender partner in the past year; only 5.3 percent of the men, and 3.5 percent of the women, said that they had done so since the age of 18; only 9 percent of the men and 4 percent of the women said that they had done so since the onset of puberty. These figures are a small fraction of those that were obtained by the Kinsey reports of roughly 50 years earlier (Kinsey et al., 1948, 1953).

A third set of findings uncovered by the University of Chicago sex survey that the media and the public (and the researchers) found surprising related to sexual *frequency*, which was considerably *lower* than many observers had anticipated. Only one-third of the sample (34 percent) had sex as often as twice a week; of that total, only

8 percent said that they had sex as often as four or more times a week. One out of ten of the men in their fifties (11 percent) and three out of ten of the women of that age (30 percent) did not have sex *at all* during the past year. Perhaps even more surprising, the *married* members of this sample were significantly *more* likely than the single members to have had sex twice a week or more (41 versus 23 percent); however, cohabiting partners who were living together but unmarried were even more likely to have had sex that often (56 percent). In addition, the marrieds were most likely to report being physically and emotionally pleased with their sex and its frequency. The image of the wild and free and easy sex lives of the "swinging singles" received a serious body blow from the findings of this study.

A fourth set of findings from this survey pertained to the sexual *activities* that were most appealing to the sample. Traditional penile-vaginal sex turned out to be the only sexual activity that was almost universally appealing: 83 percent of the men and 78 percent of the women said that it was "very" appealing to them. And 80 percent of the sample said that *every* time they had sex during the past year, they had vaginal sex. Half the men and a third of the women said that watching their partner undress was very appealing; the same proportion said that receiving oral sex was very appealing to them. Of the remaining sex acts, only giving oral sex (37 for the men, 19 percent for the women) was appealing for a substantial proportion of the sample. All the other activities attracted only a tiny fraction of these figures. For instance, only 5 percent of the men (and only 1 percent of the women) said that having sex with a stranger was very appealing to them. All in all, the activities the respondents said they found appealing were quite traditional and conventional. Unusual, far-out, or "deviant" activities attracted very, very few positive evaluations (Laumann et al., 1994; Michael et al., 1994).

How much confidence can we have in the findings of this survey? Some observers criticized the study because they assumed that respondents would lie about their sex lives—for instance, that men would exaggerate the extent of their sexual behavior while women would minimize it. Some critics claimed that many people simply forget about a great deal of what they do sexually, and hence leave it out of their answers to an interviewer. (Let's keep in mind that we can't always be sure whether the relevant questions and categories *mean* the same things to the researcher and the respondent.) It is too early to tell whether the results of this study can be taken as definitive; it will be a while before its validity will be sorted out by later researchers. Nonetheless, it is certainly the best survey ever conducted on sexual behavior in the United States. Its answers are as close as we'll get to the true picture of sexual behavior for some time to come. The fact that the researchers used a variety of techniques to cross-check the answers respondents gave (asking the same question twice, in different parts of the survey, in different ways, or having respondents fill out a questionnaire for especially touchy and sensitive subjects) gives us more confidence that the answers they received are accurate. And the fact that similar surveys have been conducted elsewhere—for instance, in Britain (Wellings et al., 1994) and France (Spira et al., 1992, 1993)—and reached similar conclusions for a number of behaviors, again, imparts confidence to the study's conclusions.

A comparison of the findings produced by the Kinsey reports and those produced by the University of Chicago sex survey is extremely instructive. Such a comparison tells us a great deal about the problems and pitfalls of conducting a survey, especially one on controversial, sensitive, or deviant activities. The much lower levels of unconventional sex produced by the survey conducted in the 1990s, as compared with those produced by Kinsey's survey, show us that selecting a sample is *extremely* important for our findings. If researchers base their findings on questions asked of respondents in a biased sample, those findings will be misleading, even worthless. Again, each person may be telling the truth, but added together, the overall results from such a survey will not reflect or represent the views or behavior of the population at large. And the reason why nearly all researchers believe that the findings turned up by the survey conducted by the team from the University of Chicago are more reflective of the sexual behavior of American society than Kinsey's survey roughly 50 years earlier is that the more recent study is based on a randomized

sample of the population, while its earlier counterpart was not.

Surveys on Deviant Behavior: An Overall Assessment

Tens of thousands of surveys and polls have been conducted, one or more of whose questions have asked about deviant or criminal behavior, beliefs, or traits. Most of them have been mainly concerned about more conventional matters; they devoted only a small number of questions to issues directly of interest to the deviance specialist. Of those that have been focused on deviant matters, only a minuscule percentage were based on large, randomized samples. As I said above, any descriptive statistics issuing from such a survey do not convey any meaningful information about behavior, beliefs, or traits in the general population. However, such samples are probably adequate, although not ideal, for testing relationships between key factors or variables and inquiring about the cause of deviance and crime, or what's referred to as their "etiology."

Probably the most useful function of survey research is to investigate attitudes *about* deviant behavior, beliefs, and conditions. Indeed, this is what many public opinion polls do. Surveys have also been conducted on the public's attitudes regarding the "seriousness" of a range of crimes, a phenomenon that is very closely related to the concept of deviance. Crime victimization surveys produce very useful information about the likelihood that Americans will become victims of a variety of criminal acts during a given period of time. From such surveys, estimates can be made about the national crime rate, and such estimates can be compared with official information about crimes reported to the police (Rennison, 2001). Drug use surveys are useful if the samples are large and researchers recognize that estimates of the use of relatively rare, exotic drugs are likely to be off the mark, especially if we are interested in rates of addiction and dependence (SAMHSA, 2002; Johnston, O'Malley, and Bachman, 2003a, 2003b). Surveys on sexual behavior are probably useful, since most of the questions in such a survey will be asked about fairly conventional acts; determining the extent of deviant sexual expression is a by-product of such surveys, not its explicit aim (Laumann et al., 1994; Michael et al., 1994). Estimates of the extent of crime in the population drawn from self-report surveys decline in accuracy as the seriousness, and hence the rarity, of the acts asked about increases. Surveys on criminal and delinquent behavior are much better for examining relationships between and among variables than for determining the extent of crime and delinquency in the population.

Surveys are also useful for learning about a variety of unconventional, unacceptable acts, beliefs, or traits that take place within more or less conventional settings, such as school and college, marriage and the family, community and neighborhood, hospitals, and work settings. Some examples include student cheating on exams; violence within the family; levels of alcohol consumption; holding unconventional— for example paranormal—beliefs; Internet-related or cyber deviance, for instance, the consumption of cyber-porn; automobile-related deviance (speeding, driving without a license, and so on); legal and illegal gambling; the use of tobacco products; and mental health and disorder in the noninstitutionalized population at large.

Whether fortunately or unfortunately, however, many, perhaps most, of the matters in which a deviance specialist is interested cannot be investigated via survey research. Researchers have learned that they cannot go door-to-door or telephone people randomly and ask questions about many, perhaps even most, deviant activities. Some activities are too shameful for participants to discuss with a researcher. Others are so rare that even a large randomized sample would yield only a handful of potential respondents. Still other activities do not yield their most interesting secrets via the interview or questionnaire. Some activities, organized belief systems, or collectivities of possessors of undesirable traits and characteristics need to be studied from the inside, *in situ* as it were—on the ground, on the site where their participants, believers, or possessors are located. We need to live the lives they lead; share the air they breathe; eat meals with them; find out what they do on a day-to-day basis; listen to them explain and justify what they do, what they believe, and who they are. In short,

we may need to engage in a particular type of qualitative research—*participant observation*.

PARTICIPANT OBSERVATION

Unlike sociologists in general, most deviance specialists make use of some form of participant observation as their primary research tool. The pages of the journal most centrally devoted to the study of deviance, *Deviant Behavior*, are filled with participant observational studies of strip clubs, tattoo parlors, biker gangs, rodeo groupies, Mardi Gras celebrations, prisons, homosexual bathhouses, meetings of Alcoholics Anonymous, and dozens of other less-than-respectable scenes. What is this research method sociologists refer to as participant observation?

Some kinds of behavior can only be studied by direct, firsthand, face-to-face, natural observation. Imagine conducting not just one interview but many. Imagine that these interviews are very much like ordinary conversations: spontaneous, free-flowing, informal. Imagine too that you not only converse with the people you are studying but that you do just about everything else with them as well: go bowling, play cards, attend weddings, visit families, go out drinking, and so on. Participant observation thrusts researchers right into the day-to-day, minute-by-minute behavior they are studying. They examine social life "in the field," in its "natural habitat," observing behavior as it takes place, more or less around the clock, over a period of many months or even years. Studying behavior in its natural setting is referred to as *participant observation, field work,* or *ethnography*.

This methodology entails that the researcher acquire a huge mass of information and write down his or her observations in the form of what's called *field notes*. There is no need to rely on a single question or even several questions to find out about behavior or attitudes, as is true of surveys. The many observations the researcher makes cross-verify one another and ensure the validity of conclusions that are drawn. The participant observer also profits from the richness of this mode of research. Any idea or hypothesis may be confirmed and reconfirmed with many different indicators, questions, and observations. The researcher does not have to rely on a single question in a single interview or questionnaire. "In general, multiple observations convince us that our conclusion is not based on some momentary or fleeting expression of the people we study, subject to ephemeral and unusual circumstances" (Becker, 1970, pp. 53–54).

The informant in the field faces the sociologist in many different situations: at home, on the street, at work, with friends and relatives, and so on. This makes it "difficult for people to tell a coherent lie and even more difficult for them to act on it. Because they are unwilling to be caught in a lie or an incoherence, they eventually reveal their true beliefs" (p. 54). Of course, informants can and do lie to participant observers, just as husbands and wives can and do lie to one another. But the more you know about someone, the harder it is for that person to lie to you.

Another advantage of participant observation is that it maximizes the chances that what the researcher hears and sees will reflect real-life behavior and beliefs. All other research methods are several steps removed from the actual behavior itself. By going into the streets, into factories, into homes—into the lives of informants—sociologists remove many of the barriers between what they want to know and what they can—and do—observe. More than almost any other research technique, participant observation gives access to the insider's point of view.

Along with its strengths, participant observation has a number of drawbacks as well. One such drawback is that it forces us to rely on a case study. If you rely on only one street gang, one bar, one corporation, or one house of prostitution, how do you know what gangs, bars, corporations, or houses of prostitution are like *in general*? How can you be sure that the group, scene, community, or organization you study is typical? Answer: You can't. Unlike survey research, participant observation does not employ formal sampling procedures, so the issue of nonrepresentativeness is an even more serious problem. You can never really know whether what you have seen in your research site is a cross-section of the whole picture or merely a very narrow and unusual slice of it.

Second, field work tends to yield *qualitative* rather than quantitative data. Qualitative data cannot be measured precisely, while quantitative data can. Usually, the results of participant observation cannot be worked up into numbers or statistics, tables, charts, or graphs. Data from questionnaires and formal interviews can be systematized and standardized, and the results can be analyzed statistically. This is typically not the case with quotes from informants or observations of people's everyday lives.

In addition, participant observation cannot resolve questions of cause-and-effect. In general, it suits description better than explanation. Participant observers are not likely to answer the question "Why?" definitively. They are, however, able to accurately describe the details of a particular social setting.

One important distinction among participant observers is the matter of the actual participation of the researcher in the behavior under study. The roles the researcher may adopt while engaging in this method of study range from a *complete participant* to a *complete observer* (Adler and Adler, 1994). Some observers believe that actual participation in deviant and even illegal behavior by the researcher is not only desirable but necessary (Ferrell and Hamm, 1998). Others believe that observation alone is not only sufficient but the wisest and most productive strategy—that the researcher should most decidedly *not* engage in deviant or illegal behavior (Williams, 1996). As I said above, all researchers strongly believe that no one should be harmed by their research. But most deviant and illegal activities entail no direct harm to anyone.

If one is conducting a participant observational study of the homosexual community, does one engage in homosexual sex to get closer to one's informants? Some researchers think so (Styles, 1979; Bolton, 1995, 1996). If one is studying strippers firsthand, does it help to become a stripper oneself? Some researchers would nod assent to that question (Ronai and Ellis, 1989; Ronai, 1995). If one is studying drug dealers in their natural habitat, in the field, is it wise to use drugs oneself? It is not only wise, it may be necessary, say some researchers (Adler, 1985, 1994). There is probably no definitive or cut-and-dried answer to the question of researcher participation.

Certainly no participant observer believes it is necessary to murder someone in order to study murder. Where does one draw the line? It's not clear.

By participating in deviant or illegal behavior, no researcher should make it impossible for other researchers to conduct their own studies in the field. And again, no informants should be harmed by the researcher's participation in questionable behavior. Administrators at universities most emphatically *do not want* the researchers who teach at their institutions to engage in questionable or illegal activity. All universities house IRBs (Institutional Review Boards) that oversee research that is conducted by their faculty and students, and *no* IRB anywhere would approve the sort of full participation research described above—that is, research that entails homosexual sex with informants, stripping, or drug use. Hence, the researcher must make a decision whether or not to conduct research that his or her university considers completely unacceptable. I'll have more to say about the question of ethics in social research later in this chapter. But ultimately, the resolution of this issue comes down to the researcher's own personal ethics, sense of morality, and predilections. But if one does engage in such behavior, one had better be prepared for the consequences. As any study of deviance and crime will tell us, such behavior is never risk-free.

Researching Drug Dealers: Conducting a High-Risk Participant Observation Study

For many behaviors or scenes, a survey of the general population is not feasible. Most of us recognize the difficulty of obtaining truthful and complete answers when the behavior asked about is as deviant, supersensitive, and illegal as drug dealing. Patricia Adler (1985, 1994) goes so far as to argue that the only way to acquire accurate, valid knowledge about deviant behavior is to interact with informants on a face-to-face, day-to-day basis in real-life or naturalistic situations, that is, to engage in participant observation research. That way, she argues, we get an *insider's* perspective. This is especially the case with drug dealing; given the "highly illegal nature of their occupation,"

dealers have become "secretive, mistrustful, and paranoid. To insulate themselves from the straight world, they construct false fronts, offer lies and misinformation, and withdraw into their group" (Adler, 1985, p. 11). The reason why sociologists have so little information on how drug dealing is conducted is that sociologists have had such a difficult time "penetrating into their midst" (p. 11). Only by entering the social circle of drug dealers, becoming friendly with them, and adopting a "peripheral" role in that circle, was Adler able to conduct her research on drug dealing.

Patricia Adler and her husband, Peter, both at the time graduate students at the University of California at San Diego, became friendly with a neighbor who had an abundant supply of drugs, including cocaine, which is (and was) extremely expensive for graduate students. He also seemed to be very knowledgeable about drugs and their prices. And his apartment seemed to attract a large number of well-to-do visitors, yet he and his friends didn't seem to have what could be called a job or a visible means of support. When the Adlers asked him what he did for a living, he was vague and evasive. It soon became clear to them that the man was a drug dealer. This presented them with an opportunity to conduct a study of drug selling in the local area, so they discussed the matter with their faculty advisor, Jack Douglas, an expert both on deviance and participant observation. Douglas agreed that they ought to do it; they had some experience with drug use research, they were in their twenties, and their attitudes were sufficiently tolerant toward recreational drug use and unconventional lifestyles that they could easily move in a setting dominated by the distribution and sale of illicit, controlled substances. Consequently, they became friendly with their dealer-neighbor, "Dave," and got involved in his social network.

One day, in a casual conversation, one of Dave's companions let it slip that they were engaged in drug selling and were part of a smuggling crew. After some embarrassment, Dave finally agreed to allow the Adlers to observe his world. The research that ensued is an example of *serendipity*—a fortunate or "happy accident." The Adlers' research was opportunistic; they capitalized on a situation that, in a sense, they had stumbled into. They became friends with Dave and his friends, and for six years they conducted detailed, formal interviews, which were tape-recorded. They did favors for them, acted as character witnesses for them (in non–drug-related trials, for instance), lent them money when they were down and out, and helped Dave's wife take care of their kids. Their research branched out when Jean, Dave's wife, left him and began dealing herself, engaging in transactions with a different circle of clients. Dave was briefly incarcerated for writing bad checks, and when he came out of jail broke, he lived with the Adlers for seven months and they watched, close-up, his transformation from a scared ex-convict who swore never again to deal drugs to a reentry into full-time dealing.

Day by day, year by year, the Adlers' circle of informants "snowballed" into an expanded study, with more and more dealers and customers, and more and more dealing operations. With new people in the study, Patricia and Peter took a "covert" or *hidden* research role, not informing them initially that they were engaged in research, waiting until they were accepted as peers, at which time they informed them of their role. In general, they were accepted as cool friends of dealers who could be friendly with other dealers. When they built up the trust of new acquaintance-dealers, they could inform them about what they were up to, then ask them more detailed, probing questions. Some sociologists believe that this "covert" phase of conducting field research is unethical, that all persons should be aware that researchers are conducting a study at all times, that all informants should be allowed to freely grant their "informed consent." (See the section on page 133, on "Ethical Issues in the Study of Deviance.") When the Adlers established the trust of new acquaintances and told these informants of their role, they moved from the "covert" to the "overt" or open research role. Sometimes this was done directly (they told them themselves) and sometimes it was done indirectly (their friends told them). This plan presented them with a series of problems—for instance, coming on to potential informants too fast; "blowing it" or saying the wrong thing to potential informants and having them refuse to cooperate; and juggling their two different roles, covert and overt, with different people.

After the Adlers had children, their involvement with the research diminished considerably. The study culminated in a PhD dissertation and a book for Patricia Adler, *Wheeling and Dealing: An Ethnography of an Upper-Level Drug Dealing and Smuggling Community* (1985, 1994). It is considered something of a classic in participant observation research on deviance.

Obviously, research of this type is more difficult and stressful than constructing and administering a questionnaire or interview schedule and then analyzing the data it generates. The problems the Adlers faced in conducting their research were myriad. Here are a few.

• *The effect of drug use on the research process.* Under the influence of marijuana, respondents became sleepy, disoriented, distracted, and uninterested in being interviewed. The authors believe, in contrast, that under the influence of cocaine, their interviews were superior to those that were conducted when their informants were not under the influence of any drug. Interviewees under the influence of cocaine were alert, sharp, and focused.

• *Assuming risks while doing research.* The research posed special dangers for the researchers. Dealers were not infrequently moody and erratic; the Adlers' fear was that they might become dangerous and violent. Dealers also became paranoid about the Adlers' use of the tape recorder during interviews. And the Adlers were fearful of being arrested by the police or subpoenaed by the authorities. Obviously, by observing crimes and not reporting them to the police, the Adlers were committing crimes themselves. Drug deals took place in their house and thus, they were aiding and abetting crimes—which was itself a crime. And of course, they possessed and consumed drugs with their informants. All of which created concerns for the researchers.

• *A clash in values and attitudes between the Adlers and their informants.* The Adlers were graduate students, working toward a doctoral degree in sociology at a major university. Hence, they lived a life that was organized, disciplined, and future-oriented; they had schedules, deadlines, appointments; they had to work, study, convince their advisors that they were making progress toward their degree; they had a solid marriage, a stable family life. In contrast, their informants tended to be self-indulgent, spontaneous, present-oriented, and, from the Adlers' perspective, irrational in much of their behavior. In conducting their research, they had to maintain good relations with their informants, with whom they had developed friendships, yet continue to perform in the other realms of their life.

• *Ethical problems.* The Adlers also found that there were ethical problems in conducting their research, which I alluded to above and will discuss in more detail below. Is deception of informants ethical? Some researchers do not believe it is (Erikson, 1967). How much deception is necessary? How much should they lie to some of their informants to protect others? And which ones? How much detail should they go into in writing up their research report, which would inevitably reveal intimacies to others about the scene they studied? Would their informants feel they had been exploited by the Adlers' research? And was violating the law really necessary to gather the information they got? As we've already seen, some researchers feel it is unacceptable (Williams, 1996); clearly, the Adlers disagreed.

Participant Observation: An Assessment

As I said above, the Adlers strongly believe that participant observation is not only the best but the only methodology that should be used to study deviance. Survey methods are preferred by researchers with a more positivistic or natural science bent; participant observation or field methods are favored by social constructionists. I do not regard either method as superior *overall.* Each has strengths and weaknesses *for certain purposes.* Participant observation is stronger on the basis of *validity*—that is, researchers can be confident that what they say is true. Field workers get into the intimate, day-to-day lives of their informants in a way that no other technique can. And participant observation can study phenomena that survey methods cannot hope to approach—dangerous scenes, extremely illegal or deviant behavior, activities in which a very small proportion engages. In contrast, survey methods are superior on the basis of *reliability*—that is, they can be confident that their findings will be reproduced or replicated by other researchers using the same methodology. Certainly the survey method gets a good cross-sectional view; that is, surveys are based on randomized samples that reflect the population as a whole. But survey

methods cannot study many, perhaps *most*, of the issues that participant observers study. Neither can be said to be better as a whole; the question of which is superior depends on what the researcher is attempting to find out.

Narratives, Autobiographies, Life Histories, and Personal Accounts

The use of personal or autobiographical narratives or accounts has been both embraced and rejected by sociologists for a century. A classic work by W. I. Thomas and Florian Znanieki, *The Polish Peasant in America* (1918–1920), a five-volume work of 2,500 pages, devoted 800 pages to personal life histories from informants. But with the growing emphasis in sociological research on quantitative, statistical methods, biographical accounts fell out of favor in the field. It has only been in the last decade or two that the use of narrative and biographical materials has once again come into its own as a legitimate research method. Several journals are entirely devoted to the study of human behavior by means of the biographical method; *Narrative Inquiry* is an outstanding example.

The narrative method encompasses a range of research modes, stretching all the way from the detailed, informal interview, conducted by the sociologist, to the formal, detailed autobiography, written by the subject. As a general rule, narratives are accounts rendered by informants about their own lives. They give minimum control over the content of the material to the researcher and maximum control to the subject. Moreover, of all research methods, the narrative technique is the most *democratic,* in that it gives subjects who have traditionally remained marginal and powerless their own voice, a forum, the means of expressing themselves in ways that, to a major degree, they have chosen themselves. In a sense, unlike all other research methods, in the biographical method the subject is the "star of the show." The narrative technique is probably the prime example of constructionist reasoning, one in which *the subject* defines or constructs his or her own reality. Of course, that reality is always filtered through the researcher's perspective.

Three decades ago, overwhelmingly, personal accounts were examined by researchers and scholars more or less exclusively with respect to their factual accuracy. The issue that guided such investigations was whether accounts could be used to determine "what happened" in the literal, concrete sense. "Good" accounts were those that were empirically accurate; "bad" accounts were those that were factually false or distorted. But in the 1970s, an Italian historian, Alessandro Portelli, noticed that the oral histories of the people whom he interviewed contained systematic omissions, distortions, and imaginary embellishments of events that had taken place 20 or more years before. He decided that the construction of the stories told by his informants was *itself* a historical datum worth investigating. Instead of simply being factually accurate or inaccurate, accounts are also social and historical creations in their own right. They represent testimonies that are organized according to principles that convey cultural, social, and personal truths. This recent stress on "subjectivity" does not mean that the issue of empirical or concrete facticity must be abandoned altogether. But it does mean that the value of an account does not lie in its factual accuracy alone.

All contemporary observers who study the subject of personal accounts agree on at least one basic assumption: Narratives are *not* a simple *reflection of* or *window on* material reality—that is, the events that are narrated. All students of narrative argue that "Just the facts, ma'am" is quite literally an impossibility—in effect, a fiction. Events and experiences do not simply imprint themselves on our brains and come out in the telling, intact and identical for all narrators. The meaning of events and experiences is unstable, liable to interpretations that vary from one teller to another. Stories get told in particular ways, both with respect to a particular cultural and social setting and with respect to individual predilection.

Why do we tell stories in a particular way? Why do we include *these* events in our narrative and leave *those* events out? Which events get recalled? Which ones are forgotten? Everyone who studies narrative assumes that a great deal of variation prevails from one teller to another in the stories that are told. Even the same set of events

will be narrated in radically different ways. For instance, if we were to ask Alan and Sarah, a divorced couple, about their marriage and why it broke up, we would receive two very different accounts of supposedly more or less identical events. Yet, those two accounts are not necessarily contradictory. Both may be literally and factually true; if we had videotaped the events each describes, chances are, we would have seen more or less exactly what Alan said and more or less exactly what Sarah said. But Alan's account left out much of what Sarah's account included, and vice versa. Again, their accounts are factually true—but highly selective, a particular *spin* or *interpretation* on the events that took place.

In the words of Jerome Bruner (1993, p. 46), all autobiographical accounts possess "both verisimilitude and negotiability." As for "verisimilitude," there are the "bare bones" of the events themselves, not subject to interpretation. Did these events take place or didn't they? *For certain purposes*, the verisimilitude of these "bare bones" matters. As with history, explains Bruner, there are "matters of consensual public record to be taken into account" (p. 46). Certain versions of a life are constrained by the events that take place in the material world. Just as ignoring matters of record makes bad history, subverting the factual record makes bad autobiography. Setting aside or falsifying the "bare bones" of a life lends an aura of unbelievability to autobiographical accounts.

Thus, an autobiographical account by a supposed alcoholic would make no sense whatsoever if he or she had been drinking grape juice all those years rather than bourbon. One by a man claiming to be a devotee of S&M (sadomasochism) would be utter nonsense as autobiography if he actually were a happily married heterosexual who engaged only in "missionary" sex with his wife. And if a woman weighing a svelte 120 pounds wrote about her life as an obese woman, her account would make no sense whatsoever as a rendition of her lived experiences. We would be forced to say, as Bruner does when the autobiographer's account is alienated from the "bare bones" of his or her life: "It just doesn't make sense" (p. 47). Hence, one is forced to strongly disagree with Norman Denzin, who claims: "True stories are stories that are believed in" (1989, p. 25). Believed in by whom? one wonders. If half the population believes a story and half disbelieves it, which half decides? How can two contradictory beliefs both be "true"? "The dividing line between fact and fiction," Denzin continues (p. 25), "becomes blurred in autobiographical and biographical text, for if an author can make up facts about his or her life, who is to know what is true and what is false?" If this assertion is true, why should anyone take statements that are likely to be *made up* seriously? Is anyone willing to base decisions on practical matters on made-up stories? Moreover, we already know that many autobiographical claims have been unmasked as false. "Since all writing is fictional," Denzin adds, "it is necessary to do away with the distinction between fact and fiction" (p. 25). Necessary in what sense? To whom? According to what purposes? As determined by what criteria? one wonders. Hence, in autobiographical narratives, factual correctness or verisimilitude is crucial—but it is not the only issue.

Many of the assertions contained in autobiographical accounts can be checked against the documentary record: photographs; hospital records; employment records; school records; college transcripts; physicians', psychiatrists', and psychologists' diagnoses; arrest records; DNA tests; blood and urine tests; and so on. In addition, we are free to consult co-participants in the events being described to seek independent confirmation. Many autobiographical claims are unmasked as false after the historical record is checked. And for many autobiographical accounts, the question of whether the narrated events actually took place *is* important and interesting. After all, if some people *really were* abducted by extraterrestrials (Mack, 1995), the world would be a very different place from the way it is had those stories been imagined or invented. But for *most* narratives, literal facticity is *not* the most interesting issue. Once again, the reader *assumes* a core of verisimilitude.

Bruner reminds us that, just as there must be a foundation of "verisimilitude" in a valid autobiographical account, there is "negotiability" as well. What are some crucial dimensions of negotiability? In short, what explains the "same events, different accounts" phenomenon? Here again, slant, emphasis, and focus loom large. Several sources of negotiability come readily to mind, including individual and cultural variation. *Individual* variation refers to how and why

different people narrate different stories about the same set of events—the personal, idiosyncratic reasons all of us select certain events to tell others about and filter out others. *Cultural* variation refers to how and why norms about life stories that are appropriate (and inappropriate) to tell are disseminated throughout a society and influence the content of what is narrated.

How do people *define* and *experience* unconventionality? What is the experience of being stigmatized? How do conventionals regard, think about, and act toward persons whom they define as socially unacceptable? And how do such experiences shape the content of the accounts that these persons contribute? These and other questions are addressed in deviance accounts.

It is probably in the sphere of *vocabularies of motive* or deviance "accounts" that the narrative method has been most employed—and has been most productive—in the study of deviance. Every human on earth—and that includes you and me—indulges in "vocabularies of motive." That is, we all explain ourselves *to* ourselves and to others in a way that presents us and our actions in more-or-less acceptable, positive terms. All of us, as functioning members of society, learn to use certain phrases to explain what we are doing and why. For the most part, these phrases make us and our actions seem reasonable. Not all vocabularies of motive are appropriate for every action, nor are they acceptable to all audiences. We learn the circumstances under which a particular explanation is acceptable, and to which audiences (Mills, 1940). Of course, we are, ourselves, one of our many audiences, and accounts are frequently directed at convincing ourselves that we are decent, worthwhile human beings.

Which actions require accounts or vocabularies of motive? We do not have to explain to ourselves or others why we tie our shoelaces in the morning. That action seems straightforward, commonsensical, obvious, and strictly utilitarian; no one is going to challenge us on it. But other actions are regarded as problematic. Scott and Lyman (1968; Lyman and Scott, 1970, p. 112) define an account as a statement that is offered for an "untoward" action. An "untoward" action is one that is regarded as unacceptable, improper, blameworthy. When others find out that we engaged in the behavior, we are likely to be challenged or questioned about it; we are likely to be called on to provide an explanation, an account, or a justification. Hence, even in advance, we have to give some thought to why we engaged in a particular behavior.

A major type of vocabulary of motive centers around deviance, since the violation of norms is, by its very nature, problematic to the members of the society in which it takes place. People who engage in actions, hold beliefs, or possess characteristics that are widely regarded as unacceptable are frequently called on to provide some sort of account of them. Even if we do not interact in face-to-face encounters with conventional others who challenge them, we are rarely so insulated from the norms of the society that we are unaware of what those challenges are likely to be. At the very least, we usually formulate mental responses to hypothetical objections to our deviant actions, beliefs, and characteristics.

Most deviance accounts or vocabularies of motive entail *stigma neutralization*. This is a special type of explanation used by persons who anticipate being condemned. Specifically, it reduces or obliterates the anticipated condemnation. Indeed, some versions even find positive qualities in what others find objectionable. For instance, acts that others consider wrong are seen as *not so bad*—or not as bad as others say; beliefs that others condemn are *for a higher cause*—indeed, the beliefs of the condemners are wrong; conditions that others regard as repulsive are a product of fate—or become a *badge of honor*.

Stigma neutralization has a long history in the study of deviance. It is a basic component of how discredited persons, or persons with potentially discrediting secrets about themselves, present themselves to the audiences they have met or are likely to meet.

The professional fence explains his participation in selling stolen goods by emphasizing that he is not a thief. Says one fence: "I don't do nothing wrong. . . . The way I look at it, I'm a businessman. Sure, I buy hot stuff, but I never stole nothin' in my life. Some driver brings me a couple a cartons [of merchandise], though, I ain't gonna turn him away. If I don't buy it, somebody else will. So what's the difference? I might as well make money with him instead of somebody else" (Klockars, 1974, p. 139).

Convicted rapists, too, resort to vocabularies of motive in order to advance the claim that they are acceptable, self-respecting human beings. Many admit having had sex with the women they were sent to prison for having assaulted, but they "disavow" that a rape took place. It was consensual, they claim: "She wanted it," "She was willing," "She was asking for it." Others admit having raped but regard having unlimited sexual access to women as a man's prerogative: "Rape is a man's right. If a woman doesn't want to give it, the man should take it. Women have no right to say no. Women are made to have sex. It's all they are good for" (Scully and Marolla, 1984; Scully and Marolla, 1985, p. 261; Scully, 1990).

Male street hustlers, who have sex with homosexuals for pay, deny that they are engaged in "real" sex. Instead, they justify the act by claiming that they engaged in it solely for the money; they did not initiate it; they remain emotionally aloof from the parties with whom they engaged in it; they received no gratification from it; and, above all, their participation in it does not indicate in any way that they are homosexuals (Reiss, 1964; Calhoun, 1992).

An extremely high proportion of college students admit they have cheated. In fact, more than half say they have done so at least once during their undergraduate careers. The majority of these cheaters use one or another of a variety of stigma neutralization techniques and choose to blame others and/or the situational context for their behavior. Many feel they aren't responsible; it's the system that's at fault: "It's the only way to keep up," "In today's competitive world you do anything to keep up," "Most of the class cheats." Others deny that there is a victim—in effect, "No one gets hurt." Some blame the fraternity and sorority system for organized cheating, which puts nonmembers at an unfair disadvantage; others blame the special coddling of athlete-students. In short, most of the cheaters feel that they have very good reasons for breaking the rules (McCabe, 1995).

Nurses who steal drugs from hospital cabinets justify their behavior by saying that the drugs improve their "disposition" and, hence, make them better caregivers. Moreover, they make a sharp distinction between stealing less potent, nonnarcotic drugs, such as Valium and Darvocet, and stealing the more potent narcotics, such as morphine. Hence, their minor thefts fade into insignificance while their opposition to the theft of the major drugs seems virtuous, almost saintly (Dabney, 1995).

In short, stigma neutralization is a major component of deviance. While all of us engage in vocabularies of motive, persons who have been or are likely to be challenged, criticized, or condemned for their behavior, beliefs, or physical characteristics are especially prone to do so. Indeed, accounting for their unconventional behavior is a central task for deviants or potential deviants; the enterprise of deviance is almost inconceivable without it.

In a society such as ours, conventionals and unconventionals mingle shoulder-to-shoulder. Almost no rule violators could be unaware of the views of the majority toward their deviations or toward themselves *as* deviators. All are forced to conduct a kind of internal dialogue with the conventional majority that goes something like this: "I am aware of the fact that you consider prostitution—or homosexuality, alcoholism, obesity, sadomasochism, dealing drugs, child molestation, or being a dwarf—as abnormal, offensive, or reprehensible. Since I belong to one of these categories, you consider me to be the sort of person who deserves to be stigmatized, shunned, and condemned. The fact is, I believe I do not really deserve this stigma; I feel you do not have the right to direct it at me, and here are some very good reasons why." Vocabularies of motive are born out of precisely this internal dialogue of someone whose behavior, beliefs, or traits may be challenged (a real or potential "unconventional") by an audience (real or potential "conventionals"). The more influence conventionals have over unconventionals, and the more intimate they are with them, the more necessary these stigma neutralizing accounts become. In the world of deviance, they are everywhere.

Deviance vocabularies of motive often challenge the legitimacy of conventional accounts of deviance, occasionally to the point where they offer a viable and plausible cultural alternative to how behavior is explained and understood. In the accounts that follow each chapter of this book, we should pay close attention to the vocabularies

of motive of our contributors. (I adapted the previous four or five pages from Goode, 2002, pp. 249–262.)

It should be said at once that not all deviance accounts are successful. For instance, the National Association to Advance Fat Acceptance (NAAFA) is an organization that attempts to define fat or deviant bodies as acceptable. Most of the fat women in the organization continue to diet—that is, regard their fat bodies in negative terms; are attracted to average-sized, not fat, men; and are contemptuous of the men who are attracted to them because they are fat (Gimlin, 2002, pp. 110–140). Hence, the ideology of the organization has failed to convince its members that "fat is good." Indeed, even to its members, a fat body is a *failed* body (p. 113). In short, though vocabularies of motive are practically universal among deviants, as an effective means of reducing the stigma of deviance they don't always work.

Please notice that accounts and vocabularies of motive are not the *cause* of the behavior they address; stigma neutralization is not an *explanation* of deviance, as many observers mistakenly believe (Siegel, 2003). Delinquents cannot be distinguished from nondelinquents, homosexuals from heterosexuals, prostitutes from nonprostitutes, or tattooed from tattoo-free persons by virtue of the fact that the former have managed to justify a form of behavior before committing it while the latter cannot. An examination of the facts simply does not support such an explanation. The fact is, neutralization techniques are part and parcel of the deviance process, almost inevitably arising when we engage in a mental dialogue with conventional others who are likely to undermine our respectability and decency. They may be verbalized before, during, or after the questionable behavior is enacted, the controversial belief is expressed, or the discrediting trait is acquired, and they may be learned from a subculture or formulated independently. But *whenever* and *however* stigma neutralization is formulated, it cannot be thought of as a reason *why* an actor engaged in deviant behavior. I propose a very different view. All persons who face being defined as deviants face the menace of stigma, potential or real, and all likewise find neutralizing that stigma appealing. And it is through the narrative method that researchers are likely to uncover techniques of stigma neutralization.

ETHICAL ISSUES IN THE STUDY OF DEVIANCE: TEAROOM SEX, A CASE STUDY

In the 1960s, Laud Humphreys, an ordained Episcopal priest, enrolled in Washington University's graduate department of sociology. Captivated by Howard Becker's admonition to study deviance firsthand, animated by the realization that, as a married man, he was gay, and seized by the desire to shatter the image of academia as a cloistered, ivory-tower profession, Humphreys decided to carry out his dissertation research by conducting a participant observation study of sexual transactions in "tearooms." A "tearoom" is a public urinal where anonymous male homosexual contact is common. Humphreys was acquainted with an inside informant, a man who frequented tearooms—"David." Humphreys assumed a nonsexual role in his study, that of "watchqueen"—a lookout who observes when the police or strangers approach a restroom, then warns the persons inside who are participating in sexual activities. During the course of his study, Humphreys observed 134 sexual encounters in urinals, and recorded and wrote up his observations in the form of a doctoral dissertation and a classic book, *Tearoom Trade* (1970). As we might expect, the research on which the book was based was extremely controversial; among other things, by conducting his research in the way he did, Humphreys was accused of violating the sociologist's code of ethics. One faculty member at Washington University was so outraged by Humphreys' research that a verbal altercation between them resulted in a fistfight.

Most sociologists who commented on the study regarded Humphreys' research as unethical less because of his observation of homosexual encounters in public toilets than because of the deception he used in his follow-up interview study. He wrote down the license plates of cars parked near the urinal he studied (it was located in a public park accessible to vehicular traffic) and convinced a police officer that he was conducting

"market research" and needed to obtain the addresses of the owners of these cars. A year after his observational study, he interviewed 50 of the men who had participated in the sexual acts he observed. (None remembered him.) Why was this unethical? Because Humphreys lied to his interviewees. He told them he was conducting an innocuous "social health" survey, not a survey about homosexual behavior. (Remember, this study took place in the 1960s.) In fact, in the interview, he did not deal with the topic of homosexual behavior at all. Many sociologists believe that deceiving one's interviewees, informants, or subjects is profoundly unethical and should not be done in any study that social scientists conduct. Says Kai Erikson, "it is unethical for a sociologist to *deliberately misrepresent* the character of the research in which he [or she] is engaged" (1967, p. 373). Non-sociologists, including journalists and university administrators, were also distressed by the fact that Humphreys hung around public toilets and watched homosexuals engage in oral copulation. The book received a *torrent* of criticism for its supposed unethical research methods. Five years after Humphreys' study was published, a new edition appeared (1975) that reprinted a few of the criticisms it received. These comments summarize much of the opposition to the deception in which the researcher engaged.

Says Nicholas von Hoffman, a journalist: Humphreys was a "sociological snooper" who violated the privacy of his subjects. We find "social scientists behind the hunting blinds . . . peeping into what we thought were our most private and secret lives . . . , studying us, taking notes . . . , indifferent . . . to the feeling that to be completely human involves having an aspect of our lives that's unknown" (1975, p. 177). Donald Warwick, a social scientist writing in an academic journal devoted to discussions of "ethics and the life sciences" (1973), accused Humphreys of "deception, invasions of privacy, and harmful uses" of his research findings. The researcher, he says, was guilty of a "concatenation of misrepresentation and disguises [that] . . . must surely hold the world record for field research." More specifically, says Warwick, the researcher *lied*: (1) about the fact that he was a homosexual; (2) about his "watchqueen" role (he was there primarily as a researcher and voyeur, not as a watchqueen); (3) about the fact that he recorded his observations by hiding a tape recorder in the front seat of his car; (3) to the police about his "market research" to obtain addresses of tearoom participants; (5) to his interviewees that he was conducting a "social health" survey; (6) to his interviewees about his identity (he changed his car, his hairstyle, his attire); (7) to his interviewees that they were part of an anonymous, randomized sample when in fact, their names were known to him in advance and they had already been preselected for the study by virtue of their participation in tearoom sex. All in all, says Warwick, the costs of Humphreys' deception to human freedom, to privacy, to his informants and interviewees, and to social science as a whole, were too great; the study should never have been conducted in the way it was done. Arlene Kaplan Daniels claims that "no one in the society deserves to be trusted with hot, incriminating data. Let me repeat, *no one*" (Glazer, 1972, p. 219). And in a textbook on research methods, sociologist Myron Glazer states that he would "attempt to dissuade others" from the research path that Humphreys followed. "The dangers to respondents, to the researcher, and to the precious sense of respect for the privacy of others seem too great for the returns. Had Humphreys faltered, had his data been secured by police officials or unscrupulous blackmailers, Humphreys would have been branded a rogue and a fool" (1972).

Are these critics correct? In 1968 and again in 1997, the American Sociological Association issued policy statements stipulating that sociologists should not conduct research "without the informed consent of subjects." It also issued qualifications; "waivers" may be obtained under certain circumstances. As I said above, Institutional Review Boards (IRBs) pass judgments concerning the "protection of human subjects," including the matter of deception. Had there been an IRB in place at Washington University when Humphreys conducted his study (1965–1968), its committee would *not* have permitted him to do it the way he did. On the other hand, the actual membership of the American Sociological Association (ASA) is more divided on the issue. Two sociologists (Long and Dorn, 1983) conducted a survey of ASA members and found that six out of ten agreed with the statement "It is ethically acceptable for sociologists to deceive research subjects and to expose them to temporary 'harm' so long

as care is taken to eliminate long-term post-research effects" (p. 283). According to Long and Dorn, sociologists favored neither "restrictions in research in the name of ethics, nor did they favor unrestricted research—an apparent inconsistency" (p. 283). What are sociologists "willing to do" about unethical research? Long and Dorn's data suggest "not too much"—except write and talk about the subject (p. 297).

Many sociologists, including the Adlers (Adler, Adler, and Rochford, 1986), Jack Douglas (1976), and myself (Goode, 1996a), are not as distressed about these ethical issues as Humpreys' critics are. It is true that Humphreys did not debrief his informants and interviewees about the true nature of his research. However, he *did* take *extreme* measures to ensure their anonymity, to make sure that their names would not fall into anyone's hands. Von Hoffman compares "sociological snoopers" to police undercover agents, but he ignores the fact that the police do take names and have one purpose in mind—to make arrests—whereas sociologists keep identities anonymous and names a secret, and are dedicated to ensuring that no one is *ever* arrested as a result of their research. Daniels claims that no one in our society should be entrusted with "hot, incriminating evidence," but journalists, psychiatrists and psychologists, physicians, and the clergy *do* have such information. And sociologists are the only profession among this list whose practitioners are *not* involved in pinning such evidence to specific persons. Instead, they are more-or-less exclusively involved in depicting patterns and drawing generalizations from such "evidence"— *without* the names of specific persons.

Glazer's more nuanced warning makes sense, however: Only the brave and extremely competent researcher should undertake research that poses serious risks for both informants and the researcher. As with most ideological, political, and moral issues, the matter of ethics in social research cannot be resolved with a simple, cut-and-dried answer. It depends on the skill of the researcher, the nature of the research, the risks involved, the seriousness of the ethical violation, and the possible rewards to the society of the publication of the research. In my view, a democratic society can afford to tolerate a little "snooping" from a tiny number of researchers engaging in controversial research methods for the purpose of disseminating findings about unconventional behavior. To close down such behavior would have a chilling effect on the freedom of expression guaranteed by the Constitution. It would in fact make this society a more repressive, boring, and stultifying—and less free—place in which to live.

And yet, I must emphasize, all human behavior should be guided by a sense of moral conviction, and this behavior includes social research. The fact is, the researcher of deviance and crime is faced with moral and ethical dilemmas. Once we admit that IRBs typically protect the interests of the university at the expense of the interests of social researchers, and once we agree that if researchers were to follow the law to the letter of the law, a great deal of controversial research would be prohibited, we are still left with a great many unanswerable questions.

Clearly, the sociologist should not condone rape, murder, and harmful corporate crime. Ferrell and Hamm urge sociologists not only to observe and condone but in some cases even to participate in deviant and illegal behavior. But what if this entails condoning a female minor being "kept by [a] crack-house owner for sex with clients" (1998, p. 3)? What about studying by observing and even taking part in the operation of a "chop shop," a garage that receives stolen cars that are cut up and sold, piecemeal? What if the researcher finds out that white supremacists burned down houses and businesses owned by African Americans? At that point, what is one's moral obligation?

If one agrees that, as a citizen, one has an obligation to report serious and truly harmful crimes to the police, how serious and how harmful do they have to be? These days, in Iraq, practically daily, network television journalists are interviewing terrorists and protecting the identity of their sources. Is this ethical? At what point is one able to say, "My research is more important than my obligations as a citizen"? Can one truly retreat to the position that one has an obligation to protect the identity of one's sources *at all cost*? I have no glib, pat answers to these questions. After all, prosecutors can and do force journalists, physicians, psychiatrists, and the clergy to reveal evidence in criminal cases where the overriding interests of society compel that revelation. Sociologists and other researchers have the same obligations as the

members of these other professions to act morally and ethically. But where is that point reached? I can't decide for other researchers where that point is reached *for them*. A definitive statement on exactly where social research becomes unethical and immoral will have to be made by a sociologist braver than I am. The issue is fraught with dilemmas and contradictions, and sociologists who work at the front lines of these dilemmas and contradictions will have to test and re-test these boundaries. Contemplating the issue of ethics and morality reminds us that social research is, after all, an all-too-human enterprise.

SUMMARY

Deviance is a subject whose study poses special problems but, at the same time, yields special rewards. The subject has been studied by means of a variety of research methodologies. Some are *quantitative*, that is, they generate data that are easily measured, that can be reduced to numbers and statistics. Others are by their very nature *qualitative*, that is, they produce data that are not easily reduced to numbers but reside in the form of apposite and revealing quotes, metaphors, and examples. Survey methods, laboratory experiments, and the use of official data tend to be quantitative. In contrast, participant observation or field methods and autobiographical accounts tend to be qualitative. A method that entails the close examination of texts or cultural documents—content analysis—can be conducted in such a way that the researcher generates both quantitative and qualitative data.

Information generated by government agencies for administrative purposes can be referred to as "official" data. Sociologists often use such data for theoretical, descriptive, and analytic purposes. Three major sources of data used by sociologists of deviance, crime, and drug use are the Uniform Crime Reports, DAWN (the Drug Abuse Warning Network), and ADAM (the Arrestee Drug Abuse Monitoring Program). The Uniform Crime Reports are tabulations made by the FBI of crimes reported to the police and arrests that take place each year in nearly all the police jurisdictions in the United States. Clearly, neither crimes reported to the police nor arrests accurately reflect the actual commission of crime, and so sociologists and criminologists have figured out limited ways of using these flawed data. DAWN examines both nonlethal and lethal drug "overdoses" in urban areas around the country; such tabulation tells us a thing or two about changes in drug abuse over time as well as how dangerous and widely abused different drugs are. ADAM looks at drug use among arrestees. It tells us about the strong relationship between drug abuse and criminal behavior as well as about regional differences in the use of various drugs.

Survey methods represent the most important and prominent methodology for sociologists in general as well as for criminologists, but are not not as important for the sociologists who study deviance. Ideally, surveys are conducted on large, randomized samples that "represent" a cross-section of the country as a whole. Researchers attempt to ensure that the answers of their respondents are honest and that the response rate of their surveys is high. Most researchers go beyond a simple description of the social world; they want to explain *why* things are the way they are. They establish cause-and-effect explanations by controlling for or holding constant the relevant variables. Hence, in sociology, survey methods are the positivist's method of choice. Survey methods are not ideal for the study of all, and possibly most, deviant phenomena. Attitudes held by the general public about deviant behavior are one possible subject that is amenable to the survey method, as is the study of crime victimization, sexual behavior, and drug use. However, many other subjects either require too large a sample or involve too touchy a subject to be amenable to survey methods.

Participant observation entails the direct, face-to-face observation of the intimate, day-to-day lives of informants in their natural habitat. It is a method that is based on getting as close to the people one is studying as possible, being with them around the clock, and engaging in as much of their behavior as ethics and legality will allow. This method generates mountains of rich descriptive data, called field notes. The many observations by the researcher, and behavior and statements by the informants, maximize validity, or the confidence that what is observed is true.

But the scene, the group, the social circle selected by the researcher may not be typical or representative of such scenes, groups, or circles in general. Some field workers prefer to be observers only and do not participate in the behavior under study; others prefer to participate in the behavior under study.

Narratives, autobiographies, life histories, and personal "accounts" represent a major means of studying deviant scenes. In the past, personal statements by subjects were looked at as valuable only insofar as they were factually truthful. However, more recent researchers have focused on the *social construction* of life stories—what is included and what is left out, the *slant* of a particular narrator. Contrary to what some commentators have argued, literal facticity cannot be dismissed as irrelevant. Nonetheless, it is not the only issue; indeed, *how* life histories are told has been the central focus of most researchers who use this research method. The study of vocabularies of motive or techniques of stigma neutralization probably represent the most interesting line of inquiry of this particular methodology.

Since the 1960s, researchers and university administrators have been increasingly interested in the matter of research ethics. (Actually, IRBs are more concerned about preventing their parent institution from being sued than about the rights of human subjects, but that is another matter.) Central to the official interpretation of research ethics are the twin matters of *informed consent* and *deception*. A strict interpretation of ethics requires that all subjects, informants, and interviewees be informed as to exactly what the researcher is doing, what his or her aims are: No deception or disguised observation is regarded as acceptable. Not all researchers agree. In fact, a survey of the members of the American Sociological Association revealed that most sociologists regard deception as acceptable under certain circumstances. According to the strictest interpretation of research ethics, as interpreted by most IRBs, the majority of participant observation studies on deviance would quite literally be impossible, since researchers cannot inform each and every person they observe from moment to moment what they are up to. Indeed, had they been operative at the time, university IRBs would not have permitted most of the classic participant observation studies discussed in this chapter, and that includes Patricia Adler's study of drug dealers and Laud Humphreys' study of tearoom sex. Many conservative university administrations— and not a few sociologists—do not feel this would represent a great loss to scholarship. I do not agree, and have argued that IRB regulations are too strict to accommodate many types of research on deviance (Goode, 1996a).

Field Experiment: Public Reactions to Normative Violations

Field experiments are a rarely used method of social research in the sociology of deviance. Nonetheless, they can be an interesting and productive means of studying normative violations. One idea is to engage in behavior openly and publicly and then observe and record the reactions of witnesses or audiences. Whenever actions consistently elicit negative reactions, we know we have a case of deviance on our hands. And by systematically varying the conditions of the experiment, we test the factors that elicit, versus those that do not elicit, negative reactions. For instance, are onlookers more likely to chastise a man, as opposed to a woman, for a given normative violation? Do they chastise women more for certain normative violations? Are the residents of cities more likely to chastise norm-violators than residents of small towns? These and other questions can be addressed by the field experiment. I got the idea of assigning the following field experiment from R. H. Potter, who assigned it to the students enrolled in his deviance courses at the University of New England, Australia (1999).

Here are the instructions I gave to my students. (This assignment was only one out of a dozen paper options; hence, only a small proportion of the class chose to do it.)

You will commit a deviant act in a public place, or have someone else commit a deviant act in a public place. You will observe, record, and write in detail the reactions you observed to the deviant act. Engage in the act again, in another public place, varying systematically from the first in some meaningful way. For instance, do the same thing—same act, two different settings—on a college campus versus in a shopping mall; in a very public place versus only in the presence of a few friends who do not know you are engaging in an experiment; indoors versus outdoors; in a city (D.C. or Baltimore) versus a small town; etc. Interview people who have observed or reacted to your unconventional behavior and ask them why they reacted as they did, or how they feel about your behavior if they did not react, or why they didn't react at all. Analyze these reactions by using the theoretical, analytic, or conceptual perspective(s) you believe best explain(s) or illuminate(s) the act. Possible issues to discuss: Why did you expect this act to be deviant in this particular setting? Why did the people react as they did? Any interesting observations? "Deviant" reactions? Did these reactions and/or your analysis give you any insight into the processes of deviance and social control? Did the settings you chose make any difference? Be as detailed in your descriptions as you can. Possible deviant behaviors: eating at the dinner table with your hands; wearing bizarre clothes; attempting to haggle over price in a store that sells items for a fixed price; standing in a particular spot and reading aloud from a book; standing in a particular spot and staring intently at nothing in particular; ostentatiously picking your nose; swearing repeatedly; drinking water out of a vodka bottle or tea out of a whiskey bottle; standing in front of a class in which you are not enrolled as the lecture is about to begin and staring vacantly into space; smoking in a non-smoking area; constantly interrupting someone in an ordinary conversation or asking for clarification for simple, commonplace words; walking

Field Experiment: Public Reactions to Normative Violations (cont.)

backwards through the campus; etc. I'm sure you can think of others. *Under no circumstances are you to do, or ask someone to do, anything that could be construed as dangerous or criminal. I will not bail you out if you are arrested, or serve as a character witness at your trial.* (Potter, 1999)

During one semester, I received a half-dozen papers from students who chose this option. ("This is gonna be fun!*" shouted one student after I explained the assignment.) Below we have an example of one of these papers.*

PERSONAL ACCOUNT: Two Guys Holding Hands in Public
Steven M. Clayton

Randy, my best friend, and I conducted our field experiment in New York City in November 2001. My study centered around the notion that we were homosexual partners. My goal was to demonstrate that fact to the people who saw us in the public places where we carried out our project, and to observe their reaction and interview them about how they felt about what we did. We conducted this study in two locations. One was in public on 42nd Street, in Times Square in midtown Manhattan. The other site was in a restaurant in Greenwich Village in downtown Manhattan. In a city as diverse as New York, we were eager to observe and understand the reactions of people on the street when they saw what was depicted as homosexual tendencies and behavior.

We hit the streets on November 3rd. We began by walking along 42nd Street, holding hands—holding one another more closely than friends hold one another. Throughout that day, we were never more than a few feet from each other. We also drank from the same soda cup and shared food from a hot dog vendor on the street. It was our hope that these actions showed to the people around us that we were homosexual partners. Our aim was to determine what their naturalistic reactions would be to our (perceived) acts of homosexuality.

Throughout the day we got many different reactions from different people. Some of them seemed unfazed by our behavior. We even had a few people come up and wish us good luck in our relationship. However, the great majority of the people we observed reacted negatively. One reaction that stands out above the rest was when we saw a mother pull her children away from us, yelling "Didn't I tell you to stay away from these type of people!" A substantial number of others didn't say a word to us but gave us dirty looks and stares.

One middle-aged man came up to us and stated, "You know what you are doing is wrong." When I asked him if I could ask a few questions, I was pleasantly surprised when he accepted the offer. The first question I asked was, "Do you find homosexual acts to be deviant?" The man replied, "To be frankly honest, yes I do. Well, at least in public areas such as this. What you do behind your bedroom doors is none of my damn business, but don't come out here to corrupt the straight, moral ones in our society!" Then I asked him a follow-up question: "By engaging in such actions in public how do you feel we are corrupting society?" The man replied: "History will teach you that every action people engage in is done for copycat reasons. Heck, the reason why you and your buddy over there are

PERSONAL ACCOUNT: Two Guys Holding Hands in Public (cont.)

gay is probably because of some fucked up stuff you saw in your childhood. At least have the morals not to do the same stuff to the millions of people walking every day in this congested area."

I also had the opportunity to interview one of the women who wished us good luck in our relationship. I asked her the same question as I asked the gentleman: "Do you find homosexual acts to be deviant?" Her response was very interesting. She said: "I would have to say yes, I do believe that homosexuality and homosexual actions are indeed deviant, from my perspective. However, who am I to tell you what you can and can't do. It's your life, so I wish you the best of luck in whatever endeavors you choose to pursue, whether I may personally approve of them or not."

I expected the perceived homosexual acts that Randy and I were engaging in to be deviant, in Times Square particularly, because of the very large crowd of people there. By sheer probability alone, there being a range of different perspectives on homosexuality, chances were that someone would react in almost any imaginable way. Still, the majority in our society in the present day view homosexual acts in public as deviant. I felt comfortable that in a crowd or a space that large, we would have little trouble drawing reactions from people who thought the perceived homosexual acts we were supposedly engaged in were deviant. . . . .

Our second day of the project brought us downtown to Greenwich Village. This time, instead of being on the street, we did our study in a restaurant that was about six blocks from New York University. We engaged in many of the same activities that we had on the street in Times Square, such as holding hands, being physically close to one another, drinking out of the same cup, and so on. However, we did add a few activities.

Part of the reason why we were drawn to Greenwich Village was that we understood that the area had a high percentage of homo-

sexuals and that overt homosexual acts in public were accepted much more than they would be had they taken place in other locations in New York. We were curious to see if this theory was correct. For the most part, it was. We received many fewer dirty looks or stares than we did on 42nd Street and more people communicated freely regarding homosexual issues and asked questions on the supposed homosexual relationship that my friend and I were having. However, it should be noted that we did receive some negative reactions, especially from one tourist in particular. In fact, we experienced something of an altercation. I'll describe his reaction momentarily.

The first person I interviewed happened to be a gay male who lived in the Village. I was intrigued to have at least one of my interviews be with a homosexual, since I felt it vital and necessary to get their perspective in my study. I asked him, "Do many people who are regular customers of this restaurant regard public acts of homosexuality as deviant?" He responded: "Most people in the area don't give it a second thought, since it [homosexuality] has become such an important and vibrant part of the Village community." He went on to say: "You [referring to homosexuals] will always be safe here." I then asked him: "Do you believe that is why the Village has such a high population of homosexuals—because of the established success of homosexuals in the past and possible support networks here that wouldn't be found in other places?" The man answered: "To be honest, that is why I came here. I'm from Toronto, so I wasn't even an American at birth. The Village, however, can honestly be viewed . . . as a Disney World for gays and lesbians."

Not all reactions we received were quite as positive, however. A tourist from Oklahoma approached us and yelled at us, "This is hell and you fools are the Devil's servants! Burn in hell, you cocksuckers!" Somehow, I summoned up the courage to ask this gentleman if I could ask him a few questions in an attempt to understand

PERSONAL ACCOUNT: Two Guys Holding Hands in Public (cont.)

his perspective. He agreed, his hope being for him to save us, to convert us to moral and productive heterosexuals. That way, he said, we could be "one of God's loving children." The first question I asked him was: "What is your reason for your feelings toward homosexuals?" He responded: "Well, the truth is that those of you, who are different from the rest of us, started off as God's children, but you fell along the path. You are not to blame—it is because of your stupid culture. From where I am from [Oklahoma], we have such things as values and morals that will not allow one of us to stray such as you folks have." The second question I asked him was, "Saying that New York culture is to blame, would that prevent you from doing anything more than simply to visit as a tourist?" His answer was: "Most definitely yes. Come on, honestly, how am I supposed to raise my family and try to teach them what is right and moral in God's eyes, when all of this [homosexuality] is going on around us? That would fight the good my wife and I instill in our children."

Negative reactions to our actions gave Randy and me an inside look into the workings of social control. Like many forms of deviance, homosexuality and homosexual behavior for the most part are perfectly legal. They are in New York State. So, forms of social control other than the police and the courts are used to effect social control. Homosexual acts are controlled by informal means, such as receiving the negative reactions we observed and even threats from individuals. This certainly operates in public areas, as we found out.

But on the other hand, the proportion of people who don't seem bothered at all by homosexuality, or those who respond positively, have increased because of the influence of gay liberation in the 1990s. We expected that in Greenwich Village, but to be honest, we were surprised that we found some similar feedback in Times Square as well. Before the gay liberation movement, you would rarely if ever see anyone engaging in homosexual acts in public. Today, one can go to almost any

major city and observe the kind of behavior that Randy and I exhibited on those November days in New York City. It can be that exposure of homosexuality to the majority is beginning to overcome the preconceived stereotypes and produced more favorable reactions toward homosexuality and homosexual behavior.

There are also sociological reasons why some people gave us bad looks or stares as well as the negative feedback we received to our supposed homosexual behavior. There are still many who view homosexuality as a major sin. Thus, when they see such behavior, it causes them to condemn such acts and even speak against or abuse persons who engage in those acts. A significant proportion of this country, especially those living in rural areas of the South and the Midwest, view homosexuality in a very negative and very deviant light. This prompts them to openly condemn the people they perceive as homosexuals. The belief that homosexuality is the ultimate sin has been spurred on by fundamentalist Christians such as Jerry Falwell, who said: "What was considered a deviant lifestyle is now considered by many Americans to be an alternative lifestyle. . . . The entire homosexual movement is an indictment against America and is contributing to its ultimate downfall" (Falwell, Dobson, and Hindson, 1996, p. 13). It is no wonder that some people condemned us openly and publicly.

Another reason we elicited the negative reactions we received was that there is a great deal of negative, anti-homosexual literature out there in American society, educating the way the public thinks about the matter. For instance, as Mary McIntosh said of the male homosexual, as of the 1960s, in American culture, there is "the expectation that sexuality will play a part of some kind in all his relations with other men, and the expectation that he will be attracted to boys and very young men, and probably willing to seduce them" (1968, p. 185). It is through such beliefs, which are passed on through the media, that negative images of the homosexual lifestyle are expressed and in turn this

PERSONAL ACCOUNT: Two Guys Holding Hands in Public (cont.)

influences how they would react to us engaging in perceived homosexual acts on the street. Such media and religious influences that cast a negative light on homosexuals and homosexuality combine to produce a negative and sustained stigma. Many of the negative reactions we got were as a result of this stigma that people have entrenched in their minds. They don't even have to think about it before coming to a negative judgment on the actions they saw my friend and me supposedly engage in. . . . The tourist from Oklahoma felt we were deliberately offending God and heaven by engaging in our supposed homosexual acts. . . .

With respect to the question, "What makes our actions deviant?" the answer is that the majority perceives the actions as deviant and reacts to them negatively. If the act were not deviant, people would not have condemned us for what they thought we were doing. From both a normative and a reactive perspective, what we were doing was deviant. We violated the majority's norms about proper sexuality and many condemned us for it. That makes what we did deviant.

In conclusion, this study was very compelling for Randy and me. Being straight men who are not personally bothered by seeing homosexual acts, we were given a unique and inside view on how overt homosexuals are treated on a daily basis. We found that while there were some positive reactions, and some places were better suited for our activities than others, it is difficult to engage in those activities and not face a harsh backlash. . . . Should homosexual acts be considered deviant? We don't think they should, but clearly others disagree. All the different opinions we got to that question were extremely interesting.

QUESTIONS

Do you think that Steve Clayton's experiment is an interesting method of investigating whether and to what extent homosexuality is deviant? What other methods might be used? Of the methods discussed in this chapter, which one is most productive? Or is any one most productive in the abstract? Are some methods more productive for certain purposes, and others more productive in different ways? Can you imagine yourself conducting research on deviance by using one or more of the research methods we looked at here? Which one might be the most enjoyable and interesting to conduct? Of the many forms of deviance you can think of, which one would you most like to study? Which research method would you use?

CHAPTER
6

Criminal Violence

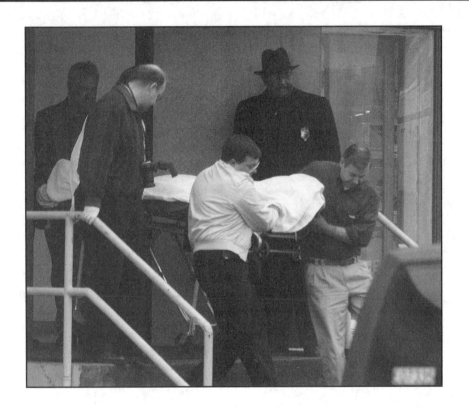

A study of "conventional" crime—that is, the kinds of criminal acts that come to mind when the word "crime" is encountered—is instructive for both the positivist and the constructionist. "Crime" is both an objective reality whose causes and consequences can be investigated, and a concept that people have in their heads, a subject about which people talk and about which they try to do something.

What's criminal behavior? When is a crime committed? And what's the relationship between crime and deviance? And what specifically is criminal *violence*?

A man walks into a bank brandishing a shotgun and demands cash. A teenager jimmies open the window of a parked car, pops the ignition, and drives off. A woman in a department store slips several blouses into her shopping bag and walks away. A couple has a furious argument and both begin throwing objects at one another; the man grabs the woman by the throat and begins choking her. A teenager sneaks to the back of a neighbor's house, crawls through an open window, pulls open all the dresser drawers, finds cash and some jewelry, runs downstairs, and exits through the back door. A man meets a woman in a bar and she agrees to go home with him; in the car, he parks, holds a knife to her throat, and sexually assaults her. At a party, a dozen people in their twenties sit in a circle and snort cocaine, brought by one of the guests. Two men, drinking in a bar, begin an altercation; they step outside and, on the sidewalk, one pulls out a knife, the other smashes a whiskey bottle against the curb, and within minutes, one of them lies dead in the gutter. A man working for a restaurant uses the credit card number of a customer to charge tens of thousands of dollars' worth of merchandise against the cardholder's account. At a meeting, the executives of a factory agree to violate the state's antipollution laws; over the following months, their factory releases poisonous chemicals into a nearby stream. A secret military operation assassinates the leader of a political movement opposed to the government's policies.

Are these crimes? How do we know? And who decides?

More to the topic of this chapter, what's violence? And what's the difference between criminal violence and noncriminal violence?

The most valuable lesson we learn when we contrast the findings of the positivist criminologist's and sociologist's studies with the perspective gained by looking at reality through the constructionist's eyes is the *discrepancy* between them. In other words, *the truth of science is not always the truth of belief.* When the discrepancy between them is huge, the inquiring sociologist wants to know why. *What accounts* for the fact that people believe things that are not factually correct? For instance, if people are concerned about and fear a given condition much more than is warranted by that condition's objective threat (Jenkins, 1998; Glassner, 1999; Fenster, 1999; Cohen, 2002), we are alerted to the fact that *something is going on* that we should find out about.

When it comes to crime, most people are concerned about and fear "street" crime, the Index Crimes, stereotypical or "conventional" criminal behavior—especially violent crime. But the fact is, in the United States, we are far less likely to be murdered (16,000 victims in 2002) than to die of tobacco-related causes (440,000 deaths). Our chances of being robbed are minuscule (about a million victims a year) compared with being a victim of a corporate crime (which includes the entire population, considering the fact that the public has to pay for corporate schemes that are paid for by tax dollars). And the classic stranger rapes that are thought of as rape and reported to the police are far less common than date or acquaintance rape that is often not even regarded as rape and is reported in only a minority of cases. Yet the vast majority of us are concerned about, and fear, murder, robbery, and stranger rape far more than we fear these other, far more common, sources of victimization.

The fact is, the public fears violence at the hands of a stranger far more than violence at the hands of intimates. Yet intimates are *far more* likely to inflict violence on us than strangers are. For instance, studies show that family violence— wife battering and child abuse, including sexual abuse—is extremely common (Pryor, 1996; Barnett, Miller-Perrin, and Perrin, 1997; Arriaga and Oskamp, 1999). All incidents of serious family violence, most of which are not reported, are many times greater than all the cases of aggravated (or serious) assault that are reported to the police. In 2002, where the police knew the relationship between victim and killer, more than one murder victim in five (22 percent) was killed by a family member; another 7 percent involved a killing by a boyfriend or girlfriend. When the killing involved a husband and wife or boyfriend-girlfriend, in nearly eight out of ten cases, it was the male who killed the female. In other words, the total number of family members we have is small in number but they make up a *huge* proportion of the total picture of violence. Of all the violence that takes place, a substantial proportion stems from the very people we are closest to—and yet, for most of us, they are the very people we fear the least. Strangers are much less likely to commit violence against us, yet we fear them the most. Again, to the sociologist of deviance, paradoxes such as these are interesting and very much in need of investigation.

CRIME AND DEVIANCE: A CONCEPTUAL DISTINCTION

To begin with, it is clear that crime and deviance are *not* the same thing. Earlier, we found out that crime is not a *defining criterion* of deviance. Many deviant acts, beliefs, and conditions are not criminal: obesity, being a creep, a loser, a geek, and a dweeb, being an eccentric, an atheist, and an alcoholic, are all deviant—but they are not crimes.

What about the other way around? Are all crimes deviant? Most of the conventional or mainstream public regards having been convicted of and, even more so, imprisoned for a crime as stigmatizing. True, in some social circles, being an ex-convict brings a certain measure of hip, edgy, romantic cachet. But the more conventional the person, the more discrediting having been imprisoned is likely to be. In that sense, yes, all crimes are deviant—though, again, crime is not a defining criterion of deviance; it is one specific *type* of deviance. In other words, by itself, *being* a criminal is deviant because it is a stigmatizing status.

But independent of its stigmatizing character, is violating the criminal code a form of deviance? Are laws a type of norm the violation of which

constitutes deviance? Sociologists answer this question in different ways. One, fairly broad, definition of deviance sees *any and all* negative reactions—regardless of whether they come from a friend or from the criminal justice system—as the defining criterion of deviance. According to this definition, a crime is a violation of one *specific* kind of norm—a law—which generates formal, state-supported sanctions, including conviction and imprisonment. Clearly, then, according to this definition, all crime *is* deviant (Clinard and Meier, 2004, pp.130–133). But keep in mind that here, again, crime does not *define* deviance; instead, this definition sees laws as a *type* of norm, and criminal punishment a type of condemnation. Hence, crime is a *form* or *subtype* of deviance.

A second, somewhat different definition of deviance is offered by other observers. By this definition, deviance is *solely and exclusively* informal and interpersonal in nature, while crime is *specifically* the violation of formal norms and hence, is conceptually *separate* and *distinct* from deviance (Quinney, 1965; Robertson and Taylor, 1973). According to this definition, crime is *not* deviance. They are two different things. Of course, once again, the *informal* stigma that the status of being a criminal tends to generate is a separate matter; to the extent that criminality is stigmatizing, crime is a form of deviance by any definition.

In sum, then: One, criminality is not a *necessary* defining criterion of deviance according to *any* definition. Two, to the extent that crime is stigmatizing, it is a form of deviance by *all* definitions. And three, according to *some* definitions of deviance, crime is a form or variety of deviance and according to *others*, crime is separate and distinction from deviance. Clearly, then, deviance and crime are intertwined in interesting and important ways. They overlap, albeit imperfectly.

It follows from the fact of the far-from-perfect overlap of deviance and crime that a course on the sociology of deviance does not deal with precisely the same topics as a course on the sociology of crime. Behaviors that are against the law, whose enactment is likely to result in the perpetrator being arrested, are discussed in the field known as criminology. As we saw in Chapter 1, it would be repetitious to discuss each and every one of them in a deviance textbook. Therefore, in this book, I shall not devote a great deal of attention to topics that are likely to be discussed in a criminology course—such as murder, rape, robbery, burglary, and corporate crime. However, the *analytic* or *theoretical* concepts that run through any course on deviance—and which will run through this book— may also apply to any number of illegal actions. Such concepts include the social construction of reality, deviance neutralization, vocabularies of motive, stigma, stigma management, condemnation, identity, subculture, moral panics, moral entrepreneurs, power, social conflict, and contingency. In addition, many theories of deviance are *also* theories of crime; I discussed them in Chapters 3 and 4. The most important thing about both deviance and crime is not the specific details of each activity—important though they be—but the insight that studying them gives us concerning how society works. What the study of both deviance and crime are "about" is, primarily, the dynamics of normative violations, and ultimately, social life in general. The details about each should serve the concepts, not the other way around.

In short, there is a kind of rough "division of labor" between the fields of the sociology of crime and the sociology of deviance. By that I mean that a somewhat different set of scholars focus on somewhat different subject matters. Deviance specialists tend to focus on behavior, beliefs, and conditions that generate *informal* sanctioning, as well as the origin, dynamics, and consequences of the informal sanctioning itself. (Examples: Rubington and Weinberg, 2002; Adler and Adler, 2003.) Specialists in crime, often referred to as criminologists, tend to focus on behavior (rarely on beliefs, and *never* on physical conditions) that generates *formal* sanctioning, as well as the origin, dynamics, and consequences of the formal sanctioning itself. (Examples: Siegel, 2003; Adler, Laufer, and Mueller, 2004.)

COMMON LAW AND STATUTORY LAW

The legal system of the United States is based on English common law. Prior to the Norman Conquest of 1066, the Anglo-Saxon legal system was extremely decentralized, with a somewhat different set of rules and customs prevailing in different counties or "shires." Moreover, wrongs committed by one person against another were mainly considered disputes between and among private parties, who were the offender's and the victim's families. Rather than the offender being punished, the families of offenders had to pay victims or their families a specific sum, depending on the offense. The compensation received tended to be in the form of cows, sheep, or other such things of value. Separately, the church courts adjudicated offenses the church considered sins, and punished the sinners accordingly.

During the reign of King Henry II (who ruled 1154–1189), judges were sent out into the shires around England and heard cases that previously had been adjudicated more informally by local authorities. As a result of the rulings of these traveling or circuit judges, a codified "common law" developed, that is, a set of legal precedents that were national rather than local in scope, which applied equally (or "in common") to all English subjects, in all shires, without regard for local custom. Eventually, these decisions acquired the status of precedent for later cases. *Common* law came to be *national* law. Hence, common law is technically *case* law or *judge-made* law—law decided in court, albeit law that is restrained by the weight of precedent.

The decisions of these traveling judges were not arbitrary. Common law stemmed from ancient custom, tradition, and precedent. This is sometimes referred to as "primal law," that is, a set of laws that defines as crimes acts that violate norms that have existed for thousands of years. Its existence is based on the *unwritten* law (or, later, court decisions *based* on these norms, which were decided on by a courtroom judge rather than adjudicated by a legislature). Laws against murder, robbery, and rape are examples of "primal" law. Their violations are referred to as "high-consensus" crimes because practically everyone in a given society agrees that laws against them should exist and are valid and legitimate. The implication of common law is that it does not come into being as a result of the pressure of special-interest groups, but has the force of tradition behind it. In the United States, nearly all common law has been transformed into *statutory* law; that is, laws have become enacted into law by a legislature, a formal body of elected or appointed officials. The history of common law, then, is a three-step process. First, the laws *began* as tradition (that is, their violations were "primal" crimes), then (at least in England) they were codified judicially, in the courtroom, by legal precedent, and finally, they were enacted into statutory form.

In contrast, laws whose existence *began* as statutes (known collectively as "statutory law") have a history that is completely different from laws that began in the common-law tradition. Most statutory laws refer to crimes for which there are *no* roots in historical or cultural tradition. Most also tend to have less than complete public consensus concerning their legal status. Statutory laws arose because technological change made certain controls necessary (those regulating computer crimes, for instance), or because conflict between social categories in the population resulted in the triumph of a more moralistic group's views over those of more permissive groups (the laws governing sexual behavior, for example).

While many societies developed informal norms concerning gambling, even where they existed they were often ignored, and they rarely mobilized the sentiment of the entire community. Our current gambling laws are statutory laws. The public remains divided about whether gambling should be a crime in the first place. (Moreover, the government permits many forms of gambling, which further dilutes the legitimacy of the gambling statutes.) And gambling laws do not have the force of thousands of years of tradition behind them—that is, unlike murder, forcible rape, and robbery, gambling was not always considered a crime.

Corporate and white-collar crimes, likewise, do not carry the force and authority of historical tradition. They came to be defined *as crimes* only in the twentieth century and only as a consequence of statutes, that is, the decisions of a legislature. In fact, many of the very activities proscribed by the laws against white-collar crime *did not even exist* as recently as a decade or two ago. Many statutes addressing corporate malfeasance are extremely technical, and a violation of them can be understood only as a result of

knowledge and training not available to the general public.

The drug laws, likewise, are statutory in nature. The use of psychoactive substances was legal until a century or so ago. In the United States, the vast majority of the drug laws did not exist before the twentieth century. And while something like nine Americans out of ten believe that possession and sale of the "hard" drugs (such as heroin and cocaine) should remain a crime, nearly three-quarters of the public believes that marijuana users should not be imprisoned. And a majority (about 80 percent) of voters believe that the *medical* use of marijuana—by federal law, a crime—should be legal. In short, there is disagreement over the criminal status of many statutory crimes.

Unlike primal or common law that has come down to us after thousands of years, most illegal behavior defined by a set of statutes ("statutory law") is subject to change over time and often varies from one jurisdiction to another. Prior to 1973, abortion was illegal in the United States; today it is legal. Before the 1930s, the possession and sale of marijuana was legal; after that decade, it became illegal in every jurisdiction in the country. In the early 1960s, homosexual acts between consenting adults were against the law; today, the majority of the states have abolished their laws against such behavior. The legislative status of the sale of alcohol has come full circle over the years, from legal to illegal to legal. For many years, every form of gambling was a crime in every state except for Nevada; today, most states administer government-sponsored lotteries. Nevada licenses prostitution in all but a small handful of counties; in that handful and in the other 49 states, selling sex for money is illegal. Moreover, in each jurisdiction, the absence or presence of a law addressing each of these behaviors is under attack; each one could change at some time in the future.

It is crucial to emphasize that, even for the primal or common-law crimes, a measure of relativity exists (Curra, 2000; Chapters 4, 5, and 7), not so much with respect to whether the actions should be against the law or whether they are wrong, but regarding the judgment as to *when, by whom*, and *under what circumstances* such crimes were committed. By that I mean that ancient societies often permitted one party to inflict a harmful action against another party, but punished that same action against a different party. For instance, if a man inflicted forcible or violent intercourse on a woman, the judgment of the members of the society as to whether or not that act constituted an instance of rape depended on a variety of factors, including the power and social standing of the family of both the man and the woman. Likewise, the killing of a member of a society other than one's own was often considered acceptable—indeed, it may even have been encouraged—but if the killing involved a member of one's own society, it was punished. Moreover, during periods of turmoil and widespread bloodshed—for instance, in Vietnam in the 1960s and early 1970s; Cambodia in the 1970s; Rwanda, Kosovo, Somalia, and Ethiopia in the 1990s; in Liberia in the early part of the twenty-first century—killings on a mass scale have been condoned by the regimes in power.

Hence, while primal crimes have existed for thousands of years, the judgment that such a crime did in fact take place has varied according to local custom and tradition. Even today, the taking of human life is condoned under certain conditions—for instance, legal execution, warfare, and in some jurisdictions, euthanasia. On one side of a border between Israel and the West Bank and Gaza, for instance, a killing is regarded as an act of heroism; on the other, murder. Is abortion murder? It depends on whom you ask. Is a specific killing justifiable, excusable, an accident, self-defense—or a crime? Again, different observers will answer the question in different ways; moreover, under exactly the same circumstances, the answer will vary from one society to another. Murder may be a primal crime, condemned everywhere and at all times, but even *what murder is*, is socially constructed.

WHAT IS OUR MISSION?
CONSTRUCTIONISM VERSUS POSITIVISM

The fact that even common-law crimes are interpreted differently according to who the perpetrator and actor are tells us that *crime is a social construct*. It is constructed by definitions—called laws—and interpretations *of* those laws that regard

certain actions as unlawful, worthy of punishment, and others as acceptable, noncriminal. And, as we saw, even the same action may be regarded as a crime or not a crime because of the circumstances of the act. Clearly, the constructionist is very interested in these circumstances—what makes an act a crime *here* but a law-abiding action *there*. For many criminal statutes, consensus simply does not exist, and the laws change from one decade to another. Should abortion be a crime? As we saw, prior to 1973, it was. And Americans are deeply divided on this issue, with a substantial minority seeking to return to the days when it was illegal to abort a fetus. The point is, legislation is not simply a product of abstract right or wrong but the outcome of conflict, of one segment of the society gaining the upper hand and passing a law favorable to its views. If circumstances were to change, matters could reverse, and the law would be rewritten to reflect that fact. How laws change, how they are interpreted, how they vary from one jurisdiction and society to another, how the circumstances of the act and the characteristics of the actor influence arrest, conviction, and incarceration—in the realm of crime, answering these questions is the social constructionist's mission.

There is a saying, "everything is relative," but this is not *completely* true of crime. *In addition* to the relativity we see from one time period to another and from one society to another in what's a crime, there is also a *common core* to crime. As we saw, some crimes have existed—*as crimes*—for many thousands of years. Hence, crime remains a mixed bag. Many crimes look more-or-less the same the world over, in all societies that exist now or that have ever existed. (But again, just which specific actions committed by which specific actors against which specific victims is highly variable.) Murder is illegal and is prosecuted the world over, just as it has been from the dawn of humanity. Taking property not one's own by force is a crime everywhere. Having sex by force with a woman, likewise, is criminal behavior in all jurisdictions known to criminologists. It is true that it is possible to find small, exotic locales or circumstances where these generalizations do not hold; nonetheless, *as a general rule*, there is a set of statutes that exist everywhere and there is a high likelihood of arrest, prosecution, and imprisonment if those statutes are violated. One of the positivist's missions is the study of these widely prosecuted acts, this behavior that is regarded as criminal everywhere.

The majority of criminologists study the causes, consequences, and control of common-law or *street* crimes, acts that are defined as criminal throughout history and in most or nearly all places of human habitation. As we saw in Chapter 5, the Federal Bureau of Investigation (FBI) collects and publishes information on crimes known to the police, and on arrests. The data on crimes known to the police are collected only for what are referred to as Part I offenses, that is, Index Crimes. These are the classic street crimes—murder (or criminal homicide), aggravated (or serious) assault, forcible rape, robbery, burglary, motor vehicle theft, and a grab-bag category of stealing that is referred to as "larceny-theft." (An eighth Index Crime, arson, was added by congressional mandate in 1979; criminologists very rarely study arson and rarely discuss it as an Index Crime.) The study of these Index Crimes is the "meat and potatoes" of the positivist's mission. To repeat, most criminologists investigate the causes, consequences, and control of the street or Index Crimes. In addition, a very high proportion of incarcerated offenders were convicted of the Index Crimes; the vast majority of those who were convicted of other crimes *also* committed one or more Index Crimes. And there is a remarkable consistency the world over in what are regarded as street or Index-type Crimes. To repeat: There is a "common core" to what's considered criminal behavior.

Criminologists also study non–Index Crimes. Just because statutes came into existence only in the past century or the past few decades does not mean that their violation is not harmful to the society, or that their understanding is not important for the criminologist's mission. Drug laws are statutory laws, and understanding the whys and wherefores of substance abuse is just as crucial as understanding why the drug laws came into existence and how they are enforced. Chapter 8 is devoted to an understanding of the use and distribution of illicit drugs. Laws governing white-collar and corporate crime are of historically recent vintage, but in many ways, the violation of those laws has an even greater impact on the society than the violation of street crime. One of the more interesting facts about the relationship of deviance and crime is that while corporate crime steals more money from, and inflicts more bodily harm on, the public, committing such offenses is not as stigmatizing as engaging in street crime. We'll take a look at this paradox in Chapter 13, on organizational crime. In a like fashion, organized crime, political crime (such as treason), offenses against children, violations of the laws against weapons possession, driving under the influence, the sale of alcohol to minors, and fraud—none of which are Index Crimes—all have important consequences for the society, and are studied by criminologists.

As I said, the study of deviance is not the same as criminology; hence, in this chapter, I will focus on a fairly small roster of criminal behavior: murder, rape, and robbery. The so-called "public order" or "moral" crimes (mainly drug and alcohol offenses and sex crimes) are discussed throughout this book. Each in its own way highlights the relationship between deviance and crime.

VIOLENCE: AN INTRODUCTION

It might seem that everyone knows what violence is and nobody likes it. To begin with, violence, as with every other concept in this book, is a social and cultural construct. What different observers mean by "violence" varies from one to another. When a police officer shoots and kills a struggling suspect, many observers would say that that killing is justified and hence, not a legitimate instance of violence—and yet the suspect is still dead. Most people would argue that a punch thrown in the boxing ring or a block that levels a would-be tackler on the football field are not violent, even though they involve a great deal of force, and the man on the receiving end of each may experience pain for a while. When intergroup conflict breaks out and members of one group kill or beat members of another, they rarely see the violent acts their own group inflicts on the other as violence; violence is what is done to members of their own group. At least one observer has argued that racism, classism, warmongering, and exploitation constitute a class of violence that he referred to as "covert, institutional" violence, that inflicts harm on the victim's body, dignity, autonomy, and freedom (Liazos, 1972). In short, a person may be harmed by an act someone else inflicts, and some observers may not refer to that act as violent. What audiences label as violence is not dependent on the harm that is inflicted. Instead, what observers regard as instances of violence are illegitimate, unjustified, inexcusable—or *deviant*—actions taken by one person or set of persons against another. In other words, violence is a loaded, biased, socially constructed concept.

MURDER

Paramount among the primal crimes is murder. Of all prohibitions, we might expect that the prohibition against murder is the one that is completely universal. Every society on earth—every single one, and at all times—has had a taboo against murder. If a primal crime can be said to exist, surely this is it. In other words, it might seem that, for murder, the constructionist's mission is irrelevant, that only the positivist would have something to say about the subject. The matter is not quite this simple, however. To understand this, we have to make a distinction between "murder" and "killing."

The Social Construction of Murder

It is true that murder is universally condemned. The word *murder* is a loaded, evaluative term. It *already* implies a negative judgment. *By definition*, murder is a deviant, criminal sort of killing. To say that murder is universally a crime is like saying a dog is a mammal. Since that is how murder is defined, murder is *always and by definition* deviant, as well as a crime. Saying that murder is always and universally a crime is a *definitional*, not a descriptive or an empirical statement. *Of course*, murder is always and everywhere considered wrong, deviant, a crime—that is how it is defined. The relevant question is, is the taking of human life—that is to say, *killing*—always and everywhere a crime? And the answer is, "Of course not."

Presumably, the Sixth Commandment says "Thou shalt not kill." Or so the commandment reads, in English, in the King James Version of the *Holy Bible*. As we saw earlier, however, this is a serious mistranslation. In Hebrew (as in English) there are two entirely different words for the taking of human life: *laharog*, which means "to kill," and *tirtzach*, which means "to murder." The verb "to kill" is objective and descriptive. It simply refers to the taking of human life, regardless of motive or circumstances. In contrast, "to murder" is subjective, that is, a judgment that killing belongs to a certain category—that is, as I said, an unauthorized, deviant, and criminal form of killing. In Hebrew, the Sixth Commandment actually reads: "*Lo tirtzach*"—that is, "Do not murder." King David, who was certainly aware of the Sixth Commandment, killed in battle; he was a warrior, he took human life—he *killed*. And he did so, according to Jewish tradition (and, as later interpreted by Christian theologians), not *in violation* of God's law but *in pursuit* of it. David's slaying of Goliath, the Philistine, was a righteous killing, most certainly not one prohibited by the Sixth Commandment. David *killed* but he did not *murder* Goliath. (I would like to thank Nachman Ben-Yehuda for making this distinction clear to me.)

All societies accept, tolerate, authorize, legitimate, and even encourage certain sorts of killing. In other words, a very hard, concrete, and seemingly indisputable fact—the taking of human life, the death of a human being—is judged very differently, is subjectively evaluated and placed into vastly different categories according to how it is seen by observers and audiences surrounding the killer and the victim. The legal status of a killing is determined by the law, the criminal justice system, and the courts. But in addition, we all have our own opinion on the matter. And whatever that opinion is, it is the result of a certain *judgment* that is made about the termination of human life. Making a judgment one way or another will transform a given act, in the blink of an eye, from criminal to noncriminal behavior, and vice versa. The point should be clear: *The taking of human life is tolerated, even encouraged, under certain circumstances. Some* killings are not seen by certain observers or audiences as murder, as criminal, or as deviant. Human life has never been an absolute value in this or in any society in human history. What is evaluated as murder, as criminal homicide, or as a deviant form of killing, is the result of a socially and culturally based judgment. In other words, what is or is not murder is *socially constructed.*

Many Americans do not consider human zygotes (newly fertilized eggs), embryos (developing organisms roughly eight weeks or less following conception), or fetuses (developing organisms from the third month on following conception) as full-fledged human beings. Therefore, they do not regard abortions—which *kill* zygotes, embryos, and fetuses—as murder. Yes, they would say, an abortion destroys human *tissue*, but it does not kill *a human being.* Hence, to the pro-choice advocates, abortion is not murder. To others, the "pro-lifers," the instant a human sperm penetrates and fertilizes an egg, that is, beginning with the zygote, a full-fledged human being exists; it is a "baby" or an "unborn child." Therefore, the abortion of zygotes, embryos, and fetuses is murder. Which position is correct cannot be determined empirically, with the tools of science. Whether abortion is or is not murder is socially constructed by the contestants in the abortion controversy.

When someone jumps in front of a car and is run over and killed, the law usually considers the killing an accident. However, during times of intergroup tension, if the driver belongs to one group and the deceased another, unruly mobs have deemed such seemingly accidental killings as murder, and have attacked, even killed the driver. Justifiable homicide is a killing that results from the dictates of a legal demand, such as a police officer shooting a felon "in the line of duty" or a citizen taking action against a felon, presumably to protect his or her life or the life of another. But up until the 1970s, shooting a fleeing suspect was legal; today, it is not, and the officer who engaged in such a killing could be prosecuted. Are "assisted suicides" criminal or noncriminal—acts of murder or mercy? In Switzerland and the Netherlands, such actions are legal; in the United States, they are not. An absolute pacifist would see all killings, including those that take place in warfare, as murder.

These examples illustrate the fact that we should keep in mind just *how* homicides are categorized, and *why.* A basic question we have to ask here is: *What sorts of killings are judged as criminal—and deviant?* And which ones are tolerated, accepted, condoned—*not* considered criminal or deviant? These are some of the issues that a constructionist would deal with in studying murder as a social construct.

Murder: The Positivist's Mission

In spite of the importance of the social construction of murder, many killings *are* legally classified as murder. And there is a social *patterning* to illegal killings. According to the FBI, 16,204 criminal homicides took place in the United States in 2002, a rate of 5.6 per 100,000 in the population for that year. The FBI refers to criminal homicide as "murder and nonnegligent manslaughter" and defines it as the *willful* killing of one or more human beings by one or more others. Not included in the classification "are deaths caused by negligence, suicide, or accident; justifiable homicides; and [unsuccessful] attempts to murder or assaults." Although legally the terms "murder" and "criminal homicide" refer to slightly different phenomena, from here on I'll use them interchangably.

The category criminal homicide is a social construct, but once we've agreed on a definition and we've encompassed the actions included within that definition, as I said, we notice that those actions so encompassed are *socially patterned* (Harries, 1997; Holmes and Holmes, 2001; Beeghley, 2003). By that I mean that the willful taking of human life is not a random event; it conforms to a set of sociological generalizations. For our purposes, these generalizations can be boiled down to eleven.

One: *The public and media image of murder is extremely distorted.* The image of criminal homicide that is conveyed in the news, television crime dramas, and murder mysteries, as well as the image most people have of the typical or modal murder, bears very little relationship to the real thing. The public and media image exaggerate the role of mass and serial murders, murders committed during the course of a felony such as a robbery or a rape, intentional or premeditated murder, murder for hire, murder for material gain, gangland slayings, and murders committed either by deranged, psychotic killers or truly evil human beings. These tend to be rare; they do not describe the modal or most common murder.

Two: *Most murder takes place "in the heat of the moment."* Very few killings are premeditated. Explosive altercations or escalating interpersonal disputes represent the circumstances of the vast majority of all criminal killings.

Three: *Most murders are justified by killers as a form of vindication, a way out of an intolerable situation.* They feel that in the killing they are obliterating or defending themselves against hostile circumstances. They have defined the source of their oppression or humiliation as an evil that *demands* retaliation. ("He was in my face," "She slept with every guy in town," "He was my best friend—how could he *do* that to me?" "What the hell makes you think you can say that to *me*?" "You lookin' at me, *suckah*?" "You think you can get away with *that*?" "Waddaya think—you can dis *me*?" "Hey, Mac, you just stepped on my *foot*!") Only through a violent expression of rage are these killers capable of wiping away the disgrace of stigma, shame, and humiliation. In the words of Jack Katz (1988, pp. 12–51), much murder is "righteous slaughter."

Four: *The more intimate the relationship, the greater the likelihood that one person will kill another.* On a person-for-person basis, intimates—friends, acquaintances, neighbors, relatives, spouses, and lovers—are much more likely to kill one another than strangers are. Of course, murder is an *exceedingly* rare event; it very, very rarely happens. Hence, the vast majority of intimates do *not* kill one another. But of the willful killings that *do* take place, intimates figure in them extremely prominently. There are only a few dozen or a few hundred intimates in our lives, but many millions of strangers; but, according to the FBI, roughly half of all criminal homicides take place between and among intimates. Two plausible explanations: One, we are in the company of, or *with*, intimates, on an hour-by-hour basis, much more than we are with strangers; and two, while intimates are much more capable of stimulating positive emotions, they also stimulate our negative emotions, including rage.

Five—and this is an extension of our fourth generalization: *Murderers and victims look remarkably alike.* The stereotype is that the

murder takes place like a bolt out of the blue, the murderer selects a totally innocent victim and inflicts undeserved violence on him or her. Of course, no one *deserves* to be a murder victim, but the fact is, given the circumstances and interpersonal dynamics of murder as well as the social circles in which people who kill travel, in the majority of cases, the person who kills and the person who is killed are often difficult to distinguish—with respect to age, race, social class, residence, prior criminal record and background, the use of drugs and alcohol, the locales they frequent, and lifestyle. There are exceptions, of course, but the majority of homicide victims resemble their killers in most important ways.

Six, and this is also an extension of both our fourth and our fifth generalizations: *Murders tend to be overwhelmingly intraracial.* This means that Blacks tend to kill Blacks, whites tend to kill whites. There are many exceptions to this rule, of course, but in the United States, roughly 90 percent of all intentional killings by both Blacks and whites conform to this rule. It is true that the intraracial factor is weaker in large cities than in smaller communities, and it is also true that interracial killings—those that take place between persons of different races—are on the rise. But in all communities and even today, intraracial killings remain in the vast majority. The reason makes a great deal of sense: People who know one another stand a higher likelihood of killing one another than people who are more socially, emotionally, and physically distant. And people tend to be more intimate with persons of the same race and more distant from persons of different races. People of the same race interact more with one another, they spend more time with one another, they are emotionally more significant to one another, they tend to marry one another, and they tend to kill one another.

Seven: *African Americans are both more likely to kill and more likely to be the victims of criminal homicide than whites are.* In the United States in 2002, just over half of all murderers and just under half of all murder victims were Black, which means that, relative to their numbers in the population, African Americans are overrepresented as both killers and victims by a factor of four. Most criminologists argue that the reasons are demographic—that is, poverty, urban residence, and residence in more socially disorganized neighborhoods are the explanatory factors, not race per se.

Eight: *Murder is related to social class.* Socioeconomic status (or SES)—that is, occupational prestige, income, and education—is *very* strongly correlated with criminal violence generally and with homicide specifically. Murders are *typically* committed by people toward the bottom of the SES ladder, that is, men who are relatively uneducated and are unemployed or who work at poorly paid, low prestige jobs. (Let's keep in mind, however, that murder is an extremely rare event and so very, very few members of the lower class ever commit murder.) When a murder is committed, it is extremely uncommon for someone at the upper end of the SES continuum—a successful lawyer, corporate executive, or physician—to have committed it. Just about every study that has ever been conducted on this relationship finds the same correlation. It is one of the most robust findings in the field of criminology (Beeghley, 2003, pp. 73–74). Researchers cite a number of factors to explain the relationship: being at the bottom of the heap; experiencing sharp social and economic inequality and its attendant deprivations, inadequate parental socialization, the relative absence of fathers or, more generally, intact families; having poor impulse control; living in neighborhoods and communities with high levels of disorganization and disintegration; being socialized into a "subculture" of violence; and living in an environment that combines continual challenges to one's manhood with physical prowess, strength, daring, and a resort to violence as tests of one's manhood.

Nine: Everywhere, *men are much more likely to kill than women.* In the United States, roughly nine out of ten killers are men; in 2002, the figure was almost exactly 90 percent. And men tend to kill men (in the United States, 75 percent of all the criminal homicides that men commit are committed against another man); women also tend to kill men (again, three-quarters of the time that women kill, they kill a man). And when men are killed, they tend to have been killed by a man (this is true 90 percent of the time); when women are killed, they tend to have been killed by a man (again, this is true 90 percent of the time). In other words, men loom much larger in the criminal homicide pic-

ture, both as killers and as victims. Whenever the exceptional woman kills, it is usually a man whom she kills; whenever the exceptional woman is killed, it is usually a man who kills her. The explanation? Men tend to be more directly governed by matters of dominance, hierarchy, competition, rivalry, rank, altercation, confrontation, and physical risk than women. And it tends to be other men with whom these rivalries and confrontations are involved. In contrast, when women kill men, they are most often defending themselves, whether directly or indirectly, in a physically abusive relationship.

Ten: *Rates of criminal homicide vary enormously from country to country, from one society to another.* Admittedly, the crime data from many countries is not very reliable. And legal definitions of criminal homicide are somewhat different the world over. Still, a few generalizations can be formulated. A number of Latin American countries, such as Colombia, Mexico, and Brazil, have extremely high rates of criminal homicide. In general, the murder rate is also very high in Africa; currently, South Africa has one of the highest murder rates ever recorded. Murder tends to be relatively rare in Arab countries. Poverty is *related* to high rates of criminal homicide, but Egypt, a poor country, has a low murder rate, while the United States, an affluent one, has a high rate. As a general rule, the murder rate is lower among fully industrialized countries, and especially those in northern and western Europe, than in industrializing Third World nations. Among industrialized countries, the United States has the highest rate of criminal homicide. Some experts attribute the high rate of criminal homicide in the United States to the widespread availability of guns, but guns are also readily available in Canada, Switzerland, and Israel—countries with much lower rates. Among all industrialized societies, the United States has the strongest tradition of resolving conflicts with violence.

And eleven: *In the Western world, violence, especially lethal violence, has declined enormously since the Middle Ages* (Johnson and Monkkonen, 1996). Europe prior to industrialization was an extremely dangerous place in which to live; violent death at the hands of another was a very common event. One estimate has it that medieval Europe's homicide rate was ten to twenty times what it is today (Gurr, 1989, p. 31). Nearly everyone at the time went about armed with a knife, a staff, a sword, or a club. Violence as a solution to disputes was routine; "murderous brawls and violent deaths . . . were everyday occurrences" (Givens, 1977, pp. 28, 34). Historians argue that the reason for the decline in the homicide rate over the past half-millennium or so includes the growing power of a central authority, that is, the monarchy; the expanded role of courts of law to settle disputes; and what's called the "civilizing process" (Elias, 1994)—that is, through the educational process, learning manners, civility toward others, propriety, and restraining expressing one's emotions through physical actions (Beeghley, 2003, pp. 45–46). In addition, the higher the level of economic development, the lower the rates of criminal violence (p. 46), although, as we saw, the United States is a major, although partial, exception to this rule.

Positivists take the constructed nature of murder for granted—they put it on the back burner, so to speak—and examine criminal homicide as a consistent, coherent, materially real form of behavior rather than a socially defined and judged phenomenon. Clearly, as we've just seen, murder possesses enough internal consistency to reveal social patterning; certain categories of people in the population, certain types of societies, and certain eras in history, exhibit higher rates of criminal homicide than others. As a result, positivists argue that specific conditions are consistently and causally related to the likelihood of committing violence. It is the job of the positivist social scientist to locate those conditions, establish relevant generalizations, and explain *why* murder takes place.

FORCIBLE RAPE

The FBI defines forcible rape as "carnal knowledge of a female forcibly and against her will." Most statutes regard any forced penetration of a woman's mouth, vagina, or anus by a man's penis as rape. Men can be raped by men, and it does take place frequently in prison, but it is far less often studied, and, unfortunately, is less likely to be taken seriously by the public.

Currently, among criminologists and other social scientists, forcible rape is regarded primarily a violent rather than a sexual act. ("Forcible" rape may be distinguished from "statutory" rape, or consensual sex with an underage female.) Rape is an *assault*. It employs force, violence, or the threat of violence. This is not to say that sex is not involved in any way whatsoever—after all, there is a difference between beating a woman and sexually assaulting her. If there were no difference, acts of rape would be classified as assault, and rape would not exist as a separate category. In rape, there is, to be technical about it, genital contact, or an attempt to effect genital contact, while there is no such element in assault by itself. But what defines an act as rape is that it is nonconsensual, a sexual act *forced on*, or *against*, a woman, against her will. *In this respect*, it is no different from being physically assaulted. Legally and by definition, forcible rape entails the use of force, violence, or the threat of violence. Thus, rape is *always* and *by definition* a violent act. Rape is *never* free of its violent character. Even if the victim, the offender, the general public, or law enforcement did not regard a specific rape as violent, legally, *if it is forced*, it is rape. What *defines* or *constitutes* it *as* a rape is that it is, *by definition and by its very nature*, against the victim's will— and therefore violent, and therefore rape. As we might expect, however, even this clear-cut and emphatic formulation hides a swarming host of social constructions.

The Social Construction of Rape

As Diana Scully says, the arguments that stress the violent and aggressive character of rape often "disclaim that sex plays any part in rape at all" (1990, p. 142). The fact that rape is—always, by definition, and by its very nature—violent, does not mean that it cannot be *other* things as well. The "rape isn't about sex—it's about violence" cliché is a bit too simplistic for sociological purposes. It sets up a false dichotomy, which assumes that rape is "about" *either* violence *or* sex—it cannot be "about" both. This formulation assumes that there is one and only one way of looking at rape, that there is an inner concrete or objective "essence" contained by rape, which is violence, that manifests itself to all reasonable and unbiased observers under any and all circumstances. *And* that this essence precludes other, very different, essences, such as sex—whose essence is mutual consent. Since rape lacks the latter essence, it cannot, by definition, be "true" or "real" sex. But, as we've already seen so often, the same phenomenon can be seen, defined, or experienced in different ways. What is rape to the woman and to the law *may* be sex to the man. This does not mean that it is any less violent—and therefore not rape. What it does mean is that it may be experienced differently by the rapist.

Scully argues that rape can be sex *in addition to* being violence. First, for some men, violence and sex are fused. For them, violence against women has become sexualized. There is something erotic and sexually exciting about inflicting violence upon women. To these men, sex and violence do not exist in separate worlds. To the contrary, they are fused. Rape is sexual because it is violent. Of course, for their female victims, there is nothing erotic at all about rape. And second, for many men, rape is instrumental—to gain sexual access to otherwise unattainable women (Scully, 1990, pp. 142–144). For these men, rape was not "about" violence because they did not imagine that what they did was particularly violent. "When a woman is unwilling or seems unavailable for sex, men can use rape to seize what is not offered" (Scully, 1990, p. 143).

The social construction of rape is "relative" (Curra, 2000, pp. 85–103). Different audiences define it in different ways. This is the legal definition of rape. But two persons or audiences could watch a videotape or hear a description of exactly the same act—both of which qualify by the FBI's definition *as* rape—and one would regard it as an instance of rape and the other wouldn't. This does not mean that we cannot settle the issue of what rape is legally. In fact, the law is quite specific concerning its definition of rape. What it means is that social, cultural, group, and individual conceptions vary as to just what constitutes rape (Estrich, 1987; Bourque, 1989). What rape *is thought to be* is partly a matter of definition. What we have here is a striking contradiction between how the law defines rape ("the carnal knowledge of a female forcibly and against her will") and

how many people judge concrete cases *that actually qualify as rape* according to the law. As a result, it is absolutely necessary to examine *how rape is seen, defined, and judged by audiences.* The absolutely central importance of these varying judgments becomes clear when we examine their role in subjective judgments of rape made by three crucial audiences: *the general public, the criminal justice system*, including the police, and *victims of rape.*

The general public can be divided according to a *spectrum* or *continuum* of judgments of what is rape. At one end, we have those that are extremely *exclusive*—that is, the definition is very narrow—which judge very few acts of sexual aggression by men against women as rape. At the other end, we have judgments that are very *inclusive*—that is, they are extremely generous, very broad—which include *many* acts as rape.

Perhaps the most extremely exclusive definition would be held by rapists, many of whom believe, in effect, that rape does not exist—that all or nearly all charges of rape are false. One convicted rapist expressed this view when he denied the existence of rape on the grounds that "if a woman don't want to be raped, you are not going to rape her." Said another, rape is when a woman says, "No, you're not going to get it and you're going to have to beat me senseless to where I can't fight you" (Williams and Nielson, 1979, p. 131). An extremely minuscule number of acts of intercourse against a woman's will would qualify as rape by the exclusivistic or extremely narrow definition, which sees men as having nearly unlimited sexual access to women, regardless of their resistance, and women as having no rights at all—only the choice between death or being beaten unconscious on the one hand and being assaulted on the other. In one study of convicted, incarcerated rapists (Scully and Marolla, 1984), nearly a third said that they had sex with their victims but denied that it was rape. "As long as the victim survived without major physical injury," these men believed, "a rape had not taken place" (p. 535).

At the other end of the spectrum, equally extreme, is the completely *inclusive* definition, held by some radical, militant, lesbian feminist separatists, who believe that *all* intercourse between men and women, however consensual it may appear on the surface, represents an assault, an act of aggression, an invasion, a violation—in a word, rape. Men exercise power over women—*every* man has power over *every* woman—and consequently, *no* sexual relationship between any man and any woman can be freely chosen by the woman. Consequently, *all* heterosexual sex is coerced—that is, is not freely chosen by the woman—and hence, qualifies as rape. Heterosexual sex is, *by its very nature, tainted* by patriarchy, *saturated* with its sexist essence. In a patriarchal society, women are brainwashed to think they want male companionship and all that goes with it. In a truly equalitarian society, no woman would want to have sex with any man. In short, *all* heterosexual sex is rape (Dworkin, 1981, 1987).

Both the extremely *exclusive* view, held by most rapists, and the extremely *inclusive* view, held by a few radical feminist separatists, represent very tiny minority views. Very few Americans would agree with them. Between these two extremes, we will find the *moderately exclusive* and the *moderately inclusive* definitions, which, together, encompass the views of the overwhelming majority of the American populace.

The moderately exclusive definition tends to be held by sexual and gender-role *traditionalists* and *conservatives*. Persons who hold to the moderately exclusive definition believe that a woman's place is in the home, and that she must have a man to protect her from the advances of other men. In this view, if she puts herself in a vulnerable position, such as going to bars, acting flirtatiously or seductively, going alone to a man's apartment and allowing one in hers, wearing "provocative" clothing, dating a number of men, hitchhiking, or walking on the street alone at night, or even remaining single too long, well, perhaps she is responsible for provoking men's sexually aggressive behavior—maybe she provoked men into forcing intercourse on her. In fact, maybe she wanted it all along—maybe it wasn't force at all. This definition does not see very many acts of coercive intercourse as rape because it does not accept the view that women should have the freedom, especially the sexual freedom, that is granted to men. This view is summed up in the saying, "Nice girls don't get raped." In other words, if women don't engage in

all these sexually provocative activities, they won't bring on men's sexual attention in the first place. The corollary of this saying is that if a woman is raped, maybe she wasn't so nice after all. It is possible that some version of this definition is held by a majority of the American public. It is possible, in other words, that most Americans hold a moderately exclusive definition of rape. Many, perhaps most, Americans—to a degree and under a number of circumstances— will blame a woman for a sexual attack against her. They restrict their notion of what rape is to a relatively narrow set of acts.

The *moderately inclusive* definition tends to be held by sexual and gender-role *liberals*. They believe that a woman has the right of sexual determination—the right to choose where she wants to go and whom she wants to go with. Thus, she cannot be blamed for an attack against her. If a woman makes it clear she is not interested in a man's advances, and he persists, then he is forcing himself on her; she is being coerced, the act takes place against her will, and it is a case of rape. Moderate inclusionists feel women should not have to be "protected" by a man to live a life free of assault. A woman has the same rights to go where and when she wants as a man has. And she has the right of control over her own body, whom she chooses to go to bed with, and whom she refuses to bed down with. Men have no right to force her to do anything sexual; if they do, it's rape. Men do not have the right to threaten harm, or pin a woman's shoulders down, twist her arm, force her legs open, physically restrain her, jam an elbow into her windpipe—or do *anything* to physically overpower or coerce her—in order to have intercourse with her. If they do, it's rape. The moderately inclusive definition is probably held by a minority, albeit a substantial minority, of the American public.

Judgments made by the criminal justice system—the police, prosecutors, and the courts— reflect the same discrepancy between what rape is legally (or "objectively") and how it is defined by various audiences. Each year in the United States, hundreds of thousands of women are victims of coerced intercourse; they are raped, according to the legal definition, but are not *regarded* as having been raped by the criminal justice system. Sexual violence inflicted against women is tolerated by the criminal justice system under certain circumstances. To understand how this happens, it is necessary to grasp the distinction between two kinds of rape—*simple* and *aggravated* rape. These categories correspond roughly, but not perfectly, with *acquaintance* and *stranger* rape (Estrich, 1987, pp. 4ff.).

Simple rape is forced sexual intercourse in which there is little overt, clear-cut violence (that is, there is no weapon and no beating), there is a single assailant, and he has some prior relationship with the victim. *Aggravated* rape—to the law, "aggravated" means serious—is defined by overt violence (a weapon and/or a beating), or multiple assailants, or no prior relationship between victim and assailant. The American criminal justice system is schizophrenic about rape. Even though, by law, there is only one kind of rape, the way that sexual violence is prosecuted—or not prosecuted—makes us realize that, in fact, there seem to be two kinds of rape: simple and aggravated rape, as spelled out above.

If our definition of rape is limited to aggravated cases, then rape "is a relatively rare event, is reported to the police more than most crimes, and is addressed aggressively by the police." On the other hand, if the cases of simple rape are included, "then rape emerges as a far more common, vastly underreported, and dramatically ignored problem" (Estrich, 1987, p. 10).

Almost no one "has any difficulty recognizing the classic, traditional rape—the stranger with a gun at the throat of his victim forcing intercourse on pain of death—as just that" (Estrich, 1987, p. 13). In such cases, victims usually report the crime to the police, who record it as a crime and undertake an investigation to discover and apprehend the perpetrator. If the offender is caught and the evidence against him is compelling, he will be indicted and prosecuted. Chances are, he will be convicted. Given our system of plea bargaining, the likelihood is high that he will be convicted on a less serious charge than rape; nonetheless, there is a better than even chance that he will serve jail or prison time for the offense.

On the other hand, when the case is one of simple rape—say, when a man has forced himself on a woman he knows, especially in a dating situation, when he is in her apartment, or she in his, willingly and voluntarily, and when there is no

overt violence and no weapon—the criminal justice outcome is almost always different. Women who are victims of such attacks rarely report them to the police. If they do, the police are not likely to pursue the case, or sometimes even to officially record it as a rape. Even if the suspect, by some accident, is arrested, he is very unlikely to be indicted. If he is, the case is unlikely to go to trial. If it does, he is not likely to be convicted. And if he is, he is unlikely to go to jail or prison.

The crucial importance of the subjective dimension becomes even clearer when we look at definitions of rape *used by the victims themselves*. Research indicates that the *majority* of women who are victims of forced intercourse *do not see themselves as having been raped*! *Any* time a man coerces, forces, or threatens violence against a woman to have sex with her, it is rape. But most women who are so coerced, forced, or threatened do not define themselves as the victims of rape. One study asked 595 undergraduates at a large Eastern university several questions about rape and forced intercourse. One question read: "Have you ever been forced to have sexual intercourse when you did not want to because some degree of physical force was used (e.g., twisting your arm, holding you down, etc.)?" Sixteen percent of the sample answered this question in the affirmative. But when they were asked, "Have you ever been raped?," only *2 percent* said yes. (In addition, not all of those who said yes to the second question also said yes to the first.) In other words, only about one out of 7 of the women (or 15 percent) who said that they had been forced to have intercourse saw themselves as having been raped! For most of them, there was a failure to perceive forced sex *as* rape. "There seems to be a tremendous confusion among these victims regarding their experiences and their legal rights. They were legally raped but they do not understand this behavior to be rape, or they are not willing to define it as such" (Parrot and Allen, 1984, p. 18).

Rape: The Positivist Approach

The FBI recorded a total of just over 95,000 rapes in 2002, for a rate of 64.8 for every 100,000 females in the population. All criminologists recognize that this figure *hugely* underreports the frequency of sexual assault in the United States, since most rape victims do not report the crime, or even, as we just saw, recognize forced sex, when it occurs, *as* rape. Victimization surveys find that of all serious violent crimes (rape, robbery, and aggravated assault), rape is *least* likely to be reported; in the period between 1992 and 2000, only 32 percent of all female rape victims reported the crime to the police (Hart and Rennison, 2003, p. 3). Rates of reporting were *higher* when the offender was a stranger to the victim, was armed, and when the victim was physically injured, and *lower* when the offender was known to the victim, was not armed, and when the victim was not physically injured (p. 1). Hence, from official police statistics, we receive not only a distorted view of the *frequency* of rape, we also receive a distorted view of its *nature* as well. *Unreported* forced sex—in comparison with *reported* forced sex—is much more likely to be acquaintance or date rape, and much less likely to involve a weapon and to result in serious physical injury. With information on rape, as with all other social phenomena, we must pay close attention to *how* the researchers gathered that information and thus, what *aspect* of reality is included—and excluded.

Perhaps the three major types or broad categories of rape theories are *individual, sociocultural,* and *situational.* "Individual" explanations of rape are those that argue that some men have a higher *tendency* or *proclivity* to sexually assault women than others do. Rapists are different from nonrapists, and men who rape have different personalities or a different upbringing than those who don't. "Sociocultural" explanations of rape are those that argue that the content of certain *cultures* or *subcultures* influences men to be sexually aggressive toward women; men influenced by these cultural messages are more likely to force women to have sex than is true of men who learn to treat women in a more equalitarian and less aggressive manner. And "situational" explanations are those that focus on factors that place women in vulnerable situations. A certain proportion of the men in those situations will sexually aggress against these women because the women are available and there is nothing to prevent them from committing the act.

The most *extreme* form of the individual explanation of rape is the *psychopathology* theory. It holds that rapists are disordered, mentally ill, or "sick." (For a moderate and sophisticated version of the psychopathological approach, see Groth, 1979.) It is clear that this perspective cannot explain the actions of *most* rapists. Most are, in fact, depressingly "normal." Most are able to function in the everyday world—attend school, hold down jobs, interact with others in a conventional fashion. As an explanation for the typical or most common rapist, the psychopathology theory is clearly wrong. This does not mean that no rapist is mentally disordered. In fact, the more violent and brutal the rape, the greater the likelihood that a mental disorder comes into play. And the further from conventional male-female courtship a given rape is, the greater the likelihood that it was motivated by psychopathology.

More moderate individual explanations argue that the personalities and backgrounds of rapists are not so much sick or disordered as they are *different* from those of the men who do not rape women. Psychologist Neil Malamuth more or less conclusively demonstrated that rapists are different from nonrapists. He asked a group of undergraduates to fill out questionnaires and say whether there was "some" (on a sliding scale) or "no" chance that they would rape a woman, if they could get away with it. Then he played (fictional) audiotapes of a variety of sexual encounters, including sexual aggression by men against women without the woman's sexual consent. The men who said that there was "some" chance that they would rape a woman were significantly more sexually aroused (as measured by a monitoring device) by the sexual aggression tapes than the men who said that there was "no" chance. Then Malamuth played these tapes to convicted, incarcerated rapists—who presumably actually *had* raped women. The college men who said that there was "some" chance that they would rape a woman and the rapists had arousal patterns that were similar to one another, while the arousal patterns of the "no chance" men were very different. In addition to looking at arousal patterns, Malamuth found that, like the convicted rapists, the "some" chance men were also more likely to believe in "rape myths" (women enjoy rape, women who were raped were "asking for it," and so on), and more likely to have admitted to having personally used force against women to have intercourse with them. In short, there is a cluster of individual factors that indicate that some men have a higher "proclivity" to rape women and that men characterized by these factors have in fact raped women (Malamuth, 1981).

Gottfredson and Hirschi (1990) agree that rapists are a particular type of individual. (They *also* support the situational or opportunity theory, elaborated below.) As we saw, their "general theory of crime" argues that crime is a product of poor parental socialization, which in turn leads to low self-control. Recall from Chapter 3 that Gottfredson and Hirschi argue that criminal acts "provide immediate gratification of desires. . . , *easy* or *significant* gratification of desires," including "sex without courtship." In addition, such behavior is *"exciting, risky, or thrilling."* Moreover, crime "often results in pain or discomfort for the victim." People who lack self-control and who commit predatory crimes against others "tend to be self-centered, indifferent, or insensitive to the suffering and needs of others" (p. 89). In other words, Gottfredson and Hirschi's "general theory of crime" is an example of an individualistic explanation of rape. They argue that it is the early childhood experience of males growing up in an inadequate parental or child-care environment that determines their likelihood of sexually aggressing against women (and a great deal more as well). Their rape "proclivity" is an *aspect* or a *feature* of their more general tendency to grab, take, steal, exploit, satisfy themselves at the expense of others—regardless of the consequences. The gratification that Gottfredson and Hirschi see as motivating the rapist is primarily sexual rather than political or ideological. That is, rapists do not seek to subdue or humiliate women, as feminists claim. Instead, they correspond to one of Scully's rape characterizations; they "seize what is not offered" (1990, p. 143). And they do this because they lack impulse control, and they lack impulse control because their parents or caretakers did not monitor or penalize their deviant behavior when they were growing up. In short, they rape because they are different kinds of individuals from conventional, law-abiding, nonrapist males.

Sociocultural theories argue that the norms, values, and beliefs held by the members of a given society, or social group, circle, or category, are *conducive* to men raping women. In other words, men *learn* to rape in much the way that, in our society, they learn to play football or eat pizza. According to this perspective, rape is *conventional* behavior. Sanday (1981) analyzed ethnographic data from 95 small, tribal societies and found a substantial proportion in which rape was extremely uncommon or unknown (which she called "rape-free"), while in a few, rape was a much more likely event ("rape prone"). The norms of the rape-free societies discouraged sexual aggression and encouraged sexual equality, while those of the rape-prone society encouraged sexual aggression and male dominance. Similarly, Sanday (1996) believes that different campuses also vary with respect to how "rape-free" or "rape-prone" they are. Some college campuses urge norms that are conducive to female equality, friendship between men and women, and acceptance of homosexuality; discourage heavy fraternity drinking; and severely punish sexual assault. In contrast, other campuses are characterized by male dominance, heavy drinking, taking advantage of intoxicated women, male sexual promiscuity, the ridicule of homosexuals, and ignoring or "slap-on-the-wrist" penalties for sexual assault. On the former campuses, we can expect low, and on the latter, high incidences of rape. Sanday also argues that, in general, the vast majority of college fraternities teach their members values and norms that are conducive to rape: drinking heavily, sexual inequality, exploiting and taking advantage of women, and sexual promiscuity (1990). In short, Sanday's explanation for rape is sociocultural; she argues that the relevant factor accounting for sexual aggression by men against women is the socialization process itself. In some societies or groups, men *learn* to rape women; in others, they do not.

In spite of what some observers have argued, the sociocultural explanation is not mutually exclusive or contradictory with the individual explanation. Neither can be expected to explain all or most rapes. In fact, in the vast majority of rapes, neither is the only valid explanation; both operate simultaneously. Feminist proponents of the sociocultural model argue that in American society, rape is common because rape-positive values are an essential component of American culture. We live, it is said, in a patriarchal culture in which men are dominant, a sexist culture in which women are devalued and relegated to an inferior status, and an androcentric culture in which men are center-stage and women occupy a secondary, servile, and marginal status. Men learn that they deserve to be served and gratified by women; women exist to cater to men's needs. It is inevitable that in such a society, men would be imbued with a culture that fosters rape. In fact, some feminists argue, not only are women systematically victimized by rape; rape is also a political instrument for keeping women servile, subservient, and submissive (Brownmiller, 1975; Russell, 1975). To cite one spokesperson for this view: "All men are socialized towards an aggressive masculinity and encouraged to see women as inferior to themselves." Thus, she says, all men are capable of rape, the only missing element being an "individual man's decision to become a rapist" (Roberts, 1989, p. 28).

This simplistic model of rape holds a mistaken conception of culture. No culture is ever a seamless, unified whole. All members of all cultures are exposed to, and learn, somewhat different strands of an elaborate, complex mix of teachings. There is practically no value or norm that is swallowed whole by all members of any society. While the eroticization of dominance and subordination exists in our society, as it does in many others, this is not necessarily a cultural strand that is picked up and adopted by all, or even most, of its male members.

We live in a society, it is true, in which many, and very likely the majority of, men learn that women are inferior and should be expected to serve them. There is a sexual double standard that accords men more sexual freedom than women, that dictates that men are free to come and go as they wish, but that if a woman takes on the same freedoms, well, she should expect the consequences, rape being one of them. A society that discourages women from seeking their own destiny, freedom, and autonomy—from wanting to have some of the mobility and privileges that men enjoy—will be one that will excuse certain forms of rape as justified or provoked by the woman.

But conventional, mainstream cultural values do not *directly* encourage men to rape women. They may (for some men) provide the raw material that some men use to justify hostile, exploitative

attitudes and behavior against women. By themselves, they dictate no rape-related behavior. To repeat: There is no doubt whatsoever that sociocultural factors influence rape. But since most men, even in a society with sexist values, never rape women, clearly this theory is not a complete explanation. You cannot explain a variable (some men rape and some don't) with a constant (American society is sexist and hence, encourages rape). Mainstream American values do not support, condone, or encourage violence against women to the point of rape. What they do support, in varying degrees, is masculine dominance over women which, *if taken to a behavioral extreme*, can find an outlet in rape. They key to an adequate explanation is finding what causes some men to push such values to their behavioral extreme. Saying that rape has a cultural component does not imply that there is no difference between conventional and deviant sexual aggression, or that "all men are rapists," or that there are no detectable differences between men who rape and those who do not, or that mainstream American values directly encourage the rape of women by men. Just as violence is a cultural value for some American males, not all men are violent to the point of homicide, or even assault. Cultural values are adapted, shaped, transformed—or ignored—by each individual living in every society.

In many ways, rape is the extreme end point of several American values. The kinds of violent sexual attacks on women that are nearly universally judged by the law and perceived by the members of the society to be instances of rape are the end product of values that many of us accept, although in more diluted form. We expect the man to take the initiative in matters both sexual and nonsexual. Many of us believe that the woman is indecisive in making up her mind and often needs the assistance of a man to help her along. To many men, "no" means "maybe" or "later" or even "yes." In other words, if exaggerated and interpreted through the lens of individuals whose background and personalities favor hating, abusing, exploiting, and humiliating women, such values could translate into sexual aggression and rape.

Situational theories argue that the key to rape is *opportunity*. Clearly, routine activities theory fits in here. To the extent that a "motivated offender" (the potential rapist), a "suitable target" (that is, a vulnerable, available woman), and the "absence of a capable guardian" (a locked door, a snarling dog, the police or others who would protect the woman from attack) are in conjunction, rape is more likely to take place. To the extent that these three do not come into conjunction with one another, it is less likely (Cohen and Felson, 1979). Malamuth's research, which supports the individualistic theory of rape, also suggests the importance of opportunity, since 35 percent of his male subjects said that there was "some" chance they would rape *if they could get away with it*. In fact, this figure rose to 50 percent if they were asked about the likelihood of "forcing a woman to have sex" (Malamuth, 1981). In other words, the chances are, a lot more men would rape if they had the chance. The fact that many are deterred by the fear of arrest or other sanctions keeps the incidence of sexual assault lower than it would otherwise be. In short, men are deterred from rape as a result of the *cost* to them, and that cost includes both arrest and social stigma. If both are low, the likelihood that a certain proportion of men will rape women is increased; if both are high, that proportion is correspondingly higher.

Tedeschi and Felson (1994, pp. 336–337) argue that women who date a number of different men, and who spend a substantial amount of time outside the home, especially at night, especially in cars, and especially in situations that are not supervised or monitored, are more likely to be rape victims than those who date no men, or only one man, and spend more time at home. Of course, as we know, some women are raped by dates, boyfriends, and even husbands, and being at home is no protection from sexual assault (Johnson, 2002). Moreover, focusing on women's behavior as an explanation for the rapes that are committed against them can be construed as *blaming the victim* (Ryan, 1976). But some observers have argued that there is a clear-cut distinction between blame, which is a *moral* concept, and cause, which is a *scientific* concept (Felson, 1991). Saying that women who date different men and go out a lot at night *do* have a higher than average statistical likelihood of being sexually assaulted is completely different from saying that they *should be blamed* for their behavior. If I take a plane to Los Angeles and the plane

crashes and I die, my taking that plane is one *cause* of my death—but I should not be *blamed* for my death. In a society based on equal rights for all, women should have the right to come and go as they please. But the fact is, opportunity is one cause of crime, and to the extent that women place themselves in situations in which motivated offenders face an absence of capable guardians, rape is more likely to take place. Of course, one way of cutting down on the odds is for women to become *their own* "capable guardians," that is, by carrying a weapon or learning karate. And one day—who knows?—we may live in a society free of "motivated offenders."

Clearly, these three factors—individual, sociocultural, and situational—have to be taken into account to explain a phenomenon as complex as rape. After summarizing the available literature as well as their own research, a team of psychologists (Malamuth, Heavey, and Linz, 1992) present a perspective they refer to as the "interactional" model. It argues that for a male to commit an act of sexual aggression against a woman, several factors must converge in the same man: (1) becoming sexually aroused at the sexual assault of women; (2) being angry or hostile toward women; (3) holding attitudes that support violence against women; and (4) engaging in impersonal, promiscuous sex. These factors, the authors say, "interact" with one another. When presented with an available opportunity, a male who ranks high on a scale consisting of these four dimensions is substantially more likely to force a woman to have sex than the male who ranks low on it.

These four factors may be regarded as *proximate* causes of sexual aggression against women—that is, they stand near, next to, or immediately prior to the physical act of rape. They motivate or disinhibit some men to inflict sexual violence or aggressive actions against women. But what factors or forces encourage these orientations? Malamuth and his collaborators locate a number of earlier, prior, or more *distal* factors that stand out as crucial: being abused, especially sexually, as a child; experiencing poor, conflictual, violence-ridden parent-child interactions; and observing violence between parents.

Malamuth et al. also argue that a specific subculture—the delinquent subculture—acts as an intermediary between early conflictual experiences and the later, four-part constellation discussed earlier. A subculture of delinquent peers may contribute to the development of these attitudes and values. Youngsters are socialized by the delinquent subculture; it may exaggerate incipient attitudes they already have, as a result of their childhood experiences. "Subcultures and societies that regard qualities such as power, risk-taking, toughness, dominance, aggressiveness, 'honor defending,' and competitiveness as 'masculine' may breed individuals hostile to qualities associated with 'femininity.' For these men 'aggressive courtship' and sexual conquest may be a critical component of 'being good at being a man.' Men who have internalized these characteristics are more likely to be controlling and aggressive toward women in sexual and non-sexual situations" (Malamuth, Heavey, and Linz, 1992). Sanday (1990) argues that college fraternities facilitate much the same socialization process.

ROBBERY

Most people use the term "robbery" very loosely. They say, for example, "My apartment was robbed yesterday." To criminologists, robbery has a very specific meaning. Robbery entails *victim confrontation*; it is a theft involving force, violence, or the threat of violence. There is some controversy among criminologists as to whether robbery is a property crime or a crime of violence; clearly, it has some elements of both. In fact, it is the one crime that is *both* a property crime—since the perpetrator takes money or goods from the victim—*and* a crime of violence—since the perpetrator uses force, violence, or the threat of violence. Four out of ten of all robberies entail the use of firearms, one out of eight entails the use of a knife, and four out of ten are strongarm or weaponless robberies.

Because of the confrontational nature of the offense and because both robber and victim might be injured in the course of the offense, robberies are much less common than other property offenses. Few who contemplate theft have the daring and recklessness to face a victim and demand property or cash; most thieves prefer

stealth and secrecy. One need only compare the 420,000 robberies tabulated in 2002 by the FBI with the 2.1 million burglaries and 7 million simple thefts or larceny-thefts to appreciate that robbery is a *vastly* less common offense than the other forms of stealing property. The fact is, most offenders simply do not wish to engage in robbery. It is a dangerous, high-risk activity. Of course, a minority of offenders do engage in robbery, but this minority is very atypical of property crime offenders in general. And, perhaps equally important, robbery, like murder and rape (for women), is one of those crimes that is most highly feared by the citizenry.

The total financial take for all robberies reported to the police in the United States in 2002 was $539 million—not much of a haul for such a well-publicized crime. Cash or property worth an average of $1,281 per incident was taken, although bank robbers ($4,763 per incident) did better than robbers of gas or service stations ($679 per incident) or convenience stores ($665). The clearance or arrest rate for robbery was 25 percent in 2002. Although this might seem low, consider that, if a typical robber steals only $1,200 per offense, and assuming his crime is reported half the time, and he is arrested only a quarter of the time his crime is reported, he will earn under $10,000 for each arrest. (Of course, consider two additional facts: One, the more that is stolen, the greater the likelihood that the incident will be reported, and two, commercial robberies are *almost always* reported.) Stated this way, robbery doesn't seem like a very promising way to make a living. Naturally, the FBI's statistics include a great many young, inept, unprofessional robbers who do not plan their jobs and who are very likely to get caught, and relatively few older, professional robbers who do plan their jobs carefully. Robbery may very well be a lucrative career for a small professional elite, but for the average robber, it represents an extremely risky and unlucrative means of earning a decent income. Its appeal is that it yields a fairly substantial amount of cash in a very short period of time.

Robbery is overwhelmingly a big-city offense. The likelihood of being a victim of a robbery in a big city is *stupendously* greater than in a small town or a rural area. In 2002, the robbery rate for rural areas was 17.7 per 100,000 in the population;

in cities with a population of a million or more, the robbery rate was 416 per 100,000—*almost 24 times higher*. Moreover, the robbery rate for nearly every category increased as community size increased; mid-sized cities were also in-between with respect to their robbery rates. It is unlikely that there is any crime that increases so sharply in concert with community size as robbery does. The reason should be obvious: Since robbery is a crime that entails victim confrontation, the victim typically sees—and can identify—the perpetrator. In a smaller community, the likelihood of identification is vastly greater than in a larger one. What big cities offer to the robber is *anonymity*. The two other offenses, both crimes of violence, that entail victim confrontation—rape and aggravated assault—also increase with community size, but not nearly so sharply. Assault is usually a crime that takes place between intimates, and it is almost never planned. Thus, anonymity rarely figures into the perpetrator's calculations as to when, where, and with whom to commit the offense. And rapists rely on the victim not to report the offense to the police, an assumption to some degree valid for acquaintance rape but increasingly less so for stranger rapes. Clearly, anyone who wants to understand robbery must understand big-city life.

In most cases, then, the robbery victim is confronted by a stranger. In a victimization survey of robbery victims (Harlow, 1987), this was true in just under seven out of ten cases of robbery by a single offender (69 percent) and just over eight of ten cases involving multiple offenders (82 percent). For single offenders, not quite one in ten (9 percent) was a casual acquaintance, just under one in eight (12 percent) was well-known to the victim, but was not a relative; 4 percent of all single-robbery offenses entailed one *spouse* robbing another (usually a husband robbing a wife), and 2 percent entailed other relatives robbing one another.

The fairly high proportion of acquaintances and relatives—including spouses—among the victims and perpetrators of robbery might seem to contradict my point about the crime being one in which anonymity is an essential ingredient. What these statistics show us, however, is that robbery is not a completely homogeneous category. In fact, robberies between relatives and

acquaintances are less likely to be reported to the police than robberies that take place among strangers, because they often represent disputes between parties over the legitimate ownership of money or a given article of property. For instance, two friends may have made a $20 bet, which the loser refuses to honor; to force the loser to pay up, the winner may simply take what he sees as rightfully his—by force. Or a separated couple may have an argument about who owns a television set or compact disc player; one night, the husband may come to the wife's apartment and simply take the item—again, by force. Such offenses will not be reported to the police, but may be reported to an interviewer in a victimization survey. Because such offenses are not uncommon—although, nonetheless, in the minority among all robberies—our point about robbery and anonymity must be modified, albeit only slightly. The original point still holds, however: Robbery *tends to be* a crime between strangers, in which the offender is not usually known to the victim. As a consequence, it is a crime *vastly* more likely to take place in large cities rather than in small towns and rural areas.

Who is victimized by robbery? In the 1940s, Hans von Hentig (1948), a German criminologist, launched the study of the relationship between criminals and their victims. Hentig argued that much of what victims *do* or *are* leads to their victimization; crime is a product of an *interaction* between offender and victim, he said. The field of "victimization" was born. The earliest victimization studies were heavily influenced by Freudian psychology, which argued that victims *yearned*, and were in some way *responsible*, for their victimization; such an assumption came to be dubbed "blaming the victim" (Ryan, 1976). However, current criminologists are much more careful to make a distinction between *blame* and *cause* (Felson, 1991). Victims may be selected by offenders in part because of what they do or who they are, but they should not be *blamed* for their victimization. *Blame* is a heavily value-laden term, whereas *cause* is a more objective, readily determinable sequence of events. For instance, young women are more likely to be victims of sexual assault than older women—this is a causal, not a moral, statement—but younger women must not be *blamed* for being raped. Poorer households are more likely to be burglarized than more affluent households, but, again, to assign blame to their criminal victimization is both causally suspect and a confusion of analytically separate dimensions.

What do the victimization surveys tell us about robbery? Members of what categories in the population are most likely to be victimized by robberies? Males are twice as likely to be robbery victims—a rate of 2.9 per 1,000 in the population for 2002—as females, 1.6 per 1,000 (Rennison and Rand, 2003, p. 8). Of all age categories, teenagers (age 16 to 19) and young adults (20 to 24) are most likely to be robbery victims, 4.0 and 4.7 per 1,000, while the elderly, age 65 and older, are least likely—in fact, roughly one-fourth as likely as these younger categories, 1.0 per 1,000 (p. 8). The rate of robbery victimization for African Americans, 4.1 per 1,000, is over twice as high as the rate for whites, which is 1.9 per 1,000 (p. 8). Lower-income persons (with household incomes under $7,500) are *six times* more likely to be robbed than are the more affluent (incomes over $75,000)—6.3 versus 1.0 per 1,000.

One of the reasons robbery is so important to criminologists is that, typically, it is a much more serious crime than the other property offenses; it is a far better predictor of an offender's overall rate of involvement in crime. Given its relative rarity and the strong inhibitions most potential offenders have against forcing, or attempting to force, a person to hand over money or property, it tells us a great deal about someone who overcomes those inhibitions and does the deed. An offender who robs is highly likely, statistically speaking, to have previously engaged in a number of other types of offenses. On the other hand, someone who engages in larceny-theft, for example, or even burglary, is significantly less likely to have engaged in other offenses. In other words, robbery is a very powerful *indicator* or *measure* of someone's involvement in or commitment to criminal behavior; it is a good predictor of future criminal activity in general.

Although robbery is technically a property crime *and* a crime of violence, most of the time, the concrete violence is more potential than actual. Usually the robber *threatens* his victims with harm rather than actually harming them. However, victims are harmed a fair proportion of

the time—a minority, but a significant minority nonetheless. In a summary of a number of victimization surveys, victims were injured in 33 percent of all robberies; of these, they required hospital care in 15 percent of the cases, and in 2 percent, robbery victims required hospitalization at least overnight (Harlow, 1987, p. 7). In 2002, according to the FBI, more than 2,000 murders (2,314) were committed while the offender was committing a felony, such as a rape, a burglary, or a robbery, of which half (1,092) were committed in the course of a robbery. In other words, of all the murders that took place in the United States in 2002 whose "circumstances" could be determined by the police, robbery-murders made up 1 out of 14 of the total (1,092 out of 14,054).

The likelihood of being injured during a robbery varies with the nature of the weapon used. As a general rule, robberies committed with a gun are the *least* likely to result in injury, and strong-arm or weaponless robberies are the *most* likely to result in injury. Though the victim, statistically speaking, is unlikely to be killed during the course of a robbery (out of roughly a million personal robberies and perhaps 150,000 robberies of commercial and financial establishments in the United States in 2002, a bit more than a thousand resulted in the death of a victim, or less than one out of a thousand robberies), it is also true that, if the perpetrator uses a gun, death is more likely than for any other type of robbery, strong-arm included (Conklin, 1972; Cook and Nagin, 1979; Wright, Rossi, and Daly, 1983, p. 208). The use of a weapon and the occurrence of injury strongly influence whether a robbery will be reported to the police. In one victimization study, 45 percent of all strong-arm robberies, 54 percent of all robberies in which a knife was used, and 73 percent of those in which a gun was used, were reported to the police. Only 49 percent of noninjury, 61 percent of minor injury, and 76 percent of serious injury robberies were reported (Harlow, 1987, p. 9).

Who is the robber? The statistics on arrest compiled by the Uniform Crime Reports for 2002 paint the following portrait of the robber—at least, the *arrested* robber. He is overwhelmingly male—90 percent, according to the Uniform Crime Reports. Just over half of all arrested robbers (54 percent) were Black; only four out of ten

(44 percent) were white. For no other Index Crime are African Americans so overrepresented. And he is young: 61 percent were under the age of 25, 26 percent were under the age of 18, and 5 percent were under the age of 15; a total of 85 robbery arrestees in 2002 were under the age of 10. The problem with these statistics, as anyone might guess, is that they represent *arrested* robbers, not robbers in general. We suspect that robbers who aren't caught will differ in important ways from those who are. For instance, almost certainly the younger, less experienced robber is more likely to be caught than the older, wiser, more cautious, more professional, and more experienced robber.

One way of verifying this suspicion is to compare the FBI's arrest figures with the *perceived offender characteristics* supplied by robbery victims in the victimization surveys of the National Crime Victimizations Surveys. The two sources of data generally agree with one another on robbers' characteristics, with some minor inconsistencies.

In nine out of ten robbery victimizations (89 percent), the offenders were male; in 5 percent of all cases, they were female; and in 4 percent, the victim was robbed by both male and female offenders—that is, at least one male and at least one female were said by victims to have committed the crime. Clearly, then, there is nearly perfect agreement between the FBI's statistics on arrest and victims' reports with respect to gender. In about half of all robbery victimizations, the offenders were identified as Black (51 percent); in a third, they were white (36 percent); in 4 percent, they were members of some other racial category; in 4 percent, the offenders formed a "salt-and-pepper" team of mixed-race offenders; the rest of the victims weren't sure of the race of the offenders. Here, there is less than perfect agreement: Nearly 10 percent more *arrested* robbers were Black than were robbers identified in victimization surveys.

In four out of ten of all cases of robbery (41 percent), offenders were described as 20 years old or younger; in another four out of ten, they were identified as 21 or older; and in not quite one in ten, they were described as being of mixed ages (Harlow, 1987, p. 2). Here, the correspondence between arrest and victimization figures is fairly close.

In a nutshell, then, the portrait we received from the FBI's figures on arrest and the characteristics

as identified in victimization surveys is that, relative to their numbers in the population, robbers tend to be young, male, and Black—and, of course, overwhelmingly urban.

Clearly, any explanation of robbery focusing on the offender must make use of at least two factors: *daring* and *poverty*. Robbery is not a crime for the fainthearted; it entails a great deal of risk, both to the victim and to the perpetrator. Robbers, therefore, tend to be (unrealistically) confident that they won't be injured or caught. Such misplaced confidence is more characteristic of males than of females, the young than the older.

The race of robbery offenders is probably largely a function of a combination of the economic position of Blacks in the United States and the fact that African Americans tend to live in large cities. Black family income is roughly 60 percent of that of whites, and Black unemployment is twice as high. Moreover, although a growing proportion of Blacks earn incomes that, increasingly, approximate those of whites, a substantial proportion of the African-American population is seemingly permanently stuck in the "underclass" (Wilson, 1996). In addition, since 1973, the poor have been getting poorer and the rich have been getting richer; hence over the past two decades or more, the economic situation of the "underclass," of whom a disproportion are inner-city minority members, is not only stagnating, but deteriorating (Cassidy, 1995; Krugman, 2003). Added to the economic picture is the demographic factor: African Americans are much more urban than whites. Nearly three out of ten whites live in a rural area, whereas only 15 percent of Blacks, half the white figure, live in rural areas. At the other end of the scale, only a quarter of all whites in the United States live in central cities (25 percent); for African Americans, the figure is more than twice as high—between 50 and 60 percent. The combination of a lower per capita income and a far more urban residence makes it almost predictable that Blacks will have a higher rate of robbery than whites. In addition, there is the factor of age; while only 30 percent of the white population is under the age of 20, 40 percent of the Black population is that young. Since the African-American population is so much younger than the white population, this factor alone would tend to boost its robbery rate.

SUMMARY

The contrast between the findings of positivist criminology and the constructionist's perspective provides an interesting paradox: The classic crimes of violence, which we fear the most, tend to be relatively rare, while other, more common, sources of harm tend to be feared far less. The sociologist of deviance is interested in paradoxes such as these.

Deviance and crime overlap, but imperfectly. Many forms of deviance are not crimes—witness eccentricity and obesity. Some forms of crime are not deviant in the narrow sense; at least, they do not generate a great deal of informal condemnation, even though they may lead to arrest; many white-collar offenses qualify here. The field of criminology focuses on criminal behavior. Rather than repeat what's in that course, in this book I will devote my discussion mainly to acts, beliefs (and traits) that are interesting mainly because they generate *informal* negative reactions. However, it should be kept in mind that *conceptually* and *theoretically*, deviance and crime share much of the same territory; hence they cannot be cleanly separated.

Criminal behavior covers as diverse a collection of activities as does deviant behavior. As with deviance, what is against the law is determined by judgments of an audience. The audience that decides what a crime is consists of *agents of formal social control*—the police and the courts, including prosecutors, judges, and juries.

Some acts have been punished by formal judgments of a society or tribe for thousands of years, even before such a thing as a law-making body existed. It is custom, not legislatures, that has determined their criminal status. These are the *primal* crimes, which have existed pretty much everywhere and throughout human history. They include murder, rape, robbery, and theft. It is difficult to refer to these offenses being "relative" to time and place, since there is a *common core* of such offenses that exists everywhere and has always existed. However, even for the primal crimes, judgments of *who* committed *what* offense against *what* party are variable, relative to time and place.

During the reign of King Henry II of England in the twelfth century, judges standardized the diverse jumble of law and custom that prevailed in the country's many shires. Their judgments came to be referred to as "common law." Later, legislatures passed laws, based both on the common or court-derived law and on the need to punish behaviors that emerged out of situations and contexts that were new. Most of the instances of the latter type of law have existed only since the twentieth century. Legislature-created law is called "statutory" law; it rarely has the force of sentiment that is as strong as that behind common law.

Murder has been a primal crime since the existence of humanity, and it was one of King Henry's common-law crimes nearly half a millenium ago. Even though there has been a common core to the acts that are judged as murder nearly everywhere and at all times, exactly what specific acts are deemed murder has varied from one time and place to another. In this sense, there is cultural relativity for even the most reprehensible and heinous of acts.

Even though it is condemned in one form or another pretty much everywhere, rape exhibits even more relativity than murder. In the contemporary United States, a distinction is made between "aggravated" and "simple" rape. The law, the general public, and the legal system distinguish two types of forced intercourse, one of which is regarded as reprehensible, criminal, and deviant, the other of which is regarded simply as a somewhat aggressive form of sex. Audiences vary with respect to how "inclusive" (or broad) versus "exclusive" (or narrow) their definitions of rape are; the variation is sociologically patterned.

Robbery is both a property crime and a violent crime. It entails victim confrontation, putting the victim in fear, or forcing the victim to relinquish money, property, or things of value. Since it is dangerous both for the perpetrator and the victim, in comparison with theft and the other property crimes, robbery is relative rare. The victims of robbery, in comparison with the population at large, are more likely to be male, young, urban, poor, and African American. The perpetrators of robbery tend to be male, young, urban, poor, and African American. The positivist criminologist is interested in explaining the whys and wherefores of robbery.

PERSONAL ACCOUNT: Having a Deviant Father

The following account was written by Danielle Fritze. When she wrote it, she was a 21-year-old college senior at the University of Maryland. She describes her life with her father, Arnold. In the following account, Danielle explains, "I aim to recollect the deviant life of my father through the experiences I have had with him, and from what I have been told by others whose recollections precede my memories of him."

My parents were married in 1978. The marriage was rocky from the start. About a year into the relationship, my father became physically abusive. I have seen a picture of my mother with a black eye my father gave her. . . . I was born in 1982. During the three years after my birth, life was relatively stable for my mother and father. . . . In 1986, my little sister, Jeannie, was born. My mother told me that my father was very upset that he did not have a son. . . . To support his family of four, my father picked up a second job. . . . With the added stress of a second job, and a second child, my father's [previous] drug habit resurfaced. Although his drug use had basically [just] been marijuana from the time he and my mother were married, [after my sister was born] he started doing PCP and LSD again. My mother was extremely disapproving of my father's drug habit. This was often the subject of many fights between them. One fight in particular I remember being told about resulted from an incident when my father neglected my sister. One day, while my father was off from work, he and his friend did drugs in the basement of our house. My father left the house, abandoning my two-year-old sister for a few hours.

I recall many confrontations during which my father became violent toward my mother. The worst fight I witnessed between my parents happened when I was about six years old and my sister was about three. My sister and I were on the first floor of our house playing with toys when we heard our parents yelling upstairs. We went upstairs to find my father, a two-hundred-pound man, sitting on top of my mother, a one-hundred-pound woman, strangling her against the headboard of their bed. Despite the pleas of my sister and me for my father to stop choking my mother, he did not stop. This incident of abuse ended when I crawled up onto the bed and bit my father until he bled. Additional episodes of abuse I remember witnessing include my father threatening to throw my mother down the basement stairs, him holding her up by her hair and shaking her, and him throwing a dining room chair on top of her after knocking her down. Despite my father's constant abuse of my mother, he never abused my sister or me. . . .

After twelve years of abuse, my mother and father separated. My father moved out of our house into an apartment. At first, it was hard for my sister and me to deal with the separation, but my mother explained to us that it wasn't safe for her and my father to remain married. My sister and I saw our father on Tuesdays and Thursdays after school and spent the night at his apartment every other weekend. During my visits with my father, he often sat me and my sister down and had long conversations with us. For the most part, these conversations were about the fact that my father thought my mother was trying to brainwash us into hating him. Although she never did anything of the sort, my father was convinced that because she had ended their marriage, my mother would try to end his relationship with his children. For about four years, my sister and I were having steady visits with my father, and he held those "brainwashing" conversations with us.

The first time I remember my father being admitted into a mental institution was when I was in the fifth grade. My mother received a call from my father's sister, Becky, and she told her that my father was unable to see my sister and me for a while, explaining the events leading to my father's hospitalization. Apparently, one day after work, Aunt Becky stopped by my father's apartment to give him something. When she entered his apartment, she found him, heavily armed, hunched behind his sofa, wearing a helmet. When my aunt asked my father what he was doing, he explained to her that it was

PERSONAL ACCOUNT: Having a Deviant Father (cont.)

Armageddon and he was preparing himself to fight for his life. He also revealed delusions that his mother was the Virgin Mary and that his father was Joseph, implying that he thought himself to be Jesus Christ. After seeing my father in this state, my aunt had him committed to a mental hospital. . . . There, he was diagnosed as bipolar, or manic depressive. During this time, my father maintained a correspondence with his work supervisor, who was very forgiving of his leave of absence, promising him his job back once he was mentally stable. Finally, my father was discharged from the facility after his condition was stabilized with lithium.

For a few months after my father left [the psychiatric facility], my mother supervised his visits with my sister and me. During the first few weeks after my father was out of the hospital, he was a wreck. He had random crying spells. His voice was very high-pitched and he gave very long, inspirational life-lesson speeches. A few weeks after being discharged, he went back to work. Shortly after his return to work, because he felt normal, my father stopped taking his medicine. This led to his first relapse. At the time of my father's first relapse, I was in the sixth grade. His superiors at work were on the lookout for symptoms of mental irregularity. After seeing some signs that he was no longer on his medication, they made him recommit himself in order to keep his job. He was readmitted, this time for a longer stay than the first. My mother took my sister and me to visit him a couple times during his stay, thinking it might help get his spirits up and encourage him to stay on his medication. Shortly after leaving [the hospital the second time], my father returned to work, and once again he stopped taking his medicine, feeling his condition was regulated.

After stopping his medication for the second time, my father stopped working as well. My mother received no child support payments for over a year. Because my mother earned very little, my father's child support payments were necessary to make ends meet. Finally, my mother went to court. Since my father was not in any condition to work and since symptoms of a mental illness were apparent, my mother convinced him to file for disability payments from the government. That way, she would receive payments from Social Security in place of child support. My mother had realized that my father would never get better. She revoked his right to unsupervised visits with my sister and me. He was unhappy with this arrangement. Because of the return of income to his life [in the form of disability payments], my father started doing drugs again. Because he did not keep track of his spending habits—including indulgences in drugs, stereo equipment, and lottery tickets—he filed for bankruptcy and moved in with his parents. Eventually, he stopped seeing my sister and me. At some point, my grandmother, thinking that the beach would help my father get well, moved them into a trailer near the beach.

My mother, sister, and I heard nothing from my father for two or three years. The first news we got of him came late September when I was in the ninth grade. . . . The phone rang at six in the morning. . . . My sister answered the line and eavesdropped. [I didn't hear this until she got home from school when] she told me that our aunt called to tell our mom that there had been a murder. I insisted that my sister was mistaken, but she was persistent in her claim that she had heard correctly. When I asked for details, my sister told me to ask our mom because she wanted to go outside and play. . . . When my mom got home from work, I told her that my sister claimed that there had been a murder. After I told her that Jeannie was playing at a friend's house, my mother explained what happened. My aunt had called that morning to explain that my father had killed his mother and then attempted to kill himself. She did not elaborate and in fact she did not know the details, so she was unable to answer many of my questions. When my mom explained the contents of the phone call, I began having a panic attack.

It was extremely difficult for me to accept what my father had done and what had happened to my grandmother. After about a month, my aunt came to our house to explain the situation.

Sparing no detail, my aunt told me the complete story leading to my grandmother's murder. Apparently, my father's mental health had drastically deteriorated. Although he was still receiving disability checks, his mother controlled the money, and this was often the cause of arguments. A few weeks before the murder, my grandmother called my Aunt Becky and explained to her that she was becoming increasingly afraid of my father. She often saw him sharpening knives and witnessed him talking to someone when there was no one in the room but himself. My aunt told my grandmother to have my father committed [to a mental institution] but she didn't listen. On the day of the murder, once again, my father and grandmother had been arguing about money. My grandmother was afraid of my dad, and she walked out of the trailer, but my father chased her and knocked her to the ground and threw a heavy metal object, a ring to contain campfires, on top of her. My father went back into the trailer and when he came back, wielding the knives he had been sharpening, he repeatedly stabbed my grandmother in the chest and abdomen. My grandmother's cries for help attracted an audience of concerned neighbors, fellow residents of the trailer park who had come outside to see what was going on. My father sat on the hood of his car, smoked a cigarette, then stabbed himself in the abdomen.

My father and grandmother were taken to a local hospital. My grandmother died shortly after arriving at the hospital and my father was treated for his wound and sent to the infirmary at the nearest hospital. Tests revealed that my father had some kind of foreign substance in his body which turned out to be medicine for his fish, which he was using to get high. When Aunt Becky asked my father why he had murdered their mother, he said that "The voices told me to" and "She is out of this horrible world now." My aunt told him not to think he did anyone any favors. After the incident, my grandfather was approached by the district attorney as to whether or not he wanted to pursue the death penalty against my father, but he refused their offer. My grandfather then went to live with my Aunt Becky because he was unable to deal on his own with the shock of what had happened.

About a year after my father was sent to jail, he began communicating with my sister and me both by mail and by phone. He was never particularly interested in talking to my sister because he thought my mom had successfully brainwashed her. . . . Nonetheless, they engaged in meaningless chit-chat. In my conversations with him, my father and I didn't mention his crime very much. The subject matter of our correspondence revolved around his trial—whether he was competent to stand trial, his lawyer, his lawyer's defense strategy, and other aspects related to his trial. At the time, the prison system held him in a psychiatric ward. He was more or less coherent, although he still heard voices. He was diagnosed as having a drug-induced condition characterized by symptoms similar to paranoid schizophrenia. At his trial, my father pled not guilty by reason of insanity.

The trial returned a verdict of guilty but insane; he was sentenced to life in prison without parole. When he could, he called or wrote and asked us to come and visit him in prison. My sister and I haven't gone to visit him since he has been incarcerated because, for the most part, he still isn't sane. He talks about creating a perpetual motion machine, and thinks his ticket out of prison is his invention of a magnet-powered automobile engine. My father thinks that if he can get someone to build his invention and get it patented, he will win the Nobel Prize for science and receive a presidential pardon from his prison sentence. He also believes that because he saw a cloud that looked like a human face, he is a spiritual messenger, with three half-brothers in heaven. Until last year, my sister and I indulged my father by listening to what he had to say without voicing our doubt about his delusions. The last few times my dad called, when he started speaking about his ideas, we just changed the subject. My father's calls have recently become few and far between, and he rarely writes us any more.

QUESTIONS

What's your reaction to reading this account? Clearly, the behavior and condition of Danielle's father exemplify what is defined as deviance in this chapter. His drug use—to the point where its effects interfered with the conventional demands of his life; his violence toward his wife; his delusions—all violate the norms of this society. In addition, societal reactions toward him as a result of his behavior and his delusions point to their deviant character. His behavior and delusions generated both *official* reactions—Arnold was arrested, convicted, and incarcerated—and unofficial or *interpersonal* reactions, that is, his daughters have become increasingly estranged from him. In other words, what Arnold did and how he thought are both deviant and criminal. Has Arnold been labeled as *a* deviant? How do you feel about his daughter writing an account of her father's deviant behavior?

PERSONAL ACCOUNT: Omar's Story

It seems a life of deviance was predestined for me. From conception, I was out to beat the odds. I was born out of wedlock from parents who had sex only once. My father stumbled upon me on the street, as my mother was pushing my stroller, when I was two years old. He immediately recognized the resemblance. When he showed my mother a picture of himself at two, she realized that he was my biological father. Unfortunately, my father lived in the Caribbean and was unable to guide my life as he wished. . . .

Looking back, I can recall being involved in deviant behavior at a young age. Once, in nursery school, I was caught in the girls' bathroom. . . . In the second grade, I stole some money; I walked into an empty classroom and saw a purse lying on the desk with the corner of two $20 bills sticking out. . . . I went home and put the money in an envelope and wrote the words "From the Devil" on the envelope. After my mom got home, I got the envelope where I had stashed it and took it to my mom and said, "Look what I found!" That was a mistake. She spanked me with a belt until I confessed where I had gotten the money. I was so stupid. I should have just kept the money and had a ball at the candy store for two weeks.

I went to a predominantly white middle school in Capitol Hill. I took the Metro to get there. Outside the station, I bummed money. I realize that I was exploiting my attractiveness, innocence, and youth. I used the money I received to purchase a Metro ride, a pepperoni sub, and an ice cream.

From a young age, I believed I could find a way to get what I wanted. I always found a way to sidestep conventional ways of obtaining things. Sometimes the conventional ways simply weren't available. Once, I heard my mom tell me she had to steal food to eat. Maybe I learned something from this, I can't say for sure. Anyway, my tendency to get what I wanted by however means I could increased as I got older.

When I was 11 and 12, I got caught twice for stealing, once at 7/Eleven and once at Toys 'R' Us. At the 7/Eleven, I was even arrested. Stealing wasn't the only way I could earn money. One time, a thirty-something Spanish guy solicited me to take a ride with him. He told me if I took a ride with him, he would give me money. I took the ride, he touched my leg, and I walked away with $40. In high school, I worked at the school store. A girl who worked there taught me how to embezzle money. She'd steal $30 a day from the store. I took more modest amounts, knowing she was already ripping them off. Still, I got pretty good money by embezzling from the store, considering I was only a ninth grader.

It was in the ninth grade that I started dealing drugs. . . . This involved being away from home a lot of the time. Still, I did abide by *some* of my family's rules—I just couldn't stay out all night, every night. Believe it or not, through all this, I was a pretty good student, I just missed a lot of classes. . . . In my senior year, I missed 48 days of school.

Can you imagine how independent I felt? I was making my own money—and good money at that. And the girls that came along with my deviant behavior! Don't get me wrong, I know I am a little attractive, but I think the money attracted girls, too. I'd flash a wad of money in front of the girls, buy breakfast and school lunches for them. It was cool. Hell, I began having sex at 12 or 13. By the time I graduated from high school, I am sorry to say I contributed to three abortions. I threw a party once to raise money for an abortion. Sex was a huge part of my high school years. My best friend and I skipped school a lot to find action with some girls. I did it alone, too. Looking back, I was moving pretty fast. I used to keep a few girlfriends. Once I had sex with three different girls, one after the other, in the same day. I really don't know how I got the attitudes and beliefs that allowed me to act the way I did. I know now that my behavior wasn't that normal compared with the other kids at my school. I also know that my behavior led to a lot of unfortunate situations.

By the time I graduated from high school I had sold drugs, stolen cars, committed an armed robbery (it was a carjacking), and had a baby on the way. Soon after I graduated from high school, I was incarcerated for a robbery that I committed earlier that year. Looking back, it seems that I had grown up in a rebellious era in which Black males, including myself, followed along with the rebellion. I mean, "gangsta rap" was born and the crack epidemic was at its peak. Instead of following the examples laid out by my parents, I wanted to follow the social trend and be one of the thugs on the street. I don't understand why I didn't go along with being at home at a certain time. The fact is, I respected the street life and the people in it. And it was fun. I felt a sense of exhilaration. Breaking the rules provided an edge to my life. I felt I wasn't your average "Joe." I gained respect for taking risks. Ironically, my dad used to tell me not to compare myself with people who had less than me, always compare myself with those who had

better. My problem was that I didn't look at street people as having less than I did. They showed me love, and they had culture and spirit.

My deviant behavior continued after my two-year incarceration. Before long, I began peddling drugs again. In the year after my release, I was arrested twice for cocaine distribution. I also caught a maiming charge that was dropped. I worked for a while in a job my mom hooked me up with, a day treatment center for the mentally retarded. That was an experience in itself. Those employees really used to beat up on their clients. I guess they just got frustrated sometimes. While I worked there, I managed to engage in unconventional activities. For a month, I operated a strip club out of my apartment. It was a big party where I got to control and interact with the women as I wished. I saw some wild things! I also sold drugs as a kind of side job.

I began college at the age of 22. I started at a small Black college in the South. I only stayed there for a year, but the drug dealing followed me there. I used to transport weed and crack from DC to South Carolina. Once, when I was traveling south, the bus stopped at a town in North Carolina and was searched by the police. I had a quarter pound of weed on me, and it had a strong smell. Luckily, I was seated in the middle of the bus and I had time to see what was going on. I got the weed out of my bag and put it on my body, so when the police checked my bag, I had nothing but books in it. That was a close call!

I believe if it hadn't been for my unconventional behavior, I wouldn't have been able to reach the goals I've reached. [I managed to graduate from college at a very good university and I'll be applying to law school.] Maybe that is backwards, maybe if I had followed the rules more my life would have been simpler. However, I cherish my experiences and believe that they have given me valuable insights about human behavior and the ways of the world. After interacting with drug addicts, dealers, inmates, prostitutes, the police, and being arrested, as well as being acquainted

PERSONAL ACCOUNT: Omar's Story (cont.)

with the world of violence, going to college and finding out why these things exist gives me a dynamic spin on the way I look at them. I wouldn't say I am cynical, but many things don't surprise me. I'm glad I deviated as a youngster. I'm glad I didn't have certain constraints that would have kept me narrow-minded, which would have given me a fictitious understanding of the world. After coming to college, I realized that there was a reason why I broke society's rules. . . . I realize, though I had no business doing the

things I did, my deviance allowed me to connect with underprivileged people, people I would have had little sympathy for if I hadn't lived their reality and shared experiences with them. I am glad I was deviant and I had the courage to break the rules. Still I'm fully aware of the consequences. Now I am able to make calculated risks that give me high rewards. I am a risk-taker. I pray that God continues to lead me in the right direction. I give Him and my parents all the credit for the successes I've had.

QUESTIONS

Omar engaged in what was clearly criminal behavior. Yet his account does not convey quite the same flavor of deviantness that Danielle's account of her father's behavior does. Why? If there was any stigma in his background, Omar seems to have gotten rid of it—that is, being labeled as a criminal

did not seem to lead to a lifetime identity as a "gangsta." In fact, he went to college after his incarceration, graduated, and intends to go to law school. Do you have faith that Omar will "go straight"? Do you sense a feeling of remorse for his earlier criminal behavior? Does Omar's case tell us anything about the process of "exiting" from a deviant status?

CHAPTER
7

Legal Drugs: The Use of Alcohol and Tobacco[1]

[1]This chapter has been adapted from Chapter 8 of my other book, *Drugs in American Society* (sixth edition), McGraw-Hill, 2005. Reproduced with the permission of The McGraw-Hill Companies.

In this chapter we'll look at *legal* drugs as deviance. For our purposes, the legal drugs are tobacco and alcohol. Why not coffee, which contains a stimulant, caffeine? The answer: The effects of caffeine, in the levels that the drug is consumed, are too mild to consider substances such as coffee, tea, cola drinks, and chocolate (which contain caffeine) as drugs. Moreover, in this society, drinking coffee is almost never associated with deviant behavior. (It has been, at different times and in different places.) Another question: Why not consider prescription drugs as drugs in this chapter? Actually, there is a fair amount of misuse, abuse, and overuse of prescription drugs, and a consideration of the pharmaceuticals would make an interesting chapter in itself in a deviance textbook. Here's my reasoning for sticking to alcohol and tobacco: I see the illicit drugs (marijuana, cocaine, heroin, Ecstasy, methamphetamine, and so on) and alcohol and tobacco as sharing an important quality, one that sets all of those drugs off as separate and distinct from prescription drugs. This quality is the *purpose* for their use.

Prescription drugs (most of which do not influence the mind) are taken to return the body or mind to what is regarded as a state of "normalcy" or ordinariness. Something is perceived to be wrong—a malfunction, a disease state which the administration of a pharmaceutical substance "fixes." The illicit drugs—*as well as* alcohol and tobacco—have exactly the opposite function: They are taken to *depart from* a state of "normalcy," ordinariness, or everyday consciousness. They are used to *step out of* our routine ways of thinking and feeling. In Greek, this desired state is called *exstasis* (similar to the English word "ecstasy")—a condition that is out of or beyond the static, ordinary, everyday, or "normal" mentality. (Addiction—and most cigarette smokers are nicotine addicts—changes this picture quite a bit, since when someone is addicted, taking the drug *becomes* a state of normalcy. Most drug users, however, are not addicted.) To put the matter a bit differently, *even though they are legal*, alcohol and tobacco, exactly like the illicit substances, are *recreational* drugs. (Of course, prescription drugs can be *used* as recreational drugs, in which case, they are illegal.) In contrast, pharmaceuticals are used as medicine—to restore the body and mind to what's considered a "normal" state—or *stasis*. It is this difference in purpose, use, or function that leads me to consider medications in a different light, and to group alcohol, tobacco, and street drugs together in the same category.

What's the difference between alcohol and tobacco on the one hand and those substances we usually refer to as drugs—the illicit substances such as LSD, heroin, and cocaine on the other? Are alcohol and tobacco *drugs* in the same sense that the illegal substances are? Do alcohol and tobacco belong in their company? And what relevance does the answer, one way or another, have for the study of deviance?

The substances we generally refer to as "drugs" have a wide range of effects. What is it that they all have in common? The answer is, there is *no* property that *all* drugs have in common. Penicillin (an antibiotic) is a drug, as are Prilosec (an antacid), methamphetamine, Claritin (an antihistamine), Ecstasy (MDMA), and heroin. Three of the substances I just named have effects that are useful in the treatment of medical conditions, while, in the United States, three are *banned* as medicine. Three do not get the user "high," that is, they have no—direct—pleasurable effect on the mind, while three, obviously, do. And three are legal if obtained by means of a prescription, while three are illegal substances, the possession and sale of which is a crime. So, where's the common thread?

There is no such thing as a drug in the abstract. A substance is a "drug" only within a particular social context.

Within the context of medicine, a "drug" is a substance that has effects that have been legitimated by the medical profession, and is *defined* and *used* by physicians *as* a drug. But here's a wrinkle in this equation: *Which* physicians? *How many* physicians? And in *what country*? At least one substance is endorsed *as medicine* by a substantial proportion of physicians, but is not approved by the federal government. And it is approved by 10 state governments but, again, not by the federal government. That drug is marijuana. Is marijuana a drug because it is a medicine? Or is its medical status bogus? The answer cannot be simple or straightforward; it depends on whom you ask.

Within the context of the law, a "drug" is a controlled substance—that is, a substance whose possession and sale is either completely illegal or illegal if taken for purposes defined by criminal statutes as illicit. But again, *which* jurisdiction's laws one consults will determine whether a given substance is illegal. Small-quantity marijuana possession is not a crime in 12 states of the United States; it is in the remaining states and according to federal law. (Constitutionally, federal law trumps state law.) But substances such as LSD, heroin, and Ecstasy are illegal in all states and by federal law. In addition, the sale and purchase of tobacco is illegal to someone under the age of 18, and the sale and purchase of alcohol is illegal to someone under the age of 21.

Within the context of psychopharmacology—the study of the effects of substances on the workings of the mind—a "drug" is a substance that is *psychoactive*, that is, it influences mood, emotion, feeling, and cognition.

In this chapter, we'll take a look at two substances that are psychoactive but legal: alcohol and tobacco. Neither is a drug to the medical profession. Neither is illegal to nonincarcerated adults. But both are "drugs" specifically within the context of pharmacology—they both influence the workings of the mind. And in the next chapter, we'll consider those substances that are also psychoactive but whose distribution and possession are illegal: marijuana, cocaine, heroin, methamphetamine, and the "club drugs," including Ecstasy.

Why is the use of drugs an interesting topic to study *as deviance*? And why look at the use of the *legal* drugs in a course or book on deviance?

As we just saw, psychoactivity is not the only definition or criterion of what a drug is. Substances are also socially and legally *constructed* or defined and dealt with *as* "drugs." Society—and different societies—decide that specific psychoactive substances are "drugs," and that others are not. For instance, as we just saw, marijuana is accepted as medicine in some states of the United States but not in others; heroin has accepted medical uses in the United Kingdom but not in the United States. Thus, the medical definition is not simply a matter of a drug's effects but also of how a society *constructs* the reality of medical utility and acceptability. Thus, as students of deviance,

we have to understand just what observers *mean* when they say that one substance is a drug and another isn't. Likewise, the law dictates whether certain substances are or are not "controlled substances," the sale or possession of which is illegal—that is, *drugs*. And this legal designation both changes over time and varies from one country to another, even from one state to another. Thus, as sociologists of deviance, we have to understand the process of the criminalization of drugs, which means *passing and enforcing laws prohibiting and controlling psychoactive substances*. How does it come to pass that it is illegal to possess, use, and sell one psychoactive substance but not another? This is the sort of question a constructionist would ask. And it is just as interesting to ask why the possession, use, and sale of certain psychoactive substances are *not* illegal and deviant as it is to ask why other substances *are* illegal. Alcohol and tobacco have been defined at certain times and in certain places as medicine, and their possession, sale, or use have been defined as a crime and as deviant behavior, hence our interest in these substances.

As we saw in Chapter 1, harm is *not* a defining criterion of deviance. Much physically harmless behavior is deviant, and a great deal of harmful behavior is conventional. But if we were to ask a cross-section of the public (I have done this with my students) *why* the use of certain drugs is banned, a very common answer would be "Because their use is harmful." But are alcohol and cigarettes so much less harmful than the illicit drugs? Right now, we should keep an open mind on the subject, but I'd like to suggest that *in some ways*, the use of alcohol and cigarettes may be more harmful than that of the illicit drugs. (Just as, in some ways, several of the illicit drugs are much more harmful than others.) If a given activity is *harmful but not deviant*—as is true of the use and sale of alcohol and tobacco—as students of deviance, our curiosity should be aroused. We are led to take a look at this discrepancy.

Here are my answers to the question, "Why should a sociologist of deviance study legal drug use?":

First, there's a parallel between using (the *psychoactivity* dimension) legal and using illegal drugs. While taking, and experiencing the effects of, legal drugs is tolerated, taking illegal drugs is condemned. Since they belong to the same category with respect to psychoactivity, the discrepancy in their legal status should be interesting to any student of deviance.

Illegality is one possible measure or indicator of the deviant nature of illicit drug use; it is a major point of departure between legal and illegal drugs. But we should also be led to ask: Why is the distribution and use of some substances legal and socially tolerated while that of others is both illicit and deviant? Why does the criminal status of some substances change over time? For instance, during Prohibition, the distribution of alcohol was illegal, and it remains illegal in some jurisdictions ("dry" counties, for instance). During most of U.S. history, it has been legal for most jurisdictions. Why? Shortly after tobacco was introduced into Europe in the 1500s, it was banned. Today, its sale and use are legal for everyone above a certain age. Why is it possible to walk into shops in the Netherlands and purchase marijuana, but legally impossible to sell and purchase it for recreational purposes everywhere in the United States? These are not rhetorical questions; again, the student of deviance finds such questions intriguing.

The *behavioral overlap* dimension (the correlation between legal and illegal drug use) tells us that the people who use legal drugs and those who use illegal drugs are similar in many ways. It is possible that their motives are also similar; chances are, using one category of drugs and using the other represent *points along a continuum*. This indicates that the line between legal and illegal drugs is artificial. If there were striking differences between legal and illicit drug use, why are users of tobacco and alcohol so *much* more likely to use illegal drugs than people who abstain from tobacco and alcohol? This wouldn't make any sense if the two activities existed in separate universes.

And lastly, both in the United States and worldwide, alcohol and cigarettes do more total harm than the illicit drugs. Hence, it is not harm alone that causes illicit drug use to be condemned; clearly, other factors are at work as well. If tobacco and alcohol cause so much more harm than the illicit drugs, then why is the distribution of the latter illegal and deviant and that of the former legal? Are societies "rational" in criminalizing and condemning the activities they've targeted? Again, these are not rhetorical questions; they are not intended to argue for the legalization of the currently illicit drugs. Rather, they are points of departure for any investigation of the social construction of psychoactive substances.

PSYCHOACTIVITY

In the sense that they are psychoactive, alcohol and tobacco (that is, the nicotine *in* tobacco) are drugs. If we drink enough alcohol, we become drunk, "high," or intoxicated. In other words, alcohol influences how our mind works. Likewise, nicotine, a substance that is in all tobacco products, alters the way the mind works. Like alcohol, nicotine is psychoactive; it constricts blood vessels and increases heartbeat rate, deprives the lungs and the blood of oxygen, causes the skin to flush, generates an arousal or alertness state, decreases appetite, is a mild painkiller, and in large quantities, if efficiently absorbed, will cause dizziness and nausea and, in massive quantities, paralysis and death. And alcohol and tobacco are drugs for another reason as well: They can induce an "addiction" or *dependence*—that is, heavy users engage in extraordinary measures to continue using in spite of the day-to-day or potential harm they experience, or know they will experience.

In fact, our two most common addictions or dependencies are with alcohol and tobacco consumption. There are roughly 10 million alcoholics in the United States—and many more worldwide—who continue to drink heavily in spite of the social cost to themselves and others. In 2002, over 70 million Americans had used tobacco—cigarettes, cigars, pipes, chewing tobacco, and snuff—in the past month. For cigarette smokers specifically, the median level of tobacco consumption is more than 15 cigarettes (or "doses") a day (SAMHSA, 2003). By any measure, the vast majority of smokers are drug *addicts*. The toll this drug use takes on consumers is enormous, but smokers seem to be powerless to stop.

Thus, if we refer to their psychoactive properties, the questions, "Is alcohol a drug?" and "Is tobacco a drug?" can be answered in a straightforward fashion. In the *objectivistic* sense, *yes*, alcohol, tobacco, and psychoactive medications *are* drugs: They influence the workings of the mind. When introduced into the body, they produce physiological changes that are not qualitatively different from those produced by the category of substances we refer to as drugs. There is no distinguishable difference between legal and illegal drugs with respect to psychoactivity. Of course, different drugs and drug types have different effects, but *on the dimension of psychoactivity*, what makes a substance a drug is that it alters consciousness. In that respect, alcohol and tobacco are in the same kettle of fish as marijuana, cocaine, and Ecstasy. In this sense, we see parallels between the legal drugs—alcohol and tobacco—and all the illegal drugs.

BEHAVIORAL OVERLAP

In spite of their different legal status, the behavioral worlds of the users of these two types of substances, legal and illegal, do *not* exist in separate and distinct realms. There is substantial overlap between them. Far from being mutually exclusive, many of the same "cast of characters" use both. One interesting clue to the parallel between the consumption of alcohol and the use of the illegal drugs is that there is a remarkably powerful correlation between them. The 2000 National Household Drug Abuse Survey revealed that, among 12-to-17-year-olds, nearly six in ten (59 percent) of the "heavy" drinkers (that is, respondents who said they had consumed five or more alcoholic drinks on the same occasion five or more times during the past month) had also used marijuana within the past 30 days, but only 2.4 percent of respondents who had *not* used alcohol at all during the past month had also used marijuana during this period—a difference of 25 times! "Heavy" 12-to-17-year-old drinkers were *100 times* more likely to have used cocaine in the past month (10.6 percent) than was true of nondrinkers (0.1 percent)! The same correlation prevailed for *all* drugs and *all* levels of alcohol consumption (SAMHSA, 2001, p. 157). If the National Household survey had tabulated

substance consumption among the other age categories, no doubt much the same correlation would obtain. The fact is, the recreational consumption of psychoactive substances, taken as a whole, tends to be of a piece. People who drink, especially heavily, are much *more likely* to use controlled substances, and, to turn the equation around, people who use controlled substances *overwhelmingly* drink alcohol.

The same relationship prevailed between smoking tobacco cigarettes and illicit drug use. Again, in the 2000 National Household survey, among 12-to-17-year-olds, *15 times* as many smokers as nonsmokers had used marijuana in the past month (37.5 percent versus 2.5 percent), and *38* times as many smokers as nonsmokers had used cocaine (3.8 percent versus 0.1 percent). And the same relationship with smoking prevailed for all the illicit drugs (SAMHSA, 2001, p. 156). Clearly, illicit and legal drug use do not exist in separate realms; in fact, they heavily overlap. The impulse to alter one's consciousness with *one* substance—whether legal or illegal—is strongly related to altering it with *other* substances, again, whether they are legal or illegal. The fact that licit and illicit drug use are correlated with one another indicates that their social and behavioral worlds are not radically distinct from one another. The people who engage in one are statistically similar to those who engage in the other. We should keep this fact in mind when contemplating the deviant character of illegal drug use and the conventional nature of legal drug use. This does not (necessarily) mean that legal drug use *causes* illicit drug use—that is a matter to be investigated separately—but it does mean that the two exist in similar behavioral universes.

HARM VERSUS SOCIAL CONSTRUCTIONISM

Here's an interesting statistic, one that relates directly to the dual themes that have run throughout this book, positivism versus social constructionism. More than a hundred epidemiologists and biostatisticians from the World Health Organization surveyed the available data and isolated roughly 20 leading risk factors for premature death in countries around the world. The risk factors were somewhat different for "developing" (that is, economically less industrialized, less affluent) countries as compared with "developed" (economically more industrialized, more affluent) countries. In the developing or Third World countries, like Nigeria, Indonesia, and Bolivia, factors such as malnutrition and poor sanitation were the leading causes of premature death. But in the developed or industrialized countries such as France, the United States, and Japan, tobacco consumption accounted for 12.2 percent of the years of life lost to all the risk factors, while excessive alcohol consumption accounted for 9.2 percent. For these countries, tobacco and alcohol were the number one and number three factors in this respect. In contrast, the use of illicit drugs only accounted for 1.8 percent of years of life lost. In other words, in the industrialized world, the legal drugs, taken together, contribute more than *five times* as much to premature death than is true of the illegal drugs (Krug et al., 2002; Brown, 2002). Clearly, then, *objectively speaking*, legal drug use is a *far* more serious social problem than illegal drug use. At the same time, illegal drug use is *socially constructed*—that is, it is *subjectively*, in the way the public regards it and the government deals with it, the more serious social problem. It is dilemmas such as these with which we have to grapple throughout this book.

ALCOHOL: AN INTRODUCTION

Alcohol has an ancient and checkered history. Fermentation was one of the earliest of human discoveries, dating back to the Stone Age. Alcohol emerges spontaneously from the fermented sugar in overripe fruit; the starch in grains and other food substances also readily converts to sugar and from sugar to alcohol. Because this process is so simple and basic, the discovery of alcohol by humans was bound to occur early. Alcohol consumption, in all probability, began when a prehistoric human consumed fermented fruit and experienced its effect. Alcohol can induce pleasure, euphoria, intoxication, a sense of well-being, a state of relaxation, a relief from tension, a feeling of good will toward others, the

alleviation of pain, drowsiness, and sleep. As a result, it is an almost universally acceptable beverage. Consequently, as paleontology tells us, humans have been ingesting beverages containing alcohol for at least 10,000 years, and it is, coffee excepted, the most widely used drug in existence—ubiquitous, almost omnipresent the world over.

Societies differ vastly in their average level of alcohol consumption. Every society that has some acquaintance with alcohol has devised and institutionalized rules for the proper and improper consumption of alcohol. These vary systematically from society to society and from one social group or category to another. Although alcohol does have objective or biochemical "effects," both short-term and over the long run, most of them can be influenced, mitigated, or drastically altered by the belief in and observance of cultural rules. The extent to which intoxication leads to troublesome, harmful, or deviant behavior varies considerably from society to society. In many places, alcohol use poses no problem to the society according to almost anyone's definition; the drug is consumed in moderation and is associated with no untoward behavior. In other places, alcohol use has been catastrophic by any conceivable standard. The overall impact of alcohol, then, is not determined solely by the biochemical effects of alcohol, but by their *relationship* to the characteristics of the people drinking it. This is not to say that alcohol can have *any* effect the members of a society expect it to have. There is a great deal of latitude in alcohol's effects, but it lies within certain boundaries.

ACUTE EFFECTS OF ALCOHOL

The potency of alcoholic beverages is measured by the percent of alcohol (sometimes referred to as "absolute" or *pure* alcohol) they contain. Pure ethyl alcohol is 100 percent absolute alcohol. Beer contains about 4 or 5 percent alcohol. Wine contains about 10 to 13 percent; it is the most potent drink we can concoct through the natural fermentation process. "Fortified" wine, in which alcohol is added to wine, is legally set at no higher than 20 percent alcohol. (The wines skid-row alcoholics drink are usually fortified. Sherry is a wine fortified with brandy.) Most wine coolers contain about the same percentage of alcohol as beer, 4 or 5 percent. The process of distillation (boiling, condensing, and recovering the more volatile, alcohol-potent vapor from the original fluid, and adding an appropriate quantity of water) produces drinks like Scotch, vodka, gin, rum, and tequila, that are about 40 to 50 percent alcohol, or 80 to 100 "proof." Consequently, in order to consume roughly an ounce of absolute alcohol, someone would have to drink two 12-ounce cans of beer, or one 8-ounce glass of wine, or a mixed drink containing about 2 to 2½ ounces of Scotch or gin.

According to *the rule of equivalency*—which states that the effects of alcohol are determined principally by the volume of pure alcohol that is drunk, rather than the type of drink itself—these drinks would be roughly equal in strength and would have approximately the same effects on one's body. The "rule of equivalency" denies that different drinks—separate and independent of their alcohol content—have different levels of potency, as well as the assertion that mixing different types of drinks is more potent than consuming the same drink. Other things being equal, alcohol is alcohol is alcohol; nothing else makes a significant difference.

Alcohol, it has been said, is "the only addictive drug that dangerously alters behavior yet at the same time is freely and legally available without a prescription" (Goldstein, 2001, p. 137). When it enters the body, alcohol translates into what pharmacologists call *blood-alcohol concentration* (BAC), or *blood-alcohol level* (BAL). This corresponds fairly closely to the percent of the volume of one's blood that is made up alcohol after it is ingested. A given BAC or BAL has been described as "bathing the brain" in a given alcohol concentration (p. 137). There is a relationship between blood-alcohol concentration and behavior. The effects of alcohol are, to a large degree, dose-related: With some variation, the more that is drunk, the greater the effect.

The effects of alcohol are, however, influenced or *mitigated* by many factors in addition to the total volume of alcohol in the drinker's body. Some of these factors are directly physiological. Since alcohol registers its impact via the blood-

stream, the *size* of the drinker influences blood-alcohol concentration; other factors are the presence of food and water in the stomach; the speed with which one drinks; and last, sex or gender. (Women seem to be more sensitive to the effects of alcohol, and manifest effects at lower doses, or greater effects at the same dosage, than is true of men.) In addition, as with practically all drugs, alcohol builds up pharmacological *tolerance*: It takes more alcohol to achieve a given effect in a heavy or regular drinker than in an abstainer or infrequent drinker.

Alcohol is a depressant, much like the sedatives such as the barbiturates. Alcohol depresses, slows down, retards, or *obtunds* many functions and activities of organs of the body, especially the central nervous system. In other words, organs become more sluggish, slower to respond to stimuli. If the dose is too high, the body's organs will shut down altogether, and death will ensue. Alcohol also disorganizes and impairs the ability of the brain to process and use information and hence, impairs many perceptual, cognitive, and motor skills needed for coordination and decision making. One ounce of alcohol, or roughly two mixed drinks, consumed in less than an hour will result in a blood-alcohol concentration of roughly .05 percent in a person of average size. This produces in most people a mild euphoria; a diminution of anxiety, fear, and tension; a corresponding increase in self-confidence; and, usually, what is called a "release" of inhibitions. Decreased fear also typically results in a greater willingness to take risks; this effect has been demonstrated in laboratory animals. Alcohol is, for most people, at low doses, a mild sedative, antianxiety agent, and tranquilizer. This is by no means universally the case, however. There are many people for whom alcohol ingestion results in paranoia, distrust, heightened anxiety, and even hostility. These effects, however, typically occur, when they do, at moderate to high doses.

Alcohol's effects on motor performance are familiar to us all: clumsiness, an unsteady gait, an inability to stand or walk straight, slurred speech. One's accuracy and consistency in performing mechanical activities decline dramatically as blood-alcohol concentration increases. And the more complex, the more abstract, and the more unfamiliar the task, the steeper the decline. The most noteworthy example is the ability to drive an automobile. It is crystal clear that drinking, even moderately, impairs the ability to drive and contributes to highway fatalities. How intoxicated does one have to be to lose the ability to perform mechanical tasks? What does one's blood-alcohol level have to be to produce a significant decline in motor coordination? And how many drinks does this represent? The answers depend on a number of factors, as I just said. All drinkers experience a loss of motor skills at a certain point, and it occurs at a fairly low BAC. At about the .03 percent blood-alcohol level, that is, after finishing a single alcoholic drink, some very inexperienced and particularly susceptible individuals will display a significant decline in the ability to perform a wide range of tasks. At the .10 level, even the most experienced drinker will exhibit some impairment in coordination; this is roughly four drinks each containing a half-ounce of alcohol. However, many drivers are quite willing to get behind the wheel while intoxicated: According to the FBI's Uniform Crime Reports, in the United States in 2002, there were roughly a half million arrests for drunk driving.

ALCOHOL CONSUMPTION: ACCIDENTS, DISEASE, AND SOCIAL COST

The fact that alcohol causes discoordination leads us to the subject of one of this drug's more harmful consequences: its role in causing accidents, especially on the highway. Zador (1991) estimates that, compared with someone who is sober, a driver with a BAC between .02 and .04 has a 1.4 increased chance of having a fatal single-vehicle crash. This risk increases to *11 times* for drivers with a BAC between .05 and .09, *48 times* at the .10 to .14 level, and *385 times* for drivers with a BAC over .15! The risk increases even more sharply among younger drivers, and for females.

But there is a ray of hope: In the United States, over the long run, alcohol-related automobile fatalities have been declining. Each year, the National Highway Traffic Safety Administration compiles, tabulates, and publishes data on motor vehicle accidents. In 1982, 53 percent of all auto-mobile fatalities involved one or more drivers who had a blood-alcohol concentration of .08 or higher—a total of 23,246 deaths. This figure continued to decline through the 1980s and mid-to-late 1990s, reaching a low of 34 percent and 14,421 deaths in 1997. Unfortunately, during the late 1990s and the early 2000s, the numbers plateaued, even creeping up slightly; in 2001, of all fatal crashes, 35 percent or 14,953 involved an alcohol-impaired driver. (It must be kept in mind that twice as many miles are driven on America's roadways today as compared with two decades ago; hence, the number of fatal alcohol-related accidents per 100 million miles has consistently declined over time.) In roughly half of all fatal crashes, the driver had a BAC of .16 or higher. Thus, in spite of the long-term decline, alcohol's effects are distinctly discoordinating, and at the legal level of driving while impaired (0.08 percent in two-thirds of the states), drivers are most decidedly a danger to themselves and others. The overall decline is partly due to the fact that, in the United States, alcohol consumption has been declining since its twentieth-century high in 1980, and partly because today, law enforcement and public attitudes toward drunk driving are significantly less tolerant and more punitive.

Motor vehicle accidents are not the only source of alcohol-related death. Alcohol consumption is also causally related to violent crime. In approximately one-third to one-half of incidents of criminal violence, both offenders and victims were legally under the influence of alcohol (Pernanen, 1991; Parker, 1995). In addition, compulsive alcohol consumption, if it takes place over a long period of time, is medically harmful and, typically, results in premature death. Since 1971, every three years or so the U.S. National Institute on Alcohol Abuse and Alcoholism (NIAAA), a division of the Department of Health and Human Services, has issued summary reports assessing alcohol's impact on health. At this writing, the most recent volume was released in 2000. To put its findings in perspective, it should be kept in mind that just under half of the American population consumes a dozen or more alcoholic drinks a year, and approximately 7 percent of the population drinks abusively, according to NIAAA's criteria. Alcohol is used by more people than any other drug (caffeine excepted), although tobacco is consumed more often. Alcohol is consumed five to ten times as often as is true of all the illicit drugs combined. According to NIAAA's summary of the available data:

- The total cost of alcohol abuse in the United States is $185 billion.
- Alcohol alone is involved in substance-related violence in one-quarter of all incidents, a total of 2.7 million acts of violence per year; in a substantial proportion of the remainder, alcohol is used in conjunction with one or more illicit drugs.
- About 900,000 residents of the United States suffer from cirrhosis of the liver, mainly caused by the heavy use of alcohol, and 26,000 die of the disease each year.
- Excess alcohol consumption is related to immune deficiencies, causing a susceptibility to certain infectious diseases, such as tuberculosis, pneumonia, HIV/AIDS, and hepatitis.
- Heavy drinkers (those who consume 29 or more drinks per week) have twice the risk of mental disorder as compared with abstainers.

These highlights do not exhaust NIAAA's list of harms caused by alcohol. In 2004, the Centers for Disease Control and Prevention (CDC) estimated the total number of people killed each year in the 2000s in the United States by the consumption of alcohol to be at 85,000; a third to half of these deaths are caused by accident, suicide, homicide, and other nondisease-related sources (Stein, 2004; Ravenholt, 1984; NIAAA, 2000). Alcohol is one of the "Big Three" drugs, along with heroin and cocaine, that causes or is implicated in overdose deaths, as tabulated by the Drug Abuse Warning Network (DAWN), a federally funded data-collection project that tallies all lethal and nonlethal overdoses in the major metropolitan centers of the United States. Many experts believe that, in the United States, roughly 10 percent of all deaths can be attributed to alcohol consumption. In comparison with that of a moderate drinker, an alcoholic's life is shortened by roughly 15 years. To be brief about it, human life is undermined, threatened, corrupted, and destroyed by alcohol abuse.

However, NIAAA does point out that *moderate* alcohol consumption is not only *not* harmful but may actually confer distinct and measurable health benefits on the drinker. All

studies on the same subject say more or less the same thing (Zuger, 2002): For a number of diseases, the morbidity of moderate drinkers is actually *lower* than that of abstainers—and moderate drinking is vastly far more common than heavy drinking. It is entirely possible that, taken as a whole, from a public health standpoint, the positives of alcohol consumption outweigh the negatives. Nonetheless, as a psychoactive substance, alcohol stands below only tobacco as a major source of death and disease, and stands virtually alone as a source of violence and accidents.

ALCOHOL CONSUMPTION TODAY

Today, Americans age 14 or older consume an average of 2.21 gallons of absolute alcohol per person per year, according to the National Institute on Alcohol Abuse and Alcoholism. This is a fairly "hard" or reliable statistic because it is based on sales and not what people *say* they drink. This figure is called "apparent" alcohol consumption, because not every drop of the alcohol that is purchased is actually drunk during a given year. Still, the possible sources of error are small, mere blips on the radar screen; they do not change the big picture at all. The fact is, the figures on alcohol sales are very close to actual consumption levels. In any case, 2.21 gallons of absolute alcohol per year works out to just under 1 ounce of absolute alcohol per person age 14 or older per day. Of course, some people drink a lot more than that, some less, and some not at all. Roughly one-third of all Americans are more or less total abstainers; that is, they did not consume a single drop of alcohol during the previous year. Thus, it makes sense to tabulate the quantity of alcohol consumed specifically *for drinkers*, and leave abstainers out of the picture altogether. On average, adult drinkers consume roughly 1.5 ounces of absolute alcohol per day. This represents two and a half 12-ounce bottles or cans of beer *or* one and a half 8-ounce glasses of wine *or* three 1-ounce drinks of hard liquor per day for every drinking adolescent and adult in the country.

Recorded yearly alcohol sales (a "hard" statistic) can be backed up with information on the proportion of the American population who *say* they drink (a "soft" statistic). Every year or so, the Gallup Poll asks a sample of Americans age 18 and older the following question: "Do you have occasion to use alcoholic beverages such as liquor, wine, or beer, or are you a total abstainer?" This question was first asked in 1939, when 58 percent defined themselves as drinkers, 42 percent as abstainers. In 1947, 63 percent said that they drank. The percentage rose steadily through the 1950s and 1960s, and reached a peak of 71 percent in 1976, 1977, and 1978. After that, the figure declined slightly. In Gallup's latest poll at this writing (2001), just over six Americans in ten (62 percent) said that they "have occasion to use alcoholic beverages." A quarter of its 2000 sample (26 percent) said that they had drunk an alcoholic beverage within the past 24 hours.

The National Household Survey on Drug Abuse (SAMHSA, 2002) and the National Survey on Drug Use and Health (SAMHSA, 2003) questioned respondents on their alcohol consumption in addition to their drug use. The questions this survey asked are a bit different from Gallup's; they are more specific about the time periods in which the alcohol consumption took place—that is, has the respondent *ever* drunk alcohol, drunk it within the past *year*, and drunk it within the past *month*. In 2001, just over half, or 51 percent of the population age 12 and older, had consumed one or more alcoholic drinks in the past month. The comparable figure for 1991 was exactly the same, 51 percent (NIDA, 1991, p. 85).

The claim that under-21-year-olds are drinking at least as much as, if not more than, they did since the 21-year-old drinking age limit was imposed (Ravo, 1987; Mooney, Grambling, and Forsyth, 1992) is not borne out by the evidence. The Monitoring the Future survey verifies what other systematic studies tell us. The annual prevalence of alcohol use for high school seniors stood at 88 percent in 1979; in 2002, it was 72 percent. The 30-day prevalence was 72 percent in 1979 and by 2002, it was 49 percent. For the study's full-time college subsample, the annual prevalence dropped only 8 percentage points between 1980 (when the first survey of college students was conducted) and 2002—91 versus 83 percent—but the decline in the 30-day prevalence was a bit more substantial, from 82 to 69 percent

(Johnston, O'Malley, and Bachman, 2003a, p. 47). Given the weight of the evidence, it seems difficult to deny the decline in alcohol consumption by adolescents and young adults—indeed, for the population as a whole—in the past half-generation or so. Some critics have pointed out that, though teenagers' overall level of alcohol consumption may have declined, *binge* drinking among the young has increased—a distinct possibility (Hoover, 2002).

One beneficial consequence of the nationwide prohibition on the sale of alcohol to persons under the age of 21 has been a decline in alcohol-related highway fatalities among drivers in the 16-to-20-year-old age range. As we can see from Table 7.1, between 1977 and 1999, the number of alcohol-related fatal crashes among 16-to-20-year-olds declined from just under 4,000 to just over 1,500. The decline in alcohol involvement in fatal crashes among young drivers (60 percent) is *three times* the decline among drivers age 21 and older (18 percent)—a clear indication that something positive is happening on the teenage drinking-and-driving front. It is possible that the American public is aware of this development. In a 2002 Gallup poll, the vast majority of the respondents questioned (77 percent) said that they opposed lowering the drinking age to 18; only 18 percent were in favor. When asked whether penalties for underage drinking should be more strict, less strict, or remain as they are now, 60 percent said more strict, 6 percent said less strict, and 33 percent said they should remain as they are now. Clearly, the laws are doing some good, and the majority of the public supports them.

WHO DRINKS? WHO DOESN'T?

Just as interesting as the overall figures on alcohol consumption and their changes over time is group-to-group variation in drinking. Who drinks and who doesn't? Are certain groups or categories significantly and consistently more likely to drink than others?

There are at least two crucial measures of alcohol consumption: drinking at all and drinking to excess. Drinking varies dramatically from one

TABLE 7.1

ALCOHOL-RELATED TRAFFIC FATALITIES PER 100 MILLION VEHICLE MILES TRAVELED, UNITED STATES, 1977–1999

1977	1.19
1999	0.47
Percent Change	−60.8

ALCOHOL-RELATED FATALITIES PER 100,000 REGISTERED VEHICLES, UNITED STATES, 1977–1999

1977	11.71
1999	5.69
Percent Change	−51.4

ALCOHOL-RELATED FATALITIES PER 100,000 LICENSED DRIVERS, UNITED STATES, 1977–1999

1977	12.61
1999	6.70
Percent Change	−46.9

ALCOHOL INVOLVEMENT IN FATAL CRASHES AMONG YOUNG DRIVERS AND DRIVERS AGE 21 AND OLDER, UNITED STATES, 1977–1999

	AGE 16–20		AGE 21+
1977	3,912	1977	11,989
1999	1,554	1999	9,787
Percent Change	−60.3		−18.4

PER CAPITA ALCOHOL CONSUMPTION, UNITED STATES, 1977–1999 (EXPRESSED IN GALLONS OF ABSOLUTE ALCOHOL CONSUMED)

1977	2.64
1999	2.21
Percent Change	−16.3

Source: http://www.niaa.nih.gov/databases

category in the population to another; likewise, drinking heavily, compulsively, and abusively—that is, to excess—varies along sociological lines. We might expect that categories in the population that have a high proportion of drinkers (and, contrarily, a low proportion of abstainers) would also rank high in the likelihood that their members are alcoholics, that is, those who drink to excess. The opposite side of the coin should be expected as well: The lower the proportion of drinkers in a social category, the lower the likelihood that the members of that category will be abusive drinkers. This is not always the case, however; some groups in the population have extraordinarily high proportions of drinkers but low propor-

tions of alcoholics, while other groups are more likely to abstain, but its drinkers are more likely to drink compulsively and abusively (Armor, Polich, and Stambul, 1976). For instance, persons of Jewish and Italian ancestry are highly likely to drink, but their rates of alcoholism are extremely low. In contrast, men over the age of 60 have higher than average rates of alcohol abstention but also higher than average rates of alcoholism.

Social class or socioeconomic status (SES), which is usually measured by income, occupation, and/or education, correlates strongly and consistently with the consumption of alcohol. As a general rule, in the Western world, including the United States, the higher the social class or SES (which includes education), the *greater* the likelihood of drinking at all. This generalization is confirmed by the 2001 National Household Survey on Drug Abuse, which found a remarkably strong correlation between education and drinking during the previous year. Among respondents 26 and older, only 46 percent with less than a completed high school education drank during the prior year; 54 percent of high school graduates had done so; 64 percent of respondents with some college had; and a whopping 77 percent of college graduates said that they had drunk an alcoholic beverage once or more during the past year. The same finding is consistently turned up by the annual Gallup poll in its question about whether respondents "have occasion" to use alcoholic beverages: The higher the income, education, and socioeconomic status (or social "class") of the respondent, the greater the likelihood that he or she drinks alcohol.

Gender or sex, too, correlates strongly with drinking. In fact, of all variables (except age), perhaps gender correlates most strongly with alcohol consumption. Men are consistently more likely to drink than are women, and they drink more when they do drink. The 2001 National Household Survey found a sizeable male-female difference in drinking: 55 percent of the males but only 42 percent of the females in the study had drunk alcohol during the past year; over a quarter of the men (28 percent) said that they were "binge" drinkers, or drank five or more times on at least one occasion over the past month, while only 13 percent of the women did; and 9 percent of the men but only 3 percent of the women were, according to the criteria of the survey, "heavy" drinkers.

As we've already seen, age is also strongly correlated with drinking. Drinking tends to be extremely low in early adolescence, shoots up in the middle-to-late teenage years, reaches a peak between 19 and the early twenties, and declines slowly after that. In the 2001 National Household Survey on Drug Abuse, drinking in the past month increased from 2.6 percent among 12-year-olds to a peak of 67.5 percent among 21-year-olds, and remained at something of a plateau after that, diminishing only very slightly into middle age: 66 percent at the age of 22, to 53 percent among 50-to-54-year-olds, then 46 percent between the ages of 55 and 64, then to

33 percent at the age of 65 and older. This is a very different pattern from drug use and very different from that hypothesized for a wide range of criminal and "deviant" behaviors (Gottfredson and Hirschi, 1990, pp. 124–144). Of course, drinking during the past month is not as "deviant" as illicit drug use; in fact, in American society, it is conventional, very much in the mainstream.

TOBACCO: AN INTRODUCTION

Is tobacco a drug? Like marijuana, tobacco is a plant product that *contains* a number of naturally occurring ingredients—chemicals—that have psychoactive properties. The principal psychoactive drug in tobacco is nicotine; the tobacco leaf contains roughly 1 percent nicotine by weight. In the dosages normally taken, nicotine does not produce a profoundly psychoactive effect on users. The short-term or acute effects of small doses of nicotine are fairly mild and transient; Goldstein refers to the effects of nicotine as "a low-key high" (2001, p. 121).

Of course, as we've seen so many times before, *route of administration* is crucial here: Smoking is such an efficient means of taking a drug that, by this factor alone, nicotine's impact is heightened over and above that obtained with other methods of use, such as chewing or inhaling snuff. In addition, keep in mind the fact that cigarette smokers almost always inhale—and inhalation is an extremely effective means of use—while pipe and cigar smokers almost never do. So, the consequences of tobacco use will be very different according to *how* it is used. Also keep in mind that smoke is airborne, which means that nonsmokers may have to inhale the tobacco smoke generated by the people in their presence (this is referred to as passive, "sidestream," or "secondhand" smoke) and thus, in a sense, they are *forced* to use the drug nicotine.

TOBACCO: MEDICAL HARM

Nicotine is a poison; if injected directly into the bloodstream, roughly 60 milligrams is the lethal dose, that is, sufficient to kill a human being.

Since cigarettes are smoked, a substantial proportion of its strength is dissipated into the air. A cigar contains about 100 to 120 milligrams of nicotine, but, as we saw, its smoke is not inhaled. Nicotine kills as a result of muscular and hence, respiratory, paralysis. Fortunately, not enough of the drug is absorbed in a brief period of time for it to be lethal. Perhaps the most noticeable acute effect of cigarette smoking is that it releases carbon monoxide, which reduces the body's supply of oxygen to the blood, causing shortness of breath and, in more substantial doses, dizziness. (Over the long run, this chronic oxygen deficit will damage the heart and the blood vessels of smokers.) The same effect in expectant mothers can damage her fetus and increase the likelihood of birth defects (Goldstein, 2001, pp. 126–127). Nicotine is a vasoconstrictor; that is, it constricts the blood vessels, causing the heart to work harder to maintain a sufficient supply of blood and oxygen. It also inhibits the stomach contractions that are associated with hunger; hence, the belief that if one stops smoking, one may gain weight has some validity. More broadly, the drug does not produce profound behavioral changes or impairment; nicotine (along with caffeine) is the only drug that passengers do not have to be concerned about if their pilot is using it (Goldstein, 2001, p. 122). Intellectual and motor ability do not decline significantly under the influence; indeed, at certain doses, they may even improve slightly.

Is nicotine addicting? In the 1980s, Philip Morris, a major cigarette manufacturer, commissioned a study on whether tobacco produces an addiction in rats. The results of this research showed that, indeed, nicotine is an addicting drug. Was this study published? No; when the company reviewed the research findings, the researchers were fired and the lab was closed down (Ray and Ksir, 2002, pp. 320–321). In 1994, tobacco executives testified before Congress to the effect that nicotine is not addicting. Today, most pharmacologists agree that nicotine is addicting and the primary, and very possibly the only, reinforcing substance in tobacco. However, as Goldstein (2001, p. 121) points out, the addictive properties of nicotine were difficult to establish in the laboratory since animals found the drug so unpleasant that it was difficult to

induce them to self-administer it. It took researchers many years to figure out a way of getting laboratory animals to become tolerant enough to the effects of nicotine to take it regularly; this was possible only through a slow and gradual process. Years of research with both humans and animals have shown that nicotine does produce a physical dependency, and its strength depends on the size of the tobacco "habit," that is, the quantity of nicotine consumed per day. What evidence do we have for this generalization?

Specifically, with respect to nicotine, there are at least six indications of nicotine's addicting or dependency-producing properties. First, as we've already seen, of all drugs, tobacco is the one that is used *most frequently* by smokers. In the United States, smokers take their drug 15 times a day, indicating that the drug has a strong hold over its users. In addition, of all drugs, users of tobacco cigarettes display the strongest yearly-to-monthly "loyalty" rate—they use it most regularly. Second, if we were to plot use during the day with levels of nicotine in the blood, their correspondence would resemble a thermostat. That is, the nicotine level in the smoker's body rises during and immediately after smoking, declines soon afterward; when it falls below a certain level, the smoker lights up again, elevating that level once again (Goldstein, 2001, pp. 118–121). A line depicting the presence of nicotine in the smoker's body during the course of a day would resemble a sawtooth pattern, rising and falling over time. Third, once laboratory animals have been induced to take nicotine regularly, they work extremely hard to continue self-administering it. If smokers switch to a low-nicotine cigarette, they inhale more deeply and/or smoke more cigarettes to obtain the same level of nicotine in their body. Fourth, smokers who quit describe feeling a strong "craving" for cigarettes that persists as long as years after the onset of abstention. Fifth, the statistics on relapse show that, although many smokers do quit, they do so only with great difficulty and as a result of repeated efforts; as many smokers return to their drug of choice as heroin addicts do. And last, there are the physical effects produced by nicotine abstention: headaches, fatigue and drowsiness, shortened attention span, irritability, anxiety, insomnia, hunger, heart palpitations, and tremors.

Smokers are *much, much* more likely to die a premature death than nonsmokers are. In fact, the federal Department of Health and Human Services estimates, a *nonsmoker* is more likely to live to the age of 75 than a *smoker* is to live to 65. A two-pack-a-day smoker is 23 times more likely to die of lung cancer than a nonsmoker is. In what was no doubt a carefully crafted public relations move, in 1999, Philip Morris executives publicly admitted that medical research indicates that smoking causes cancer. The fact is, long before this date scientists had accepted the fact that cigarettes cause disease and death. The latest estimate issued (in 2002) by the federal Centers for Disease Control and Prevention (CDC) estimates that tobacco causes roughly 440,000 premature deaths in the United States each year. This means that tobacco causes more deaths *than all other drugs combined*, and by a wide margin. Currently, the annual death toll in the United States from alcohol, according to the CDC, is 85,000 (Stein, 2004); for illegal drugs plus the illegal use of prescription drugs, it may be in the territory of 20,000 or so. Moreover, tobacco kills more than its smokers. The Environmental Protection Agency estimates that 50,000 Americans die each year as a result of "passive" smoke, that is, smoke inhaled by a nonsmoker from a smoker's cigarette. And, according to an extensive review of the literature, more than 5,000 infants die each year as a result of their mother's smoking habit; this does not include an estimated 19,000 to 141,000 spontaneous abortions (or "miscarriages") directly or indirectly induced by tobacco smoke (DiFranza and Lew, 1995).

The CDC estimates that, in the United States, *one out of five* of all deaths can be traced to smoking. And, as we've seen, medical experts affiliated with the United Nations estimate that in the industrialized countries of the world, 12 percent of all years of premature death is caused by the consumption of tobacco. The CDC estimates that, while cigarettes cost about $3 a pack nationwide, because of the multiple harms that they cause—an immense loss of life, health, medical costs, and productivity—they actually cost society about $7 per pack. (But as we'll see, some

economists calculate that society *saves* money by the premature deaths of smokers, since they tend not to live long enough to collect retirement benfits! See Viscusi, 2002). In short, tobacco is *by far* the country's number one drug menace. Smoking shaves an entire decade off one's life. Moreover, it reduces the quality of life as well, since the last few years of the smoker's life are likely to be marred by diseases such as lung cancer, stroke, emphysema, heart disease, and bronchitis. The harmful effects of cigarettes have been known for many years.

TOBACCO: A BRIEF HISTORY

The tobacco plant is indigenous to the Western Hemisphere; prior to the 1490s, its use was completely unknown in Europe and Asia. The native inhabitants of San Salvador, an island in the Caribbean, presented Columbus with a sheaf of tobacco leaves. When first introduced into Europe, the practice of tobacco consumption generated a great deal of hostility, as well as legislation outlawing the sale and use of this plant product. Some of these laws even called for the death penalty against offenders. In 1604, King James issued a "Counterblaste" condemning the consumption of tobacco; he referred to smoking as "a custom loathsome to the eye, hateful to the nose, harmful to the brain, [and] dangerous to the lung." Nonetheless, within a decade, the English decided to live with the "stinking weede." Tobacco's story was essentially the same everywhere the plant was introduced—the Ottoman Empire, Russia, China, Japan, Hindustan: condemnation, followed by legislation, and, eventually, legal and public acceptance.

Today, cigarette smoking is such an overwhelmingly favorite method of tobacco consumption, it is difficult to imagine that, just a bit more than a century ago, cigarettes were smoked hardly at all. The earliest recreational use of tobacco involved inhaling the fumes of the combusted leaf through a tube or a straw. By the 1700s, sniffing or snorting powdered or shredded tobacco snuff came to be far more popular. In the United States in the 1800s, the most popular method of tobacco consumption was chewing, but as the society became more urban, more middle class, more fashionable and sophisticated, this unsightly and unaesthetic habit declined in popularity. Still, as late as 1920, three out of four pounds of tobacco were devoted to cigar and pipe smoking, snuff, and chewing.

Smoking tobacco in the form of cigarettes did not become popular until well into the first half of the twentieth century. The change was partly cultural and partly due to technology. In 1880, according to the U.S. Department of Agriculture, the total American sale of cigarettes was only half a billion; on a per population basis, consumption was only *one three-hundredths* as great then as it is now. In 1881, the cigarette-rolling machine was patented. It could manufacture 120,000 cigarettes a day—the work of 40 hand rollers. By 1900, 2.5 billion cigarettes were sold in the United States, an average of 54 cigarettes per adult. In only a dozen years, by 1912, the total number manufactured shot up by more than five times, to 13.2 billion, and the per capita average increased by four times, to 223 cigarettes. By the end of the decade, the consumption of cigarettes had tripled, to 44.6 billion. During the decade between 1920 and 1930, the number of cigarettes consumed in the United States more than doubled, to 119.3 billion. Between 1900 and 1963, the number of cigarettes sold in the United States increased from 2.5 to 523.9 billion, an increase of more than 200 times, and the per capita consumption jumped from 54 to 4,345, an increase of 80 times. Today, about six out of seven pounds of tobacco consumed in the United States are devoted specifically to cigarette smoking.

THE DECLINE OF SMOKING

In 1964, probably the most influential document in the history of the tobacco industry was published—the Surgeon General's Report, entitled *Smoking and Health*. Summarizing the research current at that time, this report argued that the use of tobacco products represents a serious health hazard to smokers. The impact of this report was immediate; in 1964, the per capita consumption of cigarettes declined slightly, and continued to fall throughout the remainder of the twentieth

century and into the twenty-first. From its 1963 high of 4,345, by 2002 America's per adult tobacco consumption for the population age 18 and older had declined to 1,979. The total number of cigarettes sold continued to rise decades after 1964, of course, since the American population continues to grow; 1981 represents the peak year for total tobacco sales, when 640 billion cigarettes were sold. By 2002, the total had fallen to 420 billion. (See Table 7.2.)

Perhaps the factor most closely tied into the cessation of smoking is education. According to the information supplied on the Internet by the Epidemiology and Statistics Unit, today, high school dropouts are more than two and a half times more likely to smoke (36 percent) than college graduates (14 percent); persons with at least three years of college are 20 percentage points more likely to be *ex*-smokers (65 percent) than persons without a high school diploma (45 percent). Between the 1970s and the late 1990s, smoking declined 51 percent among college graduates but only 19 percent among persons with less than 12 years of education. Educated people are much less likely to smoke, and if they do smoke, much more likely to give up the habit, than is true of less well-educated persons. In the United States, only 14 percent of college graduates smoke, while 34 percent of adults without a high school diploma do so, with the in-between educational levels also in-between in the likelihood of smoking (SAMHSA, 2002, p. 37).

It is important to know that tobacco is a $45-billion-a-year industry, one of the largest in the country (Greenwald, 1997); executives, employees, communities, stockholders—and governments—profit from the sale of tobacco products. Indeed, since, economically speaking, the sale of tobacco is an industry just like every other industry, it generates wealth that indirectly benefits the entire country, not just persons directly involved with it. In 1997, according to the Federal Trade Commission, the industry's advertising budget was $5.66 billion—adjusting for inflation, more than a three-and-one-half times increase since 1970 (Feder, 1997a). While most agricultural products yield about $4,000 an acre, the annual gross for tobacco is over $200,000 an acre (Torregrossa, 1996). Factor in, too, a bizarre and

TABLE 7.2   CIGARETTE CONSUMPTION, AGE 18 AND OLDER, UNITED STATES, 1900–2002

YEAR	BILLIONS SOLD	PER CAPITA CONSUMPTION, 18 AND OLDER
1900	2.5	54
1908	5.7	105
1912	13.2	223
1918	45.6	267
1929	118.6	1,504
1935	134.4	1,564
1941	208.9	2,236
1945	340.6	3,449
1963	523.9	4,345
1975	607.2	4,123
1980	631.5	3,851
1985	594.0	3,370
1990	524.0	2,926
1995	485.0	2,470
2002	420.0	1,979

Sources: Economic Research Service, U.S. Department of Agriculture; various year-by-year publications.

grim statistic: State and federal governments *save* about 33 cents per pack on Medicaid and Social Security benefits that don't have to be paid out because smokers generally die before they are able to collect them (Gravelle and Zimmerman, 1994; Viscusi, 2002). All in all, the incentives to protect tobacco from legal, political, and economic assault are massive. In 1996 alone, the tobacco industry spent $600 million, employing 350 separate law firms, to protect their business from lawsuits (Feder, 1997b). On the basis of these facts alone, one might predict that tobacco was an impregnable fortress.

The crack in the egg was caused by a variety of factors, perhaps none so powerful as a growing concern for the fate of teenage smokers. Over 90 percent of adult smokers began their habit before the age of 18; some experts argue that, if people do not begin smoking as teenagers, they are unlikely to begin at all. Consider, too, the fact that the earlier the smoking habit begins, the greater the likelihood that tobacco will kill the smoker. Experts estimate that, today, roughly 3,000 American teenagers will take up the habit *every day*; of these,

one-third will eventually die of a tobacco-related illness (*New York Times*, August 18, 1996, p. 14E). The CDC estimates that roughly five million American teenagers age 17 and younger now smoking will die of one or more diseases caused by cigarette smoking; if the downward trend that began in the late 1980s had continued, perhaps as many as four million of them would have survived (Feder, 1997b). Contemplating the horrific loss of life in the decades ahead has led many policy analysts to seek drastic measures to curtail the consumption of tobacco.

Fortunately, a decline in smoking among adolescents has taken place during the early years of the twenty-first century. Monitoring the Future's (MTF) 1995–1999 30-day prevalence figures for high school seniors were in the 33.5-to-36.5 percent range. In 2000, this declined to 31.4; in 2001, to 29.5; and in 2002, to 26.7 percent. In other words, in spite of the rise in smoking during the 1990s among secondary school students, the current level is lower than it has been since MTF began conducting its surveys. If present trends continue, the decline that took place between the late 1990s and the early twenty-first century will translate into several millions of lives saved. Public health figures hope for a continuation of the recent decline well into the remainder of this century.

SUMMARY

Objectively speaking, alcohol is a drug; it is psychoactive, it is taken for its effects on the mind, it is physically and psychologically addictive, and it can cause a lethal overdose. In fact, again, judging strictly on the basis of objective criteria, alcohol (along with tobacco cigarettes) represents this society's most serious drug problem. In addition, many of the same people who use alcohol also use illicit drugs, indicating that the alteration of one's consciousness characterizes both drinkers and users of controlled substances. But *subjectively* or in the constructionist sense, alcohol is not a drug at all; that is, its possession and sale are legal, and it is not *regarded* or socially or mentally "constructed" as a drug by much of the public.

The use of alcohol dates back thousands, possibly tens of thousands, of years; humans were drinking alcohol longer ago than they were fashioning metals. The members of nearly every society on earth consume alcohol. At the same time, the way it is used varies from one society to another. In some societies, its use has become a serious problem; in most, moderation is typically the rule.

Alcohol's effects are closely related to the concentration of alcohol in the bloodstream. Perhaps its most well-known effect is discoordination, which results in a substantial increase in the likelihood of accident and death while engaged in a wide range of activities. Violence, too, is associated with intoxication, although the causal dynamics here are not altogether clear. In addition, a wide range of medical pathologies are associated with heavy alcohol consumption.

Since 1980, the use of alcohol has been declining on a year-by-year basis; it now stands at slightly above two gallons of "absolute" alcohol per year per teenager or adult, roughly an ounce and a half per drinker per day. Though some observers claim that the 21-year-and-older law has stimulated drinking among teenagers, the evidence suggests lower teenage alcohol use after the law than before. (Binge drinking may have increased since the law was passed, however.) Drunk driving and automobile fatalities under the influence have decreased as well, especially for teenagers but also for the population as a whole.

The consumption of alcohol is distributed unevenly in the population, with some groups and categories drinking significantly more than others. As a general rule, drinking is *positively* related to social class or socioeconomic status (SES)—the higher the income, education, and occupational prestige, the greater the likelihood that someone will drink. However, though upper-SES persons tend to drink, they are highly likely to do so moderately. The lower the SES, the lower the likelihood that someone will drink—but, among drinkers, the higher the likelihood that he or she will drink heavily and abusively. Men are more likely to drink than women and the men who do drink have a higher likelihood of doing so in greater volume. Of all age groups, young adults under the age of 35 are most likely to drink; the likelihood of drinking declines with age, although slowly.

As with alcohol, whether or not the nicotine in tobacco can be regarded as a drug depends on our definition. By objectivistic criteria, nicotine most decidedly is a drug; it is psychoactive and it can generate a serious dependency. In the past, however, nicotine was not regarded as a drug either by the law or by the public. In the 1990s, the awareness that smoking cigarettes is a drug-taking behavior began to grow; in addition, legal restrictions on the sale and consumption of cigarettes have multiplied as well. Objectively speaking, among all psychoactive substances, tobacco causes the most damage; experts at the federal Centers for Disease Control and Prevention estimate that roughly 440,000 Americans die prematurely each year as a result of cigarette smoking; the heavy consumption of tobacco cuts an average of 10 years off the life of the smoker. The United Nations estimates that, in the industrialized countries of the world, roughly 12 percent of all the years lost to premature death are caused by tobacco consumption.

PERSONAL ACCOUNT: The Bar Scene

The contributor of this account is Nancy, a 23-year-old college student. She describes past behavior she no longer participates in, which, she now feels, was deviant—although a learning experience. Her account illustrates the fact that the heavy consumption of alcohol often accompanies other nonnormative activities, including illegal drug use and casual sex. In other words, lurking beneath a conventional facade of certain styles of alcohol consumption, we find a most decidedly deviant reality.

It started, strangely enough, with a sociology course I took in community college. I was innocent at the time, straight out of high school. I hadn't experienced much of the bar scene at all. I took a sociology course in which a major theme was the instructor's insistence that if you had experienced a variety of forms of sexual intercourse with different partners, then you would learn exactly what desires you had and pleasures you wanted to receive; you would become sensitive to both your and your partner's needs. This rang a bell with me. I hadn't had the variety of sexual experiences the instructor had talked about, so after one of my night classes, I strolled into a nearby bar, "Gold Coast," for a few drinks. It was different from any bar I had ever gone to—not that there were that many—because the clients there were mainly men who were between 25 and 30 years old. As I walked in by myself, all the men turned around and looked at me. I realized how exciting it was to receive that much attention from so many men. At first, I felt guilty because I had a boyfriend I planned to marry. But deep in my heart I knew there was something he wasn't giving me. I had one drink and left.

Two nights later, I went to the same sociology class, walked out, and, as I passed "Gold Coast," I felt an urge to go back in, but I didn't, not at first. I went to my girlfriend Lynette's house. At that time, she wasn't seeing anybody, so I told her I wanted to go to "Gold Coast," so we fixed ourselves up and left. As we got there, I felt an urge to have sex with another man

besides my boyfriend. We went in; all the customers were men, and they all watched us as we walked in. I drank my drink slowly. When I finished it, different men bought me drinks, I played darts, and listened to some great classic rock music. I became half loaded, but I was still pretty much on the ball. The place became packed with people, both men and women. But I felt as if I was the greatest thing in the bar because all the men wanted to pick me up. Unfortunately, none of them turned me on except for Jim, one of the bartenders. He was soft-spoken and wore jeans and a vest. He looked great, and he hit a nerve in me. I found out he knew my brother and his friends, which hit another nerve because I always got along with my brother's friends. I figured he must be good, too—and he was.

At four in the morning, my girlfriend wanted to leave. I told Jim that I wanted to leave, and he walked me to my car and asked me to come back tomorrow night. I said yes right away. I loved the way he kissed. The next night, I went back again, and again Lisa came with me. This time I made sure I looked great, so that when I walked in, Jim would notice me—and he sure did! He came over to me and talked for a while, then he went back behind the bar. So I talked to the other customers, mainly men. I soon found myself outside with a clique of men smoking pot, really getting high. Jim came out and joined us. He knew some of the guys I was smoking with. When he put his arms around me, I felt a tremendous rush. He stimulated me in every possible way. I knew that this was the night I was going to have sex with him.

Later, "Gold Coast" began to clear out. At some point, Jim came from behind the bar and told me to stay. I asked Lynette if she could get a ride from someone else because I was staying. No guilt was in my mind at all. Then Jim began cleaning up the place, lowered the lights, and we began to hold one another very, very close. He locked the door of the bar while I waited on a stool. He came back over to me and started to kiss me again. I felt a strong rush of pleasure

PERSONAL ACCOUNT: The Bar Scene (cont.)

that I had not felt in a long time. I soon found myself on top of one of the tables, stark naked, having intercourse with Jim. After we were done, I told him I would see him tomorrow.

I went back to the bar a couple of nights later, but I didn't feel the same way about Jim. I wanted someone else, but I still wanted Jim to come after me. I liked this game a lot. I started to wander around the bar, talking to other guys, getting them all hot and bothered. For some reason, I loved doing this. A few weeks before this, I would never have believed that I would have become a woman who would excite such lust in men. I always considered myself a home girl—but not now, not this time. I loved it, the flirting, exciting these men. I began talking to a man who had some roofies [Rohypnol, a tranquilizer], and he gave me some. I only took one because I was drinking. I soon found myself on cloud nine, in heaven, coming and going with the pleasure of walking around and arousing men to want to take me to bed. Then, Jim noticed me and he walked over to me. When he was close, I touched him in his crotch. I didn't even care if anybody saw me. It felt great. After arousing Jim, I told him I'd be back. I began hanging out outside with some more men. I found myself going home with some guy I didn't even know. After having sex with him, I told him I wanted to go back to "Gold Coast." He took me back. I was still wasted. I left him, too. I called my girlfriend Lynette and told her I was leaving. She met me in the bar around 3:45, and we left together.

I started to make this a habit I could not break. It was fun because it was something that not my parents, friends, nor I myself would ever have believed. It was only under the influence of alcohol or drugs that I would get this urge to have sex with someone else. I wanted to enjoy sex that was different from the boring sex I had with my boyfriend. For once, I was getting pleasure instead of giving it.

Summer came around, and I began going to a different bar, "Places," because Friday is ladies night. It felt great getting dressed up and doing the same things I was doing at "Gold Coast." I was dancing with a lot of men, playing the field, and still dating my boyfriend. It had become a habit to have sex with other men, but I was always the one who picked who I was going to have sex with.

I met a man who had a house on the beach where my girlfriend Crystal and I went for the weekend. Chris had a lot of money and his house was fantastic. He had a swimming pool, a tennis court, and an ocean beach as his back yard. He worked as an actor and has been in some very famous movies. He was different from the other men I had sex with. Chris was into kinky sex. He always had a lot of people sleeping over at his summer house. One night, Crystal and I went to his house, and I found myself sleeping with Chris. My friend Crystal was in the same room, having sex with Ted. They left, and just as Chris and I were finished, a couple of his friends entered the room and started to undress. I soon found myself having sex with three men at the same time. I thought it was a big turn-on because they all wanted me. They did kinky things I had never experienced before in my life. Before, I might have fantasized doing these things; now I was actually doing them. After two hours of this, we went to the bathroom and showered.

I got dressed and went downstairs where Crystal and Ted were, and we all began snorting coke. There was about an ounce of it, and it was really great. I'll never forget that weekend. I had engaged in sexual acts that, before, I never imagined I would have engaged in. I used to be so innocent, I thought, and yet here I am, this lustful woman, going from flirtations to barroom pickups to kinky group sex. If my boyfriend, my friends, or my parents knew about what I did, they would have disowned me.

I began having very negative feelings about myself as well. In a sense, I began to disown myself. I had become someone I didn't like. I saw myself engaging in sex just for the fun of it, but I knew that was not really me. I had forgotten about my morality. Once, I lived by such

PERSONAL ACCOUNT: The Bar Scene (cont.)

high standards. Then I played out all my fantasies. The urge to do wild things like the weekend at the beach had left me.

Meanwhile, the relationship I had with my boyfriend fell apart. Even though he never found out about what I had been doing, deep down, I felt I wasn't right for him. I decided I couldn't have sex with him any longer because I did these things behind his back, felt guilt about it, and secretly wished that he had found out about them and left me. After what I did, things could never be the same between us again.

I dated my boyfriend for four and a half years. We had a commitment and plans to marry.

I risked all this for experiencing a year of lust in the bar scene. Now I feel I have fulfilled every fantasy about sex I ever had. Now I want and can handle having sex without feeling I've missed out on anything. I had my variety. Now I shall make my choice of who I want to be with. I'm glad I got this out of my system. I know that I could never in my entire life tell anyone about what I did. I really don't think that anyone would believe me. They wouldn't believe me because I just don't appear to be the kind of person who would have engaged in the sexual encounters I experienced during that year of my life.

QUESTIONS

Do you think that the consumption of alcohol in a bar setting had something to do with the sexual behavior Nancy engaged in? Do you accept her statement that she is glad she got the experiences she had out of her system? What do you predict for her future behavior? Does her behavior illuminate any of the theories of deviance we looked at in Chapter 3? If she is not "the kind of person who would have engaged in the sexual encounters" she experienced, then why did she do it? If they taught her that her relationship with her fiancé would not work out, were they worth it? What did her experiences tell her about what kind of person she is? What role did alcohol play in this process?

CHAPTER 8

Illicit Drug Use

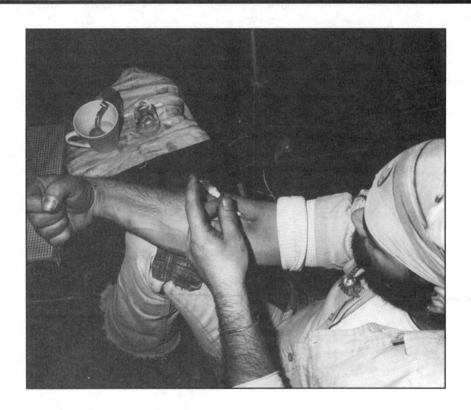

Drug use as deviant behavior can be looked at from both the positivist and the constructionist perspectives. With each approach, the questions I raised earlier must be asked about illicit drug use: *What is our mission? What is to be explained?*

From a strictly positivistic perspective, the issue that needs explaining is *why some people use illegal substances.* This perspective regards the deviant nature of drug use as unproblematic, that is, an issue that need not be considered. It is assumed, or remains in the background. To the positivist, why the use of certain drugs is deviant is not the question that most needs to be answered. In contrast, "Why do they do it?" *is* the question that needs to be answered.

Of course, each positivistic or explanatory theory answers the "Why do they do it" question in a somewhat different way. Some focus on individual explanations—for instance, biological or personality factors. Other perspectives examine differences between and among people living in certain types of social and economic structures. In other words, it is the *structural conditions* that influence the rates of drug use of persons subject to them. Still others ask not "Why do they do it?" but "Why *don't* they do it?" This amounts to much the same "why" question, only in reverse. But all take drug use as the *dependent* variable, that is, the variable that needs to be explained, and the factor their theory focuses on as the *independent* or explanatory variable. Hence, all positivist theories have the same basic structure or form: A (their key factor) causes B (drug use). Another positivist line of inquiry is captured in the question: "What are the *consequences* of drug use?" In the form this question is asked, positivists assume that specific drugs have specific consequences—at a certain dose, if used in a certain way, for a certain length of time, and so on.

In contrast, for the constructionist, the very issue that for the positivist is intellectually and theoretically unproblematic becomes central; this issue is: *"Why is the use of certain substances deviant?"* And here, it is the "Why do they do it?" question that is in the background. And the "consequences" question, while not irrelevant, is held in abeyance for the moment. The constructionist raises questions such as: Why are certain substances regarded as "drugs" while others aren't?

Why is the possession and sale of some drugs legal while others are illegal? Why does the public sense of danger and threat from and concern about drug use vary from year to year? What are the processes through which influential segments of the society mount an antidrug campaign to convince the public that substance abuse is wrong? Why does so much of the public believe that the "drug war" should be fought with ferocity? Why is the use and distribution of heroin and cocaine widely seen as evil while the use of alcohol and tobacco are regarded as acceptable, recreational—or a bad habit, or an illness? These are not political, ideological, or rhetorical questions, but inquiries that demand serious, systematic investigation.

Drug use is a type of behavior with causes and consequences. To explain why people use drugs, it is necessary to explore a range of social, psychological, biological, and economic factors or variables. Likewise, to understand the impact of drug use, we have to look at the links between the ingestion of certain substances and what it does to users and to the persons that the behavior of users influences. In other words, to examine drug use as a type of *behavior*, it is necessary to adopt the point of view of the positivistic sociologist.

But in addition to being a form of behavior with real-life causes and consequences, drug use is also a social construction; the two approaches are complementary, not contradictory. Members of the society hold social beliefs about drugs—indeed, create the very category "drug" in the first place; define their use and users in certain ways; regard and treat users in a certain way; and take steps to "do" something about the problem they believe their use has created. These are central matters for investigation to the constructionist sociologist.

One of the more interesting things about social deviance is how a given form of behavior and its social constructions—and the social constructions of its enactors—mutually influence one another. Social constructions are based in part (but not completely) on the concrete or so-called objective features of the behavior they supposedly typify. But they are also based on *ideas* or *assumptions* that are to some degree arbitrary, often entirely inaccurate, even invented. How accurate are social constructions about deviance? Well, they aren't created out of whole cloth, but they tend to depart significantly from what we would see if we observed the behavior very closely. Hence, an interesting issue is whether and to what extent social constructions of deviance vary from what facts would reveal about them. Likewise, to what extent do social constructions *influence* the concrete features of deviant behavior? Even though inaccurate, some false beliefs may exert a strong influence on events that take place in the material world. That is, certain ways that deviants are *seen* and *treated* by the society at large may turn around and influence the lives of enactors of deviance in many crucial and relevant ways. In other words, definitions that are *believed* to be real often have real *consequences* (Thomas and Thomas, 1928, p. 572). Hence, once again, these two realms of deviance—what a positivist and what a constructionist looks at—are not entirely separate; they continually feed back on one another.

DRUG USE: THE SOCIAL CONSTRUCTION OF A SOCIAL PROBLEM

Humans have been ingesting drugs for thousands of years. And throughout recorded time, significant numbers of nearly every society on earth have used one or more drugs to achieve certain desired physical or mental states. Drug use comes close to being a universal, both worldwide and throughout history. It is possible that the Eskimos (or Inuit), prior to the arrival of Europeans, are the only society on earth whose members did not use mind-altering substances (Weil, 1972).

Drugs are most often used in a culturally appropriate and approved manner (Edgerton, 1976, p. 57). Sometimes drug use is regarded as unacceptable to the society's more conventional members: The wrong drug is taken; it is taken too often, or under the wrong circumstances; or it is taken with undesirable consequences. In such cases, we have instances of deviant behavior.

"Execute Drug Dealers, Mayor Says," "Brutal Gangs Wage War of Terror," "Flood of Drugs—A Losing Battle," "Surge of Violence Linked to Narcotics," "War on Drugs Shifting to Street," "Drug Violence Erodes a Neighborhood," "Drug Production Soars"—these and similar headlines

fairly scream out the public's anxiety over the drug abuse issue.

These newspaper headlines tap a certain *fear* and *concern* felt by the public about drug abuse. (More specifically, they tap the fear and concern that journalists, editors, and newspaper publishers *believe* the public feels—a belief that is often justified.) Drug use, like every existing social condition, has a socially constructed or *subjective* dimension: the public's feeling or attitude about it; what is believed about it; what the public, or segments of the public do, or want to do about it; and the public's feelings, attitudes, and beliefs about the individuals who engage in it.

Likewise, as we saw, drug use and abuse have an *objective* side: what drugs actually do to humans who use them, how widely and frequently they are used, and what kind of impact they have on the society.

As we might expect, as with most other behaviors, conditions, and issues, the constructed and the objective sides of drug use overlap, but extremely imperfectly. That is, we may be concerned about behavior and conditions that, objectively speaking, are not threatening or damaging at all; and we may be unconcerned about behavior and conditions that are objectively *very* threatening or damaging. Moreover, these two dimensions—the subjective and the objective—may be out of sync with one another over time, with concern rising when damage from drug abuse is dropping, and declining when it rises. It is wise, when investigating deviant behavior and conditions, to keep the subjective and the objective dimensions separate in one's mind. (Even though, as I said, in real life they influence one another.) Regarding a given condition or behavior as threatening, damaging, as deviant, or as a social problem (the subjective or socially constructed dimension) could be completely unrelated to the physical or psychological damage it does (the objective or positivist dimension). In other words, the connections between these two dimensions cannot be assumed; they have to be investigated empirically.

In short, we can define a social problem in two ways—subjectively and objectively. The subjective definition of a social problem is captured in the *fear* and *concern* people feel about a given condition (or supposed condition) and the steps they take to deal with it. In other words, subjectively, a social problem is what people *think* or *feel* is a problem. In contrast, objectively, a problem is the *harm* that a condition actually inflicts on the society—for instance, death, disease, and monetary cost.

Fear of and concern about the threat of drug use and abuse have waxed and waned over the years in the United States. One measure of that fear and concern is the number and content of news stories on the subject. In the 1930s, hundreds of sensationalistic newspaper and magazine articles were published nationally that detailed the supposed horrors of marijuana use. In the 1940s and 1950s, such stories declined sharply in number and stridency. In the second half of the 1960s, literally thousands of news accounts were published and broadcast on LSD's capacity to make users go crazy and do dangerous things to themselves and others. By the early 1970s, LSD had ceased to be news, and heroin stormed into the headlines. In the mid-1970s, the media had quieted down on the drug front. But the mid-to-late-1980s witnessed a rebirth—indeed, something of an explosion—of public concern over the use and abuse of illegal drugs.

For instance, between the early and mid–1980s, the number of articles on the subject of drug abuse published in all the popular national magazines that are indexed by *The Readers' Guide to Periodical Literature* increased by some eight times. In the single year between 1985 and 1986, the number increased more than two and a half times, from 103 to 280. Clearly, although it had been building up in the two or three years prior, 1986 was the year that drug use and abuse fairly *exploded* as a social problem in the United States, subjectively speaking. However, into the 1990s, this concern, although it remained high, had declined significantly. Into the twenty-first century, drug use remains a focus of media attention, but that attention is only moderate compared with the peak years of the mid-to-late–1980s. Other concerns—such as the economy and the war in Iraq—crowded drug abuse off the center stage of media attention.

Another measure of the subjective dimension is the public's designation of a given condition or behavior as a serious problem. Each year, and several times during some years, the Gallup Poll asks a sample of the public what they regard as the "number one problem facing the nation today." As with the articles published in the *Readers' Guide*, the Gallup Poll provides a very rough measure of subjective public concern over a given condition at a particular time. The public's concern over drug abuse rose and fell, and rose and fell again, between the early 1970s and the early 1990s. In February 1973, 20 percent of the respondents in the Gallup Poll felt that drug abuse was the nation's number one problem. However, between that date and 1985, the percentage mentioning drug abuse as the country's most serious problem was so low it did not even appear among the top half-dozen problems. During 1985 and into January 1986, between 2 and 3 percent of the American public mentioned drug abuse as the country's most important problem; in April 1986, in a set of parallel polls conducted by *The New York Times* and CBS News, again, 2 percent mentioned drugs as the country's number one problem. In a July 1986 Gallup Poll, the figure was 8 percent; in an August *Times*/CBS poll, it was 13 percent. The figure continued to rise throughout the remainder of the 1980s until, in September 1989, a whopping 64 percent of the respondents in a *Times*/CBS poll said that drugs constituted the most important issue facing the country at that time. This response represents one of the most intense preoccupations by the American public on the drug issue in polling history.

The September 1989 figure proved to be the pinnacle of public concern about drugs; it is unlikely that a figure of such magnitude will ever be achieved for drug abuse again. After that, said one media expert, intense public concern simply "went away" (Oreskes, 1990). By November 1989, according to a *Times*/CBS poll, the figure had slipped to 38 percent; in July 1990, to 18 percent; in August 1990, to only 10 percent (Kagay, 1990; Oreskes, 1990; Shenon, 1990). Between November 1990 and December 1991, the figure remained in the 8-to-12 percent range; between March 1992 and August 1994, it had dipped slightly into the 6-to-8 percent range; and in May 1998, it was 12 percent. Since that time, the figure has wobbled on either side of 10 percent. (For these figures, see George Gallup, Jr., *The Gallup Poll: Public Opinion*, Wilmington, Del.: Scholarly Resources, for the relevant years.)

What we saw during late 1980s, then, was a period of *intense* public fear of and concern about drug use and abuse. It was so intense that observers referred to it as a drug "scare" or "moral panic" (Ben-Yehuda, 1986; Kerr, 1986; Jensen, Gerber, and Babcock, 1991; Goode and Ben-Yehuda, 1994a, 1994b; Reinarman, 2000). A *moral panic* is an intense, widespread, explosively upsurging feeling on the part of the public that something is terribly wrong in their society because of the moral failure of a specific group of individuals, a subpopulation that has been defined as the enemy, a "folk devil" (Cohen, 1972, 2002). In short, a category of people has been *deviantized* (Schur, 1980). This is precisely what happened with drug use and abuse between 1986 and 1989. During this period, American society was undergoing something of a moral panic about drug use; drug abusers were defined, even more intensely than was true in the past, as deviants. Of course, illegal drug use was seen as deviant before 1986, and continues to be so regarded today, but the *intensity* of this feeling reached something of an apex during that relatively brief three- or four-year period.

This does not necessarily mean that, objectively speaking, by the late 1980s and early 1990s drug use had ceased to be a problem in the United States. In fact, by some indicators, such as drug overdoses, in the late 1980s the drug problem actually increased in seriousness. But the important point is this: Moral panics and the fear of and concern about a given behavior or condition do not emerge solely as a result of public awareness of an objective threat. There are usually far more serious conditions or more dangerous behaviors that attract little or no concern compared with those that generate fear during a given moral panic. In fact, as a rule, the public has an extremely hazy notion of how threatening or damaging certain conditions or forms of behavior are, and the world of drug abuse is no exception.

Why is illegal drug use, including the illicit use of prescription drugs, a source of far more public concern than the use of legal drugs (alcohol and tobacco cigarettes), when the former kills no more than 20,000 or so Americans each year, while the latter kills over 600,000 (Horgan, Skwara, and Strickler, 2001)? Why are illegal drug users deviants while legal drug users are not? There may be concrete reasons for this greater concern that relate to the concrete, objective, or real-world

impact of illegal drugs as opposed to legal drugs. Perhaps it is based, in part, on the fact that the victims of illegal drugs are *younger* than the victims of alcohol and tobacco, and hence, far more years of life are lost per death. Perhaps there is the feeling that drug dealers destroy communities and corrupt law enforcement in a way that is quite unlike the way that purveyors of legal drugs work. (Of course, the very illegal status of some drugs may contribute to the harm they cause.) There may very well be a wide range of objectivistic factors influencing this relationship. But the fact remains, legal drugs kill more than 30 times as many Americans as illegal drugs, yet Americans are *far* more concerned about illegal drug abuse than about legal drugs. This paradox is central to any examination of drug use as a form of deviance. As a general rule, the public formulates judgments about the seriousness of certain conditions, behaviors, and issues, and regards certain behaviors as deviant, on the basis of criteria that are to some degree *independent* of estimates of their objective harm. In fact, the public's estimates of the objective harm of specific conditions, behaviors, and issues are extremely faulty, and are influenced by a wide range of extraneous factors (Slovic, Fischoff, and Lichtenstein, 1980; Erikson, 1990; Slovic, Layman, and Flynn, 1991).

WHAT IS DRUG USE?

As we saw in Chapter 7, substances can be defined as "drugs" according to four different criteria or within four specific contexts.

One such criterion is *psychoactivity*: What makes a substance a drug is that when ingested, it influences the workings of the brain. Clearly, psychoactivity is an objectivistic definition: Substances are classified as drugs according to their action, and that is an objective fact that is determined by the scientist.

Another is *medical utility*: Medically, substances that are used to heal the body or mind are considered drugs. Medical utility is partly a social construction and partly an objective fact. Substances are judged to be useful as medicine by physicians—and, interestingly, by the law as well—but presumably, physicians make this judgment according to the scientific evidence available to them.

A third criterion of "drugness" is *legal status*, which is largely a social construction. Legally, any substance whose possession and sale is prohibited by law is a drug. Hence, according to the lights of this definition, it is the law that dictates what a drug is. Presumably, the more dangerous the effects of the substance (an objective property) the more likely it is to be criminalized and hence, declared a drug. As we've already seen, this is not quite the case, since alcohol and tobacco, which kill far more users than LSD, PCP, marijuana, and Ecstasy, are legal.

And lastly, according to the criterion of public opinion, substances are drugs if they are *thought to be* drugs by the general public—that is, if they are talked about, thought about, looked upon, and judged to be drugs. Ask a cross-section of the public to name a half-dozen "drugs." Ask people to provide an example of drug "users." The users of *which* substances are offered as examples? Alcohol and tobacco are rarely regarded as or thought to be drugs by the general public; heroin and cocaine are nearly always on the public's mind as drugs.

Constructionist definitions of drugs assume a certain measure of *independence* between objective properties and how substances are defined, seen, and dealt with. For instance, these definitions would argue, it is not *only* the most harmful drugs whose possession and sale are against the law, it is not *only* the most medically efficacious that are used by physicians to heal the body and the mind, it is not *only* substances that have "drug-like" effects that are regarded as drugs by the general public. It is this independence between the objective properties of substances— that is, their *effects*—and the way that substances and their users are thought about, dealt with, and treated by the medical fraternity, by law enforcement, and by the general public, that is the central issue for sociologists who are interested in drug use and sale as deviant behavior.

Sociologists use *all* of these definitions of what a drug is: those based on a substance's psychoactivity, medical utility, legal status, and public definition. As students of deviance, psychoactivity is useful because it tells us that substances that offer users pleasurable sensations—a way of getting "high"—are likely to be used in ways that violate the norms of the society. Using substances as medicine that are not authorized for that purpose is clearly deviant, that is, a violation of the norms of the medical profession. Using substances whose possession and sale are a violation of the law is clearly a deviant act. And using substances that the public regards as drugs is, again, a normative violation and hence, deviant behavior. Hence, when contemplating drug use, the sociologist of deviance is confronted with a gold mine of opportunity.

A CLASSIFICATION OF DRUGS AND THEIR EFFECTS

There are many ways of looking at drug effects. For our purposes, one of the most important is the distinction between those that are *psychoactive*, that is, that influence the workings of the mind, and those that are not. Drugs that have effects only on the body (such as those for "heartburn," ulcers, allergies, and so on) are not psychoactive and are not used recreationally; hence, in a society such as ours, their users usually don't attract a deviant label. In contrast, drugs that are psychoactive tend to be taken for recreational purposes, that is, to get high. When substances are taken recreationally, in societies that condemn hedonism and self-indulgence, this tends to attract condemnation, and the users of these substances may become deviants.

It must also be recognized that a variety of factors influence drug effects. *Dose*, or how much is taken, is one such factor; some drugs may have mild effects when taken in small doses, and much more powerful ones when larger doses are taken. *How* a drug is taken, or *route of administration*, is also crucial. Injected intravenously or smoked, drugs tend to have a stronger, more immediate effect; swallowed, their effects will be weaker, more muted, much slower to take place. *Experienced* users will manifest somewhat different effects than drug *novices*; *expectations* of what effects a drug will have may influence the effects themselves; the *setting* in which a drug is taken, likewise, may alter drug experiences; whether a drug is *mixed*, or taken simultaneously with, other drugs will also determine the effects it has. All in all, a wide range of factors and dimensions influence or determine the effects drugs have.

All classifications of drugs and their effects are at least a bit misleading. A drug does not "belong" together with other drugs in a certain category and apart from others as a result of an edict from reality, science, or medicine. In fact, humans *construct* drug classifications. We latch onto certain traits, characteristics, or effects as a relevant basis for a classification scheme. One of the basic principles in pharmacology—the science that studies drug effects—is that *all drugs have multiple effects*. There is no drug with a single effect. This means that one effect of a given drug will lead a scientist to place it in one category, while a second effect of that same drug will cause another scientist to place it in an altogether different category. Which scientist is right? In which category does the drug "belong"? The answer is that there is no correct answer to this question—it depends on what is of interest to the observer; it does not depend solely on the objective characteristics of the substance.

Still, while drug classifications are fuzzy around the edges, the picture is not totally without a certain pattern. Several drugs classified in one way do have some properties and effects in common. So, classify we must, for, as misleading as classification is, it is also necessary; the human mind thinks in terms of categories. Table 8.1 offers a classification of most well-known psychoactive drugs.

The drugs in which we are interested are psychoactive. However, psychoactive drugs have a vast range of different effects. One way of classifying drugs is to look at their effects on the central nervous system (CNS)—that is, the brain and the spinal cord. Some drugs directly stimulate or speed up signals passing through the CNS; others depress or slow down these signals; still others have little or no impact on the speed of CNS signals; and lastly, some have a complex and contradictory effect.

Central nervous system *stimulants* produce arousal, alertness, even excitation; they inhibit fatigue and lethargy. Stimulants speed up signals passing through the CNS. Strong stimulants include cocaine, amphetamine, and Ritalin.

Caffeine is a weak stimulant—so weak that most of us do not think of it as a drug at all.

Depressants have the opposite effect: They inhibit, slow down, retard, or *depress* signals passing through the central nervous system. There are two basic types of CNS depressants. The first is the *analgesics*, which inhibit mainly one principle action of the CNS—the perception of pain. For the purposes of the observer of deviant behavior, the most important type of analgesic is the *narcotics*. This category includes the *opiates*—opium and its various derivatives: morphine, heroin, codeine. They are very *strong* and *highly addictive* analgesics. This category also includes the various synthetic and semisynthetic narcotics, called *opioids* (or "opium-like" drugs), such as Percodan, methadone, and meperidine (or Demerol), and oxycodone (including OxyContin). In addition to their painkilling property, all narcotics are also physically addicting, that is, they generate a physical dependency on regular, long-term use. There are also several weak, nonaddicting nonnarcotic drugs that have some of the narcotics' painkilling properties, but do not induce dependence, mental clouding, or euphoria. It is their euphoria-generating property that causes many people to use narcotics recreationally, that is, for the purpose of getting high. Nonnarcotic analgesics include aspirin, ibuprofen, Tylenol (acetaminophen), Talwin, and Darvon; they are rarely used recreationally. As might be expected, nonnarcotic analgesics are far less potent painkillers than the narcotics.

Unlike the narcotics, which have a depressive effect principally on one bodily function—the perception of pain—*general depressants*, while not effective painkillers, have a depressive effect on a *wide range* of body organs and functions. They tend to induce relaxation, inhibit anxiety, and, at higher doses, result in drowsiness and, eventually, sleep. The most well-known of the general depressants is alcohol, which is known to scientists as ethyl alcohol or ethanol. Other examples include sedatives (or sedative-hypnotics), such as barbiturates, methaqualone (once sold under brand names like Quāālude and Sopor), and GHB; and tranquilizers, such as Valium, Xanax, Librium, lorazepam, and Rohypnol ("roofies"). In sufficiently high doses, general

TABLE 8.1   A CLASSIFICATION OF PSYCHOACTIVE DRUGS, WITH EXAMPLES

SEDATIVE-HYPNOTICS/GENERAL DEPRESSANTS

alcohol (ethyl alcohol or ethanol)
barbiturates: Nembutal, Tuinal, Amytal, Seconal, phenobarbital, pentobarbital
benzodiazepines (Librium, Valium, Xanax, Halcion, Rohypnol, Ativan)
miscellaneous sedatives: meprobamate (Miltown, Equanil);
     methaqualone (Quāālude, Mandrax, Sopor); GHB (gamma-hydroxybutyrate)

ANTIDEPRESSANTS OR MOOD ELEVATORS

Prozac, Elavil, Zoloft, Sinequan, Tofranil, Paxil

ANTIPSYCHOTIC AGENTS

phenothiazines: Thorazine, Stelazine, Mellaril, Haldol

HALLUCINOGENS/PSYCHEDELICS

LSD ("acid"), mescaline ("mesc"), psilocybin (" 'shrooms")

NARCOTICS

opiates (opium and its derivatives): opium, morphine, heroin, codeine
opioids (synthetic narcotics): methadone, oxycodone (OxyContin), Darvon,
     Percodan, fentanyl, Dilaudid, Demerol

STIMULANTS

cocaine ("coke"), crack cocaine
amphetamine (Adderall, Benzedrine, Dexedrine, "speed")
methamphetamine (Methedrine, Desoxyn, "meth," "crank," "crystal," "ice")
Ritalin (methylphenidate)
caffeine

DISASSOCIATIVE ANESTHETICS

PCP (Sernyl, Sernylan, "angel dust")
ketamine ("K," "special K," "super K")

NICOTINE

DRUGS NOT EASILY CLASSIFIABLE IN A GENERAL CATEGORY

marijuana
MDMA (Ecstasy, "XTC," "E," "X")

Note: A number of these substances are classified as Schedule I drugs (those that are completely illegal according to federal law) and therefore are not legally available. Hence, their trade names, referred to here, are those that were used when they were sold as prescription drugs; they are not currently manufactured under these trade names. The first letter of trade or brand names is capitalized; the first letter of generics is not.

depressants induce mental clouding, drowsiness, and physical dependence; an overdose can produce unconsciousness, coma, and even death. Some users seek the woozy, cloudy, drowsy feeling that depressants or "downers" generate. Since such a psychic state is potentially dangerous, such drugs are controlled. Still, let's recognize that alcohol has many of the same effects as the other sedatives, and it is available to anyone over the age of 21.

Hallucinogens (also referred to as psychedelics) have effects on the CNS that cannot be reduced to a simple stimulation-depression continuum. These are the drugs that induce *profound sensory alterations*. They occupy their own unique and distinct category and include LSD, peyote and mescaline, and psilocybin or "magic mushrooms" (" 'shrooms"). The principal effect of the hallucinogens is not, as might be expected from their name, the inducement of hallucinations, but extreme psychoactivity, a loosening of the imagination and an intensification of emotional states. MDMA or "Ecstasy" is sometimes referred to as a hallucinogen, but it does not produce sensory alterations; a more accurate term to describe it would be "empathogen," that is, capable of inducing empathy, or an emotional identification with others. Most recent classifications include a drug called PCP or Sernyl, once referred to as "angel dust," as a hallucinogen. Once used as an animal tranquilizer, this drug has almost none of the properties associated with hallucinogens, such as dramatic sensory transformations. More sophisticated classification schemes see it as a *disassociative-anesthetic*. Ketamine ("special K") is a milder version of PCP.

Marijuana has, at different times, been classified as a depressant, a stimulant, and, as late as the 1970s, a hallucinogen. Most observers nowadays feel that it belongs in a category by itself.

THE EXTENT OF DRUG USE IN THE UNITED STATES

There are four fairly readily identifiable types or categories of drug use in the United States: (1) medical or *legal/instrumental* use, (2) *legal*

recreational use, (3) *illegal instrumental* use, and (4) *illegal recreational* use.

Medical Use

Medical use includes the use of drugs, called *prescription* drugs or *pharmaceuticals*, that are prescribed by physicians to patients and taken within the context of medical therapy, as well as the use of the weaker over-the-counter (or OTC) drugs purchased directly off the shelf by the general public, without the need for a prescription. Over three billion prescriptions are written for drugs in the United States each year, about half of which are new prescriptions and the other half are refills. Roughly one in seven prescription drugs is psychoactive; psychoactive drugs influence mood, emotion, and other mental processes. The majority act more or less entirely on the body rather than on the mind. In 2002, prescription drug sales represented a $192 billion-a-year business in the United States. OTC drugs, for the most part, are not significantly psychoactive, do not produce a strong dependency, and have a fairly low level of toxicity—that is, it is fairly difficult to overdose on them; they are hardly ever taken for recreational purposes. Examples include aspirin, Nō-Dōz, Sominex, Allerest, and Dexatrim. The annual retail sales of OTC drugs in the United States is roughly $20 billion.

The medical use of prescription and OTC drugs is not regarded as deviant by most Americans. These drugs can be abused or misused, of course. Unscrupulous physicians can overprescribe pharmaceutical drugs, particularly those that are psychoactive, to patients who seek their effects; such practices were extremely common in the 1960s and 1970s. Aspirin and acetaminophen (Tylenol) are responsible for hundreds of overdose deaths in the country each year (mainly either through children accidentally ingesting them, or through intentional suicides), and thousands more nonfatal overdoses. Still, the vast majority of prescription and OTC drug use is safe, conventional, ethical, legal, legitimate, and most decidedly nondeviant.

For the well-known psychoactive prescription drugs that were widely used on the street in the 1970s, the number of prescriptions written in the early years of the twenty-first century is significantly lower than that written in the 1970s. For instance, roughly *one-fifteenth* as many barbiturate prescriptions, and *one-seventh* as many amphetamine prescriptions are being written today as was true 20 to 25 years ago. (Dexedrine is an exception, since it is being prescribed in the absence of Benzedrine, which is no longer prescribed at all.) In 1985, methaqualone, a sedative, was discontinued altogether as a prescription drug. Because of the negative publicity that resulted from both medical misuse and overuse and street use, pressure was put on the medical establishment to reduce the practice of over-prescribing psychoactive pharmaceuticals. For instance, in the 1960s and 1970s, amphetamines were widely prescribed by physicians to combat obesity. (Many of their patients were adolescents, and most were only slightly overweight, if at all.) Today, because of such abuses and their attendant medical consequences, prescribing amphetamines for obesity has been brought to a virtual halt. Methaqualone (whose trade name in the United States was Quāālude), hugely prescribed in the 1970s and widely used on the street—once billed as an aphrodisiac, the "love drug"—is not legally permitted by prescription at all today. In short, overprescribing came to be defined as deviant behavior by the medical fraternity. As a consequence, the excesses of the 1960s and 1970s were brought under control by both formal and informal sanctions, including the arrest of physicians who continued to overprescribe. In contrast, the number of prescriptions for *non*psychoactive drugs is stable, even increasing a bit, because ours is an aging population, and as people grow older, their need for medication tends to increase.

Halcion and Prozac, two prescription drugs whose use, in contrast, *increased* between the late 1980s and early 1990s, offer an instructive morality tale to the student of deviance. The use of both Prozac, an antidepressant, and Halcion, an antianxiety agent, attracted accusations of untoward effects and a great deal of bad publicity, and were defined by the medical profession as deviant. As a result, their sales declined sharply.

Prozac is a mood elevator, that is, a drug designed to combat depression; introduced on the market in 1987 by Eli Lilly, it quickly became the nation's number-one-selling antidepressant, with nearly a million prescriptions written per month.

Between 1988, its first full year of commercial availability, and 1990, its sales increased by more than five times. In its earliest years of use, the drug seemed to be a promising treatment for depression (Cowley et al., 1990). As its popularity increased, however, anecdotal horror stories detailing the destructive behavior of Prozac patients—including self-mutilation, suicide, violence, and murder—began to mount. Some of these patients ("Prozac survivors") have sued Lilly for multimillion-dollar damages, and some who have murdered have claimed in court that "the drug made me do it" (the so-called "Prozac defense"). Lilly claimed that some untoward behavior is to be expected of a certain proportion of depressed patients, whether or not they take Prozac; in Lilly's clinical studies, patients taking the drug displayed fewer suicidal tendencies than those not taking it (Cowley et al., 1991). In spite of the negative publicity surrounding Prozac, some physicians who prescribed the drug, and many patients who took it, remained staunch supporters. Some observers have claimed that there is a Prozac "culture," whose members sing its praises at every opportunity (Kramer, 1993; Cowley, 1994). Still, by 2002, Prozac dropped off the list of the 200 most widely dispensed drugs in terms of total number of prescriptions written. Prozac has been replaced as the nation's most popular antidepressant by Zoloft, which is seventh in sales for all prescription drugs (31 million scripts written). Paxil, another antidepressant, at number two for antidepressants, is ninth overall—28 million scripts (www.pharmacytimes.com/article.cfm?ID=338).

In 1982, the Food and Drug Administration (FDA) approved the sale of the sedative-hypnotic Halcion in the United States by its manufacturer, Upjohn. In 1983, Halcion was marketed and, within a short period of time, it became the best-selling sedative on the market, with seven million prescriptions filled in the United States each year; in 1991, 8 percent of Upjohn's $2.5 billion in sales worldwide derived from Halcion. In the late 1980s and early 1990s, the then-president of the United States, George Bush, used it. However, soon after doctors began prescribing Halcion, they began noticing peculiar things happening to their patients. A Utah woman taking the drug shot her mother eight times and placed a birthday card in her dead mother's hand; she claimed the drug made her do it. Patients reported symptoms of paranoia, depression, nervousness, and an obsession with suicide. Termination of the use of the drug usually resulted in a cessation of the symptoms. One physician, Ian Oswald, working on behalf of patients who are suing the company, began reanalyzing the data Upjohn submitted to the FDA and claimed that some of the results of the studies were falsified. Upjohn's spokespersons admit that mistakes were made in some of these experiments, but they say that there was no pattern of falsification. The implication that Halcion was responsible for untoward reactions in depressive patients, Upjohn claims, is false and misleading, since many of them would have felt and done the same things without the drug (Kolata, 1992a, 1992b). Concludes one observer: Halcion is a drug that has been shown to cause "extreme and frightening side effects in a small number of people if taken in large quantities for extended periods of time" (Byron, 1992, p. 18). As a result of the unfavorable publicity about the drug and its effects, Halcion's sales went "into a tailspin. Physicians simply don't want to take the risk of prescribing the drug any more" (Byron, 1992, p. 18). By 1994, Halcion was not even on the list of the nation's 200 most often prescribed pharmaceutical drugs.

Legal Recreational Use

Legal recreational use is the legal use of psychoactive substances to achieve a certain mental or psychic state by the user. As we saw in Chapter 7, the most commonly used legal recreational drugs in the United States—caffeine excepted—are alcohol and the nicotine in tobacco products. In each case, a mood-altering substance is consumed in part to achieve a specific, desired mental or psychic state. Of course, not every instance of use of these drugs is purely for pleasure or euphoria. Still, alcohol, tobacco, and even caffeine are consumed for a desired psychic state. Coffee drinkers do not achieve a high with their morning cup, but they do use caffeine as a "pick-me-up" to achieve a mentally alert state, a slight "buzz" to begin the day. Thus, coffee drinking can be described as both

recreational and instrumental. Many—perhaps most—cigarette smokers are driven to smoke by a compulsive craving at least as much as by the pleasure achieved by inhaling a psychoactive drug; still, the two dimensions are far from mutually exclusive. If smokers do not achieve a true high, then at least they achieve a psychic state that is more pleasurable to them than abstinence. And drinkers, of course, consume alcohol for the effects it has on their mind.

According to the 2002 National Survey on Drug Use and Health, conducted in the general population, sponsored by the Substance Abuse and Mental Health Services Administration (SAMHSA), slightly over half (51 percent) of the sample, roughly 120 million Americans age 12 and older, said that they drank alcohol within the past month, and were therefore defined as "current" drinkers. Between a quarter and a fifth (22.9 percent, or 54 million people) age 12 and older had engaged in "binge" drinking—consuming five or more drinks on one occasion—in the past month. Three Americans in ten age 12 and older (30 percent), or 71.5 million persons, can be considered current users of cigarettes (SAMHSA, 2003, pp. 23ff.). These figures represent significant declines from those of the 1980s, which, in turn, were smaller than was true of the late 1970s. However, they represent a slight though significant upturn between the 1990s and today.

Thus, the extent of legal recreational drug use is immense (although for the population as a whole it is declining—albeit slowly—over time). With the exception of caffeine, the most popular legal recreational drug is alcohol, which is used by a majority of the adult American population. Even tobacco, the second most commonly consumed legal recreational drug (again, with the exception of caffeine products), is used by more individuals *than are all illegal recreational drugs combined*. In fact, of all drugs, tobacco, in the form of cigarettes, *is used most frequently*. Taking the number of cigarettes sold in the United States last year (more than half a trillion), dividing that figure by the number of current smokers (71 million), we arrive at an average of 15 cigarettes per smoker per day. In contrast, current drinkers consume one or two alcoholic beverages per day. (Most drink less than this, some drink a lot more.) In other words, smokers consume *ten times* the number of "doses" of their drug of choice than drinkers do theirs. Thus, while alcohol is the legal drug that is used *by the greatest number of people* (caffeine excepted, of course), nicotine is the drug that is used *most frequently*. Clearly, in the total picture of drug use, legal recreational use looms extremely large.

At the same time, the moderate use of the legal recreational drugs, alcohol and tobacco, by adults is not typically considered a form of deviant behavior in most quarters of American society. We looked at the use of alcohol and tobacco as deviant behavior in more detail in the previous chapter. The use of the legal drugs, as we saw, may be considered in a discussion on deviance for the following reasons.

First, the *excessive* and *inappropriate* use of alcohol—which overlaps heavily with the condition referred to as alcoholism—*is* regarded as deviance. Second, the use of alcohol *by minors* is against the law and is condemned in most social circles. Third, alcohol is often used *in conjunction with* a great deal of criminal and violent behavior, which is deviant. Fourth, the sale of alcohol was outlawed once in this country's history, during Prohibition (1920–1933); in addition, the use of alcohol is both deviant and criminal in some other countries (such as Iran and Saudi Arabia), even to this day. Fifth, both in the past and currently, efforts have been instituted to criminalize and *deviantize* the sale, possession, and use of tobacco cigarettes (Troyer and Markle, 1983); at the present time, these efforts are escalating. They tell us a great deal about the circumstances under which certain definitions of deviance are constructed and enforced. Sixth, there are more arrests (though not more imprisonments) on alcohol-related charges in the United States than on illegal drug-related charges. In 2002, according to the Federal Bureau of Investigation, arrests for drug abuse violations totaled 1.5 million. But there were also 1.4 million arrests for driving while under the influence of alcohol, over 650,000 for violations of the liquor laws, and over 570,000 for public intoxication. Whenever law enforcement swings into action, clearly, we have a case of deviance on our hands. In addition, as we saw in Chapter 7, there is substantial behavioral overlap between legal and illegal drug use; many of the same people consume both categories of substances. And lastly, more people are killed as a result of alcohol and tobacco consumption than through the use of illicit drugs. Although harm is not part of our definition of deviance, high levels of harm from legal drug use points to the fact that the reason why illicit drugs are banned cannot be based on harm alone.

Illegal Instrumental Use

Illegal instrumental use includes taking various drugs without benefit of prescription for some instrumental purpose, such as driving a truck nonstop for long distances, studying for exams through the night, calming feelings of anxiety, improving athletic performance, and so on. Individuals who purchase pharmaceutical drugs illegally, without a physician's prescription, do not think of themselves as "real" drug users. They do not seek a high or intoxication, but rather a goal that most conventional members of society approve. These users regard their behavior as only technically illegal and therefore not criminal in nature, and decidedly nondeviant. They do not make a sharp distinction between the use of legal over-the-counter drugs and the use of pharmaceuticals without a prescription; both are for the purpose of attaining a psychic or physical state that permits them to achieve a given socially approved end. In our society, however, using psychoactive pharmaceuticals without benefit of a physician's prescription happens to be illegal and, in most quarters, deviant as well.

Illegal Recreational Use

It is in the realm of illegal recreational use that we encounter our most harshly condemned instances of deviant drug use. The illegal drug trade is an enormous economic enterprise, variously estimated to represent a $65-billion-a-year business in the United States (Rhodes et al., 2001, p. 3). Other estimates vary somewhat from this one, but clearly a great deal of money is spent on illegal drugs in the United States—certainly tens of billions of dollars a year. And these huge sums represent a correspondingly huge demand for illicit drugs.

Roughly a third of the American population have used one or more illicit drugs at least once during their lifetimes. The Substance Abuse and Mental Health Services Administration's National Survey on Drug Use and Health cited earlier found that, in 2002, 8.3 percent, or 19.5 million people, had used an illicit drug within the past 30 days and can be regarded as "current" users. As we might expect, of all age categories, young adults age 18 to 25 were most likely to have used illegal drugs: for 2002, for use in the past month, a fifth (or 20.2 percent) of 18-to-25-year-olds did so at least once (SAMHSA, 2003, p. 14).

The most frequently used illegal drug in America is, as we might expect, marijuana; in 2002, 6.2 percent of the population age 12 and older used marijuana—a figure six times as high as for cocaine and 12 times as great as for hallucinogens (p. 12). In fact, 75 percent of all consumers of illicit drugs use marijuana and 55 percent use *only* marijuana (SAMHSA, 2003, p. 11). For cocaine, the next-most-popular illicit drug, 0.9 percent of all adult Americans (2.0 million people) said that they used it in the past 30 days. About 2.5 percent of Americans had used one or more of the psychotherapeutics—stimulants, analgesics, tranquilizers, and sedatives—nonmedically in the past month. According to this survey, crack cocaine, a highly publicized drug, was used, ever, by only 0.2 percent of Americans during the past 30 days—just over half a million people. Heroin, like crack a well-known and highly publicized illegal drug, was used by only 0.1 percent, or 166,000 people (SAMHSA, 2003, p. 11). However, the National Survey on Drug Use and Health is almost certainly *least* useful for estimating the drug consumption of heavy users of crack and heroin, because of the problem of locating them. Hence, these figures for crack and heroin are probably substantial underestimates. (Table 8.2 spells out these incidence figures in detail.)

A study of drug use among high school seniors, college students, and young adults not in high school or college (the "Monitoring the Future" survey) found much the same picture with respect to illegal drug use, except that their level of use was slightly higher than is true for the population as a whole (Johnston, O'Malley, and Bachman, 2003a). In 2002, a quarter of high school seniors (25 percent) had used one or more

illicit drugs at least once in the past 30 days, and a fifth of tenth-graders (21 percent) and a tenth of eighth-graders had done so (10 percent). For students in all grades, as with the population as a whole, marijuana was *by far* the most popular illicit drug.

Whatever the drug, as a source of illegal and deviant behavior, illicit drug use is formidable and impressive. But three qualifications are in order at this point: *One*, the use of nearly all illegal drugs declined significantly after the late 1970s. *Two*, illegal drug use is not nearly as high as many sensational media stories claim. *Three*, illicit drug use is considerably less widespread than the use of alcohol and tobacco.

Both legal and illegal drugs vary considerably in user loyalty or continued use. Users are much more likely to "stick with" or be "loyal to" certain drugs, while with other drugs, users are much more likely to take them episodically or infrequently, or to abandon them after a brief period of experimentation.

As a general rule, *legal* drugs tend to be used much more on a continued basis, while *illegal* drugs tend to be used more infrequently, and are more likely to be given up after a period of time (Sandwijk, Cohen, and Musterd, 1991, pp. 20–21, 25; Goode, 2005). Of all drugs, legal or illegal, *alcohol* attracts the greatest user loyalty: Just over six persons in 10 (61 percent) who said that they ever drank, even once, did so within the past month. For cigarettes, just over a third (or 38 percent) of all at least one-time smokers are still smoking. For illegal drugs, marijuana tends to be "stuck with" the longest—15 percent of all Americans who have tried it remain users. In other words, the more legal the drug, the more "loyal" users are to it, the more they "stick with" it, the more likely they are to continue using it over time, and the less likely they are to give up its use. Turning the equation around, the more illegal or illicit the drug, the less likely it is that one-time users will stick with it or continue to use it. In fact, this generalization works even with illicit drugs. Marijuana, the "least illicit" of the illicit drugs is the one that users tend to be most "loyal" to, the one that one-time users are most likely to continue using. For cocaine and methamphetamine, the figure is 6 percent (SAMHSA, 2003, p. 200).

TABLE 8.2   ILLICIT DRUG USE, LIFETIME, PAST YEAR, AND PAST 30 DAYS, AGE 12 AND OLDER, 2002 (%)

	TIME PERIOD		
DRUG	LIFETIME	PAST YEAR	PAST MONTH
Any Illicit Drug	46.0	14.9	8.3
Marijuana	40.4	11.0	6.2
Cocaine	14.4	2.5	0.9
Crack	3.6	0.7	0.2
Hallucinogens	14.6	2.0	0.5
LSD	10.4	0.4	0.0
PCP	3.2	0.1	0.0
Ecstasy	4.3	1.3	0.3
Psychotherapeutics	19.8	6.2	2.6
Analgesics	12.6	4.7	1.9
Tranquilizers	8.2	2.1	0.8
Stimulants	9.0	1.4	0.5
Methamphetamine	5.3	0.7	0.3
Sedatives	4.2	0.4	0.2
Any Tobacco	73.1	36.0	30.4
Cigarettes	69.1	30.3	26.0
Alcohol	83.1	66.1	51.0

Note: "Psychotherapeutics" includes the nonmedical use of the drugs indicated in the table. Does not include medical use, or use of over-the-counter drugs. The category "hallucinogens" includes LSD (a true hallucinogen), PCP (a disassociative-anesthetic), and Ecstasy (an empathogen); however, the incidence of LSD, PCP, and Ecstasy is tabulated separately.

Source: Substance Abuse and Mental Health Services Administration, 2003, p. 200.

MARIJUANA'S EFFECTS: HARMFUL OR INNOCUOUS?

With marijuana, as with every other drug, we must juggle the positivistic and the constructionist approaches. The positivistic approach tells us things such as how many people use the drug, why, and with what effects. The constructionist approach tells us about marijuana's public image, its place in the media, public attitudes about the drug's users—more specifically whether they are regarded as deviants or not—the drug's legal status, and attitudes about its legal status.

One of the interesting things about the use of drugs whose use is regarded as deviant is that, in different periods of history, different claims are made as to their harmful effects. In the 1930s, it was the acute or immediate, short-term effects

that attracted attention: Newspaper and magazine stories alleged that marijuana caused users to go crazy, engage in promiscuous sex, and commit violent acts. Today, these claims are hardly ever made, even by the strongest anti-marijuana propagandists. It is not the *acute* or short-term effects of marijuana that now attract the most critics, but the *chronic* or long-term effects. Today it is feared that the long-term use of marijuana will prove to be medically damaging. Even so, these effects remain controversial. Are the chronic effects of marijuana harmful to the user?

One should keep in mind the fact that no drug is *completely* safe. There is no chemical substance, no drug, no activity known to humankind, that is completely without harm to anyone who has ever used or engaged in it. *Some* damage can be found with the ingestion of every drug on earth—that is, in some people, at some time. Aspirin, one of the safest drugs known, causes hundreds of deaths a year in the United States. So the question for a given drug should *not* be: Can *some* damage be found if we look hard enough? After all, one can die of an "overdose" of water; it's called drowning—a source of thousands of deaths in the United States each year. Does that mean that water is a dangerous and damaging substance? Of course not. Thus, with the use of any drug, the question should be: What is the *likelihood* of damage—both acute and chronic—in a wide range of situations and instances of use? Moreover, when assessing studies that claim to show damage caused by one drug or another, we would want to have an ingredient that is essential to all scientific research: *replication*. That is, studies are often conducted whose findings are not duplicated by any later researchers; to a scientist, a study that lacks replication lacks confirmation and thus, lacks validity. If other scientists can't come up with the same findings using the same methods, scientists reason, perhaps they aren't valid; perhaps the first study was flawed, faulty, invalid. Over the years, numerous propagandists have insisted that marijuana is a dangerous drug and that its legal status is justified. True or false?

What is called marijuana is made up of the flowering tops and leaves of the cannabis plant. The psychoactive ingredient in marijuana is the chemical THC—tetrahydrocannabinol. Cannabis has been used by humans both as medicine and for the purpose of intoxication in hundreds of cultures around the world for thousands of years. Many thousands of studies have been conducted on the effects of the drug. Hence, scientists know a thing or two about what the drug does to the human mind and body.

To assess the conclusions of studies on the dangers of marijuana use, however, we'd need to know the answer to a number of crucial questions. Was the study conducted on humans or animals? What were the doses administered? Were they realistic, that is, similar to the doses that are taken in real life? Or were they so high that humans never ingest the drug at those levels? What was the potency of the marijuana that was administered? Is the drug that is administered pure THC (the active ingredient in marijuana) or is it administered in the form of marijuana cigarettes of variable potency? Again, do these experiments replicate real-life conditions or do they administer the drug at a level that is so high as to test a potential rather than a reality? And what sorts of comparisons were made in these studies? Were the effects of marijuana compared with other substances, such as tobacco and alcohol? Or were the dangers of marijuana compared with zero effects, that is, not taking a drug of any kind? When advocates of the "marijuana is a dangerous drug" position make their points, these considerations are rarely raised.

To emphasize the point: In the sense that marijuana has the potential to cause damage to the human organism at some levels of use over a long enough period of time, yes, marijuana is a dangerous drug. But as compared with what? Sky-diving? Mountain climbing? Stock car racing? Or even compared with what drugs? Heroin? Cocaine? Tobacco? Alcohol? These are not easy questions. They demand complex, nuanced answers, not pat, propagandistic formulas.

What does the available research on the effects of marijuana's dangers tell us?

One thing on which all researchers agree is that marijuana is perhaps the *least toxic* drug known to humanity. It is practically impossible to die of a drug "overdose" on cannabis. This is because the drug does not link up with the brain centers that control breathing and heartbeat. One researcher estimated that it would require consuming 900 high-strength marijuana cigarettes for 15 consecutive hours to reach a lethal dose (Earleywine, 2002, p. 144). In effect, the drug "is incapable of creating an overdose" (p. 143). Summarizing thousands of studies on the effects of marijuana on medical and health problems ranging from brain to lung damage, this researcher concluded:

> These results confirm that marijuana is neither completely harmless nor tragically toxic. Compared to other drugs that are currently legal, its impact on health is minimal. People with psychotic disorders should probably avoid cannabis. Chronic daily use obviously creates potential problems for the quick performance of complex tasks. Smoking every day undoubtedly taxes the lungs. Men attempting to impregnate women may have more luck if they abstain from cannabis. Pregnant women should probably avoid all drugs. Nevertheless, occasional use by

healthy adults does not appear to create dramatic mental or physical illness. Cannabis seems to have fewer health effects than legal drugs, like alcohol, caffeine, or tobacco, and kills far fewer people. (Earleywine, 2002, pp. 164–165)

• School performance? Some critics of the drug charge that it causes what's called the "amotivational syndrome"—the loss of desire to achieve, to accomplish, to perform, to seek goals most of us value, such as doing well in school and on the job (Mann, 1985; Jones and Lovinger, 1985). It is true that high school students who use marijuana do less well—as measured by grades—than those who do not use marijuana, and the earlier use begins, and the more that is used, the greater the disparity between users and nonusers (Kandel and Davies, 1996). But when all the other factors are taken into account—patterns of rebellion, overall patterns of deviance, the use of other drugs in addition to marijuana—the independent contribution of marijuana seems to be minimal or nil. Youngsters who use marijuana tend to have been academically unmotivated even before they began use (Donovan, 1996).

• Intellectual ability? Marijuana influences the workings of the mind; it is a *psychoactive* drug. One of its many acute effects is an impairment of intellectual processes, including memory. Under the influence, users experience a deterioration in short-term memory—the ability to learn new information and perform cognitive tasks. However, the drug's impact on chronic or long-term memory and other cognitive functions is less clear. It is possible that long-term exposure to marijuana decreases the capacity to perform "complicated tasks that require speedy responses" (Earleywine, 2002, p. 95). These deficits imply "some alteration in brain function" (p. 95).

• Highway fatalities? It is true that marijuana use has a detrimental effect on motor coordination; under the influence, people tend to perform less well at tasks such as driving (Barnett, Licko, and Thompson, 1985). It makes sense, since THC attaches itself to areas of the brain that control coordination. But most users say they compensate for the effects of the drug and force themselves to drive more slowly and carefully. It is true that among young drivers involved in a fatal accident, a significantly higher than average number had THC in their bloodstreams (Williams, Peat, and Crouch, 1985). But the majority also had alcohol in their systems. In fact, several studies indicate, *marijuana-only* drivers have a lower than average likelihood of having an automobile accident that leads to injury or death (Williams, Peat, and Crouch, 1985; Terhune, Ippolito, and Crouch, 1992; Drummer, 1994).

• Crime, aggression, and violence? While this accusation was common in the 1930s, today it has all but disappeared in criticisms of marijuana. It has been known for some time that, unlike alcohol, cocaine, and amphetamine, marijuana does not activate the centers of the brain that control aggression. In the early 1970s, I was asked by the National Commission on Marihuana and Drug Abuse to analyze the data from an interview study on marijuana use and crime (Goode, 1972), and I found that, though the two were correlated, the relationship disappeared when the use of other drugs was controlled. Marijuana users were more likely to use drugs other than marijuana than nonusers were—hence, the correlation between marijuana use and crime. The use of marijuana itself had no impact on crime whatsoever.

• Is marijuana a "gateway" drug? Does the use of cannabis "lead to" the use of more dangerous drugs? The *correlation* is clear: The use of marijuana is statistically correlated with the use of other drugs, including cocaine, methamphetamine, and heroin. But, as we've already found out, so is the use of tobacco and alcohol. While the *vast majority* of users of cocaine, methamphetamine, and heroin once used marijuana, only an extremely *tiny* minority of marijuana users "go on" to the use of these more dangerous drugs. Most researchers believe that the correlation that does exist is not caused by the effects of marijuana as such but by the lifestyle of the users who do progress and the friendships they make in using marijuana. The statistical associations that are observed, say Morral et al., are a product not of marijuana use per se but of the age at which users take marijuana versus harder drugs and differences among individuals with respect to their willingness to alter their consciousness, that is, to take any drug. "The people who are predisposed to use drugs and have the opportunity to use drugs are more likely than others to use both marijuana and harder drugs," Morral says. "Marijuana typically comes first because it is more available. Once we incorporated these facts into our mathematical model of adolescent drug use, we could explain all of the drug use associations that have been cited as evidence of marijuana's gateway effect" (Morral, McCaffrey, and Paddock, 2002). Morral and his team believe that the results of their study demonstrate that reducing marijuana consumption will have no impact whatsoever on reducing hard drug use, since persons who use the harder drugs are *already* predisposed to do so—whether or not they use marijuana. In short, argue Morral et al., the "gateway" hypothesis is a myth. In September 2002, after surveying the available literature, the Canadian Senate issued a report on marijuana, *Cannabis: Our Position for a Canadian Public Policy.* On the issue of the "gateway" hypothesis, the report concludes: "We feel that the available data show that it is *not cannabis itself that leads to other drug use* but the combination of the following factors: Factors related to personal and family history that predispose to early entry on the trajectory of use of psychoactive substances starting with alcohol; early introduction to cannabis, earlier than the average for experimenters, and more rapid progress towards a trajectory of regular use; frequenting of a marginal or deviant environment; availability of various substances from the same dealers" (p. 126). The Canadian Senate Special Committee on Illegal Drugs rejected the "gateway" theory that the use of marijuana per se "leads to" or causes the use of harder drugs.

In short, most of the claims for most of the damaging, even ravaging chronic effects of marijuana have not been supported by the scientific literature. Yes, the drug is psychoactive and thus, takes the mind away from practical matters such as studying, learning, and performing motor tasks. Most users take the drug recreationally, on a weekend or once-in-a-while basis, so this isn't a serious problem for the modal or typical marijuana consumer. And yes, on average, users do perform less well in school and on the job than nonusers, but this is related to their lifestyle and personality—which causes them to use in the first place—rather than to the direct effects of the drug. Yes, lung functioning is reduced by the inhalation of the drug's combusted, hot, potentially harmful smoke—as is true with smoking tobacco cigarettes. But most researchers do not find that the majority of the claims of medical damages once attributed to marijuana use are

supported by strong, incontrovertible scientific evidence. The sensitive observer must be struck more by the enterprise of producing anti-marijuana claims than by the drug's damaging medical effects. Certain propagandists, some of them extremely sophisticated and well-informed, have made something of a career of campaigning against this relatively nontoxic drug (Nahas, 1973; Mann, 1985; Jones and Lovinger, 1985). And clearly their message resonates with what much of the public and many officials wish to hear. Here we see the process of the social construction of marijuana's deviant image in action.

MARIJUANA USE IN THE UNITED STATES, 1960–2002

We already know that behavior, beliefs, and conditions that are widespread are not necessarily unconventional, and behavior, beliefs, and conditions that are rare are not necessarily deviant. In other words, infrequency of occurrence is not a *defining characteristic* of deviance. Still, knowing how rare or widespread something is is an interesting and relevant piece of information in any investigation of deviance.

At the beginning of the 1960s, very, very few Americans used illegal drugs. Even the use of marijuana, by far the most widely consumed illicit substance, was at an extremely low level. In 1960, less than 1 percent of youths age 12 to 17, and less than 5 percent of young adults age 18 to 25, had even tried marijuana. By 1967, these figures had nearly quadrupled, to over 5 percent for youths and over 15 percent to young adults (Miller and Cisin, 1980, pp. 13–16). The percent trying and using marijuana increased throughout the decade from the late 1960s to the late 1970s, and reached its peak roughly in 1979, when nearly a third of youths age 12 to 17 (31 percent) and two-thirds of young adults age 18 to 25 (68 percent) had tried marijuana. The use of marijuana declined during the 1980s but then rose again after the early 1990s. In 2002, in the most recent National Survey on Drug Use and Health available at this writing, only 21 percent of 12-to-17-year-olds and 54 percent of 18-to-25-year-olds said that they had ever *tried* marijuana (SAMHSA, 2003, p. 3). For the

TABLE 8.3   MARIJUANA USE, HIGH SCHOOL SENIORS AND COLLEGE STUDENTS, 1980–2002 (%)

	1980			1990			2002		
	EVER	YEAR	MONTH	EVER	YEAR	MONTH	EVER	YEAR	MONTH
High School Seniors	60	49	34	41	27	14	48	36	22
College Students	65	51	34	49	29	14	50	37	22

Source: Johnston, O'Malley, and Bachman, 2003a, pp. 40–48; 2003b, pp. 32, 39.

population as a whole, this figure was four out of ten.

This up-and-down pattern was revealed by surveys conducted by the Monitoring the Future study. (Table 8.3 summarizes these findings.) In 1980 (the first year that this survey interviewed college students), a solid majority of high school seniors (60 percent) and college students (65 percent) had at least tried marijuana, roughly half had used the drug within the past year (49 and 51 percent, respectively), and a third had used it in the past month. But in the decade that followed, the percentages who had used marijuana for each of the three periods asked about had declined significantly, to 41, 27, and 14 percent for high school seniors and 49, 29, and 14 percent for college students. During the 1980s, it seemed as if the use of marijuana was diminishing; many commentators argued that marijuana specifically, and illegal drug use generally, would decline to the point at which they would cease to be a problem in the United States.

But after the early 1990s, for both high school seniors and college students, the percent who used marijuana increased to the point that, in 2001 and 2002, roughly half had used the drug once or more, well over a third had used it during the past year, and roughly a fifth had used it in the past 30 days (Johnston, O'Malley, and Bachman, 2002b, pp. 217–219; 2003a, pp. 40–48). Clearly, then, among high school seniors and college students, during the decade of the 1990s, the use of marijuana had become more widespread, more common. (In 1991, the Monitoring the Future study began surveying eighth- and tenth-graders, and exactly the same increases prevailed in these younger age brackets.) While the prevalence of marijuana use today does not reach late 1970s to

early 1980s levels, it is significantly higher than it was in the early 1990s and much, much higher than it was in the late 1960s. Marijuana use would have to decline drastically to reach the vastly lower figures that prevailed in the 1960s. This is extremely unlikely to take place within the first decade or two of the twenty-first century. The fact is, in spite of the declines from its peak in 1979, among the young, a sizeable volume of marijuana use is *deeply* entrenched in American society.

MARIJUANA USE AS DEVIANCE AND CRIME

In the United States, the use and the criminal status of marijuana have had a remarkable and extremely complicated history. In the 1920s, very few Americans had even heard of marijuana or even knew anyone who used it and, consequently, very few thought of it as deviant. Until well into this century, the few who did know of the drug thought of it as a kind of medicinal herb. George Washington grew marijuana plants on his plantation, probably for this purpose. During the decade of the 1930s, however, marijuana became the subject of hundreds of sensationalist newspaper and magazine articles. The drug was dubbed the "killer weed," the "weed of madness," a "sex-crazing drug menace," the "burning weed of hell," a "gloomy monster of destruction." Journalists and propagandists gave almost unlimited reign to the lurid side of their imaginations on the marijuana question. Every conceivable evil was concocted concerning the effects of this drug, the principal ones being, as I said, insanity, sexual promiscuity, and violence. A popular film distributed in the 1930s, *Reefer Madness*, illustrates this "marijuana causes you to go crazy, become promiscuous, and want to kill people" theme. In the past few years, this movie has been shown a number of times to pro-marijuana audiences, who find it so ludicrous as to be hilarious.

By 1937, partly as a result of the hysterical publicity surrounding the use of marijuana, laws criminalizing its possession and sale were passed in every state and at the federal level as well. Several observers argue that racism against Mexican-Americans was one of the principal reasons for the white majority's belief in the drug's evil effects, as well as for the swiftness with which these laws were passed (Musto, 1987, pp. 219, 245). The majority of states that passed the earliest anti-marijuana laws were Western states with the largest concentration of Mexican-American populations. At times, an activity can be condemned, even criminalized, less as a result of a sober assessment of its objective impact than because of the majority feeling about the group that is thought to practice it.

Marijuana remained completely illegal and deviant throughout the remainder of the 1930s, and during the 1940s and 1950s. During the course of the 1960s, as we saw, the popularity of this drug increased dramatically. Along with this increase in use came the widespread awareness that it was not simply the poor or members of minority groups but also the sons and daughters of affluent, influential, middle-class folk who used it. Marijuana acquired a mantle of, if not respectability or conventionality, then at least not complete deviance either. Attitudes began to soften, and in the 1970s, 11 states comprising one-third of the U.S. population decriminalized the possession of small quantities of marijuana. Then, beginning roughly with the election of Ronald Reagan as president in 1980, the tolerant sentiment toward marijuana that had been growing during the 1960s and 1970s dissipated, and a new, more condemnatory mood set in. For a time, no states decriminalized marijuana possession after 1980 and, in fact, in popular referenda held in 1989 and 1990, two—Oregon and Alaska—*re*criminalized the possession of marijuana. Increasingly, the public saw the drug as dangerous, and a decreasing proportion of Americans, as we saw, actually used it. The tide had been

reversed: Marijuana, its possession, use, and sale, had become deviant once again. For certain activities, deviance and crime display something of a cyclical pattern.

One measure or indicator of the growing deviant status of marijuana use is the growing percentage of high school students who say that marijuana use should be illegal, that the regular use of marijuana is harmful, and that they disapprove of regular marijuana use. As with use, the late 1970s represented an era when tolerance and acceptance of marijuana were at their peak. After 1978, a growing percentage of Americans said that the drug's use should be against the law, that the use of the drug is harmful, and that they disapproved of its use. In 1978, the Monitoring the Future survey showed that only a quarter (25 percent) believed that adults should be arrested for smoking marijuana in private; only a third (35 percent) believed that people who smoked marijuana "regularly" risked harming themselves; and well under half (44 percent) disapproved of the occasional use of marijuana.

What happened roughly after the late 1970s and throughout the 1980s was truly remarkable. Tolerance of marijuana use among high school seniors evaporated and a far more condemnatory attitude replaced it. By 1990, their belief that private marijuana use among adults should be illegal more than doubled, to 56 percent; the belief that one risks harming oneself by smoking marijuana regularly, again, more than doubled, to 78 percent; and the percent saying that they disapproved of the occasional use of marijuana nearly doubled, to 81 percent (Johnston, O'Malley, and Bachman, 2002a, pp. 297–304). In short, marijuana use came to be seen as *more deviant* over the course of the 1980–1990 period. In the sense of supporting the arrest and imprisonment of users, believing that regular use is medically dangerous, and disapproving of regular use, American's high school seniors moved *away from* seeing marijuana use as conventional, acceptable, safe, and ordinary *to* seeing it as unconventional, unacceptable, dangerous, and out of the ordinary—in short, as deviant.

As with use itself, after the early 1990s, a significant reversal in attitudes toward marijuana occurred. The 1990s and the early years of the new century witnessed a growing tolerance and

TABLE 8.4 ATTITUDES TOWARD MARIJUANA, HIGH SCHOOL SENIORS, 1978–2001/2002 (%)

	1978	*1990*	*2001/2002*
Illegal	25	56	39
Harmful	35	78	53
Disapprove	44	81	63

Note: Results of "Illegal" question not tabulated for 2002; 2001 figure is presented here. All others are 2002 data.

"Illegal": Do you think that people (who are 18 or older) should be prohibited by law from smoking marijuana in private? (percent agreeing)

"Harmful": How much do you think people risk harming themselves if they smoke marijuana regularly? (percent agreeing)

"Disapprove": Do you disapprove of people (18 or older) who smoke marijuana occasionally? (percent agreeing)

Source: Johnston, O'Malley, and Bachman, 2002a, p. 297; 2003a, pp. 49ff.

acceptance of the drug. Between 1990 and 2001, the proportion of high school students saying that smoking marijuana in private should be illegal declined from 56 to 39 percent; between 1990 and 2002, those saying that people who smoked marijuana regularly risked harming themselves declined from 78 to 53 percent; and those who disapproved of people who smoke marijuana occasionally declined from 81 to 63 percent (see Table 8.4). Acceptance and tolerance of marijuana at the turn of the twenty-first century was not as great as it was during the late 1970s to the early 1980s, but clearly, it is significantly—and strikingly—greater than it was just a bit more than a decade ago. We can assume that this pattern is not confined to high school seniors because, after 1980, the same questions were posed to young adults and precisely the same results were obtained (Johnston, O'Malley, and Bachman, 2003a, pp. 50–55; 2002a, pp. 297–304). In short, the deviant status of marijuana use reached an all-time low in the late 1970s, grew throughout the 1980s, then retreated again during the 1990s and into the first few years of the twenty-first century. One indication: The decriminalization movement is back on track, energized by the issue of medical marijuana. Today, a dozen states permit small-quantity marijuana possession without arrest. The decline in the deviant status of marijuana consumption among teenagers and young adults will probably continue throughout the first decade or two of the new century. After that, it's anybody's guess.

Among adults, the polls indicate complicated attitudes toward marijuana legalization. During

October 2002, CNN and *Time* magazine conducted a poll that indicated qualified attitudes both for and against legalization (see Table 8.5). The straight question, "Do you favor or oppose the legalization of marijuana?" yielded a 34 percent favorable and 59 percent opposed response. When asked about the legalization "of small amounts," the opposed response dropped to a bare majority, 51 percent. But when respondents were asked if people should be jailed for the possession of small amounts or pay a small fine "but without serving any jail time," only 19 percent favored jail time, while 72 percent favored a fine without jail time. And 80 percent of the respondents in this poll favored legal marijuana for medical purposes (http://www.norml.org/index.cfm?Group_ID+555 0). Pretty much the same findings were obtained by 20 other surveys conducted after 2000. Hence, today, the possession of marijuana, although not quite legal, isn't entirely deviant, either. Again, though illegality is not a defining criterion of deviance, when a growing and substantial proportion of the population favors the decriminalization of a previously illegal act, clearly, that act is losing its deviant status.

Here is a nutshell summary of the deviant and criminal status of marijuana use in the United States during the course of the twentieth century. During the 1920s, marijuana use was practically unknown to most Americans. During the 1930s, it became publicized, illegal, and deviant. During the 1940s and 1950s, it remained illegal and deviant, but was not widely mentioned in the media. During the 1960s and 1970s, it grew dramatically and its

TABLE 8.5   ATTITUDES TOWARD MARIJUANA LEGALIZATION (%)

"Do you favor or oppose the legalization of marijuana?"

	1983	1986	2002
Favor	24	18	34
Oppose	73	78	59
Not sure	4	4	7

"Do you favor or oppose the legalization of marijuana? What about in small amounts, for example, three ounces or less? Do you favor or oppose the legalization of marijuana in small amounts?"

	2002
Favor	34
Favor, but only in small amounts	6
Oppose	51
Not sure	9

"Assuming marijuana is not legalized, do you think people arrested for possession of small amounts of marijuana should be put in jail, or just have to pay a fine but without serving any jail time?"

	2002
Put in jail	19
Fine without jail time	72
Both*	2
Neither*	4
Not sure	3

*Volunteered response

"Do you think adults should be allowed to legally use marijuana for medical purposes if their doctor prescribes it or do you think that marijuana should remain illegal even for medical purposes?"

	2002
Yes, should be allowed to use marijuana medically	80
No, marijuana should remain illegal, even for medical purposes	17
Not sure	3

Source: Data from CNN/*Time* magazine poll conducted October 23–24, 2002; found at http://www.norml.org/index.cfm?Group_ID=5550

deviant status diminished. During the 1970s, its illegal status was terminated in some states and it became more widely tolerated and accepted. During the 1980s it declined dramatically, its deviant status grew, and, in two jurisdictions, its illegal status was reinstated. Finally, during the 1990s (and, predictably, during the early years of the twenty-first century), marijuana use as well as tolerance became more widespread, although falling far short of the watershed years of the late 1970s. And, though marijuana possession and sale remain a criminal offense, the public voted to approve of the use of the drug for medical purposes in more than a dozen states. (But even in these states, medical marijuana is still illegal according to *federal* law.) These shifts demonstrate that the deviant and criminal status of an activity is a dynamic, labile affair, one that is usually accompanied by changes in the social, political, and economic landscape. And just as activities can become *more* deviant and *more* criminal over time, likewise, they can become *less* so. Historically, we are witnessing fluctuations in the deviant and criminal status of marijuana use, possession, and sale. The most substantial change was the huge, unprecedented increase in the use of marijuana, and a corresponding decline in its deviant status, throughout the 1960s and 1970s. The decline in its use, and the increase in condemning it that took place throughout the 1980s, did not come close to offsetting the earlier changes. During the 1990s and the early 2000s, again, we see a shift in the wind, a shift that is likely to continue in the early years of the new millennium.

HALLUCINOGENIC DRUGS

Hallucinogenic drugs are substances that produce severe "dislocations of consciousness" (Lingeman, 1974, pp. 91–92), that act on the nervous system to produce significant perceptual changes (O'Brien and Cohen, 1984, p. 114). While all psychoactive drugs, by definition, influence the workings of the mind, hallucinogens are specifically, powerfully, and *exquisitely* psychoactive in their effects. They are the exemplary or *preeminent* example of a category of psychoactive drugs.

There are many hallucinogenic drugs, but most are not widely used. In the United States, nearly all hallucinogenic drug use is with LSD. Psilocybin mushrooms (or " 'shrooms"), and, among devotees of the Native American Church, the peyote cactus (which contains mescaline), are also used in some social circles. As I said above, Ecstasy (or MDMA) is commonly referred to as a hallucinogen, but it produces almost none of the profound perceptual changes caused by LSD and the other psychedelics. Some experts prefer the term *empathogen* to categorize Ecstasy—that is, it stimulates the capacity to empathize or identify with others. In addition, some observers classify PCP (or Sernyl), once referred to as "angel dust," as a hallucinogen. However, as with the Ecstasy-type drugs, PCP or Sernyl causes none of the florid, flamboyant, or extravagant psychic effects

that the hallucinogens produce. Respecting both effects and use patterns, then, when I refer to hallucinogens, I will be referring *mainly* to LSD. In the 1960s, hallucinogens were commonly referred to as "psychedelics," a term that implied that the mind is "made manifest"—or works better than ordinarily—under the influence. Today, the term "psychedelic" is used less frequently among drug experts than "hallucinogen."

It is in the mental, psychic, and "subjective" realm that the effects of LSD and the other hallucinogens have their most profound, dramatic, and interesting effects. Experiences take on an exaggerated emotional significance under the influence. Moreover, huge, emotional mood swings tend to dominate an "acid" trip. On the other hand, in spite of their name, hallucinogens typically do not generate full-blown hallucinations, that is, cause users to see things in the concrete world they know "aren't really there." More often they will have experiences or visions they know are a product of the drug, that is, that are in their minds rather than a reality that is located "out there" in the material world. (These visions are sometimes referred to as "virtual" hallucinations.) Many users will experience *synesthesia*, or the translation of one sense into another—that is, "hearing" color and "seeing" sounds. Many LSD users, under the influence, experience the world as in flux— fluid, dynamic, wobbling, flowing. The effects of LSD are experienced as *vastly* more incapacitating than those of marijuana (depending on the dose, of course); many users imagine that they can cope (drive a car, converse, interact with others, especially parents and the police) on marijuana, whereas very few will say that they can do so at the peak of the LSD trip. In spite of the sensationalistic media reports, very, very few users of hallucinogens experience a psychotic outbreak sufficiently serious as to require hospitalization. Such reports reached their peak in the 1960s (when use was actually quite low) and declined sharply after that.

Psychedelic drugs have been used for thousands of years: psilocybin, or the so-called "magic" mushrooms, by Indians in Mexico and Central America; the peyote cactus by the Indians of northern Mexico; the Amanita (or "fly agaric") mushroom among the indigenous Siberian population;

the mandrake root among pre-Christian Europeans, to name only a few (Schultes and Hofmann, 1979). In 1938, a Swiss chemist named Albert Hofmann discovered the chemical that was later to be called LSD. Hofmann did not experiment with it until 1943, when he ingested a minuscule quality of the substance himself. He experienced an extraordinary and intense "play of colors," a sense of timelessness, depersonalization, a loss of control and fears of "going crazy." The early researchers on LSD thought the drug might be the key to unlock the secrets of mental illness, especially schizophrenia. Later they found that the differences outweighed the similarities, and this line of research was abandoned. In the 1950s, the English writer Aldous Huxley, author of the classic novel *Brave New World*, took mescaline (the psychoactive ingredient in the peyote cactus) and wrote about his experiences in a slim, poetic volume, *The Doors of Perception*. Huxley drew the parallel with insanity, but he added a new dimension not previously discussed. Psychedelic drugs, he claimed, could bring about a view of reality that washes away the encrustation of years of rigid socialization and programming. These drugs, Huxley argued, enable us to see reality without culture's blinders—reality "as it really is." Taking psychedelic drugs could bring about a kind of transcendence, much like religious insight.

Huxley's book was read by Timothy Leary, holder of a PhD in psychology and lecturer at Harvard University. Leary took a dose of psilocybin and had a "visionary voyage." Soon after, he began a series of experiments that entailed administering the drug to convicts, theology students, and undergraduates; he claimed the drug "changed their lives for the better." Authorities at Harvard felt the experiments were casually administered, lacked sufficient safeguards, and were aimed mainly at proselytizing. Leary brushed off such concerns as so much "hysteria" that was hampering his research. In the spring of 1963, Leary was fired from his job, an event that touched off national headlines. In the decade prior to Leary's firing, a total of fewer than a dozen articles on LSD had been published in the national magazines indexed by *The Readers' Guide to Periodical Literature* (excluding *Science*, which is not really a popular magazine). These articles exploded after the Leary incident;

publicity surrounding his firing focused an intense public glare on the use of LSD and the hallucinogens.

Prior to 1967, nearly all the articles discussed the drug's supposedly bizarre effects, especially those that seemed to indicate that it caused users to go insane. The effects of LSD were described as "nightmarish"; "terror and indescribable fear" were considered common, even typical experiences under the influence. *Life* magazine ran a cover story in its March 25, 1966, issue entitled "The Exploding Threat of the Mind Drug that Got Out of Control." *Time* magazine ran a feature essay on LSD emphasizing the "freaking out" angle. "Under the influence of LSD," the story declared, "nonswimmers think they can swim, and others think they can fly. One young man tried to stop a car . . . and was killed. A magazine salesman became convinced he was the Messiah. A college dropout committed suicide by slashing his arm and bleeding to death in a field of lilies." Psychic terror, uncontrollable impulses, violence, an unconcern for one's own safety, psychotic episodes, delusions, and halluciniations filled the bulk of the early news stories on the use of LSD.

On March 17, 1967, an article was published in the prestigious journal *Science*, which seemed to indicate that LSD damaged chromosomes (Cohen, Marinello, and Back, 1967). The media immediately surmised that the drug would cause birth defects; this wave of media hysteria was not quite as intense or as long-lasting as that touched off by the "insanity" angle, but it did convince much of the public—some users included—that the drug was uniquely and powerfully damaging and dangerous. An article that appeared in the *Saturday Evening Post* (Davison, 1967) was perhaps typical. It explained that "if you take LSD, even once, your children may be born malformed or retarded" and that "new research find it's causing genetic damage that poses a threat of havoc now and appalling abnormalities for generations yet unborn." Scientists learned soon after that the whole issue was a false alarm; in the doses taken on the street, LSD is an extremely weak mutagen or gene-altering agent, extremely unlikely to cause birth defects (Dishotsky et al., 1971).

In the 1960s, LSD use appeared to many to pose *a uniquely deviant potential*. In 1966, the New Jersey Narcotic Drug Study Commission declared LSD to be "the greatest threat facing the country today" (Brecher et al., 1972, p. 369). And yet, this hysteria and fear evaporated in what was probably record time. Today, the use of hallucinogens is no longer a public issue, at least not apart from the use of illegal drugs generally. LSD has been absorbed into the morass of drug-taking in general—less seriously regarded than crack and heroin use, but more so than that of marijuana. LSD never really materialized into the threat to the society that many observers and critics (or, for that matter, its supporters) claimed it would. The drastic, dramatic, cosmic, philosophical, and religious claims originally made for the LSD experience now seem an artifact of an antiquated age. The psychedelic movement—whose members glorified the drug as a superhighway to an astoundingly new vision, perhaps a new way of life for the society as a whole, but who never made up a majority of even regular users in the 1960s—simply disappeared. The fear of the conventional majority that users would go crazy, drop out, or overturn the social order never came to pass. LSD became simply another drug taken on occasion by multiple drug users for the same hedonistic, recreational reasons they take other drugs—to get high.

One of the most remarkable aspects of the use of LSD and the other hallucinogens is how *episodically* or *sporadically* it takes place. In fact, of all drugs or drug types ingested currently in the United States, it is possible that, among the universe of everyone who has taken the drug at least once, the *lowest* percentage are still *current* or *recent* users. Recall that alcohol generates very high continuance or loyalty rates: Over six out of ten of at-least-one-time drinkers consumed one or more alcoholic beverages in the past month. But only one out of 20 persons who ever used LSD had also taken it within the past month— *one-twelfth* the figure for alcohol and *one-tenth* that for cigarettes. LSD is simply not a drug that is taken very often or regularly—even among users. Psychopharmacologists rank the "dependence potential" of the hallucinogens as extremely low—in fact, aside from PCP, dead last among all drugs and drug types.

There is a perception of the 1960s as a "psychedelic" era, a period of history when the use of LSD was not only widespread but characteristic of

the period. The fact is, evidence points to the fact that the incidence of LSD use was extremely *low* (although climbing) in the 1960s; it reached something of a peak in the 1970s; it declined into the 1980s; and it has remained at a fairly stable level for the past 20 years or so. In 1967, according to a Gallup Poll, only 1 percent of American college students (in all likelihood, the category that was *most* likely to have taken the drug at that time) said that they had tried LSD, even once; by 1969, this figure had grown to 4 percent. But by 1970, this had increased to 14 percent, and by 1971, 18 percent. In other words, precisely at a time when media attention to LSD had dropped off, its use was mushrooming. In 1980, the lifetime prevalence figure among high school seniors for LSD was 9 percent; by 1985, this had declined slightly to 7.5 percent; in 1990, it was 8 percent. In 2002, the latest year for which we have data at this writing, it was 8.4 percent (Johnston, O'Malley, and Bachman, 2003a, p. 40). For college students and noncollege young adults, the trend lines are similar. Thus, although again, LSD and the psychedelics are used extremely *episodically* by those who use it, its use has not disappeared. In fact, as many young people use LSD today as was true a generation ago.

The use of LSD in the United States should teach us some very important lessons about the perception of social problems and the imputation of deviance to an activity. First, the public hysteria generated over an activity, a belief, or a condition may be totally disproportionate to its objective threat to the society. Some activities or conditions attract considerably more than their fair share of public hysteria, while others attract far less. Second, media attention does not necessarily reflect how common or frequent an activity is; some commonly enacted behaviors receive little or no media attention, while some rare or infrequent activities receive a great deal. Media attention to an activity could very well *increase* at a time when it is declining in frequency, or *decline* when its frequency is increasing. Third, it is likely that people base their notions of the frequency or commonness of behaviors, beliefs, and conditions and the threat they pose to the society more on how *well-known* they are than on the objective, concrete facts of the matter. In many ways, a study of LSD is more instructive for what it tells us about deviance in general than for what it tells us specifically about drug use.

COCAINE AND CRACK

Cocaine is a stimulant. Its most commonly described effect is exhilaration, elation, euphoria, a voluptuous, joyous feeling. Probably the second most frequently described effect by users is a sensation of mastery and confidence in what one is and does. And third, users most commonly report a burst of increased energy, the suppression of fatigue, a stimulation of the capacity to continue physical and mental activity more intensely and for a longer than normal period of time.

In the nineteenth century, before its effects were fully understood, cocaine was used by physicians for a variety of ills, ailments, and complaints—first, to offset fatigue and depression; later, to cure morphine addiction (Spillane, 2000). Today, one of its very few medical uses is as a local anesthetic, that is, to kill pain when applied topically to delicate tissues and organs, such as the eye or the gums. The earliest papers of Sigmund Freud were devoted to singing the praises of this drug; when he became dependent on it, he realized his mistake (Byck, 1974; Andrews and Solomon, 1975; Ashley, 1975, pp. 21–28). At the end of the nineteenth and the beginning of the twentieth centuries, cocaine, like morphine and opium, was a major ingredient in many patent medicines. In fact, cocaine was contained in many "soft" drinks—including Coca-Cola—until 1903, when it was removed because of pressure applied "by Southerners who feared blacks' getting cocaine in any form" (Ashley, 1975, p. 46).

A major reason for the criminalization of cocaine after the turn of the twentieth century, many observers feel, was racism. Although there is no evidence whatsoever that African Americans were any more likely to use cocaine than whites, or that those who did were any more likely to become dangerous or violent under the influence, the fear among many whites that both were true may have been responsible for bringing the drug under state and federal control. Numerous articles published just after the turn of the twentieth cen-

tury made the claim that cocaine stimulated violent behavior among Blacks.

In 1903, the *New York Tribune* quoted one Colonel J. W. Watson of Georgia to the effect that "many of the horrible crimes committed in the southern states by the colored people can be traced to the cocaine habit." A Dr. Christopher Koch, in an article that appeared in the *Literary Digest* in 1914, asserted that "most of the attacks upon white women of the South are a direct result of a cocaine-crazed Negro brain." *The New York Times* published an article in 1914 entitled "Negro Cocaine Fiends Are a New Southern Menace," which detailed the "race menace" and "hitherto inoffensive" Blacks' "running amuck in a cocaine frenzy" (summarized in Ashley, 1975, pp. 66–73; Grinspoon and Bakalar, 1976, pp. 38–40). "All the elements needed to ensure cocaine's outlaw status were present by the first years of the twentieth century: It had become widely used as a pleasure drug . . . ; it had become identified with [groups that were] despised or poorly regarded [by middle-class whites] . . . . [that is], blacks, lower-class whites, and criminals; and it had not . . . become identified with the elite, thus losing what little chance it had of weathering the storm" (Ashley, 1975, p. 74). By the time of the passage of the Harrison Act in 1914, which included cocaine as a "narcotic" (which, as we saw, pharmacologically, it is not), 46 states had already passed state laws attempting to control cocaine. (By that time, only 29 had done so for opiates, such as morphine, opium, and heroin.) This indicates that cocaine was seen at that time as a serious drug problem. It is entirely likely that a major reason for the criminalization of cocaine was racial hostility toward African Americans on the part of the dominant white majority.

Most experts argue that the use of cocaine declined sharply during the 1920s and remained at an extremely low level until the 1960s (Ashley, 1975; Spillane, 2000). The increase in cocaine use during that decade and into the 1970s paralleled that of marijuana use, although on a much smaller scale. Although no systematic, nationally representative surveys were conducted on drug use in the United States until 1972, a 1979 study "reconstructed" estimates for the 1960s based on dates interviewees gave for when they began drug use (Miller and Cisin, 1980). This study estimated that only 1 percent of all Americans who were 18 to 25 in 1960 had used cocaine even once in their lifetime; by 1967, this had doubled. In 1972, when a full-scale survey was conducted, lifetime prevalence figure for young adults stood at 8 percent, and in 1979, it shot up to 27 percent (p. 17). According to the national survey I've cited earlier, the figures for at least one-time use for the population as a whole age 12 and older declined significantly during the 1980s and into the 1990s: 1991, 18 percent, and 1998, 11 percent; however, into the twenty-first century, this lifetime figure increased slightly—in 2002, to 14 percent.

The point is this: Practically all surveys show a decline in the use of cocaine in the general population over time since the late 1970s. This sounds encouraging, but yearly, even monthly, use may not present a serious problem to the society. Even the once-or-twice-daily use of cocaine is not intrinsically or necessarily harmful to the user, nor does such a level of use pose an unambiguous threat to the non-using majority. What most expert observers are most concerned about are the problems posed by cocaine *addicts*—the frequent, chronic, heavy, compulsive abusers who stand a high likelihood of causing medical damage to themselves as a result of overdoses and heavy use, and of victimizing others in the form of property crime and violence. The problem is that such users are extremely difficult to locate. What indicators we do have, however, indicate a trend line that is not nearly so encouraging as for casual use. While the casual, recreational use of cocaine in the general population *has* declined in the past decade or two, it is possible that the heavy, chronic abuse of the drug has actually increased. What we see is something of a *polarization* in cocaine use, with the *least* involved (and least criminal and least deviant) user *most* likely to give up the drug, and the *most* involved (and most criminal and deviant) abuser *least* likely to abstain. Abusers who are most likely to harm themselves and victimize others are also most likely to stick with cocaine over an extended period of time.

One indicator of this increase comes from a program that is referred to by its acronym, DAWN—the Drug Abuse Warning Network. DAWN is a federal data-collection program that plots two drug-related events over time: nonfatal drug-related emergency-room admissions, and medical examiner reports on lethal drug-related deaths. While there are many reasons why these figures would change over time (including changes in drug potency, trends with respect to taking different drugs simultaneously and taking drugs via different routes of administration, and an aging addict population), one reason is the change in the number of very heavy abusers, resulting in changes in the medical problems they exhibit. Between 1990 and 2001, the number of cocaine-related emergency-room episodes that took place in the United States increased a bit more than 20 percent, from about 141,000 to 174,896. The number of cocaine "overdoses"—deaths attributed by medical examiners to the use of cocaine—increased nationally from just over 3,000 in 1991 to just under 4,500 in 1996—just shy of a 50 percent increase. Between 1996 and 2000, however, there was more or less of a leveling off, to just 4,782. In short, patterns that hold for occasional or even regular users may not be valid for heavy, frequent, compulsive abuse. In fact, what we see with cocaine is that, while relatively *infrequent* use has been declining in the past few years, relatively *frequent* use may have increased or at least remained stable.

In its powdered form, cocaine is usually sniffed or snorted, that is, inhaled sharply through a nostril. Often the drug is chopped on a smooth surface; then it is arranged in the form of a fine line. The user snorts each line up one nostril with a tiny tube, such as a short, cut-off soda straw or a rolled-up bill. Some users prefer to scoop up the powder with a tiny spoon (or a long fingernail), place it in the vicinity of the nostril, and then snort it. Snorting cocaine is slower, less efficient, less reinforcing, and less intensely pleasurable than smoking it. Perhaps nine users out of ten will snort cocaine most of the time that they use it. Until 1985 or 1986, pure cocaine, in the form of "freebase," was smoked. After 1986, crack became the cocaine substance that was smoked. Crack is an impure crystalline precipitate that results from heating cocaine with baking soda; it contains only 30 percent or so cocaine.

The difference between powered cocaine and crack is mainly in route of administration, or the way these substances are taken. Taking powdered cocaine intranasally produces a high that takes roughly 3 minutes to occur and lasts perhaps 30 minutes. There is no real "rush" or intense orgasmlike explosion of pleasure. Injected, the rush will take only 12 to 15 seconds to appear, and it is described as a vastly more voluptuous feeling than the high that occurs when cocaine is snorted. Powdered cocaine is rarely smoked, since the combustion temperature is extremely high. When cocaine is smoked in the form of freebase or crack, the onset of the drug's impact is even faster, a matter of 6 to 8 seconds, and the intense, orgasmlike high or rush lasts for perhaps 2 minutes, followed by an afterglow that lasts 10 to 20 minutes. The euphoria achieved in this experience is extreme—in the terms of the behaviorist psychologist, it is highly *reinforcing*—and, often, this impels users to want to take the drug over and over again.

However, to say that smoked crack cocaine is highly reinforcing—more so, in fact, than almost any other drug—is *not* to say that most users become chronic abusers. As with nearly every newly introduced drug, sensationalist exaggeration in the media accompanies its widespread use. In the mid-1980s, newspaper headlines and television reports implied that all teenagers in the country had used crack or were in imminent danger of doing so—that every community nationwide had been saturated by the drug. The reality is not nearly so terrifying. The first year the Monitoring the Future study asked about crack (1987), only 5 percent of high school seniors questioned said that they had used crack even once in their lives; in 1998, the figure was 4 percent; and in 2002, it was, again, 4 percent (Johnston, O'Malley, and Bachman, 2003a, p. 40). The figures for annual and 30-day prevalence are, of course, much lower. (Unfortunately, high school dropouts, whose crack use is likely to be considerably higher, could not be included in this survey.) For college students, in 2002, the lifetime figure was only 2 percent (Johnston, O'Malley, and Bachman, 2003b, p. 34).

Just as the incidence or frequency of crack use was exaggerated by the media, the drug's demonic addictive power was sensationalized as well. A June 16, 1986, story in *Newsweek* claimed that using crack immediately impelled the user into "an inferno of craving and despair." "Try it once and you're hooked!" "Once you start, you can't stop!" These and other slogans were repeated so often that they seemed to take on a life of their own. In fact, they are a serious distortion of reality. Crack may be among the most reinforcing drugs we know, and it is possible that a compulsive pattern of abuse builds more rapidly than for any other known, widely used drug. Still, only a fairly small minority of users take the drug compulsively and destructively. In one Miami study of over 300 heavily involved drug users age 12 to 17, 96 percent of whom had taken crack at least once and 87 percent of whom used it regularly, only a minority, 30 percent, used it daily, and half used it weekly or more but not daily. A majority of even the daily users limited their use to one or two "hits"— "hardly an indication of compulsive and uncontrollable use. Although there were compulsive users of crack in the Miami sample, they represented an extremely small minority" (Inciardi, 1987, p. 484). While there is unquestionably a certain *risk* of dependence in smoking crack, the hellish experiences that were described in the media in the 1980s did not typify what most users went through when they took this drug. Once again, drug users are often characterized as extreme deviants by the media, a characterization that assumes a reality in the way they are pictured by much of the public.

A good example of the way that cocaine and crack use was demonized in the media is provided by the "crack babies" phenomenon of the late 1980s and early 1990s. In his *Folk Devils and Moral Panics*, Stanley Cohen (1972, pp. 77–85; 2002) refers to the process of *sensitization* in the early stages of a moral panic—that is, "the reinterpretation of neutral or ambiguous stimuli as potentially or actually deviant" (p. 77). Thus, a familiar, nondeviant source that causes a certain measure of harm does not generate much concern, while an unfamiliar, deviant source that causes the same level of harm will touch off a *firestorm* of concern, fear, and hostility. We already saw the sensitization process at work in the 1960s with LSD: Panic reactions were interpreted as an epidemic of psychotic episodes, and peculiar-looking chromosomes drawn from one mental patient who was administered LSD were interpreted as a future tidal wave of malformed, abnormal children.

The findings of the initial studies on children born to cocaine-dependent mothers were extremely pessimistic. Babies whose mothers were exposed to crack and powdered cocaine during pregnancy, compared with those whose mothers were not exposed to the drug, are more likely to be born prematurely, have a lower birth weight, have smaller heads, suffer seizures, have genital and urinary-tract abnormalities, suffer poor motor ability, have brain lesions, and exhibit behavioral aberrations such as impulsivity, moodiness, and lower responsiveness (Chasnoff et al., 1989). Findings such as these were picked up by the mass media with great speed and transmitted to the general public; within a short period of time, it became an established fact that crack babies made up a major medical and psychiatric problem for the country; it is possible, some argued, that they could never be cured. Crack babies could very well become a catastrophe of monumental proportions. William Bennett, then federal drug "czar," claimed that 375,000 crack babies annually were being born in the United States in the late 1980s—one out of ten births!—a figure that was echoed by *Washington Post* columnist Jack Anderson and *New York Times* editor A. M. Rosenthal (Gieringer, 1990, p. 4). One reporter, in a major and widely quoted article published in *Time* magazine, claimed that the medical care of crack babies would cost society 13 times as much as normal babies. There is fear, she said, that these children will become "an unmanageable multitude of disturbed and disruptive youth, fear that they will be a lost generation" (Toufexis, 1991, p. 56). A Pulitzer Prize–winning columnist describes the crack baby crisis in the following dramatic, heart-wrenching words: "The bright room is filled with baby misery; babies born months too soon; babies weighing little more than a hardcover book; babies that look like wizened old men in the last stage of a terminal illness, wrinkled skin clinging to chicken bones; babies who do not cry because their mouths are full of tubes. . . . The reason is crack" (Quindlen, 1990).

It was not until the early 1990s that enough medical evidence was assembled to indicate that the crack baby "syndrome" was, in all probability, mythical in nature (Neuspiel et al., 1991; Coles, 1992; Richardson and Day, 1994). The problem with the early research on the babies of mothers who had used cocaine and crack was that there were no *controls*. Most of these women also drank alcohol, some heavily—and medical science has documented at least one damaging outcome of heavy drinking by the expectant mother: fetal alcohol syndrome. Likewise, no controls were applied for smoking, which is associated with low birth weight in infants; nutritional condition; medical condition of the mother; medical attention (receiving checkups, following the advice of one's physician—indeed, even seeing a physician at all during one's pregnancy); and so on. In other words, factors that vary with cocaine use are known to determine poorer infant outcomes; mothers who smoke crack and use powdered cocaine are more likely to engage in other behaviors that correlate with poorer infant health. Is it the cocaine or these other factors that cause these poorer outcomes? Expectant mothers who use cocaine are more likely to get sexually transmitted diseases; such mothers are less likely to eat a nutritious, balanced diet, get regular checkups, and so on. Were these factors at work in their children's poorer health? Or was it the independent effect of the cocaine itself that produced these medical problems?

When the influence of these other factors was held constant, it became clear that the poorer health that was observed in very young babies was not caused by the effects of cocaine use itself. Instead, it seemed to be a function of the impact of the other drugs these pregnant mothers were using, including alcohol and cigarettes, and a lifestyle that included an inadequate diet and insufficient medical care. In short, it is entirely possible that the crack babies issue was a "hysteria-driven" rather than a "fact-driven" syndrome. In the late 1980s and early 1990s, the public, the media, and even the medical profession were sensitized to believing in the harmful effects of cocaine on newborns with scanty, skimpy evidence; at the same time, the possible influence of the more conventional factors was normalized and ignored. Such processes are characteristic of the moral panic; it is in the moral panic that hostility to and condemnation of deviant behavior and deviant actors are invigorated, intensified, reaffirmed.

As we saw, for the general population, cocaine use declined during the 1990s: In 1991, 18 percent had taken the drug even once during their lifetime; in 2002, this figure was down to 14 percent. For college students, the comparable figures were 9 and 8 percent (Johnston, O'Malley, and Bachman, 2003b, p. 34). But as we saw, the story is not quite the same for all categories or groups in the population. In fact, among schoolchildren, cocaine use actually increased during most of the 1990s, then leveled off and even declined after that. Between 1991 and 1998, the lifetime prevalence of cocaine use among eighthgraders doubled—from 2.3 to 4.6 percent; the percent using it in the past 30 days nearly tripled, from 0.5 to 1.4 percent. But between 1998 and 2002, the figure for lifetime prevalence dipped very slightly, to 3.6 percent. The comparable changes for high school seniors were more modest—from 7.8 to 9.3 percent for lifetime prevalence (1991–1998), and 7.8 percent in 2002; and from 1.4 to 2.4 percent for use in the past 30 days (1991–1998), and 2.3 percent in 2002 (Johnston, O'Malley, and Bachman, 2003a, p. 41). These numbers are small, and the plateau in the past few years is encouraging, but the fact that these increases run so completely counter to the declines that have been taking place in the adult population should give us cause for concern.

HEROIN AND THE NARCOTICS

Of all well-known drugs or drug types, heroin ranks lowest in popularity. Assuming the polls are reasonably accurate, just under 1 percent of the American population has even *tried* heroin, and a fraction of that figure (two-tenths of one percent) has used it, even once, in the past month. The percentages for high school seniors are about twice those for the general population—less than 2 percent has at least tried it and one-half of one percent has done so in the past month (Johnston, O'Malley, and Bachman, 2003a, pp. 40, 45). Less than 2 percent of college students are at-least-one-time heroin users (1.2 percent, to be exact) and less than one-tenth of one percent did so in the past 30 days (Johnston, O'Malley, and Bachman, 2003b, p. 41).

Remember, however, that school surveys do not interview dropouts; in addition, infrequent school attenders and truants are less likely to show up in a survey's sample. And it is almost certain that dropouts and truants are significantly more likely to use heroin. In addition, studies of the general population are based on households. Homeless people and the incarcerated do not live in households; and the chances are, they are more likely to use heroin than members of stable households. All things considered, however, heroin nonetheless ranks extremely low on America's list of the illicit drugs that are most likely to be used.

The question that arises, then, is: Why study heroin use at all? If, compared with marijuana, cocaine, and the hallucinogens, it is used with such rarity, why study it? Why discuss heroin in a general overview of drug use and abuse as a form of deviance? One answer is that, until the advent of crack in the mid-1980s, heroin use, and especially addiction, has been the most *deviant* form of drug use in the public mind. It is usually regarded as the *ultimate* or *most serious* form of drug use known. In addition, although many users take heroin once, twice, a dozen times, and abstain from it from then on, and many use it occasionally, or, if regularly, confine their use to weekends or special occasions, still, a very substantial proportion of heroin users become addicts. As we saw, LSD is a drug that is taken by many Americans, of whom an extremely *tiny* proportion use it with any regularity. In contrast, heroin involves a far higher proportion of users in frequent, compulsive, abusive, and harmful use. Most estimates of the number of narcotic addicts in the United States hover in the half-a-million range. It is possible that, according to a more generous definition, there may be as many as a million American heroin addicts or abusers. (It must be stressed that defining just who is an addict or an abuser is not as obvious or straightforward as might be supposed.) In contrast, virtually *no one* is an LSD "addict."

One reason why heroin is such an important drug for sociologists to study (aside from its strongly negative image in the public's mind) is that its use seems to generate social problems of great seriousness and magnitude. This is not merely a matter of socially or subjectively *constructing* a problem in a certain way; objectively speaking, heroin causes a great deal of damage to users and nonusers alike. As we've already seen, it is clear that alcohol and tobacco kill more Americans than the illegal drugs. Still, among the *illicit* drugs, heroin ranks at or near the top in objective seriousness. Heroin causes a great deal of *medical* damage. In 2000, heroin ranked second (after only cocaine) in DAWN's medical examiners' reports, figuring in four out of ten (39 percent) of all lethal drug-related deaths, or drug "overdoses" (SAMHSA, 2002). Heroin also ranked third in nonlethal emergency department episodes as well, during 2001, figuring in complications leading to just under 100,000 trips to hospitals and clinics nationwide (SAMHSA, 2002).

Considering that heroin is used about *one-tenth* as often as cocaine, its contribution to these overdose figures is truly remarkable—in fact, astounding. It is possible that, on an episode-by-episode basis, objectively speaking, heroin is the most dangerous of all the well-known drugs. It remains an interesting and vexing question as to whether it is the *direct action of the drug* or the way the legal system *deals with* heroin users that causes such extensive medical havoc. But clearly, *given the way that heroin is currently used*, its contribution to medical harm justifies attention to its use as sociologically important.

Another reason why a study of heroin is crucial in any course on deviance is that the potency of the drug sold on the street has been increasing dramatically over the past decade. Through the 1960s and 1970s, the heroin available on the street at the retail level had remained stable at only 3 to 5 percent pure; the rest was made up of relatively inert and nonpsychoactive fillers such as mannitol, lactose, and quinine. During and after the 1980s, however, the New York City

police were confiscating heroin with a purity of 30 to 70 percent. Today, a packet of heroin purchased on the streets of our large cities averages 25 percent. Currently, a substantially greater range of ethnic and national groups is importing heroin than was true in the past; partly as a consequence, it is being imported from a far greater range of countries of origin. Most of the heroin consumed in the United States comes from Latin America, principally Colombia. The drug's hugely abundant supply has brought its purity up and its price down. During the 1990s, the collapse of the Soviet Union served to expand the countries of origin of heroin to include Afghanistan and the central Asian republics. Given the diversity of its origins, halting heroin distribution by stamping out the drug at its source seems a fool's errand.

Some reports indicate that, while heroin use in the general population remains low, the heavy or abusive use of heroin among a small minority may be on the upswing. Certainly the increase in DAWN's figures on lethal and nonlethal overdoses suggest increases in heavy use and abuse. (Another possible explanation: an aging addict population, leading to more deaths and medical complications. A third explanation: the increase in the potency of heroin has led to more overdoses.) Between 1990 and 2001, nationwide, heroin-related visits to emergency rooms increased from 33,000 to 97,000, while lethal drug-related overdoses in which heroin was present doubled between 1990 to 1996 from just under 2,000 to just under 4,000; between 1996 and 2001, however, that figured leveled off. Applications to drug treatment programs likewise have increased significantly in the past half-dozen years. Some journalistic reports suggest that the use of heroin in chic, trendy, "fast lane" clubs and scenes and among the more avant-garde professions, such as fashion and the arts, may be increasing (Gabriel, 1994). In 1994, River Phoenix, a young actor, died of a multiple drug overdose with morphine in his bloodstream (heroin breaks down into morphine in the body), and the same year, Kurt Cobain, a rock star, committed suicide, also with morphine in his body. Today, heroin is far more likely to be smoked (or, more properly, it is heated and its vapors are inhaled, a practice that is called "chasing the dragon"), or sniffed, than was true in the past. The fear of needles—and of AIDS—kept many middle-class druggies away from heroin; with an increase in the popularity of these other methods, this barrier has been dissolved.

SUMMARY

Drug use has both an objective and a subjective side. On the one hand, it is an identifiable form of behavior; it has certain concrete, measurable consequences; and it is caused by and has consequences that are a product of specific, discoverable factors. On the other hand, drug use is also categorized in a certain way by the general public, by the law, and in the media, and users, likewise, are thought about and dealt with in certain ways. In addition, drug use generates a certain level of public concern. These two dimensions, the objective and the subjective, overlap extremely imperfectly. By this I mean that the *magnitude* of public concern is not always an accurate reflection of the degree of objective danger or damage represented by drug abuse. Often there is great concern at a time when the harmful effects of drug abuse are declining and, contrarily, concern is often relatively low when these drug effects are on the rise. In addition, the specific drug that attracts public concern has shifted over time—from marijuana in the 1930s, to LSD in the 1960s, to heroin in the early 1970s, and to crack cocaine in the later 1980s. Sociologists refer to a period in which concern over a given condition, such as drug abuse, is intense and disproportionate to its concrete danger as a *moral panic*. Usually, in a moral panic, a specific agent is held responsible for the condition or threat—a *folk devil*.

Humans have ingested psychoactive or mind-altering substances for thousands of years. Drug use is very close to being a human universal in that nearly all cultures use psychoactive substances. Sometimes the wrong substance is ingested, or it is taken too often, or under the wrong circumstances, or with undesirable consequences. In such cases, we have instances of deviant behavior.

Most definitions of drugs have focused on the objective or concrete properties of substances. The fact is, however, no property exists such that *all* substances that are referred to as drugs share it and that, in turn, *no* substances that are *not* called drugs do not. In contrast, a *subjective* definition of drugs recognizes that, though substances that are referred to as drugs do share certain properties in common, they do so only within specific contexts. In other words, some substances referred to as drugs are psychoactive; some are not. Some "drugs" are useful as medicine; some are not. Some are taken for the purpose of getting high; some are not. Some are addicting; some are not. The possession of some drugs is illegal; some are completely legal. Each of these dimensions defines "drugness," but only in certain contexts. No single objective or concrete quality covers all substances that are known as drugs; each is useful in a limited fashion. Thus, the subjective definition emphasizes that whether a given chemical substance is a drug or not is in part in the eye of the beholder. Still, the "objective" definition of what a drug is that seems to make the most sociological sense is *psychoactivity* or the capacity to induce mental and psychic changes.

Since all drugs have multiple effects, they may be classified in different ways, according to different criteria. Still, by focusing on a limited number of effects, certain drug classifications have come to be widely accepted as standard. One classification, useful for psychoactive drugs, focuses on the effect of substances on the central nervous system, or brain and spinal column. *Depressants* retard or slow down, or "obtund," signals passing through the central nervous system. *General depressants* inhibit a wide range of functions and organs of the body. *Narcotics* tend to act more specifically on dulling the brain's perception of pain, and they are popularly known as "painkillers." Narcotics also produce euphoria and all are addicting. *Hallucinogens* (or "psychedelics") produce profound and extreme alterations in perception, especially those of a visual nature. Most classifications put marijuana into a distinct and separate category.

Four categories of drug use may be distinguished: legal medical, or instrumental use;

legal recreational use; illegal instrumental use; and illegal recreational use. In the past two or three decades, for several important categories of drugs, psychoactive prescription drug use has declined sharply. Legal recreational drug use (mainly the use of tobacco and alcohol) has declined as well. Illegal instrumental use—for instance, taking amphetamine to stay up all night to study for an exam—represents a substantial part of the drug picture. It is the illegal recreational use of drugs—taking psychoactive substances for fun, that is, for the purpose of getting high—that defines the drug problem for most of the public. Studies show a huge increase in illegal drug use between the early 1960s and the late 1970s; 1979 or 1980 represented the peak year for the use of most illegal drugs. During the 1980s, drug use declined in the United States, but it began to increase again in the early 1990s. After about 1996 or so, it may have leveled off, at least among the young.

Marijuana use has gone through several drastic changes as an illegal and deviant activity. In earlier centuries, marijuana was used as a medicine. Early in the twentieth century, the recreational use of marijuana was not well-known; users were rarely condemned as a separate category of deviants. During the 1930s, numerous articles in popular magazines and newspapers created something of a marijuana scare or panic; in that decade, possession and sale of the drug became a crime in all states of the United States and at the federal level as well. Harmful medical effects of marijuana have been asserted but never fully documented; the jury is still out on this question. In the United States, during the 1960s and 1970s, marijuana use became much more common, more accepted, and less deviant, and the drug has been decriminalized in a dozen states. In addition, it is legal as medicine in ten states. Since 1990, marijuana use has become more common and less deviant among the young.

Hallucinogens or psychedelics include LSD as their most well-known representative. During the 1960s, an LSD scare or panic erupted. Users were said to suffer temporary insanity and irreparable chromosome damage. The first effect is now regarded with suspicion by experts, while the second has been entirely discounted. LSD use has not disappeared. If anything, it has stabilized over the past decade or two. LSD is taken extremely sporadically, with great infrequency. It very rarely becomes a drug of serious, heavy, or chronic abuse.

Although an ingredient in some medicines and beverages, for recreational purposes cocaine was never a drug of widespread popularity in the United States until the 1970s. Cocaine was criminalized, along with narcotics, in the aftermath of the Harrison Act. In the 1980s, a new form of cocaine, "crack," became popular. Crack is smoked and thus produces an intense and extremely rapid high. Never widespread in the country as a whole, crack quickly became popular among a minority of poor, inner-city youth. Its use declined during the course of the 1990s. Crack use, while far from safe, was demonized by the media; its harmful effects were hugely exaggerated. Babies born to cocaine-dependent mothers were said to be permanently disabled mentally and physically. In fact, it is now clear that their medical problems were due more to the lifestyle of their mothers than to the effects of cocaine per se. In other words, the fear that crack will severely harm the fetuses of dependent mothers was a "fear-driven" rather than a "fact-driven" syndrome. Crack abuse became another in a long line of drug panics. During the 1990s cocaine use declined in the general population but increased among the young.

Heroin is perhaps the least popular of all widely known drugs in America. As it is used, on an episode-by-episode basis, with respect to lethal overdoses, it is also one of the most dangerous. (Although, interestingly, if used in a medically controlled fashion, heroin does not seem to harm the body at all; that is, it does not damage organs or bodily tissue.) Considering the small number of heroin users in the United States, an astonishingly high number of addicts die of heroin overdoses and other related ailments. It is possible that this has as much to do with the legal situation as to the effects of the drug itself. Since the early 1980s, heroin sold illegally on the street has become increasingly pure and abundant. It is now imported from a much wider range of sources than was true in the past.

PERSONAL ACCOUNT: Barbiturate Abuse

William, the author of this account, is 44 years old. His father was a successful executive, and his parents divorced when he was young. He was convicted for the manufacture of amphetamine and has served 24 months of a 15-year sentence in Oklahoma, "which translates into about six calendar years." In addition, until 2003, he had a 60-year sentence to serve in Texas, for which he already served 10 years; in that year, he was paroled. William is eligible for parole in Oklahoma in 2005. He received a college degree in prison.

I committed many burglaries when I was a teenager. At a certain point in my career as a burglar, when was 15, I began hitting doctors' offices. The first one I hit was my own oral surgeon. I knew he had good dope, since he had knocked me out with it when he operated on me. Here's how it happened. The big night arrived. I worked with one of my buddies. We dressed like ninjas. Dressed all in black. . . . Plastic bags to haul off our bounty. Mace spray cans in case we were caught. Off we go. The building was unlocked. Up the elevator, down the hallway. I went into the men's room, climbed onto the sink, got up into the hanging tile ceiling, crawled a few feet, and dropped down into the doctor's office. Apparently the doc was moving—everything was boxed up and properly labeled. Anesthetic? Load it up, set it by the door. A tank of nitrous oxide? We'd have to think about that one. After all we're on foot. We bagged up everything we wanted to take and set it all by the office door. Ding-a-ling! The alarm went off. Arrrggghhh!! We dropped the goods and took off running down the hall, hitting those stairs two by two. Heart racing, blood pumping. The police will be here any second! Why did I do this crazy burglary? Thoughts were racing through my mind as I reached the door to the street. Hey, wait a minute! There's no more ringing alarm, no bell, no sirens. What we heard was the bell on the doctor's door that announced to the receptionist that someone came into the office. We laughed and went back and got our dope.

At home, we checked out our haul. We had a lot of liquid Valium. Not bad. Frankly, I preferred barbs [barbiturates], not tranquilizers. Actually, we also had some liquid barbiturates— Sodium Brevital [an ultra-fast-acting barbiturate] and Sodium Pentothal [a slow-acting barbiturate], both which have to be mixed with water. I read the instructions on how to dilute the liquid barbiturates with water. Not good enough, I thought—too diluted. I increased the barbiturate-to-water ratio suggested by the instructions by 10 times. I got the solution, one-third of a cc [cubic centimeter] into a needle and injected it. It gave me the best barb rush I *ever* felt! Whooosh! Up and down—total euphoria. Then, boom! I opened my eyes to find my partner in a panic. He thought I had overdosed. I gave him a quarter of a cc. His eyes rolled back in his head, he grinned, then slumped over. Eureka! I had found the right dosage. These barbs were great! Shooting barbiturates is the best rush! Better than speed [amphetamine], better than cocaine. Eventually, I shot every kind of dope I got my hands on, and by far the barb engulfment does it best. Hard to encapsulate in words. It's warm, overwhelming, almost like a sexual orgasm.

The Sodium Brevital was a killer barb— very fast-acting, very short duration. This translates into a bigger, better rush, but it doesn't last very long, you come down quickly. When you take it, the problem was getting up to do another shot. You'd wake up, and the others may be awake, or not. Usually, they'd be laid out, dead-looking. Rig [needle] in their arm, sometimes a trail of blood running down their arm, and they'd be drooling. So you'd grab a rig, pull up a shot, and hit it again. Wham! That killer rush! After about 30–45 seconds, you'd slump out. It was like you were in a horror film—everyone was dead around you. You didn't care, you'd just look for the bottle and do it again. Once the bottle was dry,

PERSONAL ACCOUNT: Barbiturate Abuse (cont.)

you'd pull yourself together. You'd be wiped out afterwards. Your arms would hurt bad, you'd be so disgusted, you'd swear off the "Brevey" forever. Then after a few months, I'd get that call from my customers, "Hey, you got any more?" I'll bet I was 20 before I ran out of that supply. The stuff was that good. And strange. And dangerous.

Years later, I went to someone's house to score some dope. When I got there, the guy I was dealing with was the only one awake. There were five or six people passed out in the living room. One got up, did a shot, passed back out. I asked my dealer what it was they were

shooting. He brought the bottle over to me. The label called it "sleepy time." The picture on the label showed a dog with X's for its eyes. It was Brevital, full-strength, used to euthanize dogs! I just burst out laughing. Next time I found it, it was one of the three drugs used in the cocktail for executing prisoners in the Texas death house. Kinda weird, kinda sickening. I laughed because I know those poor saps on death row go out with a smile, a good rush goodbye. I wonder if any of my friends who spent a whole day jamming a needle in their arm and flopping onto the floor had any idea what the state of Texas uses to kill people with.

PERSONAL ACCOUNT: Smoking Marijuana

One interesting aspect of illicit drug use is that there is a gulf between what the law says on the one hand, and public opinion and law enforcement on the other. Illegal is illegal. Though penalties vary from drug to drug, the fact is, both in a number of states and according to federal law, one can receive a lengthy sentence for the possession of a usable quantity of marijuana—a crime most of the American public thinks should not draw a jail or prison sentence at all. In Arkansas, possession of an ounce or more draws a sentence of four to ten years in prison; in Connecticut, a second conviction of simple possession of any amount draws a sentence of five years; and in Florida, possession of 20 grams (less than an ounce) calls for imprisonment for five years. Moreover, while the federal government seems adamant about retaining marijuana's criminal status, possession of small quantities of the drug is extremely low on law enforcement's radar screen. As we saw in this chapter, 80 percent of the population favors medical marijuana and 72 percent is opposed to

incarcerating recreational pot smokers. Hence, we observe a disconnect between the law on the one hand and how the public feels and what the police and prosecutors are willing to do to enforce the law, on the other.

Brad is in his forties and is a recreational pot-smoking parent. His daughter, Tiffany, is a college student. In the eighth grade, she took a drug education course under the auspices of D.A.R.E., and was shocked, angered, and appalled when she discovered that her dad smoked marijuana.

"I had been force-fed the notion that people who used drugs are all criminals," she explains, "and addicts. It angered me that he would want to do that to his body. To me, smoking pot was the equivalent of shooting heroin. A drug was a drug, and I was ashamed to have such an out-of-control father who was stuck in his little seventies world. Somehow, the fact that he took me skating every day, went to work, helped my mom, made dinner, and cleaned the house, did

PERSONAL ACCOUNT: Smoking Marijuana (cont.)

not matter. . . . Granted, he never smoked in front us [Tiffany and her brother]. It was just always there in the background somewhere in a smoked-filled bathroom. . . . In my family, as well as our family's friends, my dad is not considered deviant. Some of his musician friends do much harder drugs than he does. . . . In our neighborhood, though, as well as in America as a whole, his marijuana use would definitely be seen as deviant. I think this is because of the belief that fathers and mothers should set a good example for their children and that parents who use drugs are not good parents. A lot of conservative people would argue that Brad's drug use is irresponsible and immature." Tiffany adds: "Brad is an example of a person who shatters the stereotype of a parent who uses marijuana. He is hard-working, family-oriented, and responsible. That is not my own personal opinion, it is a fact. The proof is the roof still over my house, the wedding ring on my mom's finger, and the diploma I will receive in a year."

In this interview, Tiffany is asking her dad questions.

TIFFANY: How regularly do you smoke?

BRAD: Daily. I stop drinking alcohol when I'm stoned. I get my stuff from one of my fraternity brothers from college. He gets me a whole bunch so I don't have to go through some dealer I don't know. I don't think I'd do it half as much if it was hard to get. But it's cheap and easy for me. I don't smoke a lot at a time. I just pack a bowl with about half a gram, about the size of a dime [there are 28 grams in an ounce], watch TV, and don't remember what I saw, I kind of zoom out. Anyway, pot's so strong nowadays, I get much higher with less than I used to. I don't have to smoke as much pot to get the same effect that I got years ago. Strong stuff.

TIFFANY: What kind of jobs have you had?

BRAD: I've worked in the telecommunications field for a long time for a lot of different companies. I also helped my wife when we ran a daycare business out of our house. It was a great little thing we had. Just a handful of infants and toddlers—we were great at it.

TIFFANY: Were you ever high at work?

BRAD: Usually I don't smoke until I get home. I have to get up too damn early for that.

TIFFANY: How is smoking [marijuana] seen in those circles [that is, among the people Brad works with]?

BRAD: I only talk about it with people I know smoke too. Like, you could tell who did it and who didn't. The people who didn't, yeah, they probably have a big stick up their ass about it, but I really don't care. I don't advertise that I smoke or anything.

TIFFANY: So if everybody knew you smoke, how do you think they'd react? Do you think they would consider you somehow deviant?

BRAD: By a small percentage, I'd be seen as a deviant.

TIFFANY: Do you think you'd be fired?

BRAD: I don't know. I guess it depends on the boss. I don't really think about getting fired or not. That's not why I keep it hidden. It's more the fact that I don't want people judging me on their limited knowledge. . . . They lump pot in with heroin. I think pot's not even in the same galaxy as the hard drugs. It's like alcohol or cigarettes. But a lot of people think that way because they haven't had the same experiences as I have. Ignorance is bliss and there's a lot of blissful people in the world.

TIFFANY: How do you think you have been as a parent?

BRAD: Above average. I've come home every night, done laundry, washed dishes, haven't fooled around, haven't beaten my kids or sexually abused them, I've encouraged them to excel in whatever they were interested in. I've been open, honest, and supportive. We've lived within our means, sometimes above our means.

PERSONAL ACCOUNT: Smoking Marijuana (cont.)

We always ate well, and my kids' friends were always welcome and fed. I have the greatest relationship with my kids. They're awesome. Much better than I could have hoped. They know self-reliance, they know they can trust me with a secret, and I've continued to earn that trust by not revealing any of those secrets. They know that they can come to me with anything, day or night as a dad, friend, nurse, sounding board for ideas, devil's advocate, accountant, or a resource for information. I think I'm just a nice guy.

TIFFANY: Has being high ever affected your parenting?

BRAD: No, I don't think so. I've always been there for my family. They're the most important thing in my life. Career's a distant fifth, and pot's a little after that.

TIFFANY: If your drug use were public and obvious, how do you think people in the community would see you?

BRAD: In our community, about 10 percent would think I'm extremely deviant and the rest would think I'm normal. I know there's a ton of people out there who do a whole lot worse shit than I do. I think I'm somewhere in the middle there.

TIFFANY: How about how you're seen in your social circle?

BRAD: In my private social circle there's marijuana use and some limited cocaine use. You know, wussy stuff. And [with the cocaine], it's just snorting. I'd say a lot of my friends go further than I do. We're a diverse mix of guys, and I'd say that in that mix, I'm one of the more conventional ones.

TIFFANY: If it's no big deal to you and you don't think that most people would care, why do you keep it a secret? Do you have any fear of stigmatization?

BRAD: Not fear of stigma really. I just don't need the hassle with cops or anything. I don't want rehab, parole, or community service. Cops are the biggest hassle [with using an illegal substance]. There's just no reason for me to flaunt anything in front of them or anybody else. I don't want to be the poster boy for middle-aged marijuana use.

TIFFANY: Would you consider yourself an addict?

BRAD: Hell, yes. Just like I'm addicted to cigarettes. I quit for nine years, but when I wanted to smoke again, I did. I don't need pot to live, but it doesn't hinder my life or change how I act, so there's no need for me to quit.

TIFFANY: If your life were put into a newspaper, how do you think a lot of people would react to your drug use?

BRAD: If my life were put into a newspaper I guess I'd be considered deviant. But I don't believe in organized religion, and that's deviant too. Let me put it this way. On *Dr. Phil* or *Oprah*, yeah, I'd be considered deviant. On *The Man Show*, I'd be a minor hero.

TIFFANY: Do you think you're a part of a small group of people who do this? Do you feel connected to adults like you who smoke pot—maybe feel like you belong to a subculture?

BRAD: No. I'm just a guy who likes to drink beer and get high in my basement. Life is short and some things are fun.

QUESTIONS

The two above accounts present different views of illicit drug use—William, a convict and former barbiturate addict and amphetamine distributor, and Brad, a regular pot smoker, parent, and unconventional though not entirely deviant parent. Try to imagine the drugs reversed: Could marijuana have produced the kind of life William had, and the regular use of barbiturates, the kind of life Brad experienced? In other words, is there or is there not *something about the drug* that makes certain lifestyles possible, and precludes others? Is the regular use of certain drugs more demanding and forceful in intruding into the life of the user, making certain ways of life necessary, and others impossible? Do you buy Brad's claim that he could quit any time he wanted? What sense do you get from William's account about how he feels about his experiences as a barbiturate addict? Does he feel he has learned anything? Do you feel Brad was irresponsible for smoking marijuana while parenting his children? Do you accept Tiffany's defense of her dad's use of pot? If you were to guess, would you agree with her that the fact that he has performed in a number of conventional roles while continuing to smoke pot indicates that the stereotype of a marijuana smoker is inaccurate?

9

Sexual Deviance

A half-dozen years ago, I had occasion to correspond with a sociologist who had decided not to teach a course on deviance any longer. He had stopped teaching it, he explained, because it had become overly focused on sexual deviance. I suggested he cut down on those portions of the course that dealt specifically with sex, and expand his discussion of other forms of deviance. I doubt if he followed my suggestion. As we saw in Chapter 1, more than a generation ago, a critic (Liazos, 1972) attacked—indeed, made fun of—sociologists of deviance who studied "nuts, sluts, and deviated preverts," which in his mind included prostitutes and homosexuals. He regarded the emphasis on actors who engaged in the violation of society's sexual norms as a "bias" that ignored the truly important and influential forms of deviance—such as the evil deeds of powerful corporate and government actors. The message of these two sociologists seems to be: No more sex in deviance courses! (Well, at least, less than was taught in the past.)

But the fact is, it *is* more interpersonally discrediting—and therefore more *deviant*—to engage in the "nuts, sluts, and preverts" forms of behavior than in, let's say, corporate crime or most political wrongdoing. As a result of this "misguided" and "biased" emphasis, sociologists of deviance still focus on the study of, and continue to discuss, sexual deviance far more than the "big bang" deviant behaviors, such as corporate crime and high-level political malfeasance. The fact is, sexually unconventional behavior remains a central topic of discussion in most courses in deviance. And with good reason: It is a prime example of *deviant*—that is, discrediting—behavior.

Critics who claim that sociologists focus too much on sex in their courses on deviance are asking the wrong question. Two *right* questions are: *Why are there so many norms about sexual behavior?* And: *Why are the punishments for violating sexual norms so severe?* The ways that we violate mainstream society's norms by engaging in variant sexual acts is almost infinite. And the *severity* of society's punishment for many sexual transgressions is quite substantial. How many husbands or wives divorce their spouses for committing corporate crime? How many people become the butt of gossip as a result of bribing an

official? In contrast, *many* sexual acts are "off limits" or unacceptable to most of the members of this—indeed, almost any—society. The fact is, societies pretty much everywhere have laid down, and enforce, an *immense* number of norms dictating acceptable and unacceptable sexual behavior. The do's and don'ts of sex are staggering in their number, variety, and complexity. And these do's and don'ts usually carry with them stiff penalties.

Moreover, we construct almost uncountable *social identities* on the basis of what we do, or have done, sexually. We have—and we construct for ourselves—*categories* for people as a result of the fact that they, or we, engage, have engaged, prefer, want to engage, try to engage, or can't engage, in certain types of sexual acts. Think of these categories: homosexual, heterosexual, bisexual, adulterer, cuckold, faithful husband, faithful wife, impotent man, frigid woman, necrophiliac, pedophile, child molester, rapist, rape victim, "pervert," "dirty old man," "slut," "tramp," whore, prostitute, pornographer, sadist, masochist, lap dancer, stripper, nude dancer, "tease," a "lousy lay"—the list goes on and on. Obviously, sex plays a very *central* role in defining who we are in this—and probably every—society. And its importance, so intricately and intimately tied in to social relations generally, is indicated by the number and strength of the norms attempting to govern it. Clearly, sexual deviance is an *important* type of deviant behavior. It would represent a "bias" to ignore it. Indeed, viewed in this light, corporate crime is an extremely *minor* form of deviance, since only a *small* number of people can engage in it, the sanctions for transgressions are usually *minor*, and it is *rarely* relevant to corporate actors' identities. Precisely the opposite is true of sexual deviance.

Consider the Bible's sexual prohibitions. It is true that, for most people, the Holy Bible is not the primary source of all sexual norms. In fact, many people ignore most of the injunctions in the Bible as irrelevant for their lives. For instance, most of us eat shellfish (shrimp, lobster, crab, and clams), touch articles of pigskin (a football, for example, or leather gloves), wear garments made of different types of materials (say, a cotton-nylon blend), and don't worry about crops that come from fields with "mingled" seed—all of which are prohibited in the Bible. Still, when we want to understand how sexual norms work, a good place to start is the Old and New Testaments; at the very least, these texts give us a clue to what's considered sexually wrong.

The fact is, a perusal of the Bible tells us a great deal about sexual norms. The number of injunctions and prohibitions against sexual acts considered wrong by the ancients, and the severity of the punishments for violating them, are impressive. Consider the fact that the Bible contains 69 different passages that refer to "adulterer," "adulterers," "adulteress," "adulteresses," "adulteries," "adulterous," and "adultery," and 44 that refer to "fornication," "fornications," "fornicator," and "fornicators." In addition, the holy book prohibits sex with one's father's wife, daughter-in-law, mother-in-law, sister, father's daughter, mother's daughter, mother's sister, father's sister, uncle's wife, and brother's wife—not to mention animals, another man, and one's own wife, during menstruation. (It is interesting that these prohibitions are spelled out mainly for men, less often for women; those governing women's sexual acts are more likely to have been taken for granted.) Several of these injunctions carry a penalty of death: "And the man that committith adultery with another man's wife. . . , the adulterer and the adulteress shall surely be put to death. . . . If a man also lie with mankind, as he lieth with a woman, both of them have committed an abomination: they shall surely be put to death. . . . And if a man lie with a beast, he shall surely be put to death: and ye shall slay the beast. . . . And if a woman approach unto any beast, and lie down thereto, thou shalt kill the woman, and the beast: they shall surely be put to death" (Leviticus 20:10, 13, 15, 16).

Clearly, the control of sexuality and the punishment of deviant sexuality were major tasks of the prophets. And the fact is, the importance of sexual prohibitions remains true to this day.

IN WHAT WAYS IS SEXUAL BEHAVIOR DEVIANT?

In contemporary society, what are the *ways* in which sex may be considered deviant? One observer (Wheeler, 1960) isolated four main dimensions or *aspects* of sexual behavior that our laws are designed to govern. Although laws represent an extremely imperfect reflection of attitudes and morality, it happens that some of the same dimensions are relevant to sexual deviance as to sex crimes. With sex norms, as with laws governing sexual acts, there are the *who, what, how, where,* and *when* questions. Who one's partner is is clearly an important source of prohibition; "what" one's partner is, likewise, determines right and wrong in the sexual arena; how the sex act takes place also can determine its inappropriateness; where and when sex is performed, too, can be a source of right and wrong. According to Wheeler, what *makes* a sexual act illegal, and by extrapolation, deviant, is an *inappropriateness along one or another of the following dimensions*: (1) the degree of consent, or one aspect of the *how* question; (2) the nature of the sexual object, or the *who* and *what* question; (3) the nature of the sex act, another aspect of the "how" question; and (4) the *setting* in which the sex act occurs, or the *where* question.

Rape, which is regarded by most expert observers as more an act of violence than a type of sexual behavior, and which is discussed in a bit of detail in Chapter 6, is deviant along dimension (1)—*consent* on the part of the woman is lacking; force, violence, or the threat of violence is used to obtain sexual intercourse.

All societies on earth proscribe certain sex partners as unacceptable, and sex with them as deviant—dimension (2), or *nature of the sex partner*. The number of sex partners who are regarded as inappropriate for all members of societies around the world is enormous. In addition, all societies deem certain partners for designated persons off-limits, while those partners may be acceptable for other persons. In our society, close relatives may not have sex with one another (again, the "who" question); if they do, it is automatically an instance of deviance. The same applies to members of the same sex, strangers, partners who are married to someone else, or anyone except our spouse if we are married, and so on. Adults may not have sex with underage minors; Catholic priests may not have sex with anyone; on many university campuses, professors should not have sex with students; psychiatrists may not have sex with their patients; and so on.

Many of these restrictions pertain to the relationship we have (or don't have) with certain persons—brothers and sisters, strangers, and so on. Dimension (2), the nature of the sexual partner, also includes nonhuman sex objects, such as animals or sex dolls. (This is the "what" rather than the "who" question.)

"Kinky" sex, encompassing dimension (3)—the nature of the sex act, or the "how" question—represents a broad umbrella. It is made up of sexual behavior that is unusual and bizarre to many people, constituting what used to be referred to as "perversions." Some people receive a sexual charge out of receiving an enema; this is regarded as "kinky." Others like to be tied up when they have sex, or to tie their partner up; this too may be referred to as "kinky." Sadomasochistic practices (giving or receiving pain during the sex act) likewise fall under the "how" umbrella of dimension (3). Some acts that were once considered kinky or perverted are more likely to be accepted and considered normal today—for instance, oral and anal sex. "Kinky" sex is condemned or considered deviant specifically because what is done—the nature of the act—is considered weird, unwholesome, and worthy of condemnation. Sex with a partner of the same gender is condemned in many social circles of Western society. Another sexual activity that is widely controlled—by custom, if not by law—in this society is masturbation. Adolescent boys and girls are admonished not to "touch" themselves, and adults are very rarely willing to discuss their participation in it, even to their close friends.

And lastly, some people find sex in public and semipublic places exciting and practice it because they have a certain chance of being discovered by others. Pushed to its extreme form, this is referred to as exhibitionism, and it is regarded as deviance because of dimension (4), the "where" question—sex in an inappropriate setting. Judging from the sexual fantasies (male fantasies, at least) that researchers have elicited from respondents, sex in an inappropriate setting excites the imagination of a substantial number of the members of this society.

There are other dimensions that are not covered by the law or are less strongly governed by law than by custom that, nonetheless, dictate the inappropriateness of certain sexual behaviors.

There is, to begin with, the *how often* question: The desire for sex that is widely deemed *too frequent* may court the charge of being a "sex addict" (Carnes, 1983) or being "sexually compulsive" (Levine and Troiden, 1988). On the other hand, desiring or having sex *not often enough* may result in being labeled "impotent" or "frigid." Next, there is the *when* question; a wide range of cross-cultural taboos attend intercourse at certain times (Paige, 1977), such as during pregnancy (63 percent of all societies), menstruation (73 percent), and the postpartum period (95 percent). Generally, sex at *too young* an age, even if the partners are the same age, generates condemnation and punishment among conventional others, parents especially. Not uncommonly, persons who are deemed *too old* will experience some negative, often condescending, reactions from others—often their own children! Sex with *too many* partners (a pattern that is conventionally referred to as "promiscuity," a loaded and sexist term) will attract chastisement, although more often for women than for men, and more often for homosexual men than for heterosexuals. Sex with too many persons in the same place at the same time (called an "orgy"), likewise, is regarded as a deviant practice by much of the public. Watching others have sex or undress (voyeurism or "peeping") is deviant and, under certain circumstances, illegal as well. As we saw, exposing one's sex organs to an unwilling, coerced audience (exhibitionism), too, qualifies as an unconventional sex act, and is illegal as well. Selling, acting in or posing for, making, or, in some quarters, purchasing and consuming material that is widely regarded as pornographic is regarded as deviant. And selling and buying sexual favors is a clear-cut instance of sexual deviance in most people's eyes; prostitution is one of the more widely known and condemned forms of sexual deviance.

ESSENTIALISM VERSUS CONSTRUCTIONISM

Positivism is related to a perspective that in philosophy is referred to as "essentialism." There is perhaps no arena of human life in which a contrast between essentialism and constructionism is starker and more glaring than in sexual behavior. The *essentialist* position sees sexuality as "real," as something that exists, in more or less standard form, everywhere and for all time. Sex is a "thing," a pre-given entity, a concretely real phenomenon, much like an oxygen molecule, an apple, an orange, or gravitation. For both the sexual conservative and the sexual libertine, sex is an immanent, indwelling force; it is *there*; it exists prior to human consciousness. "Everyone knows" what sex is; sex is sex is sex. Essentialists recognize that sex norms and sexual customs and behavior vary the world over and throughout recorded time. But the conservative would say that certain variations are a perversion of "true" or legitimate sexual expression, and the libertine would say that sexual *repression* is a perversion of a "true" or legitimate sexual expression. Both agree, however, that the essence of sexuality is a "thing" that can be characterized in a more or less standard fashion. In other words, both are essentialists.

As we might guess, a completely different view of sex is offered by *constructionism*. Constructionism asks questions about *construction* and *imputation of meaning* (Gagnon and Simon, 1973; Plummer, 1975, 1982). Instead of assuming beforehand that we already know what phenomena in the world bear an automatic sexual meaning, the constructionist asks: *How is sexuality itself constructed?* What *is* sexuality? How is the category put together? What is included in it, what's excluded? What are the *meanings* that are attached to it? How is sex thought about? Talked about? What rules do societies construct for appropriate and inappropriate sexual behavior? Constructionists argue that these meanings vary from person to person, from setting to setting, from one social circle to another, from one culture or society to another.

Constructionists insist that behaviors or phenomena that are superficially, mechanically, and outwardly the same—that might seem *formally* the same to an external observer—can have radically different meanings to the participants. And the opposite is true as well: Actions and other phenomena that, if examined externally and mechanically, are objectively radically *different* can actually bear very *similar* meanings to observers or participants.

What is sexual to one person may be totally *lacking* in sexual content or meaning to another.

Is being strangled with a nylon cord sexually exciting? Very few of us would feel that way, but sexual asphyxia—strangling oneself to achieve sexual excitation—is common enough be to be well-known to every coroner and medical examiner in the country. Does wearing rubber and leather arouse our passion? What about engaging in dominance and submission games with your partner? Are children your sexual cup of tea? Do strippers become "turned on" when they perform? Many members of their audiences certainly do; in contrast, these performers are often simply going through the motions, utterly unmoved by their act. Receiving an enema or watching an entire family playing volleyball at a nudist camp may be sexual to one observer or participant and totally asexual to another. Is a vaginal examination by a gynecologist "sexual" in meaning? To repeat: An act that sickens one person leaves another cold, and causes a third to become aroused to the point of orgasm.

The point is, sexual meaning does not exist intrinsically or inherently in a given act. Rather, sexual meanings are *read* or *infused into* phenomena or behaviors in the world; they do not lie there, inert, immanent, ready to be noticed and picked up, much as we might reach down and pick up a rock.

Consider the following roster of behaviors, all of which may be regarded as "sexual" by some actors or observers but not by many others:

> When a child plays with his genitals, is this "sexual"? When a person excretes is this sexual? When a man kisses another publicly, is this sexual? When a couple are naked together, is this sexual? When a girl takes her clothes off in public, is this sexual? When a lavatory attendant wipes down a toilet seat, is this sexual? When a boy has an erection climbing a tree, is this sexual? When a morgue attendant touches a dead body, is this sexual? When a social worker assists her client, is this sexual? When a man and woman copulate out of curiosity or out of duty, is this sexual? The list could be considerably extended. . . . Most of the situations above could be defined as sexual by [some] members [of the society]; they need not

be. Sexual meanings are not universal absolutes, but ambiguous and problematic categories. (Plummer, 1975, p. 31)

A crucial extension of this point is that, to the constructionist, if the sexual meaning of activities cannot be translated in an automatic, glib, superficial, and mechanical fashion from one person to another, then they likewise cannot be translated from one culture to another. Actions that are *outwardly* similar are *experienced* in radically different ways; "the same" mechanical action will inhabit an entirely different internal or subjective landscape. Consider same-gender sexual behavior in ancient Greece. In this case, same-gender sexual behavior was accepted, even expected, if one male was older and the other was an adolescent and the older male continued to have sex with women as well. Now consider same-gender sexual behavior in the contemporary United States, where it is more likely to be stigmatized, the partners tend to be age peers, and it is not typically accompanied by heterosexual activity. Can we equate the two? Are they "the same" sort of behavior? Can we refer to both as "homosexuality"? To do so would make many constructionists extremely uncomfortable. In Eskimo (or Inuit) society, a custom exists of husbands offering their wives sexually to male guests; in contemporary United States, in some social circles, married couples "swap" or "swing" or engage in "co-marital" sex. Are these two practices very similar to, or very different from, one another? They are likely to serve entirely different functions and be experienced by the relevant parties in radically different ways. Hence, to the constructionist, they are entirely different acts; their similarities are likely to be more superficial than meaningful.

The point is, in comparing these and other sets of objectively or externally similar genital activities, vastly different *meanings* are attached to them, depending on the social context in which they take place. (Indeed, much behavior that is not even *initially* genital in nature may *generate* a genital response, so symbolic or constructed is this thing we refer to as sex.) Moreover, vastly different actions can be interpreted as having a sexual content or meaning. The meaning does not arise automatically from the nature of the act; it is the meaning that *makes* the act sexual in nature.

In contrast, constructionists argue that *sexuality is in the service of the social world.* Sexuality does not shape our social conduct so much as social meanings give shape to our sexuality (Plummer, 1982, p. 232). We are sexual because we are social. It is social life that *creates, motivates,* and *shapes* our sexuality. Some men seduce women to gain the admiration of their peers; in prison, sex acts as a power broker, a source of masculinity and affection (Gagnon and Simon, 1973, p. 258); one teenage girl dates many boys in search of admiration and respect, while another dates very few, seeking the boy of her dreams; the prostitute has intercourse in pursuit of cash; the health faddist has sex as part of a rigid schedule of vitamins, exercise, and fat-free foods; another health faddist avoids sex altogether in pursuit of "purity" and physical conditioning. In each case, "sexual experiences are constructed from social motives and settings" (Plummer, 1982, p. 233).

In short, the social constructionists argue, sex is not a given, a hard-and-fast reality, a bedrock biological constant—something that simply "is"—but something that is created or *fashioned* out of our biological "raw material," partly by our culture, partly by our partners and our interaction with them, and partly by the richness of our imagination. It is not sex that makes us who we are but *we who make sex what it is.*

The constructionist argues that the categories that many of us think of as clear-cut and hard-and-fast are much more ambiguous and subjectively problematic than we realize. For certain categories, there is a great deal of disagreement about their meaning. Two people may use the same words, but they may understand very different things by those words. Concepts like "freedom," "justice," "democracy," "racism," "exploitation," "love," and so on, are social constructs. People who hold every conceivable position along the political, ideological, and moral spectra interpret them in radically different ways. The same is true of sex. Sex "is" whatever we make of it.

The importance of how categories are socially constructed by different parties in a controversy exploded in the public consciousness in 1998 and 1999, during the impeachment hearings of then-President Bill Clinton, when the president claimed not to have "had sex" with Monica Lewinsky. The hearings made it clear that Clinton and Lewinsky did engage in oral-genital contact. Was the president lying? Did the fact that they had oral-genital contact (more specifically, that she performed oral sex on him) mean that they "had sex" or not? Agreement was far from universal.

Survey researchers ask questions about what people do, what they believe, for whom they plan to vote, what drugs they use or have used, and so on. But how can we be sure that the meaning of the categories researchers ask about and the answers their respondents give agree with one another? If researchers conduct a survey that asks if its respondents "had sex" or not, do their respondents have the same *understanding* or *interpretation* of that category, "had sex," as the researchers? An illustration of the constructionist position toward sexual behavior is the varying answers researchers receive to the question, "Have you had sex?" Respondents vary with respect to what they mean when they answer this question. Some respondents will answer "yes" to the question that others will answer "no" to—even though they have engaged in exactly the same physical behavior. This does not necessarily mean that lying is involved; again, it may be a matter of interpreting the meaning of the categories differently.

Stephanie Sanders and June Reinisch, researchers at the Kinsey Institute for Research in Sex, Gender, and Reproduction, decided to address the question of varying interpretations to the question, "Have you had sex?" They asked a sample of undergraduates, "Would you say you 'had sex' with someone if the most intimate behavior you engaged in was. . . ," followed by a series of specific behaviors. It might seem that everyone would agree on the interpretation of the word "sex," that any and all who use the word refer to a specific, concrete set of actions that has a stable, more or less universal meaning. To the contrary, as the Clinton-Lewinsky case made clear, there is a substantial amount of disagreement when it comes to regarding some of these actions as "sex."

Only 2 percent of the sample's respondents would say that they "had sex" with someone if the most intimate act with them was "deep kissing." Clearly, there was almost universal agreement that deep kissing did *not* constitute having

"had sex." And only 15 percent of the sample said that they regard the manual stimulation of the genitals (either giving or receiving) as having "had sex." At the other end of the spectrum, 99.5 percent of the respondents said that they would say that they "had sex" if the most intimate behavior was "penile-vaginal intercourse." Hence, there was a nearly universally agreed-upon meaning attached to penile-vaginal intercourse: For nearly the entire sample, it *does* constitute having "had sex."

The most disagreement came in when the respondents were asked about oral sex: 40 percent of the sample said that they would say that they "had sex" with someone if the most intimate act they engaged in was oral contact with that person's genitals and 40 percent said the same about another person having oral contact with their genitals. Contrarily, 60 percent said that they do *not* regard having oral contact as having "had sex." Just under one respondent in five would *not* consider having engaged in penile-anal intercourse as having "had sex." For many respondents, having engaged in everything *except* penile-genital intercourse constitutes "technical virginity" (Sanders and Reinisch, 1999).

Another issue, not explored by the researchers, is why respondents regarded certain activities with their partners as more intimate than others. Why did they feel that penile-vaginal intercourse was more "intimate" than oral-genital contact, and so on? What went into the construction of this intimacy hierarchy, with "deep kissing" at the bottom and penile-vaginal intercourse at the top? Again, what this study shows is that sex is constructed by the society, the culture, and subgroup and individual interpretation.

GENDERING SEXUALITY

It might seem odd to emphasize the specifically gendered aspect of sex generally and heterosexual deviance specifically, since our reaction is likely to be: "*Of course* heterosexual sex is gendered— that is, anchored to the sex of the participant. That's so obvious it's trite, trivial, and banal. Why bring it up?" But the point may be so obvious that we lose sight of it.

How do we "gender" heterosexuality? What about sexual deviance?

"Heterosexuality," writes Diane Richardson (1996, p. 2), "is a category divided by gender." Obvious as it is, heterosexual behavior takes place between men and women. This means that when men engage in heterosexual behavior, it is influenced—some would say entirely determined—by their physical equipment and their male gender role. Likewise, when women have sex with men, they do it as women. An obvious point? Perhaps not, since its implications seem to have escaped many observers when they write about heterosexual sex and heterosexual deviance. To understand our subject fully and in all its complexity, we need to ground it in male-female gender roles. More specifically, we need to understand what Weitzer (2000) calls the "gender disparity" in heterosexual deviance—that is that male sexual behavior "is less subject to social strictures" than female sexual activity (p. 7). For example:

- Evaluations of sexual behavior vary according to the sex or gender of the actor. Thus, a sexually active teenage girl is condemned more strongly than a teenage boy; an adulterous wife is condemned more harshly than an adulterous husband. Hence, the very foundation of deviance—that is, stigma or condemnation—is dependent on who is being stigmatized or condemned, which, in turn, is based on the sex or gender of the enactor.
- Standards of beauty, tightly linked to sexual desirability, are much more stringent, far narrower, and less pluralistic for females than for males. Girls and women are evaluated much more stringently on the basis of their looks than boys and men are, they are much more likely to be painfully aware of their inadequacies in the appearance department, they suffer more because of it, and they are more likely to take drastic measures—including bulimia, anorexia, life-threatening diets, and surgery—to measure up to those exacting standards (Freedman, 1986; Schur, 1984, pp. 66–81). An unattractive girl or woman is regarded as something of a deviant; an unattractive boy or man is simply an expression of variation along a spectrum.
- The problem of teenage sex, pregnancy, and subsequent out-of-wedlock births is widely

regarded as a problem almost exclusively of the behavior of girls. The sexual behavior of boys is considered natural, understandable, inevitable, and beyond society's control. When the authorities attempt to "control" teenage sex, it is specifically the sexual behavior of teenage girls that is the target of such control.

- Comarital sex, "mate swapping," or "swinging" is generally initiated by the husband and complied with by the wife. It is the husband who pressures his wife into engaging in sexual exchanges with other couples (although it is often the wife who enjoys it more and the husband who is made more uncomfortable or insecure about the experience). Swinging generally involves translating masculine sexual fantasies, retained from adolescence, into reality; for the wife, swinging "represents the fulfillment of the social-romantic demands that she makes upon her mate" (Bartell, 1971, p. 47). In fact, most exotic forms of sexual behavior are initiated by the man, who pressures or forces the woman into participating in them (Rodmell, 1981, p. 207).
- The vast majority of "sex work"—jobs that involve being paid to take part in one or another sex-related activity, such as prostitution, telephone sex, acting in pornographic videos, nude or "exotic" dancing—is enacted *by* women *for* men. More specifically, women are paid to gratify the sexual demands of men to engage in actions they otherwise would not choose to do. Thus, sex work is a creation of the sex role of and the vastly greater power exercised by men; for the most part, women go along with such importunings because their options are more limited than those that men face.
- Even more specifically, "female sex workers are [regarded as] quintessential *deviant women*, whereas [their] customers are seen as essentially *normal men*" (Weitzer, 2000, p. 7). Condemnation for participating in sexual deviance is much stronger for women than for men. (Of course most of the time, for women, the behavior is more central: it is a full-time paying job; whereas for men, it is little more than a part-time recreation.) The stigma of having to pay for sex is vastly less than the stigma of being paid. "The very terminology used [for women]—whore, hooker, harlot, slut—is heavily laden with opprobrium." By contrast, the terms used for male customers are "fairly tame labels." In short: "You may be a bit surprised to learn that a male friend has visited a prostitute, but shocked to learn that a female friend *is* a

prostitute" (p. 7). The same applies to a one-time experience.

• This "gender disparity" applies to the research literature as well. Female sex workers are studied vastly more than their male customers—or, for that matter, than males involved in any way in the sex industry. (Interestingly, the reverse is true of homosexuality: Gay men have been studied much more often than lesbians.) The exceptions are few and far between (Milner and Milner, 1972; Monto, 2000). One major exception: male sexual arousal in response to erotic or pornographic materials (Donnerstein, Linz, and Penrod, 1987; Linz and Malamuth, 1993). Much more research needs to be conducted on male participation in the sex industry.

The list could be multiplied almost endlessly, but the point should be clear: Sexual behavior generally, and sexual deviance more specifically, are expressions or manifestations of the roles of men and women. Sex as behavior cannot be understood independent of sex as a role. In short, sex is "gendered," and our understanding of sex, sexual deviance included, must incorporate gender as its foundation. It is naive to assume that a given sexual encounter between a man and a woman means the same thing to the two participants, has the same consequences, or is interpreted by members of the society in the same fashion. While men and women act and interact together, in a way they inhabit social worlds that are in large measure separate and distinct. Gendering must always inform our view of sexual deviance.

WHAT CONSTITUTES SEXUAL DEVIANCE?

The constructionist position goes considerably beyond the insight that understanding symbolic meaning is necessary to understand sexual behavior. It argues further that not only is the very *category* of sexuality constructed; in addition, a specific *evaluative* meaning is read into it as well. By "evaluative" I mean that sexual categories are rendered "good" or "bad"—that is, conventional and norm-abiding, or deviant, in violation of the norms—through the construction process. For instance, not only are the categories "homosexual" and "heterosexual" constructed (and in some societies, they are not even constructed at all!), and constructed at different points in different societies, but they are *infused with positive or negative meanings*. Each is regarded in a certain way—as "abnormal" or "normal," "evil" or "acceptable," "an offense in God's eyes" or a "tolerable practice," "repulsive" or "straight, boring, vanilla sex," "liberating" or "repressive," an "alternative lifestyle" or "conformist," "nonhierarchical" or "patriarchical," "compulsive" or "freely chosen"—depending on the society or social circle rendering the judgment. It is these social definitions we have to pay close attention to; they are what social deviance is built on. Different forms of sexual expression do not bring with them an automatic response or evaluation; they do not drop down from the skies as a reaction to their essence or basic reality. What *creates* the phenomenon of deviance is these reactions; they are variable in societies the world over, from one historical time period to another, and from one social circle or context to another in the same society. It is the construction process that is the very stuff of deviance.

Of all areas of deviance, it is perhaps in the sphere of sexual deviance that the idea of sickness and pathology has been and remains most prominent. Historically, the imputation of pathology has been part and parcel of the construction process in the study of deviance. Until the 1970s, the vast majority of research and writing on nonnormative sex cast it beyond the pale of normality. Sexual deviants, these early researchers and authors were saying, are distinctly *not like the rest of us*. When the words "sexual deviant" are used to describe someone, the image that comes to mind is someone who is impelled to act as a result of uncontrollable, unfathomable, and distinctly abnormal, motives—someone whose behavior is freakish, fetishistic, and far-out.

Although, for the most part, the behaviors on the American Psychiatric Association's list of sexual disorders, described in its *Diagnostic and Statistical Manual* (1994), would qualify as sociologically deviant sexual behavior, most also represent *extreme versions* of what is in fact a *continuum* or *dimension*. The *full range* of sociologically deviant sexual behavior, although by definition condemned, is considerably more mundane or *ordinary* than these extreme and spectacular cases. It seems especially necessary to remind ourselves when discussing sexual behavior that deviance refers specifically to *socially disapproved* behavior and characteristics—and that only. It includes no taint of pathology or disorder whatsoever, no implication of harm; it does not assume that we are discussing the *more extreme* end of a continuum that runs from mildly to extremely deviant.

Practitioners of certain forms of deviance will often respond to the term by saying: "We're not deviants! There's nothing sick or wrong with what we do!" A sociologist would respond by asking if said persons *do* or *would* receive negative, punishing, or condemnatory reactions from others as a result of what they do. "What would your parents do or say if they found out? Your friends, acquaintances, fellow students, teachers, your boss, co-workers, relatives, neighbors—the general public?" If the answer is that their reaction is likely to be negative, that they would condemn or socially reject you, ridicule or gossip about you, punish or humiliate you, then we have a clear-cut case of deviance on our hands; if not, we don't.

Let's put the matter another way: *psychological* and *social* (or sociological) deviance are not the same thing. They delineate two separate and independent dimensions. They overlap, of course; the chances are that nearly all cases of *psychological* deviance would qualify as *sociological* deviance. But the reverse is not the case. Psychologically, sexual deviance implies a *disorder*, a *dysfunction*; socially and sociologically, sexual deviance simply refers to a violation of norms and a subsequently high likelihood of condemnation. No disorder and no dysfunction are implied. What violates the norms in a given society may in fact be quite normal psychologically. (Although it may not.) What is accepted, practiced, and even encouraged in one society may be savagely condemned and harshly punished in another. What is a normative violation at one time may be the norm at another. Again, because the link between sexual deviance and psychological abnormality is so strong in many observers' minds, we have to be reminded of their conceptual independence.

Once again, I'd like to emphasize that *condemnation* is not the same thing as *disorder*; *punishment* is not the same thing as *dysfunction*. (And remember, too, that which is regarded as a disorder or a dysfunction at one time may be accepted as normal at another time.) For something to qualify as social deviance, all that is necessary is that it be condemned in some social quarters or circles, and this may include behavior that clinical psychologists and psychiatrists agree is quite normal. No doubt some forms of sexual deviance harm others, or the actors involved, or are the product of a clinically disordered or abnormal psyche; the majority do not. Many practitioners of sexual deviance—homosexuals and prostitutes perhaps especially—will insist that they are not "deviants," meaning, of course, that they are psychologically normal. Yet they will agree that much of the public views them as somewhat less than respectable. It is easy to become ensnared in a squabble about what words mean. Reminding ourselves that, sociologically, "deviant" simply means "unconventional" and "likely to be condemned" will put us back on the right track.

HOMOSEXUALITY

Of the many ways that humankind is divided into categories, it is possible that sexual behavior and orientation are among the most basic and important of those categories. Why is the sex of one's sexual partners such a crucial part of our identity? Why do we divide humanity into "straight" and "gay"? Why is such a division so much more important for us than one that, let's say, divides us into "egg eaters" and "people who don't eat eggs"? And why does this division include an evaluative component? Not all societies condemn sex with members of the same gender—although many do—but virtually all recognize that men who prefer to have sex with other men and women who have sex with other women represent a different category of humanity than heterosexuals. In the United States, a sizable—although shrinking—percentage of the population believe homosexual acts to be an "abomination," and support the laws banning them.

Fundamentalist Christians and political conservatives point to the Bible to justify their opposition to homosexuality. As we saw, Leviticus clearly states that homosexual behavior is an "abomination." "It's God's judgment, not just mine!" these opponents will state. But, as I also said above, this conveniently omits the fact that the Bible also condemns many other actions that these opponents of homosexuality completely ignore, including eating shellfish, mixing different fabrics in one's garments, growing different crops in the same field, handling pigskin, and eating pork. In addition, the Bible condoned slavery, patriarchy, and polygamy. In other words, homosexuals must feel that strict Bible Christians *pick and choose* certain biblical injunctions, but pretend that others don't exist. *Today*, they wonder, why is homosexuality an abomination, while so many other actions that are also condemned in the Bible are regarded as perfectly acceptable?

And yet, for the society as a whole, things are changing. Perhaps the most interesting and significant development that has taken place in the past decade with respect to homosexuality as deviance has been the fact that homosexuality is "departing from deviance" (Minton, 2002). This development has accelerated hugely since the previous edition of *Deviant Behavior* (2001), and even more so in the past decade or two. A substantial proportion of Americans still regards homosexuals as deviants and feels that homosexual behavior is abnormal, unnatural, and unacceptable. But that proportion is dwindling. The segment that is consistent in its strong condemnation of homosexuality is increasingly confined to political conservatives and fundamentalist Christians. This remains a huge segment of the public, but it is soon to become practically the only segment that feels and acts this way.

Perhaps a kind of scorecard of recent developments will place this issue in perspective.

Public Opinion

For starters, public opinion has become *much* more accepting of homosexuality than was true a generation ago. Today, as compared with 20 or more years ago, the public is significantly, and in some cases, strikingly, more likely to believe that:

homosexual relations should be legal (54 percent versus 45 percent); homosexuals should have equal job opportunities (85 percent versus 59 percent), should be hired as salespersons (91 percent versus 70 percent), in the armed forces (72 percent versus 52 percent), in the clergy (54 percent versus 38 percent), and as elementary school teachers (56 percent versus 32 percent); and that homosexuality is an "acceptable alternative lifestyle" (52 percent versus 34 percent). In a number of these cases, opinion has shifted over the past 20 or so years from a majority *against* to a majority *for* homosexual rights. In short, *in many important respects*, a majority of Americans no longer regards homosexuality as a form of deviance, or homosexuals as deviants. (See Table 9.1.)

Homosexual Behavior as a Crime?

Until June 2003, 11 states of the United States had laws on the books criminalizing what was referred to as "sodomy," which applied equally to homosexual and heterosexual acts; 4 states had sodomy laws that applied only to homosexual acts; and 35 states had by then repealed their sodomy laws. In that month, the Supreme Court of the United States ruled that the Texas sodomy laws were unconstitutional, a decision that repealed the sodomy laws everywhere. This decision, referred to as *Lawrence v. Texas*, overturns a 1986 ruling, *Bowers v. Hardwick*, that affirmed the right of states to criminalize homosexual sodomy. The 2003 Supreme Court decision, say legal scholars and movement spokespersons, represented a "landmark victory for gay rights" (Lane, 2003b). It is likely to have far-reaching legal and social consequences.

Homosexual Marriage and Civil Unions

In September 2003, Canada's Parliament endorsed homosexual marriage. The vote was close (137 to 132) but binding; the ruling went into effect the moment it was rendered (Brown, 2003). American public opinion is largely opposed to homosexual marriage; in 2000, according to a Gallup Poll, respondents were

TABLE 9.1   ATTITUDES ON HOMOSEXUALITY, 1982–2002 (%)

"Do you think homosexual relations between consenting adults should or should not be legal?"

	1982	2001
Should	45	54
Should not	39	42

"In general, do you think homosexuals should or should not have equal rights in terms of job opportunities?"

	1982	2001
Should	59	85
Should not	28	11
No opinion	13	4

"Do you think homosexuals should or should not be hired for the following occupations?"

	1982		2001	
	SHOULD	SHOULD NOT	SHOULD	SHOULD NOT
Salespersons	70	18	91	6
The armed forces	52	36	72	23
The clergy	38	51	54	39
Elementary school teachers	32	59	56	40

"Do you think that homosexuality should be considered an acceptable alternative lifestyle or not?"

	1982	2001
Yes	34	52
No	51	43

Note: "No opinion," "Don't know," "Not sure," etc., deleted from table.
Source: Data from Gallup Polls, 1982, 2001.

opposed to making gay marriage legal by a margin of almost two to one (62 percent opposed, 34 percent in favor). In the United States, Vermont's "civil union" law went into effect, authorizing a marriage-like bond between partners of the same sex. Couples joined in civil union "shall have all the same benefits, protections and responsibilities . . . as are granted spouses in a marriage" (http://www.sec.state.vt.us/otherprg/civilunions/civilunions.html). In November, the Massachusetts Supreme Court ruled that homosexual marriage is a constitutional right (Von Drehle, 2003). Americans are more or less evenly split on the issue of favoring (46 percent) and opposing (51 percent) civil unions, according to a Gallup Poll

administered in May 2002. The consequences of these changes are too recent to determine, but the fact that they took place is remarkable, given the country's recent past.

The Media

In its September–October 2003 issue, *Bride's* magazine published an article about homosexual weddings. The appearance of this article was such a radical departure from tradition that *The New York Times* devoted an article to reporting the event. It was the first time that any of the five top-selling bridal magazines had devoted a feature to the subject (Carlson, 2003, p. C2). On October 1,

A Congressman Accepts a Lesbian Daughter

Social change takes place not only structurally, cataclysmically, on the big stage, but also microscopically, individually, on a person-by-person basis. Often individual changes reflect or *symbolize* the larger changes. Looking at the changes in a single politician's life may say a great deal about how the society is changing as a whole.

In December 2002, Congressman Dick Gephardt, a Democrat from Missouri who was a contender for the Democratic nomination for president in 2004, sent out 2,000 Christmas cards to friends, relatives, and constituents. On the card was a photograph—the usual family portrait consisting of Representative Gephardt; his wife, Jane; his single daughter, Kate; his son Matt and Matt's wife Tricia; and his other daughter, Chrissy—with her arm around another woman. The other woman, it turns out, was Amy Loder, Chrissy's lover. Dick Gephardt and his wife were publicly acknowledging that their daughter was "proudly and openly" a lesbian. Indeed, the Christmas card seemed not only to accept but to *endorse* his daughter's sexual orientation (Swarns, 2003, p. A1).

It is extremely unusual for a politician from a conservative state to endorse a child's homosexuality. Barney Frank, a member of Congress, is an open, acknowledged homosexual, but he represents a district in Boston with a liberal constituency. Dick Cheney, George W. Bush's vice president, has a lesbian daughter, but the Cheneys have never spoken publicly about the sexual orientation of their daughter. Gephardt is in fact "the first presidential hopeful to give a gay relative such a prominent and public platform" (p. A1). What is so remarkable about the Gephardt endorsement is that it comes from a politician whose views began at the conservative end of the political spectrum.

Representative Gephardt, 62, the son of a milk-delivery driver, grew up in a segregated St. Louis. He never knew anyone who was openly gay, he says, and then, people ridiculed homosexuals. "It was seen as abnormal behavior," he explains (p. A11). Gephardt grew up in a religious household and was a youth leader in the Baptist church, and his mother hoped he would become a minister. In the early 1980s, Gephardt opposed abortion and federally financed legal services for homosexuals. However, his views on homosexuality began to shift even before his daughter came out to her parents as a lesbian. In 1992, Gephardt hired an openly gay man as his chief of staff. The Gephardts have joined a gay advocacy group, Parents, Families, and Friends of Lesbians and Gays, which publishes, displays, and distributes family portraits with captions that read, "We love our gay son" and "We love our lesbian daughter." Although Gephardt does not support gay marriage, he has come a very long way from where he was on this issue.

What happened? What caused the change? "You learn as you go through life," he says. "You meet people, and you listen to people—and I do try to listen to people—you can really learn. And I've learned" (p. A11).

Is Gephardt emblematic of changes that have been taking place in American society generally? Public opinion polls, as well as sector-by-sector changes in American institutions, suggest that this may be the case. It is possible that on the individual scale, what Representative Gephardt has experienced reflects what the country as a whole is going through.

2003, on its "Weddings, Engagements, and Anniversaries" page, *The Washington Post* announced the marriage of James Gasser and Gregory Ramsey in Toronto, Canada. A month later, the announcement said, the couple would also celebrate their twenty-fifth anniversary together. Both Gasser and Ramsey are "active parishioners" of All Souls Memorial Episcopal Church. Two months later, on November 30, 2003, *The New York Times* announced the wedding of two men in their fifties (in Canada), Richard Mohr and Robert Switzer. Whether this portends a developing trend can only be speculated on at this point. Still, these announcements certainly indicate a radical change of media representations that have taken place over the past two or three years.

The early years of the twenty-first century witnessed the release of a remarkable array of gay-oriented television programs. To appreciate how truly remarkable this development is, consider the fact that 30 years ago, prime-time television tended to depict homosexuals as mentally disordered. The hero of *Marcus Welby, M. D.* urged a "tormented patient" of his to "win that fight" against his homosexual impulses. An episode of *Police Women* portrayed three lesbians murdering the residents of a retirement home. As late as 1995, *Serving in Silence*, the first sympathetic depiction of a homosexual character, Colonel Margarethe Cammermeier, who was dismissed from the Washington State National Guard for her lesbianism, elicited a refusal of many sponsors to advertise, and a kiss between the two main characters brought forth protests against the stations that aired the show. All that has changed. In January 2001, Showtime launched *Queer As Folk*, a remarkably sexually explicit program depicting gay men and women living in Pittsburgh—with a great deal of homosexual kissing, caressing, nearly total nudity, and bedroom scenes. Buoyed by its success, in January 2004 the cable channel Showtime released *The L Word*, which is centered around a social circle of lesbians living in Los Angeles. In 2003, Bravo launched *Queer Eye for the Straight Guy*, a program depicting five gay men who each week give style and fashion advice to a different (and usually clueless) heterosexual man. The audience watching the first two broadcasts of this show was the largest in Bravo's history. So successful has the program been that NBC, Bravo's parent station, broadcast the program; it was the network's second-most-watched program in that time slot in more than two weeks. Advertisers—including Bausch & Lomb (an optical company), Levis, Volkswagen, and the movie *Seabiscuit*—lined up to sponsor the show; none objected to its content. This development is not without its critics, including representatives of the Parents Television Council, a conservative lobby group. Interestingly, some homosexual spokespersons also object to such programs, contending that they feed into gay stereotypes. "You're not seeing diverse images on these shows," said Martin Duberman, a historian of the homosexual rights movement. But Randy Barbato, co-creator of *Gay Hollywood*, an AMC program that aired in August 2003, disagrees. "There are a few visible stereotypes right now. That'll open the door for different kinds of characters" (Weintraub and Rutenberg, 2003, pp. A1, C5).

Homosexual Clergy

In 2003, an openly gay New Hampshire priest, Gene Robinson, was elected bishop of the Episcopal Church. The Episcopal Diocese is affiliated with the Anglican Union, a denomination with 80 million members worldwide. As we saw earlier, the book of Leviticus declares homosexual acts to be an "abomination." In Romans, Saint Paul refers to same-sex acts as "unseemly," "unrighteous," and "unnatural," depending on the translation. These and other biblical passages—for instance, in Timothy, Corinthians, and Genesis—are what gay rights activists refer to as "clobber passages," that is, they have been used to denounce homosexuality. An increasing number of Christian theologians, however, are redefining homosexuality in ways that challenge traditional views of Scripture. For instance, Robert Goss, a former Jesuit priest and an advocate of what's called "queer theology," argues that God created humans in His image; hence, homosexual behavior, an expression of that humanity, is a blessing, not a sin. Several theologians have even gone so far as to argue that Jesus's relationship with his disciples was "homoerotic." Christians "have so much baggage around sexuality, so much shame that short-circuits pleasure," explains Professor Goss; it's time, he says, for Christians to "reconnect with their lovers, their community, and their God" (Broadway, 2003, p. B8).

Holdouts

Such pro-gay interpretations of Christian theology are controversial, however. If we are to compile the "scorecard" I mentioned earlier, detailing the many ways that homosexuality is "departing" from deviance, to be balanced, such changes would have to be compared with those ways in which the deviant status of homosexuality is not changing. Who are the "holdouts," those segments of American society that continue to regard homosexuality as deviant?

Conservative Clergy

One such segment is, as we might expect, conservative Christianity, both among the clergy and the laity. Contemplating the election of Bishop Robinson, Richard Land, head of the Southern Baptist Convention's Ethics and Religious Liberty Commission, stated: "Homosexual behavior is deviant behavior according to the clear and consistent teaching of Scripture, from the Book of Genesis to the end of the New Testament." Bishop Robinson's election is, he said, "the antithesis of Scripture" (Broadway, 2003, p. B8). The fact is, the election of Bishop Robinson threatens to split the Episcopal Church right down the middle. Regardless of which interpretation prevails—or whether the impending split actually takes place—it is clear that these issues were not seriously discussed a decade ago, nor was the traditional perspective so seriously challenged. Christianity has moved from monolithic opposition to homosexuality to a consideration of overturning at least a millennium of that opposition. If such a change were to be institutionalized, it would be as momentous and far-reaching in its impact as the Protestant Reformation of the sixteenth century.

The Laity

The laity also has its views on the deviance of homosexuality. A nationwide poll conducted by *The Washington Post* in August 2003 revealed that a clear majority (63 percent) felt that their own denomination should *not* bless "committed relationships of gay or lesbian couples." Only a third (31 percent) approved. Evangelical Protestants, most of whom have a literal interpretation of the Bible, were more likely to disapprove (81 percent) than the majority. Respondents who were members of a congregation were evenly

split on the question of whether, if their local church did bless homosexual unions, they would continue to attend (48 percent) or look for another church (47 percent). Not quite six in ten (58 percent) opposed a law "that would allow couples to legally form civil unions, giving them some of the legal rights of married couples"; roughly a third (37 percent) favored such a law. Interestingly, public support favoring civil unions or marriage-like arrangements for homosexual couples *declined* in the aftermath of the Supreme Court's decision repealing the sodomy laws nationwide. Earlier polls showed roughly half the population in favor of such unions (Morin and Cooperman, 2003). Clearly, both the church's and the general public's views on homosexuality are in transition.

The Boy Scouts

In 1990, James Dale, a 19-year-old Eagle Scout and unpaid assistant scoutmaster, gave a talk at a conference of high school teachers about his difficulties as a homosexual boy growing up in New Jersey. After his talk was reported in a local paper, he was dismissed by the Scouts. He sued to be reinstated, and the Supreme Court of New Jersey agreed, finding that his constitutional rights had been violated by the dismissal. But the Boy Scouts of America (BSA) appealed, taking the case all the way to the nation's highest tribunal. In 2000, in a five-to-four ruling, the Supreme Court found that the Scouts had the right to exclude homosexuals. Over 110 million boys have joined the BSA; 3 million are current members. The Boy Scouts of America is an extremely traditional, family-oriented organization; most members believe that gay Scouts do not support "basic moral values." Said one Scout: "A lot of people don't feel comfortable around homosexuals" (France, 2001, p. 45). According to a Gallup Poll conducted in 2000, by a two-to-one majority, the American public felt that the Boy Scouts should not be "required to allow openly gay adults" to serve as Boy Scout leaders (64 percent vs. 31 percent).

But in scouting, as with nearly all areas of social life, "there is no easy consensus" (p. 45). The BSA is sponsored by organizations, including businesses, voluntary associations such as local parent-teacher organizations, Lions Clubs, and the United Way, and religious bodies. For instance, the Church of Latter-Day Saints (the Mormons) sponsors 26,000 troops; the Roman Catholic Church sponsors 17,000 (Rimer, 2003). Both institutions are staunch supporters of the gay ban, and a reversal would result in the withdrawal of hundreds of thousands of Scouts. On the other hand, institutions opposing the ban are gradually withdrawing support. In the past decade, funding from the United Way has declined by over $20 million. In just the single year since the Supreme Court ruling, membership in the Scouts declined nationally by 4.5 percent; in the Northeast, the decline was 7.8 percent (France, 2001, p. 47). The Scouts engage in a certain proportion of their activities in affiliation with federal and local government institutions—for instance, stocking trout ponds for the Department of the Interior, or, in New York, working with the New York City Police Department. This opens the door to the charge that the BSA is not a private organization but one dependent on public support, and hence subject to the same nondiscrimination rules that apply to government employment.

Some local troops are adopting their own nondiscrimination policies. For instance, the website of the Greater New York Councils states: "Prejudice, intolerance, and discrimination in any form are unacceptable" (p. 50). In 2001, New York troop leaders called the ban on gays "stupid" and "repugnant" (Lipton, 2001). In Cleveland, the leaders of the troop sponsored by the Pilgrim Congregational United Church of Christ decided not to discriminate against gays. But the council leaders in the Cleveland area declared that they would not back up the decision, and soon after, all the canoes, tents, flags, and plaques the church stored were removed, "stripping the church bare of its Scout troop" (France, 2001, p. 50).

Although the ban against homosexuals in the BSA continues, it is not without opposition. Scouting for All, a national organization, is currently challenging the gay ban. The very fact that this controversy exists, and that opposition to excluding gay Scouts is widespread, indicates that, in one of the country's oldest and most conservative institutions, the definition of homosexuality as deviant is receding.

The Military

The United States military is another institution in which homosexuality is regarded as unacceptable—by its very rejection of gays, dealt with as deviant. In 2001, a total of 1,200 men and women were discharged for declaring themselves as homosexuals or for being caught at engaging in homosexual acts, the highest figure in 14 years. In addition, the number of incidents of anti-gay harassment in the four services increased by 23 percent over 2000. At one base, roughly a third of all military discharges are for reasons relating to homosexuality (Marquis, 2002). But like the ban on gay Scouts, the prevailing military policy ("Don't ask, don't tell") has come under fire. *Lawrence*, the Supreme Court's 2003 decision overturning the sodomy laws, will very likely be applied to military personnel. If, as *Lawrence* ruled, criminalizing sodomy is unconstitutional because of the fact that it both restricts individual liberties and, at the same time, serves "no legitimate state interest," then, in principle, the same applies to military personnel. Article 125 of the Uniform Code of Military Justice prohibits "unnatural carnal copulation with another person of the same or opposite sex or with an animal." While Article 125 is very rarely directly invoked, its application is implied in the discharge of gay military personnel. Such discharges raise the obvious question, "What interest do you have in regulating private consensual activity?" Clearly, a court challenge to the military's definition of homosexuality as deviant is likely to be brought very soon (Lane, 2003a). As we saw, more than seven Americans out of ten (72 percent) believe that homosexuals should be allowed to serve in the military.

The exclusion of gays in the military is also under fire from another source: the empirical evidence. A "think tank" located at the University of California at Santa Barbara, The Center for the Study of Sexual Minorities in the Military has investigated the impact of including homosexuals in the armed services in Canada, Israel, Great Britain, Australia—and the United States. (A total of 24 nations allow gays to serve openly in their military forces.) The conclusion of all these studies is that allowing gays to serve in the military does not decrease military performance or undermine combat effectiveness (Frank, 2002; Belkin,

2003; these studies are available online at http://www.gaymilitary.ucsb.edu/Publications/ PublicationsHome.htm). One military sociologist, Charles Moskos, claims that the "empirical data" demonstrate the opposite, but the evidence he cites consists of a Roper Poll conducted a dozen years ago which shows that 45 percent of military personnel who served in mixed-sex units said that "there was enough sexual activity to degrade military performance" (Frank, 2002). Notice that this was an opinion, not a fact, and that this applied specifically to male-female sexual relations—and the fact is, hardly anyone questions the presence of women in the military. Notice, too, that similar claims of lowered troop performance were made about the integration of African Americans into the military before they achieved equal footing with whites (Evans, 2003), claims long since regarded as ludicrous.

Before Canada permitted gays to serve in the military, 62 percent of the personnel questioned said that they would refuse to share showers, undress, or sleep in the same room as a gay soldier. In Britain, two-thirds of male personnel said they would not serve if gays did. But in neither country did any service member resign in protest when the ban was lifted (Belkin, 2003). Increasingly, the American military brass will have to deal with the fact that the evidence does not support the exclusion of openly gay personnel in the military, and that their closest allies have accepted homosexuals in the ranks without serious negative impact. As far as the armed forces of the countries that have lifted the gay ban are concerned, inclusion has been a "non-event" (p. 110).

Mainstreaming Homosexual Identity

If we are to consider whether and to what extent homosexuality is departing from deviance, we have to look at the behavior and attitudes of homosexuals themselves. Countless observers have noticed that the gay culture has become less isolationist, less militant, and more desirous of participating in mainstream society and conventional institutions. *Outweek* was a radical, hard-edged, "bitchy" magazine, filled with "libido and rage," whose orientation, by the late 1990s, was considered passé; *Outweek* is now defunct. In contrast, *Out* "looks

pretty much like any other glossy monthly with a middle-class American readership—surprisingly tame, its libido kept carefully under control. . . . The closest thing you get to libido among *Out*'s advertisers is the nice boys cuddling in the new Abercrombie & Fitch ads" (Mendelsohn, 1996, p. 29). Michelangelo Signorile, who once wrote for *Outweek* and now writes for *Out*, produces columns that are "notably more domestic, quieter, more couch-potato-ier than the semi-hysterical screeds he used to produce for *Outweek* " (p. 29). Some of his recent columns include meditations on monogamy and "the difficulties of reconciling a gay lifestyle with traditional family life . . . stuff that isn't all that different from what you find in *GQ* (*Gentleman's Quarterly*) or . . . *Esquire*" (p. 29). As Signorile's columns make clear, there are distinctive features of gay culture.

Perhaps the most remarkable indication of this trend is the increase in the number of gay couples with children. Of course, gay men and women— especially women—have (usually secretly) raised children for generations. But in recent years, the practice has become much more open and much more common. No precise figures are available, but journalists have noticed the trend; homosexuals have begun writing about their own experiences with raising children (Mendelsohn, 2000; Strah et al., 2003), and handbooks on how to be a gay dad are being published (Barret and Robinson, 2000; McGarry, 2003). A Google search turned up over 9,000 entries for "gay dads," many of them websites for support groups for homosexual fathers; the same search for "lesbian mothers" turned up over 20,000 entries. Says one journalist: "Even ten years ago, the only certain thing about a gay couple's future was that it wouldn't include children. But gays and lesbians are now becoming parents in record numbers, and it's changing how they think about themselves—and each other" (Usborne, 2003, p. 28). Daniel Mendelsohn, author of a book on his experiences with, among other things, gay parenthood (2000), said that ten years ago, in his twenties, what his life and the lives of most of his peers looked like "was a lot of clubbing" and "a lot of dating." Today, he says, gay men in their twenties are looking at not only clubbing and dancing but also "a time when you might get married and have children. And that is not all that different from the paradigm that all my straight peers were dealing with—that at some time they would settle [down]" (Usborne, 2003, pp. 30–31). In the future, this trend will be more fully documented, but anecdotally, its beginnings have been noticed; what was once a trickle has become a flood, and it is likely to continue.

Is Homosexuality Departing from Deviance? A Summary

In short, as I said earlier, in many respects, homosexuality is "departing from deviance" (Minton, 2002). Gay couples are, increasingly, permitted to adopt children (Brody, 2003); as we saw, the media are depicting homosexuals in a more realistic, less negative light; three-quarters of gays and bisexuals "feel more accepted by society today than a few years ago" (Associated Press [AP], 2001); an increasing percentage of Christians, both clergy and laity, believe that homosexuals should be accepted on an equal basis as co-religionists; sodomy laws outlawing homosexual acts have been struck down as unconstitutional; the majority of psychiatrists and psychologists no longer believe that, in and of itself, homosexuality is the manifestation of a mental disorder (American Psychiatric Association [APA], 1994; Minton, 2002); as we saw, gay marriage is legal in Canada, and marriage-like "civil unions" between two persons of the same sex are legal in several states of the United States; gay proms, complete with "pride and corsages," are becoming increasingly common (Baker, 2001); today, heterosexuals are vastly more accepting of homosexuality than was true even a decade ago; and in society's more traditional sectors and institutions, monolithic opposition to homosexuality has given way to open conflict, dissension, and schisms. In short, the deviant status of homosexuality is eroding. "The war for acceptance" of gays, says a New York magazine writer, "is practically won" (Green, 2001, p. 27). Consider the fact that a deviance textbook published as recently as 1976 included a chapter on premarital sex (Bell, 1976, pp. 37–59). Today, no one would think of writing such a chapter because premarital sex is no longer regarded as a form of deviance. Although, as we saw, in some sectors of the society, homosexuality is still seen as an "abomination," those sectors are shrinking, and this position is becoming, increasingly, a minority view, much

like belief in creationism, masculine dominance, and uncompromising opposition to abortion. In other words, if we look at deviance in *horizontal* terms, we will still be able to find categories in the population—political conservatives and strict Bible Christians—who retain the view that homosexuality is immoral, a sin, and hence, deviant. However, within a generation, for the society as a whole, homosexuality's deviant status will shrink to the point where it will no longer be a form of *societal* deviance. By that time, in all probability, homosexuality will no longer be discussed by sociologists as a form of deviance.

SEX WORK

New York magazine is much like its beat, the city of New York—sophisticated, sleek, and slick. Its back pages feature advertisements that appeal to a wide range of interests—for instance, Boats and Yachts, Town and Country Properties, Entertaining, and "Strictly Personal," or the magazine's personal ads. Two pages advertise services with a distinctly sexual angle; they headline "Massage" and "Role Play." One massage ad offers "Pure Delight," another, "Pure Bliss," a third, a "Euro-Asian model—Exotic, Sensual," yet another, "Asian Sweethearts—The best to fulfill your dreams," and still another, "The Perfect Private Interlude." The 100 or so "Role Play" ads promote a variety of offerings, including "Polite Mistresses" who will "Play Out All Your Fetishes & Fantasies," "Hot, Sensual, Elegant Models and Adult Film Stars [who] Await You!", and an "Exquisite Mistress—Sensual, erudite, upscale, discreet."

Who are the women (and men) who place these ads? Who are the men (and a few women) who answer them? And what does this whole enterprise of commercial sex—whether real or symbolic—or sex for pay add up to? What does it mean for the society in which we live? To the people who participate in them?

Sex workers sell sexual services. For them, sex is a job, a source of income. For the most part, their motive is financial, not sexual. Prostitution is a major form of sex work, but it is far from the only variety. In fact, the street (or "outdoor") prostitute has been studied extensively and in great detail, while a variety of "indoor" sex workers, such as call girls, women who work in a house of prostitution, masseuses, telephone sex workers, actors and actors in pornographic videos and films, and topless dancers have received much less attention (Weitzer, 2000, p. 5). It is entirely possible that five to ten times as many sex workers are employed in "indoor" enterprises than is true for "outdoor" or street prostitution. This exclusive emphasis on a single variety of sex worker is very likely to yield a biased and distorted picture of the job situation of women who sell sexual services. To put together a more accurate picture, therefore, it is necessary to examine a full range of sex work.

Sex work—mainly prostitution—has been approached or analyzed from a variety of perspectives. Throughout history, perhaps the most common of these perspectives has been the *moralistic* perspective: Sex work and its workers are evil, immoral, vile corrupters who deserve the contempt and condemnation they receive. A variety of this perspective might be called the "social worker" approach: Sex *work* is evil but sex *workers* have been corrupted and need to be "saved" or "salvaged," shown the straight and narrow path, shown the error of their ways, offered a decent job at a decent wage so that they don't have to demean or debase themselves by selling their bodies. *Marxism* has argued that prostitution is a manifestation of class exploitation; since capitalist society offers working-class women few opportunities to earn a living, many are forced to sell themselves to survive. *Functionalism* argues that prostitution offers many hidden benefits to the society that no other institution can supply.

Most recent writings on sex work fall into one of four perspectives: *radical feminism, "pro-sex" feminism, sexual libertarianism*, and *sexual radicalism*.

Radical Feminism

The defining feature of radical feminism is the view that *all* heterosexual sex is patriarchal or male-dominated and therefore oppressive. Sex work generally, and prostitution and pornography specifically, represent the most *extreme forms* of patriarchy and sexual oppression. As long as patriarchy exists, the sexual oppression of women will endure. It is absurd, radical feminists argue, to distinguish between "good" sex and "bad" sex,

since *all* sex under patriarchy is bad, that is, oppressive to women. Prostitution and pornography are not only manifestations or expressions of patriarchy—they also contribute to men's domination over women. Men exploit and demean prostitutes by patronizing them; they exploit and demean the women who act in pornographic videos. In fact, *all* women are exploited, demeaned, and brutalized by pornography: Men who are exposed to it carry over this exploitative stance into their relations with all the women in their lives. If the institutions of prostitution and pornography were eliminated, several major bricks in the wall of patriarchy would be removed (Russell, 1998). Eventually, the entire wall must be dismantled.

Radical feminists divide into two camps: those who acknowledge that some measure of equality can be negotiated on the micro level between and among couples, whether heterosexual or homosexual, who are more enlightened and liberated than the majority and have, to a degree, transcended society's macro-level patriarchy; and those feminists who believe that *all* sex in a patriarchical system is tainted, indeed, *saturated* by patriarchy.

The most extreme version of the radical feminist perspective—all sex is saturated by patriarchy—is often referred to as the "anti-sex" position. This is the position that *all* heterosexual sex is sexual slavery. Prostitution and pornography are merely *models* or *paradigms* of all sexual interaction between men and women. Sex is "contaminated" by patriarchy and cannot be separated out from it. Hence, it is necessary to do away with all sex. (Some radical feminists would include homosexual sex in this summary judgment.) Say the Southern Women's Writing Collective, who organized under the banner of "Women Against Sex": "All sex acts subordinate women. . . . Any sex act which did not subordinate women would literally not be a sex act." To Andrea Dworkin, perhaps the most prominent of all radical feminist "anti-sex" theorists, in a patriarchal system sex is synonymous with male supremacy and female objectification; in such a system, all women are whores (Dworkin, 1987; Chapkis, 1997, pp. 18, 19). Says Dworkin: "Force—the violence of the male confirming his masculinity—is seen as the essential purpose of the penis, its animating principle as it were. . . . The penis must embody the violence of the male in order for him to be male. Violence is male; the male is the penis; violence is the penis. . . . What the penis can do it must do forcibly for a man to be a man" (1981, p. 55). Since all behavior taking place in a patriarchal society is "saturated" with patriarchy, even homosexual sex partakes of patriarchy. There is no escaping the "system"; the only way out of it is no sex at all.

Pro-Sex Feminism

Pro-sex feminism believes that "good" sex can be separated from "bad" or bogus sex. This position offers "an eros free of the distortions of patriarchy, prostitution and pornography" (Chapkis, 1997, p. 13). Prostitution and pornography as well as other forms of sex work are not really an expression of sexuality at all but a *corruption* of sex that must be excised from the body social (Chapkis, 1997, pp. 13–17). This position is exemplified by Gloria Steinem's distinction between "erotica" and pornography (1982); Robin Morgan's distinction between "female-centered sexuality," with its emphasis on love, tenderness, and mutuality, and the "male sexual style," with its emphasis on promiscuity, objectification, and emotional noninvolvement (1977); and Kathleen Barry's distinction between "positive sex" and prostitution and pornography, sex which is purchased—sex which is not worthy of the name (1984, 1995).

This camp argues that one of feminism's tasks is to enlighten the members of the society about the exploitative nature of commercial sex. Men must learn that every time they patronize a prostitute or watch a pornographic videotape, they are contributing to the exploitation of women. Women must learn that by working in such enterprises they are oppressing not only themselves but all womankind by reinforcing certain patterns of behavior in the men who pay for their services. In addition, women bear the responsibility of teaching their husbands and boyfriends the truth about patriarchy and the role that prostitution and pornography play in upholding it. In several Western cities, there is mandatory instruction for men arrested for soliciting undercover police officers posing as prostitutes (Monto, 2000, pp. 69–71; see also Davis, 2000). Pro-sex femi-

nists, unlike "radical" feminists, do not throw out the baby with the bathwater; they believe that heterosexual sex can be salvaged, tamed—or feminized.

Sexual Libertarianism

The sexual libertarian argues that sex work is empowering, not degrading; that the woman is not a slave or a victim but a free agent who chooses a path that not only defies society's normative restrictions but also makes her a dominant party in sexual transactions (Chapkis, 1997, pp. 21–25). It is the man who has to pay for the sex. Far from representing power, offering money for sexual services is an expression of weakness. Camille Paglia offers the most flamboyant and outspoken version of this position (Kirshenbaum, 1991; Chapkis, 1997, pp. 21–22). To the sexual libertarian, each person has more-or-less absolute agency, or will, and is responsible and accountable only to himself or herself. If consent is granted and the actors are not minors, any act is acceptable. This position is characterized by two basic assumptions: one, all sexual acts, including sex work, have meaning independent of the culture or social structure; and two, each sexual encounter is an isolated, independent act.

Sexual Radicalism

Sexual libertarianism blends into our fourth position, *sexual radicalism* (Chapkis, 1997, pp. 21, 26–32). Sexual radicals are "pro-sex" feminists who argue vigorously and vociferously against what they see as the anti-sex position of the radical feminists. But they also set themselves apart from sexual libertarianism in arguing that the meaning of sex generally and sex work specifically is negotiated within the framework of a patriarchal system. Unlike sexual libertarians, sexual radicals deny that each person is independent of every other, deny that everyone has absolute agency, and deny that social structure can be ignored. Unusual sexual practices can be liberating, sexual radicals argue, but *only* if they are designed to subvert the dominant system of patriarchy. Prostitution and pornography, like other forms of commercialization, can be interpreted "in more complex ways than simply confirmation of male domination. They may also be seen as sites of ingenious resistance and cultural subversion." They are sites or places of agency "where the sex worker makes active use of the existing sexual order"; they may be seen as symbols of sexual autonomy and, as such, potential threats "to patriarchical control over women's sexuality" (Chapkis, 1997, pp. 29–30). Sexual radicalism is expressed by:

- Wendy Chapkis (1997) and Frederique Delacoste and Priscilla Alexander (1998), who permit a full and unabridged range of female sex workers to speak for themselves (unlike the proponents of the "anti-sex" position, who search out testimony of "victims" and "survivors" of commercial sex; see MacKinnon and Dworkin, 1998);
- Laura Kipnis (1996), who argues that pornography is not only an integral and indestructable element of Western society, but it also offers something positive for the society as well;
- Linda Williams (1989), who argues that, increasingly, women are using porn for their own purposes and that this tendency is more often liberative than oppressive;
- Kate Ellis and her colleagues, who edited a volume, *Caught Looking* (1988), whose pages are chockfull of pornographic photographs;
- Margot St. James, former prostitute and leader of COYOTE (Call Off Your Old, Tired Ethics), a social movement organization dedicated to the legalization of prostitution;
- Annie Sprinkle, a former stripper, masseuse, prostitute, nude model, and actor in pornographic films, who performs or acts out in explicit detail her sex career on stage (Williams, 1993);
- Pat Califia, who celebrates commercial sex, including pornography and prostitution, as locales in which actors learn about and engage in nontraditional or deviant sexual activities—such as bondage, threesomes, anal sex, and so on—which undermine traditional, straightlaced "vanilla" practices that are not only restrictive but truly oppressive (1988).

In short, sexual radicalism is a vigorous and diverse voice among feminists on the question of sex work and its meaning. It argues that sex workers do not need to be "saved" or liberated from their current mode of employment. Indeed, these writers and theorists argue, sex workers have a great deal to teach us about the nature of sexuality and gender. It is they who may very well liberate us from the oppressive bonds of patriarchy.

It almost need not be said that most traditional feminists, especially radical feminists, do not even consider sexual radicals as feminists at all. In *Faces of Feminism: An Activist's Reflections on the Women's Movement*, Sheila Tobias (1997, pp. 182–185) ignores all other feminist approaches to porn aside from radical feminism and "pro-sex" feminists, and even pretends there are no theoretical differences between these two sharply divergent perspectives. In the light of a flood of recent writings by feminist theorists, this stance seems naive, ill-informed, and erroneous.

EXTRAMARITAL SEX

According to Jewish and Christian tradition, Moses received the Ten Commandments directly from God. Among them, the seventh is "Thou shalt not commit adultery." Like the other proscriptions, it forbids an action that is tempting to many and hence frequently engaged in, and deviant as well. In fact, *because* it is so tempting—and because of its potentially harmful consequences—it *had to be* prohibited. In the absence of the prohibition, adultery would be far more commonplace than it is.

"It used to be, I'd get in the shower and my wife would come in there, too, impulsive and sexy and all," says Anthony. Not long ago, he snuck up on her in the shower. "What are you doing?" she asked. "Grow up. The kids will hear us." Anthony and his wife no longer have sex. He has had three extramarital liaisons; they only take place on business trips, far from home. "I've cheated because I just wanted to have sex and that was something my wife and I weren't doing. . . . And if what I did was away from home it doesn't count" (Konigsberg, 1998).

We already know a thing or two about the deviance of adultery.

One: Most Americans disapprove of it. In the "Sex in America" survey, as we saw, three-quarters of the sample (77 percent) agreed with the statement "Extramarital sex is always wrong." This condemnation is even more widespread than that for teenage sex and same-gender sex. The same finding turned up in a comparable survey conducted in Great Britain (Johnson et al., 1994, pp. 238–240, 471). Interestingly enough, however, given how widespread the condemnation of adultery is, the strength of this condemnation is rather muted and qualified. In a recent national poll, only a third of the population (35 percent) said that adultery should be a crime (Goldberg, 1997), and a majority of the American population opposed the impeachment of President Bill Clinton, an event that was launched by his lies, under oath, about an extramarital liaison with a White House intern. In a *Newsweek* poll, only a third of the sample (35 percent) considered the adultery of a political candidate a sufficient reason to vote for someone else (Adler, 1996).

Two: In every Western society in which a nationally representative survey has been conducted—France, the United Kingdom, Finland, and the United States—the vast majority of married respondents were faithful to their spouses for the entire length of their marriages. In the United States, only a quarter of the men (25 percent) and a bit more than one-seventh of the women (15 percent) in intact marriages said that they had ever had even one "extramarital affair" (Laumann et al., 1994, p. 216). If this survey is valid, it is clear that adultery is far less common than most of us imagine.

Three (and related to point two): As we just saw, men are significantly more likely to engage in extramarital sex than women. However, the gap may be closing: Among the *oldest* respondents (age 54 to 63) in the "Sex in America" survey, the male-to-female infidelity gap was three to one (37 versus 12 percent), whereas among the *youngest*, the gap was much smaller—12 percent versus 7 percent (Adler, 1996, p. 60).

And *four*: In most of the societies of the world, a double standard exists; women are more likely to be condemned for adulterous sex than men are. As we saw, it is extremely common for societies around the world to completely tolerate (43 percent of all societies studied did so) or at least condone (22 percent) extramarital sex for the man but condemn the same behavior for the woman (Broude and Greene, 1976, pp. 415–416). Recently, however, some observers have argued that the reverse has become true: "When men cheat, they're pigs. When women do it, they're striking a blow for sexual freedom" (Roiphe, 1997, p. 54).

The motives for extramarital sex are many and varied (Hunt, 1971; Wolfe, 1976; Atwater, 1982; Lawson, 1988). The simplest reason for men and women straying from the marital bed is as a response to a failing marriage. This is indicated by the fact that couples in marriages that end in divorce are vastly more likely to have adulterous sex than those in intact marriages. In this case, extramarital sex may be both cause and consequence of marital instability. At the same time, it is clear that a substantial number of stably married men and women (though not, as we saw, a majority) have intercourse with partners other than their spouses. Why? Why risk getting into trouble, being defined as a deviant, disrupting a marriage that is more or less satisfying? Does anyone believe, for example, that had Bill Clinton known that he would run into the kind of trouble he encountered as a result of his fling with Monica Lewinsky, he would have gone along with her importunings? What possessed him to take such a risk?

Evolutionary psychologists think they have found the answer. The key, they say, can be located in the tendency of organisms, humans included, to act in such a way that they maximize the transmission of their genes to later generations. And one way of understanding this process, they claim, is the difference between males and females in response to questions about what would be most upsetting about the infidelity of their spouse or partner. "What would distress you more," these researchers ask respondents, "discovering that he or she has formed a deep emotional attachment" to another person, or discovering that your spouse or partner "is enjoying daily passionate sex with the other person"? As it turns out, women are much more likely to be distressed by the emotional involvement of their partner, while men become more upset at their partner's sexual infidelity. Evolutionary psychologist David Buss has asked this question of samples of respondents in Germany, the Netherlands, and the United States; the differences between the sexes in these three countries are, says Buss, "quite solid."

The reason for the findings? This "jealousy gender gap" is encoded in our genes, say Buss (1994, pp. 125–131). Think back to the early ancestors of humans, these researchers argue. Since men can never be certain of the paternity of their children, they are most threatened by their partner having sex with another man; if their partner becomes pregnant by him, they will thereby end up being tricked into supporting offspring who are not biologically their own. Moreover, when the male's partner is pregnant with another man's child, he is thereby prevented from impregnating her himself. What heightens a man's chances of ensuring the survival of his genes is a faithful wife. It is the winners in this competition to keep their female partners faithful who are our ancestors, evolutionary psychologists claim.

The female has a different task, they argue. If a woman's partner strays, the sexual aspect of the encounter could be over in minutes, or even seconds, and that may very well be the end of it. No threat to the long-term relationship need be implied by such a liaison. But if he were to become emotionally involved with another female, he might abandon his long-term mate and thus threaten her likelihood of survival and that of her children as well—and therefore, the survival of her genetic material. In short, women are "evolutionarily programmed to become more distressed at emotional infidelity than sexual infidelity" (Begley, 1996/1997, p. 58).

Not all observers agree that jealousy is genetically encoded. Enormous variation exists from one society to another with respect to how jealous its members are at the infidelity of their partners. The male-female gap predicted by the evolutionary biologists is found everywhere, it is true, but the size of the difference varies considerably. In the United States, three times as many men as women are upset at their partner's sexual faithlessness versus their emotional infidelity; in Germany, the gap is only 50 percent. Moreover, while the *relative* differences between men and woman support the theory, the absolute *size* of the percentages runs counter to it. Evolutionary biologists predict that more men would care about sexual than emotional fidelity; in fact, *most* men are *not* disturbed more by sexual than emotional infidelity, which is totally contrary to the theory (p. 58).

What triggers sexual jealousy, many observers argue, is how members of each sexual category picture the connection their partner has in his or her mind between sex and love. Men's conception of the female sex has it that her sexual infidelity implies emotional infidelity as well. In other words, if she has sex with another man, he assumes, that pretty much means that she loves him, too. In addition, some women can be in love with another man but not have sex with him. Hence, the man loses twice when his partner is sexually unfaithful, a more threatening situation than simple emotional infidelity, which may imply nothing beyond that. In contrast, women are aware of the fact that their male partner can have sex with another woman without loving her. But when a man forms a romantic or loving attachment to another woman, it is much more likely to be a serious threat to his relationship with the first woman.

In short, it is our awareness of what sex and sex roles *mean* to our partners that determines the differences researchers observe. In other words, the jealousy gender gap, critics of evolutionary psychology argue, is the result of a cultural, intellectual, and to some degree "rational" process, not the nagging and largely unconscious demands of our genes. Regardless of which explanation is correct, we can be certain that marital infidelity is not likely to be accepted any time soon. It remains a major form of sexual deviance.

SUMMARY

The constructionist position toward human sexuality argues two points. One, sex is *constructed* by the society and social contact through the *imputation of meaning*. And two, the sex drive itself is, in large part, a *product* of human contact. Constructionists argue that social dynamics are lurking behind all things sexual; sexuality is *in the service of* the social world. Sexuality does not shape our social conduct so much as social meanings *give shape to* our sexuality. We are sexual *because* we are social; it is social life that *creates*, *motivates*, and *shapes* our sexuality.

The construction process applies not only to infusing phenomena and behavior specifically with *sexual* meaning, but also to filling the content of "sexual" definitions with a certain type of evaluation—positive, negative, or neutral, "normal" or "abnormal," conventional or deviant. How deviance is socially constructed is central to any understanding of sexual behavior. It is likely that sexual deviance is more likely to be regarded as "sick," abnormal, and pathological than any other type of deviance. A central feature in the psychiatrist's and the psychologist's conception of sexual deviance is *dysfunction* or *disorder*—an undesirable condition in need of treating or curing. However, the notions of dysfunction and disorder are alien to the sociologist's, particularly the constructionist's, notion of sexual deviance. Sociologically, what defines sexual deviance, as with all varieties of deviance, is that it is *nonnormative* and *likely to result in the condemnation of the actor*. No implication of dysfunction or disorder whatsoever is implied. Hence, the sociological conception of sexual deviance overlaps extremely imperfectly with the psychiatric and psychological conceptions.

Sexuality is "gendered." By that, sociologists mean that it is impossible to understand heterosexuality (or for that matter, sexuality of any kind) apart from men's and women's gender roles. Everything that we do sexually is informed or saturated by our maleness or femaleness. What are seemingly the same acts mean very different things if performed by men versus by women— both to the participants and to the society at large. We cannot understand sexual behavior without simultaneously considering who we are as males and females.

A variety of dimensions determine judgments of deviance with respect to behavior in the sexual arena. Several of them include degree of consent; who (or what) the sexual object or partner is; specifically what behavior is engaged in; where it takes place; who engages in the sex act; how often, when, with how many partners; and so on. These dimensions proscribe or render deviant a substantial number of sexual acts. How does the sociologist of deviance decide which ones should be studied? How strongly a given behavior is condemned (some acts are not deviant enough), how frequently it is enacted (some acts are not common enough), whether it makes up a category that is well-known enough to be a form of deviance in the public's mind (some acts are not conceptualized as a deviant category, and some are too obscure to be thought about or condemned), and whether it generates a social structure (some acts are enacted by scattered, isolated individuals), will all influence the decision made by the sociologist of deviance.

Sociologically, a sexual disorder or pathology is not the same thing as sexual deviance. The sociological concept of deviance emphasizes that certain behavior is condemned by the majority. Of the countless sexual activities that sociologists might study as deviance, sex work and extramarital sex are both fairly widespread and widely condemned.

In Western society, homosexuality is decreasingly regarded as a form of sexual deviance. Over time, a decreasing proportion of the American population believes that homosexual relations should be against the law; the media are increasingly depicting gays in a non-demeaning, non-stereotypical fashion; a growing number of Christian denominations are accepting gays both as members and as clergy; the sodomy laws have been struck down as unconstitutional; Canada has legalized gay marriage; and in a growing number of jurisdictions, "civil unions," which grant partners the same rights as married couples, have been legalized. Even in sectors of society that hold to traditional views on homosexuality (for instance, the Boy Scouts and the military), the exclusion of gays is under fire. In other words, increasingly, homosexuality is "departing from deviance."

Sex work encompasses a wide range of sex, both simulated and real, for pay: prostitution, massage, pornography, telephone sex, nude dancing, and being an escort. In the past, the vast majority of research has been conducted on street prostitution or "outdoor" sex work. In contrast, "indoor" sex work has rarely been studied; this deficiency is currently being corrected. Sex work has been approached from a variety of perspectives, including feminism and libertarianism, which draw very different conclusions about it.

Extramarital sex is widely condemned and far more rarely practiced than most of us believe. Men and women differ in their response to their partner's infidelity. Women are more likely to be distressed by their partner's emotional faithlessness, while men are more likely to become upset about their partner's sexual infidelity. Evolutionary psychologists believe that these responses are dictated by messages encoded in the genes; social psychologists argue that they are a result of reasonable inferences about the meaning of sex roles in our society.

PERSONAL ACCOUNT: Bondage and Discipline Sex

The following account was written by Jackie, a college student at the University of Maryland. She describes her participation in "bondage and discipline" sex. (A film released in 2002, entitled Secretary, *depicts a sexual relationship much like the one Jackie describes in this account.)*

I am a 21-year-old bisexual female, who, in the BDSM [bondage-discipline-sadism-masochism] community, is known as a "switch." I was raised Catholic in an interesting sort of family life. My mother is a diagnosed antisocial psychopath. My father raised his siblings because his mother was the town drunk while his dad abused both him and his siblings; he then in turn grew up to be a rage-aholic, a verbal and physical child abuser. I lived off and on with my "grandmother"—one of my half sister's grandparents—who has been more of a parent than anyone else. I began studying psychology in an attempt to work with children so I would be able to remove them from the sorts of abusive situations I had to endure as a child. . . .

I have always thought women were attractive. I remember watching beautiful women when I was younger. My mother was a beautiful woman. . . . My mother was a very sexual woman, and there was a constant stream of men in the house. She used them to get things, not for sex—that was part of her disorder. Because of this I grew up seeing men and women in much the same light. I don't think I fully admitted this to myself until I was in college. I have always done a lot of nudes in my paintings, females preferably because I like their lines better. When I visited my high school art teacher—also a close friend—because I was having a crisis over the stress of admitting I was gay, she informed me she had known that since she met me. Even my guy friends in high school knew. Recently, I asked John how he knew about me. He said the whole time he had known me I had looked at men and women with the same interest and desire, whereas usually, people choose one or the other. Specifically, he said, most men look at women and drool, whereas he looked at other attractive men and wished he looked more like them. John said I looked at attractive women *and* men with a drooling look. . . .

At one point, I tried telling my grandmother. I could never tell my mother—she was a gay-basher—or my father, whom I don't feel close to. My grandmother said it was a phase. At some point or another, every woman had fantasies about other women. She "knew me," she said. I'd meet some knight in shining armor and get married; I'd live in a nice house surrounded by a picket fence. Besides, she'd say, even if I were a lesbian—it wasn't possible to like both sexes, she believed—I could never marry another woman. And I couldn't live in sin—I was a Catholic, after all. And so I'd have to live my life alone.

I've had relationships primarily with men, but a few with women. Men are easier to come by. There is more of a selection of males to choose from, and I am picky with the people I date. It's harder finding same-sex partners, although it's easier living so close to a big city than in a less urban area. I'm not openly gay. My first gay relationship was with Emily, my best friend in high school. I was at her house, fooling around with a guy friend. I was young and most definitely stupid. I remember feeling uncomfortable with this guy. . . . I really wasn't into fooling around with this guy, but he was and he kept going. Finally I called Emily over and she began kissing me on the neck and breasts and I felt exhilarated. We drove our friend home and she and I talked. Apparently, we have been attracted to each other since we had met but we were just afraid to act on your desires. Within the week, we were dating and were constantly with one another. My family knew that she was my best friend, so they didn't suspect anything. Her mom knew about us but she also knew how much we cared for each other as friends, so she never minded me staying over, although we never had sex when we stayed over. There are some things I just considered too uncomfortable.

I've always believed in monogamy no matter who my partner was. I always hated the stigma that bisexuals are "easy," into having sex with as many people as possible simply because they

PERSONAL ACCOUNT: Bondage and Discipline Sex (cont.)

like both sexes. . . . Even now most of my friends don't know I am bisexual. Definitely not my roommates or my mother. My roommates are a little more tolerant than my mother, but when you're living in a house full of girls, they start getting uncomfortable. One of my housemates in particular, Jennifer, whom I love dearly—in a strictly platonic way, mind you—had a run-in because one of her past roommates was bi and told her not to worry because she wasn't attracted to her. Instead of feeling less anxious, she got insulted. It's like me saying, I am not going to grope you in your sleep so you can rest easy and not live in terror.

During my freshman year of college, I worked in an office in a work-study program. I didn't think anything of being bisexual until one day my supervisor began talking about a guy in the department she thought was gay. I couldn't believe it when I heard her refer to this kind, intelligent man as a "fag," then she began making jokes about the fact that he was a homosexual. I wanted to crawl into my skin or a deep hole and never come out. I knew if anyone at my job found out I would be harassed or, even worse, I'd lose my job. . . . Sometimes the nicest people make a complete change of face when they find out someone is gay. There is a lot of stigma associated with being bisexual. Most people think we are lascivious, can't make up our minds, sick, perverse—you name it, we are pretty much labeled it. . . .

I think about who will be reading this account. I hardly share any of this with outsiders. If anyone were to find out how I lead my sexual life, I could lose all credibility as a therapist simply because of the stigma of how perverse I am. . . . The things I do would shock anyone I guess. For as long as I can remember, seeing men and women tied up, spanked, smacked, or interacting in violent or sexually aggressive ways has always been a turn-on [for me]. No one else I knew seemed to have these feelings. Having had the background I did, I couldn't tell if it was my own form of self-abuse, mental illness, or seeking the familiar. My childhood was very

abusive. . . . I thought it may be possible that I seek humiliation, abuse, and power in relationships because I was trying to act out familiar patterns. That didn't really make sense, though, since in sex, I played the dominant or dominatrix role. I have always had some form of a power dynamic in my relationships, even with partners who weren't into being kinky. The first woman I dated I told her that I had a surprise. I came home blindfolded and I tied her up and tickled and teased her as I watched her writhe until I was satisfied that her release and satisfaction were completely dependent on my will. In the beginning, I didn't really consider it kinky, I saw it mainly as experimentation.

Most of the time my actions got really negative responses. I can remember one guy I dated in high school. When I pulled his hair and tried to bite his neck, he kinda freaked out. From then on in that relationship, I never tried anything out of order again. I did remain the "top" partner, though, the person who causes the sensation. That was doing what I wanted—getting my way, staying in control, and enjoying every minute of it. I wanted to take the dominant role in pleasing a partner. At the time, I didn't realize there was a community and a literature about all this that explained that what I was doing could please both me and my partner. Women were a lot more welcoming with my tendencies than men. Men never seemed to understand what I was up to, or they would see my dominance as challenging their masculinity. The women I dated liked being tied up, blindfolded, bitten, degraded, smacked, and used sexually. I guess this is one reason why I always like to dominate women. I don't think another woman could ever dominate me. I just don't have that mind-frame. I enjoy watching them too much.

You could look at this and say that I am trying to assume a power role because I was badly abused in childhood. Being dominant in my sexual relationships is safer because I call the shots. But the fact is, I never really saw myself as a victim. In school, when I was living with my parents, I thought these behaviors—shaking, hitting, punching, being thrown across the room,

PERSONAL ACCOUNT: Bondage and Discipline Sex (cont.)

leaving bruises—happened to everyone. When I was living with my mom, I hadn't known anything different. My sense of what should happen in a family was kind of skewed. I've thought a lot about it, though. Maybe my whole reason for seeing this as interesting and arousing is that it uses sex as manipulation as my mom did. It's a possibility; she was my earliest role model. No one can be born liking this, right? When I was younger, I still viewed this as sick and twisted.

Every time I was abused at home, I swore I would never hurt anyone like that. So I went through extreme bouts of cognitive dissonance. I was thinking along one track while trying to do the exact opposite. For me, sexual activity was fun, but without certain elements, I never really got fulfilled. There came a time when I knew I wanted to try something different. I wanted to be in the other role. I wanted to be subservient. I craved it. I tried prompting boyfriends at the time by bringing up non-scary items, such as scarves. I could tell there was something wrong with me. I still wasn't fulfilled because those boyfriends were terrible at doing what I wanted them to do, but I was also terrible at trying to explain how to do it in a way that wouldn't send them running. So I continued to remain dominant.

Don't get me wrong: Bad things can happen both during sex and during a relationship. There is a population of people who believe that bondage and discipline is all about force—real abuse, real rape. I had a relationship with a guy. For a while, things were pretty good. I was usually dominant, but occasionally, things switched the other way. He became verbally and emotionally abusive, taking out his anger at his exes on me. He eerily reminded me of my father. We were very volatile, providing catalysts for one another. We went through phases when we would cut things off and end up sleeping with one another, over and over again. I thought maybe we could be just friends, but I realized I was being naïve and foolish. One night, I went to his place thinking that he was going to help me find parts for my car. When he wanted to have sex, I told him no. I tried to pull away from

him but couldn't because he was stronger. He tied me up from hand to foot. Before, we had played with handcuffs and ropes, but I just never thought he would use them without my consent. I felt very violated that night. I walked home, shaking. I couldn't sleep. I sat on the fire escape outside my bedroom, smoked two packs of cigarettes, and watched the sun rise. . . . I thought that if I kept doing these bad things I would end up with more people who would take advantage of me. My next relationship was with a very conventional guy. I guess there's a Catch-22 situation here: When I engaged in bondage and discipline, bad things happened; when I didn't, bad things happened.

The conventional guy, we talked about marriage and kids, but he hated anything even remotely kinky, even the non-scary things. He saw bondage and discipline as abusive to women. He accused me of being a nymphomaniac—apparently all I wanted was sex. I became extremely depressed and began taking antidepressants. I realize now that I wasn't satisfied with the sex I engaged in, so I tried to make it up with quantity. He ended the relationship, and I got upset because he was perfect for leading the life my family wanted me to lead: the husband, the family, a two-car garage, a good income—and most definitely no collars or handcuffs. I felt guilty about the failure of the relationship. I had screwed up what would have been perfect if I could just be normal. This was everything I was supposed to want by conventional standards. I won't ever have a normal life, I thought. . . .

I started visiting specialty adult stores. I accumulated a little collection of the toys I enjoyed. This is part of me, I realized. When I fight who I am, I end up miserable. It didn't take me long to get over this guy.

Through a friend, I met Jason, the guy I've had my most recent relationship with. I completely brushed him off, and he thought I was a total bitch. We met again three months later. We decided to change our stances toward one another. At first, we talked as friends online.

PERSONAL ACCOUNT: Bondage and Discipline Sex (cont.)

He told me things about myself no one had ever bothered to notice. He was supportive when we were talking about sex. He felt the same things. He had problems with sex earlier because he didn't want to see himself as abusive. He took the teacher role, showing me books and answering my questions. He wasn't sickened by me and he gave me an opportunity to fulfill my need for being submissive. He became my friend, lover, and above all, master. He explained what being submissive entails. The dominant partner has to earn the trust and respect from the submissive to play the role. He told me that whatever may go on in the bedroom—degradation, humiliation—they happen because the submissive partner wishes to fulfill the role that involves those activities. He would treat me in this way because he respects the dynamic between us. In turn, I would allow him to treat me like that because I would have the control to say who treats me as such and when. He also set up what's called a "safe word" for me. Sometimes things can become so intense that the words you might speak in a typical dialogue during a scene won't stop the action. You need a safe word that you would never say during a scene that would be a signal to stop the action so that the participants can try to fix anything that may be going wrong. S&M is all about communication. My safe word is "blue." I think I picked it because I think primarily in colors and it reminds me of feeling scared. It seemed right.

We have a library of books that explain techniques of the bondage and dominance "lifestyle." Occasionally, when I'm reading one of them, one of my roommates will walk in and see my book, and so I explain it away as a book for research on deviance or aesthetics or some other such thing. As for my toys, they are usually kept in a duffle bag or in drawers in my closet. . . . One aspect of the bondage and discipline lifestyle is covering up evidence of how we live, including bruises and bite marks, or simply putting away the toys so that no one will ever find out about it and accuse us of abuse. We have many friends in the bondage and discipline

community because it tends to be very tight-knit. We choose to keep it private among ourselves. . . .

Some people in this community find romance in pieces of glass—that is, bloodletting, cutting the skin to achieve sexual arousal. I enjoy many different things. Sometimes the simple act of being tied or having something placed around my neck will send me into a frenzy of arousal, wanting to do anything to please to earn pleasure. Sometimes I surprise Jason by setting up a scene for him when he comes home from work. One such scene involved twelve lit candles lining each side of the corridor to the bedroom door and red rose petals scattered on the floor. Inside the bedroom, I trailed petals up to the bed with candles lighting the windowsill. A rope trailed zig-zag through the petals under the door and onto the bed, there, connected to the collar I was wearing. It was then my turn to wait, having mentally prepared myself for him to come home, when he would decide what happened next. One night, paddling or flogging; the next night, maybe hot wax, anal intercourse, or bondage and teasing.

There is a sensation called "floating" a lot of submissives describe. It's when you get so far into your personal head-space that sensation floods you and everything feels like soft pillows. After we have a vigorous scene, my master usually gathers me into his arms or holds me and we talk about everything we felt and went through in our minds, things that happened—and maybe didn't happen—during the session. This is the most fulfilling and loving relationship I have been in. . . . In the morning, we're like every other couple. We get up and shower, brush our teeth, dress, and the like, and go about our normal lives, for him it is his work, for me to school and therapy sessions—where we await the next time we see each other. When we get together, we're distinctly not like other couples. . . .

It excites me to think I will be able to spend the rest of my life with someone who fills me with such joy—emotionally, intellectually, and physically. Someone who pushes me to be the

Personal Account: Bondage and Discipline Sex (cont.)

best I can, someone who makes me dinner when I am stressed or gives me a backrub or surprises me by putting up Christmas lights, or bringing my favorite candies for a devious blindfolded study break. Someone who won't judge me. To me that doesn't seem deviant. It's really all in the way you look at it.

I have a job I enjoy tremendously, trying to make the lives of children better. I am in my last year of college. I won't talk about private members' clubs for bondage and discipline participants in my deviance course because all eyes would turn to me in accusation. If people in my everyday life knew about my sex life, they would accuse me of being sick, being just like a child molester, accuse me of doing things with my clients with the same ignorant thought processes that lead people to think you can "catch" homosexuality. I won't discuss anything that happened the night before, when I subjected myself to any number of abuses and perversities. I will put on the mask of a confident, conventional, heterosexual woman. I will hope that I remembered to put

all my toys away, that I haven't left a trail that may lead to being scrutinized, judged, evaluated, stigmatized. And I will love being comfortable, finally, with who I am.

Everyone wants to feel accepted. I spent most of my life either not admitting things to myself or thinking I was a bad person because I felt a certain way. Now that I feel accepted in one area of my life, I have a much easier time separating the two halves of my life and not worrying about one affecting the other as much. Now that I have confidence in my sexual self, I am much more confident in my social self. Jason says it is funny that my family never liked any of the guys I dated in the past who were supposed to be so acceptable. Now that my family knows Jason—the one person who shouldn't be acceptable—they've fallen in love with him. Jason says, "Being comfortable allows other people to be comfortable with you." I don't consider myself "normal" in the way that the "American dream" is normal, but I am the way I want to be.

Questions

What's your reaction to Jackie's sexual behavior? Do you accept her notion that it should be regarded as "normal"? Does it challenge the very meaning of the concept "normality"? Sociologists do not use the term "normal"; instead, they prefer to refer to such behavior as "nonnormative" or deviant. Jackie's behavior would certainly be regarded as nonnormative or deviant by the majority of the American public. She is aware of that fact by keeping her sexual activities a secret from others. How would a psychologist or psychiatrist regard this behavior? If the behavior causes no distress in her or her partner, what's wrong with it? Is such behavior likely to disrupt conventional social arrangements? Or, if it is kept

secret, is it more likely to have no impact on them at all? Why have radical sociologists such as Alexander Liazos argued that the attention sociologists of deviance pay to behavior such as Jackie's is a kind of "bias"? Do you agree? Is the kind of corporate crime Liazos refers to as stigmatizing as Jackie's sexual activities? Do sociologists of deviance pay too much attention to what Liazos (1972) contemptuously referred to as "nuts, sluts, and deviated preverts"? Or is that attention appropriate, given the subject matter? What theories might positivist sociologists and psychologists have about the behavior of devotees of S&M sex such as Jackie? Was the key factor here the influence of her "rage-aholic" father? Her alcoholic mother? The fact that she was raised by her half-sister's grandmother?

Cognitive Deviance: Holding Unconventional Beliefs[1]

[1]Portions of this chapter were adapted from sections of two of my previous books: *Paranormal Beliefs: A Sociological Introduction,* Prospect Heights, IL: Waveland Press, 2000, and *Collective Behavior,* FT. Worth, TX: Harcourt Brace, 1992. Permission to make use of this material is gratefully acknowledged.

Is holding unconventional *beliefs* a form of deviance? Doesn't everyone have a right to believe whatever they please? Isn't what you believe "nobody's business but your own"? The answer to the latter two questions is: apparently not; to the first: clearly. The fact is, almost as many—and in some eras of history, even more—people have been punished, stigmatized, and condemned for their beliefs as for their behavior. Erving Goffman's classic formulation of "blemishes of individual character" includes "treacherous and rigid beliefs" (1963, p. 4)—and a belief that what one person regards as "treacherous and rigid," another sees as just and righteous, and vice versa. *Of course* holding beliefs that wander off the beaten path is a form of deviance! Not only are certain beliefs deviant to the members of the general society; many beliefs that are deviant to the general society are acceptable in some social circles, and, again, vice versa. Hence, we encounter a process in which two parties engage in "the mutual construction of deviance"—or *diabolize* one another (Aho, 1994, pp. 50–67).

- Matilda believes God created the world out of nothing in six days less than 10,000 years ago. Mark disagrees; he thinks that about 15 billion years ago the "big bang" generated matter that coalesced into stars, then planets; on earth, he believes, out of primordial ooze, primitive life formed that evolved into the plant and animal species, humans included, that now exist.
- Luke believes that unidentified flying objects (UFOs) are really space vehicles from another planet, and that the government is aware of this fact but keeps it a secret from the American public. Joanna sees that belief as totally wrong and feels that all UFO reports can be explained by strictly routine causes—sightings of satellites, conventional aircraft, swamp gas, northern lights, ball lightning, the planet Venus—or hoaxes, or an overactive imagination.
- Paula believes in the existence of God, the divinity of Jesus, an afterlife—that is, heaven and hell as literal, concrete places where the soul is transported when the body dies—and in the resurrection of the body upon the Second Coming of Christ at the Last Judgment. Timothy is an atheist and holds that God is merely a concept invented and maintained by humans who are too insecure and frightened to face the inevitability of death and the absurdity of worldly existence.

- James believes that the Jews control the media and the government and want to take the guns, the property, and all political rights away from white Christians and herd them into concentration camps. Linda couldn't disagree more; she feels that James is a crackpot whose belief is paranoid, delusional, false, and insane—nothing more than a pretext for blatant anti-Semitism.

What makes some of these beliefs—or the people who hold them—deviant? What makes other beliefs and their believers conventional? And how do deviant *beliefs* differ from deviant *behavior*?

Cognition refers to knowing—that is, what one believes to be true. It encompasses "beliefs, disbeliefs, guesses, suspicions, judgments, and so forth" (Douglas and Waksler, 1982, p. 364). It includes the view that ghosts exist and the view that they do not exist; that there is a heaven and hell—and that there is no afterlife whatsoever; that John F. Kennedy and Martin Luther King were assassinated by conspirators, and that they were killed by lone gunmen; that Catholicism is the One True Religion, and that Mahayana Buddhism is the path to enlightenment; that communism is the solution to society's problems, and that a free market or laissez faire economic policy will bring the greatest good to the greatest number of people. When sociologists refer to "knowing," we do not imply that these views are empirically correct. (Or that they are wrong.) What we mean is that people *think* that they are true. Cognition refers to the *belief* that a given assertion or claim is valid. Cognitive *deviance* refers to holding beliefs that are unconventional and nonnormative, which, in some social circles, causes their believers to be shunned, isolated, marginalized, rendered powerless, criticized, condemned, or punished.

With respect to the central analytic features of deviance—what makes something *deviant*—in principle, deviant beliefs are identical in all basic respects to deviant acts. The same basic principles apply: Someone, or a category of persons, is regarded by the members of one or more audiences as violating a rule or norm. The content of the belief is less important than the fact that that belief is deemed normatively unacceptable. Thus, being an atheist violates a rule that says one must believe in God; belief in creationism violates the principles of scientific reasoning; belief in evolution violates a literal reading of the Bible; belief in alien spaceships violates a law that says that objects cannot travel faster than the speed of light; and so on. Because specific audiences hold certain beliefs to be nonnormative, unconventional, unacceptable, scandalous, heretical, vulgar, unseemly, improper, and/or just plain wrong, they isolate, stigmatize, condemn, and/or punish the persons who hold them. Of course, precisely the beliefs that *one* audience finds unconventional *another* accepts as normatively correct. In these respects, holding unconventional beliefs is no different from engaging in unconventional behavior. Both result in stigma and condemnation. In other words, social rules apply "not only to how one behaves but also *how and what one thinks*" (Douglas and Waksler, 1982, p. 366).

It is not always a simple matter to separate beliefs from behavior. Often, unacceptable beliefs *translate into* or *become a basis for* unacceptable behavior. Someone who holds a certain belief announces to the world that he or she has the potential to act in a certain way. In other words, the *believer* can become an *actor*.

The belief that Jews are parasites who are organized into an international conspiracy to enslave the Christian world (Abanes, 1996, pp. 175–178; Lamy, 1996, pp. 118–134) is far more than a "mere" belief: A number of the members of organized groups who hold such beliefs have committed overt violence against Jews. In the 1950s and 1960s, many politically mainstream Americans feared and stigmatized communists not merely because of their unconventional ideology but because they sincerely believed that communism was actively dedicated to the destruction of everything they valued: religion, spiritual values, the conventional family, democratic elections, the work ethic, a free press—in other words, that which defined the "American way of life." Hence, audiences may label or condemn people who hold unconventional beliefs because they fear that these believers pose a clear and present danger to the way of life—indeed, the very physical existence—of right-thinking people everywhere. Hence, many cognitive belief systems are not deviant *merely* because they violate mainstream notions

of what's true. Their proponents are *also* regarded as deviants because of the behavior those beliefs could call forth. The nature of Timothy McVeigh's deviance (and his crime) was not that he criticized the United States government; it was that he blew up the Alfred P. Murrah Building in Oklahoma City, killing 168 innocent victims.

In this chapter I'll emphasize the forms of cognitive beliefs that are *unlikely* to translate directly into deviant behavior—that are, insofar as this is possible, cases of "pure" cognitive deviance. Those cognitive belief systems that are regarded as being much more likely to translate into deviant behavior will not be discussed here.

Audiences do not *necessarily* see unconventional beliefs as threatening to their worldview, nor do they regard persons who hold such unconventional beliefs as potentially dangerous to life and limb. While *in practice*, it is difficult to separate the threat that deviant beliefs represent to the mainstream from their mere unconventionality, *in principle*, the two are analytically distinct. Many deviant beliefs are regarded as silly, laughable, ludicrous, and absurd—by no means either a concrete or a symbolic threat—but the persons who hold them are nonetheless stigmatized, condemned, and socially isolated. Even if audiences do fear them, the threat that these unconventional beliefs pose may be largely symbolic; that is, they may threaten to undermine a worldview, a way of thinking about reality, rather than life and limb.

In an earlier era, certain beliefs were regarded as proof positive that their holders had consorted with the devil or other evil spirits. More recently, as we'll see in Chapter 11, psychiatrists and clinical psychologists have regarded the expression of certain beliefs as a manifestation or an indicator of mental disorder. For instance, schizophrenics are said to suffer from *delusions* and *hallucinations*. One man describes a transmitter that has been implanted in his teeth that receives signals from a distant galaxy commanding him to deliver a message to everyone on earth about a coming catastrophe. A woman believes that her thoughts have been "sucked out" of her mind "by a phrenological vacuum extractor" (Davison, Neale, and Kring, 2004). A man believes that x-rays have entered his body through his neck, passed down to his waist, and settled in his genitals, preventing him from getting an erection. A woman claims that she is "just a puppet who is manipulated by cosmic strings. When the strings are pulled my body moves and I cannot prevent it." Clearly, then, people who are diagnosed as having a mental disorder often hold deviant or unacceptable beliefs.

Just as there are parallels between mental disorder and cognitive deviance, however, there are differences as well. Schizophrenia is nearly always accompanied by a number of other disturbances in addition to cognitive delusions and hallucinations. Some of these include flat or inappropriate emotions, bizarre motor activity, and the use of jumbled words ("word salad") and thoughts. Clinical depression, too, is marked by inappropriate beliefs, but in addition, it is a *mood* disorder characterized by feelings of sadness, dread, apprehension, worthlessness, guilt, and anhedonia, or an inability to take pleasure in life (Davison, Neale, and Kring, 2004). In contrast, *by itself*, cognitive deviance, or holding unconventional beliefs, is not necessarily linked with any psychiatric disorder. Mental disorder and cognitive deviance are *empirically* related but *definitionally* separate and distinct. In other words, while mental health professionals would classify many cognitive deviants as mentally disordered, and many of the persons they classify as mentally disordered would also be regarded as cognitive deviants, neither category demands nor necessitates the other.

One last point on our definition. Beliefs are not deviant simply because of their content. No belief, however bizarre it might seem to us, is *inherently* or *objectively* deviant. A belief is deviant in two ways—one, normatively and two, reactively. In other words, one, because it violates the tenets of the dominant belief system, and two, because its adherents are likely to be condemned or punished by the members of the mainstream culture. A belief is deviant only because it is *considered* wrong and its believers are *treated* as socially unacceptable—*in* a given society, group, or collectivity. To repeat a point I've made throughout this book: Deviance makes sense *only* with reference to the beliefs of certain audiences. Beliefs that are regarded as wrong, unacceptable, and deviant in one social circle may be considered right, good, proper, and true in another. Among political radicals, conservatism is

anathema—unacceptable and deviant. Contrarily, among conservatives, radicals are on the hot seat. To the fundamentalist Christian, the atheist is the spawn of Satan, most decidedly a deviant. Turn the picture around: To the atheist, fundamentalist Christians are ignorant, narrow-minded fools. Again, we encounter the process of "mutual deviantization."

But let's be clear about this: Deviance is never *solely* a matter of the word of the members of one social category against the word of another. Yes, we live in a society that is a loose assemblage of different and mutually antagonistic belief systems. But society is as much a ladder as a mosaic. This means that some beliefs are more *dominant* than others; their adherents have more power and credibility, and hence can legitimate their beliefs and discredit those of their opponents. To the extent that a particular belief is taught as true in the educational system, it is dominant, legitimate, and credible; to the extent that, when a belief is expressed in schools, its proponents tend to be *disparaged*, that belief is deviant. To the extent that holding a certain belief is a criterion among a majority of the electorate to vote for a given political candidate, it is a dominant belief. To the extent that a substantial segment of the electorate *refuses* to vote for a political candidate because he or she is known to hold a certain view, that view is deviant. To the extent that a given belief is taken for granted as true in the mainstream media, it is dominant; to the extent that holders of a given belief are scorned, rebuked, and ridiculed—that belief is deviant. In each of society's major institutions, we can locate beliefs that are mainstream, "inside the lines," conventional, dominant, or hegemonic; *and* we can locate those beliefs that are nonmainstream, outside the lines, beyond the pale, unconventional—in a word, from the societal point of view, *deviant*.

THE SOCIAL FUNCTIONS OF BELIEF SYSTEMS

Are beliefs just beliefs? To put the matter another way, are beliefs *ever* just beliefs? How does the sociologist approach deviant beliefs? More generally, how do *we*, as students of the sociology of deviance, approach beliefs? As Berger and Luckmann say, the task of sociologists who study beliefs is not to look at beliefs for their own sake, to take them as "just" beliefs and attempt to prove them right—or, on the other hand, debunk or prove them wrong. Instead, sociologists attempt to understand the social conditions that *generate* or *encourage* them (1966, p. 12). The basic insight of sociology is that beliefs serve social functions that *transcend* their uniqueness *and* their empirical validity or truth value. We argue that the way humans think is rooted in the material and social world. Beliefs usually grow out of real-world conditions, and tend to have real-world consequences.

For thousands of years, theorists, philosophers, and other observers of social reality have commented on the relationship between the *ideational* world—the world of thoughts, beliefs, and ideas—and the material world. Many theories have been proposed to account for that relationship. (And these theories have *themselves* become an essential part of the ideational world, and some of them have had major real-world consequences.) The central thrust of the bulk of these writings is that beliefs *do* spring from social conditions, they *do* serve social functions, and they *do* have social consequences.

Most of us think that what we believe comes from our own special and unique individuality. We convince ourselves that our beliefs would be the same even if we had been subject to very different social influences. Sociologist Joel Charon asks the question "Why do we believe what we believe?" To answer it, he invites the reader to imagine the following: "If my life had been different, if I had been born at a different time or place, would I still believe in God? Would my beliefs about God be the same as they are now?" (1995, p. 99). Do you really think your beliefs would be the same if you had grown up in a different time and place? If you had grown up two centuries ago the child of a white slaveholder, would you have believed that slavery is evil? If you had been a gentile child in Nazi Germany, would you have believed that Jews are good, decent people who deserve the same rights as everyone else? If you had been an Aztec half a millennium ago, would you have believed that human sacrifice is wrong? If you had been born a

thousand years ago in the New Guinea highlands, would you have had the same religious beliefs you have now? Or had you been born 300 years ago on a Polynesian island, would you have thought that public nudity was immoral? Do you really believe that, in a very different society in a very different time period, you would have had exactly the same notions of right and wrong and true and false that you have now? "Can you think of *any* idea you believe that does not have primarily a *social* foundation? Is there anything we believe that has not arisen primarily through *interaction* with others?" (p. 99). Thus, the first and more-or-less universally accepted sociological principle of beliefs is that they arise through social interaction with others. In other words, *human consciousness is determined by social existence* (Berger and Luckmann, 1966, pp. 5–6).

Karl Marx, a nineteenth-century German intellectual who, for more than 150 years, had a profound impact on sociology, philosophy, history, and economics, argued that the way we think at a particular time and place is a *reflection* of the economic arrangements of the society in which we live. "Morality, religion, metaphysics, all the rest of ideology and their corresponding forms of consciousness," Marx wrote, "thus no longer retain the semblance of independence. . . . Life is not determined by consciousness, but consciousness by life" (1846/1947, pp. 14, 15). And by "life," Marx meant *economic* life. It is the nature of the economy that determines the nature of a society's art, politics, religion, science, system of justice— in short, the ideational world, the world of beliefs and ideas. Moreover, in any society, it is the dominant social class whose ideas tend to be most influential. "The class which has the means of material production at its disposal, has control at the same time over the means of mental production. . . . The individuals composing the ruling class . . . rule also as thinkers, as producers of ideas, and regulate the production and distribution of the ideas of their age: thus their ideas are the ruling ideas of the epoch" (p. 39).

The influence of Marx's theories has declined considerably during the past generation. Most social scientists and intellectuals see a much more complex and less deterministic relationship between the economy and beliefs. They argue that ideas can influence the economy as much as the economy can influence ideas, and they see the many institutions, including art, religion, and politics, as "codeterminate," or equally capable of influencing one another. For instance, Max Weber, an early-twentieth-century sociologist, argued that religious beliefs influence the economic life of a society as much as the other way around. It was ascetic, rationalistic seventeenth-century Protestantism, he said, that stimulated industrial capitalism—a case of ideas generating material conditions rather than the reverse. The Industrial Revolution could not have been born in a society dominated by religions such as Hinduism and Buddhism because they denied rationality and the central importance of the material world. Moreover, today most observers regard ideas and beliefs as much more than simple justifications for the dominant economic system.

Max Weber wrote of the *elective affinity* people have for certain ideas and beliefs (1946, pp. 62–63, 284–285)—that is, the social and material conditions in which they live influence the likelihood that they will be receptive to certain ideas. They do not choose (or "elect") their beliefs—their social and material conditions do. The privileged classes tend to be attracted to religions that assure them that their status is justified and legitimate. For the poorer strata, religious beliefs (or, alternatively, political beliefs) will be appealing to the extent that these beliefs offer a salvation of compensation, that is, righting the wrongs they feel have been inflicted upon them, either in this world or the next. The prophecy of seventh-century Islam was especially appealing to warriors. The religious expression that middle-class urban-dwellers during early Protestantism found compatible with their way of life was practical, rational, based on a mastery of nature and relations with others. Members of the bureaucratic class—whether in ancient Rome or in the contemporary West—have found irrational, ecstatic, or completely otherworldly religious expression unappealing, but were comfortable with a religion that offered ways of controlling the masses (Weber, 1922/1963, pp. 89, 107, 108, 265). Clearly, Weber sees much more diversity in the ideas of the many social classes in the society than Marx—who only pictured two social classes—did. Weber neither sees the ruling class so overwhelmingly dominant that their ideas are the

"ruling" ideas of the era, nor does he see liberation as the only function of the ideas of oppressed peoples. Ideas and beliefs may serve many functions aside from their economic interests.

In other words, unlike Marx, Max Weber saw a *two-way street* between the ideational world—the world of beliefs and ideas—and the material conditions of people's lives. People are attracted to beliefs because those beliefs are compatible with the way they live. But "the way they live" is much more than economic circumstances alone. It includes the many and myriad facets of our existence. And ideas and beliefs, in turn, can act back on material conditions. For instance, a religion can generate ideas that either stimulate or inhibit a certain kind of economic system. Buddhism, practiced in Tibet and Bhutan, actively rejects materialism—and therefore the very basis of industrial capitalism. In contrast, as we saw, according to Weber the beliefs of seventeenth-century Protestantism actively encouraged the Industrial Revolution. So, to Weber, there is reciprocity here. In contrast, to Marx, it was more of a one-way relationship—economic circumstances cause beliefs. On this issue, most contemporary theorists prefer Weber's way of thinking to that of Marx.

The functions that deviant belief systems serve can be looked at from two different approaches—one, the functions they serve for the believer, and two, the functions that *opposing* unconventional beliefs and *condemning* their believers serve for the society at large or, more specifically, for their condemners.

For each of the belief systems discussed in this chapter, we should think about the strata or social circles or segments of the society for whom each functions in one way or another. Each affirms the believer's way of life or upholds a certain vision of the way things are. Each is supported by a specific epistemology or "way of knowing" and each points to an unacceptable way of looking at things, a belief system that it rejects or that rejects it. Some are backed up by a *demonology*—the designation of an immoral, fiendish wrongdoer who represents evil in the flesh—while others merely point out the errors perpetrated by persons who fail to see things the way the believers see them. Either way, beliefs respond or correspond to issues that are a vital part of the way their believers live their lives; all answer questions and provide solutions to problems that make them believable or credible to some of the members of a society rather than others.

Thus, in cognitive deviance there are usually two sets of deviants—to each side of the controversy, the *other* side. To Martin Luther, Catholicism was deviant—indeed, evil. To the pope, Martin Luther and his Protestant followers were deviant, representatives of the devil himself. To the person who believes that UFOs are spaceships from another planet, anyone who denies that belief is wrong, cognitively in error—or part of the cover-up to hide the fact that aliens are all around us. Looked at from the other end of the controversy, the viewpoint of those who are wedded to the mainstream institutions, UFO believers are wrong, silly, irrational, and most decidedly deviant. To the fundamentalist Christian, proponents of evolution are secular humanists and hence the spawn of Satan; to the traditional scientist, creationists are ignorant, closed-minded enemies of reason and enlightenment. The list could be multiplied endlessly. In this sense, we are talking about looking at definitions of deviance in horizontal terms—from one group, category, or social circle to another.

But I'd like to reemphasize another, absolutely crucial, point: What's central in any controversy is which side has the influence to legitimate and validate its own special view of right or wrong and true or false. *Whose* notion of right and wrong are we talking about here? is the central issue. It is true that *in* creationist circles and *to* creationist audiences, evolutionists are considered deviant. But it's also true that with respect to power, influence, legitimacy, and credibility, creationists are *marginalized*; their views are *not* mainstream in the society at large. This is what makes creationism a deviant belief system—not because it is empirically wrong. (That is a separate issue.) In the event that the mainstream institutions were to legitimate creationism and stigmatize and marginalize evolutionist thinking, then it would be the evolutionist whom the sociologist would designate as the cognitive deviant. The same applies to the belief that UFOs are real. The belief that unidentified flying objects are alien spaceships is held by just under half of all Americans; the belief that they are not is held by

the same proportion. What then makes the belief, "UFOs are real," deviant? It is deviant *societally* because it does not have hierarchical legitimation. The most influential media (the news divisions of the television networks, *The New York Times, The Washington Post*), the relevant departments of major universities, and the major, mainstream churches do not accept the belief as true. If a political candidate were to announce the belief in a speech—or to urge that its truth be adopted by educational curricula—he or she would be made fun of by the media. When John Mack, a Harvard professor, published a book asserting his belief that people had been kidnapped by aliens (1995), a shock wave of horror shot through the university community. When Minister Louis Farrakhan announced that he had visited an extraterrestrial spaceship, observers said that he was a crackpot (Brackman, 1996). Again, charges of deviance can more easily be legitimated by influential representatives of social institutions than by those who are weaker and more marginal. But once again, *within* those weaker, more marginal sectors of the society, the dominant definitions of right and wrong may nonetheless be regarded as deviant. To repeat, as students of deviance, we need to think in terms of *both* the vertical *and* the horizontal dimensions of deviance.

RELIGIOUS DEVIANCE

Throughout most of recorded history, the majority of cognitive deviance has been religious in nature. Persons or groups holding unorthodox or heretical views of the sacred, that is, views that challenged dominant theological interpretations, tended to be shunned, condemned, and persecuted. In past centuries, the dominant religious bodies in a given society usually had powers of arrest, imprisonment, and punishment—including torture and even execution. Hence, during the majority of the history of humanity, religious unorthodoxy was not only deviant—it was also a crime. Today, at least in Western society, religious beliefs are not criminal but they may be deviant. (Of course, if a religious belief becomes the *basis* for illegal behavior, the actor may be arrested. Human sacrifice may be demanded by your particular god, but in the eyes of the law, if you engage in it, it is still murder.) Currently, the reactions that the expression of deviant religious beliefs generates are *informal* rather than formal, but they are real nonetheless.

It is almost impossible to imagine the violence that has been inflicted on religious dissidents over the centuries. And in many, if not most such conflicts, both sides resorted equally to violence. In other words, which religious group inflicted violence on the other depended on which one had the power. Had the weaker side in a given religious conflict been the more powerful side, it would have been the one inflicting the violence, rather than the other way around. Because religion invokes divine sanction, it lends to its believers and adherents a special aura of righteousness, an *absolute* righteousness that dictates that the heretic is not only wrong but unholy, unclean and defiling, a devil in the flesh, a threat to godliness—and hence worthy of annihilation. Why is this?

It is the task of every religion to create a worldview, construct a "sacred canopy," carve an encampment of "meaning . . . out of a vast mass of meaninglessness, a small clearing of lucidity in a formless, dark, always ominous jungle" (Berger, 1967, p. 24). If, as many philosophers and social and natural scientists believe, life has no inherent meaning; if it is, as some say, inherently *absurd* (Lyman and Scott, 1970); if it is *humans* who create *God* rather than the other way around; if reality is a *social construct* rather than an absolute, a given, a concrete, bedrock, taken-for-granted cosmos (Berger and Luckmann, 1966)—then any threat to this fragile social construction, this socially fabricated religion, this imaginary God, is a threat to reality itself.

If religion really was created to alleviate the terror that comes with the awareness of meaninglessness, then any threat to a society's religion generates that self-same terror. The institutional order was created out of nothing, ex nihilo; it was, in fact, socially constructed. But teaching that life is absurd and that society, including religious beliefs, are nothing more than arbitrary social conventions is not likely to create a great deal of commitment on the part of believers. We do not want to hear that our most cherished beliefs were contrived for the purpose of social utility. Instead, we are most comforted by being told that these beliefs have an eternal, inevitable, *cosmic* quality. In other words, religious beliefs must be *clothed in an aura of sacredness*. We want to hold them because they are true and valid—*not* because they make people feel better and help hold the society together. Hence, the socially constructed character of religion must be *masked*, hidden, concealed in a wrapping of certitude and absolutism—given a *cosmic* status (Berger, 1967, p. 36). In other words, to be legitimated, religion must *pretend* that it is sacred and convince its adherents that it is sacred. Any challenge to established religion must be seen as a challenge to the cosmos itself. Enemies of established religion must be demonized because they threaten to unmask the very foundation of society, the bedrock on which all social life rests (or substitute an entirely different cosmology or way of thinking about the world). These enemies announce that the whole enterprise on which one's beliefs rest is a lie. Hence the fury and bitterness of the many religious conflicts in which we humans have participated over the centuries.

For instance, consider the Crusades. In the seventh century, the forces of the Muslim Caliph Umar seized Jerusalem. For centuries thereafter, the Muslim rulers of the Holy City respected the rights of their Christian (and Jewish) subjects and permitted pilgrims to visit its sacred shrines and churches. But in 1009, Caliph Hakim ordered the Church of the Holy Sepulcher—one of Christendom's holiest sites—demolished, and he launched an era of persecution against Christians. Although this persecution diminished after Hakim's death in 1021, warfare with the Seljuk Turks led the leaders of the Byzantine forces to appeal to European Christians to wrest Jerusalem from the hands of the infidel. Thus began nearly 200 years of religious warfare between Christians and Muslims in the Middle East, as well as in the lands that served as the corridor between Western Europe and the Middle East. Just for good measure, Crusaders considered Jews the enemy and killed them along with Muslims. In addition, the armies and populations of lands ruled by princes and kings who did not support the campaign were likewise slaughtered. In Hungary, observers claimed, the Danube was dyed with blood for miles downstream. According to the Crusader belief system, the deviants were, first of all, Muslims, who ruled the Holy Land, Christ's dominion, and supposedly desecrated holy Christian shrines; secondly, Jews, whose sin was that they were not Christians, that they denied Christ; and thirdly, opponents of the Crusades. Crusader invasions came in nine separate waves between 1095 and 1272.

During the Crusades, Christian violence against Muslims and Jews was justified by divine mandate. To slaughter the infidel was God's will and Christ's desire, theologians at the time proclaimed. The Middle East is Christ's holy dominion, they stated; the Crusades would return to the Lord what was rightfully and properly His. Unbelievers menaced and threatened the very seat and soul of Christendom itself. The Crusades—and therefore the butchery of non-Christians—was "Christ's own enterprise. . . , regarded as positively holy" (Riley-Smith, 1987, p. xxix). Crusaders bragged that because of their righteous slaughter, the streets of Jerusalem ran red with the blood of Muslims and Jews. Perhaps they were exaggerating, but their boast captures the flavor of the furious passion that frequently fuels religious conflict and the persecution of the heretic. Hundreds of thousands of people, in all likelihood as many Christians as Muslims and Jews, perished in the ill-fated Crusades. When the Crusaders were finally driven from the Middle East, the Holy Land remained in the hands of Muslim rulers.

Another example: the Old Believers, who were persecuted for over 200 years in Russia. For the better part of a millennium, the Russian Orthodox Church had relied on devotional manuscript texts that contained numerous translation and transcription errors. In the seventeenth century, the Orthodox hierarchy decided to edit and retranslate a number of their holy texts, including prayer books, rather than continue to rely on the error-ridden versions they had used for so long. To the Zealots of Piety, a reform group of Orthodox clergy whose members held a strict, fundamentalist interpretation of Orthodoxy, the implication that the texts they had relied on for so long contained errors was unacceptable. God's reasoning, they maintained, is mysterious and unknowable; to attempt to decipher the word of God was a mortal sin, a substitution of man's reasoning for

divine. And since prayer itself was the word of God, to alter His message one iota was blasphemous—a sacrilege. Hence, the Zealots of Piety staunchly opposed this retranslation of the original Greek texts. Their leader, archpriest Avvakum, was arrested, imprisoned, exiled, and, in 1682, burned at the stake. His followers became a splinter or schismatic sect, an archipelago of religious communities scattered across Russia and Siberia that came to be called the Old Believers. In 1667 they were excommunicated from the Russian Orthodox Church by a synod of Eastern Orthodox patriarchs. At its height, roughly 20 percent of what would have been Russian Orthodoxy was composed of Old Believers.

What might seem to the outsider subtle or inconsequential differences of worship and ritual—a disagreement over esoteric, obscure, even irrelevant points of faith—became the basis for one of the more violent controversies in the history of Russia. Adherence to the old texts and rituals was only the tip of the iceberg; Old Believers also resisted all Western cultural and religious influences, resisted the power of the Tsar and the central government, and held expectations of the coming apocalypse. When supporters of church reforms managed to enlist the Tsar's support when Old Believers had been excommunicated and much of their leadership had been imprisoned and executed, it became clear that Old Belief had lost out in a worldly struggle with mainstream orthodoxy. When Old Believers failed to recant their faith, thousands were put to the torch. The faithful among them believed that Satan had seized control of the church; hence, to renounce their beliefs would be to make a pact with the devil. Moreover, many Old Believers held that the struggles with mainstream orthodoxy indicated that the Second Coming of Christ was just around the corner. Far from dousing the flames of heresy, the execution of the faithful only acted to fan them. In a single year, 1687–1688, in two monasteries in Siberia, over 6,000 Old Believers voluntarily burned themselves to death rather than continue to live under what they considered a corrupt regime (Torke, 1997); thousands more were to follow. Bloody purges continued for hundreds of years, and the Old Belief has survived to this day.

To the Old Believer, the Orthodox clergy and especially its hierarchy were demons in the flesh, minions of Satan—deviants in the most extreme form possible. But to the Orthodox mainstream, it was the Old Believers who were in error; they were heretics, schismatic troublemakers, apostates who refused to grant to the holy Tsarist throne the reverence God demanded it be given—in short, they were deviants who deserved to be burned at the stake. The struggle between the Old Belief and the mainstream Russian Orthodox Church is one of the most interesting religious conflicts in human history. It is a clear example of religious deviance on both sides of the controversy. To each side, adherents on the other side of the fence were deviant, but since Orthodoxy triumphed in this struggle, it was its definition that prevailed. After all, it was the Old Believer zealots who went up in flames—not the Orthodox clergy.

THE PERSECUTION OF WITCHES IN RENAISSANCE EUROPE

Between the early 1400s and the mid-1600s, a fever of persecution clutched Continental Europe. Roughly half a million souls, the vast majority of them women, were denounced, tortured, and executed. Their crime: consorting with the devil. Much of Europe, especially France, Switzerland, and Germany, was in a turmoil of suspicion, accusations, trials, and the punishment of supposed evildoers. A kind of craze or panic about witchcraft and accusations of witchcraft swept over the land. Once an accusation was made, there was little the accused could do to protect herself. Children, women, and "entire families were sent to the stake. . . . Entire villages were exterminated. . . . Germany was covered with stakes, where witches were burning alive." Said one inquisitor, "I wish [the witches] had but one body, so that we could burn them all at once, in one fire!" (Ben-Yehuda, 1985, pp. 36, 37; Goode and Ben-Yehuda, 1994a, p. 150; Goode and Ben-Yehuda, 1994b, p. 155).

Although witches, sorceresses, warlocks, magicians, and shamen who supposedly possess special spiritual and magical powers have existed since the beginning of humanity, in Europe it was not until the early fifteenth century that a theology of demonology was fully developed and promulgated. Witchcraft came to be regarded as totally negative, unholy—a kind of antireligion. Witches came to be seen as Satan's puppets, handmaidens of the devil. The witch myth came to assume the dimension of a kind of religion, a quasi-religion, a coherent, unified, rationalized system of beliefs, assumptions, rituals, sacred texts, and the like. The struggle against witchcraft came to be regarded as the equivalent of the struggle between good and evil, light and darkness, Christianity and the forces of Satan. The Dominican order was especially emphatic in insisting that the evil of witches was precisely the reverse of the good of God, that witchcraft was the exact opposite of the true faith—that is, Christianity itself (Goode and Ben-Yehuda, 1994b, p. 150).

The Witches' Sabbath—the ceremony presided over by Satan and participated in by his diabolical minions—represented an exact mirror image of the holy Mass. Christians pray during the day; witches conduct their ceremony at night. Christians pray in the holy church; witches celebrate their perverse Sabbath in a terrifying place. In church, people kiss the crucifix; in the Witches' Sabbath, they kiss the posterior of a male goat, the symbolic representation of Satan. In the Mass, the wine and wafer—the blood and body of Christ—are revered; in the Witches' Sabbath, the wine and wafer are mocked and desecrated and instead, participants feast on unbaptized, aborted, or strangled babies, or bodies stolen from graves. At Mass, holy water is sprinkled; during the Witches' Sabbath, filthy water is sprinkled by stinking toads. At Mass, heavenly music is played; during the witches' ceremony, grotesque, macabre music is played on bizarre instruments, such as bones, skulls, and logs (p. 151).

What caused these outlandish accusations to be made? Why these charges of deviant behavior that were completely imaginary? And why were they believed? How did they become the basis of the persecution, torture, and execution of hundreds of thousands of innocent people? Why did this orgy of witch-mania erupt when it did? And why were women its principal target?

According to some observers, the Renaissance witch-craze broke out at precisely a time when the medieval order, including the absolute dominion of the Catholic Church, was under challenge. During the Middle Ages, society's moral boundaries were clearly defined. But by the end of the fourteenth and the beginning of the fifteenth centuries, Western Europe was experiencing massive changes that threatened to overturn the worldview that had reigned during the Middle Ages. Commerce, economic growth, a huge expansion of the money economy, a rising standard of living, population increases, ubanization, worldwide exploration and geographical discoveries, the beginning of the scientific revolution, peasant rebellions, increasing contact with non-Christian peoples, the stirring of the Reformation, the separation of the sacred from the profane—these and other developments began to tear away at the strictly hierarchical feudal structure that once was "firmly embedded in a finite cosmic order ruled by God" (pp. 166–168).

These threats to the traditional social and moral order called for the creation of a scapegoat who could be vilified and persecuted, whose vilification and persecution could firm up the moral boundaries of the society. By identifying, condemning, and punishing fictitious deviants, the Catholic Church attempted to reestablish its former power, dominance, and ascendancy. The witch-craze represented the Church's need for an enemy that could be hated with divine vehemence and fury. It was precisely at the dawn of the modern era that a crumbling traditional society needed to fabricate and persecute an imaginary enemy to rejuvenate the faith and rebuild the very foundation of the society. Europe was in crisis, suffering the "painful birth pangs of a new social order" (p. 183); something had to be done. So profound was this crisis that even in Protestant regions, witches were burned at the stake in equal numbers.

Witchcraft, as the developing consensus at the time held, was mainly the province of women. Why? Why were women the principal targets of the Renaissance witch-craze? Women, whose sexuality in a patriarchal society had been demonized for centuries, offered a convenient, relatively powerless target—because women are more credulous and gullible, as the stereotype had it; because they are subject to "carnal lust, which is in women insatiable"; and because "women have a slippery tongue and tell other women what they have learned" (Goode and Ben-Yehuda, 1994b, p. 150). Accusations of witchcraft took on a sexual thrust; the accused were seen not merely as consorting with but engaging in perverse, unholy, and barren sexual intercourse with the devil. Evil spirits assumed human form; voluptuous, hyper-sexual female-appearing beings ("succubi") and attractive, super-sexual male beings ("incubi") would attempt to seduce opposite-sex partners, corrupting them with debauchery.

By the mid-1600s, the witch-craze had been discredited. European society and the Catholic Church had learned to adapt to the encroachments of secularization and theological heterogeneity. With the dawn of the new era, the persecution of witches ceased.

SATANIC RITUAL ABUSE

Beginning in the early 1980s, a belief began to circulate to the effect that a conspiracy of Satanists was kidnapping (and breeding) children in order to use them in satanic rituals, which include sexually molesting, torturing, mutilating, then murdering them. These practices are taking place on a vast scale, some observers claim. It is claimed that 50,000 to 60,000 children are being murdered each year in satanic rituals. The conspiracy is being covered up at the local and even the national level because of a combination of ignorance, fear, and complicity on the part of officials. Police officials, teachers and day-care workers, newspaper editors and reporters, judges, and politicians are part of the conspiracy, this legend proclaims.

Circles of Satanists do exist, of course, but they number no more than a thousand members nationwide. Violence has not been connected with these groups. And many teenage "dabblers" take on the trappings, symbols, or language of Satanism, and a few do commit murders, occasionally in the "name" of Satan, but hardly any of them murder children, and the number who have done so over the past decade or two can probably be counted on the fingers of one person's hand. No one has ever turned up evidence of the kind of conspiracy that is being claimed, or that children are being kidnapped or murdered on such a vast scale—indeed, even on a minuscule scale. The Federal Bureau of Investigation (FBI) tabulates a total of fewer than 20,000 murders in the United States each year from all sources; in any given year, typically, not one involves satanic ritual abuse. Fewer than 600 children are kidnapped by strangers each year for as long as overnight; during any one five-year period, the total who are still missing is roughly 500. In contrast, the vast majority of child kidnappings are committed by the child's parent, usually in a custody dispute with his or her estranged spouse, and roughly 2,000 children are murdered each year by their parents. Not a single satanic ritual abuse–child murder claim has been borne out by the facts (Richardson, Best, and Bromley, 1991; Hicks, 1991; Goode, 1992, pp. 337–342; Victor, 1993).

The most interesting aspect of the Satanism story is not its falseness, however; remember, the sociologist of beliefs is not primarily interested in debunking or disproving claims. (At the same time, the fact that this claim departs so *radically* from the facts tells us that an examination of who believes it, and why, is likely to be interesting and revealing.) The most important thing about these assertions is that they are believed, for the most part, among fundamentalist Christians with relatively low levels of education who live largely in rural areas and small towns. These beliefs take deepest roots in areas hit hardest by economic changes that have transformed the society in the past generation. It is people who have experienced the most severe erosion of their traditional way of life and values who find these assertions credible. Moreover, such people are experiencing an institutional crisis (Bromley, 1991): It is they who are losing out as a result of the economic changes that have been sweeping over the globe, while the winners in these changes are the very segments of the society whose way of life is most alien and repugnant to them. The term *left behind* most emphatically applies to them.

A generation ago in traditional circles, the husband was the head of the family; he worked

and the wife and mother stayed home and raised their children. Today, husband and wife both work and many of them put their children in day-care centers. In the early 1970s, abortion was illegal and strongly condemned. Today it is legal, and nearly a million are performed every year. Indeed, it is possible that abortion is a *metaphor* for satanic murder—that is, huge numbers of fetuses (to the fundamentalist Christian, *children*) are being killed by "the forces of Satan" (that is, the physicians who perform the abortions). So what happens in real life is *very much like* the satanic legend, even if it isn't literally true. In other words, a righteous, Christian way of life is being subverted by embodiments of ultimate evil (Bromley, 1991), such as blasphemy, secularism, humanism, irreligion, pornography, prostitution, drugs, and the unpunished murder of innocent children. And meanwhile, huge segments of the society who support or are part of these changes are growing more prosperous and influential.

In short, here we have a belief—a *deviant* belief, with deep and strong religious roots. In this belief system, the supposed deviants who are designated are in fact imaginary, since the behavior that is charged never actually took place. In American society, this belief is deviant because holding it demarcates its powerless, marginal believers off from the mainstream. It is not valorized by the mainstream media, the educational system, or the political hierarchy. It is held by members of the society whose interpretation of reality is not granted legitimacy in the mainstream. In fact, this interpretation is not merely ignored but derided by that mainstream—as are holders of that interpretation. But to the persons charged in the cover-up, the reverse is true: the charge is not only false but deviant. What's important here is that the belief functions in a certain way for a specific segment of the society. (It may also function in other ways for different segments of the society.) It is an atrocity tale that permits rural, uneducated, fundamentalist Christians to wax indignant about forces that seem to be robbing them of their birthright, their traditional way of life, their comfortable position in the community. This horror story provides a concrete reason for the fundamentalist Christian to oppose secular humanism. It is a way of affirming a belief system in the face of just about the most horrifying act that can be imagined (Goode, 1992, pp. 337–342).

PARAPSYCHOLOGY

We receive a phone call from a friend about whom we were just thinking; simultaneously, two people blurt out exactly the same sentence; someone predicts that an event will take place, and it does. "That must have been ESP!" we declare. Does such a power exist? Can two people communicate with one another without the use of words? Can we picture things miles away, in our mind, without devices of any kind? Is it possible to predict the future? Or "see" events that took place in the past that we did not witness and no one told us about?

Although different observers define parapsychology somewhat differently, common elements that are most often included in definitions are *telepathy*—mind-to-mind communication; *remote viewing* (sometimes referred to as "clairvoyance")—the ability to "see" or perceive objects from a distance without the aid of technology or information; *precognition*—seeing the future; *retrocognition*—seeing the past without the requisite information; *psychokinesis* (PK)—the ability to move physical objects solely with one's mind. All or some aspects of these parapsychological powers are known as "psi" (Pronounced "sigh"). The terms other than psychokinesis are also referred to as *extrasensory perception* (ESP) or, less commonly (and a bit confusingly), *clairvoyance*. Psychokinesis is sometimes referred to as "telekinesis"; clairvoyance (again, confusingly) sometimes refers to seeing the future and the past. The essence of psi is mind-to-matter and mind-to-mind influence or communication.

A very high proportion of the public believes that ESP or other parapsychological powers exist. In 1996, *Newsweek* sponsored a poll that asked respondents whether they believe in "ESP or extra-sensory perception." Two-thirds of the sample (66 percent) said they believed that the power of ESP is real. The proportion saying they believed in "telepathy" or the ability of some people to "communicate with others through means

other than the five senses" represented a slight majority (56 percent). For "clairvoyance, or the power of the mind to know the past and predict the future," the figure was slightly above a quarter of the sample (27 percent), and for "telekinesis, or the ability of the mind to move or bend objects using just mental energy," it was 17 percent. (The figures for a similar Gallup Poll taken about the same time were slightly lower.) Interestingly, except for the fact that residents of the West were considerably more likely to believe in these powers than residents of other geographic locations, correlations between social characteristics and these beliefs seem to be practically nonexistent. Worldwide, the proportion believing in some type of parapsychological power almost certainly adds up to roughly three or four billion souls. A belief this widespread demands attention.

Professional Parapsychologists

For our purposes, even more interesting than the beliefs of the rank-and-file or grassroots is the small social grouping whose members are engaged in conducting systematic research on this belief. Internationally, there are a few hundred parapsychologists, professionals with PhDs, who use the techniques of conventional science—that is to say, controlled experiments— to conduct research designed to test or verify the existence of psi. This is not true of any other paranormal belief system. Very few scientific creationists are professional scientists with PhDs in relevant fields; nearly all "ufologists" (people who publish articles and books arguing that UFO are alien space-craft) are self-taught in their chosen field; and there are no programs in higher education that offer an advanced degree in how to be a psychic, a horoscope reader, or an astrologer.

In contrast, parapsychology researchers conduct scientific investigations on the reality of psi, a particular type of paranormal power. While astrologers and psychics claim to possess psi themselves, parapsychologists study or examine psi in others. The research methods of parapsychologists are far more science-like than is true of the practitioners of any other area of paranormalism. As a result, mainstream scientists are less likely to reject the tenets of parapsychology out of hand. These facts make this belief system interesting for a variety of reasons. I'd like to look at the research-oriented parapsychologists as a sociological collectivity whose members study a set of ideas that contradict what more conventional scientists believe is possible or at least likely.

One of the most remarkable aspects of the research of parapsychologists is that it manifests the *form* but, according to most scientists, not the *content* of science. In other words, the research *methods* of parapsychologists are no less rigorous and "scientific" than those of conventional, mainstream psychologists. And, if the research were to deal with a conventional subject, the *findings* of these studies would be convincing to most scientists, at least to most social scientists. But scientists find two problems with parapsychology research.

One is that parapsychologists offer no convincing conventional explanation for *why* their findings turn out the way they do. Moving objects with the mind? *How?* the conventional scientist asks. What is the *mechanism* by which someone can bend a spoon without touching it? *How* do subjects view faraway objects without the aid of instruments? *In what way* do minds "communicate"? What *causes* psi or parapsychological powers? The problem is, parapsychologists give no answers that satisfy the conventional scientist. Since the latter consider only *material* forces or mechanisms within their explanatory scope, they find it difficult to accept the parapsychologist's arguments. (The same objection can be raised for some features of conventional or cutting-edge science. For instance, why do superstrings exist? No physicist alive has any idea, but most believe in them.)

Physicists make use of material forces such as velocity, mass, friction, gravity, and heat; biologists invoke molecules, cells, genetics, biochemistry, and anatomy; social psychologists and sociologists speak of socialization, peer influence, prestige, power, and social sanctions. These concepts, forces, or factors can be readily understood in a straightforward, naturalistic, cause-and-effect fashion. (Or so scientists say. Poke too far into the structure of any natural and especially social science, and inexplicable forces begin to appear.)

What is the parapsychologist's cause-and-effect explanation for psi? Even if their studies of

empirical regularities demonstrating that *something* is going on were accepted, what *material* explanation for such effects do parapsychologists offer? Some resort to theories of electromagnetic forces (Irwin, 1994, pp. 167–169), "energy field" explanations (p. 169), the action of "elementary particles" (p. 170), or quantum mechanics (Radin, 1997, pp. 277–278, 282–286). Still others "treat psi as a negative 'wastebasket' category. . . , atheoretic anomalies in need of an explanation" (Truzzi, 1987, p. 6). But none has an explanation of how these forces generate or cause the effects their findings point to that is plausible to most scientific observers. In the words of Dean Radin (who holds a doctorate in educational psychology), "The only thing we can do is to demonstrate correlations. . . . *Something* is going on in the head that is affecting *something* in the world." To most scientists, this assertion is not sufficient until a convincing explanation is supplied.

Traditional scientists have a second problem with granting a scientific status to parapsychology: its inability to *replicate* findings, or what Truzzi calls "psi on demand" (1982, p. 180). Scientists take replication seriously. When a scientist produces a finding in an experiment or study, if the principle on which that finding rests is valid, another scientist should be able to conduct the same research and come up with the same finding. Findings should be repeatable, experiment after experiment, study after study. (Replicability is taken more seriously in the natural sciences than in the social sciences, however, and more seriously in psychology than in sociology.) If entirely different results are obtained in repeat experiments, something is wrong with either the experiment or the finding. Radin (1997, pp. 33–50) argues that parapsychology does not display replication any less than traditional science. In addition, he claims that psi is elusive, subtle, and complex and that our understanding of it is incomplete. Hence, experiments demonstrating psi are difficult to replicate.

Conventional scientists are not likely to find his argument convincing because parapsychology is an experimental field and parapsychologists have been unable to replicate the findings of their experiments. In some experiments, psi "effects" appear, while in other almost identical experiments, they do not. Psi seems fragile and elusive.

The assumption that forces are consistent throughout the universe is the bedrock of science itself.

To most scientists, the lack of a plausible explanation and the inability to replicate research findings are serious deficiencies in parapsychology that "will probably prevent full acceptance" of the field by the general scientific community (Truzzi, 1982, p. 180). Hence, many observers refer to the field as a "pseudoscience" (for instance, Hines, 1988, pp. 77–108). In contrast, Truzzi prefers the term "protoscience" (1980, p. 180).

When paranormalists say that the field is "scientific," they mean that the evidence demonstrating some sort of effect is strong, convincing, statistically significant. (While psi is not predictable in the sense of consistently appearing across subjects and experimenters, in the aggregate of *many* experiments, psi "effects" *do* appear vastly more often than by chance.) Says Dean Radin, "the strength of the scientific evidence . . . stands on its own merits" (1997, p. 5).

In contrast, when mainstream scientists say that the field is *not* scientific, they mean that no satisfying naturalistic cause-and-effect explanation for these supposed effects has yet been proposed and that the field's experiments cannot be consistently replicated. "Is there such a thing as mind over matter? Can energy or information be transferred across space and time by some mysterious process that on the face of it seems to confound the principles of biology and physics?" asks journalist Chip Brown. "Most scientists believe the answer is no—no, no, no, a thousand times no" (1996, p. 41).

Does psi exist? Most scientists say no, and the "effects" observed in the laboratory have been explained away as due to experimental error and bias (Gardner, 1957, pp. 299–314). Departures from chance *have* been recorded by parapsychologists in their experiments. Do these departures represent the effects of psi? Whether they do or not, the "effects" described by parapsychologists are not massively greater in frequency than random occurrences. If psi exists, far from being infallible, it sometimes "produces" results that are a bit better than guessing and sometimes does not. Over the course of thousands of experiments, the cumulative likelihood of these differences becomes massively greater than chance. But in a single experiment, this is rarely the case. Consequently, it is unfair and premature of skeptics and debunkers to insist that psi achieve more than its advocates claim it is capable of achieving.

Research Conducted by Parapsychologists

The earliest systematic research was conducted by J. B. Rhine. Rhine's experiments demonstrated that, more or less consistently, subjects intuit the identity of cards more frequently than chance. For instance, in one set of 800 trials conducted between 1931 and 1932, subjects got 207 hits, or slightly better than 25 percent (Irwin, 1994, p. 72). While this effect occurred only slightly more often than chance, the departure from randomness was statistically significant, and it was fairly consistent over a large number of trials.

Even more remarkable, a number of experimental subjects displayed a *strikingly* higher than average ability to select the correct card. For instance, Hubert Pearce, a graduate student in theology, participated in a series of four runs. He averaged a mean number of 8.3 hits per run (Irwin, 1994, pp. 81–82), substantially above the average of five. Moreover, Pearce's ability to select the cards did not diminish over time.

What should we make of this finding? Between 1934 and 1940, Rhine's research met with "vehement criticism" from conventional psychologists (Irwin, 1994, p. 73). Some of the critiques were strictly rhetorical; these critics refused to accept that anything significant was happening and reduced Rhine's work to "superstition and mysticism" (p. 73). But some of it was substantial, usually of a methodological nature. For instance, what if the backs of the cards became marked or scuffed and their identity could be discerned by subjects? What if subjects counted the cards and developed the ability to determine which ones had a higher than chance likelihood of appearing next? Was there any "sensory leakage," cues from researchers concerning upcoming cards, in the experiment? That is, did researchers emit information to subjects about the identity of the cards? Was shuffling adequate? Was fraud possible? Was the erroneous but unconscious recording of wrong answers as right likely to take place by researchers who wanted to demonstrate the power of psi (Gardner, 1957, pp. 199ff.)?

One particularly controversial methodological aspect of the study was the "suppression of null results." Many subjects consistently guessed at the random or 20 percent level; they were classified as "not sensitive," and their trials were discontinued. At the .05 level of statistical significance, simply as a result of random variation, positive results can be obtained 1 out of 20 times. If the researcher saves the results of the one trial that produced positive results and throws away the 19 that produced no differences, significance can be fabricated out of simple random variation. Were Rhine's findings a product of saving what seemed significant and throwing away what did not? It is true that discontinuing trial runs of "not sensitive" subjects was common practice in Rhine's experiments. But since the results of all their experiments were saved, a check reveals that this practice does not account for most of their results. Moreover, it does not account for the extraordinary success of those especially "sensitive" subjects such as Hubert Pearce (Irwin, 1994, p. 75). It is clear that *something* was happening. Exactly what that "something" was, no one knows for sure.

Since Rhine conducted his card-intuiting experiments, numerous parapsychologists have engaged in systematic investigations into the validity of psi in a variety of ways.

Remote Viewing

Between 1978 and 1987, a series of studies was conducted at PEAR, the Princeton Engineering Anomalies Research Laboratory. A "percipient" (remote viewer) was asked to describe the physical or geographical site or setting in which an "agent" (an individual known to the viewer) was located. Some possible descriptions included whether the agent was inside or outside; whether the setting was light or dark; whether animals were present or not; what nearby structures, if any, looked like; whether there were sounds at the site; and so on. The agent filled out a 30-item form and, in most cases, took a photograph of the scene. Experimental conditions included

agent-selected sites ("volitional") and sites the experimenter instructed agents to go to ("instructed"). Of the 334 trials, the odds against the correspondence between what the remote viewer described and what the agent saw directly at the site were 100 billion to one. Interestingly, correspondences were greater for the instructed than for the volitional sites (Radin, 1997, pp. 103–105).

Perception through Time

Honorton and Ferrari (1989) summarized over 300 studies reported in over 100 articles published between 1935 and 1987 that were concerned with the phenomenon of "future-telling" or "forced-choice precognition." More than 50,000 subjects participated in almost two million trials. They were asked to tell the experimenters what they thought would happen in the future. These "targets" included average daily low temperatures in cities around the world, the value of the numbers on dice about to be tossed, ESP card symbols, and the appearance of randomly generated numbers. Twenty-three of the 62 investigators produced successful results; the odds against successful results being obtained by all of the studies, taken as a whole, were "ten million billion billion to one" (Radin, 1997, p. 114).

Telepathy

Between the late 1960s and the early 1970s, a series of 25 "dream" studies were conducted, which reported on 450 sessions. In these studies, one subject selected a picture from an envelope while a second slept in another room. When sleeping subjects manifested REM (rapid eye movement) sleep, they were awakened by a researcher and asked to describe the content of their dreams. In 19 out of the 25 experiments, the outcome was positive; that is, there was a better-than-random chance that the subject of the picture corresponded in crucial ways to the content of the sleeper's dreams. With the 450 sessions added together, the odds against the number of hits obtained was, Radin claims, 75 million to one (1997, pp. 72–73), ruling out any likelihood of chance.

Ganzfeld

Ganzfeld (in German, "whole field") experiments entail placing subjects in a low-stimulus environment, taping a halved ping-pong ball over their eyes and, after a period of relaxation, asking them to think about the target imagery. This may be a picture placed in an envelope in another room (which could entail remote viewing) or the thoughts of the experimenter or another subject who is located, again, in another room (which could entail telepathy). Researchers claim a remarkably high correspondence or hit rate and hence, impressive evidence for psi (Irwin, 1994, pp. 103–105). According to Radin (1997, p. 84), Honorton's summary of 25 Ganzfeld studies (1985), which ran 762 trials, demonstrates a hit rate of 37 percent, corresponding to odds of a trillion to one.

Mind-Matter Interaction

In 1991, parapsychologists Dean Radin and Diane Ferrari summarized all the systematic studies published in English that were conducted over the previous half-century on the outcome of tossed dice (1991). The outcome of experimental conditions (solely with the power of the mind, attempting to control the value of the die face) versus control conditions (not attempting mentally to control the value on the die face) were compared. Seventy-three relevant publications were located; over 2,500 subjects took part in these experiments, and they threw the dice 2.6 million times when they applied "mental influence" and 150,000 tosses without mental influence. For the outcomes stipulated, the hit rate for the control conditions was 50 percent and for the experimental conditions, it was 51.2 percent. While the percentage difference between them is small, the odds against it occurring in this many trials is one billion to one (Radin, 1997, p. 134).

Research by Parapsychologists: Summary and Conclusions

By now, the number of published studies conducted by scientifically oriented parapsychologists runs into the thousands. Several professional,

peer-reviewed journals are devoted more or less exclusively to parapsychology—for instance, the *European Journal of Parapsychology*, the *Journal of the American Society for Psychical Research*, the *Journal of Parapsychology*, the *Journal of the Society for Psychical Research*, and *Research in Parapsychology*. A substantial proportion of the researchers who have conducted these studies are competent, honest, and dedicated to convincing the scientific community that their results are real. Many, although not all, of these studies meet adequate scientific standards; that is, controls are applied and efforts are made to rule out contaminating influences. The "effects" observed tend to be small, but taken cumulatively they are hugely above and beyond what could be obtained by chance or random variation. In other words, *something* is undoubtedly happening. What is it? Is it the elusive psi? And how does psi work? Answers to these questions await a later generation of researchers.

Skeptics and Debunkers

Skeptics and debunkers of parapsychology abound. The pages of the journal *Skeptical Inquirer*, the organ for The Committee for the Scientific Investigation of Claims of the Paranormal (or CSICOP), are filled with critiques of parapsychology. In one of its articles, Paul Kurtz (1978) delivered something of a standard critique of parapsychology, arguing that the field is a pseudoscience; it is lacking in experimental rigor, a coherent testable framework, and a scheme that is replicable; it is subject to experimenter bias; its central concepts are unexplained, inexplicable, and deny a fundamental law of science, namely, the conservation of energy principle; it has been a handmaiden to fraudulent psychics, magicians, and mediums, who have been uncritically endorsed by professional parapsychologists; its proponents hold a mystical, spiritual, and metaphysical worldview that they are motivated to vindicate; they deny the basic principle that extraordinary claims need to be verified by extraordinary evidence, and this is what they are unable to supply. "Is parapsychology a science?" Kurtz asks. Unless its proponents manage to convince its skeptics, "their claims will continue to be held suspect by a large body of scientists" (Kurtz, 1978, p. 31; see also Truzzi, 1980).

Parapsychology as a Deviant Science

From a sociological perspective, perhaps the most interesting feature of parapsychology is that it is an excellent example of a deviant science. This does not mean that it is wrong, invalid, pathological, or a "pseudoscience," only that it tends to be condemned or ignored by mainstream scientists. Dean Radin's question, "Why has mainstream science been so reluctant merely to admit the existence of psi?" (1997, p. 202) says it all. While he argues that this is changing, the fact remains that the conventional sciences reject "extraordinary anomalies," and, given the laws of physics, chemistry, and biology, the findings of parapsychology represent anomalies; they cannot be incorporated into the existing theoretical framework. Hence, they must be debunked or neglected.

McClenon (1984, pp. 128–163) conducted a survey among the council members and selected section committee representatives of the American Association for the Advancement of Science (AAAS). His sample was made up of elite scientists in that they are in positions of leadership and hence can influence whether parapsychology is granted full scientific legitimacy. His final sample (N = 339) includes social as well as natural scientists. Overall, a minority, only 29 percent, consider ESP "an established fact or a likely possibility" (p. 138). Moreover, disbelief in ESP is strongly correlated with denying legitimacy to the very subject of its investigation. Thus, "parapsychologists are labeled as deviant because scientists do not believe in the anomaly that they investigate" (p. 145). Being a skeptic versus a believer is also related to reporting one or more personal paranormal experiences (p. 150). Still, half as many of these scientists report having had an ESP experience (26 percent) as is true of the American population as a whole (58 percent).

McClenon (pp. 164–196) also conducted interviews with parapsychologists, attended their meetings, and read their journals. Before conducting his study, he hypothesized that the field of parapsychology was a kind of science-like cult that righteously defended its belief in psi and actively proselytized outsiders to its position. Contrary to his expectations, parapsychologists did not believe that proselytizing was necessary and felt that, eventually, because of the rigor of their research methods and the robustness of their findings, the "truth will be revealed" (p. 165). In this respect, parapsychologists are traditional or positivistic scientists. They accept the scientific ideal.

The vast majority of parapsychological research is excluded from the mainstream natural science and psychology journals. In fact, says one of McClenon's interviewees, the *best* work in the field "can't get published there. The editors reject it because it was conducted by people within the field of parapsychology. . . . The editors of most [mainstream] journals aren't that knowledgeable about parapsychology. They don't know what to look for in a piece of research" (p. 167). According to the field's proponents, the best work is published in the specialty or parapsychology journals, thereby contributing "to the oblivion to which this body of information has been committed" (pp. 167–168).

The few exceptions prove the rule. Beloff, an Edinburgh psychologist, selected his seven best examples demonstrating the existence of psi (Beloff, 1980); only one of them received even brief mention in a mainstream journal. When Harold Targ and Russell Puthoff (1974) published the results of a remote viewing experiment in the prestigeous journal *Nature*, they were accused of fraud and incompetence. The vehemence of their critics was characteristic of the heat generated by assertions of psi. Neither a recalculation of a minor methodological flaw nor a more tightly controlled subsequent study attracted any commentary from scientists. Critics continued to pick apart the earlier, slightly flawed, study (McClenon, 1984, p. 168). Later replications by other researchers, published in parapsychology journals (Dunne and Bisaha, 1979; Schlitz and Gruber, 1980), are likewise ignored.

In addition to being virtually frozen out of the mainstream science journals, and in spite of the scientific rigor of its experiments, parapsychology "has no professor/graduate-student training like that which exists for the rest of science" (McClenon, p. 171). Parapsychologists "are often discriminated against in academic circles and find it difficult to gain legitimate teaching positions, promotion, and tenure." As a result, few are in academic positions that are necessary to train graduate students (p. 171). The prospective parapsychologist "is advised to become something else" (p. 172): "Conceal your interest in parapsychology," they are told. "Get a doctorate in whatever subject interests you. Then you can be of value to the field" (p. 173).

Common sense would tell us that parapsychologists would react to their outsider status, as many deviant groups do, by becoming even more deviant and far-out and by enlarging their ranks as much as possible. In this case, common sense is wrong; neither is the case. Parapsychologists have stuck to a rigorous scientific methodology and rationale. And the membership policy of the Parapsychological Association (PA) is highly restrictive. Full members generally hold the PhD degree, and to be admitted prospective members must demonstrate evidence of having conducted scientific research in the relevant area (p. 174). Said one parapsychologist who talked with McClenon: "The PA is one of those organizations that was founded with the intention of keeping people out rather than letting them in" (p. 174).

The socialization process that apprentice parapsychologists go through makes them more rather than less cautious and conservative (McClenon, 1984, p. 176), more skeptical, more attuned to fraud and unfounded enthusiasm. Many parapsychologists argue that valid research can be conducted only under tightly controlled laboratory conditions, thereby cutting the field off from the very real-life conditions which, presumably, the field wishes to investigate (p. 177). Interestingly, parapsychologists reject the validity of the personal and anecdotal experiences that lead much of the general public to believe in psi. McClenon says that this suspicion often extends even to the work of other parapsychologists, an effect he refers to as "paranoia in defense of science" (pp. 178, 181). Said one researcher: "I can only be sure of the people I have worked with in the past" (p. 181). The "symbolic hardware" (that is, exceptionally rigorous methodological strategies) used by parapsychologists "often goes beyond that of normal scientists" (p. 182), extending, for example, in some journals, to submitting the design of a planned study "before it is carried out" (p. 182) and the publication of nonsignificant results (p. 183).

UFOs Are Real: The Roswell Incident

The facts of the matter, at least as they appear to most scientists and reputable journalists, can be related fairly briefly. On June 14, 1947, ranch foreman W. W. ("Mac") Brazel found the remains of what appeared to be an aircraft of some kind in the desert 80 miles from Roswell, New Mexico. Material was strewn along a 200-yard path. In an interview conducted on July 8, Brazel described it as consisting of tinfoil, wooden sticks or struts, strips of rubber, tough paper, and tape, some of it with a floral design. He said he initially "did not pay much attention to it," and continued on his rounds around the ranch.

Eleven days later, pilot Kenneth Arnold's report of seeing "flying saucers" was broadcast across the nation. The news touched off hundreds of similar sightings nationwide. However, Brazel, living in a shack in the desert with no radio, was unaware of the furor the Arnold sighting had touched off. He did not consider his discovery important enough to report until several weeks later. On July 4, he collected the debris, rolled it up, and tossed it underneath a bush. On July 5, Brazel drove to Corona, New Mexico, where he may have heard a rumor floating around that there was a reward for anyone who located the remains of a crashed saucer. He returned to the desert and, with his wife and two children, gathered up the debris, which weighed about five pounds, and brought it home.

On July 7, Brazel drove back to Corona for the purpose of selling some wool. He brought along the material he found in the desert, taking it to Sheriff George Wilcox, telling him that he "might have found a flying disk" (Jaroff, 1997, p. 68). Wilcox then called nearby Roswell Army Air Field and got in touch with a Major Jesse Marcel, the base's intelligence officer. Marcel, thinking the material could be the remains of a flying craft, drove to Corona with another officer, Captain Sheridan Cavitt, picked up Brazel, followed him to the ranch, collected the debris, put it into the trunk of his car, and brought it to the base. Cavitt stated on public record that there was nothing out of the ordinary about the material. In addition, Marcel stated that there were no crash or scoop marks on the ground where the material was found. Back at the base, Marcel and Brigadier General Roger Ramey were photographed with the debris. Officials at the Roswell base then shipped the wreckage to a regional command center, Carswell Army Air Force Base in Fort Worth, Texas. From there, it was shipped to what is now Wright-Patterson Air Force Base in Ohio. It is crucial to emphasize that, at the time, very few observers thought of flying "disks" or "saucers" in terms of extraterrestrial craft. Nearly everyone assumed that they were secret military aircraft, possibly Soviet in origin.

On July 8, authorities at the airfield issued a press release stating that the debris from a "flying disk" had been recovered. This prompted an article in *The Roswell Daily Record* entitled "RAAF Captures Flying Saucer." The news created a sensation, and inquiries flooded in from around the world asking about the craft. The night of July 8, General Ramey called the media, issuing a statement asserting that the remains were from a high-altitude weather balloon, not a flying saucer. We now know that the general's statement was false, a story to cover up Project Mogul, an airborne system of spying on Soviet atomic explosions. The next day, the *Daily Record* ran the headline: "General Ramey Empties Roswell Saucer." The disclaimer quieted things down, and for more than 30 years, the matter was largely forgotten.

In 1978, Stanton Friedman, a former nuclear physicist, interviewed Major Marcel, who remained convinced that what Brazel gave him was the wreckage of an unusual craft of some kind. Unfortunately, Marcel's accounts reveal the decay of memory over time. For instance, he could not recall the year when the incident took place, the fact that he had appeared in two press photos and not just one, that a total of seven photographs had been taken, and that the material in all of these photographs is identical. These details assume enormous importance later on. Friedman ignored these problems and interviewed several other witnesses; he coauthored a book with Charles Berlitz and William Moore (coauthors of the infamous and now-discredited *The Bermuda Triangle Mystery*), entitled *The Roswell Incident*, which was published in 1980.

Two features of the Friedman/Berlitz/Moore book were remarkable. The first is that it put forth the contention that the debris discovered in the desert near Roswell was the wreckage from an alien craft. Note that the first three published claims of crashed alien ships (in 1948 and 1950) were either a hoax or a joke (Peebles, 1994, pp. 47–50; Ziegler, 1997, pp. 13–14), indicating the rarity with which this belief was held at the time of the collection of the Roswell material.

The second remarkable feature of the claims made in this book was a story, told secondhand, of a man who died in 1969. The man claimed he had seen another crash site on the plains of Saint Agustin, 150 miles from where Brazel had found the debris. The story is that this other site was littered with tiny humanoid bodies. At the time, no one, Friedman included, placed much credence in the secondhand story from a deceased man, since it seemed to have no relation to the Roswell crash. But eight years later, the second tale assumed prominence in a book written by two science fiction writers, Kevin Randell and Don Schmidt. *UFO Crash at Roswell* claimed that the government had found and "spirited away" the extraterrestrial bodies. New alleged Roswell eyewitnesses emerged, including a mortician, who had been asked for "child-sized coffins," and a nurse, who claimed to have seen an autopsy performed on "strange-looking, small bodies" (Jaroff, 1997, p. 69).

Since that time, dozens of books claiming that alien spaceships crashed in the desert near Roswell have been published; in all likelihood, dozens more are in the works. With each succeeding book, new witnesses turn up, claiming to have seen extraterrestrial bodies. It has become a full-time job to track down each and every claim. According to a poll conducted by *Time* magazine, among the segment of the public accepting the idea that UFOs are alien airships, two-thirds believe that a UFO "crash-landed near Roswell"; four-fifths believe that the U.S. government "knows more about extraterrestrials than it chooses to let on" (Handy, 1997, p. 63).

The fact is, contrary to the conspiracy theorists, the U.S. military was actively seeking to locate physical evidence of an alien crash after the Roswell incident. Secret documents that the government was forced to release under the Freedom of Information Act contain statements by top Air Force officials to that effect. For instance, in a document dated March 17, 1948, Colonel Howard McCoy, chief intelligence officer at the air force base, where the remains of the Roswell crash were supposedly shipped, stated: "We are running down every [UFO] report. I can't tell you how much we would give to have one of those [mysterious craft] so we could recover whatever they are" (Handy, 1997, p. 70). Moreover, if the materials from Roswell were extraterrestrial and were vastly superior to earthly materials, it makes sense that the military would have conducted a huge research project to unlock their secrets. (Remember, the "Cold War" with the Soviet Union had begun just a year before the Roswell incident.) Yet engineers who worked on military contracts at that time were not aware of the existence of any such research (Klass, 1997, pp. 226–231). Clearly, the military was aware of the fact that the material collected in the desert was not of extraterrestrial origin.

In 1994 and 1997, the Air Force released two reports on the Roswell incident. (They are summarized in Broad, 1994, 1997; Weaver and MacAndrew, 1995; MacAndrew, 1997.) Both admitted that the weather balloon story had been a cover-up for top-secret Project Mogul, which was designed to monitor Soviet atomic tests.

The materials used to assemble Mogul's balloons match perfectly Brazel's 1947 description of what he found in the desert, as well as the seven photographs taken of the debris before they were shipped from the Roswell base. The balloons were fitted with "corner reflectors" that were held together with beams made of balsa wood and coated with glue; the seams were reinforced with the same tape (with "pinkish-purple . . . flower-like designs") which Major Marcel interpreted as bearing "hieroglyphics" (Ziegler, 1997, pp. 8–9). Records show that one train of balloons was released in the first week of June (p. 4), about a week before Brazel found the debris. The object disappeared off the radar screen that was monitoring its movement just 20 miles from the ranch where Brazel found the debris. Moreover, military records show that there were no unusual operations, movements, or maneuvers during the period in question, nor did pilots assigned to the Roswell base at the time report any rumor or hubbub occurring just after the discovery of the debris.

According to the Air Force reports, the small bodies some witnesses claimed to have seen may have been test dummies, 67 of which were released in projects High Dive and Excelsior, which took place in the area between 1954 and 1959. Some critics charge that these projects took place *after* the Roswell incident. But remember, in 1947 *no one* reported having seen alien bodies. In all cases, the recollection of supposed eyewitnesses of extraterrestrials took place well after the Roswell incident; the passage of time collapsed their recollection to 1947. For instance, the autopsy that the nurse-eyewitness reports could not have taken place until 1956, when she was first assigned to the Roswell base (Gildenberg and Thomas, 1998). In 1978, a man told author Friedman that another man, who died in 1969, had told him about dead bodies that he claimed to have seen in 1947, but clearly this story cannot be verified. In other words, we have no evidence that is unassailably contemporaneous to 1947 that says anything about alien bodies. This part of the tale was tacked on much later, after the notion of extraterrestrials had become believable to the American public.

Thus, the interesting questions about the Roswell incident are not physical and forensic, but sociological and anthropological. In other words, what is important about Roswell is not what happened, because we already know what happened. (At least, we know the version that is most credible to scientists, historians, and journalists.) I am not attempting to verify the scientific, historical, or journalistic account, but to show how different it is from that believed in by the ufologists. What is important from the perspective of a social scientist is how and why the tale that aliens crashed in the desert arose and what role it plays in contemporary culture. The official version of the crash is questionable only if one buys into the notion of a vast government conspiracy. But if one believes that the government released false information to cover up the real story, that there was an alien craft, one is free to construct any story one might choose. After the 1970s, alien crash stories became essentially unfalsifiable; that is, no amount of discrediting information could possibly falsify any assertion because that information is inevitably believed to be part of a government cover-up of the truth (Ziegler, 1997, p. 15). This mythical story needs close examination.

According to anthropologist Charles Ziegler, there are at least six separate, distinct, and partly contradictory although overlapping Roswell tales (1997, pp. 17–29). All have tidied up their assertions so that they are consistent with the alien angle. For instance, in several versions of the tale, Dan Wilmot and his wife saw a flying saucer in the air on July 2. In these versions, Brazel is supposed to have discovered the wreckage in the desert after July 2, not on June 14, when he said he found it. But all contain the same core elements. Our intellectual puzzle is this: What makes one or another version of the Roswell story plausible to some observers but not to others? Why do close to 75 million Americans believe that the debris Brazel collected in the desert near Roswell was extraterrestrial in origin?

Ziegler classifies the six versions of the Roswell incident that assert the alien origin of the crash as myths. By this he does not mean they are necessarily false, only that they follow a stereotypical or folkloric structure, much like the tales told in tribal and folk societies. The Roswell myth contains themes that have been embedded in stories for thousands of years. The central motif of the Roswell tale is that "a malevolent monster (the government) has sequestered an item essential to humankind (wisdom of a transcendental nature, i.e., evidence-based knowledge that we are not alone in the universe)." The tale has a hero as well as a villain: "The cultural hero (the ufologist) circumvents the monster and by investigative prowess, releases the essential item (wisdom) for humankind" (1997, p. 51). Hoarded-object folk narratives in which the hero, through intelligence, bravery, and zeal releases or liberates the hoarded object "are truly ubiquitous and geographically widespread" (p. 52). Once again, the folkloric quality of the Roswell story does not automatically invalidate it, but it does shed light on its appeal. According to Ziegler, the Roswell incident "is a folk narrative masquerading as an exposé" (p. 155).

- In addition, the Roswell UFO story is appealing to many believers because: It represents a "vehicle for social protest" against the government; it is an expression of "antigovernment sentiment," dramatic testimony to ongoing government conspiracies (p. 68).
- It is unfalsifiable; it cannot be disproven. Any fact that is presented to counter its validity is interpreted as a government cover-up.
- It contains a strong religious element. For many observers, aliens are contemporary angels possessing wisdom humans need but lack (pp. 70–74).

- It is an ingredient in affirming group solidarity and distinguishing believers (who are wise and virtuous) from nonbelievers (who are fools, knaves, and narrow-minded dogmatists) and stressing the superiority of the former over the latter (p. 66).
- It is a means by which the "we are not alone" notion is made manifest and, simultaneously, an assertion that our earthly imperfections could be rectified by the wisdom of infinitely superior, superhuman, almost supernatural beings.

Ziegler argues that the image that scholars and scientists hold of the Roswell incident is based on a "way of knowing" that is radically different from that which believers use (p. 154). Scholars and scientists tend to have different, and usually stricter, standards regarding acceptable and decisive evidence. Issues that concern them tend to assume less importance to advocates, believers, and ufologists.

For instance, scientists and scholars place far more emphasis on physical and forensic evidence, while believers have more faith in eyewitnesses (if they agree with their own version of the truth). Discrepancies in different versions of the Roswell tale (indeed, as I said, some of them are contradictory) are more distressing to the expert and less so to the believer. The fact that the tale follows well-worn traditional and stereotypical folk idioms that have existed for thousands of years arouses more suspicion in the scientist and the scholar, less so in the believer. The fact that some supposed eyewitnesses have come forward decades after the event, or have been shown to have been dishonest in other matters, or changed their stories over time, is far more discrediting in the view of the scientist and the scholar than in that of the believer.

In contrast, believers more readily discount evidence that issues from the government, assuming that it is "tainted" by a conspiracy; scientists and scholars are less likely to do so, arguing that conspiracy theories are an excuse for protecting a theory that cannot be falsified.

Once again, as we have so often seen, the ways that scientists "know" something to be true are very different from the ways that believers or laypersons "know" their version of the truth. Each is based on an epistemology that *cancels the other out*. Given their incompatability, it is almost unimaginable that the mystery of Roswell can be solved to the satisfaction of all parties any time soon.

It must be emphasized that the account I render here does not represent a validation of the skeptic's version of Roswell and a critique of the ufologist's. It does, however, represent an effort to emphasize that *different sorts of evidence* are accepted by the two sides. Believers feel that the fact that the government has covered up in the past is crucial evidence in the Roswell mystery; given the fact of a cover-up, it *must have been* about aliens. In contrast, skeptics argue that, in principle, the cover-up could have been about anything; in fact, it was about a secret anti-Soviet surveillance program. The fact that six *entirely different* and, in large measure, contradictory extraterrestrial Roswell stories circulate is crucial for the scientist, almost irrelevant for the believer. (After all, *at least one* has to be true, they reason.) The fact that these tales resonate with and address cultural and societal concerns is important for the scientist, a mere distraction for the believer. Once again, a narration of the events of Roswell underlines the fundamental differences in epistemology between ufologist and scientist; it does not prove that one version is right and the other is wrong. At this point, neither side could possibly be successful in convincing the other of the validity of its position. But to emphasize a point made about the previously discussed belief systems, even though roughly half of the American population supports the view that the Roswell crash entailed extraterrestrials, this belief is deviant to the extent that it is rejected by the high-prestige media, the educational system, and the other influential, mainstream social institutions, and its adherents are marginalized, depicted as kooks, derided, and stigmatized.

Summary

Cognitive deviance refers to holding beliefs that relevant audiences consider unacceptable, unconventional, and discrediting. It is not always an easy matter to distinguish beliefs from behavior, since beliefs so often manifest themselves in or become the basis for action or behavior. In this chapter, I focus on those unconventional beliefs that are unlikely to translate directly into deviant behavior—that remain more or less in the ideational realm. Many deviant beliefs are held by persons who are deemed psychiatrically

disordered. However, mental illness usually manifests itself in a variety of other symptoms aside from belief. Again, here, I focus on beliefs that typically lack the component of mental disorder.

Beliefs have been examined by social observers at least as far back as the ancient Greek philosophers. Social scientists argue that beliefs grow out of social position and material condition. Marxists tend to emphasize economic factors as the wellspring of ideas and beliefs. In contrast, Weberians stress the mutual influence between and among a variety of social institutions, including the economy, emphasizing that the material and the ideational realm mutually influence and act back upon one another.

Religious differences have contributed some of the most important and bloodiest controversies in human history. Typically, each side of a religious conflict brands its opponents as deviants; which side successfully defines the other depends on which has the most power, influence, and resources. The Crusades, the Russian Old Believers, the Renaissance witch-hunt, and charges of Satanic ritual abuse in contemporary America represent historical instances of religious—and more generally, cognitive—deviance in action. In each case, one category—a circle of co-religionists—believes certain things to be true, while a larger, or more powerful, category of the society believes something else. In the power struggle, the first of these categories is "left behind" and hence, regarded as unconventional—in a word, deviant.

Parapsychology offers an example of cognitive deviance. Professional parapsychologists argue that forces that conventional science cannot understand operate in nature. Parapsychology adopts the form but not the content of science; hence, it is branded by mainstream researchers as a deviant science.

The claim that unidentified flying objects (UFOs) are real is a deviant belief system. Ufologists—supporters of this claim—argue that the mysterious crash in the desert near Roswell, New Mexico, in 1947 is clear-cut proof that the earth is being visited by creatures from other planets. Conventional scientists, journalists, and much of the American public do not validate this claim; they regard its claimants as "kooks"—in a word, cognitive deviants.

PERSONAL ACCOUNT: The Belief That Extraterrestrials Are on Earth

Steven, 35, who works as an office manager in a physician's office, holds a belief in paranormal phenomena. He was interviewed by Gretchen Kowalick, a student at the University of Maryland. Steven, says Gretchen, "has a family and a job and seems to live a normal life. But he has beliefs that are considered to be deviant. They stray from mainstream beliefs and the beliefs of the scientific community."

GRETCHEN: What are your beliefs about aliens and UFOs?

STEVEN: They have been here and are still here. They may just be in the skies, not actually living in the population. I think it has to do with some type of technology exchange between the government and the aliens and we want to keep the upper hand in the situation. There are multiple groups of aliens visiting the earth. Ancient texts speak of multiple beings visiting the earth.

GRETCHEN: What type of technology?

STEVEN: I believe we allow them to abduct people and do experiments on them in order to get technology from them. Some of the technology we have gotten from them has been night vision and the stealth bomber. I think we have been close to developing this type of technology but we were missing things and they gave us the missing links to add it all up. I also believe they have given us the technology that can end our dependence on fossil fuels, but that's the global economy so they don't want to tell us they know. The people who are in charge want to stay in charge so they can't allow the technology to come out. In 1947, the government came out and said they had a crashed saucer, but 24 hours later they took back the statement . . . .

GRETCHEN: Where do you get your information?

STEVEN: I read a lot. I watch the History Channel, Discovery Channel, and the Learning Channel. With Internet access, there is a lot of information out there and I can even check some of the sources out. There are a lot of firsthand witnesses so either there is mass hysteria or people are telling the truth. There are even pictures that can't be explained, or the explanations that are given aren't feasible. For example, for one picture, they said it was swamp gas that made the image.

GRETCHEN: Are you in any [UFO] clubs?

STEVEN: No. Many of them are dangerous and take this to extremes and kill themselves [such as the "Heaven's Gate" UFO cult, 39 of whose members committed suicide in 1997]. I don't like to think of myself as an extremist. My views can be considered extreme. But I just look at things with an open mind and a lot of things get explained.

GRETCHEN: Do you ever go to conventions or [listen to] speakers?

STEVEN: Absolutely. Stephen Greer and Jim Marrs are two speakers I have been to see. Jim Marrs is a journalist who came from Texas and wants to get at the truth. They have over 400 government witnesses on videotape who are talking about their experiences and say they were told by the government not to talk about it. There are generals and colonels, not just average citizens. People with high-ranking positions talking about things they have seen and experiences they have had with UFOs. . . . Dr. Geer spoke about government secrecy, about 9/11, and our dependence on fossil fuels. . . . I also went to a conference with multiple speakers who talked about alien abductions, crop circles, and ancient Sumerian texts. There were a variety of people there, from all walks of life. Of course, there were some extremists there who would believe anything they were told. In order to understand this phenomenon, you have to understand that it's . . . been here since we've been here. Indian texts talk about beings coming and building anti-gravity vehicles. Most are dismissed as myth, but if you put this together with the stories in the Bible, it makes sense.

GRETCHEN: But are all aliens good?

STEVEN: No. Some have good intentions and some have bad intentions. I relate this to

PERSONAL ACCOUNT: The Belief That Extraterrestrials Are on Earth (cont.)

when you go to the doctor when you are a young kid. You don't know what the doctor is going to do to you, but you let him do it because you think it's going to be OK. It's the same way with aliens. If you get abducted, you don't know exactly what they are doing to you because you really don't have a choice. The aliens are crafting a new race. They have done this before, and this explains gaps we've found in the fossil records. There was a type of being already here, and the aliens manipulated what was here to help humans get to where we are today. We got our jump-start from another race of beings. This is another reason why the government doesn't want us to know. Again, a lot of ancient texts speak of this. People who have been abducted have had sperm taken from them and they are taken back afterwards to see what they have helped to create. . . . [In 1938, Orson Welles broadcast a radio drama of the novel by H. G. Wells, *War of the Worlds*, about an invasion from Mars] and people thought that it was really happening, that aliens were invading. There were people committing suicide. It was just mass hysteria. Some say this was a test to see if we were ready to know all that the government knew about the aliens here, but that proved we weren't ready. In the 1960s, there was a report that was done that said we would be likely to find alien artifacts on the Moon, on Mars, and on Saturn, and that this information should be kept from the public. Many believe that Roswell was the first crash of an alien craft, but it wasn't. One time in California [during World War II], they thought they were being invaded by the Japanese, and they shot at the thing in the air, but this was never explained. There are some very famous paintings that have pictures of UFOs in the background.

GRETCHEN: Why do you think the government has kept everything a secret?

STEVEN: People begin to question reality when they talk about all this. The amount of evidence is overwhelming. In a court of law, the evidence would be enough. The cover-up may be grander than we can ever understand. . . . The two main reasons for the cover-up are, one, people can't handle change in their belief system, and two, the change it would cause in the economy.

GRETCHEN: Does everyone you know know about the beliefs you have?

STEVEN: No, not everyone. The ridicule factor is very high and I know that. If you are going to discuss this, you have to sneak it in through the back door. Global politics is a good subject to talk about and then sneak the discussion in about aliens and UFOs.

GRETCHEN: What about your family? How do they feel about your beliefs or do they even know about them?

STEVEN: I talk to some of them about it. I'm more comfortable with my family. We talk about religion and I can slip in the UFO topic. Some of them believe it to a certain extent but they think I go too far with it, especially when it comes to religion. My mom knows I believe in aliens and UFOs and stuff, but she doesn't believe in it at all. This is more than a hobby to me and they know that. . . . I just want to know the truth.

GRETCHEN: When did this all begin for you?

STEVEN: It was like a ball of yarn unraveling. I was watching the TV show, "Sightings." It showed a face on Mars, just a quick glimpse, and it intrigued me, so I started reading. NASA [the National Aeronautics and Space Administration, a government agency] said it was a trick of light and shadow. So they found another picture at another time of day and the face was still there. They have done research on the picture and the eyes were in the right place, and the nose was in the right place, so I don't think it was just a coincidence. There have also been pictures of a five-sided pyramid, and as of today, there is no natural explanation for a five-sided pyramid. The aliens used pyramids as beacons.

PERSONAL ACCOUNT: The Belief That Extraterrestrials Are on Earth (cont.)

They came here to mine for gold to help fix their atmosphere. Sumerian texts say that man got started this way, because aliens made humans mine the gold for them.

GRECHEN: What have you done to get this information out?

STEVEN: I volunteered for Stephen Basset in the last election. He was an independent who ran for Congress in the Eighth District in Maryland. He was the first person to run with UFOs as his main platform. He knew he wasn't going to get elected. His main goal was to get exposure for the subject. The other people running wouldn't even let him take part in the debates. . . . I volunteered for him and helped by handing out flyers and things like that.

GRETCHEN: Does it bother you that people think you are crazy?

STEVEN: It doesn't bother me. If they stopped to listen, they will hear that I know what I am talking about. I have made people begin to question reality. . . . This is serious and I am serious about it. Why all the secrets? That's what I want to know. What is so secretive that you have to make up stories to explain things? You have to gather all the information before making credible judgments [and I've done that]. It is part of our mental conditioning that when you believe in this [sort of thing] you are [supposed to be] crazy.

GRETCHEN: What do you think about crop circles?

STEVEN: They are real. Some paranormal thing makes them. There is no man-made reason for them. They go back three hundred years. . . . The government puts out misinformation [about them].

QUESTIONS

Do you agree that belief in UFOs is a form of cognitive deviance? If so, why? If not, why not? Is the government concealing evidence that extraterrestrial spacecraft crashed on earth? What motive would officials have to do something like that? Is it possible for the government to keep something like that a secret? And, since there are so many people who work for the government—and who hold conflicting views on almost every imaginable subject—who exactly is "the government" that is keeping this important fact a secret? And if the evidence is as "overwhelming" as Steven says, why are so many scientists—any one of whom who supplied such evidence would be regarded as having made the most important discovery of all time—dubious about the claim of aliens on and around earth? And why are scientists spending so much time and money to communicate with intelligent beings in other solar systems when extraterrestrials are in our backyard? Is Steven someone you would want to talk to? Hang out with? Do you buy his beliefs in a range of different paranormal phenomena? If nearly half of the American public shares Steven's belief in the reality of UFOs, why do I refer to that belief as deviant?

CHAPTER 11

Mental Disorder

The schizophrenic is a perfect machine of self-destruction.

—Elizabeth Swados (1991)

One day in October, in a remote valley in Colorado, Margaret Ray, age 46, knelt on the railroad tracks in front of a speeding coal train. She was killed instantly and, it is to be hoped, painlessly, but her entire life before that moment had been filled with little else but pain. In her tragically brief life, Ms. Ray had achieved a sort of notoriety—the kind that is celebrated by sensationalistic tabloid journalists—by being a David Letterman stalker. She repeatedly broke into the comedian's house, camped out on his tennis court, and once, even stole his Porsche. Although Letterman joked about Ms. Ray's shenanigans, her life was far closer to tragedy than to comedy. Her older brother committed suicide at the age of 22 by driving full speed into a tree. At the age of 23, her younger brother walked into a garage, turned on the ignition of a car, lay down on the floor, and succumbed to carbon monoxide fumes. Ms. Ray, her suicidal brothers, and her father—who died more than 20 years ago of a heart attack—had all been diagnosed as schizophrenics. Tom, her middle brother and the only one who lived a normal life, spent much of his life on the lookout for telltale signs of mental disorder. Once, he thought he was hearing nonexistent voices—a sure sign of schizophrenia—but quickly realized that a radio was playing in the next room. "I'm kind of the oddball in the family," he said. "The genetic lot missed me." So fearful is Anna-Lisa Johnson, Ms. Ray's 22-year-old daughter, a law student in Washington, about the genetic inheritance she will pass on that she is extremely uncertain about having children. Once she was ashamed of her mother and sought to conceal her tainted identity. She has since had a change of heart. "Right now," she says, "I'm not embarrassed of who my mother was. . . . She was a sick woman, and people made it a joke" (Bruni, 1998, p. 50).

Michael Laudor breezed through Yale, receiving a bachelor's degree *summa cum laude* in three years. But in his twenties, he became, in his own words, a "flaming schizophrenic." After working at his first job, he was seized with the idea that his phone lines were tapped. He quit the job, left abruptly, and settled into his home town. He became convinced that the musicians with whom he played were part of a suspicious cult. Soon after, he imagined that neighbors were ringing bells outside his bedroom window on a deathwatch until dawn. Institutionalized, he became certain that "at any moment," the psychiatrists in the hospital "would surgically cut me to death without any anesthesia." After he was administered antipsychotic drugs and placed in a halfway house, Michael's hallucinations and paranoia "became manageable." He was offered a job at Macy's; instead, he decided to attend Yale Law School, which had accepted him before his disorder. Acquiring a reputation for being something of a genius among a number of faculty and students, in his senior year he acted as editor of *The Yale Law Review*. Discussing his condition with a reporter, he said, "I feel that I'm pawing through walls of cotton and gauze when I talk to you now. . . . I'm using 60 or 70 percent of my effort just to maintain the proper reality contact with the world" (Foderaro, 1995, p. B4). Michael wanted to work as a law professor, but was afraid that his mental condition would discourage schools from hiring him.

For a time, Michael seemed to have his condition under control. He received a $600,000 book contract and a $1.5 million movie contract for his life story. He became engaged and was living with his fiancée, Caroline Costello, who, friends said, loved him. Said a friend, "Michael was the golden boy. He is handsome, kind, spiritual, a wonderful conversationalist, a wonderful sense of humor and he was destined for what everyone thought was greatness" (Berger, 1998, p. B4). The couple was expecting a child. But in 1995, Michael's father—who had been a stabilizing influence in his life—died of cancer. Michael was unable to land a job as a law professor and couldn't seem to get motivated to write his book. Within several years of his father's death, the antipsychotic drugs he had been taking no longer seemed to be effective; his psychiatrist struggled in vain to find the right medication and dose. At some point, a friend said, he stopped taking his drugs altogether. One day in June, Michael flagged down a police car and told an officer he thought he might have hurt his girlfriend and possibly even killed her. Taken into custody, he was alternatively calm and agitated. At one point, he hit a police officer, who had to be taken to the hospital. When police entered the couple's apartment, Ms. Costello's body was found in the kitchen with a dozen stab wounds in her neck and back. Michael was arrested and taken into police custody (Berger, 1998).

Released from Rikers Island, New York City's jail, Barry McCrea, age 40, clutches a Metrocard good for two fares. The card is the "parting gift" inmates receive when they are dropped off on the street. "I got no meds now," says Mr. McCrea, who has a long history of mental disorder. At the jail, he says, "I kept asking about it [receiving medication after his release], but they were too busy" (Bernstein, 1999, p. B1). The New York City penal system treats more than 15,000 seriously mentally ill patients each year, but discharges them in the same way it does all other inmates. While advocates for the mentally ill are suing the city to provide medication and expedite Medicaid, referrals, and shelter to homeless mentally ill former jail and prison inmates, city officials are fighting the suit. Said one government official, "No law says the city has to provide medicine for mentally ill inmates after they leave jail" (p. B1).

In jail for six days for shoplifting two bottles of hair dye and selling two bags of marijuana, Mr. McCrea received Dilantin, an antiseizure medication; Haldol, an antipsychotic agent; and another drug to control trembling, a side effect caused by Haldol. Unlike mental hospitals, psychiatric units in jails have no control over when and how their patients leave. Said a spokesperson for a city hospital: "We treat them while they're there, and when they're gone, they're gone" (p. B6). Previously, short-term jailings produced no disruption of Medicaid payments. But five years ago, in an effort to save money, the city searched through the jail rolls and terminated the medical benefits of inmates upon release. On the street, Mr. McCrea had no money, no prescription, and no Medicaid card to cover the cost of medications. He has been taking prescription drugs for 20 years. After his wife and twin sons were killed in an automobile accident, Mr. McCrea threw himself in front of a car. He

lay in a coma for 18 days. Since then, he has taken prescription drugs, albeit irregularly, for his mental problems. After his most recent release, Mr. McCrea managed to locate a black-market bottle of Dilantin, but it quickly disappeared. It "might have fell out of my pocket," he explained, "while I was sleeping on the [park] bench" (p. B6).

We all know someone who seems odd or bizarre, who acts in a totally inappropriate fashion. A stroll down many streets in the nation's larger cities will reveal men and women who look disheveled and who scream or mutter incomprehensible phrases to no one in particular. Some people are so fearful of lurking, unmentionable forces that they are literally incapable of walking out of their front door. Others are unable to hold a conversation anyone else would regard as intelligible. Still others are so depressed that they lie curled up in a fetal position for hours or days—or even weeks, or more—on end. Some make it a point to be abusive and offensive to practically everyone they meet, insulting them, physically striking them, engaging in actions that seem almost designed to shock, hurt, or outrage others at every opportunity. Persons we may have read about hear voices from another planet commanding them to kill, to become dictator of the world, or to deliver an urgent message to the residents of North America. Some people are convinced that their dentist has implanted an electronic receiver in a filling in their teeth that is sending bizarre messages into their brain. Some people wear a perpetual, peculiar smile, and seem to exist in "their own little world."

In everyday language, we have terms for such persons. "He's wacko," we say. "She's out of her mind," "He's a nut," "She's completely cracked," "He's a weirdo," "She's a sicko," or "He's off his rocker," we declare, pointing to the people who display what we regard as manifestations of a mind that's "not right." More formally, the condition such people suffer from is referred to as *mental illness* or, more broadly, *mental disorder*.

What is mental illness? In what way can a mind be said to be "ill"? What is a mental "disorder"? How can a mind be said to be "disordered"? Is mental illness or disorder an instance of deviance? If so, in what specific ways?

WHAT IS MENTAL DISORDER?

Defining mental disorder is not as easy or as straightforward a task as might appear at first glance. As we've seen, even defining deviant behaviors that manifest themselves in *specific* actions, such as murder, homosexuality, drug use, and prostitution, proves to be an extremely thorny matter. Mental disorder presents a much more formidable definitional problem because, first of all, it is not a type of behavior as such; instead, it is seen as a mental condition that presumably manifests itself in certain behaviors, thought patterns, and verbal utterances. Second, even the behavior supposedly associated with it cannot be pinned down to any one type of action with much precision. (Of course, certain specific *categories* of mental disorder have more clear-cut symptoms than others, but mental disorder *generally* does not.) Rather, mental disorder is a set of conditions that exhibits itself in a *wide range* of behaviors. Consequently, no general definition of the phenomenon can be completely satisfactory.

The term mental *illness* does not appear in the table of contents or the index of the latest edition of the American Psychiatric Association's *Diagnostic and Statistical Manual*, its fourth, or DSM-IV (1994), nor is it in the leading textbook on abnormal psychology (Davison, Neale, and Kring, 2004). Psychiatry and clinical psychology, the "healing professions" that deal with and attempt to treat persons who are emotionally troubled, prefer the term "mental disorder" to "mental illness." It is possible that the term "illness" is seen as stigmatizing while "disorder" is regarded as more clinical, descriptive, and "scientific." On the other hand, the term "mental illness" is still used among sociologists; witness the titles of two textbooks in the field—*A Sociology of Mental Illness* (Tausig, Michello, and Subedi, 2004) and *The Sociology of Mental Illness* (Gallagher, 2002). But clearly there is a world of difference between the classic mental "illnesses" (for instance, schizophrenia and clinical depression) and the grab bag that is covered by the term

mental "disorder," including impotence, the inability to stop smoking and drinking coffee, "transient tic disorder," "mathematics disorder," "reading disorder," and "disorder of written expression." It is possible that sociologists are more likely than psychiatrists and psychologists to study *epidemiology*—the distribution of mental disorders in the population—and hence, are acutely aware of the fact that the broader the category the lower the likelihood that any single generalization can cover all disorders. Clearly, no single factor or variable correlates consistently with all mental disorders. On the other hand, a number of social characteristics are statistically related to mental "illness," which is much narrower and more specific a phenomenon.

Mental *disorder* encompasses a wide range of conditions or supposed conditions, while mental *illness* is a much more specific category. Although itself a fairly broad category, mental illness is clearly a *subcategory*, or one specific *type*, of mental disorder. All mental illnesses are disorders, but not all mental disorders are illnesses. Clearly, clinical depression is both a disorder and an illness. However, mental retardation, or the possession of a measurably low intelligence, is *not* a form of mental illness, at least as the term is most commonly understood—but it *is* clearly a disorder or *malfunction* of the mind. The same is true of autism, Tourette's syndrome, dyslexia, stuttering, hyperkenesis, and a number of other disorders that are not mental illnesses as such. Throughout, I'll be using these two terms, "disorder" and "illness," more or less interchangeably, but their conceptual distinction should be clear. When I refer to mental disorder, I'll be referring *mainly* to mental illness, such as schizophrenia and clinical depression. On the other hand, if I refer to mental illness, I do not necessarily mean to include any of the non-illness disorders such as retardation or dyslexia. In this chapter, I will not discuss the various "non-illness" disorders in any detail. Most discussions mean mental *illness* when they use the term mental *disorder*.

The American Psychiatric Association (APA) issues a standard reference work, previously mentioned, entitled the *Diagnostic and Statistical Manual of Mental Disorders*. Its first edition (referred to as DSM-I) appeared in 1952; it was thoroughly revised in 1968 (DSM-II) and in 1980 (DSM-III), partially revised in 1987 (DSM-III-R), and thoroughly revised again in 1994 (DSM-IV). We might expect DSM-IV to be a good place to find a coherent framework for understanding mental disorder. In this expectation we would be sorely disappointed. DSM-IV does not so much *define* mental disorder as *enumerate* a range of mental disorders. In fact, this "manual" of mental disorders is descriptive, atheoretical, inductive, and lacking in any explanatory framework. It provides a long list of symptoms the clinician is likely to encounter in therapeutic practice, and leaves matters at that. DSM-IV (as with two of its predecessors) offers what one observer has referred to as a "Chinese menu" (Thio, 1995, p. 256). In fact, so useless is the *Diagnostic and Statistical Manual of Mental Disorders* as a means of understanding mental disorder generally that two critics write that it "applies no coherent standard of what constitutes a mental disorder"; "few clinicians actually use it as a basis for psychotherapy." Instead, they say, its popularity is guaranteed "because insurance companies use it to determine reimbursement for psychiatric services" (Kirk and Kutchins, 1994). It is the stranglehold that the American Psychiatric Association has over the field of mental health, not the utility of its diagnostic and statistical manual, that determines DSM-IV's widespread use, these critics argue. Not all observers agree, of course; there exists a lively controversy over the utility of DSM-IV.

With all its shortcomings, DSM-IV does offer a sketchy definition of mental disorder. Each of the disorders enumerated in the manual "is conceptualized as a clinically significant behavioral or psychological syndrome or pattern that occurs in an individual and that is associated with present distress (e.g., a painful symptom) or disability (i.e., impairment in one or more important areas of functioning) or with a significantly increased risk of suffering, death, pain, disability, or an important loss of freedom" (APA, 1994, p. xxi). The manual stresses that such suffering is not the manifestation of a mental disorder if it is in response to a temporary event, such as the loss of a loved one. Moreover, the manual stresses, mere *deviant behavior*—for example, political, religious, or sexual activities or beliefs that run counter to the norms—is *not* to be included as a mental disorder *unless* such behavior is a "symptom of a dysfunction in the individual" (p. xxii). *By itself*, the manual stresses, political radicalism, religious heterodoxy—or atheism—or homosexuality does *not* indicate a mental disorder. (Although such beliefs and practices do not *preclude* that the individual is suffering from a disorder, either.) In addition, the manual states, different cultures, subcultures, and ethnic groups have somewhat different customs. Hence, the clinician must make sure to avoid making judgments of psychopathology that ignore the "nuances of an individual's cultural frame of reference" (p. xxiv). For instance, in some societies, bereavement for the death of a loved one may include seeing visions of the deceased. If the patient has grown up in such a society, this experience may be well within the boundaries of what is considered normal.

The original edition of DSM listed 100 disorders. There are 300 disorders listed in DSM-IV— far too many to enumerate, let alone describe in any detail here. There are those that are "usually first diagnosed in infancy, childhood, or adolescence," such as mental retardation, learning disorders, autism, attention deficit disorders, and Tourette's syndrome. There are "delirium, dementia, and amnesiac and other cognitive disorders," including Alzheimer's and Parkinson's syndromes. The list includes all the "substance-related disorders," that is, abuse of and intoxication and dependence on, a variety of psychoactive substances (including caffeine and nicotine). Schizophrenia "and other psychotic disorders" are listed, as are mood disorders, both simple depression and bipolar disorders (manic-depression). A variety of other syndromes follow: anxiety disorders (panic disorder, agoraphobia, obsesssive-compulsion, and so on); somatophorm disorders (such as hypochondriasis); sexual and gender identity disorders, including sexual dysfunctions (a lack of sexual desire, male impotence, an inability to achieve orgasm), "paraphilias" (exhibitionism, fetishism, masochism, sadism, voyeurism); eating disorders, sleeping disorders, impulse-control disorders, and personality disorders. (See the boxed insert on pp. 290–292, which summarizes some of the most common disorders.) This represents a remarkably diverse and miscellaneous grab bag of mental disorders. DSM-IV represents little more than a listing of syndromes, as I said, and a description of a wide range of disorders the clinician is likely to encounter. But it has no internal logic, and it is atheoretical: that is, it *sidesteps* the issue of etiology or causality—what it is that generates disorders in general, or these disorders in particular.

Most of us recognize that there are *degrees* of mental disorder. This dimension is commonsensically captured in the distinction between *neurosis* and *psychosis*. (But keep in mind the fact that the distinction may also be qualitative, or one of *kind*, as well as one of degree.) Most people think of the neurosis as less serious than the psychosis. We all recognize that there are neurotics in our midst; we ourselves may even be one of them. Many of us engage in behavior that is regarded as eccentric, excessive, annoying, compulsive, and unacceptable. Neuroses often entail anxiety that is, from a "rational" point of view, excessive, even needless. (This is why tranquilizers such as Valium are effective against many disorders, because they depress anxiety.) Other neurotic disorders entail a compulsion—a ritualistic action that is repeated without apparent aim—for instance, washing nonexistent germs from one's hands, over and over again, for hours on end. To the man and woman on the street, neurotics engage in a wide range of unusual and annoying behaviors. Someone who has to take six showers a day; is excessively tight with money; is overly compulsive, neat, and tidy; has an uncontrollable fear of spiders; can't go outside without swallowing a Valium; feels the need to insult or demean others; or vomits or breaks out in a rash upon taking multiple-choice exams would probably be referred to as a neurotic by most of us. Nonetheless, in most ways, neurotics maintain contact with reality; while psychotics have lost contact with reality, neurotics recognize reality but can't accept certain aspects of it. Consequently, neurotics can function in most areas of life—get an education, hold down a job, carry on meaningful relationships. In contrast, psychotics can very rarely function in any area of life, at least not without medication. Hence, popularly, we tend to reserve the concept of the psychosis for those cases that are considerably more serious, and vastly less common, than the neurosis. Again, without medication, the psychotic's condition, unlike the neurotic's, is almost always a barrier to academic and occupational achievement and social relationships, including marriage and family. In addition, although the outbreak of a psychosis is frequently grounds for institutionalization in a mental hospital, that of a neurosis almost never is. DSM-IV does not mention psychosis or the psychotic, and the term "neurosis" does not appear in its index. Still, the neurosis-psychosis distinction captures most laypeople's thinking about the dimensional quality of mental disorders. Moreover, *each* of the disorders listed must be regarded as a matter of degree.

Clearly, then, there is no assumption among experts that mental disorders can be sharply and cleanly separated from the condition of mental health. Mental disorder is not a "completely discrete entity with absolute boundaries dividing it from other mental disorders or from no mental disorder" (APA, 1994, p. xxii). In reality, most experts argue, extreme or "textbook" cases can be detected when encountering the most florid or stereotypical symptoms such as those enumerated in the *Diagnostic and Statistical Manual of Mental Disorders*. Clinicians are emphatic in insisting that the fact that mental disorder is a continuum or dimension does *not* mean that therefore most of these disorders cannot be diagnosed or do not exist. One observer criticizes "the idea that if it is difficult to make a distinction between two neighboring points on a hypothetical continuum, no valid distinctions can therefore be made even at the extremes of the continuum. There are thus persons who would argue that the existence of several variations of gray precludes a distinction between black and white" (Rimland, 1969, p. 716). This reasoning is invalid, argues this critic. "While I will agree that some patients in mental hospitals are saner than nonpatients, and that it is sometimes hard to distinguish between deep unhappiness and psychotic depression, I do *not* agree that the difficulty sometimes encountered in making the distinction between normal and abnormal necessarily invalidates all such distinctions" (p. 717). In short, most clinicians feel that the fact that some distinctions are difficult to make—for example, deciding whether sundown is day or night—does not mean that it is impossible to distinguish grosser or cruder distinctions, such as that between noon and midnight (Davison, Neale, and Kring, 2004).

Some Common Mental Disorders Listed in DSM-IV

In the fourth edition of its *Diagnostic and Statistical Manual of Mental Disorders* (DSM-IV), the American Psychiatric Association (1994) spells out the most common symptoms for 300 mental disorders. Some of them are fairly rare, while others are more common. Here are descriptions of several of the most common mental disorders.

Schizophrenia Schizophrenia is considered a *thought* or *cognitive* disorder. While no single set of symptoms alone is indicative, it tends, among other things, to be characterized by distortions of perception, that is, "distortions or exaggerations of inferential thinking (delusions), perception (hallucinations), language and communication (disorganized speech), and behavioral monitoring (grossly disorganized or catatonic behavior)" (pp. 274–275). Delusions are "erroneous beliefs that usually involve a misinterpretation of perceptions of experiences" (p. 275). Often, such delusions entail a feeling of being persecuted; "the person believes he or she is being tormented, followed, tricked, spied on, or subject to ridicule" (p. 275). Often, the person believes that words in songs, books, newspapers, and other media sources refer directly to him or her. DSM-IV cautions that "bizarreness" is difficult to determine, given the cultural component of beliefs; nonetheless, many schizophrenics' beliefs are bizarre in that they "are clearly implausible and not understandable and do not derive from ordinary life experiences" (p. 275). An example would be the belief that someone has removed all the person's internal organs and replaced them without leaving any traces. Hallucinations, common with schizophrenia, most commonly entail voices separate from the person's own thoughts; "pejorative or threatening" voices are most common. Speech is usually disorganized, with words jumbled, one upon the other ("word salad"), and with thought associations frequently incomprehensible to the listener.

Mood Disorders While a wide range of mood disorders are specified by DSM-IV, two stand out as frequently encountered by clinicians: *depression*, or "major depressive disorder" (a "unipolar" depressive disorder), and *bipolar* disorder. Clinical depression is diagnosed by a period of two or more weeks during which there seems to be a total loss of pleasure "in nearly all activities" (p. 320). This is usually accompanied by a feeling of worthlessness, deep guilt, an inability to concentrate, recurrent thoughts of death or suicide, decreased energy, a loss of appetite, and/or an inability to sleep. The person suffering from depression is typically described as feeling sad, hopeless, and discouraged. Irritability or extreme crankiness sometimes accompanies depression, along with agitation. The person often neglects previously pleasurable activities and describes himself or herself as "not caring anymore." A lack of interest in or desire for sex is also frequently experienced. Fatigue is common; even minimal exertions, such as getting out of bed in the morning or putting on clothes, will be described as exhausting. The person will often blame himself or herself for past failures. While all of these symptoms may be found in clinically normal persons, in a major depressive episode they become so pronounced that the person is unable to function in a wide range of necessary activities.

In *bipolar* disorders, the above depressive episodes are alternated with periods of extreme and abnormally elevated, expansive, and giddy euphoria. Symptoms include "inflated self-esteem or grandiosity, decreased need for sleep. . . , flight of ideas, distractability. . . , psychomotor agitation, and excessive involvement in pleasurable activities with a high potential for painful consequences" (p. 328). When the person's wishes are frustrated, irritability and anger characteristically follow. Delusions are common. The person will often make serious pronouncements or undertake projects on subjects on which he or she has no special expertise: writing a novel, running the United Nations, conducting a symphony orchestra, inventing a perpetual motion machine. The person usually has little need for sleep, feeling alert and full of energy after going days without

Some Common Mental Disorders Listed in DSM-IV (cont.)

sleep. Manic speech "is usually pressured, loud, rapid, and difficult to interrupt. . . . Individuals may talk nonstop, sometimes for hours on end, without regard for others' wishes to communicate" (p. 328). Poor judgment and an unrealistic optimism will frequently lead to "an imprudent involvement in pleasurable activities" (p. 329)—for instance, casual sex with strangers, shopping sprees that cannot be paid for, reckless driving. To others, the person will seem "out of control."

Personality Disorders   DSM-IV lists 10 specific personality disorders, including the following: "paranoid personality disorder," or "a pattern of distrust and suspiciousness such that others' motives are interpreted as malevolent"; "antisocial personality disorder," or "a pattern of disregard for, and violation of, the rights of others"; "histrionic personality disorder," or "a pattern of excessive emotionality and attention seeking"; "narcissistic personality disorder," or "a pattern of grandiosity, need for admiration, and lack of empathy"; "dependent personality disorder," or "a pattern of submissive and clinging behavior related to an excessive need to be taken care of"; and "obsessive-compulsive personality disorder," or "a pattern of preoccupation with orderliness, perfectionism, and control" (p. 629). Only when these personality traits "are inflexible and maladaptive and cause significant functional impairment or subjective distress" do they constitute personality disorders, says DSM-IV (p. 630). The personality disorder that is most likely to come to the attention of authorities is the "antisocial personality disorder," which not infrequently manifests itself in violence.

Substance-related Disorders   These are the disorders that are "related to the taking of a drug of abuse" (p. 175), "despite significant substance-related problems" (p. 176). While the precise symptomatology varies according to the nature and effects of the drug in question, some common features include dependence; tolerance (a need to increase the dosage to achieve the

desired effects); withdrawal upon discontinuing the use of the drug; an inability to remain abstinent after withdrawal; persistent unsuccessful attempts to give up the drug; investing an inordinate amount of time, energy, and emotion in obtaining the substance in question; giving up important activities as a consequence of use; and continuing to use despite the harm the drug causes (p. 181). Several of the drugs listed cause acute intoxication, which may be accompanied by "belligerence, mood lability [extreme mood swings], cognitive impairment, impaired judgment, [and] impaired social or occupational functioning" (p. 183).

Sexual and Gender Disorders   "Sexual dysfunctions" are characterized by a lack of sexual desire or incapacity for arousal, including erectile impotence for men and an inability to achieve orgasm for women. "Paraphilias" are characterized by "recurrent, intense sexual urges, fantasies, or behaviors that involve unusual objectives, activities, or situations," that cause severe distress or impairment in other important areas of life. They include exhibitionism, fetishism, pedophilia (an erotic attraction to children), voyeurism, masochism, and sadism. "Gender identity disorders" are characterized by strong and persistent "cross-gender identification" combined with a "persistent discomfort with one's assigned sex" (p. 493).

Disorders First Diagnosed before Adulthood   DSM-IV lists a wide range of disorders that are "usually first diagnosed in infancy, childhood, or adolescence" (pp. 37–121). They include mental retardation (a measured IQ of 70 or below); various learning disorders (academic achievement substantially below age level); autism (impaired development in social interaction and communication, and markedly restricted activities and interests); hyperactivity (severe and maladaptive inattentiveness); conduct disorder (a persistent pattern of behavior that entails a violation of either the rights of others and/or basic rules of conduct); and Tourette's disorder (uncontrollable

Some Common Mental Disorders Listed in DSM-IV (cont.)

and compulsively repetitive physical and/or verbal tics, such as yelps, barks, snorts, clicks, grunts, squatting, retracing one's steps, and twirling).

DSM-IV does not use the term "mental illness." Clearly, however, only some of the 300 disorders it lists would colloquially be referred to as a mental "illness"; certainly schizophrenia and, if sufficiently severe, depression and manic-depression, and some of the personality disorders. (On the other hand, most of us know someone who displays a fairly mild version of these disorders. Where to draw the line between a serious and a less serious condition, between a person who is "neurotic" and one who is clearly mentally "ill," is not an easy task.) In contrast, most of us would not refer to one of the other disorders as a mental *illness*. Is someone who is dependent on cigarettes (APA, 1994, pp. 242–247), coffee (pp. 212–215), or marijuana (pp. 215–221) *mentally ill?* Almost certainly not. Is dyslexia, hyperactivity, Tourette's syndrome, autism, or mental retardation a mental illness? Again, very few of us would say so; they are disorders of the mind, but are not "illnesses" as we popularly understand the term. Most of us associate mental illness with extreme thought (schizophrenia) or mood (depression) disorders. Once again, the American Psychiatric Association does not use the term mental "illness," and prefers to focus on disorders, malfunctions, dysfunctions, and disabilities of the mind in a wide range of respects. Nonetheless, in the lay or popular mind, the conceptualization of mental illness as distinct from intellectual dysfunction retains a strong measure of influence.

MODELS OF MENTAL DISORDER

Two questions have to be answered in order to characterize the various approaches to or models of mental disorder. The first is: *How is the reality of mental disorder defined?* And the second is: *What causes mental disorder?* To distinguish among the various perspectives, theories, or "models" of mental disorder, let's look at a concrete example.

In 1722, John Hu, a Chinese convert to Christianity, accompanied a Jesuit missionary to France; only two Chinese before him had ever visited that country. By European standards, Hu behaved oddly. During his first ride in a coach, he jumped from the moving vehicle, rushed over to a clump of blackberry bushes, and gorged himself on the fruit. Acquiring a fine, coffee-colored suit, he promptly gave it to a beggar. And once, he marched through the streets of Paris, banging on a drum and waving a flag with the message, "Men and women should be kept in their separate spheres" written on it. After too many such incidents, the French authorities committed Hu to an insane asylum, where he remained for three years (Spence, 1988).

How would the question of Hu be approached? Is it possible to refer to mental disorder across such vast cultural and national boundaries? Was Hu sane or insane? Is it even possible to make such a judgment? If we can, and if he was insane, what was the cause? If he was not, why was he institutionalized? If we cannot make such a judgment in the first place, why was one made in his case? Different models of mental disorder answer these questions in different ways.

By the question, How is the reality of mental disorder defined?, I do not refer to a formal definition such as that proposed by the American Psychiatric Association. Instead, I mean something much more basic and more general: *Wherein does its reality lie?* On this question, expert observers can be divided into two camps, the same two that have approached all the phenomena we've looked at so far: *essentialists* and *constructionists*. "Essentialism" is the belief that phenomena in the world, whether physical or social, fall into pregiven, universal pigeonholes, categories that can be agreed on by all reasonable, knowledgeable observers. (Positivism is a variety of essentialism.) And "constructionism," as we know, is the view that categories are created not by nature or reality or God, but by the human mind. The essentialist believes that mental disorder is "real," independent of the social label, while the constructionist believes that it is the social label that is the most important feature of mental disorder.

To the essentialists, what is important is not the label but the *condition*. What they look at is the *concrete reality* of mental disorder. Mental disorder is a condition that can be determined by means of objective tests or indicators. Determining what mental disorder is is much like picking an apple off a tree or a rock from the ground; it is "there" to be discovered by the expert or specialist, with an objective reality all its own. It does not matter what a society *calls* the condition or how it is *reacted to* or *treated*—it has a concrete reality *independent* of these judgments and reactions. At different times and in different societies, the condition may very well have been misdiagnosed, just as, say, in earlier times, porpoises might have been thought a type of fish. But however it is regarded at a given time or in a given society, its reality remains intact nonetheless. Moreover, it is *caused* by specific conditions in the material world; those conditions may be social, biological, or psychological—but we can determine what brings this condition into the world. With enough medical and psychiatric knowledge, we can cure or treat mental disorders—we can make sick people healthy.

In contrast, *constructionists* see the reality of mental disorder in the label, the reaction, the judgment, the definition, in a set of practices; they are far more concerned with *the social enterprise of mental disorder labeling and treatment* than with the condition itself. To the constructionist, what counts is *how what is seen* as mental disorder is *judged and treated* by professionals and laypersons. What social constructionists look at and study is a certain *discourse*, a narrative—in short, what we *do* and *say* about what we refer to as mental disorder and those persons we refer to as the mentally disordered. Whether there is a concrete reality "there" in the material world that we refer to as mental disorder is a secondary or even irrelevant question; what's important is *how judgments of mental disorder are made*.

Hu's unfortunate encounter with European society highlights these two perspectives toward mental illness. The strict *essentialistic* or positivist model would argue that what counts most is Hu's condition, not how it was diagnosed.

However Hu was treated by the psychiatric establishment in eighteenth-century France, he either *was*, or *was not*, mentally disordered. Some essentialists would say that Hu's behavior was so bizarre, so floridly disordered and dysfunctional, that the contemporary clinician cannot but see him as mentally ill. The cultural differences between France and China, however great they were in the eighteenth century, do not explain Hu's peculiar behavior. Hu was hospitalized because *he really was crazy*. It didn't matter that he was only one of three Chinese who had ever visited France at the time; it didn't matter that the French then were unacquainted with the rules of proper Chinese conduct, or that Hu was unacquainted with the rules of proper French conduct. The behavior that caused the French to hospitalize Hu would have caused him to be hospitalized everywhere—or, at least, *should have*. Hu would have been regarded as mentally disordered in all cultures, China included; culture had nothing to do with his condition. The process of differential labeling of mental conditions is uninteresting, nonproblematic, and more or less straightforward. Some other essentialists might have argued that it is entirely possible that eighteenth-century French psychiatry was so crude and error-prone that Hu was *misdiagnosed*. Perhaps the condition of mental disorder was not fully understood then, and hence, Hu's misdiagnosis. But as societies cast off ignorance and superstition, there will be a fuller understanding of what mental disorder is and how to diagnose it. What *counts* is the objective facts of Hu's disorder, not how it has been diagnosed in different societies.

In contrast, the social constructionist would say that what is most important about the question of Hu was that he was treated by eighteenth-century French psychiatry in a certain way. These are the facts of the case, not Hu's putative or supposed "condition." The reason why this is so crucial is that definitions of mental disorder are culture-bound; what is called crazy in one society or social context may be seen as perfectly normal in another. Hu's behavior was regarded as a sign of mental disorder simply because the French expected the man to act the way the French acted; when he acted quite differently, he was labeled crazy. The constructionist would examine the enterprise of *defining* and *dealing with* Hu, and all others defined and dealt with as mentally disordered in eighteenth-century France, as *itself* a subject to be investigated, *not* as an approximation or a departure from an "accurate" or scientifically valid definition of mental illness. For constructionism, the most interesting question is not whether psychiatrists are scientifically accurate when they define and treat the mentally disordered. Instead, they look at these definitions and treatments as interesting in and of themselves. Why one judgment rather than another? How and why do judgments vary from one society to another, from one professional to another, from one time period to another? Would Hu be regarded as insane today? Would he be hospitalized? How do popular and expert views of mental illness differ from those of physical illness? How does the public view the mentally disordered? Why do certain treatment modalities come into and fall out of vogue? Why is mental disorder so much more stigmatizing than physical illness? Is the psychiatric establishment acting as a means of social control? These and other concerns animate the constructionist. The "soft" or "moderate" constructionist puts condition in the background and emphasizes judgments; the "hard" or "strict" or "radical" constructionist argues that *all* judgments, including those made by psychiatrists, are by their very nature equally subjective and problematic—in effect, that *there is no such thing* as mental disorder aside from the label.

Our second question, What *causes* mental disorder?, marks off a related although analytically distinct dimension—*etiology*. Social constructionists are not especially interested in the question of causality; if mental disorder is socially constructed rather than an objectively identifiable condition, then it cannot be said to be "caused" by factors external to these social definitions. In contrast, etiology is the essentialist's *primary* concern. As we might expect, we have a variety of etiological theories of mental disorder. Some observers are eclectic, and believe that different explanations can account for different sorts of disorders, or that a *combination* of factors can explain mental disorders generally or a specific disorder. Other observers are more monolithic and argue for a *single* theory or explanation, either for a given condition or for all disorders generally. As we've seen with other phenomena,

there are almost as many explanations as experts. Still, three rough, broad theories or explanations of mental disorder can be identified: the sociological, the psychological or psychodynamic, and the biological. Within each broad category, there are a host of variations. Thus, the biological theory might have argued that Hu suffered from pathological genes, or a hormonal imbalance, or a neurological disorder. The psychological theory might have looked into Hu's childhood experiences, especially with his family, or what rewards and punishments he experienced through his life. Social theories might have looked at the stress he suffered as a member of a certain social category. One variant of the sociological theory, the labeling perspective, might have argued that, having been *labeled* as crazy, Hu actually *went* crazy after his institutionalization.

ESSENTIALIST APPROACHES TO MENTAL DISORDER

As we've seen, the essentialist approach defines mental disorder as an objectivistic condition that can be located in the real world, in the concrete behavior or verbalizations of persons who are disordered. Such behaviors or verbalizations are clear-cut signs or manifestations of a disordered mind, in much the same way that the height of a column of mercury on a thermometer indicates or measures temperature. As I said with respect to the question of Hu, we can define mental disorder and lay our hands on it in much the same way we can pick an apple off a tree. True, defining and locating mental disorder is a bit more complicated, difficult, and intellectually challenging than picking an apple, but the principle is the same: The essential reality of "appleness," as with the reality of mental disorder, is an objective fact, identifiable by pointing to specific properties that the fruit possesses to all observers. In the same way, to identify mental disorder we would point to specific properties that persons designated by the label manifest—that is, concrete, real-world behavior or verbalizations. Of course, mental disorder manifests itself in somewhat different ways in different societies, but there is an *inner* or *common core* to all mental disorder everywhere.

A severe schizophrenic in Zambia would be a severe schizophrenic in Thailand, Panama, or Norway. What counts is not social definitions or constructs of the condition but the nature of the condition itself (Murphy, 1976).

The hardest or most extreme version of the essentialistic approach is often referred to as the *medical* model. It argues that mental disorder is very much like a medical disease; a disease of the mind is very much like a disease of the body. The bizarre and inappropriate behaviors exhibited by mentally disordered persons are symptoms of an underlying or internal pathology of some kind. Mental patients present *symptoms*, those symptoms can be *categorized*, and the sane are *clearly distinguishable* from the insane (Rosenhan, 1973, p. 250). More colloquially: "Some people *are* more crazy than others; we can tell the difference; and calling lunacy a name does not *cause* it" (Nettler, 1974, p. 894). The medical model emphasizes the *intrapsychic* forces in mental disorder—that is, it is an internal *condition* within the psyche of the disordered person. Once someone has "become" mentally disordered, that condition will manifest itself in *any and all* situations and contexts, at least until psychiatric intervention treats or cures that person. Much as a physical disease is internal to the sufferer, likewise, a mental disorder is a disease that is "in" the insane.

Essentialists are interested in, and study, the *epidemiology* and the *etiology* of mental disorder. "Epidemiology" refers to how mental disorders are distributed in categories in the population; "etiology" refers to explanations of the *causes* of mental disorder. Essentialists would argue that there is a "true" rate or incidence of mental disorder in a given population and a given society. They investigate whether men or women have higher rates of mental disorders, and more specifically, *which* disorders. Are married or unmarried men and women more likely to become mentally disordered? Blacks or whites? Urban or rural dwellers? How is socioeconomic status or social class related to mental disorder—again, to *which* disorders? Are lower-class people more mentally dysfunctional because lower-class life is more stressful than middle-class life? Or because, if you're disordered, it's very difficult to become successful? These and other questions are asked by epidemiologists who regard mental disorder as

a concretely real phenomenon with essentialistic qualities. Essentialists hold that there exists a pre-given entity or syndrome that researchers can define, identify, locate, lay their hands on, and eventually explain or account for. Mental disorder is not merely a label or a social construction. *It does not matter* how the disorder is socially defined—the reality exists *independently* of that definition. The application of the label and the society's response to persons so labeled are not the most interesting things about it or even interesting at all. The most interesting thing about mental disorder is what it is, its dynamics, how it works, what causes it—and how we may cure it and restore the mentally disordered to mental health.

Epidemiology is usually seen as being in the service of etiology. The purpose of studying how diseases are distributed in the population, many experts feel, is so that an explanation of illness can be devised and tested. Someone with an essentialistic orientation sees the primary task of anyone who studies mental disorder as devising a valid theory or account of etiology: *What causes it?* Again, whether this theory is sociological, psychological, or biological does not determine the essentialist's model. The sociologist of mental disorder would argue that it is caused, at least in large part, by social factors: stress, for instance, brought on by lower-class status, gender membership, or racial and ethnic prejudice. Most sociologists agree that social factors combine with genetic, neurological, hormonal, and/or psychological factors. Certain persons who are *genetically predisposed* could experience socially induced stressful conditions, which push them over the edge into mental disorder. Still, these sociological etiologists would say, social factors are *crucial* in the causal dynamics leading to mental illness. Again, simply because a theory is sociological does not mean that it is any the less essentialistic: Even sociological theories of mental disorder hold that mental disorder is an identifiable clinical entity. What counts is how the condition is caused, how it came about, what brought it on. And what does not count, what is not interesting or problematic—or at least is of secondary significance—is the creation and application of the label. The enterprise of mental health diagnosis and treatment is crucial only insofar as it relates specifically to the success of treatment outcomes. It is important to know which treatments work and which ones don't, but it isn't important to study treatment as an intellectually or theoretically problematic dynamic in its own right, as a phenomenon to be explained and understood for its own sake.

The strict medical model argues that mental disorder is largely or always a manifestation of abnormal biophysical functioning—brain damage, a chemical imbalance, pathological genes, neurological malfunction, and so on (Torrey, 1994). This school suggests that environmental factors, such as stress or early childhood experiences, have little etiological significance. At most, they may act as "triggering" mechanisms that exacerbate an already established susceptibility to mental disorder. Consequently, any legitimate and effective therapy for psychic disorder must be physical in nature, such as drugs, electroshock therapy, or surgical intervention. The strict medical model has been gaining adherents in recent years. Electroshock therapy has been making a comeback in the past decade, while the use of psychoactive drugs has almost literally overtaken all other forms of therapy since their introduction in the 1950s. (In contrast, surgery, such as prefrontal lobotomies, has been almost completely discredited as a treatment for mental disorder.) At the other end of the spectrum, psychoanalysis, the "talk" therapy introduced by Sigmund Freud, has plummeted in popularity since the 1950s; in some professional circles, it has been completely discredited (Gruenbaum, 1993; Esterson, 1993; Torrey, 1994; Crews, 1995; Webster, 1995).

Just as biological and genetic theories of mental disorder, which hold that sociological factors are of secondary importance, could be seen as "hard" essentialistic theories, psychological and sociological theories could be seen as "soft" essentialistic theories. Both agree that the clinical entity, mental illness or mental disorder, is concretely real; that diagnoses tap or measure something in the real world. Both agree that mental disorder represents a genuine malfunction or dysfunction, a true or real disorder above and beyond the mere label or diagnosis itself. But these approaches—the biological on the one hand and the psychological and the sociological on the other—part company on the *cause* of mental disorders. Psychological and sociological theories

emphasize that they are caused by the patient's experiences, not by an inherent or inner biological or chemical condition. That is, they stress *nurture*, or environment, rather than *nature*. A mentally disordered person may have nothing physically wrong, yet, as a result of his or her experiences, still have a dysfunctional mind. Since physical, biological, or congenital theories posit causes that are more indwelling, more inherent, the only way that mental disorders can be cured or treated, in this view, is by changing the very physical factors that caused them. That means surgical, chemical, hormonal, genetic, or electrical treatment. Merely changing the conditions of the patient's life, or attempting to cure by means of "talk" therapies, will not change that pathological mental patient's condition. Still, these approaches or theories agree that, because the condition is concretely real, researchers can identify and explain it and, possibly, eventually, treat and cure it. The sociological and psychological theories of mental disorder argue that certain experiences exist in some peoples' lives that cause or influence them to "go crazy." And being disordered can be measured by means of certain concretely real objective criteria or indicators. So the psychological and sociological essentialists don't differ on this particular point with the biological essentialists: Mental disorder is concretely real; it is not simply a label.

Earlier, I introduced the term "medical" model. The medical model sees mental disorder as a condition that is internal to, or "in," the mental patient, just as cancer, say, is "in" a medical patient. Once a person "has" a mental disorder, it manifests itself under any and all conditions. The medical model is the most *extreme* version of essentialism. Not all essentialistic models of mental disorder conform strictly to the medical model, however. Many sociologists and some psychologists believe that mental disorder will manifest itself more under certain conditions than others. For example, some persons who are vulnerable or susceptible to mental disorder may be perfectly normal or healthy under certain conditions—those that are less stressful, or when they have a social support network.

Essentialists who adhere to the nonmedical model stress that mental disorder may be a *temporary* condition, one that is not solely "in" the individual, one that is as much dependent on the social environment in which the individual interacts as on the individual's internal condition. Again, nonmedical essentialists retain the idea of mental disorder as a real "thing" in the material world as well as a disorder. But they see its appearance as much more heavily dependent on external factors than do proponents of the strict medical model. Biogenetic and biochemical theories of mental disorder most definitely adopt a medical model; mental disorder is a condition "in" the individual, a condition that manifests itself pretty much everywhere. Psychoanalysis, too, adopts a medical model, although it could be seen as a "softer" version, since it views mental disorder as a condition that can be treated by means of a form of therapy that does not entail physical or strictly medical intervention. Once someone has gone through certain pathological childhood experiences, again, one will remain mentally disordered until treatment intervenes. Thus, though psychoanalysis holds that the environment *causes* mental disorder, once it has been set in motion it manifests itself pretty much regardless of the environment.

CONSTRUCTIONISM

A social constructionist model would argue that whether or not there is a "common thread" or "common core" to mental disorder is not especially interesting or intellectually problematic. What counts is the *enterprise* of mental disorder—again, what is *said* and *done* about persons who are *defined* as mentally disordered. One major reason why this is such a crucial question is that diagnoses differ in societies around the world; hence, the reality of mental disorder varies along with them. Definitions of mental disorder are culture-bound; what is labeled dysfunctional in one society or social context may be seen as perfectly normal in another—or as possessed, extraordinary, saintly, inspired by the holy spirit.

The constructionists regard mental disorder as socially defined, both by the general public and by the psychiatric profession. In other words, as with deviance, constructionists do not think that mental disorder can be defined "objectively" by focusing on the common thread that all disorders share. Instead, they argue, what mental disorder

"is" is how it is seen, judged, reacted to, treated, and evaluated in a given society. There exists a mental illness *enterprise* or, in the words of Michel Foucault, a mental illness *discourse*: the psychiatric, legal, and social machinery designed to deal with persons designated as mentally disordered; the writing, the research, and the diagnostic manuals that the mental health industry and the drug industry built around administering medication to the mentally disordered; not to mention public attitudes focusing on mental disorder, the popular beliefs, stereotypes, prejudices, legend and folklore, media attention, and so on. Thus, what mental disorder *is* is what we *say* and *do* about it, what we say and do about persons designated as mentally disordered. Mental disorder has no "essential" reality beyond these social constructions, this "discourse," these reactions, the social enterprise surrounding it.

The constructionist model of mental disorder argues the following points: one, that *it is a form of deviance*; two, its reality is *called into being* by the labeling process; and three, the application of the label is influenced at least in part by a variety of *extrapsychiatric* factors or variables. The mentally ill are derogated and stigmatized, excluded from full social acceptance; the process of judging persons *to be* mentally ill makes their behavior or mental states sociologically relevant (although, of course, such judgments do not *create* the condition in the first place); and these judgments are influenced by a number of factors *in addition to* the severity of their condition. In a nutshell, these are the basic assumptions of the constructionist approach to mental disorder. It is not a theory that attempts to explain *why* some people are or become mentally ill (but see the labeling theory below); instead, it is an approach or framework, or set of "sensitizing concepts" that help to understand one major aspect of the phenomenon.

One observer argued that mental patients suffer not so much from mental illness but from *contingencies*. Whether someone becomes a patient in a mental hospital, for instance, depends on the person's social and economic status, the visibility of the offense committed, his or her proximity to the hospital, the treatment facilities that are available, and so on (Goffman, 1961, pp. 134–135). Another sociologist, not associated with the labeling or constructionist school, argues that "the diagnosis, categorization, and labeling of mental disorders are themselves profoundly social acts and that other social factors besides the behavior itself affect the informal and formal processes whereby persons are judged to have a mental pathology" (Akers, 1985, p. 314). One study (Simon and Zussman, 1983) examined a legal case involving the victims of a flood who were suing a coal company for creating conditions that made it possible for the flood to ravage a community. The plaintiffs claimed "psychic damages" as one of the harmful consequences of the flood. Countering their argument, the defendants, representatives of the coal company, argued that the flood had no such impact. Two sets of psychiatrists, one hired by the defense and the other by the plaintiffs, examined 42 flood victims. Not surprisingly, the defense's psychiatrists found little evidence of psychopathology, while the plaintiff's found considerable psychic impairment. If mental disorder were as closely analogous to physical disorder as the medical model argues, such extreme discrepancies would seem hardly possible.

Consider the fact that, in the first edition of the *Diagnostic and Statistical Manual of Mental Disorders* (1952), homosexuality was deemed an instance of a "sociopathic personality disturbance." In the second, it was listed as belonging under the category "sexual deviance." In 1973, under pressure from movement activists and militants, the American Psychiatric Association decided that, in and of itself, homosexuality was not a disturbance; it represented a disorder only if it created conflict and generated the wish to change one's sexual orientation. In the third edition (1980) this was further modified to apply only to persons for whom such a wish was a "persistent concern"; the APA referred to this condition as "ego-dystonic homosexuality." In the revised third edition (1987, p. 426), an explanation as to why this condition was dropped was offered ("it suggests to some that homosexuality was considered a disorder"). In the fourth edition (1994), there is no mention of homosexuality whatsoever as a disorder of any kind. It is difficult to imagine such contortions taking place for a physical state or condition.

The influence of extrapsychiatric factors is in large part due to the vagueness of psychiatric diagnosis. Although certainly more precise and reliable today than in the past, diagnoses of mental disorder are considerably less so than are strictly medical diagnoses, that is, those concerning strictly physical conditions. It is clear that agreement among psychiatrists as to patients' conditions is high only when they present "classic" or "archetypical" symptoms. In contrast, agreement is low for patients who present symptoms that are less clear-cut and more ambiguous. In fact, the majority of cases psychiatrists see are less classic and more ambiguous in their symptomatology (Townsend, 1980, pp. 270–272). A summary of the reliability of psychiatric diagnoses found it to be high only when the categories were extremely broad or the symptoms extreme and clear-cut; where the categories were specific or detailed or the symptoms less than clear-cut, disagreement between and among psychiatrists was high (Edgerton, 1969, pp. 68–69). Two commentators conclude that "art far outweighs science" in psychiatric judgments (Stoller and Geertsma, 1963, p. 65). An author of a textbook on psychiatric methodology states that expert judgments on mental disorder "are of a social, cultural, economic and sometimes legal nature" (Loftus, 1960, p. 13).

In one study (Kendall et al., 1971), videotapes of diagnostic interviews with patients were shown to a large number of psychiatrists in the United States and Great Britain. Those patients presenting "classic, textbook" symptoms generated almost unanimous agreement as to psychiatric condition. However, patients manifesting less than clear-cut symptoms touched off less than unanimity in diagnosis. One patient was deemed schizophrenic by 85 percent of the American psychiatrists, but by only 7 percent of the British; another was judged to be schizophrenic by 69 percent of the Americans, but only 2 percent of the British. Clearly, the American concept of schizophrenia is much broader than is the British. Again, it is difficult to imagine such disparities in the diagnosis of a strictly medical disease, such as cancer or tuberculosis.

Examining *informal* mental disorder labeling around the world, even greater variation prevails. Cross-culturally, certain terms or labels are applied everywhere to persons "who are thought to be conducting themselves in a manner that is inappropriate, abnormal, or unreasonable for persons in that culture who occupy a similar social position; that is, to persons who can provide no otherwise acceptable explanation for their conduct" (Edgerton, 1969, p. 50). Every culture has a label that indicates some version of mental disorder or illness. How are these labels applied? A summary of the available anthropological literature points to two conclusions. First, the recognition and labeling of persons "who are both severely and chronically psychotic" typically occurs with a high degree of consensus "because persons such as these are typically so dramatically, and enduringly, far beyond the pale of everyday rationality" (p. 51). And second, most people who act strangely or "crazily" do not do so in an extreme or chronic fashion; consequently, being labeled for these persons is a complex matter, influenced by a wide range of contingencies. As to whether someone is or is not regarded socially and publicly as psychotic is open to *negotiation* (pp. 51, 65)—that is, decided in a give-and-take interaction between two or more parties on the basis of factors unrelated to objective psychiatric condition.

Thus, the constructionist is more likely to be concerned with the dynamics of mental disorder labeling than etiological issues. What factors are related to being labeled as mentally disordered? Is it psychiatric condition alone? Or do extrapsychiatric factors play a role in this process? And how prominent is this role? The medical model would hold that psychiatric diagnoses (although not popular or public labels) are an accurate reflection of the patient's "objective" condition. The constructionist and labeling approach argues that this process of mental disorder labeling is considerably less rational than the medical model holds—that factors other than the severity of psychiatric symptoms influence diagnoses and the decision to admit and discharge patients. (However, labeling theorists do *not* claim that this process is random, that persons are singled out randomly or capriciously, that patients do not differ in any appreciable way from the population at large.) This process is guided by a number of contingencies, they argue. There is, in other words, "a clear tendency for admission and discharge of mental patients to be related more to social than to psychiatric variables" (Krohn and Akers, 1977, p. 341). Sociocultural factors, such as family desires and living arrangements,

adequate patient resources outside the mental hospital, cultural conceptions, region of the country, and the danger the patient represents to others can be determinants of psychiatric case outcomes (Krohn and Akers, 1977; Townsend, 1978).

Thus, constructionism argues that, *independent of etiology*, independent of the *consequences* of labeling, and even to some degree independent of the "objective" *validity* of psychiatric diagnoses, the sociologist is obliged to study *the social organization of the labeling process* that *leads to* a judgment or diagnosis of mental disorder. This issue was expressed by Edwin Lemert, an important precursor of labeling theory; almost half a century ago, Lemert stated: "One of the more important sociological questions here is not what causes human beings to develop such symptoms as hallucinations and delusions, but, instead, what is done about their behavior which leads the community to reject them, segregate them, and otherwise treat them as . . . insane" (1951, p. 387). Thus, regardless of what "causes" homosexuality, there is a social organization of the condemnation of homosexuality; regardless of the etiology of obesity, again, in this society, the obese are stigmatized and condemned. *What is made* of homosexuality, obesity, and mental disorder? What factors influence this reaction? These are some of the central concerns of the social constructionist who studies deviance. As a qualification: "Hard" constructionists see *all* views of mental disorder as constructions, including those held by psychiatrists, and sidestep the issue of whether any one of them is more valid or accurate than any other. In contrast, "soft" constructionists would argue that the reality of mental disorder is not *solely* a construction, and would grant that some constructions strike closer to the empirical reality of mental disorder than others.

LABELING THEORY

A theory that has always been treated as a variant of the constructionist model, but that harbors a strong essentialistic component, is the labeling theory of mental disorder. It may sound confusing to stress the essentialistic strains in labeling theory, since I discussed labeling theory as a constructionist approach in Chapter 4. But the fact is, as with Lemert's theory of secondary deviation, the labeling theory of mental illness emphasizes the causal dynamics or etiological factors underlying mental illness, *not* the nature and dynamics of the social construction of mental illness. To be more specific, it argues that mental disorder *is* concretely real, a material phenomenon in the real world. (Remember, Lemert's theory of secondary deviation emphasizes that it is *being labeled* that often strengthens one's commitment to a deviant role and further deviant behavior.) Thomas Scheff, the primary proponent of the labeling theory of mental illness, takes this mechanism a step or two further. Being labeled as crazy for engaging in mildly eccentric, slightly bizarre behavior results in *really, actually,* and *concretely going crazy.* The definition becomes a *self-fulfilling prophecy.* One learns to act out the symptomatology of mental illness as a result of being exposed to the definitions that are prevalent in a given society; behaving like a crazy person is how one is supposed to act if one has been defined *as* a crazy person. Hence, engaging in odd, eccentric, unconventional behavior for which there is no ready label—"residual deviance"—results in being *labeled* crazy, which, in turn, results in acting the way a crazy person is *supposed* to act, which eventually results in actually *going crazy.* But note: The labeling theory argues that there really is such a thing as being crazy; although the label creates the condition, *the condition becomes concretely real.*

It should be emphasized that, although the two approaches have often been confused, Scheff's labeling theory of mental illness and the more general labeling theory of Becker (discussed in Chapter 4) and his associates are substantially different approaches. Although for Scheff the *initial* process of labeling *is* a social construction, the process of labeling actually *produces* an identifiable condition that all can point to and identify as "true" mental illness. In other words, Scheff is not quite a true constructionist, since his primary concern is etiological. In contrast, labelists' concerns are much more heavily concentrated on constructionist matters and far less on issues of causality. Becker and the other labeling theorists never *intended* their theory to be an explanation of

deviance in the sense of accounting for its origin or etiology (Kitsuse, 1972, p. 235; Becker, 1973, pp. 178–179). Nor did it insist that the process of labeling always and inevitably results in an intensification of a commitment to deviance, the deviant role, or deviant behavior; this is an empirical question and must be studied in individual cases (Becker, 1963, pp. 34–35; 1973, p. 179). For Scheff, in contrast, the whole point is to devise a theory accounting for the origin of mental illness. Note that Walter Gove, a critic of Scheff's "harder" version of labeling theory of mental illness, *supports* a "softer" version of labeling theory "that is not concerned with specific predictions [of causality] but is concerned with how social institutions function and how such functioning is related to our understanding of mental illness as a social category and as a social career" (1989). I am inclined to agree with this "softer" version.

To reiterate, then, for Scheff, the *initial* process of labeling *is* a social construction. That is, "normals" label eccentricity or "residual deviance" *as* mental illness. Clearly, to the extent that this process is arbitrary and not based on scientific or real-world criteria, Scheff adopts a constructionist approach. Why are eccentrics being labeled as crazy? Is it because of their condition? Clearly not; a variety of extrapsychiatric social and cultural factors rule this process. However, *once the labeling process has been launched* and the person who is labeled as crazy begins to take on a crazy role, a very real condition of mental illness begins to take over. What was *defined* as real *becomes* real. Thus, Scheff has one foot in constructionism and one foot in essentialism, more specifically, in etiology.

Thomas Scheff clearly states that he is *not* a constructionist (personal communication). His theory is *etiological*; it is an attempt to explain the origin of mental illness (1966, 1984). To Scheff, the *how* and *why* of the social construction of mental illness is secondary; what counts is its power to generate behavior and a condition the psychiatric profession knows as mental illness. Hence, he must be regarded as at least as much an essentialist as a constructionist. It must be said that labeling theory, in the form stated by Thomas Scheff, has very few followers among clinicians; it is of interest almost exclusively to a very small circle of sociologists. Today, the overwhelming majority of psychiatrists adopt some version of the biomedical model. Still, it has received, and continues to receive, a great deal of attention in the sociological study of deviance. Therefore, let's look at Scheff's theory in a bit more detail.

Scheff distinguishes between *residual rule-breaking* and mental illness. Residual rule-breaking is made up of all those activities, feelings, or experiences that, first, entail a violation of social norms; second, do not fall within a specific categorical realm (such as crime, drunkenness, sexual "perversion," and so on) and for which society has no specific, explicit label; and third, make up what is regarded as a sign or manifestation of mental illness. In other words, by "acting weird" (residual rule-breaking), one could be regarded as "crazy." Scheff's theory can be broken down into nine parts. First, rule-breaking has many *sources* or *causes*—temporary stress, food or sleep deprivation, drug ingestion, and so on. Second, many persons engage in residual rule-breaking; however, very few are categorized as crazy, either informally, by the lay public, by people one knows, or formally, by the psychiatric profession. There are many more persons in the general population, Scheff argues, who engage in residual rule-breaking without being labeled than those who do so and are designated as mentally ill. In other words, the rule-breaking most of us engage in is unrecognized, ignored, or rationalized. And third, most rule-breaking is of *transitory significance*. For the most part, if others don't make a big deal out of someone acting weird, eventually the behavior will go away (1966, pp. 40–51).

Yet there are some persons who do have a mentally ill "*career.*" That is, they continue to act "weird"; acting crazy does not go away. How are they different from the rest of us? Scheff's fourth point about labeling and mental illness is that *stereotyped imagery of mental disorder is learned in early childhood*; it is part of our culture's "lore" about mental illness. And fifth, it is continually *reaffirmed* in ordinary social interaction. In other words, we all learn and know what a crazy person is and does; this is part of our cultural tradition, and is woven into how we are treated and how we treat others when certain symptoms are displayed. Sixth, someone who is labeled as a mentally ill person—for whatever reason—will be *rewarded*

for playing that role, and seventh, will be *punished* if he or she attempts to return to normalcy or conventional behavior. Eighth, in a crisis, when someone who engages in residual rule-breaking is publicly labeled as a crazy person, he or she is highly *suggestible*, and will often readily accept the proffered role of being insane. In fact, Scheff argues, ninth, among residual rule-breakers, being labeled as mentally ill is the *single most important cause* of having a "career" in mental illness. In other words, if others (friends, relatives, the general public, psychiatrists, and other mental health professionals) call one crazy when one is vulnerable, one will continue to act crazy, and this label will intensify one's commitment to crazy behavior and a crazy role (1966, pp. 64–93; 1984).

THE MODIFIED LABELING APPROACH

Gove (1975a, 1975b, 1979a, 1980a, 1982) argues that the labeling theory of mental illness is empirically wrong. Gove argues that mental patients are unable to function in the real world not because they have been stigmatized but because they are mentally ill; the mentally disordered have a debilitating disease that cripples their capacity to function normally and effectively. Moreover, Gove argues, the process by which the psychiatric profession singles out someone as mentally ill is not significantly influenced by sociological or other extrapsychiatric variables. Instead, the process is almost exclusively determined by the nature and severity of the illness. Labeling, the medical model argues, is neither capricious nor arbitrary, nor is it based on such hierarchical factors as race, sex, socioeconomic status, or power. Persons who are sick tend to be labeled as such; in turn, those who are well are extremely unlikely to be labeled as sick.

With respect to *informal* (as opposed to professional) labeling, far from being eager to label someone as mentally ill, the general public is extremely reluctant to do so and, moreover, does not hold particularly strong, negative, or stigmatizing feelings about the mentally ill. (See also Clausen, 1981.) This is especially true for intimates—spouses, children, parents, close friends—of the mentally ill, who avoid labeling until the disturbed person's behavior becomes intolerable. Lastly, hospitalization and other treatment intervention, far from making the patient's condition worse, as the labeling approach claims, most often results in an amelioration of his or her symptoms. In short, a genuine healing process does seem to take place. Gove, the most outspoken and persistent of the critics of the labeling theory of mental illness, argues that these generalizations are so well-founded empirically that he states flatly: "For all practical purposes, the labeling explanation of mental illness is of historical interest only" (1979a, p. 301).

Which model is correct? Which one approximates empirical reality most closely? To begin with, we need not be forced into an either-or, black-or-white position. It is possible that there is some middle ground here; labeling theory may be correct on some points, while its critics may be right with respect to some others. In fact, what has come to be referred to as a "soft" or *modified* labeling theory approach fits the facts of mental illness most faithfully (Link et al., 1989). The modified labeling approach would accept certain aspects of the medical model without denying the importance of the labeling process.

First, mentally disordered persons, while they do have difficulty in their everyday lives because of their psychiatric condition, also suffer serious debilitation and demoralization as a consequence of stigma and labeling. Everyone who grows up in this society, including the disordered, is aware of the negative image of the mentally ill. Persons who suffer from a mental disorder anticipate negative treatment from others, and these beliefs taint their interaction with "normals" and with mental health professionals (Thoits, 1985; Link, 1987; Link et al., 1989). Often, the expectations others have of the disordered person's behavior will actually call forth the very behavior that confirms those expectations (Jones, 1986; Link and Cullen, 1989).

We've already examined a basic proposition of labeling theory under the umbrella of constructionism, which overlaps heavily with it. (Constructionism is concerned with how judgments of reality and imputations of deviance are made and put into practice; labeling theory is, in addition, concerned with the *consequences* of such judgments and imputations.) That is, there is a certain measure of arbitrariness when applying psychiatric labels to psychiatric conditions. As we saw, American psychiatrists are far more likely to apply the label of schizophrenia to patients than British psychiatrists are (Kendall et al., 1971); in a civil case that centered around psychic damages to plaintiffs, psychiatrists for the defense found no psychic damage, while psychiatrists for the plaintiffs found considerable psychic damage (Simon and Zussman, 1983); in fact, a wide range of extrapsychiatric factors have been found to influence psychiatric judgments (Krohn and Akers, 1977; Townsend, 1978, 1980). While this must be tempered by the qualification that, as the seriousness of the condition increases, the uniformity of the psychiatric judgment increases correspondingly, it cannot be stressed too much that *most* of the judgments that psychiatrists make are of patients with a less serious rather than more serious condition. Hence, it is clear that extrapsychiatric contingencies do play a major role in psychiatric labeling.

The labeling approach is clearly wrong when it comes to treatment outcomes. Enough valid, reliable studies have been conducted on treatment outcomes to demonstrate that psychiatric intervention is more likely to be beneficial to the patient than harmful. Far from entrenching the mental patient more deeply in the mentally ill role, treatment does appear to have some positive effects (Smith, Glass, and Miller, 1980; Landman and Dawes, 1982). Some of these effects are not profound, and many do not persist over time; nonetheless, "it would be difficult for societal reaction theorists to argue that the effects of [psychiatric] labeling are uniformly negative" (Link and Cullen, 1989). Not only is psychiatric intervention more likely to move the patient out of rather than more deeply into disordered behavior, but also, undetected and untreated mentally disordered conditions often persist over long periods of time (Fischer et al., 1979), refuting "the labeling theory notion that symptoms are transient in the absence of labeling" (Link and Cullen, 1989).

In short, although it is difficult to deny the impact of the objective nature of mental disorder, at the same time, stigma, labeling, and societal reaction remain potent and crucial sociological factors to be taken into account in influencing the condition of the mentally disordered. Attempting to prove or disprove the strict labeling or the strict medical model *in toto* seems a futile exercise.

More refined attempts to test these models will find that both have a great deal to offer; in short, a "modified" labeling theory approach seems to be the most productive model in understanding mental disorder (Link et al., 1989).

FAMILIES OF THE MENTALLY DISORDERED: LABELING BY INTIMATES

Deviant roles or labels vary enormously according to how swiftly or slowly they are assigned to others and how skimpy or well-documented the evidence must be for such an assignment to take place. Alcoholism and mental disorder are similar in that they are roles or labels that are very slowly assigned to someone, and then only after great and protracted efforts at denial and the accumulation of many episodes that might point in these directions. Generally speaking, the more intimate the relationship between the potentially labeled person and conventional others, the greater the effort to deny the condition and the greater the evidence necessary to pin a label on that person. This is in part because "closeness permits one to see qualities other than the flaw" (Kreisman and Joy, 1974, p. 39). Still, some labels are slower to be attached than others; perhaps of all labels, as I said, alcoholism and mental disorder require the most evidence by intimates and family members to be attached. In this sense, they could be referred to as varieties of *conventional deviance*.

In contrast, homosexuality is swiftly assigned—to others, at any rate—and typically on skimpy evidence (Robins, 1975, p. 30). There is usually no overt behavior for nondeviant adults that can be labeled by anyone *as* homosexuality that is even remotely *like* homosexuality except homosexuality itself. (This is done in prisons, by street hustlers, and by bisexuals, but these scenes are already defined by conventionals as deviant.) Locker room camaraderie, homosociality, masculine competition, athletic contests, and macho efforts to demonstrate one's manhood all tend to be kept within socially defined and acceptable limits. They very rarely resemble actual homosexuality to anyone except a psychoanalyst. But each concrete act of same-gender sexual contact would be seen *as* a homosexual act by a nonparticipant, conventional outsider.

In contrast, "normals" tend to refuse to assign a label of "mentally ill" to intimate deviant actors until their behavior has become blatantly public and burdensomely troublesome. Most of the persons who would be regarded by a substantial proportion of clinicians and therapists as mentally ill at some time during their lives are never professionally diagnosed as such. And most are not so regarded by their peers and intimates, and do not come to see themselves as such. (Eccentric, perhaps; a bit strange, maybe; but not mentally ill.) There is, in other words, a huge population of "hidden" mentally disordered persons at large in the general population. But the more trouble a person causes others, the less power and resources that person has and the more power significant others have; the more bizarre that person's behavior and/or ideas seem to others (that is, within a particular cultural system), the greater the likelihood that others will perceive his or her behavior as a manifestation of mental disorder. Likewise, the more visible a person's behavior is, the greater is that likelihood. The greater the harm that person's behavior causes to others, again, the greater that likelihood is. The greater the departure from expected, normal social relations a person's interactions with others manifest, the greater the likelihood that person will eventually be seen as mentally ill. The greater the cost of the failure to fulfill one's social obligations, the higher the likelihood of this outcome, too. And the more that the individual's interpretations of reality depart from accepted cultural standards, the greater the chances of the imputation of psychosis.

For instance, schizophrenia, which manifests itself in mental states defined as bizarre, is more readily defined as mental illness than clinical depression, whose symptoms seem less peculiar and which, moreover, many share in miniature. People do not cause trouble, nor do they exhibit a "strange" way of thinking or acting, simply because they are psychotic. People must be *experienced* as trouble, or *regarded* as strange, by others. What is experienced as trouble or as strange in one place may not be in another. Moreover, one disordered condition may cause more trouble than another. Certainly the various character disorders that result in violent behavior lead to a swifter designation by relevant others of mental disorder than those that do not. There is certainly a central nucleus of behavior that would be experienced as troublesome just about everywhere, thinking that would seem strange in almost every setting. But some variation in community tolerance is exhibited for nearly all behavior that would eventually be regarded as clinically psychotic.

All phenomena have to be mentally conceptualized before they can be understood. We see behavior around us all the time; it does not "make sense" until we sort it out with the assistance of some notions of how the world is ordered. Most of us do not "see" mental disorder as such because we look at behavior, for the most part, in terms of misleading stereotypes. And we do not "see" the psychosis of intimates for other reasons as well: We are genuinely motivated not to do so.

In a study of the wives of men who were eventually committed to mental institutions, the basic question was asked, "How were the disorders of illness interpreted and tolerated?" How did these men "come to be recognized by other family members as needing psychiatric help?" The concern of the researchers was with "the factors which led to the reorganization of the wife's perception of her husband from a *well* man to a man who is mentally sick" (Yarrow et al., 1955, p. 12). The answer is that when and how "behavior becomes defined as problematic appears to be a highly individual matter." The subjective beginnings of this perception, these authors write, "are seldom localized in a single strange or disturbing reaction on the husband's part but rather in the piling up of behavior and feelings" (p. 16). The husband's behavior must be, they say, "*organized as a problem*" (emphasis mine). The wife's initial reactions to her husband's strange and troublesome behavior float around in a sea of "fog and uneasiness." Eventually, she begins to "see" that something is wrong. Why? "In some instances, it is when the wife can no longer manage her husband. . . ; in others, when she cannot explain his behavior." Her "level of tolerance for his behavior," they speculate, "is a function of her specific personality needs and vulnerabilities, her personal and family value systems and the social supports and prohibitions regarding the husband's symptomatic behavior" (p. 18). In other words, being regarded as mentally ill is variable and not dependent solely on one's "symptoms," but on

a host of secondary or contingent factors as well. If these factors are present, one's intimates will "see" one's mental illness; if they are absent, they may very well *not* regard one as mentally ill. Note, however, that this is not the same thing as saying that the designation "mentally ill" is assigned randomly, since all the persons in this study who were designated as mentally ill displayed the appropriate symptomatology. Contingent factors can delay or speed up the recognition of mental illness, but in most cases, they cannot create such a judgment out of whole cloth.

There are several factors that "make it difficult for the wife to recognize and accept"—in other words, to regard or *label*—"the husband's behavior in a mental-emotional-psychiatric framework. Many cross-currents seem to influence this process." One is the husband's behavior itself; it is, the authors write, a "fluctuating stimulus. . . . He is not worried and complaining all of the time. His delusions and hallucinations may not persist. His hostility toward the wife may be followed by warm attentiveness. She has, then, the problem of deciding whether his 'strange' behavior is significant. The greater saliency of one or the other of his responses at any moment of time depends in some degree upon the behavior sequence which has occurred most recently" (Yarrow et al., 1955, p. 21). The nature and quality of the relationship between husband and wife also impinge on her judgment; their ability to communicate with one another also influences how she sees his behavior and what she thinks of it. In addition, it is threatening to the wife to look upon her husband as "crazy": It is possible for her to draw the conclusion that she is, somehow, *responsible* for it, clearly a painful thought. In addition, she may visualize the next few years as the wife of a crazy person, and reject, suppress, and fight against the image because, again, it is too painful to consider.

The women in the study adopted several coping strategies to deal with the anxiety stirred up by such a consideration. One was *normalization*: The husband's behavior "is explained, justified, or made acceptable by seeing it also in herself or by assuring herself that the particular behavior occurs again and again among persons who are not ill" (p. 22). A second coping mechanism is to *attenuate* the seriousness of the behavior momentarily—to discount partly or underplay the degree of strangeness of it.

She may also *balance* acceptable with unacceptable behavior, to see both "strange" and "normal" behavior displayed by her husband and come up with the conclusion that he is not seriously disturbed. A last line of defense is outright *denial* that her husband could be emotionally ill (p. 23).

Looking at the other side of the coin, three sociologists studying the *husband's* perceptions of his *wife's* disturbing, bizarre behavior conclude: "Becoming a mental patient is not a simple and direct outcome of 'mental illness'. . . . Persons who are, by clinical standards, grossly disturbed, severely impaired in their functioning, and even overtly psychotic, may remain in the community for long periods without being 'recognized' as 'mentally ill'. . . . It is clear that becoming a patient is a socially structured event." There is a "monumental capacity of family members . . . to overlook, minimize, and explain away the evidence of profound disturbance in an intimate." With regard to mental illness specifically, there is a "high tolerance for deviance" in many families. An informal judgment of a family member as mentally ill is suppressed in the minds of the others until the problems they encounter become "unmanageable" (Sampson et al., 1964).

The dynamics of this denial process are instructive because they contradict the "hard" labeling position, as Gove (1975a) points out. While Scheff correctly argues that most "residual rule-breaking" is denied (1966, p. 51), as we might expect from knowing the dynamics of mental illness labeling among intimates, he further assumes that *if* it is denied, ignored, or rationalized *it will go away.* Here we have persons who are *not* labeled by others—whose family members, in fact, *deny* the intimate's mental disorder—who nonetheless go on to manifest increasingly serious symptoms. The condition seems to have arisen *independently* of labeling—by intimates, at any rate. Hospitalization eventually took place in these studies in spite of the absence of labeling. Although Scheff denies the significance of these studies (1974a, 1974b), his argument remains unconvincing. The denial of mental illness by intimates shows us that labeling cannot possibly be a cause of disordered symptoms, nor does it appear to stabilize a person's illness "career." The labeling process is certainly an aspect of the mental illness picture, but it does not seem to play the role that the "hard" labeling model insists it plays.

On Being Sane in Insane Places

"If sanity and insanity exist, how shall we know them?" Psychologist and law professor David Rosenhan decided to answer the question by having eight normal or "sane" persons, including himself, take part in an experiment. A "varied group" of people, they included three psychologists, a psychiatrist, a pediatrician, a painter, a full-time homemaker, and a graduate student; three were women, five were men. They "gained secret admission" to 12 different mental hospitals around the country by complaining of hearing hallucinatory voices that said "empty," "hollow," and "thud." All but one were admitted with a diagnosis of schizophrenia. (That one was diagnosed as a manic-depressive.) Once admitted, the pseudopatients acted normally, that is, did not simulate any symptoms of mental illness or abnormality. No psychiatric staff detected that these pseudopatients were normal; they were hospitalized for an average of 19 days, and were released with a diagnosis of schizophrenia "in remission," that is, without signs of mental illness. Rosenhan's conclusion is that psychiatry "cannot distinguish the sane from the insane" (1973). Clearly, his view is extremely critical of the medical and psychiatric approaches toward mental illness and it supports some version of the constructionist or labeling theory.

Rosenhan's study has received a great deal of attention, the bulk of it favorable. A review of 31 psychology textbooks published only three years after the experiment was published found that 15 cited the article, 12 of them favorably (Spitzer, 1976). In addition, most of the articles that appeared in medical, mental health, and psychology journals commenting on the

On Being Sane in Insane Places (cont.)

experiment had positive things to say. The media, too, gave the Rosenhan study a great deal of attention and overwhelmingly favorable coverage—in large part, said one critic, because "it said something that many were delighted to hear." This single study, the critic stated, "is probably better known to the lay public than any other study in the area of psychiatry in the last decade" (Spitzer, 1976, p. 459).

Not all the attention paid to "On Being Sane in Insane Places" has been favorable, however. *The Journal of Abnormal Psychology* devoted its volume 33, April 1976, issue to comments on Rosenhan's piece; most were critical. Robert Spitzer (1975, 1976), a psychiatrist and co-preparer of and consultant to several editions of the American Psychiatric Association's *Diagnostic and Statistical Manual of Mental Disorders*, is perhaps the most articulate and outspoken of Rosenhan's critics. He sees the experiment and the article that summarized it as "pseudoscience presented as science"— prompting a diagnosis of "logic, in remission" (1975, p. 442). Why?

"One hardly knows where to begin," says Spitzer (1975, p. 443). The study "immediately becomes confused" on terminology. As Rosenhan should know (he is a professor of both psychology and the law), the terms "sane" and "insane" are legal, not psychiatric, concepts. The central issue for the law (inability to distinguish right from wrong) "is totally irrelevant" to the study, which is concerned with whether psychiatrists can detect a psychiatric condition. But let's assume that Rosenhan is referring to mental disorder, not "insanity." The fact is, the pseudopatient *simulated mental illness* in gaining admission to a mental hospital. Said another critic, "If I were to drink a quart of blood and . . . come to the emergency room of any hospital vomiting blood," the chances are, he would be labeled and treated as having a bleeding peptic ulcer. But "I doubt that I could argue convincingly that medical science does not know how to diagnose that condition" (Kety, 1974, p. 959).

The fact is, these pseudopatients claimed to present symptoms of schizophrenia, and that is how they were diagnosed. What reason did the admitting psychiatrists have to doubt the genuineness of the stated symptoms?

For Rosenhan, the fact that no one detected the pseudopatients as "sane" and they were released with a diagnosis of "in remission" was significant; this means, he said, that, in the judgment of the hospital, they were neither sane, nor had they been sane at any time. Spitzer argues exactly the reverse: the fact that these patients were discharged as being "in remission" indicates that the psychiatric profession is able to detect mental disorder. The fact is, the diagnosis "in remission" indicates that patients are free from any signs of mental illness, which characterizes these cases in a nutshell. It is an *extremely rare* diagnosis, appearing, in one hospital, only once in 100 discharges; in a check of 12 hospitals, 11 *never* used the diagnosis, and in the remaining hospital, in only 7 percent of its discharges. Says Spitzer, "We must marvel" at the fact that, in Rosenhan's study, the 11 psychiatrists who discharged the pseudopatients "all acted so rationally as to use at discharge . . . a category that is so rarely used with real schizophrenic patients" (1975, p. 445). *Not one* used any of the descriptions that were available to them that would have demonstrated Rosenhan's point far more effectively: "still psychotic," "probably still hallucinating but denies it now," "loose associations," or "inappropriate affect" (p. 445).

Spitzer admits that "there are serious problems with psychiatric diagnosis, as there are with other medical diagnosis" (p. 451). However, diagnosis is *not* so poor "that it cannot be an aid in the treatment of the seriously disturbed psychiatric patient" (p. 451). But, this critic of Rosenhan's experiment says, a correct interpretation of "On Being Sane in Insane Places" contradicts the author's conclusions. "In the setting of a psychiatric hospital," argues Spitzer, "psychiatrists are remarkably able to distinguish the 'sane' from the 'insane' " (p. 451).

THE EPIDEMIOLOGY OF MENTAL DISORDER

Epidemiology is the study of the distribution of diseases in the population. Psychiatry makes the assumption that the distribution of mental disorders can be determined in much the same way that the distribution of physical diseases can be determined. The field of psychiatric epidemiology is based on the idea that there is, or can be, a "true" rate or prevalence of mental disorder, just as there is a "true" rate of cancer or AIDS. Clearly, this is an essentialist assumption, that is, that mental disorder is a concrete entity on whose reality all reasonable and informed observers can agree. The constructionist, in contrast, seeing mental disorder as a socially determined judgment, does not make the assumption that a "true" rate or prevalence of mental disorder can be determined. Instead, constructionists are interested in how mental disorder is conceptualized and defined, how certain categories in the population come to be *designated* as having higher, or lower, rates of mental disorder, and what extrapsychiatric factors influence rates of institutionalization.

All epidemiologists agree that measuring mental disorder in the population, or in certain segments of the population, is problematic. The issue of how mental disorder is diagnosed and determined for the purposes of an epidemiological study has filled a substantial number of very fat tomes. The rates of admission to mental hospitals has been used as one measure or index of mental disorder in the population and among categories in the population. However, we all recognize that there are many factors that make it likelier that some persons, and persons in certain categories, will end up in a mental hospital than others, holding mental condition constant. Some conditions cause a great deal of trouble for others, while for other conditions, the mentally disordered person suffers in isolation; clearly, the first is more likely to be hospitalized than the second. Some people live among groups and categories who consider mental hospitalization a viable option only under extreme circumstances; others look to institutionalization much more quickly and readily, on signs of relatively minor abnormality or dysfunction. The point is, there is a huge noninstitutionalized

segment of the population who *would be* diagnosed as mentally disordered were they to be evaluated by a psychiatrist. Because of problems such as these, another measure of mental disorder has been developed: a diagnostic interview schedule, which, presumably, can determine mental condition in a sample of respondents. Over the years, different interview schedules have been used, and somewhat different findings have been obtained. Still, many experts believe that, over time, these research instruments are becoming increasingly accurate. Currently, a huge ongoing study, the Epidemiological Catchment Area Program survey, is measuring mental health and disorder in a random sample of the noninstitutionalized population at large (Kessler et al., 1994).

A large number of studies have been conducted that have reached conclusions concerning the differential proneness of groups and categories in the population to mental illness or disorder. Most sociologists believe that specific social processes are related to mental disorder and that these processes are more characteristic of certain groups than others. What characteristics are most important? How do members of these social categories fare with respect to mental health and disorder? Perhaps the most basic and often-studied characteristics studied by psychiatric epidemiologists have been *sex* or *gender, marital status*, and *socioeconomic status*.

GENDER: MEN VERSUS WOMEN

It is not clear that there is a consistent relationship between sex or gender and a crude, unidimensional, undifferentiated measure of mental disorder. Reviews of the literature (for instance, Dohrenwend and Dohrenwend, 1976) have revealed that some studies find that women have higher rates of mental disorder than men, while others show men to have higher rates. This is the case for two reasons.

When it comes to *surveys* of the general population, women have somewhat higher rates of mental disorder. One nationally representative study of households across the United States conducted jointly by the National Institutes of Health and the National Center for Health Statistics identified 1.94 million females and 1.32 million males as having a serious mental disorder; rates of mental disorder were 20.6 percent for females and 15.5 percent for males. The Epidemiological Catchment Area Project study mentioned earlier, which was focused on five urban centers, found rates of mental disorder of 16.6 percent for females and 14.0 percent for males (Reiger et al., 1988). A later study using the same research instrument, based on a more nationally representative sample, reached the same conclusion (Kessler et al., 1994). A major textbook sums up the recent evidence and concludes that "women have greater tendencies toward mental disorder than men" (Cockerham, 2003, p. 163).

On the other hand, males are significantly more likely to be *admitted to mental hospitals* than females (p. 164). Moreover, during much of this country's history, the ratio of males to females was increasing over time. For instance, in 1900, there were 106 males admitted to state mental hospitals for every 100 females; by 1975, this had risen to 193, and in 1985, it reached a high of 199. Since then, the ratio has subsided somewhat. In 1997, there were 162 male admissions per 100,000 males in the population, and 89.0 males versus 54.9 female admissions per 100,000 females in the population (Cockerham, 2003, p. 165). It is entirely possible that both essentialists and constructionists would have something to say on the subject. In fact, experts believe that this disparity is due to the conjunction of the specific *type* of mental disorder males are more likely to suffer from (an essentialistic phenomenon) and professional stereotyping (a constructionist phenomenon). While men are strikingly more likely to fall victim to antisocial personality disorders, women are far more likely to suffer from mood disorders, especially depression. Each of these disorders manifests itself in a strikingly different way. More specifically, the antisocial personality is highly likely to cause havoc in the lives of others—for instance, in the form of aggressiveness and violence—while depressive mood disorders are more likely to result in withdrawal and isolation. Someone who causes disruptive social and interpersonal trouble is more likely to be institutionalized than someone who withdraws.

To be plain about it, the mental disorder of men, even holding severity of disorder constant, is regarded as more disabling, threatening, and dangerous to the society than is that of women (Gove, 1972; Rushing, 1979a, 1979b). Women are regarded as more cooperative and compliant and more readily influenced by the hospital staff and, therefore, are more likely to be released (Doherty, 1978). Some researchers also feel that the social roles men and women and boys and girls are forced to play impacts on their mental health—or lack of it. Males are expected to be more aggressive, independent, and adventurous; consequently, the disorders they manifest (again, antisocial tendencies, especially toward violence) reflect that role expectation. Females are socialized to be passive, dependent, and lacking in confidence; they, too, exhibit this tendency in extreme form in their characteristic disorder, depression (Gove and Herb, 1974, p. 259).

It is hypothesized that there is something of a "double standard" among clinicians in the diagnosis, hospitalization, and release of mental patients with respect to gender (Cockerham, 2003, pp. 174–176). Psychiatrists and clinical psychologists seem to have a lower standard of mental health for women than for men. They are more likely to diagnose mental disorder for men, other things being equal; a woman's condition would have to be more severe to warrant hospitalization, and a man's less severe, to warrant release. In addition to the nature of the symptoms (disruption and violence versus withdrawal and isolation), one hypothesis that has been put forth to explain this observed regularity is that in a sexist or patriarchal society, males are expected to perform in a society to more exacting standards. Being a man in a very achievement-oriented society is incompatible with being mentally disordered; the penalties for stepping out of line are swift and strong. On the other hand, where women are relegated to an inferior and dependent role, their performance in that role is met with more indulgence and leeway. It is felt by both clinicians and the general public, male and female, that a mildly psychically impaired woman can perform in an imperfect fashion and still "get by." Ironically, these sexist values result in a higher rate of mental disorder labeling for men, supposedly the more powerful social category, and less for women, who are generally less powerful. As sex roles become more equalitarian, one would expect these gender disparities in diagnosis, hospitalization, and release to diminish and eventually disappear.

MARITAL STATUS

Another dimension that has been studied extensively to determine its relationship with or impact on mental health and disorder is *marital status.* Among men, a very consistent finding emerges from the many studies that have been conducted: Single, never-married men are strikingly more likely to score high on every available measure of mental disorder than are married men; separated and divorced men rank somewhere in between. Two hypotheses have been advanced to account for the observed relationship. The first is that men who are married and stay married are more stable, psychologically healthy, and conventional than men who never marry—and therefore, they are less mentally disordered. The experience of marriage itself, these observers argue, has little or nothing to do with this regularity: It is only that *the kind of man* who marries is also the kind of man who exhibits relatively few personality problems, while the man who does *not* marry is far *more likely* to exhibit those same problems. Getting married entails a certain degree of social competence to attract a spouse; men with severe mental problems are not considered desirable partners and thus, will be socially avoided by women (Rushing, 1979b). "The more symptomatic and/or ineffective an individual, the less likely [it is that] he will find a marital partner. . . , and the more likely [it is that] he will spend extended periods in the hospital" (Turner and Gartrell, 1978, p. 378). It is, some say, "the inadequate man who is left over after the pairing has taken place" (Gallagher, 2002, p. 203).

A second hypothesis is that marriage confers a kind of immunity on a man: Married men have fewer mental problems than do bachelors because the experience of being married is conducive to a man's mental health, security, and well-being. "Marriage does not prevent economic and social problems from invading life," two researchers argue, "but apparently can help fend off the psychological assaults that such problems otherwise create" (Pearlin and Johnson, 1977, p. 714). Bachelors are more socially isolated from others; they lack the social supports and resources that married men have at their disposal. Hence, they are more likely to be psychologically vulnerable and fall victim to mental disorders. Again, whether this is a question of social selection or differential experiences, the tendency for single men to exhibit strikingly more, and more serious, symptoms of mental disorder is well documented in the literature (Cockerham, 2003, pp. 177–179; Gallagher, 2002, pp. 203–204).

This generalization does not hold in the same way for women. Some studies show single women to have the same rates of mental disorder as married women (Warheit et al., 1976), while other studies show married women to have *higher* rates of disorders (Gove, 1979b). In short, the special protection that marriage supposedly extends to men seems to offer no special protection for women. It is even possible that the opposite is the case: Some observers argue that marriage is a stressful, anxiety-provoking, oppressive, exploitative institution, incompatible with the mental health of women (Bernard, 1982). Men have all the advantages in marriage, they feel, and thus profit from the experience; in contrast, women suffer as a result of being married because marriage is more demanding on women. It is frustrating, unsatisfying, and lacking in gratification for them (Gove, 1972). It is also possible that the social selection process that operates so strongly for men does so far less for women. That is, sexual stereotyping rejects mentally impaired men far more strongly than women (Phillips, 1964); a man who is mentally ill is seen by all women as an undesirable partner, while a woman who displays certain mental disorders may still be considered marriageable. In any case, the differences are far less strong among women than men. The evidence seems to favor few differences between married and unmarried women in mental health and disorder (Warheit et al., 1976), yet the remarkable difference in the impact of marriage on men and women should strike the observer forcefully. While it is probably a bit too rash to state that, in terms of mental health, marriage is good for men and bad for women, the evidence does at least suggest that it may be good for men and of considerably less consequence for women. In a less patriarchal society, marriage will become more equalitarian and, possibly, equally good for both sexes.

SOCIOECONOMIC STATUS

Of all sociological variables, the relationship between social class or socioeconomic status (SES) and mental disorder has probably been the most frequently studied. And the most commonly used indicators measuring socioeconomic status are income, occupational prestige, and education. The higher someone ranks on any one or all three of these dimensions, the higher is his or her socioeconomic status or social "class," sociologists hold. Mental disorder is very closely related to socioeconomic status: The higher the SES, the lower the rate of mental disorder; the lower the SES, the higher the rate of mental disorder (Kessler et al., 1994; Gallagher, 2002, pp. 168–190; Cockerham, 2003, pp. 138–155). This holds regardless of the specific measure or indicator of SES that is used—occupational prestige, income, or education. People at the bottom of the class ladder are far more likely to suffer from psychiatric distress, especially schizophrenia, than those at the top. There are a few mental disorders that are more common toward the top of the class structure, such as obsessive-compulsive neuroses and some mood disorders, but the most serious illnesses, especially schizophrenia, are most common toward the bottom of the class structure. In dozens of studies, conducted in countries on three continents, the relationship between mental disorder and SES has been studied; almost without exception, these studies find schizophrenia significantly and strikingly more likely in the lower socioeconomic strata. This generalization has been verified empirically by studies stretching back two-thirds of a century (Faris and Dunham, 1939; Hollingshead and Redlich, 1958; Srole et al., 1962; Leighton et al., 1963).

Why should this strong inverse relationship between psychopathology and SES exist? There are at least four possible explanations.

The first stresses *types* of disorder. The kinds of disorder exhibited by lower-status persons are more likely to come to the attention of the authorities than the kinds of disorders exhibited by middle- and upper-status persons. Lower-status persons are less likely to attribute their problems to a psychiatric condition, since they are more likely to feel that some stigma adheres to consultation with a "shrink" or being committed to a mental hospital. Hence, they are less likely to seek out psychiatric assistance voluntarily. Lower-status persons are most likely to come to the attention of psychiatric authorities as a result of referral by the police or a social worker. In contrast, upper- and middle-status persons are more likely to be referred by relatives or a private physician. A great many lower-status mental disorders, especially among men, manifest themselves in the form of "antisocial" behavior, particularly violence, which is likely to attract the attention of agents of formal social control—the police. This explanation does not say that lower-SES persons are more mentally disordered than middle- and upper-SES persons overall so much as it focuses on how certain conditions, differentially distributed by social class, intersect with the social structure.

The second is the constructionist explanation. Some observers have argued that the strong inverse relationship between SES and mental disorder may be due to class bias and the labeling process. Middle-class psychiatrists find lower-class behavior troublesome and are more likely to label it disordered than the behavior of middle-class persons (Wilkinson, 1975). There is something of a built-in bias in psychiatric diagnosis against lower-class subculture and lower-class persons. Mental health is measured by a middle-class yardstick; lower-class values and behavior are more likely to be regarded as disordered by the psychiatric profession, composed, as it is, of persons who are toward the middle or near the top of the social class ladder. It seems almost unarguable that class bias plays a role in psychiatric diagnosis. Nonetheless, this explanation cannot be the whole story, since much of the behavior of the psychiatrically disordered is deemed undesirable by members of *all* social classes. Characteristically, the lower-class person comes to psychiatric attention as a result of being troublesome to, and being reported by, other lower-class persons.

A third hypothesis attempting to explain why mental disorder is more heavily located at the bottom reaches of the SES continuum focuses on the greater *stress* experienced by persons located there. Economic deprivation, poverty, occupational instability, and unemployment are strongly related to psychological impairment (Liem and Liem, 1978). As a result of having to deal with living an economically deprived existence and coping with this deprivation, the lower-status person suffers a higher level of emotional stress and consequently is more vulnerable to a psychiatric breakdown (Kessler, 1979). The pressure of daily living under deprived circumstances becomes overwhelming; problems that cannot be solved mount, become unmanageable, and force the person into a break with reality (Cockerham, 2003, pp. 149–150). There is a great deal of evidence supporting the "social stress" hypothesis of mental disorder.

A fourth hypothesis attempting to explain the strong inverse relationship between SES and mental disorder is the *social selection* or *drift* hypothesis. This theory argues that social class is a *consequence* rather than a *cause* of mental disorder. The mentally disordered are incapable of achieving a higher position on the SES hierarchy *because* they are mentally disordered (Dunham, 1965). Members of the lower class who are mentally disordered are either stuck there or have drifted there because their mental disorder prevents them from achieving a higher position. Their disorder retards their social mobility (Harkey, Miles, and Rushing, 1976). The social stress and the drift hypotheses are not necessarily contradictory or mutually exclusive; one could operate in a given case, and the other in another case. However, though there is some validity to both the stress and the drift theories, it is likely that social class contributes more to mental disorder than mental disorder contributes to social class (Link et al., 1986; Fox, 1990; Cockerham, 2003, pp. 151–152).

CHEMICAL TREATMENT OF MENTAL DISORDER

By the 1950s, it had become clear to psychiatrists who worked with mental patients that conventional therapy was not working; in the treatment of the most serious mental disorders, especially schizophrenia, psychiatrists "functioned mainly as administrators and custodians" (Berger, Hamburg, and Hamburg, 1977, p. 264). In 1952 in France, and in the United States in 1954, a drug was first used that seemed to show some promise in reducing the most blatant, florid, and troublesome symptoms of institutionalized schizophrenic mental patients. Bearing the chemical name chlorpromazine and the trade name Thorazine, it belonged to a major category of psychoactive drugs that are regarded as having an *antipsychotic* effect. Antipsychotics do not produce a high or intoxication, they are not used recreationally, and they are not sold illegally on the street. Nearly all the use of the antipsychotics is legal, licit prescription use for the purpose of controlling mental illness. Antipsychotics in addition to Thorazine include Mellaril, Compazine, Stelazine, and Haldol.

It is likely that experts would say that the two most dramatic changes that have taken place in the United States since the 1950s with respect to mental illness are the degree to which antipsychotics are administered to the mentally disordered and, correlatively, the number of patients who are in residence in mental hospitals. There is some controversy concerning the role that antipsychotics have played in depopulating the mental hospitals; some observers argue that the antipsychotics were less a cause than an opportunity (Gronfein, 1985), while others hold to a more directly pharmacological explanation (Pollack and Taube, 1975, p. 49). Regardless of the exact mechanism, the fact is, in 1955, there were nearly 560,000 patients in residence in public mental hospitals; this figure dropped almost every year until, by the 1990s, it was 80,000. This decline is not due to a reduced number of *admissions* to mental hospitals; admissions actually increased from 178,000 in 1955 to 385,000 in 1970, and then declined to about 255,000 in 1992. The fact is, length of stay was roughly six months in 1955; for the past decade or so, it has leveled off at two weeks. (Data are supplied by the National Institute of Mental Health.) As a result of much quicker discharges, mental hospitals are emptying out. Regardless of the precise timing and the causal mechanism of this change, it is impossible to argue that it could have come about in the absence of the administration of antipsychotics to schizophrenic mental patients.

Roughly 85 percent of all patients in public mental hospitals are being administered some form of antipsychotic medication.

When Thorazine was initially introduced, it was described as having the following effects on agitated, manic, schizophrenic patients: The drug, an observer wrote, "produces marked quieting of the motor manifestations, patients cease to be loud and profane, the tendency to hyperbolic [that is, exaggerated] association is diminished, and the patient can sit still long enough to eat and take care of normal physiological needs" (Goldman, 1955). The emotional withdrawal, hallucinations, delusions, and other patterns of disturbed thinking, paranoia, belligerence, hostility, and "blunted affect" of patients are significantly reduced. As a result of the use of the antipsychotics, patients exhibit fewer and less dramatic symptoms of psychosis and become more manageable, and, as a result, hospitals have been able to discontinue or reduce such ineffective or dangerous practices as hydrotherapy and lobotomies. And, as a result of the administration of these drugs, hospitals have, in the words of one observer, been transformed from "zoo-smelling, dangerous bedlams into places fit for human beings to live and, at times, recover from psychosis" (Callaway, 1958, p. 82). By inducing a more "normal" psychological condition in patients, hospitals can release them into the community as outpatients, with only minimal treatment and care in aftercare facilities. This process is referred to as *deinstitutionalization*; unfortunately, what this has produced is a huge population of mentally ill homeless people who are subject to virtually no supervision or treatment whatsoever. (See the boxed insert on deinstitutionalization.)

Studies have shown that roughly three-quarters of all acute schizophrenics demonstrate significant improvement following the administration of antipsychotic drugs, and between 75 to 95 percent of patients relapse if their medication is discontinued (Ray and Ksir, 2002, p. 226). The use of the antipsychotic drugs is regarded as not only effective for most mental patients, but it is the least expensive of all treatment modalities. However, it should be added that although these drugs do reduce the most bizarre symptoms of schizophrenia, they are not a "cure" for mental illness. They calm the agitated, disturbed patient; the symptoms of mental illness are reduced, and patients are no longer as troublesome to others as they once were: They do not manifest their former signs of craziness. Antipsychotics permit the patient to behave in a more socially acceptable fashion; the patient's problems do not surface so painfully or disturbingly. Surely that represents progress of a sort. However, it is a stopgap measure rather than a genuine cure; no mental health specialist can be satisfied until a more substantial and more permanent treatment modality has been developed. Unfortunately, there is no prospect of this for the foreseeable future.

It is not known just why the antipsychotic drugs have this calming effect on mental patients. In any case, psychiatry has not been successful in treating seriously ill patients by means of any of its more conventional "talking" cures, such as psychoanalysis (which, in addition, is hugely resource-intensive, very time-consuming, and extremely protracted). Using the antipsychotics at least keeps patients out of trouble and out of the way of "normals," and enables some to function in important social roles, such as education, marriage, and occupation. Some observers see the use of antipsychotics as a "revolution" in the field of psychiatry (Gove, 1975a, p. 245). Others (Townsend, 1980, p. 272) are more cautious and see the change not as a genuine treatment but merely as the suppression of troublesome, disruptive behavior.

The antipsychotics are not addictive and very rarely result in lethal overdoses. However, there are some serious side effects that are experienced by many patients with the administration of these drugs, including abnormal, involuntary, and sometimes bizarre movements of the tongue, lips, and cheeks; facial tremors; rigidity; and a shuffling gait. These symptoms can be treated with a separate type of drug, the anti-Parkinsonian drugs. Patients also complain of feeling "doped up." At higher, often therapeutic, doses, their responses are often sluggish; they tend to be less acute mentally than usual; they display less interest in external stimuli, including other people; and they are slower in arousal and response. Thus, the reduction of the socially and culturally bizarre and unacceptable behavior and thinking of mental patients is bought at a not inconsiderable price.

Deinstitutionalization

In 1961, the Joint Commission on Mental Illness submitted a report that criticized the warehousing of mental patients in huge, dehumanizing, impersonal, and ineffective publicly funded asylums. The report stated that smaller facilities should be maintained in local communities that care for the mentally ill on a more personal and humane basis. In 1963, President John F. Kennedy signed federal legislation mandating local community care facilities for the mentally ill (Mechanic, 1989).

Any complex and large-scale change is likely to be a product of many actors and a variety of motives. Still, the desire to improve the lives of mental patients must be counted among the original reasons for deinstitutionalization—releasing the mentally ill from large hospitals into the community. In addition, some politicians reasoned, these asylums were extremely expensive to maintain (not to mention ineffective). Thus, community care facilities would save the taxpayer a great deal of money. And thirdly, as we saw, starting in the mid–1950s, psychiatric medicine had an inexpensive and seemingly effective treatment modality at its disposal: psychotropic (or mind-active) drugs. Thus, as we've seen, within a few short years, the mental hospitals were practically emptied of patients. By the mid-1970s, only the most untreatable patients remained in public mental hospitals.

Unfortunately, things did not go as these early idealists planned. The war in Vietnam (which involved U.S. troops from 1961 to 1975) drained an almost unimaginably huge proportion of resources from the public coffers. And President Richard Nixon (1969–1974) proved to be hostile to the idea of community mental health; in 1972 he announced plans to phase out federal support for its programs. Though partially restored, presidents Ronald Reagan (1981–1989) and George H. W. Bush (1989–1993) continued to put the ax to federal support for local halfway houses and treatment centers.

The upshot of these cuts was that the mentally ill were often released into the community with little more than a vial of pills and a prescription for more. Some lived with relatives (many of these were eventually ejected), while others were simply on their own. A high proportion gravitated to low-income areas where disorganization and violence were common. Hundreds of thousands became homeless. (Experts estimate that roughly a third of America's homeless are released former mental patients.) Half of all mental patients released into the community are reinstitutionalized within a year. While the majority of released mental patients prefer living in the community, even under adverse conditions, to life in a mental ward, the fact is, most do not receive the kind of care they need—the kind of care that was envisioned in the idealistic sixties. Meanwhile, city streets have become "open mental wards" (Goleman, 1986). We see the mentally ill on the streets of our cities—and even in smaller communities—wandering into traffic, looking wild-eyed and disheveled, screaming incomprehensible phrases to no one in particular. They have been dumped there, transferred from the asylum to the streets, the victims of massive budget cuts. The system has failed to help them; they are "a silent witness to the heartlessness and befuddlement that has created no better alternative for them" than the street (Goleman, 1986, p. C1).

DEVIANCE AND MENTAL DISORDER: AN OVERVIEW

Mental disorder has both parallels and dissimilarities with other forms of deviant behavior we encountered in earlier chapters, such as drug use, homicide, and homosexuality. (Some forms of deviance are also regarded as "behavioral disorders," such as drug dependence.) On the one hand, both deviance and mental disorder represent a departure from the normative order. On the other hand, being regarded as mentally abnormal by others usually comes as a result of breaking the rules of the society; one behaves in a way that is considered odd, eccentric, bizarre, and/or troublesome. One says things that others regard as "crazy," one interacts with others in ways that make them feel uncomfortable. So, to the extent that behavioral manifestations of mental illness result in normative violations, the disruption of smooth social relations, and attracting a socially undesirable label, clearly it represents a form or type of deviant behavior.

Public attitudes toward the mentally disordered are more complicated than they are toward the deviant. Although the mentally disordered may do things that are regarded as "immoral," this is not necessary to any definition of mental disorder. Toward the deviant, the dominant emotion is often outrage, anger, hostility. In contrast, the mentally disordered attract a feeling more like condescension and pity. Most conventional persons wish to punish the deviant, but keep the mentally disordered out of sight and out of mind. The deviant is feared more for the harm we suppose he or she can do to us, to the society as a whole, or to our version of truth or morality. In contrast, we do not take the mentally disordered person's version of reality as a threat to our own, but he or she is feared for reminding us of what we could become. Deviants are seen through two contradictory principles: They are sick and act out of compulsive motives, and they are immoral, act out of free will, and are responsible for their actions. In contrast, the mentally disordered person is seen as lacking a free will and hence, not responsible for his or her actions.

In addition, deviance is nearly always located in specific actions, that is, in clearly locatable behavioral and attitudinal spheres. One is not *a* deviant generally; few people even use the term. One is deviant in specific areas of life—sex, drug use, politics, harming others, and so on. The label of mental disorder is almost unique in that it is free-floating, eminently generalizable. One is considered mentally disordered not because of having done anything in a delimited area of life, but because one has done many things in many areas that are supposedly manifestations of a psychiatric disorder, dysfunction, or disorganization. This is true of practically no other form of deviant behavior.

The major thrust of psychiatric writings published in past decades has been in the direction of adopting the medical model of mental disorder—that is, regarding it as perfectly analogous to, or literally and concretely a manifestation of, a physical pathology. The implication of this model is that the mental patient should be treated in much the same way as the sufferer of a physical disease, both by clinicians and by the lay public. The social stigma that adhered to the mental patient in the past is regarded in some quarters as an archaic remnant of the past. Being regarded as crazy, this view holds, does not cause others to view the person as deviant but instead will "redefine the deviance in a fairly positive way." Commitment to a mental hospital "tends to shift the person's label from that of being obnoxious and intolerable to that of being mentally ill and in need of help" (Gove, 1975a, p. 245). Insofar as this is true, *mental disorder is not a form of deviance.* To the extent that the public sees mental disorder on a par with physical disorder, qualitatively no different from, and attracting no more stigma than, contracting cancer, and regards the mentally disordered as not responsible for their actions, it is not a form of deviance. But remember, earlier in this century the cancer patient suffered some degree of stigma, and even today certain diseases, such as AIDS and leprosy, are considered loathsome, so physical disease is not always exclusively physical. Even for some physical diseases, the sufferer is seen in some social circles as a deviant.

But consider this: Being physically sick in our society does harbor a dimension of deviance. By that I mean that it represents a departure from being self-reliant, taking care of one's obligations; it is a failure to be healthy, productive, and "normal" (Parsons, 1951, pp. 428–479; Freidson, 1970, pp. 205–223). Illness, then, is a violation of a number of strongly held values. To a degree, being mentally disordered will always be regarded as a form of deviance in the *same* sense that physic0al illness is. Falling down on the job, being unable to cope, failing to meet one's obligations, and disrupting interpersonal relations will always be despised in a society that values performance and achievement. Being mentally ill emphasizes one's incapacity and incompetence. As such, it will always be looked down upon.

SUMMARY

Of all deviant phenomena, mental disorder comprises the most diverse and miscellaneous category. Mental disorder is a set of conditions that characteristically manifests itself in actions, mental patterns, or speech utterances that are deemed bizarre and deranged by both clinicians and the lay public. Even the behaviors associated with this condition are vastly more diverse than for any other deviant behavioral category, however broad it may be, that we have discussed so far.

In the fourth edition of its *Diagnostic and Statistical Manual of Mental Disorders*, the American Psychiatric Association (1994) defines mental disorder as a syndrome or condition that is associated with distress, disability, or an increased risk of "suffering, death, pain, disability, or an important loss of freedom." Three hundred disorders are listed; however, DSM-IV does not provide a framework or a theoretical model for disorders, but a listing of them and a description for each of the symptoms the clinician is likely to encounter in practice. Schizophrenia (a thought disorder entailing hallucinations, delusions, and disorganized speech) and mood disorders (particularly depression) are two of the most commonly encountered and most often studied mental disorders.

Experts approach the subject of mental disorder through the lens of several different perspectives. *Essentialism* is the view that mental disorder is a real, concrete "thing" that the observer can identify, locate, and explicate, much as one can pick an apple off a tree. Essentialists examine issues such as etiology (a study of the causes of mental disorder), epidemiology (a study of how mental disorder is distributed in the population), and the effectiveness of treatment. "Strict," "hard," or "radical" essentialism sees mental disorder as the manifestation of a disease, much like cancer; in its most extreme form, essentialism regards the condition as an actual, literal disease, that is, a product of biophysical pathology. *Constructionism*, in contrast, focuses not on the condition but on how it is regarded, thought about, talked about, and dealt with. Here, treatment is looked at not as a means to a cure but as a social enterprise that is itself to be explained and understood. The "hard," "strict," or "radical"

constructionists deny the existence of mental disorder in the real or concrete world and focus exclusively on judgments of and reactions to a "putative" or so-called condition. Softer or more moderate constructionists either set aside the question of the reality of mental disorder, or agree that it exists and make comparisons between such judgments and reactions and the condition itself. Constructionists emphasize contingency (factors other than condition influence judgments about mental disorder), stigma (judgments of mental disorder are stigmatizing), and the conceptual creation of mental disorder through labels.

Labeling theory is a distinct perspective from constructionism. While constructionism focuses on the *conceptual* creation of mental disorder through judgments and reactions, labeling theory focuses on its *literal* creation through these processes. It is a perspective that argues that being labeled and treated *as* mentally ill is the primary *cause* of mental disorder. Labeling theory straddles essentialism and constructionism, in that the *initial* or *primary* judgments about mental condition are made to some degree independently of "true" mental condition; they act to *create* a true mental disorder. In the past decade or so, a "modified" labeling perspective has arisen that adopts bits and pieces of the approach but not all of its particulars. It emphasizes the stigma of being labeled as mentally ill, the contingency involved in applying such labels, and the fact that treatment is often effective.

Families of the mentally disordered typically attempt to "normalize" or explain away the symptoms of a mentally disordered member. Mental disorder has sometimes been referred to as "conventional" deviance in that it takes a great deal of evidence and many episodes of disordered behavior by a family member, entailing substantial trouble and suffering, before a spouse, parents, or children will regard him or her as mentally disordered and in need of treatment.

Some sociologists study the epidemiology of mental disorder. Three of the most often studied characteristics that correlate with mental disorder are gender, marital status, and socioeconomic status.

While women are more likely to be diagnosed as mentally disordered on surveys, men are much more likely to be institutionalized. It is possible that the precise conditions that men are more likely to manifest (for instance, character or personality disorder, which often leads to violence) cause more trouble for others and result in more official intervention and hence, psychiatric labeling and commitment. In contrast, the conditions that are more prevalent among women (for instance, depression) often result in withdrawal and isolation and hence, no official notice.

Married men are significantly less likely to be disordered than single men. This may be because marriage offers a kind of immunity or psychological protection for them; they receive support in times of trouble. It may also be because men who are mentally disordered can't get married, since they make undesirable marital partners. With women, the picture is not so clear-cut. Many studies show no differences in mental disorder between married and single women, and some studies actually show married women to have higher rates of disorder than single women. It could be that marriage is more stressful for women than for men, or it could be that disordered women are deemed not nearly as undesirable as marital partners by men as disordered men are by women.

Socioeconomic status (SES) is almost certainly the single social characteristic that correlates most strongly with mental disorder. Studies conducted today and in the past, and studies around the world as well as in the United States, agree: The lower the SES, the higher the rate of mental disorder—most specifically, schizophrenia, regarded as one of the most common, and perhaps the most serious, of all the disorders. Why? At least four explanations come to mind. Personality disorder, which is common among lower SES men, frequently

results, as we saw, in official and therapeutic intervention, whereas the disorders most characteristic of middle- and upper-middle status persons are less troublesome and intrusive to the society. Second, labeling may play a role: Middle-class psychiatrists may be quicker to judge pathology in lower-class persons, particularly males. Third, lower-class life is more stressful than middle-class life and hence, more likely to lead to a psychiatric breakdown. And fourth, the mental condition of the mentally disordered *precedes* achievement in the social class ladder and inhibits that achievement; hence, they "drift" into the lower class.

In 1954, psychoactive chemicals began to be used on a widespread basis to treat the mentally ill. That year, there were over half a million patients in publicly funded mental hospitals, and their average length of stay was six months. While the use of drugs was not the only cause, it was certainly instrumental in emptying out insane asylums. Today, there are only 80,000 patients, and their average length of stay is two weeks. Antipsychotic drugs make schizophrenic patients less agitated, more manageable, and their symptoms less bizarre. They also produce a number of undesirable side effects. The "deinstitutionalization" of these patients has resulted in relatively little access to medical care for many of them, and a very high proportion of those who lack family or social supports become homeless and live on the street, often neglecting to take their medication. They have been "dumped" there in large part because the society is unwilling to pay for their shelter and an adequate system of halfway houses or treatment facilities that would alleviate the problem of the huge numbers of mentally ill homeless street people.

PERSONAL ACCOUNT: Mental Illness

John is in his early forties and suffers from bipolar depression and schizophrenia, as did his parents and his brother. His father died of cancer when he was a young boy, and his twin brother committed suicide at the age of 22. He takes four different medications to control his *disorder. He has been a college student, on and off, for 27 years. At the end of the semester when he produced this account, he received his bachelor's degree from the University of Maryland. In the interview below, I am identified with the initials, "EG," and he is identified as "John."*

PERSONAL ACCOUNT: Mental Illness (cont.)

EG: Why don't you tell me a little bit about yourself? Now, you told me that you had a certain mental condition. Why don't you explain what that is?

JOHN: Well, I suffer from depression. Bipolar depression. And also, I'm schizoid-affective, which is an emotional disorder that affects the brain. I have emotional problems.

EG: How often have you been institutionalized?

JOHN: The most I've been in one place has been for six months. [Mentions the institution.] I've been in [mentions the institution] 10 times or so and the VA hospital about 10 times over the past 20 years.

EG: First of all, how does this condition manifest itself? What do you do that's different from a so-called normal person that led psychiatrists to diagnose you?

JOHN: Well, I can't put up with a lot of stress, for one thing. That's why I've only taken one or two courses in college for years now, because going to college full-time would be putting too much pressure on me.

EG: Now, when you say you can't put up with stress, what do you do? What stresses you out and what do you do if you do suffer from stress? [Long pause, then John mouths the words, "Turn that off." After I do, he explains that he isn't sure what I mean and that he doesn't want to waste the tape because of his long pauses. I explain that it's OK, that he doesn't have to worry, he can take his time, tape is cheap, there's no pressure of any kind, he should just say whatever's on his mind.] What I mean is, what is it that stresses you out? When you say you suffer from stress, there must be something that *causes* you to feel stress. Is it, as you say, too many courses? What else? What would cause you to feel stressed out?

JOHN: Well, if I'm having emotional problems or dealing with emotions during the daytime, I have a tendency to stress *myself* out, to make myself stressful. I *worry* about something. I hope I'm making that clear.

EG: Well, what do you *do* and how do you *feel* when you feel stressed out?

JOHN: Well, what I do is I start to have a panic attack. I have to call somebody, just to let them know that I'm having that problem, and they help me over the telephone. My counselor. Over the telephone. [Silence. Groping for a response. He looks at me.]

EG: That's OK. There's no pressure in this interview at all. I mean, we can wipe out the tape, we can record it with long periods of silence, you can think about things. I mean, this is not an exam, it's not a quiz. I mean, this is just two people talking about something.

JOHN: I just want to make sure that I'm giving enough information.

EG: Don't worry about it. It doesn't matter. Listen, I've conducted a lot of interviews which haven't worked out. The last three interviews I've done didn't work out. It's no big deal. [I explain why.]

JOHN: I hope I say the right things.

EG: There's no right things. There's only what you think and what you feel and what you've done. So, there's no pressure. You don't have to worry about me wasting the tape. There's *nothing*. It's just two people talking, that's all. You should just feel calm and relaxed and not nervous or pressured.

John [Laughs.] OK. Thank you, Dr. Goode.

EG: OK, now, I'm interested in the way you experience your episodes. What do you go through, how do you feel, what causes you and the people around you to be concerned about your condition?

JOHN: My thoughts become scrambled. And I feel that my mind is moving all the time. Racing. I can't concentrate on anything. Now, my mind is clear because I'm on medication. I can read, I can do anything. But when I'm off my medication, my thinking deteriorates into scrambled thoughts and delusions and psychotic behavior.

EG: What sorts of delusions did you have?

Personal Account: Mental Illness (cont.)

JOHN: Well, I had one delusion that I committed the unpardonable sin. And it seemed so real and everything.

  EG: What's the unpardonable sin?

JOHN: Well, according to the Bible, the unpardonable sin is not wanting to be pardoned [for committing a sin]. When I have delusions of psychotic behavior, it has a lot to do with my religion. About the Second Coming and everything like that. And I'm in the middle of the universe to the point where I determine the world's destiny. Whatever I do would affect the world. For example, I was born illegitimate. And Jesus Christ was born illegitimate [in the sense that, according to Christian theology, Jesus had no earthly father]. So I thought I was representative of him. And, um, what was I going to say?

  EG: The religious delusions you had.

JOHN: Oh, yes, and my brother. My brother was named Eugene and I'm named John. And his name starts with an "E" and mine starts with a "J." And my brother was real masculine and haughty and arrogant, and I was sensitive, and sweet, and kind. I have a sensitive heart. And so, therefore, I thought we were representative of Esau and Jacob. And, you know, in the Bible, Esau had lost his inheritance to Jacob. And Jacob was real kind and compassionate, he was the momma's boy, if I may say so [laughs]. And Esau was real hairy and real masculine, so to speak.

  EG: I'm very interested in your religious beliefs because you say that this figures into your condition.

JOHN: Well, I've been raised a Seventh Day Adventist since I was in the third grade. I went to their schools until I got out of high school. You want to know what our [religious] beliefs are?

  EG: What *your* beliefs are. You know, what you believe in. Because you mentioned that they kind of figured into your delusions.

JOHN: There's this verse in the Bible that says, "Be ye perfect, even as my father in heaven is perfect." That's what it says. And so our church believes, and I've always believed this. Because I always compare myself in this way, that we had to stop sinning in order to go to heaven. . . . When I was sick, I felt that I was the *cause* of the world's sin. In other words, I thought that I was the Devil. I thought that I was the original serpent that was in the Garden of Eden. In fact, I felt that way so much that my tongue kept on constricting. I felt like I was turning into a serpent. Actually, I know that's crazy. It probably is [laughs]. But when I was ill, I thought that the whole world was standing by to see if I could meet this perfectionist standard. And that I would become the Son of God if I did this, so the world was waiting for me to make my decision. And all eternity, and the world's destiny, was waiting on me.

EG: You mentioned before that you sometimes feel pressure. That sounds like something that would cause you to feel a *great* deal of pressure. I mean, what could be more pressure-filled than that?

JOHN: Yeah [laughs]. That's even worse than running for president.

  EG: That's very interesting.

JOHN: Am I answering your questions all right?

  EG: Fine, fine.

JOHN: Am I giving you enough information?

  EG: Definitely, yeah. Basically, I'm interested in what you went through, in your experiences, and how you felt about them.

JOHN: I felt [when I was experiencing my psychotic episodes] like I was being cut off from God. There's no worse feeling than to feel like you're in a living hell.

  EG: I understand.

JOHN: The reason why I've had such grandiose ideas of myself is because my grandmother's father was a politician, he ran for Congress in the 1930s. Our family seemed to just fall apart throughout the generations. My grandmother kind of feels responsible [for that decline]

PERSONAL ACCOUNT: Mental Illness (cont.)

because all she did as the daughter of a politician, she would party all night long and everything. She seduced my grandfather and got him kicked out of the Naval Academy. So throughout three generations down, my grandmother's father was a politician and her brother was a big businessman. And now we're on welfare.

EG: OK, why don't we go back to when you were growing up.

JOHN: My father died of cancer in '64 and my mother was mentally ill; she was hospitalized. I lived with this family in Florida that the state of West Virginia gave me over to. I lived with these foster parents for about 10 years. And they were very abusive. They used to beat me and everything. Yeah. In fact, we used to have to carry blocks, cinder blocks full of cement that they would use to make bins in their garden on their farm. And we had to carry those when we were 10 years old and we had to load them into a truck, and if we didn't throw them fast enough, my foster mother would hit me across the back with a belt. They made me a slave.

EG: When you say, "we," you mean you and your brother?

JOHN: Yeah. And their kids, too. They moved to Missouri. They didn't want me to live with them, so I went to a high school in a boarding academy in West Virginia. When I left the school, I moved to a nearby city in the state. But I was only 17 and I was considered underage, which was unlawful in West Virginia, so I was sent to a juvenile home. I wrote a letter to one of my former teachers who had moved to Texas. He talked to the authorities in West Virginia, and they decided to fly me to Texas.

EG: When did you have your first episode?

JOHN: When I was 17. I used to worry about my mental illness because my whole family was mentally ill. My father and mother met in a mental institution. . . . And my grandmother was institutionalized for 10 years. My mother was in for two years. And I worried about it.

Because my mind was real scrambled with thoughts so I couldn't study or concentrate or even face reality. I knew there was a chemical substance in my brain, that there was something chemically wrong with me because I would sometimes walk down the hallway and I'd have to hang onto a railing, just to keep from tripping over. My mind was preoccupied with my mental illness.

EG: OK, you said you had "scrambled" thoughts. What happened then? I mean, how did somebody *notice* your condition?

JOHN: How did I first get to see a mental health worker?

EG: Exactly.

JOHN: Yeah. When I was 17 and living in [a small city in Texas], I was living with a teacher I knew in West Virginia. But at the time, my brother was living with these people from West Virginia I told you about, the mother with the belt, and they were living in Missouri. So when he was 17, he got $70 rounded up and he flew into Georgia, where he had some friends, and lived in this abandoned shack and hitchhiked to work at a gas station. And four years later, he had a brand-new trailer paid off, a brand-new car paid off, and $10,000 in the bank. I mean, he was really *strong*.

EG: OK, now, what was your life like at the time? What brought on your first breakdown?

JOHN: I was having an affair with this bad woman in Texas. And everybody knew about it. . . . I didn't know what I was doing—I was just a teenager. But also I had this nursing teacher, she took an interest in me for nursing school. She was an older lady. And she would let me come over to her house and study. The first semester [of community college], I completely dropped out. And the second semester, I was so scrambled with my thoughts, I wasn't even paying attention to what I was supposed to read, not even to read the syllabus.

EG: Why do you say the woman you had the affair with was bad?

JOHN: Well, she was the town prostitute. And also because she hurt me real bad, where I had to have shock treatments by the time it was all over. I was in a lot of pain, I felt like my veins were in pain. And I felt my legs were on fire and everything. I had to have shock treatments to get rid of that memory of that experience.

EG: How did she hurt you?

JOHN: Well, she hurt me by putting me in the hospital.

EG: But what did she *do* to hurt you? What was it that she actually *did*?

JOHN: Well, she had the affair, like, this was her life, she—I found this out later—her life was to get boys to have sex with her for a certain amount of time, a few months, and then she would break it off with them. And then she says, "I don't want to see you any more. I have a piece of you and you have a piece of me." Yeah, she broke it off with me. I landed in the hospital. But the first time I ever came in touch with a mental health official is this nursing teacher I was telling you about. She said, "Look, you better leave that woman alone so you can have a job next week. . . . You better study, and study hard, because there's not going to be enough jobs for the uneducated." And that scared me *so bad*. I went back to my dorm room, and the next morning, I was taking a walk, with my mind scrambled. And then my mind started *racing*. Real fast thoughts. And then I thought that I had ruined the whole system. You know, and ruined my college career, and that I wouldn't be able to have a job any more. So I climbed to the top of this building, this hospital building, and tried to jump off. And they rescued me and they put me in jail. But when they put me in jail, they just gave me back to the couple I was living with. And he [the husband] was a homosexual, he was a predator of boys. He was like that woman [I had an affair with] except that he was hurting people because he was a homosexual [not a heterosexual].

EG: Did he make a move on you?

JOHN: Yeah. Uh-huh. He crawled into bed with me one night. The night I tried to jump off that building. When I got out of jail, they took me to this person, this man and his family, and then they took me to a mental health clinic and they started giving me medications. But it didn't work out because I told my mother on the phone what he did and he overheard me and so he threw me out on the street. So I moved to my aunt's house. And it happened again. My mind was racing. And I don't even remember some of the things I did. I just went berserk, they said, and I don't even remember that. . . . So they had to put me in a hospital, a state hospital. That's when I started having pains around my veins. . . . It was really a very bad physical pain. And they had to give me shock treatments. But after I got out, and I lived in my aunt's house in North Carolina, my uncle was really mean to me because I kept sleeping a lot. I was so depressed that I would try to fall asleep and keep my eyes closed even during the day, just to escape from my thoughts and my world. So my uncle kicked me out of the house, and that's when I joined the Army.

EG: How long did you serve?

JOHN: Actually, it was a three-year term, but I only served nine months. It was because they realized that I had a mental disorder before I joined the Army and they said I wasn't eligible to serve in the Army. Actually, my condition was OK at the time when they discharged me, but they said I wasn't eligible to join to begin with, so it was an erroneous enlistment, is what they called it. And so they discharged me. Even though it was an honorable discharge. But I still get my benefits because I had been in the Army more than six months. I served in [a facility near Washington, DC].

EG: So what did you do then?

JOHN: Well, I left the Army and I got a room in Maryland. I wanted to stay in this area. I got

PERSONAL ACCOUNT: Mental Illness (cont.)

a room. . . . [Long pause. He asks me to turn the tape-recorder off, mouthing the words, "I don't know what to say." I reassure him that periods of silence, when he's collecting his thoughts, are OK.] It was for $100 a month. It had a kitchenette and a room and it was carpeted and everything. And so I went downtown to the unemployment office and looked for a clerk-typist's job, which is what I was doing in the Army, and I found a job at [a major corporation]. I was a clerk-typist for a year.

EG: Did you have any episodes during that time?

JOHN: No, I didn't. I wasn't even taking any medication or anything. I wasn't even seeing a psychiatrist.

EG: So what led to your getting Social Security benefits and being put on medication?

JOHN: My brother committed suicide. He was only 22 years old.

EG: Wow!

JOHN: This was 20 years ago. Yeah. This set me back about 20 years.

EG: I can imagine.

JOHN: I got real sick. When that happened, I was in college. I had to drop out of college. Actually, when it happened, it happened in the middle of the semester. And I don't know how I did it, but I finished the semester with a 2.5 average. But after the finals were done, I went home, I lay in bed, I got real sick, and I went catatonic. They sent the emergency team to my room. . . . I could *hear* them talking to me, they were yelling at me, talking to me, trying to get me to talk, but I couldn't talk at all. They sent me to the VA hospital. They had me tied down to the bed and everything. Because I was a danger to myself. I was just completely psychotic. I began hitting people, hitting the nurses.

EG: Do you have any memory of that?

JOHN: I have a memory of pulling one nurse's hair. [Laughs.] I'm not a violent person, it's just

that I went berserk. I thought I was going to go to hell. The feelings I had felt so real.

EG: So how long were you hospitalized for that time?

JOHN: I was in that hospital for the rest of that year, 1980. From when I got out of school in May till December, around Christmas time. When I got out, I was really in bad shape, still. In fact, I didn't shave for weeks, I wouldn't take a shower or a bath. [Long pause. Mouths the words, "I don't know what to say."]

EG: That's OK. That's all right. Then what happened?

JOHN: When I got out of the hospital, I had no place to go to. I became homeless. So I broke into this friend's house while she was on vacation. And she came home from vacation and saw me in her bed, and I was sleeping. And I didn't know what to do. She wasn't mad at me or anything. But she said I couldn't stay. And so another friend of mine called her sister and brother-in-law and asked them to take me in for one month, because that's all they could allow in the apartment. They had rules. So I stayed with them. They were the last people who let me stay under their roof. And they let me in. During that month, I looked for a room and I found a room. And my social worker had applied for welfare for me. So I got welfare. It was about $250 a month. And the room was about $125 a month. I had applied for Social Security disability before, in May, before I went into the hospital. Social Security checks for the disabled. And I was approved in December 1980. That gave me $300 a month. So that helped. It's not a whole lot, but I was able to live if I was careful with my money. Just like I am now. Right now, I live on about $672 a month. The Social Security disability check has increased from $300 in 1980 till now, which is $672. Doubled over time.

EG: Well, I'm sure this apartment costs more than $672 a month.

PERSONAL ACCOUNT: Mental Illness (cont.)

JOHN: That's right. I have subsidized housing. The place only costs me $189 a month. So I'm really fortunate. A bad thing happened to me, but it turned into a good thing, because I'm able to go to school with all this help from the government. There are some people who haven't even had any tragedies or anything and had a good life and they're not able to go to school because it's just too expensive. So I'm really fortunate. I'm really grateful to the American taxpayer. [Laughs.]

EG: You mentioned that sometimes you stopped taking your medication.

JOHN: As far as medication [is concerned], in the past, I was given medication, but I would buck the system and not take my medicine. And I wouldn't cooperate with the psychiatrists because I thought I was too good to be sick.

EG: What medication are you taking now?

JOHN: Norpramin, which is for depression [and attention deficit disorder]; Haldol, which is an antipsychotic—which is a terrific medicine for me, it really clears up my mind; Zoloft, which is an antidepressant also; and Risperdal [also an antipsychotic], which helps my mood. Before, I was taking medications, but I was being real careless about it. I had been to several psychiatrists, but none of them seemed to be helpful to me. 'Course, I probably wasn't being helpful by not taking my medicine. It's like I told my girlfriend, I said, "the only time the medicine works for me is when I'm in the hospital." And she said, "Dodo, you're supposed to be taking your medicine when you're *out* of the hospital, too. If you're not taking it, that's why it's not working." But in 1992, I found this very good psychiatrist and she gave me Haldol, and that really cleared up my thinking. My mind feels real clear right now. I don't feel any illness. I don't feel as if my mind is scrambled or racing or anything.

EG: Are you still seeing the girlfriend?

JOHN: Yes. She's a very comforting person. She's obsessive-compulsive herself. We met in a hospital. We see each other about once a week.

We talk on the phone every day. She lives a few miles from here. She has her own apartment. She lived with her mother until she was around 30. Now she has a subsidized apartment that she applied for. And she seems to be doing very well now. She has more cushion than I did. 'Cause I didn't have a family. If she got sick or something, she had her mother, and her aunt, and her family to support her. I was on my own, I was just a one-man band. I've always been independent. I mean, even though I had all of that happen to me, I still managed to survive and keep a place of my own.

EG: Tell me about your college career.

JOHN: I've been a [college] student off and on for 27 years. I started in Texas, like I told you, in '75. Since that time, I've been either in a hospital, or got a job, or went into the Army. And I kept dropping out of college, at first, all the time. I would keep going back and keep fighting. At [the large state university he attends], I went back to school after my brother died, a couple years later. I took a full-time load and I had to drop out because there was too much pressure. I did that three times, three different semesters, and I had to withdraw each of those semesters because it was just too much for me. Even though I was passing the courses when I withdrew, because it was just too much pressure. So I said, look, I'm not getting anywhere this way. I left [the state university] and went to [a local community college] and took one course at a time for 11 years and got my associate's degree. I graduated with a degree in general studies, and then I came back here in 1997.

EG: You take one course a semester?

JOHN: No, I've been taking two now, because I have to get financial aid. I didn't get financial aid at [the community college] because the courses were free for the disabled. At the end of this semester, I will graduate with a BA in political science. Then I think I want to look for a part-time job.

QUESTIONS

Do you feel that it is fair to refer to John's condition as a form of deviance? Many critics of psychotropic drugs feel that mental patients are being "overmedicated." Do you believe this is true in John's case? What do you think is the cause of mental disorder? Does each of the many disorders listed in the *Diagnostic and Statistical Manual* have its own etiology or cause? Do you think that, one day in the future, researchers will locate a gene for each disorder and make all of them a thing of the past? Or is mental disorder a permanent fixture in the human condition? What would constructionists say about John's life and his condition? Is defining mental illness simply a matter of perception, judgment, and social reaction? Is there a common thread to all clinical depression and schizophrenia, worldwide and throughout human history? If John did not receive a government subsidy to enable him to live, what would become of him? What is your opinion of certain politicians' attempting to cut or eliminate programs that support people with conditions like John's?

CHAPTER 12

Physical Characteristics as Deviance

Photo by Jared Leeds © 2004.

Whoever he be . . . that hath any blemish, let him not approach to offer the bread of his God. For whatsoever man he be that hath a blemish, he shall not approach [the altar]: a blind man, a lame, or he that hath a flat nose, or any thing superfluous, or a man that is brokenfooted or brokenhanded, or crookbacked, or a dwarf, or that hath a blemish in his eye, or be scurvy, or scabbed. . . . No man that hath a blemish . . . shall come nigh to offer the bread of his God. . . . [He] shall not go unto the veil, nor come nigh unto the altar, because he hath a blemish; that he profane not my sanctuaries: for I the Lord do sanctify them. (Leviticus 21:17–23)

Judge not according to the appearance. (John 7:24)

Can undesirable physical characteristics be regarded as a form of deviance? In Chapter 1, I've already answered that question in the affirmative. But here, let's discuss the matter in more detail, laying out my rationale for this position. In 1963, sociologist Erving Goffman published one of the most influential and widely read books in the field of deviance—indeed, in sociology generally—*Stigma*. Subtitled "Notes on the Management of Spoiled Identity," Goffman's book focuses on the *grading system* of stigma based on behavior, belief, and physical characteristics. Stigma is the manifestation or outward appearance of an inner deficiency, one that either *has been* or *may be* noticed, that results or would result in *infamy* and *dishonor*. Clearly, deviance and stigma are closely related concepts; in fact, the parallels between them are so strong it is difficult to distinguish them.

Someone who has been stigmatized, Goffman writes, is "a blemished person," a person who is "disqualified from full social acceptance" (p. 1). We realize, he says, that such a person is "different from others. . . , reduced in our minds from a whole and usual person to a tainted, discounted one" (p. 3). In short, "the person with a stigma is not quite human" (p. 5).

A stigmatizing trait is rarely isolated. Hardly anyone who possesses such a characteristic is thought to have only one. A single sin will be regarded as housing a multitude of other sins—to be only the tip of the iceberg. The one stigmatizing trait that is known about is presumed to hide "a wide range of imperfections" (Goffman, 1963,

p. 5). To be guilty of one sin automatically means to be thought of as being guilty of a host of others along with it. The one negative trait is a *master trait* or a master status. Everything about the person is interpreted in light of the single trait, status, or characteristic. "Possession of one deviant trait may have a generalized symbolic value, so that people automatically assume that its bearer possesses other undesirable traits allegedly associated with it." Thus, the question is raised when confronting someone with a stigma: "What kind of person would break such an important rule?" (That is, the violation of which elicits stigma.) The answer that is offered is typically: "One who is different from the rest of us, who cannot or will not act as a moral human being and therefore might break other important rules." In short, the stigmatizing characteristic "becomes the controlling one" (Becker, 1963, pp. 33, 34).

To be stigmatized is to possess a *contaminated* or *discredited* identity. Interaction with "normals"—Goffman's term for nonstigmatized persons—will be strained, tainted, awkward, inhibited. While "normals" may, because of the dictates of polite sociability, attempt to hide their negative feelings toward the stigmatized trait or person, they remain, nonetheless, acutely aware of the other's blemish. Likewise, the stigmatized person remains self-conscious about his or her relations with "normals," believing (often correctly) that the stigma is the exclusive focus of the interaction:

> I am always worried about how Jane judges me because she is a real beauty queen and the main gang leader. When I am with her, I hold my breath hard so my tummy doesn't bulge and I pull my skirt down so my fat thighs don't show. I tuck in my rear end. I try to look as thin as possible for her. I get so preoccupied with looking good enough to get into her gang that I forget what she's talking to me about. . . . I am so worried about how my body is going over that I can hardly concentrate on what she's saying. She asks me about math and all I am thinking about is how fat I am. (Allon, 1976, p. 18)

Highly stigmatized persons walk along two possible paths.

One is to *resist* or *reject* their stigmatized status by forming subcultures or collectivities of persons who share their characteristic, and to treat their difference from the majority as a badge of honor—or at least, no cause for shame. The homosexual subculture provides an example of this path: Most homosexuals feel that mainstream society is wrong in denigrating homosexuality, that its judgment of them as tainted is invalid, illegitimate, just plain wrong. Here, the very legitimacy of the stigma—the very basis or foundation for the judgment—is rejected.

The second path the stigmatized may take is *internalization*. Here, stigmatized persons hold the same negative feelings toward themselves and their disvalued trait as the majority does. They are dominated by feelings of self-hatred and self-derogation. In these cases, persons who are put down are made to feel they deserve it; they come to accept their negative treatment as just; they feel that the majority has a *right* to stigmatize them for what they are or do.

Goffman distinguishes stigma that manifests itself in physical characteristics from stigma that appears as violations of notions of proper behavior and belief. He refers to physical stigma as "abominations of the body—the various physical deformities" (p. 4). Goffman refers to behavior and belief as "blemishes of individual character perceived as weak will, domineering or unnatural passions, treacherous and rigid beliefs, and dishonesty, these being inferred from a known record of, for example, mental disorder, imprisonment, addiction, alcoholism, homosexuality, unemployment, suicidal attempts, and radical political behavior" (p. 4). Goffman also delineated a third type of stigma, "tribal stigma of race, nation, and religion," which is rarely discussed as a form of deviance.

As I said earlier, ironically, Goffman was skeptical about the utility of the concept of deviance: "I do not think all deviators have enough in common to warrant a special analysis," he declared; "they differ in many more ways than they are similar" (1963, p. 141). Of course, as I've already pointed out, this is true of almost every other sociological concept, including stigma itself. It's also possible that Goffman did not have the same definition of "deviators" that we have of "persons who violate an important norm." He certainly did not mean by "deviators" what we mean by "deviants." No matter; what's important here is that we understand how physical characteristics qualify as a form of deviance.

In distinguishing his own perspective on deviance from that of Goffman, Ned Polsky argues that Goffman missed the fact that he and some other sociologists excluded from their definition of deviance "people who were not *morally* stigmatized; that is, we excluded from our definition (and our courses on the sociology of deviance) various kinds of people, such as those unusually ugly according to society's current standards of physical attractiveness, who might indeed be stigmatized (by, for example, being avoided socially or joked about and discriminated against in employment) but whose condition is recognized to be 'not their fault' " (1998, pp. 202–203).

Clearly, Polsky is wrong about this. *Many* negative definitions of statuses may be entirely unearned. Is the child born out of wedlock (at one time, referred to as a "bastard") responsible for his or her status? Obviously not. In the past, was he or she stigmatized? Of course. (Today, far less so than was true in the past.) Was he or she regarded as *a deviant*? Certainly. But the moral infamy from which he or she suffered did not reside in behavior he or she enacted; we have to look to the parents, not the child, for that behavior. In this chapter, I intend to indicate my strong disagreement with Polsky's position on physical characteristics as deviance. I do *not* exclude from my definition of deviance physical characteristics. Clearly, people who possess traits or characteristics that are "not their fault" *are* stigmatized and *are* treated differently—in a pejorative, derogatory, or downputting fashion—by persons who are not similarly blemished. (Goffman refers to nonstigmatized people as "normals.") In fact, the very concept, "not their fault," is not as simple as Polsky implies.

Two considerations are crucial to categorizing physical characteristics: one, their social valuation, that is, whether they are deemed good or bad; and two, whether they are acquired voluntarily or involuntarily. The acquisition of certain physical traits or characteristics that are widely regarded as undesirable is not always entirely involuntary. Some are chosen outright: tattoos, for example. And some actually are the result of engaging in risky—including deviant—behavior, for example, sexually transmitted diseases. But whether observers take note of this connection is partly a matter of interpretation, a social construction. Someone may have become paralyzed as a result of a skiing or a motorcycle accident—that is, as a result of engaging in behavior that entails a certain measure of risk—but very few of us will say that they are *responsible* for their condition. Persons who do so will be charged with "blaming the victim." But the fact is, engaging in risky behavior *is* causally related to the possession of certain undesirable physical conditions. However, "cause" and "blame" are distinct and separate notions (Felson, 1991); causality is a scientific notion, while blame is a *moral* one. And it is blame, not cause, that is intricately intertwined with condemnation, deviance, and stigma.

For instance, most (although far from all) persons infected with AIDS received the virus as a result of unprotected, high-risk sex, often anal intercourse, or through intravenous illicit drug use. Many observers believe it is unfair to blame AIDS sufferers for their plight—and I agree with this assessment—but the fact is, much of the public *does* hold this condemnatory attitude. Somehow, many people feel, AIDS sufferers *are* responsible for their plight. Early in the AIDS epidemic, fundamentalist Christian spokespersons claimed that the disease was God's retribution for engaging in wicked behavior. In 1995, Jesse Helms, then Republican senator from North Carolina, declared that the federal government should reduce funding for AIDS treatment because persons who contracted the virus did so as a result of their own "deliberate, disgusting, revolting conduct" (Seelye, 1995). In making this statement, Senator Helms—a staunch and vigorous supporter of the tobacco industry—ignored the fact that cigarettes claim many more victims than AIDS—moreover, as a result of smokers' "deliberate" behavior. (During the last year or two of his final term in office, Helms reversed himself and adopted a more compassionate stance toward AIDS victims; he has endorsed the use of public funds for treating and curing the disease.) The point is, seeing a connection between "deliberate" behavior and possessing a physical trait is a cultural and constructed phenomenon, not a simple factual matter. Some physical conditions are deemed more-or-less entirely a product of the possessor's own behavior. We have the example of obesity, to be discussed in a later section. Negative attitudes toward the obese are related to the belief that they are fat because they are gluttonous and self-indulgent—they are lazy and they eat too much; most people believe that the obese "could control their weight if they really wanted to" (Katz, 1981, p. 4).

Here, then, are a few possible routes to how a person comes by certain physical traits or characteristics. One, these traits are inborn, a result of the genetic roll of the dice; in this category we have dwarfism. Two, they are a product of accident or disease, whether in the womb or after birth—for instance, most forms of blindness. Three, they are inflicted as a result of the actor's risky behavior—for instance, the smoker's lung cancer, the addict's AIDS, the skydiver's broken neck. Four, they are acquired after birth as a result of culturally mandated norms—for instance, the Maori's tattoos. And lastly, they may be acquired after birth by being completely chosen by the person who possesses them—for instance, tattoos in Western culture, various forms of body-piercing or alteration, or shaving or dyeing one's hair into unconventional forms, colors, or patterns.

In most non-Western societies, the view that undesirable physical traits are a punishment for wicked behavior is even stronger than it is in the West. In many societies around the world, certain physical traits are seen as a retribution from God, or the gods, or whatever entity is responsible for such matters. Or as punishment for what one did in a former life. Or perhaps as punishment for what one's parents did. In any case, it is a consequence of a moral failing of some kind. For instance, among ultra-Orthodox Jews, the Haredim, it is commonly believed that if a woman does not perform a monthly ritual to cleanse herself after menstruation, she may bear children with birth defects. In 1993, I spent an academic semester in Israel. Some members of the haredi community argued that a recent school bus crash, which killed several children, was caused by improperly inscribed biblical verses that had been placed in the mezuzah, the tiny case that holds passages from Deuteronomy, attached to the school's doorway. Such beliefs are alien to science and what we in the West like to refer to as rational thought, but they are common around the world, including sectors of the United States.

ABOMINATIONS OF THE BODY: AN INTRODUCTION

In earlier eras, babies born with serious deformities were referred to as "monsters." Their appearance was regarded as an evil omen, a sign of divine retribution, a prediction of disasters and epidemics to come. In fact, the word "monster" derives from the Latin verb *monere*, which means "to warn," "to predict," or "to foretell." Throughout ancient times, many deformed children were killed or exposed to the elements and left to die. A number of Roman authors, including Cicero and Tacitus, describe the drowning or burning of deformed children, an effort to propitiate the gods. The ancient Greeks, likewise, usually put to death children with undesirable characteristics, less out of fear of the wrath of the gods than because they were ruled by an ethic that was strongly oriented to physical perfection. Aristotle opposed the feeding of handicapped children. Plato wrote: "Deformed and infirm children should be hidden away in a secret place." The ancient Assyrians believed that if a woman gave birth to a disabled child, her house would be destroyed; if a woman gives birth to twins joined at the spine, "the gods will forsake the people and the king will abdicate his throne" (Monestier, 1987, p. 13).

In the European Middle Ages, for the most part, Christianity attributed all "unexplained natural phenomena" either to God or the devil. And, medieval theologians reasoned, if God created man in His own image, monsters—who were clearly *not* in God's image—had to be created by the hand of Satan. Hence, the hunchback "bore the weight of a horrible curse on his back"; the blind baby's eyes "had surely been seared by the red-hot coals of Hell"; the "mute baby's tongue had doubtless been wrenched from his head by infernal tongs"; the deaf child "was thought to be receptive only to the murmurings of the Beast, and unable to hear the teachings of men of God" (Monestier, 1987, p. 13). In the Middle Ages, the deformed and disabled suf-

fered most distinctly from Goffman's "abominations of the body." Even today, although far less severely, and less specifically because of satanic intervention, they do so as well.

"Abominations of the body": What does Goffman mean by this term?

Two distinctly different types of physical deviance come to mind: *violations of aesthetic norms* and *physical incapacity*.

Aesthetic norms represent standards that dictate how people ought to *look*: their height, weight, attractiveness, coloration, the possession of the requisite limbs and organs (and no more), the absence of disfigurement, the absence or presence of specific more-or-less permanent body adornment or alteration (scarification, tattoos, lip plugs, elongation of the earlobes, and so on). For instance, the skin and hair of albinos lack pigmentation. In nearly all societies on earth, albinos are stigmatized, treated as "blemished," "tainted," "spoiled"; they are "disqualified from full social acceptance." Likewise, dwarfs and midgets, hermaphrodites (people born with sexual characteristics of both males and females), and persons who are extremely ugly by society's standards are treated as less than fully human. Some physical characteristics judged aesthetically deficient are present at or before birth, while others come about as a result of environmental alterations, whether self-imposed, because of accident or disease, or intentionally inflicted by another person.

The second category of bodily "abomination," physical incapacity, is made up of bodily impairments that limit one's ability to perform certain activities considered important, such as walking, seeing, and hearing. Of course, all of us are limited in our ability to perform a number of activities. Most of us are too short, or simply can't jump high enough, to slam-dunk a basketball, or too slow to run a four-minute mile. But walking, seeing, and hearing are regarded as so crucial to everyday life that persons who lack the ability to perform these functions are treated differently, and distinctly negatively, from those who possess them. Once again, some of these characteristics were present at birth, while others were acquired at some later point in time. For instance, blindness may be the result of a genetic condition or may result from an accident at any age during one's lifetime.

PHYSICAL DISABILITY

According to Eliot Freidson (1966), the possession of a physical disability or handicap is a form of deviance. This is so because it represents an imputation of undesirable difference that sets the disabled or handicapped off from the segment of the population Goffman (1963) referred to as "normals." A person so designated departs or deviates from what he or she and/or others *believe to be normal or appropriate.* It is "normal" or "appropriate" to be able to see, walk, and hear. Not to be able to do so represents an undesirable departure from what is regarded as "normal." Put another way, deviance is not merely statistical variation or difference from the average, the mode, or the statistical norm. Rather, it is that which "violates institutional expectations" (Cohen, 1959, p. 462). We are *expected* to be able to see, walk, and hear. When we are not able to do so, we violate the norms—the "institutional expectations" that others have of our performance. In recent years, a variety of euphemistic and politically correct terms have been applied to the physically handicapped—such as "differently abled"—the reasoning being that plain, straightforward, descriptive terms stigmatize persons to whom the terms apply. Simi Linton (1998, p. 14), a disabled spokesperson, refers to such terms as "nice words," "well-meaning attempts to inflate the value of people with disabilities," which are "rarely used by disabled activists and scholars (except with palpable irony)." Many deaf militants reject the label "disabled" and claim membership in the deaf culture. But the fact is, the norms in this society do call for certain kinds of performance, and persons who are unable to meet those norms are looked down upon in one way or another.

When such violations are in a significant and important sphere of life and are "persistent," persons guilty of them are "assigned a special negatively deviant role" (Freidson, 1966, p. 73) and are "generally thought to require the attention of social control agencies" (Erikson, 1964, pp. 10–11). Social agencies that work with the physically disabled and handicapped distinguish between those who cooperate and work at ameliorating their condition—who, for instance, play the role of the "good" amputee—as opposed to those

who are uncooperative and do not work toward rehabilitation (Freidson, 1966, p. 81). What these agencies hold out is not an exit from the disabled role—indeed, even after their intervention, those who are rehabilitated by them will still occupy the status and play the role of handicapped person—but an *accommodation to* that role. In other words, the "handicapped *remain* deviant, and the task of rehabilitation is to shape the form of their deviance, which is quite a different task than that of healing the sick or punishing or salvaging the delinquent" (p. 95). In the words of Erving Goffman: "The stigmatized individual is asked to act so as to imply neither that his [or her] burden is heavy nor that bearing it has made him [or her] different from us.... A *phantom acceptance* is thus allowed to provide the base for a *phantom normalcy*" (1963, p. 122).

Disability, like behavioral deviance, is socially constructed, "produced," or "created" (Freidson, 1966, p. 83). This does not mean that the *physical conditions* on which judgments of disability are based are "created" by the society. Rather, what it means is that the definition demarcating a given condition *as* a disablement, and judgment that a specific case or person *belongs* to the general category of disablement, are to some degree arbitrary and based on social and cultural criteria. These definitions are created by the agencies that deal with the disabled and by the general public as well. Disability, as with all forms of deviance, is "objectified" or "reified" (p. 83) in that every member who is classified by the category is assumed to possess all of the characteristics the category refers to. Hence, most people who are legally classified as physically "handicapped" can walk, even though the assumption is that they cannot; most people who are legally "blind" can see, even though the assumption is that they cannot. The stereotype held by normals is that the person classified as handicapped will fit the most severely impaired end of the impairment continuum, even though most are in fact at the less severe end of that spectrum (p. 84).

One of the central tasks of the person who possesses a physical handicap and who is widely regarded as disabled is dealing with the nondisabled, that is, with "normals." It is to the benefit of rehabilitation agencies to encourage the fiction that stigma does not exist in the population at large, since this fiction furthers their rehabilitative goals. But the fact is, a stigmatizing attitude of one kind or another toward the disabled is the norm among normals. True, *ambivalence* toward the handicapped is the rule—that is, compassion is mingled with the stigma (Katz, 1981, pp. 5–11). But stigma is there nonetheless. Normals generally reject and avoid the handicapped socially. A "social distance" scale reveals this rejection with crystal clarity. When samples of respondents are asked if they would "accept" persons belonging to various disvalued categories in a range of relationships—as neighbors, as coworkers, as friends—members of none of those categories are accepted, on average, as readily as persons who are normally abled. For instance, when one study asked respondents if they would "accept" members of 22 categories, "every one was rejected to some extent"; cerebral palsy sufferers, epileptics, and paraplegics (along with dwarfs and hunchbacks) were rejected even as next-door neighbors (p. 18). Anecdotal evidence backs up these systematic surveys. "In a host of written and oral accounts [by the handicapped], the theme of being pitied, subordinated, and ignored is expressed again and again" (p. 18). Content analyses of cultural materials, such as jokes, indicate the inferior status of the handicapped. In one study of jokes, the handicapped were made fun of 80 percent of the time, whereas jokes about farmers, dentists, and judges were vastly less likely to be insulting (p. 18). There is a measure of *aversion* toward the disabled, just as there is toward disfigurements, in part because they provoke anxiety in normals, reminding them that they, too, could fall victim to the same misfortune (p. 20). In other words, normals fear the handicapped as much as they pity them.

Things are changing. In 1990, the Americans With Disabilities Act, which guaranteed prohibition against job discrimination and physical access to public spaces, was passed with bipartisan support. In the late 1990s, a substantial number of books adopting the perspective of the disabled—new-style activist researchers who want to change the way things are, most of whom are disabled persons themselves—have been published (Hockenberry, 1995; Thompson, 1996, 1997; Davis, 1997; Mairs, 1997; Mitchell and Snyder, 1997; Linton, 1998; Charlton, 1999;

Fiffer, 1999). In 1997, Mattel introduced a "Barbie" doll friend in a wheelchair. In 1991, Dayton Hudson, an advertising firm, introduced a series of ads using disabled models. In 1992, the muscular dystrophy telethon hosted by comedian Jerry Lewis was protested by critics, including some who were themselves disabled former poster children for the cause, for fostering an image of the disabled as pitiable and childlike. In 1999, a doctoral program in disability studies was introduced at the University of Illinois at Chicago. Given these beginnings, the movement toward demanding acceptance and equality for the disabled is likely to gain momentum during the course of the twenty-first century.

CONFORMITY TO AND VIOLATIONS OF AESTHETIC STANDARDS

Violations of aesthetic standards offer one major type of "abominations of the body." All societies hold their members to certain standards of physical attractiveness. Says Nancy Etcoff, a neuroscientist conducting research on the role of looks in human attraction and author of *Survival of the Prettiest* (1999): "Every culture is a beauty culture. . . . I defy anyone to point to a society anytime in history or any place in the world that wasn't preoccupied with beauty" (Cowley, 1996, p. 62). Moreover, in all societies on earth, there are negative consequences for not measuring up to these standards of beauty. Naturally, these consequences vary from society to society and from one period of history to another; they vary from being an object of teasing to being put to death. Nonetheless, in one way or another, all societies reward the attractive and punish the ugly.

At one time, most anthropologists believed that aesthetic standards were completely arbitrary, that looks judged attractive in one society might be regarded as ugly in another. Most contemporary researchers and scholars reject this radically relativistic view. In fact, the valuation of looks is considerably less variable and relativistic than was once believed. It turns out that there is a fairly substantial measure of agreement in aesthetic standards from one society to another. There is some variability, of course, and it is interesting and significant; we'll be looking at some of the sources of variability in judgments of attractiveness momentarily. The crucial point to keep in mind is that the variation is much less substantial than was believed in the past, and the consensus is probably a great deal more significant than the variation. For the most part, looks that are considered beautiful in one society are regarded as beautiful in societies all over the world; looks that are considered ugly in one society tend to be regarded as ugly in societies the world over. When researchers show photographs of faces of people from all racial categories to subjects from backgrounds as diverse as Greece, China, India, and England, they find a remarkably high level of agreement as to which ones are attractive and which ones are unattractive. The ethnic background of the subjects in these studies makes little or no difference in their judgments.

Skeptics might argue that, as a result of the influence of Western—mainly American— movies, television programs, and magazines, the aesthetic standards that rule in the United States have spread to the inhabitants of every nation on earth. But when Judith Langlois projected images of the faces of "attractive" and "unattractive" persons—males and females, adults and babies, whites and persons of African descent—before three- and six-month-old babies, the same pattern prevailed. These babies "gazed significantly longer" at the "attractive" than at the "unattractive" faces. Says Langlois: "These kids don't read *Vogue* or watch TV.... They haven't been touched by the media. Yet they make the same judgments as adults" (Cowley, 1996, p. 63; Lemley, 2000; Langlois et al., 2000).

What's behind these judgments? Is there something about a face or a body that dictates that we find it attractive? Does the same process take place in reverse for the "unattractive" face? Some psychobiologists think they have the answer: evolution. They believe that many clues point to the possibility that humans are biologically "hardwired" to make specific, distinct, and universal aesthetic judgments.

Some of the rules of aesthetic judgment are commonsensical and not especially mysterious. In nearly all persons, physical good heath is more attractive than illness. "As far as anyone knows," according to Helen Fisher, an anthropologist who studies love, mating, and physical attractiveness, "there isn't a village on earth where skin lesions [sores], head lice, and rotting teeth count as beauty aids" (Cowley, 1996, p. 63). Surprisingly, *symmetry* turns out to be a major factor in determining the physical attractiveness of human faces and bodies—a balance of each side with the other, in equal proportion. (Interestingly, the same principle holds for animals, some of them as lowly as scorpion flies. Females of many species refuse to mate with males who do not display the requisite symmetry.) Other features include, for males: slightly above average height, a broad forehead, prominent brow and cheekbones, a large jaw and strong chin, slightly above average body musculature, and a waist that is 90 percent the measurement of the hips. For females, the features include youth, of course, as well as large eyes; a small nose; delicate jaw; small chin; full lips; firm, symmetrical breasts; smooth, unblemished skin; and a waist-hip ratio of 70 percent (Cowley, 1996, p. 63).

Most evolutionary psychologists believe that these judgments are genetic in origin—that, without realizing it, our bodies are telling us to seek partners who offer the maximum potential to reproduce our own genes in our children and in subsequent generations. Each of these traits, from age to smooth, unblemished skin to the flare of a woman's hips and the jut of a man's jaw, evolutionary psychologists argue are maximally related to fertility and hence, according to their theory, maximum attractiveness. We seek in a potential partner that which tells us that if we mate with him or her, our genetic material stands the highest likelihood of being propagated to later generations. Genes are "selfish"; they seek to reproduce themselves. Seeking out the most attractive available partner is a way of doing that. Our aesthetic judgments are ruled by our selfish genes.

In contrast, most sociologists, anthropologists, and other social scientists argue that it is culture—not our genes—that explains judgments of attractiveness. If judgments of beauty were a biologically "hardwired" phenomenon designed to perpetuate the judge's genes, how do we explain homosexuality? Why do same-sex partners find many of the same physical traits attractive that opposite-sex partners do? Says Micaela di Leonardo, an anthropologist who studies human attractiveness: "People make decisions about sexual and marital partners inside complex networks of friends and relatives. . . . Human beings cannot be reduced to DNA packets" (Cowley, 1996, p. 66).

Regardless of the source or cause of the consistency of aesthetic judgments about human appearance, they are a fact of life. And studies have shown that, just as *conforming* to a society's aesthetic standards is likely to bring forth rewards, *violating* those standards is likely to result in punishment. We "set narrow standards of beauty and then insult and hurt those who fall outside those standards" (Beuf, 1990, p. 1). Is the possession of an unaesthetic appearance the possessor's "fault"? Not usually. Is this punishment unfair? Most decidedly. Is such punishment a reality in the lives of many people who fail to attain the aesthetic ideal? Answering this question is precisely the point of this section.

In a classic study by social psychologist Karen Dion (1972), a sample of college women were asked to read over a teacher's notes describing the behavior of the children in her class. Attached to the notes was a photograph of the child. The notes did not describe a real child or actual behavior; in fact, they were manipulated to describe a fictional incident in which the child hurt a dog or another child in a trivial or a serious way. The photographs, likewise, were manipulated so that they depicted one attractive girl, one unattractive girl, one attractive boy, and one unattractive boy. Members of the sample were asked to evaluate the behavior and the child. Dion hypothesized that physical appearance would make a difference in these evaluations—and it did.

If the child's misbehavior was mild (stepping on a dog's tail), the women in the sample were not influenced by the children's looks. But when the misbehavior was more serious (throwing stones at a dog, causing it to yelp and limp away), for the unattractive children, members of the sample regarded this as a serious character flaw; for the attractive children, the sample of college students tended to be more lenient and indulgent, to give them the benefit of the doubt, passing off their misbehavior as trivial. One student who read the notes and saw the photograph of an attractive girl who had thrown rocks at a dog made these

comments about the girl: "She appears to be a perfectly charming little girl, well-mannered, basically unselfish. It seems that she can adapt well among children her age and make a good impression. . . . She plays well with everyone, but, like everyone else, a bad day can occur. Her cruelty . . . need not be taken too seriously" (Berscheid and Walster, 1972, p. 45).

In contrast, here are the remarks made by another student who is commenting on an unattractive girl who committed exactly the same act: "I think the child would be quite bratty and would be a problem to teachers. . . . She would probably try to pick a fight with other children. . . . She would be a brat at home. . . . All in all, she would be a real problem" (p. 45). In addition to giving different evaluations of attractive and unattractive children and of their behavior, these respondents expressed expectations that the unattractive ones would be likelier to commit similar transgressions in the future. In short, the attribution of deviance is closely tied into looks: Other things being equal, unattractive people are more likely to be suspected of engaging in wrongdoing, more likely to be evaluated negatively, and more likely to be punished.

The fact is, "uglier people are assigned all kinds of undesirable qualities. They are expected to do evil things, and their misdeeds are judged as more wicked than if the same thing was done by a better looking wrongdoer" (Jones et al., 1984, p. 53). An enormous number of studies have confirmed the impact of looks on how we are treated by others. After they have met them, people are more likely to forget about less attractive people than those who are more attractive; work done by less attractive people is evaluated more negatively than work done by more attractive people; people tend to work less hard for unattractive people than for attractive people; and something that is lost is less likely to be returned if the owner is physically unappealing (p. 53). As a result of this differential treatment, less attractive people tend to have a lower sense of self-esteem and to have less satisfactory relations with peers (p. 54). In sum, then, "ugly or physically deviant people are clearly disadvantaged both by the immediate negative effect they elicit and by the longer term cumulative consequences of coping with the avoidant and rejecting behavior of others" (p. 56).

At the age of nine, Lucy Grealy was diagnosed with cancer. To save her life, surgeons removed a third of her jaw. After the operation, when she looked in the mirror, Lucy realized she was different. She endured 30 separate operations, most of them to reconstruct her jaw so that she would look normal. The boys in her school taunted her cruelly. "Hey, girl, take off that monster mask—oops, she's not wearing a monster mask," shouted one (Grealy, 1995, p. 118). "*What* on earth is *that*?" yelled another (p. 124). "*That* is the ugliest girl I have *ever* seen," declared a third (p. 124). The taunts, which were especially frequent during lunch period, became so painful for Lucy that, in the seventh grade, she went to her guidance counselor to complain. Rather than reprimand the children who hurled them, he asked if she wanted to eat lunch in his office, an offer she decided to accept.

All societies value beauty. Hence, "the person whose appearance is impaired, who stands out because of obvious flaws and disfigurements, is perceived as a deviant." Such a person is deviant in two ways—one, by failing to live up to an ideal cultural standard of beauty, and two, by failing to live up to what is regarded as a "normal" or *unexceptional* appearance (Beuf, 1990, p. 7). Ugly or extremely unattractive persons are often stared at, teased, taunted ("How did your face *get* like that, anyhow?"), humiliated; people with average or "normal" appearance often feel disgusted, repelled, even *tainted* to be in their presence. The cruelty of children toward the appearance-impaired "seems limitless" (p. 51). It is clear that, in spite of the fact that such people have not *done* anything to deserve their appearance, they are regarded—and treated—as deviants.

BODY MODIFICATION AS PHYSICAL DEVIANCE

Some people modify their bodies in ways that elicit suspicion, stigma, and condemnation. Erik Sprague, 27, is a "performance artist" and a PhD student in philosophy at the State University of New York at Albany. Mr. Sprague "is slowly transforming himself into a reptile." Not literally, of course; but his appearance is becoming increasingly reptilian. Scalelike tattoos appear on his body from head to foot. He's having the scales filled in, one by one, with green. He convinced surgeons to implant a bony ridge on his forehead and shape his tongue into a reptile's proverbial forked tongue. His fingernails are in the form of claws, and several of his teeth are filed down to look like "crocodile-like chompers."

Sprague calls his transformation an "experiment." The idea isn't to shock, he says, but to "stimulate dialogue, to get people thinking, to make people wonder." He wants to test the limits of what it means to be human. Even after his metamorphosis, he wonders, can he still be regarded as a full-fledged human being? He says he knows who his real friends are by their willingness to remain friends with him, even after taking in his dramatically altered appearance. "I learn a lot more about a person by their reaction to me than they could ever learn about me by just looking at my physical appearance."

Sprague works as a performer with the traveling Jim Rose Circus. He swallows swords, eats live insects, breathes fire, and sticks metal skewers through his cheeks. His ongoing bodily transformation, he says, has been great for his show business career (Anonymous, 2000).

Aside from ear-piercing, which, for women, is considered conventional and normative, tattooing is probably the most widely practiced form of voluntary body alteration. No statistics are kept on the number of people who receive a permanent tattoo, but in the United States the number certainly runs into the millions. Is tattooing a form of physical deviance?

In many societies of the world, of course, getting a tattoo is not only accepted, it is normatively demanded. In Western society generally and in the United States specifically, people who "choose to modify their bodies" by getting a tattoo "violate appearance norms" and hence "risk being defined as socially and morally inferior. Choosing to be a physical deviant symbolically demonstrates one's disregard for the prevailing norms" (Sanders, 1989, p. 2). In many ways, persons who choose to be tattooed play on that unconventionality by demonstrating their "disaffection from the mainstream." For many people who are unconventional, tattooing is a symbolic affirmation—indeed, a public proclamation—of the tattooee's "special attachments to deviant groups" (p. 2). It is an "effective social mechanism for separating 'us' from 'them' " (p. 3). This separation may be partial, as exemplified by the Wall Street lawyer who receives a single, small, inconspicuous tattoo to affirm his or her *mild* unconventionality, or it may range up to *total* unconventionality, as with the person who is tattooed from head to toe in wild designs and who therefore cannot move in any social circle whatsoever without being regarded as an out-and-out deviant—and wants it that way.

Tattooing is deviant not only for its direct symbolic value; it is also deviant because people who wear a tattoo tend to be symbolically connected with deviant groups and categories. Here we have "voluntary guilt by association." Tattooing is common among convicts, prostitutes, bikers, drunken sailors, and other disreputable types. Therefore wearing a tattoo symbolizes the "general deviance and untrustworthiness of the wearer" (p. 126). Wearing a tattoo announces to the world, "I am a great deal like these other disreputable people who are known for wearing a tattoo." Hence, wearing "a stigmatizing mark by most members of mainstream society," one became aware of "the potential negative social consequences of being tattooed" from employers, relatives, one's spouse, and other representatives of "straight" society (p. 126). Many tattooed persons do belong to deviant groups for whom the tattoo is a badge of honor rather than one of shame.

In addition, tattooing represents a major commitment. Before the advent of lasers, tattoos could be removed only through conventional surgery, which was expensive and produced scarification. Hence, until recently, a tattoo, once on the body, remained there for life. In a phrase, the wearer was "indelibly marked" (p. 126). Even today, getting a tattoo is considered a "big deal." As a result, most receivers of tattoos "start small." Getting a small, inexpensive, and readily concealable tattoo is the usual way of limiting one's commitment (p. 126). By testing the waters in this fashion, one can determine whether, in one's group or circle, social reactions to the tattoo are sufficiently negative as to call a halt to further body alterations. If these reactions are mild

among their peers, more accepting than rejecting, many recipients will escalate the process, receiving larger and more conspicuous tattoos.

In short, there is a "certain level of risk" in receiving a tattoo. One may not choose an artful or reputable tattooist; the process is somewhat painful; one risks infection; the final product may not be quite what one had hoped for; one may later have a change of heart; one may be criticized or condemned by one's peers for bearing a tattoo on one's body, or one may take up with new friends or lovers who will find the connection with tattooing repugnant; one's employers may react more harshly than one had anticipated; and so on. In short, yes, tattooing is a form of physical deviance, albeit a relatively mild form of deviance. To put the matter another way, the degree of deviance of tattooing runs the gamut from mildly deviant (a small, inconspicuous tattoo) to strongly deviant (being tattooed all over one's body, including one's face). What makes it especially interesting is that, unlike many forms of physical deviance, it is voluntary. Many tattooees *choose* to receive tattoos on their body specifically because of its association with deviant social categories and groups (Sanders, 1989).

OBESITY

Obesity represents a prime example of an "abomination of the body" that violates aesthetic standards. What makes it even more interesting than most of the characteristics with which it shares this quality is that, in addition to being physical in nature, most people believe it to be the product of immoral or deviant behavior. The majority of people who are not fat feel that the obese became fat because they are gluttonous and lazy—that is, because they eat too much and don't exercise enough. Hence, obesity partakes of both of Goffman's forms of stigma: It is both an "abomination of the body" and a "blemish of individual character."

In this society, fatness is itself looked upon with repugnance because most Americans consider it unsightly and unaesthetic, and, in addition, fatness is a sign or manifestation that the person who carries the weight got that way because of a weak, self-indulgent nature. In other words, not only is obesity unfashionable and considered unaesthetic to the thin majority, it is also considered "morally reprehensible," a "social disgrace" (Cahnman, 1968, p. 283). Fat people are set apart from men and women of average size. They are socially isolated from "normal" society (Millman, 1980). Today, being obese bears something of a stigma.

In contemporary America, the obese are stigmatized. Fat people are considered less worthy human beings than thin or average-sized people are. They receive fewer of the good things that life has to offer and more of the bad. Men and women of average weight tend to look down on the obese, feel sorry for them, pity them, feel superior to them, reward them less, punish them, make fun of them. The obese are often objects of derision and harassment for their weight. What is more, average-sized persons tend to feel that this treatment is just, that the obese deserve it—indeed, that it is even something of a humanitarian gesture, since such humiliation will supposedly inspire them to lose weight. The stigma of obesity is so intense and pervasive that many, perhaps most, fat people come to see themselves as deserving of it, too.

The obese, in the words of one observer, "are a genuine minority, with all the attributes that a corrosive social atmosphere lends to such groups: poor self-image, heightened sensitivity, passivity, withdrawal, a sense of isolation and rejection." They are subject to relentless discrimination, they are the butt of denigrating jokes, they suffer from persecution; it would not be an exaggeration to say that they attract cruelty from the thin or average-sized majority. Moreover, their friends and family rarely give the kind of support and understanding they need in order to deal with this cruelty. In fact, it is often friends and family who mete out the cruel treatment. The social climate has become "so completely permeated with anti-fat prejudice that the fat themselves have been infected by it. They hate other fat people, hate themselves when they are fat, and will risk anything—even their lives—in an attempt to get thin. . . . Anti-fat bigotry . . . is a psychic net in which the overweight are entangled every moment of their lives" (Louderback, 1970, pp. v, vi, vii).

Negative feelings toward being overweight are a matter of degree, of course. If the grossly obese are persecuted mightily for their weight, the slightly overweight are persecuted proportionately less—they are not exempt. In spite of the fact that Americans are gaining weight over time (or perhaps because of it), we are also a weight-obsessed society. It is impossible to escape reminders of what our ideal weight should be. Standing at the checkout counter in our local supermarket, we are confronted by an array of magazines, each with its own special diet designed to help us shed those flabby pounds. Television programs and, even more so, advertising, display actresses and models who are considerably slimmer than average, setting up an almost impossibly thin ideal for the public. If we were to gain ten pounds, our friends would notice it and would view the gain with negative feelings; only the most tactful would not comment on it.

These exacting weight standards fall, not surprisingly, more severely on the shoulders of women than on those of men. In a survey of the 33,000 readers of *Glamour* magazine printed in the August 1983 issue, 75 percent said that they were "too fat," even though only one-quarter were overweight according to the Metropolitan Life Insurance Company's 1959 height-weight tables, and even fewer of them were deemed overweight by current standards. Still more surprising, 45 percent who were *underweight* according to Metropolitan Life's figures felt that they were too fat. Only 6 percent of the respondents felt "very happy" about their bodies; only 15 percent described their bodies as "just right." When looking at their nude bodies in the mirror, 32 percent said that they felt "anxious," 12 percent felt "depressed," and 5 percent felt "repulsed." Commenting on the *Glamour* survey, one of the researchers who analyzed the survey, Susan Wooley, a psychiatrist, commented: "What we see is a steadily growing cultural bias—almost no woman of whatever size feels she's thin enough."

Evidence suggests that the ideal female form has gotten slimmer over the years. Women whose figures would have been comfortably embraced by the norm a generation or more ago are now deemed unacceptably overweight, even fat. In 1894, the model for the White Rock Girl, inspired by the ancient Greek goddess Psyche, was 5'4" tall and weighed 140; her measurements were 37"-27"-38". Over the years, the women who have been selected to depict the White Rock Girl have gotten taller and slimmer, and have weighed less and less. Today, she's 5′8″, weighs 118, and measures 35″-24″-34″. Commenting on this trend in an advertising flyer, the executives of White Rock explain: "Over the years the Psyche image has become longerlegged, slimmer hipped, and streamlined. Today—when purity is so important—she continues to symbolize the purity of all White Rock products." The equating of slenderness with purity is a revealing comment on today's obsession with thinness: To weigh a few pounds over a mythical ideal is to live in an "impure" condition. Interestingly, today's American woman averages 5′4″ in height and weighs 140 pounds, the same as White Rock's model in 1894.

Advertising models represent one kind of ideal; they tend to be extremely thin. They are not, however, the only representation of the ideal female form as depicted by the media. There are, it may be said, several ideals rather than just one. Photographs appear to add between five and ten pounds to the subject; clothes add a few more in seeming bulk. (White Rock's Psyche wears very little in the way of clothes, however.) Consequently, fashion models typically border on the anorexic, and women who take them as role models to be emulated are subjecting themselves to an almost unattainable—and unhealthy—standard. It would be inaccurate to argue that all—or even most—American women aspire to look like fashion models, and moreover, it would be inaccurate to assert that women in all media are emaciated. Still, it is entirely accurate to say that the ideal woman's figure as depicted in the media has become slimmer over the years. And that many women are influenced by that ideal, even if it only manifests itself in how they feel about themselves.

Aside from advertising, another ideal is depicted in Miss America pageants. Prior to 1970, Miss America contestants weighed 88 percent of the average for American women their age. After 1970, this declined slightly to 85 percent. Even more significant, before 1970 pageant *winners* weighed the same as the other contestants; after that date, however, they weighed significantly less than the contestants who didn't win—82.5 percent of the average weight for American women as a whole. Similarly, the weight of women who posed

for *Playboy* centerfolds also declined between 1959 and 1979. Centerfolds for 1959 were 91 percent of the average weight for American women in their twenties; by 1978, this had declined to 84 percent. The measurements of the 1959 *Playboy* centerfold were 37″-22″-36″. In 1978, they were 35″-24″-34½″, indicating a growing preference over time for a less voluptuous, thinner, more angular, and more "tubular" ideal female figure. Interestingly, during this same period, the American woman under the age of 30 gained an average of five pounds (which was entirely attributable to a gain in height, not to an increase in body fat). The number of diet articles published in six popular magazines nearly doubled between 1959 and 1979 (Garner et al., 1980). This trend has continued unabated into the twenty-first century.

The increasingly slim standards of feminine beauty represent the most desirable point on a scale. The opposite end of the scale represents undesirable territory—obesity. If American women have been evaluated by standards of physical desirability that have shifted from slim to slimmer over the years, it is reasonable to assume that during that same period, it has become less and less socially acceptable to be fat. In tribal and peasant societies, corpulence was associated with affluence. An abundant body represented a corresponding material abundance. In a society in which having plenty to eat is a mark of distinction, heaviness draws a measure of respect. This tended to be true not only for oneself, but for one's spouse (or spouses) and children as well. With the arrival of mature industrialization, however, nutritional adequacy becomes sufficiently widespread as to cease being a sign of distinction. Slenderness rather than corpulence comes to be adopted as the prevailing aesthetic standard among the affluent (Powdermaker, 1960; Cahnman, 1968, pp. 287–288). Over time, the slim standard comes to be adopted more and more by all social classes; while more firmly entrenched in the upper socioeconomic strata, the slim ideal has permeated all levels of Western society.

Obesity is sociologically interesting, among other reasons, because it is considered by the thin or average-sized majority as both a physical characteristic, like blindness and paraplegia, and a form of behavioral deviance, like prostitution and alcoholism. The obese, unlike the physically disabled, are held responsible for their condition. Fatness, in the eyes of the nonobese majority, is viewed both as a physical deformity as well as a behavioral aberration (Cahnman, 1968, p. 293; Allon, 1982, p. 130). Being fat is regarded as a matter of *choice*. The obese have gotten that way because of something they have done, as a result of a major character flaw.

Overweight persons "are stigmatized because they are held responsible for their deviant status, presumably lacking self-control and will-power. They are not merely physically deviant as are physically disabled or disfigured persons, but they [also] seem to possess characterological stigma. Fat people are viewed as 'bad' or 'immoral'; supposedly, they do not want to change the error of their ways" (Allon, 1982, p. 131). Contrary to the strictly and involuntarily disabled:

> the obese are presumed to hold their fate in their own hands; if they were only a little less greedy or lazy or yielding to impulse or oblivious of advice, they would restrict excessive food intake, resort to strenuous exercise, and as a consequence of such deliberate action, they would reduce.... While blindness is considered a misfortune, obesity is branded as a defect.... A blind girl will be helped by her agemates, but a heavy girl will be derided. A paraplegic boy will be supported by other boys, but a fat boy will be pushed around. The embarrassing and not infrequently harassing treatment which is meted out to obese teenagers by those around them will not elicit sympathy from onlookers, but a sense of gratification; the idea is that they have got what was coming to them. (Cahnman, 1968, p. 294)

The obese are overweight, according to the popular view, because they eat immodestly and to excess. They have succumbed to temptation and hedonistic pleasure-seeking, where other, more virtuous and less self-indulgent persons have resisted. As with all forms of behavioral deviance, getting fat represents a struggle between vice and virtue. Most of us are virtuous—witness the fact that we are not fat. Some of us are consumed with vice—and the proof of the pudding, so to speak, is in the eating. Therefore, the obese must pay for their sin of overindulgence by attracting well-deserved stigma (Cahnman, 1968; Maddox, Back, and

Liederman, 1968). The obese suffer from what the public sees as "self-inflicted damnation" (Allon, 1973, 1982). In one study of the public's rejection of persons with an array of behavioral and physical traits and characteristics, researchers found that the degree of the stigma of obesity was somewhere in between that of physical handicaps, such as blindness, and behavioral deviance, such as homosexuality (Hiller, 1981, 1982). In other words, the public stigmatizes the obese significantly *more* than they do the possessors of involuntarily acquired undesirable characteristics, but somewhat less than persons who engage in unconventional, despised behavior.

This introduces a *moral* dimension to obesity that is lacking in most other physical characteristics. The stigma of obesity entails three elements or aspects. (1) The obese attract public scorn. (2) They are told that this scorn is deserved. (3) They come to accept this negative treatment as just (Cahnman, 1968, p. 293). A clear-cut indication that the obese are put down because of their presumed character defects is seen in the fact that when respondents were informed that a person's obesity was caused by a hormonal disorder—in other words, it was not his or her "fault"—they stigmatized him or her far less than if their condition was left unexplained (DeJong, 1980). Unless otherwise informed, most of us assume that obesity is the fat person's "fault." A trait that is seen as beyond the person's control, for which he or she is held not to be responsible, is seen as a misfortune. In contrast, character flaws are regarded in a much harsher light. Obesity tends to be seen as the outward manifestation of an undesirable character. It therefore invites retribution in much of the public's eyes.

In an editorial in *The New York Times*, one observer (Rosenthal, 1981) argues that obesity has replaced sex and death as our "contemporary pornography." We attach some measure of shame and guilt to eating well. Our society is made up of "modern puritans" who tell one another "how *repugnant* it is to be fat"; "what's really disgusting," we feel, "is not sex, but fat." We are all so humorless, "so relentless, so determined to punish the overweight.... Not only are the overweight the most stigmatized group in the United States, but fat people are expected to participate in their own degradation by agreeing with others who taunt them."

Are the Overweight Universally Stigmatized? Black-White Differences

Werner Cahnman (1968) captured the typical or modal American attitude toward persons who are heavier than the norm in his classic article, "The Stigma of Obesity." In study after study, article after article, book after book, the unrelenting rejection and humiliation that overweight children and adults suffer has been documented and reaffirmed (Maddox, Back, and Liederman, 1968; Louderback, 1970; Stunkard, 1976; Millman, 1980; Allon, 1982; Schoenfielder and Wieser, 1983; Goode, 1996a; Sobal and Maurer, 1999a, 1999b). Not only are the fat stigmatized, but most overweight people—especially women—tend to *internalize* their stigma, believing that the condemnation they endure is deserved (Cahnman, 1968). But is this generalization equally true for all social categories equally? Are some overweight segments of the population insulated from this harmful process of self-derogation?

It turns out that racial differences in attitudes toward weight are substantial. As a general rule, Black teenage girls and women regard heavier levels of weight as more acceptable for themselves and others than is true of white girls and women. For the most part, African Americans tend to be totally immune to the anorexic allure of Kate Moss, Gwyneth Paltrow, and Diana Ross.

These racial differences were affirmed in a study conducted by a Black and white team of researchers of a sample of junior high school and high school girls. While 90 percent of the white teens expressed dissatisfaction with their weight, 70 percent of their African-American counterparts said that they were satisfied with their weight. Nearly two-thirds of the Black teenagers (64 percent) said that it is better to be a little overweight than a little underweight. Even substantially overweight Black teenagers described themselves as "happy" with their weight. Moreover, African-American girls recognize that Black teenagers are not attracted to a skin-and-bones figure. Say two full-figured Black teenagers: "The guys at my school don't trip on skinny" (Ingrassia, 1995, p. 67). Two-thirds of the Black teenagers (65 percent) said that women become more beautiful as they age, and many offered the example of their mothers. In contrast, the white teenagers grudgingly admitted that their mothers may have been beautiful—when they were young. It was much harder for white girls to picture age and beauty as compatible. As Mimi Nichter, coauthor of the study, elaborates: "In white culture, the [time frame of the] window of beauty is small" (Ingrassia, 1995, p. 66).

Several explanations for the difference come to mind. Many Black teenagers equate a full figure with "health and fertility." After decades of African-American leaders emphasizing that "Black is beautiful," the view that Black girls should punish themselves for being overweight seems especially unappetizing; self-respect at whatever weight seems a far healthier attitude. And, according to Mimi Nichter, body image researcher, the ladder of mobility might help explain these differences. "In white, middle-class America, part of the great American Dream of making it is to be able to make yourself over," she explains. "In the black community, there is the reality that you might not move up the ladder as easily. As one girl [Nichter interviewed] put it, you have to be realistic—if you think negatively about yourself, you won't get anywhere" (Ingrassia, 1995, p. 67; Parker et al., 1995).

Whatever explanation is correct, the fact is, Black self-acceptance among fuller-figured girls and women stands in stark contrast to the white pattern of self-disparagement. The stigma of obesity among African-Americans is significantly softer, more muted, than it is among Caucasians. Hence obesity is far less *deviant* in the Black than in the white community.

INTERSEXUALITY

Emma McDonald was born on September 15, 1998; "doctors whisked her away so quickly her family barely had a chance to look at her" (Nussbaum, 2000, p. 93). For hours, they anxiously awaited the news. Was she healthy? they wondered. Then Anita Jones, Emma's grandmother, overheard a physician discussing Emma's case with a group of medical students. Hurrying back to her daughter, Anita said, "Vicki, that doctor called Emma a hermaphrodite." Emma was born with what are medically known as "ambiguous" genitals. She had a protuberance in the genital area that was much larger than a clitoris, much smaller than the average penis, but without many of the structures possessed by the normal penis. Emma had one testicle, no vaginal opening, but an enlarged urethral opening where normally the vagina would have been. Inside her body, she had "a rudimentary uterus, one fallopian horn, and an undeveloped gonad." Her chromosomes are "mosaic," an unusual pattern that is referred to as XY/XO (p. 93). Emma was an intersexual; she possessed the primary sexual characteristics of both sexes.

We all learn that there are two and only two sexes—male and female—and that everyone belongs to one or the other category—not both—and not anything else. But for a variety of reasons, one out of every 2,000 births is characterized by a distinguishable degree of *intersexuality*; that is, like Emma, they are difficult to classify as male or female because they possess both male *and* female sexual characteristics.

Like Emma, persons of intersexual status may be born with male and female attributes, that is, the category of intersexual may be thrust on them. Or, in contrast, they may choose to take on a sexual status that they do not possess at birth. In effect, they may *change* their sex.

AGNES

"Agnes" was born with the anatomical equipment and the genetic makeup of a male. But she never felt she was a boy; she felt she was a girl *trapped* in a boy's body. At puberty, she stole hormone pills from her mother, which induced female secondary sex characteristics in her body. Throughout her childhood, she was tormented for being a sissy. After high school, she left her small-town midwestern community and lived in Los Angeles, passing as a woman. Agnes had a boyfriend but she did not permit him to explore below the waist. It was his insistence on having sexual intercourse that led her to seek a sex-change operation. She convinced her physicians that she really was a woman, that her full breasts, fleshy buttocks, smooth skin, and absence of facial hair was internally induced, and that her male genitalia were an accident of nature—external and alien excrescences, so to speak—that had to be removed and replaced with surgically produced female organs. Agnes really believed herself to be a woman and that the operation would be a *vindication* of that womanhood. The surgical procedure represented the final step in her transformation; in a sense, Agnes had "accomplished" womanhood (Garfinkel, 1967).

A hermaphrodite is defined as a person born with evidence of one or more reproductive organs of both sexes; Emma was born a hermaphrodite. Agnes was not a hermaphrodite because she did not possess the reproductive or primary sex characteristics of a female, although she did induce secondary sex characteristics by taking her mother's hormone pills. Even after her operation, she could not bear children, of course; her surgical procedure merely reconstructed tissue in her genital area that permitted her to have sexual intercourse with a man. But like hermaphrodites, Agnes was a physical deviant in that, by taking her mother's hormones, she generated female secondary sex characteristics in an adolescent male body. And like hermaphrodites, she violated the masculine norm; had others known the full story of her sexual transgressions, she would have been denounced, condemned, and humiliated.

Agnes's case demonstrates that sexual status can be *accomplished*. Biologically, she was originally a "he"; born a boy, "he" turned "himself" into a "she." Not biologically, of course—as I said, Agnes does not have a womb and cannot bear a child—but socially. Agnes "passes" as a female, is taken for a female, and attracts male attention *as* a female. Moreover, initially, she was engaged in passing at the very time she was learning what it means to be a female (Garfinkel, 1967). Agnes's case demonstrates the degree to which taking on a gender status is a learning process. As we'll see, however, there are limits to this learning process. Agnes's success was dependent or contingent on some crucial biological processes.

THE TWO DEBATES: ESSENTIALISM-CONSTRUCTIONISM/NATURE-NURTURE

Hermaphroditism can be looked at through two different conceptual lenses: *essentialism* and *social constructionism*. The essentialistic perspective is the medical approach; it is held by most physicians, many psychiatrists, as well as much of the general public. The constructionist perspective is that held by many social scientists, particularly sociologists and anthropologists, as well as by some (although not all) hermaphrodites.

The essentialistic or medical perspective toward hermaphroditism is that the condition is not only objectively real but abnormal, a kind of pathology in need of correction; that there are two and only two sexes, male and female; that they are mutually exclusive—they do not overlap or intermingle; that everyone has a "true" or essential sex; and that "biology is destiny"; that is, that it is one or more biological features—chromosomes, hormones, anatomy, neurological makeup, the brain—that determines one's sexuality.

In contrast to essentialism, what might be called the social constructionist perspective toward hermaphroditism is that there may be more than one sex, that persons with ambiguous genitals may in fact manifest a "mix" of the two sexes, that it is society not nature that forces us into clear-cut sexual pigeonholes, that the possession of ambiguous sex organs is not a pathology, that it is no more a medical or psychiatric problem than being left-handed or having red hair. Rather, hermaphroditism is a problem only because the medical and psychiatric profession and the general public regard it *as a* problem; it is professionals who need to be changed—not the infant with statistically unusual genitalia. It is not pathological to permit infants born with the primary sex characteristics of both sexes to retain them, it is not pathological to accept such persons as they are, and it is not pathological to allow them to make a fully informed decision—*when they are adults*—as to whether or not to opt for medical intervention to change their physical characteristics. The binary division of the human world into two and only two mutually exclusive sexes is arbitrary, a social construction. Some societies assign intersexuals to a third, fourth, or fifth gender. Gender categories are cultural, not dictated by biology. What is needed is a *demedicalization* of hermaphroditism, this perspective argues.

Understanding a second dimension is crucial to grasp the controversies that whirl about hermaphroditism: the *nature-nurture* debate. Most (but not all) constructionists are nurturists; most (but not all) essentialists are naturists. The difference is that constructionism is a *conceptual approach to reality* while the nature-nurture debate is a *theory* about how the material world works.

"Naturists" believe that it is biology that decides who we are, including our sexuality; the "nurturists" believe that it is social learning or socialization that is the primary determinant of who and what we become. In the area of sexuality, researchers who take the "nature" side of the debate argue that a person's sexuality is fixed at birth, that one "is" a male or female as a result of an ineradicable fact of nature. Today, most naturists believe that sexuality, that is, being male or female—and *feeling* that one is a male or a female—is a product of the fetus being exposed to male or female hormones in the womb.

Nurturists believe that at birth the human organism is a *tabula rasa*, a "blank slate," onto which can be "written" practically any sexual message whatsoever. In other words, like Agnes, the child can *learn to become* male or female, according to the appropriate socialization or social learning. During early childhood, our sexuality can be altered, pushed in one or the other direction, according to how we are treated by others, what we learn about ourselves; our sexuality is malleable, flexible, or adaptable. In other words, sexuality can be "assigned" or "reassigned"

At birth, babies are psychosexually neutral, the nurturists believe. Whatever their genetic makeup, they may be socialized to be either boys *or* girls, but by the age of two or three, the socialization process which they are exposed to, either as a boy or a girl, "takes," it is "imprinted" in them and cannot be reversed. (Some anomalous exceptions like Agnes—many of whom become transsexuals—for some reason hold an opposite-sex identity at an early age in spite of same-sex socialization processes.) And second, nurturists believe that a healthy adaptation to one sex or the other is dependent on having the anatomical or genetic equipment of a boy or a girl. In other words, if at birth a penis is grafted onto a girl, she is socialized to be a boy, and she takes male hormones at the onset of puberty, *she* will develop into a *he*—a normal, healthy boy and eventually, a man. (Of course, lacking gonads, the "he" she becomes will not be able to impregnate a woman.) Likewise, if at birth a boy is castrated and his penis is removed and a surgical vagina is constructed, he is socialized to be a girl, and he takes female hormones when adolescence begins, he will be a normal she—a girl and then a woman. (And again, lacking ovaries and a womb, "she" will not be able to bear children.) In other words, sexual identity can be created through a combination of surgery, socialization, and artificial hormones.

If an infant is born with "ambiguous" genitals, to which sex do physicians assign him or her? The arbitrary nature of how hermaphroditism is dealt with by the medical profession can be seen in the surgeries that are performed on infants with ambiguous genitalia. Nine out of ten such cases are assigned to the female sex. Is this because it makes medical or psychiatric sense to do so? Is each and every case screened and evaluated as to its suitability for assigning the child to one or the other sex?

Actually, these assignments are determined largely for reasons of surgical convenience. If the physician can create an "acceptable" penis—whether through the administration of androgen or through surgical intervention—it is made into a boy. If the child does not respond to androgen or the phallus is too small, it is made into a female (Kessler, 1990, p. 18). The fact is, "physicians generally choose a sex according to the difficulty of surgery to normalize the genital appearance" (Weinberg, Williams, and Laurent, 1999, p. 436). Quipped one surgeon: "You can make a hole, but you can't build a pole" (Hendrix, 1993). Advances in surgical technology have reduced this tendency considerably; it is now possible to build a penis out of available bodily tissue that can function sexually.

Intersexuality emphasizes the importance of some features of constructionism—while, at the same time, it emphasizes that there are *limits* to constructionism. Intersexuality stresses the following constructionist points.

The utility of constructionism is affirmed by the arbitrary assignment of the sex of intersexed babies (nearly always as a female) as a result of surgical convenience rather than scientific or medical necessity. In other words, the assignment of babies with ambiguous genitals is decided not by biological or essentialistic considerations but by the relatively primitive state of contemporary medicine—a creature of sociology (and technology), not the science of genetics.

The sense that the birth of a biologically intersexed child represents an emergency that requires immediate surgical intervention likewise demonstrates constructionism in action. Why intervene at that point? Why not permit the child to choose his or her sex at a much later point in time? In fact, why force anyone to choose at all? Why shouldn't an intersex person be permitted to stay ambiguous with respect to sex and gender? Why does society force people into pigeonholes—male *or* female? The very existence of an in-between or ambiguous sexual category denies the validity of essentialism, which holds that there are two and only two sexes and that everyone *must* belong to one or the other category.

FROM BRUCE TO BRENDA TO DAVID (THE STORY OF "JOHN" AND "JOAN")

As it turns out, the material, physical, or biological world is not nearly so pliable, malleable, or *plastic* as the nurturists imagine. In fact, reality is not completely "up for grabs," capable of being defined in any way whatsoever, totally, utterly, and completely a matter of being created by socialization— a "blank slate" (or *tabula rasa*), onto which literally *anything* may be written. In fact, much of the physical world imposes itself on human life in ways that cannot be bent, twisted, or defined in any way that we choose. Intersexuality offers an excellent test case of the limits of nurturism. In what specific way? A classic case from the intersexuality literature illustrates the point.

In 1963, twin eight-month-old boys, Bruce and Brian, were being circumcised when a sudden jolt of electricity zapped off Bruce's penis. Desperate, the parents sought advice from the staff at Johns Hopkins Medical School. The parents were advised that the boy's best chance at a normal life was as a female. The boy's testicles were removed and a workable urethral hole was created out of available tissue; to complete the picture, female hormones at puberty were administered at the onset of adolescence in order to turn the genetic boy into an acceptable girl. Bruce was renamed "Brenda." Initially, medical scientists thought the transformation was a success, and the case was cited by many as a verification of the *plasticity* of gender (Money and Erhardt, 1972; Money and Tucker, 1975, pp. 95–98).

As it turned out, the case proved exactly the opposite. A follow-up study of the reconstructed girl, who in the medical literature was given the pseudonym of "John" at birth and "Joan" as a girl, showed that the sex change did not work (Diamond and Sigmundson, 1997). "Joan" never managed to adapt to her reassigned gender. Even when she was a toddler, Joan rebelled against her sex. When her mother gave her pretty dresses, she refused to wear them. She rejected dolls and instead liked playing with stereotypical boys' toys, such as gadgets, guns, and trucks. Once, when she was four or five, seeing her father shaving and her mother applying lipstick, she said, "I don't want no makeup. I want to shave." Other kids teased and picked on her about her tomboyish looks and behavior. She was suspended from school at the age of 14 for getting into a fight with another girl. Joan tried to urinate standing up, soiling herself in the process. At some point, the other girls denied her access to the girls' bathroom. When she used the boys' room, she was ejected, and so she urinated in an alleyway adjacent to the school. She rebelled at taking estrogen, saying the hormones made her "feel funny." Recalling how she felt at the time, as an adult she said, "I suspected I was a boy since the second grade" (p. 300). At 14, in a "tearful episode," her father told her about the operation. "All of a sudden everything clicked," John said in an interview in the 1990s. "For the first time things made sense, and I understood who and what I was" (p. 300). "Joan" decided to become, once again, a male. In the late 1970s, she was surgically retransformed into a male, receiving male hormones and undergoing a mastectomy to remove her hormonally induced breasts as well as a series of surgical procedures to create a penis—small although sexually functional, but obviously incapable of impregnating a woman. "Joan" became "John." At the age of 25, he married a woman several years older than himself and adopted her three children.

This case achieved an enormous amount of publicity when members of the family revealed their identity and appeared on network television to discuss the case. ("John" took the name "David" because he felt as if he were a little guy fighting a Goliath of a problem.) The case is discussed in John Colapinto's *As Nature Made Him: The Boy Who Was Raised As a Girl* (2000). The colossal failure of the nurturist position, intimately associated with the name of medical psychologist John Money, is discussed in excruciating detail in this book.

The case will cause physicians who once believed gender to be entirely amenable to socialization to rethink the role of unbendable biological and genetic factors. It forces us to realize the limits of the process of the social learning or nurturist position. Becoming male or female may not be as fluid or plastic as has been thought. Perhaps experts who now hold the assumptions of the nurturist approach to intersexuality may have to reconsider some points offered both by the naturist and the constructionist approaches. The "nature" side of the "nature-nurture" debate tells us that some aspects of human life may be fixed at birth. For most of us, sexuality—whether we are male or female—seems to be a basic and ineradicable feature of human life; that sexuality may very well be determined by factors that are not amenable to human manipulation, such as social learning. It is entirely possible that bathing the human fetus in male or female hormones is what determines sexuality—and not learning after the age of two or three. And constructionism argues that intersexed persons need not be assigned to one sex or another by surgeons who are too hasty with their scalpel. Why not leave well enough alone and permit the child with ambiguous genitals to grow up "as nature made them," and allow them to gravitate toward their own sexual destiny?

FREAKS

When he was writing his classic book on the physically different, literary critic Leslie Fiedler floundered around for a more appropriate and less demeaning term than *Freaks* (1978), the title he eventually chose. "I should be searching for some other term, less tarnished and offensive," he wrote, introducing his subject. All those that came to mind—anomalies, human "oddities," monsters, "very special people," "sports," mistakes of nature, deformities—seemed inadequate and improperly descriptive, he decided. Society's hostility toward freaks, Fiedler writes, has typically been less than a "total genocidal onslaught" (p. 21). True, in the name of eugenics, the Nazis killed dwarfs and the ancient Spartans left infants with birth defects to die on a rocky mountain ledge. But most societies, Fielder wrote, cultivated a measure of compassion and pity toward the physically different that was mixed with scorn; they manifested a kind of ambivalence that prevented an unrelieved hostility from taking root. Freaks elicited as much amusement as contempt, Fiedler argues.

For at least a hundred years, freaks were displayed in circus sideshows. But according to sociologist Robert Bogdan, author of *Freak Show* (1988), until well into the twentieth century, these human oddities were presented as awesome and amazing prodigies of nature, to be marveled at rather than ridiculed. These "prodigies" had a special niche in the society; their differences were accepted as a tolerable form of physical eccentricity rather than a source of contempt. It was not until modern medicine gained a stranglehold on definitions of normal and pathological that "freaks" were no longer exhibited. Medicine had developed the arrogance—the Greek term for it is *hubris*—to believe that all such deformities could be cured rather than tolerated; any exhibition of persons who possessed such traits was exploitative and degrading, a "pornography of disability" (p. 2). Instead of correcting such anomalies, however, modern society has relegated their possessors to the "contemptible fringe," no longer marveled at but regarded as distressing, distasteful, and repulsive.

What is it about freaks that causes such a shudder of fear among "normals," Fiedler asks. While eliciting some sympathy, freaks stir up "supernatural terror" in us for a variety of reasons, he argues. Most freaks are the children of normal parents; by what strange and mysterious chemistry—"forces we do not understand"—is the budding child in the womb transformed into a mythic beast, a creature no one of us wants to be, a being apart from the rest of us? The freak challenges the boundaries that separate male and female (the hermaphrodite, the bearded woman), large and small (giants and fat ladies, midgets and dwarfs), animals and humans (the hairy "wolf-man," humans with an apelike appearance), and the physical integrity of one human being as distinct from another (Siamese or "conjoined" twins). Consequently, Fiedler argues, what freaks do is tear down the barrier between reality and illusion, experience and fantasy, and fact and myth. Quite literally, he says, they are a threat "to those desperately maintained boundaries on which any definition of sanity ultimately depends" (p. 24).

The "myth of monsters" originates "in the deep fears of childhood"(p. 31). The need to create and maintain firm boundaries separating these cosmic categories, Fiedler writes, stems from childhood struggles with matters of size, sexuality and gender, humanness, and togetherness/apartness.

After all, children are midgets in relation to adults, and adults are giants in relation to children. Moreover, various organs, including those relating specifically to sexual functioning, change enormously in size, transforming themselves from midget-sized (those belonging to children) to giant-sized (those belonging to adults). For instance, from preadolescence to adulthood, and from flaccid to aroused, the penis changes from small to large. Moreover, boys compare penis size among themselves. (Are you a midget? Or a giant?) And the preadolescent girl simultaneously fears that her breasts will never grow—that is, will be midget-sized—or will grow much too large (will be giant-sized).

Fears and insecurities around sexuality and gender are fundamental and eternal: the little boy who is chastised for toying with his penis; the girl who is told not to kiss the little girl next door on the lips; the children who are caught playing "doctor"; the tomboy; the too-effeminate boy; the boy who catches sight of his dad's vastly larger penis; the trauma of the girl's first menstruation.

Many children are obsessed by the fear of being attacked and devoured by wild beasts, yet, at some point, they become aware of the fact that humans eat animal flesh. Hair grows in the vicinity of the genitals and in the armpits—which, in girls, is expected to be removed—and, Fiedler writes, hairiness represents our animalistic side.

Perhaps the very first intellectual realization children have is the awareness of being an entity separate from the mother whose breast they suck on. As they grow older, they fear separation from their parents, yet they desperately have the need to make that separation to maintain their own personal sense of integrity. Boys, upon understanding the nature of the female anatomy, try simultaneously to imagine emerging from and at the same time entering the vagina.

In other words, says Fiedler, the freak projects our "infantile or adolescent traumas." They manifest or dramatize our "primordial fears . . . about scale, sexuality, our status as more than beasts, and our tenuous individuality" (p. 34). Fiedler's argument seems to be that both our negative and our tempered reactions to people who are different from ourselves correspond to some sort of universal, transcultural appeal. Instead, they are based on who we are as human beings, where we stand in the scheme of things, and what we had to struggle with when we were growing up. They are

not simply learned as a result of the accident of arbitrary cultural norms, he seems to be saying. There are limits, after all, to the whimsy, caprice, and folly of social construction. Our rootedness in childhood, adolescence, sex and sexuality, humanness, and our need to be a personal entity separate from all others, transcends and overwhelms any and all local customs dictating who and what should be stigmatized. They dictate, in fact, our interactions with and posture and attitudes toward the persons who were once designated as *freaks*.

DISABILITY AND TERTIARY DEVIANCE

John Kitsuse (1980) introduces the concept of "tertiary" deviance—the notion of socially disvalued people standing up, fighting for their rights, demanding equality with "normals." Edward Sagarin refers to this phenomenon as *Odd Man In* (1969)—or "societies of deviants." Over the past few years, a growing number of militant disabled spokespersons have stepped forward and confronted the abled, demanding that the blind, the deaf, the wheelchair-bound be accorded justice and the respect and dignity they deserve. Central among their demands is that the *image* or *public presentation* of the handicapped recognize their essential humanity.

In *Nothing About Us Without Us*, James Charlton (1999) writes of "disability oppression," alienation, raising the consciousness of the disabled, and organizing "empowerment."

In *Creatures Time Forgot*, David Hevey (1992) gives us an "in your face" political argument about disability, demanding "rights not charity."

In *Freakery*, Rosemarie Garland Thompson (1996) offers an anthology of analyses by two dozen writers who argue that, over the centuries, Western society has presented "cultural spectacles of the extraordinary body."

In *Claiming Disability*, Simi Linton (1998) engages her readers, demanding that they put themselves emotionally into everyday issues and situations involving decisions about disability. "You are an architect," she says, and takes us through the decisions and emotional identifications a designer of a community center has to go through to build a facility that can accommodate the handicapped. "You are the parent of a nondisabled young woman away at college," Linton writes, and describes the experience of that parent dealing with the fact that her daughter is bringing a disabled male friend home to visit. "You are the new personnel director for a mid-sized company," she conjectures, taking us through the demands made by a disability action group to accommodate the disabled personnel. "Hidden and disregarded for too long," Linton says, "we are demanding not only rights and equal opportunity but are demanding that the academy take on the nettlesome question of why we've been sequestered in the first place" (p. 185). Academics have been "complicit" in the confinement of the disabled; it's time for that confinement to end, she argues.

In many ways, the disabled represent an example of an oppressed minority group. There are many parallels between the civil rights movement and the new and most decidedly militant field of disability studies. Where this new militancy will take persons with disabilities is anyone's guess. But its central message is clear: The disabled do not wish to be treated as deviants. Perhaps, one day, disability will no longer be discussed as a form of deviance.

SUMMARY

Undesirable physical characteristics represent a form of deviance. They tend to attract stigma and generate a contaminated identity for their possessors. Although some sociologists insist that involuntarily acquired traits cannot be a form of deviance because they are not the possessor's fault, the fact that their possessors *do* attract stigma and condemnation is what defines deviance; hence, they are deviants. In fact, there is a *continuum* of personal causality or responsibility for possessors of deviant characteristics— yet all are stigmatized. Personal responsibility is only weakly related to the dimension of deviance.

Erving Goffman referred to one form of stigma as "abominations of the body." For our purposes, two such "abominations" stand out: violations of aesthetic norms and physical incapacity.

Aesthetic norms refer to the way we look. Our appearance is judged by audiences and found normal or unacceptable. The latter condition, if extreme, is deemed worthy of condemnation. Persons who fail to meet an acceptable standard are seen as possessing a "spoiled" identity—as being "disqualified from full social acceptance."

Physical incapacity is made up of the inability to perform life's essential tasks, such as walking, seeing, hearing, and so on.

Standards of attractiveness are not nearly so relative as has been assumed in the past. In fact, from society to society, from culture to culture, many of the same standards prevail. Most of the traits or characteristics that are found attractive in one place are likewise found attractive in others. In fact, beauty is *not* "in the eye of the beholder." Very likely, some universal causal force or dynamic influences or determines what humans (and other creatures) find attractive and desirable in a mating partner. Some researchers with an evolutionary orientation believe that it is the impulse to pass on one's genetic material to later generations that explains this pan-human tendency to judge physical attractiveness. Many culturally oriented researchers are skeptical of this explanation. Whatever the explanation, unattractive children tend to bear the brunt of the negative side of evaluations of attractiveness. That is, their actions are deemed more deviant and more worthy of punishment than the same actions engaged in by more attractive actors. In a phrase, unattractiveness is a form of deviance; it attracts stigma and condemnation.

Obesity is a prime example of a deviant or undesirable physical characteristic. What makes obesity more interesting than most forms of physical deviance is that it is regarded as both physical and behavioral. That is, the obese are denigrated for being fat *and* they are denigrated for behaving in the shamelessly self-indulgent fashion—usually overeating and not being sufficiently active— that *caused* their obesity. Most nonobese people feel superior to the obese, and the obese, in turn, tend to internalize stigma, that is, they usually think that they are *worthy* of the condemnation that average-sized persons visit upon them. The condemnation of the obese operates, in scale, on people who are only somewhat above average— that is, the hugely obese receive the harshest condemnation for their weight while the merely somewhat overweight receive condemnation in proportion to their more moderate degree of overweight. Standards of weight fall unequally on the shoulders of women: Women tend to be condemned more harshly for every degree of overweight than is true of men. Over the years, the ideal standard of female beauty has gotten slimmer and slimmer.

Intersexuality—possessing ambiguous genital characteristics—is a form of physical deviance. Positions on both sides of two separate but overlapping controversies illuminate intersexuality: essentialism versus constructionism and nature versus nurture.

Essentialism sees males and females as separate and distinct, and argues that there are two and only two sexes and that they are mutually exclusive—that everyone belongs to one or the other category.

Constructionism argues that society's attitudes toward sex and gender assignment are arbitrary and culturally determined—a social construct; there are more than two sexes that are assigned by different cultures, the constructionist argues, and one person may belong to a "mixed" or intersexed category. Intersexed persons, its advocates argue, ought to be permitted to find their own sexual destiny rather than be forced into one, against their will, at an early age.

The "nature" position argues that we are as nature made us; sexuality is fixed in the womb and cannot be altered by the socialization process.

The "nurture" position argues that sexuality and sex assignment are not innate and can be learned if socialization is consistent; intersexed children can be "reassigned" to the category male or female through surgical and hormonal intervention, and can be socialized to accept the appropriate role. However, unfortunately for the latter position, cases of intersexed children "assigned" to one sex or the other have not always worked as well as the nurturist position would have predicted. Clearly, some rethinking of the applicability of the nurture position to the matter of gender and intersexuality needs to be done.

Many explanations have been offered for why the physically different are assigned to a deviant status. Many of us suspect that we could be afflicted by the same random, terrorizing forces that have afflicted the possessors of negatively evaluated physical characteristics. By interacting with them, we could, we fear, be contaminated with whatever struck them down. Hence we sus-

pect we might very well be vulnerable to such forces and we want to keep their possessors as far away from our door as possible.

In his analysis of stigma, Katz (1981, pp. 1, 5–11) introduces the notion of *ambivalence*. Granting that "there are important attributes that almost everywhere in our society are discrediting" (p. 2), he nonetheless argues that most of us temper our negative feelings toward the disabled and the unaesthetic with positive ones. In addition to stigmatizing them, Katz claims, most people feel sympathy for the underdog, distress over their suffering, and respect for persons who are able to triumph over adversity. So why stigmatize them in the first place?

The reasons are diverse, Katz argues, but they may be traced to widespread dynamics that are difficult to ignore.

The Just World Hypothesis. Interaction with persons who possess a socially undesirable trait or characteristic that is strictly involuntary ("it's not their fault") may cast doubt on the widely held belief that the world is a just place where the innocent do not suffer (Lerner, 1980). Many of us believe that we get pretty much what we deserve. The disabled remind us that there are many people out there for whom that is not true. Justice does not triumph, the wicked may not be punished, and extreme misfortune may befall the virtuous and the innocent. This is a painful lesson, one of which "normals" are reminded nearly every time they come face-to-face with someone who possesses a disability or a disfigurement.

Vulnerability. If undesirable physical traits are inflicted on people who did nothing to deserve them, the conclusion is obvious, says Katz: We are all vulnerable to sudden, catastrophic, and undeserved misfortune. The disabled and the disfigured do not merely overturn one of our ideological and moral applecarts, they also hit home with the message that we, ourselves, could be victims of the same misfortune that befell them. This is an extremely uncomfortable message, one that most "normals" do not want to be reminded of. Hence, we avoid the disabled and the disfigured, we put social distance between ourselves and them, we treat them in a pitying and condescending fashion, and the cruelest of us stigmatize them.

PERSONAL ACCOUNT: Jan, the Transitioning Transsexual

Being a transsexual can be looked at both as physical and sexual deviance. As physical deviance, it is voluntary, *in that changing one's sex is something that one has chosen to do. On the other hand, transsexuals would say it is* involuntary, *because they feel they have no choice in the matter; they are trapped in the body of the opposite sex, they say, and reassigning their sex is simply reclaiming what was rightfully theirs to begin with. Chromosomally and anatomically, "Jan" is a male who is convinced that she is a woman. (I will follow customary usage and refer to Jan as a "she.") The fact that she has a male body has bothered her "as long as I knew there was a difference between boys and girls." Chris Berry, a student in my deviant behavior course at the University of Maryland, wrote a paper on, and gathered the following written material from, Jan. "To the casual observer—a person passing her on the street," says Chris, "Jan looks like most any college-age male. She is tall and lanky, with a protruding Adam's apple..., hunched shoulders, [and] beard stubble.... Her manner is avoidant; she hardly ever talks to passersby, often averting her eyes as they go by. If one were to examine her closely, they might notice some characteristics a bit out of place—long, nicely filed fingernails..., a slightly hormonally enhanced figure, and an assortment of women's clothing worked into her regular wardrobe. Jan is 22 years old. She is poised at a very important point in her transition and in her life.... [She] has subjected herself to over 100 hours of facial electrolysis, and has been on estrogen for over two months. She is planning on continuing her transition while finishing up her college career at the University, and is going to start living full-time as a woman after graduation and, she hopes, after facial feminization surgery. The surgery, she hopes, will enable her to pass as a woman in her day-to-day life.... One semester away from graduating from college, she is looking at entering the world as a woman." These are Jan's words about the experience of reassigning her sex.*

I have a fairly typical middle-class, white, male upbringing.... I had my little group of friends that I made in school and we kept together until we all left for college. I wasn't very popular, but I wasn't picked on. I had a girlfriend throughout high school and we broke up when we left for college. I played sports in high school. I ran track during the spring and winter seasons and played football in the fall. Yes, I played football. I was reading anything I could lay my hands on from a fairly young age. I especially liked fantasy science fiction.... I loved pseudo-medieval stories. I can talk about books for days on end.... I was a smart child who didn't try very hard. I'm sure you know the type. I got mostly A's and B's through most of my early education.... I was always more interested in whatever little project I was working on outside of school than I was in my schoolwork. I was very quiet in school, stuck to my tried-and-true group of friends, hardly ever met new people, and coasted my way through. The truth is that anybody who really knew me would realize that I was a total dork. I personally don't think that's a terrible thing.... My sports were fun. I'd do them over again if I had to do the whole thing over as a guy. If I could do it over again as a girl, I'd still run, but I think I'd take a pass on football.

But my real interests were role-playing, games, and computers—Dungeons and Dragons and the like.... Role-playing ties into *identity*. And identity is, after all, sort of the basis for my gender issues. [However] I want to make one thing absolutely clear. *Role-playing games did not make me a transsexual.* ... I had these feelings even before I picked up my first manual on role-playing. That being said, I do feel that role-playing games played an integral part in understanding, and beginning to accept, my gender identity. It was a creative outlet that enabled me to try on many different sets of traits, including gender, to see which ones felt right to me. I do not believe that it is a coincidence that most of the characters I made, when I wasn't the storyteller, were female. Nor do I believe it to be coincidental that I elected

PERSONAL ACCOUNT: Jan, the Transitioning Transsexual (cont.)

to be the storyteller because I felt ashamed that so many of my characters were female. Even at that young age, I realized that it was *weird* for me to want to be a girl. It was something I should be *ashamed* of. I remember making male characters many times just so my friends wouldn't question why I was always making girl characters, even though I really didn't want to play male characters.

Looking back at my life, I cannot remember a time when I did not either want to be a girl or think of myself as one. I also cannot remember a time when I didn't realize that this was not an okay thing to want or do. Those two feelings have been there for what seems like forever. New feelings did start to develop as I grew, however. When I was really little, my identity was a personal thing. I didn't need to think of myself as being part of the "real world" as I do today. My little life *was* the "real world"—to me, then. I could see myself as a girl, and bear the fact that others did not see me as one. Why? Because my whole world, back then, was nothing more than my imagination, my stories, and my small group of friends. And two out of three of them had me as a girl. As I grew up, my identity became less of my own and more of a social entity. Suddenly, all these things started to be important. Who your friends were, what your hobbies were, how popular you were, who you liked, what sports you played. These became as much a part of my identity as my imagination. Sure, I fought against them in my *personal* identity, but there was nothing I could do about my social identity. It was being formed for me, and the fact that I was male played a big role.

My body was of particular concern once I realized that my imagination wasn't going to cut it. In my mind, I had a female body. In the mirror, I didn't. I don't blame God, I don't blame fate, I don't really blame anything. . . . It's just the way it was. However, for the life of me, I couldn't figure out what to *do* about it. Puberty was hell. Any hope I might have had—however slim—that my body would feminize was quickly lost. Since everything around me told

me that little people with male bodies became men and little people with female bodies became women, I was resigned to living as a guy. There didn't even seem to be any reason to talk about it. One, I knew people would think I was a freak if I said I was a girl, and two, even if I could tell people, what difference would it make? It had been decided that I was going to grow up into a bigger version of my male body and that socially, I would be a man. . . . [Still], I never believed I was a boy despite what I was told, shown, and assumed to be. I didn't try to convince myself of it. . . . Instead, I just tried as hard as I possibly could not to think about it. And while it was always there, hurting from the inside—sometimes very little, sometimes excruciating—I managed to get through life. . . .

[In college], I wasn't happy, and college just made things worse. I don't mean to make college sound like a terrible place. . . . There was freedom, lots of people I didn't know, and many interesting things to do. When people say college is the best four years of your life, I see where they're coming from. My experience was a bit different, however. . . . I spent the first few months learning my way around the school and meeting the people on my floor. It turns out that the people on my floor were some of the coolest people. . . . It was more of a community than you would expect from a random bunch of college students. . . . After three semesters at college, I fell apart. . . . I was a real train wreck. . . . I had tried to form a romantic relationship with a girl I met during my freshman year, and it had crumbled rather painfully. . . . I was really frustrated and starting to feel hopeless about the conflict between my gender identity and my physical body. I was [also] at odds with a lot of my peers, and had lost touch with most of the people I knew in high school. I was homesick, I was not doing well academically. . . . I contemplated suicide, and there really isn't any point in dredging up that memory for you, here. If you are contemplating suicide, *please talk to somebody.* Even—maybe preferably—a complete stranger. [And I began] skipping classes and basically doing

PERSONAL ACCOUNT: Jan, the Transitioning Transsexual (cont.)

nothing but lie in bed with a headache and the lights out for three straight days.

I would like to think that lying in bed for this long was more than just a cry for help. . . . I remember thinking that I simply did not feel like I could deal with people any more. I felt that if I had to talk to people, or go to class, or listen to anybody, or have one more assumption made about me—if I was called "Jason" one more time, or referred to as "he," or seen as just another college guy—that I would completely snap and shout at them or start crying openly or try to hurt them or myself. . . . It's kind of strange and kind of scary pulling these memories out again. I haven't felt even remotely like that in a long time. These days, I go through phases of depression, frustration, and anxiety on a more or less regular basis, but it hasn't touched near any of the extreme feelings I've had in the past.

I finally decided that I needed to escape. I called my parents and said that I absolutely needed to get out of college for a bit. . . . I want to give kudos to my parents for being understanding. I've heard so many horror stories about people going through a lot of the same things that I am [going through] only without the parental support. When she [his mother] got there, we started talking. I found myself totally stuttering over my words, locking up, and crying a whole lot. Once the floodgates were open, everything began to come out. I talked about almost everything—my feelings of not having a direction, of stress, depression, anxiety, frustration, loneliness, not being understood, assumptions, and so forth. Just about the only thing I couldn't tell my mom at that point was that I felt I was a girl. I don't know why. Maybe I was afraid of her reaction. Maybe she wouldn't like me or wouldn't understand me. Maybe—and this seemed worst of all—she wouldn't believe me. One thing was certain—I couldn't handle school the way I was. . . . I packed up some stuff and we headed home.

[When we got home], my parents had a really tough time with me sitting there telling them

that I—their only son—was a girl, not a boy. Or at least I did a really bad job at the time of describing what I'd been going through. . . . It was the hardest thing I've ever done. I think they left the conversation more confused than anything. It became . . . a silent issue. Never talked about. . . . Not one more word was spoken about sex or gender.

Over the next few months I saw several therapists—four, to be exact. They started out really general. The first few were all-purpose psychotherapists who I went to because of my depression. A running theme throughout my life has been people trying to put me on antidepressants. I have only been on them for two weeks of my entire life. It bothers me to treat the symptoms of something until you've dealt with the root of the depression itself. But when my therapists learned about my issues with my own gender identity, they couldn't do much since they didn't have much in the way of experience dealing with people like that. The second one referred me to another therapist in the area who had some background working with transsexual patients. Her name was Dr. Horvath and she was a godsend. We really started to talk about what I was feeling and we got it out in the open. Then we could discuss what to do about it. By this time I knew, somewhere deep inside, that my life needed to be changed drastically. It was becoming more and more obvious to me that I'd never be happy unless I was a woman to everybody else, too. I mean, I had been one to myself, inside, for as long as I could remember. But I was in severe need of validation from others. Up to this point in my life, it's just been one invalidation after another. You know, every single "Yes, sir!" really adds up over all those years.

[I attended some TS—transsexual—support groups.] In my opinion, they're not for me. I don't want to be a guy, and I don't want to be a guy "pretending" to be a girl. I want to be a girl. Therefore, I don't want any labels attached to me, like "transsexual" or "transgender." And finding groups of people based on those categories associates me with them. . . . My experiences with groups involving the words "transsexual" or "transgender" have been, for the most part, negative ones. I've attended three support groups and felt uncomfortable at all of them. In all three, I was the youngest person. I felt like the only person planning a transition in hopes of "passing" (I hate that word!). Therefore, I felt like everybody was too interested in me, which led to feeling pressured into attending regularly as well as [feeling that I was on a] "sinking ship." Basically, the groups I went to consisted mostly of people stuck living in male roles. Some of them were okay with this and just liked crossdressing. These people were nice but I had trouble identifying with them. Some of them were resigned to using the support group as an outlet for their needs while living unhappy lives. . . . I felt like they were resigned to being miserable and were trying to live vicariously through me. . . . So I haven't really felt like attending support groups. I get the same vibes from some online forums, too. It makes me realize where people get the notions of what "transsexual" means. Most people I know think of Jerry Springer. . . . I got the same kind of feeling in some of these forums. . . .

Because I haven't been in contact with other people going through transitions at support groups, I didn't really have anyone to talk to about the whole process. Sure, I have my therapist, but I see her once a week for an hour, and she's a professional who I'm paying to visit. It's not the same thing as having a friend. Friends. I've always had a group of friends. I can honestly say I've never truly been alone in this world. Sure, they all see me as a guy, which is a real nuisance. I've talked to almost all of my friends at one point or another about my gender identity and future transition. I've gotten more or less the same response from every single one. Basically, they say, "Oh. Okay." And that's it. Then the subject gets changed to something else. This is good. I mean, they don't hate me. They don't find me disgusting. They're still my friends. We still hang out.

This is also bad because it becomes harder to bring up the subject because it's not acknowledged. I'm still treated just as much like a guy as before. I find it increasingly difficult to discuss how my transition may affect *them* in any way. Because it will. I feel that ignoring it and pretending like I said nothing is only going to make the transition more difficult to handle. But I suppose I'll cross that bridge when I come to it. Okay, so talking to my friends about my transition is like talking to a brick wall. And believe me, it's something I have to talk about! If I said nothing, I'd go crazy. I did that for eighteen years. Once I started opening up to people, it felt like a great weight lifted from me. I'm not about to lock it back up and pretend like it never happened. But I can't really talk to my friends about it, so there we go. Now I have at least one reason why I'm reaching out to talk to other people who are going through this transition.

On the one hand, it's nice to find people to talk to who talk to me as the girl they consider me to be. It feels good to be validated by them since I don't get that from many people. On the other hand, it seems a shame to find people who accept me as a girl, and then talk about the transition, which admits my past (and present) guy role! I mean, I'm not the kind of person who is going to lie and make up a whole past in which I lived a girl's role my whole life. No, I've been very much a guy and am still quite a bit a guy. After all, it's my safety net which I am building up courage to let go of. I look forward to the day when I've been living as a girl long enough to be able to talk to people about my "past" experiences as a girl. That will be nice!

The guidelines [for the transition from being a guy to being a girl] say that you need three months of hormone replacement therapy and you need to be living in the desired gender role for a year before qualifying for sex reassignment—or genital—surgery. I like to think of it as a three-pronged transition. Along one prong, there's the physical stuff. Dressing the way a person of the desired sex typically dresses; hours and hours (I've logged over a hundred

PERSONAL ACCOUNT: Jan, the Transitioning Transsexual (cont.)

hours on the table, so far, and am planning quite a few more) of electrolysis to remove unwanted facial and body hair; and taking hormones—estrogens, progestins, and androgen blockers—to feminize the body. And of course, there are the surgeries. It's not just all about the sex-change operation. I consider FFS (facial refeminization surgery) a more important part of a successful transition. Having facial surgery does a lot more for passability [that is, the successful social passing as a female] than does genital surgery, which most people don't even see. One of my friends says that FFS is part of the "holy trinity" of passing. These are facial surgery, electrolysis, and voice feminization. Oh yeah, the voice. That's another part of the transition, and a really difficult one. Do *not* get any kind of surgery for the voice. It's got to be trained, which takes months, even years. So that's the first prong—the physical stuff.

The other two prongs are the emotional and the social. Emotionally, adjustment is the hardest part of the whole process. Not only are you dealing with the roller-coaster of adding hormones to your body, but then usually with a loss of friends and family members, and often employment, as well. There's a lot of emotional stuff I haven't experienced yet, but I'm sure it'll come over the next few years, probably for the rest of my life. Socially, there's a whole new role to learn. I mean, I've spent roughly twenty years of my life being a guy, and I hated it. But it isn't as if I've gotten any kind of training, formal or otherwise, in being a girl. I wasn't raised as one, so that's something I need to learn. And starting to learn how to be a girl at 22 is a really awkward thing, you know? It's going to be really embarrassing! One of my transsexual friends says "transitioning isn't about getting rid of fear. It's about getting rid of *doubt*. The fear is always there." Well, I'm scared, but I have no doubt in my mind that this is the right road for me.

QUESTIONS

Do you believe that there are thousands of genetic males who believe they are really females? And genetic females who believe they are males? Does this point to a more complicated view of sex and gender than the usual dichotomy of males versus females? Or does it uphold this dichotomy? If you were a friend of Jan's, would you advise her/him to complete the sexual reassignment? Do you feel that Jan could ever be a "true" female? Do you feel that sexual reassignment is a legitimate thing to do? What do cases such as Jan's tell us about physical characteristics as deviance? Picture a typical heterosexual male being attracted to Jan—as a woman—then finding out she/he is a biological male. How would he react? Does the acceptance of Jan's status as a "wannabe" female among her/his friends surprise you? How would you react? Picture Jan growing up, say, 50 years ago. Would her/his experiences have been very different?

13

Deviant Organizational Behavior

In Chapter 1, we encountered the distinction between *individual* deviance and *organizational* deviance. In principle, *any* person in the society could engage in individual deviance—incest, drug use, homosexual acts, street crime, shoplifting, and so on. (As I said there, a few forms of deviance are status-specific, such as adultery, child molestation, and underage drinking.) Likewise, anyone could hold unconventional beliefs, such as atheism, radical political views, or the belief that one has been kidnapped by aliens, or could possess stigmatizing physical characteristics (being obese, disabled, or heavily tattooed). Individual deviance corresponds to two parts of Goffman's famous trilogy—that is, first, behavior or conditions that indicate "blemishes of individual character," and second, physical traits that are considered "abominations of the body." And while I refer to it as *collective deviance*, even the third type—"stigma of tribe, religion, and nation"—likewise locates *each and every person* along an axis of degrees of acceptability versus unacceptability. These three dimensions of deviance are relevant for *everyone* (or almost everyone) in *every* society on earth.

In contrast, this is *not* the case for the behaviors described and analyzed in this chapter. In this sense, they stand outside Goffman's trilogy. Organizational deviance can *only* be enacted by persons who have a particular position in a particular organization. Only a corporate executive can engage in corporate crime. Only a police officer can engage in police corruption or police brutality. Of course, everyone in a position to grant illegal favors can engage in corruption—just not the sort of police corruption the police commit. Everyone can engage in violence—but not *police* violence. Anyone can steal, but only an employee can pilfer *as an* employee; only an employee of a firm can embezzle, for instance. Only a professor (or a teaching assistant) can demand sex for a grade from a student. And so on. In other words, with respect to *being judged as a deviant*, a given form of organizational deviance is completely *irrelevant* for most of the members of the society. (Of course, nearly all of us are members of *at least one* organization, but only a small proportion are members of *any given one*.) Unlike individual and even collective deviance, with organizational deviance, most of us stand *outside* the process that

evaluates the behavior, beliefs, and traits of the members of the society as potential forms of deviance. As *actors*, many particular forms of organizational deviance do not touch our lives at all. Actors who *don't* occupy a particular position in a particular organization can engage in *similar* or *analogous* behavior—but not *as* a representative of that organization.

This distinction has important implications not only for *judging* the behavior of persons occupying specific organizational positions; it also has relevance for explaining the *enactment* of the behavior. More on the latter point momentarily.

One of the most interesting aspects of behavior that takes place within an organization is that judgments of deviance vary considerably according to where someone stands. By that I mean that acts that are *not* regarded as reprehensible *within* the organization, or in different segments of the organization, *are* so regarded in the society at large, and by the law. In other words, as I've said throughout this book, judgments of deviance by different audiences are to some degree separate and independent of one another. For instance, as we'll see in more detail further on, the police have their own interpretation of what constitutes "normal" force required to subdue a suspect. This interpretation differs from what they learned in the academy, differs from what the law says, and differs from what members of the community regard as acceptable (Hunt, 1985). As we'll see, business executives recognize that no product can be risk-free, that all products carry a certain measure of potential harm to consumers—a position many consumers are unwilling to accept. Employees often convince themselves that a little pilfering from the company they work for is just compensation for low pay; executives in that company are likely to disagree. In other words, condemnation of the behavior—the designation or social construction that the behavior is deviant to begin with—depends on where one stands, either inside or outside the organization, as well as within the organization itself.

In addition, a great deal of organizational malfeasance is kept secret by the higher-ups in organizations. Trusted employees who are discovered to have abused financial trust by embezzling funds are rarely turned over to the police (unless the sums are very large). Instead, they are simply fired. For many years, when the criminal abuse of children by priests was reported to authorities in the Catholic Church, it was nearly always covered up; offending priests were simply transferred to another parish, and the police were almost never notified. (Now that the media have uncovered and reported this scandal, this age-old practice is no longer possible.) The "blue wall of silence" in police departments around the country is legendary (although we'll see in this chapter that the matter isn't quite as simple as this phrase suggests). In short, typically, organizations protect their own. This doesn't always occur, but it is the modal or most common response. Cover-ups are an interesting and important aspect of the deviance process.

Organizational deviance is important not only with respect to judgments made against its enactors but also with respect to its causes. The opportunity to engage in certain forms of deviance is *structured* according to occupational position. The most basic reason why the occupants of certain organizational statuses engage in specific forms of deviance is that they are in a position to do so. On the most fundamental level, as I just pointed out, some forms of behavior *cannot be committed at all* except by occupants of particular positions. Corporate crime is the obvious example. With others, a given position gives the occupants almost unparalleled *opportunities* for committing deviance. Bank tellers handle thousands upon thousands of dollars in cash every day; they have the opportunity, and the skills, to embezzle money that the occupants of almost no other position enjoy. Since employees are exposed to volumes of merchandise and office supplies, they have access to the crime of employee theft and pilferage. Professors who have a monopoly on the distribution of what is a valued commodity to large numbers of young, attractive students—good grades—are in a *structural* position to engage in an illicit, unethical exchange of grades for sex. What I'm saying is that anyone with the inclination to engage in certain forms of behavior will be tempted by the prospect—*which is generated by structural position alone.* Many occupants of these positions will *not* be tempted by the prospect of violating organizational norms. Unethical professorial threats of low grades unless a student engaged in sex were much more common in the past; because of extremely strong sanctions against such threats, they are very rare today. Only a very tiny percentage of priests are interested in, let alone have sex with, children in their pastoral care—but the position they occupy will provide opportunities for those who are so inclined. In some organizations, the norms and the sanctions against deviant actions are so strong as to minimize them.

Organizational deviance helps in our quest to explain deviance in a second way as well. In addition to the structural difference between occupants of certain organizations versus the persons who do not occupy an organizational position, causality also comes into the picture when we compare organizations with one another. Some organizations have extremely high rates of deviance within their ranks, while others have low rates. Why? While there are many reasons, it is clear that *institutional climate* influences the enactment of deviant acts within a given organizational setting. Corporations whose executives strongly and openly oppose, monitor, and penalize the illegal behavior of their underlings are likely to have less of it than those whose executives seem indifferent or even encourage such behavior. The same principle applies to police malfeasance in different precincts. Hence, if we are devising an explanation of organizational deviance, clearly, we have to look to institutional climate, which is itself largely a product of social control issuing from the top of the organization. Institutional climate also applies to changes in time. The police today are vastly less likely to use the level of force that was routine 20 or more years ago. (Of course, standards of what is considered "inappropriate" force have also changed over time.) Today, Catholic priests cannot molest children and get away with it as they did a few years ago, because the institutional climate of the Church has changed.

The members of organizations, taken as a whole, seek to perpetuate the organization in which they are located—in a phrase, to ensure that it survives and succeeds. Certain actions that are regarded as deviant *outside* the organization are actually endorsed, encouraged, and rewarded *by* and *within* the organization. They are endorsed because they are thought to further the organization's interests. Other actions are discouraged, punished, and regarded as deviant by the organization. They are believed to be (and, objectively speaking, they actually are) harmful to the organization. In the former category we find much (although not all) corporate crime, where the perpetrator *is* the organization. To be more precise, the perpetrator is made up of the top echelon of the corporation. Corporate crime is by definition illegal behavior that is enacted *on behalf of* the corporation. In the latter category we find most (although not all) embezzlement, when an employee steals *from* a corporation. Unlike corporate crime, embezzlement is a crime *against* a corporation. The police are enjoined to enforce the law, but certain law enforcement circumstances lead individual officers to engage in actions, originally thought to be a product of police mandate, that turn out to have been a mistake: firing at a suspect who *might be* reaching for a gun but isn't, stopping and frisking suspects who are completely

innocent but fit a certain "profile," searching a dwelling that turns out to have been a wrong address.

Table 13.1 spells out some of the more crucial dimensions of organizational deviance. Clearly, just as there are similarities uniting all varieties of this form of deviance, there are basic differences as well.

WHITE-COLLAR AND CORPORATE CRIME

Here, I'd like to focus on corporate crime, but to do so, I have to introduce the "parent" concept that gave birth to it—white-collar crime. Corporate crime is a subset of white-collar crime. That is, all corporate crime is white-collar crime, but not all white-collar crime is corporate crime.

TABLE 13.1 DIMENSIONS OF ORGANIZATIONAL DEVIANCE

ACTION:	EXAMPLES:
Conforms to Organizational Mandates	Catholic Church hierarchy covering up cases of pedophilia
Contradicts Organizational Mandates	The police torturing suspects
WITHIN THE ORGANIZATION, ACTION IS JUDGED:	
Normative, Acceptable, Not Deviant	Police profiling of suspects
Nonnormative, Unacceptable, Deviant	Sexual molestation of children by priests
RESPONSE BY ORGANIZATIONAL AUTHORITIES:	
Tolerance, cover-up	Before 1985, sexual molestation of children by priests
Punishment	After 2002, sexual molestation of children by priests
TO THE GENERAL PUBLIC, ACTION IS:	
Normative, Acceptable, Not Deviant	A company charging prices that are too low to sustain a profit
Nonnormative, Unacceptable, Deviant	Police lying about a confrontation with a citizen
ACCORDING TO THE COURTS, ACTION IS:	
Legal	Accidental shooting of suspects by police in high-risk situations
Illegal	Intentional torture of suspects by police
ACTION IS UNDERTAKEN:	
By a Collectivity	Nearly all corporate crime
By an Individual	Individual embezzling of funds

What is white-collar crime? As it was originally defined by Edwin Sutherland in a speech to the American Sociological Association in 1939 (and later formulated in print), white-collar crime is *an illegal action that is committed by the occupant of high occupational status in the course of his or her professional activity* (1940, 1949).

Exactly how "high" the occupational status in question must be to qualify need not concern us; clearly, we are not referring to manual laborers, but the category does include bank clerks. Even embezzlement, a relatively lowly white-collar crime, is committed by persons who work in occupations that rank in the top half of the class structure. This definition *excludes* "common" or conventional crimes. An executive who murders his wife (or her husband) has committed a crime of violence, not a white-collar crime. It also excludes theft and pilferage from the job; that is, larceny-theft, an Index Crime category in the Uniform Crime Reports. And it excludes acts that someone may see as unethical and/or harmful but are not against the law, such as manufacturing and selling cigarettes, selling legal but dangerous products, and taking "three-martini lunches." If an act is not a violation of a legal code and does not call for a punitive sanction, that is, a jail or prison sentence—or at least a punitive fine—then it cannot be a white-collar *crime.*

The stereotype of white-collar criminals is that they are all rich and powerful. In fact, this is far from true. Weisburd et al. (1991), who examined a cross-section of offenders convicted in federal court of a variety of white-collar crimes, including securities fraud; antitrust violations; bank embezzlement; and postal, tax, and credit fraud, found that these offenders did not fit the usual portrait of white-collar criminals as occupying high-status positions. True, given the fact that they are *white-collar* offenders, by definition, they were not manual laborers. But a remarkably high proportion occupied the very lowest rungs of the white-collar status hierarchy. Many were unemployed at the time of their arrest or held fairly humble jobs, did not have a college education, and did not own their own home. At the time of the arrest that led to their conviction, offenders were twice as likely to have had a past criminal record than the national average. The authors (p. 190) conclude that most white-collar offenders are ordinary people who got

into financial difficulty and who saw their way out of it through illegal and fraudulent measures. They were "struck by the banal, mundane quality of the vast majority of criminals" in their sample (pp. 45–46); the majority of their crimes "have an undramatic, local or regional quality," a "common, familiar ring." Say the authors, business fraud is "as familiar in their business context as are street crimes in poor communities" (p. 46).

I would not refer to most of the white-collar criminals who are caught and convicted as organizational deviants. Most are individual deviants—petty thieves who act on their own, outside an organizational setting; criminals who engage in acts that are not classified as street crimes. What they do, anyone can do; their actions are not specific or unique to any particular organization setting. Hence, their actions fall outside the scope of this chapter.

The fact is, what most people mean by "white-collar crime" is *corporate crime*. While all corporate crime is white-collar crime, corporate crime is a specific *form* or *subtype* of white-collar crime. To be precise about it, corporate crime entails executives and executive officers engaging in illegal actions that are intended to further the interests of that corporation; they are actions taken *on behalf of* the corporation. (In so doing, they may *also* benefit the careers of the individual corporate actors, but that is a different matter.) This type of crime clearly contrasts with individual embezzlement, which is undertaken *against* the corporation *on behalf of* a given employee or several employees. In embezzlement, the victim is the corporation. In corporate crime, the victim, or potential victim, is the *general public* (in the case of illegal pollution), the *consumer* (in the case of price-fixing or the sale of illegally unsafe products), the *employee* (such as illegally unsafe working conditions), the *government* (for instance, illegal tax avoidance), or a *competitor* (two firms forming a price-fixing conspiracy against a third). And the criminal act was performed not only *in the context of* the corporation but also *on behalf of* the corporation. While, as we saw, the majority of white-collar criminals are low-level, unsuccessful bottom-feeders who are trying to scrape by with petty, illegal scams to cheat and defraud their victims, the same is not true of corporate criminals.

Corporate crime is not a classic, clear-cut case of deviance. *In some respects*, it is a form of deviant behavior; in some respects, it is *not*. In the sense that audiences designate corporate actions that harm people physically and take money out of their pockets as serious crimes (Friedrichs, 2004), they are a form of deviance. To the extent that illegal corporate actions are likely to result in prosecution and a jail or prison sentence, they are deviant. To the extent that a conviction and a jail or prison sentence for a corporate crime is stigmatizing, *personally discrediting*, that it *taints* the character of the offender (for instance, if friends and loved ones regard mention of it in an obituary as inappropriate, a "smear"), then clearly, it is a form of deviance. To the extent that there are social circles in this society made up of persons who define executive misdeeds as serious wrongdoing, and attempt to legitimate that view in the society as a whole, then they are indeed a form of deviance *in those circles*.

On the other hand, to the extent that seeing that harmful corporate crime, however serious, does *not* result in jury conviction or stiff prison sentences for offenders (Friedrichs, 2004), then it is *not* deviant. To the extent that social circles define the actions that corporate offenders engage in as acceptable and characterize their prosecution a "witchhunt," then, clearly, in those circles, such actions are *not* deviant. Just because corporate actions are unethical, harm people, and are formally against the law, does not automatically make them deviant *to relevant audiences*. Just because we, or persons very much like us, don't like what executives do can't magically make their behavior deviant. *Are corporate misdeeds condemned by the public?* Are they commonly *prosecuted* by the criminal justice system? Can corporate wrongdoers get into *trouble* as a result of their actions? Are such corporate actors socially *stigmatized* by their actions? If the answer is yes, then absolutely—corporate crime is deviant. If the answer is no, then corporate crime is *not* a deviant act. What we see, instead, is something of an in-between case. Clearly, corporate crime has one foot in conventionality and one in deviance. This is one of the reasons why it is so interesting.

Corporate crime is wrongdoing in high places. We do not expect the executive or lawyer to engage in crime, or to be prosecuted, convicted, and sent to prison. Most of us have a conception of crime that *precludes* the respectability of the offender. "Crime" is what street people—or at least, poor people—do. There is, as many observers have pointed out, a certain *incongruity* in seeing an affluent 60-year-old banker in handcuffs and a prison uniform, being marched off to a prison cell, to serve time with murderers, rapists, and burglars. Many of us can understand the motives of poor, powerless criminals, who steal out of desperation or commit violence as a result of anger and frustration. The crimes of the rich and the powerful are puzzling to us, however; if someone can earn a sizeable income legally, why try to earn even more in an illegal fashion? Why risk one's current material comfort and freedom simply to gain an edge over one's competitors? Is it greed? To many casual observers, corporate crime doesn't make a great deal of sense.

The fact is, corporate crime is similar to all *instrumental* actions, that is, those that are designed to achieve a certain goal; under certain circumstances, achievement of the goal assumes far greater importance than the means by which the goal was attained (Merton, 1938). One major *subtype* of—but by no means all—deviant behavior takes place when the actor resorts to *illegitimate* means to achieve a *legitimate* goal. If the likelihood of detection is extremely low, resorting to *legal* or *legitimate* means to attain that goal is actually quite *irrational*, since, typically, they are less efficient and less effective. Following legal procedures usually ties the corporate actor down to rules, regulations, and restrictions that may actually prevent or frustrate the achievement of desired goals. In the corporate world, we are forced to ask: "Given the great rewards and low risks of detection, why do so many business people adopt the 'economically irrational' course of obeying the law?" (Braithwaite, 1985, p. 6).

But note: The same logic is not unique to the business world—nor even to capitalist society. Students often cheat on exams because it gets them what they want—a higher grade; shoppers may shoplift clothes, again, because it permits them to have what they cannot otherwise afford; many of us lie because, once again, in so doing, we attain what we desire—respect, admiration, or getting out of a sticky situation. When legitimate or conventional avenues make the attainment of a goal difficult or impossible, many of us, whether as individual or as corporate actors, will resort to illegitimate or deviant avenues. But the conditions that create the impulse to deviate are widespread, and again, not confined to business dealings. "Some organizations seek profits, others seek survival, still others seek to fulfill government-imposed quotas, others seek to service a body of professionals who run them, some seek to win wars, and some seek to serve a clientele. Whatever the goals might be, it is the emphasis on them that creates trouble" (Gross, 1978, p. 72). In other words, the problem here is not the worm in the apple—it is the apple itself.

CORPORATE CRIME: CORRELATIVE FEATURES

There are also some *correlative* features of corporate crime—aspects of what it is like that are a *product* of its essential defining criteria. What are they? Imagine describing corporate crime to someone who knows nothing about the phenomenon; what would our description look like? Let's look at eight of the most essential features of corporate crime.

First, as to the nature of the behavior itself: Corporate crime tends to be made up of *complex, sophisticated*, and relatively *technical* actions. Imagine witnessing or watching a videotape of a robbery or a murder; most of the time, we'd be able to unambiguously identify the act *as* a crime. In contrast, corporate crime would not be so readily identified. How do we know a corporate crime when we see one? When we watch a videotape of an armed robbery, we know an armed robbery is in process. In contrast, a videotape of a corporate crime would result in a more ambiguous judgment from an audience. It might even take an expert—an accountant, for example, or an industrial chemist, a physician, or a government official—to determine its illegal status. The way that a corporate crime is committed is complex and interactional. At a board meeting of executives, a proposal is made and discussed. Memos are exchanged; decisions are made; policies are put into practice. Much of the time, it is not clear whether a crime in fact took place. Even experts may have trouble deciding. Even *victims* may not

know that they have been victimized. Of course, the criminal status of some actions is more clear-cut than others, but for most, it is far less clear-cut than for most street crimes. This is because these actions tend to be complex, sophisticated, and technical. In contrast, the meaning of most street crime is more direct, straightforward, and unambiguous.

Second, corporate crime tends to be *intermingled with legitimate behavior*. Illegal advertising claims are made in the context of a legal, legitimate advertising industry; some exaggeration is considered acceptable and is legal. But how much is too much? Monopolistic restraints of trade are carried out in a capitalistic business environment in which all corporations attempt to capture a larger share of the market; most of such attempts are legal and are considered good business practice, while some are illegal and "go too far." Even embezzlement is enacted within the context of ordinary, routine, workday activities, such as entering numbers into an accountant's ledger. While *some* traditional street crimes are also "intermingled with legitimate behavior" (date rape, for example, is a product of extremely aggressive courtship practices), most is not. It is difficult to imagine, let's say, what legitimate behavior a robbery or a burglary is "intermingled" with. With street crime, the crime act is illegal *in its totality*.

A third characteristic of corporate crime is that *victimization tends to be diffuse*. Harm is not always conceptualized or identifiable as such because it is usually spread out over a substantial number of victims. Again, this represents a sharp contrast with street crime. A rape harms a specific woman; a robbery, a specific store; a murder, obviously, the deceased victim as well as his or her survivors. But with corporate crimes, harm is usually spread out, usually thinly to many victims. Monopolistic practices may result in our being charged, let's say, $1,000 more for the purchase of a new car, a quarter more for a half-gallon of milk, $2 more for a pair of jeans. Even where there is physical harm, victimization can usually be measured in terms of *statistical odds* and *chances* rather than in a direct, one-to-one fashion. Pollution hardly ever kills or harms everyone exposed to it. Instead, it increases our *likelihood* of getting sick and dying prematurely.

For instance, if a given factory pollutes the air in a given area at a given level for a given period of time, the 10,000 people living nearby may have a 1 in 100 lifetime chance of contracting a certain form of cancer as opposed to a 1 in 200 chance. The harm that embezzlement inflicts is usually more direct, but even there, the loss is pretty much always insured and hence is spread out over many policyholders.

A fourth characteristic of corporate crime is that the monetary sums that are involved tend to be quite large. The total amount of money that is stolen by a single extremely successful corporate criminal in a single year is usually considerably greater than, for example, the take of *all* of the robberies in the country in that same year. As we saw in the chapter on criminal violence, the FBI estimates that less than $500 million was stolen in all robberies in the United States last year; this is roughly the sum of the *fines* the government levied against convicted stock swindler Michael Milken. The savings and loan scandal resulted in the "disappearance" of well in excess of $300 *billion*, perhaps 70 to 80 percent of which was a product of illegal acts. Since the money was insured, it will be the government—and ultimately the American taxpayer—that will foot the bill. The per capita cost? Roughly $1,500 for every man, woman, and child in the United States. Sums such as these simply *cannot* be stolen by ordinary thieves. Illegal price-fixing may add as much as $250 *billion* a year to the cost of the products we purchase. It is *only* for white-collar crime that thefts entailing sums in the hundreds of millions and the billions of dollars are possible.

There are two reasons why corporate crime is so much more lucrative than ordinary burglaries, robberies, and larcenies. The first is that street criminals have to steal money in the form of a *physical object*, and hundreds of millions of dollars are rarely found in the same place at the same time; even when it is, it is usually inaccessible except to trusted employees. In contrast, corporate criminals steal by *manipulating symbols*, which means that they can steal money they don't even have to pick up and carry away; indeed, that doesn't even have to *exist* in the form of a physical object. A second reason why so much more can be stolen by the executive thief than by the street criminal: Street

crime tends to be a "one shot deal," a single theft involving a specific sum of money. In contrast, white-collar crime is usually made up of a *number* of *interrelated* actions that extend over a period of time—months, years, even decades.

A fifth characteristic of corporate crime is that it is *rarely* prosecuted; when prosecuted, and if a conviction is obtained, penalties tend to be *extremely* light. With respect to prosecution, evidence indicating that it has taken place is not as clear-cut as with street crime. Police officers do not patrol business offices looking for corporate crimes being committed. Indeed, following up on the point on the complexity of corporate crime, how would the police even *know* when one is being committed? (In addition, business offices are private property and hence, the police cannot enter them until crimes are reported.) Relative to their incidence, arrests are very, very rarely made; the ratio of violations (were this known) to arrests almost certainly approaches and may even surpass that for crimes that entail no complainant, such as drug possession and sale. In addition, even if evidence does indicate criminal behavior, arrest is rare and business executives are rarely convicted for their crimes; conviction, when it does occur, is *extremely* unlikely to lead to a lengthy prison sentence. This is especially striking in view of the amount of money that is stolen. Jail or prison time tends to be almost nonexistent.

Sixth, for the most part, corporate crime does not fit our stereotype of "real" crime; it is rarely condemned to the same degree that street crime is, and there is very little public stigma attached to white-collar crime. When harmful corporate actions are listed on rosters of actions the public is asked to evaluate the seriousness of, for corporate crimes, condemnation tends to be commensurate with harm. The public regards corporate crime in which injury occurs as *serious* crime. However, when members of the public are asked to act in the capacity of jurors and pass judgment on and sentence corporate suspects, they tend to be extremely lenient toward them. In other words, as Friedrichs says, although the public is perfectly willing to see corporate crime as having serious consequences, this does not always translate into being willing to impose harsh sentences on offenders or support legislation calling for such sentences (2004). To put the matter another way, as we've seen, in some ways, there is some question about whether corporate crime even *qualifies* as a form of deviance.

Seventh, the media tend not to cover corporate crime in as complete or detailed a fashion as is the case with street crime. True, there have been a few notable exceptions in recent years: It's hard to ignore the theft of billions of dollars. The fact is, as we've seen, corporate crimes tend to be complex and technical; they are difficult to explain and understand, they are intrinsically unexciting, and there is virtually no way to present them on television in an even remotely dramatic fashion. They do not make "good copy," as members of the media say; they do not provide dramatic "sound bites." They do not make for juicy, sensationalist stories that get page one coverage and a prominent place on the six o'clock news. When they do get space in newspapers, they tend to be buried in the back pages, usually in the financial rather than the hard news section. In order for a story of a corporate crime to appear on television news, one of three conditions has to prevail: one, as I said, the sums stolen have to be huge; two, a scandal must be connected with the theft; or three, the accused must be prominent. For the most part, the public finds news stories of corporate misdeeds boring. It is rare that we have the financial training even to understand the nature of corporate offenses; for most of us, there is little intrinsic *drama* in these stories. The shotgun robbery of a downtown bank, complete with hostages and a standoff with the police—now, that's a story! The gangland execution of a mob figure while he's eating a plate of linguine—that grabs our attention! A daring jewel heist from a famous store, again, captures our fancy and interest. We need not invoke conspiracies among the rich and powerful to account for this; the fact is, for most of us, corporate crimes just don't make it as news. Most of us would turn the channel or the page if confronted with such a story. With rare exceptions, we are just not as interested in such stories as we are in reports of meat-and-potatoes, nuts-and-bolts street crime, which most of us find exciting and entertaining. Of course, fanciful fictional depictions of supposed corporate misdeeds, complete with the murder of rivals or crusading journalists, always sells, but I'm talking about real-life corporate crime.

And eighth, because corporate crime does not correspond to a crime stereotype and is not stigmatizing, corporate criminals, even after being convicted, rarely think of themselves as "real" criminals. To say they "rationalize" away their involvement in "real" crime is not the point. They use a "vocabulary of motives" that permits them to see themselves in a respectable, law-abiding light; they tend to "deny the guilty mind" and insist that, though their actions may have been technically illegal, they did not *intend* to commit a crime. While corporate criminals use a somewhat different explanation or "vocabulary," depending on the crime in question, they are "nearly unanimous in denying [the] basic criminality" of their illegal actions (Benson, 1985, p. 591). While some persons convicted of street crimes and their defenders will insist that they "didn't do it," corporate criminals and their defenders take a different tack: They insist that, even though they engaged in the action of which they were accused, what they did *wasn't a crime*.

Another feature of corporate crime: For the majority of corporate crimes, the *intention* to do harm to a victim is absent. Instead, corporate executives expose parties to a certain measure of *risk*. Whether this risk is acceptable or unacceptable, legal or illegal, is a matter of interpretation. Some corporate actors *knowingly* expose other parties to risks that those parties, and the law, would regard as unacceptable, while other corporate actors do so in the *absence* of such awareness. But nearly all take risk into account and weigh their actions accordingly (Short, 1990). All executives would prefer that the actions they take on behalf of their corporation cause no one any harm. But in the real world, this is not possible. On the one hand, no work site, no product, no industrial waste, can be made completely safe; some level of risk is an inevitable feature of modern existence (Friedrichs, 2004); if corporate risk were to be eliminated altogether, all business activity would cease to exist (Perrow, 1984, p. 311). For instance, no automobile can ever be manufactured in which the likelihood of injury or death is zero. On the other hand, some work sites, products, or waste products are so *blatantly* unsafe, the risk so *immense*, that harm is nearly certain; some corporate actors can be said to *deliberately* expose potential victims to unnecessary, substantial, and avoidable risk.

How does the observer make a judgment that the risk was unacceptable and the action that brought it on is a crime? How do we assess risk? According to what criteria? And *who* assesses it?

Do persons who are themselves exposed to the risk of harm assess its magnitude and the acceptability of that exposure? (In effect, they often do, in civil cases, but only *after* the damage has been done, not at the decision-making stage.) One problem is that people assess risk in an extremely inaccurate fashion, exaggerating the likelihood of certain types of harm and minimizing others (Slovic, Fischoff, and Lichtenstein, 1980; Erikson, 1990; Slovic, Layman, and Flynn, 1991; Friedrichs, 2004). On the other hand, in determining the culpability of corporate actions, do we rely on corporate actors to assess what constitutes "acceptable risk"? Clearly, we do not, for it is members of the general public who sit on juries in civil trials, not hand-picked panels of corporation executives, who are likely to decide on the basis of what's good for the corporation, not what's good for the customer, the public, or the worker.

There is a second risk the corporate actor calculates in addition to the risk of harm to customers, the public, and employees. This is the likelihood of *accountability*—in the case of the criminal law, the risk of arrest and prosecution; in the case of civil and administrative law, the risk of lawsuits and punitive fines. Corporate offenses very, *very* rarely result in criminal prosecution, and administrative agencies rarely slap corporations with huge fines. But torts do result in a *great many* civil trials and, occasionally, in extremely large settlements. In fact, today, product liability is the largest field of civil law (Priest, 1990). Here, quite clearly, we see the inhibitory impact of civil law: It forces executive actors to consider in their cost-benefit analysis the cost of harmful consequences of their operations or products in the form of substantial settlements.

Let's be clear about this: We live in a capitalist society. Corporations are not philanthropic organizations; they are designed and run to earn a profit. So far, all government experiments based on a socialist economy, or any markedly noncapitalist alternative, have either collapsed or been seriously compromised. To a corporation, what counts is the "bottom line." This means that their executives make decisions based almost exclusively on *cost-benefit analysis*: They weigh potential costs against earnings to determine possible or likely profit. To earn a profit, they make decisions to engage, or not to engage, in certain business ventures that may or may not pay off. Business ventures may be costly in various ways. Some may entail huge expenditures and offer little potential reward. Still others are likely to result in extremely unfavorable and irreparable public relations, and hence, to be costly in indirect ways. Others are highly certain to result in criminal prosecution, while still others are so likely to cause damage to customers that extremely expensive lawsuits, along with the possibility of bankruptcy, loom on the horizon. Corporations do not avoid certain actions for the public good or as a service to humanity; they do so because they would be unprofitable.

At this point, a crucial issue needs to be addressed: *Who is the corporate actor?* It is often stated that corporate crimes are distinct, different from practically all others in that they are, *by their very nature*, enacted by a collectivity rather than individual persons. Decisions are arrived at in consultation with higher-ups and approved—or initiated—at the top. It is the *corporation* that acts, as a whole, not scattered, isolated actors, one at a time. Often, after conviction, it is the corporation that is fined, not specific persons working for that corporation. On the other hand, individual corporate actors may be fined, and occasionally sentenced to a term of incarceration. (Clearly, a corporate entity cannot serve a prison sentence!) When the Pennwalt Corporation was convicted and fined more than $1 million for illegally dumping a toxic substance into Puget Sound, a federal district judge insisted on seeing the company's top executive in court before he would accept a guilty plea. "Who is the corporation?" the judge asked; "I think the public is entitled to know who's responsible" (Egan, 1989). Suffice it to say that, though individual persons act, they always do so within certain social structures. In the case of corporate crime, these social structures are formal organizations or bureaucracies. Whether persons or organizations are responsible for a given corporate crime depends on the specific crime in question. But clearly, structural entities play a larger role in acting for corporate crime than, perhaps, for any other type of crime. (For a contrary argument, see Cressey, 1988, who argues that a corporate actor is a fiction—only individual executives act.)

The question of who the corporate actor is plays a central role when we attempt to determine the *incidence* or *rate* of corporate crime. If the corporation is considered as the actor (and if the entire period of its existence is considered as well), then clearly, *most* (and in Sutherland's pioneering study, *all*) corporations are guilty of committing corporate crimes at least once, since at least some executives made decisions that turned out to be illegal. Hence, their *rate* of corporate crime would be enormous. However, if all the executives are included in the total number of actors (and if a year-by-year tally is made), it is possible that rates of corporate crime would be quite low. Most observers who argue that corporate crime is rampant have not devoted much thought to determining its rate relative to the number of persons who are in a position to commit it. Sutherland's study was based on *corporations* as the unit of analysis, but his explanation for white-collar crimes that took place within them—differential association theory—was fundamentally *individualistic*, an obvious *contradiction* (Gottfredson and Hirschi, 1990, pp. 188, 191).

Four Recent Examples of Corporate Deviance

According to the Securities Fraud InfoCenter, securities fraud occurs "when one party deliberately misinforms another party during the trading of stocks, bonds, and other securities." Corporations "are required to submit particular information to the Securities and Exchange Commission [SEC]; if this information is incorrect or incomplete, the company may be liable" (www.securitiesfraudinfocenter.com/information.php).

For years, WorldCom, once the nation's number two Internet services provider, hugely overstated its profits and assets to the SEC. By late 2002, the corporation admitted that it had juggled its books by concealing $9 billion in expenses by claiming them as assets, falsely inflating the company's net worth. As of this writing, the corporation is in Chapter 11 bankruptcy and half a dozen of the corporation's top executives, including its former chief executive officer and its former chief financial officer, have been indicted for conspiracy to commit fraud; they face possible substantial prison sentences. In addition, WorldCom is in the process of settling its civil lawsuit with the SEC (http://news.bbc.co.uk/1hi/business/2407991.stm; www.securities fraud. fyi.com/worldcom_fraud.html).

In 2002, the Securities and Exchange Commission filed civil fraud charges against Dennis Kozlowski, then chief executive officer of Tyco—a conglomerate selling a variety of products including health-care products, electronic equipment, valves, and fire alarms—and two other Tyco executives. (All three have since been fired from the company.) The trio, said the SEC's Director of Enforcement, "treated Tyco as their private bank, taking out hundreds of millions of dollars of loans and compensation without ever telling investors." The complaint seeks monetary penalties, a recovery of the ill-gotten gains, and barring the three from ever serving as officers or directors of a publicly traded company. In tandem with the SEC's suit, Kozlowski and one of the other executives faced criminal charges for stealing $170 million in company loans and obtaining more than $430 million through fraudulent sales of securities, as well as avoiding the payment of sales taxes totaling more than $1 million. As of 2002, Kozlowski owned a 30-million-dollar mansion in Florida and a 5-million-dollar house in Massachusetts; he gave a 17-million-dollar apartment to his ex-wife. He also used company funds to pay for a 1-million-dollar party for his second wife (which featured an ice sculpture of Michelangelo's *David* that spouted vodka from its penis) and bought expensive trinkets for himself, including a $15,000 umbrella stand, a $2,000 wastebasket, and two sets of sheets for

Four Recent Examples of Corporate Deviance (cont.)

$5,900. Revelations caused Tyco's stock to plummet from $15.86 to six cents a share, snatching millions away from the portfolios of shareholders (www.sec.gov/news/press/ 2002-135.htm; http://money.cnn.com/2002/09/19/news/companies/koz lowskijail/; http://www.nydailynews.com/news/story/1866p-17595c.html).

In 1997, Gary Winnick took on AT&T's request to lay an undersea cable linking Europe with the United States; the job raised billions of dollars in revenue, and Global Crossing was born. Eventually, the company laid 100,000 miles of fiber-optic cable connecting four continents and 27 countries. At one time, Winnick was the richest man in Los Angeles, with $6 billion in wealth. In 1998, he bought the most expensive single-family house ever purchased in the United States, at a cost of $60 million; renovations cost another $30 million. At its height, Global Crossing traded on Wall Street for $64 a share. In 2001, saddled with a debt of $12.4 billion and with the company's stock down to 30 cents a share, Global Crossing filed for bankruptcy. During the quarter ending in September 2003, Global Crossing lost $3.3 billion as against a total revenue of only $286 million; demand for high bandwidth cable, it seems, has been plummeting. The company simply never generated enough revenue to sustain its massive debt. Several months before the company filed for bankruptcy, Winnick cashed in $120 million in

stock. In 2002, amid allegations of insider trading, he resigned from the company he had started up. Several lawsuits have been filed against the company (www.wired.com/news/business/0,1367,501 14,00.html; www.texassecuritiesfraud.com/ securities _ pages/suspect-stocks.html).

Between 1998 and 2001, executives at Enron, a company that shipped natural gas through pipelines, made false and misleading statements about the financial performance of the corporation. A growing debt problem was concealed by illegal, undisclosed transactions and partnerships; income was inflated and debts were incomplete and underestimated. The corporation's cooked books sent Enron stock to a high of $90.75 a share. But in 2001, news began leaking out that the corporation was worth considerably less than its stated value. Eventually the SEC stepped in and investigated Enron and Arthur Andersen, the accounting firm that audited the cooked books. A total of 29 Enron executives have been charged with securities, wire, and mail fraud and accused of money laundering and conspiracy; Arthur Andersen was convicted of obstructing justice, paid a fine of half a million dollars, and was placed on probation for five years. The case is so complicated that it will take years for the many cases to be decided (www.enronfraudinfocenter.com/information.php).

POLICE USE OF EXCESSIVE FORCE

Some actions grow out of organizational mandates but turn out, in retrospect, to have been a mistake. Others depart so wildly from organizational expectations that hardly anyone in the organization supports them or their perpetrators. Still others are disputed; disagreement exists within the organization as to their acceptability. In this section, we'll look at three cases of the use of excessive force by the police—indeed, all are violent actions, two of which resulted in serious injury to their victims and one of which resulted in death. From the perspective of the organiza-

tion—that is, the police—they are significantly different from one another, although much of the public saw them in a similar light.

At 12:45 a.m. on March 3, 1991, George Holliday, 33, manager of the local office of a national plumbing firm, was awakened by the sound of police sirens. Looking out his window, he saw a helicopter spotlight trained on a white Hyundai sedan surrounded by six police cars. Holliday grabbed his video camera and began shooting. What he captured on tape was astounding: Two police officers were beating a large Black man with metal truncheons while a third stomped him and ten others watched. (A fourth was later discovered to have been directly involved in the beating.) A total of 23 officers of the Los Angeles Police Department, as well as four from other departments, had been present at the scene. The man being beaten, Rodney King, had received a total of 56 blows to his head, neck, back, ankles, legs, and feet (Skolnick and Fyfe, 1993, p. 3).

The following day, Paul King, Rodney's brother, reported the incident to the police, but received a bureaucratic runaround. When King mentioned the existence of a videotape, the officer he spoke to told King he was in "big trouble" because he had been riding in the car with his brother. No complaint was taken by the desk. Independently, George Holliday, incensed at the beating, contacted his local police station to report the incident, but the desk officer he talked to was clearly uninterested. Again, the police refused to take an official complaint. Frustrated, Holliday called television station KTLA in Los Angeles. A 19-second segment of the 81-second videotape was aired that evening. Not shown in the broadcast footage was the fact that King was zapped with several jolts from an electronic Taser gun, yet got up and "advanced" on several officers. In addition, the police said that King was obviously drunk or high; King's passenger admitted that they had been drinking. None of this excuses the behavior of the officers, but these are factors that do influence police behavior.

The story attracted national and even international media attention. The tape was played repeatedly "until it was seen everywhere in the world, from Tokyo to London to Zaïre. The beating of Rodney King . . . [was] the most explicit and shocking news footage of police brutality ever to be seen on television" (p. 3). Just about everyone who saw the tape, from President George H. W. Bush to the man and woman on the street, was sickened and horrified. Police Chief Darryl Gates condemned the King beating, calling it an "aberration." But it turns out that in the three full years before the incident, over 4,000 citizen complaints were filed against the Los Angeles Police Department. In 1990, the year before the incident took place, the city of Los Angeles paid out over $11 million for police misconduct, including civil rights violations, excessive force, and wrongful death. "What made the King beating different from those earlier events was not the conduct of the police, but the presence of George Holliday's video camera" (p. 3).

King's offense? Speeding, not pulling over when told to do so, and resisting arrest. Four days after the incident, Chief Gates announced that the four officers who had beaten King would face criminal charges. Against the nonparticipants, whom Gates said should have restrained their fellow officers, no criminal charges could have been filed since their inaction was not illegal. On March 15, the four officers, Stacey Koon, Laurence Powell, Theodore Briseno, and Timothy Wind, were officially charged with the use of deadly force and assault with a deadly weapon. The venue of the trial was changed from Los Angeles to Simi Valley, a suburb. All four officers were white. The jury was entirely white. The trial began a year later, in March 1992, and on April 19, the jury rendered its verdict—an acquittal on all charges.

The decision was almost universally regarded as unjust. In a *USA Today* poll taken soon after the trial, 86 percent of the whites and 100 percent of the Blacks interviewed said that the verdict was "wrong." The outrage was felt especially acutely in the inner-city community, which exploded with six days of rioting, violence, arson, and looting. By the time the flames had died down, 54 people had been killed, over 2,000 were injured, 13,000 were arrested, and rioters had caused $700 million in property damage.

In August 1992, the four officers were indicted by a federal grand jury for violating Rodney King's civil rights. (This was not a case of "double jeopardy," since both the charge and the court system were different.) The trial began in February 1993, and in April, the jury rendered its verdict: Koon and Powell were found guilty, and Briseno and Wind were acquitted. This time, riots did not break out. The two convicted officers received a sentence of 30 months' imprisonment. Opinion was split on King's beating: 55 percent of Blacks but only 21 percent of whites felt that the officers were not punished enough by the conviction of only two officers. Some public commentary was generated by the venue of their incarceration. The prison in which they served their time is nicknamed "Club Fed" for its loose control of inmates and its well-appointed facilities (www.crimsonbird.com/history/rodneyking.htm).

*   *   *

At four in the morning on August 9, 1997, a report of a disturbance outside a Haitian social club in Brooklyn, the Rendez-Vous, was called in to the local police precinct. While attempting to disperse the crowd, several officers began pushing people around, including, some eyewitnesses reported, a pregnant woman. A verbal altercation ensued, and a fistfight broke out between an unidentified man and one officer, Justin Volpe. Volpe was knocked to the ground, and the man who hit him ran away. The police, enraged, began insulting the crowd, hurling, some bystanders said, racial insults at them. Several scuffles broke out between officers and members of the crowd.

Abner Louima, 30, was watching the melee when an officer told him to shut up. Louima was shoved to the ground, handcuffed, put into a patrol car with two officers, and driven two blocks, where he was put into another car, then kicked and beaten with police radios. Clearly, Louima had been mistaken for the man who punched Volpe. The cops proceeded to drive him to an unlighted, more deserted area, where they were joined by two more officers, at which point the beating resumed. Louima was then taken to the 70th Precinct station house, where, at the booking desk, he was stripped—supposedly in a search for guns and drugs—with his pants around his ankles, "in full view of the cops." Two officers then walked Louima to the bathroom and closed the door. Shouting racial slurs, one officer, reported Louima, said, "If you yell or make any noise, I will kill you." While one officer held Louima down, the other shoved a stick (some said a toilet plunger, others, a broom handle) up his rectum, pulled it out, shoved it into his mouth, breaking several teeth, and said, "That's your shit," ending with a racial insult (www.nubeing.com/archives/torture.htm). The police then put Louima in a jail cell.

There, Louima began hemorrhaging; his condition looked serious. A fellow prisoner managed to convince an officer that Louima needed immediate medical attention. Several hours later, an ambulance took Louima to the Coney Island Hospital emergency room. No officers accompanied him to the hospital. Louima had a punctured bladder and a severed colon, and required extensive surgery. He was handcuffed to his bed. He remained in critical condition for four days following his operation, and had to undergo several additional surgical procedures. He was not released from the hospital until mid-October, over two months after he was assaulted (www.radcliffe.edu/quarterly/199703/page25a.html).

The torture of Abner Louima touched off an international firestorm of outrage. Almost universally, without regard to race, the public deemed the station-house abuse a deviant act. Outside the Brooklyn Supreme Court building, demonstrators waved toilet plungers and Haitians held posters that read "Yes, Massa," "Close Down the 70th," and "NYPD: KKK!" Hundreds of editorials were published expressing horror at the atrocity and demanding justice. Members of the 70th Precinct were dubbed "Rapist Pigs." Johnny Cochran, famed courtroom lawyer, offered his services on behalf of Abner Louima. Don King, flamboyant boxing promoter, handed Louima a check for $5,000 (www.mariebrenner.com/articles/incident/70.html). Eventually, Louima won an $8.7 million civil settlement, $7.1 from the City of New York and $1.6 from the NYPD's Patrolmen's Benevolent Association. It was the largest settlement involving the police in the history of the city.

Five officers in the 70th Precinct were indicted for a variety of crimes, including assault, conspiracy, and obstruction of justice. In May 1999, they went on trial. Within three weeks, Justin Volpe, the man who assaulted Louima with the stick, tearfully pled guilty to the charges; he received a sentence of 30 years in prison. In June, Charles Swarz, the man who was accused of holding Louima down, was found guilty; after appeal, he was convicted again and received a sentence of five years. (Swarz's guilt was based on conflicting testimony; it remains controversial to this day.) After several trials, the other three defendants were acquitted of all charges.

*   *   *

During the evening of February 3, 1999, Edward McMellon, Sean Carroll, Kenneth Boss, and Richard Murphy, officers working for the Street Crime Unit of the New York City Police Department (NYPD), were patrolling a neighborhood in the South Bronx, looking for a reported serial rapist who was said to be in the area. All four were in plainclothes and wore bulletproof vests. At 12:45 a.m., they came upon Amadou Diallo, a 22-year-old street peddler and West African immigrant, near the doorway of an apartment building. McMellon and Carroll had mounted the steps in front of the building, Murphy was on the sidewalk, and Boss was crouched behind a parked car on the street. The officers identified themselves, flashed their police shields, and demanded that Diallo freeze and raise his hands. The young man darted toward the vestibule of the building, then stopped and seemed to reach for something in his pocket. The officers opened fire with a barrage of bullets. McMellon and Carroll fell backwards off the stairs, then unleashed another barrage of bullets. In all, 41 rounds were fired; 19 of them struck Diallo. Murphy fired four times, Boss five; both McMellon and Carroll emptied their 16-round clips.

The young man lay dead by the doorway of his apartment building.

The police officers approached the body and quickly realized that Diallo had been unarmed and was probably reaching for his wallet, presumably to provide documentation of his identity. According to an officer called to the scene of the shooting, Carroll was hunched over Diallo's body, "crying profusely." According to the police, the killing had been "a tragic mistake." Militant African-American spokespersons claimed it was the "execution" of an innocent, unarmed Black man. Even many moderates argued that had Diallo been white, the police would not have been so quick on the trigger; chances are, they say, he would still be alive. It was agreed in nearly all quarters that the 41 bullets, and the 19 that struck Diallo, were compelling evidence of police recklessness. As with the Louima case, the killing of Amadou Diallo ignited a torrent of invective against the police and cries for justice. Clearly, much of the public regarded the shooting as *deviant*.

At the end of March 1999, the four officers were suspended from the NYPD. In April, the suspected serial rapist they had been looking for was arrested. In December, the officers' trial was moved from New York City to Albany, where, supposedly, the emotions of the local public would be less heated. The officers were charged with intentional murder, second-degree murder with depraved indifference to human life, and reckless endangerment. They faced the possibility of spending the rest of their lives in prison. On February 1, 2000, a jury was selected for the trial; it consisted of eight whites and four African Americans. The next day, the trial began. Not admitted at trial was the officers' history of gunplay, civilian complaints, and brutality. Three of the four officers had fired their weapons on the job; three of the four had civilian complaints lodged against them. McMellon, who had wounded a suspect, had five such complaints, and Boss, who had three, had killed a man who was threatening people with a shotgun.

On February 25, 2000, the jury returned its verdict. All four officers were acquitted on all counts. Critics of police brutality were horrified and outraged. How could such a thing have happened? Wasn't it a clear-cut case of the murder of an innocent, unarmed Black suspect? At the very least, wasn't it a display of a reckless and depraved indifference to human life? Surely racism was involved. How could such a brutal act go unpunished? Two days after the trial was over, 1,400 people held a prayer vigil outside the United Nations in New York City to protest the decision. The same day, the foreperson of the jury, an African-American woman who used to live in the Bronx, was quoted by a reporter as saying that the verdict "has nothing to do with race" (http://crime.about.com/library/blfiles/bldiallo.htm; www.courttv.com/archive/national/diallo/02800-background_ctv.html).

*   *   *

The police are charged with protecting the public, keeping the peace, and enforcing the law. With the exception of a military situation, the police and only the police have a monopoly on *general, legitimate, coercive force*. The police are authorized to issue a lawful command to any and all citizens, and they can back up that command with the force of the state. And violence is, of course, the most *extreme* form of coercive force. Representatives of no other entity or institution in society have that power (Bittner, 1970, pp. 36ff.). Clearly, if more than one entity had that power, chaos would be the inevitable result, since all institutions have *some* goals or practices that conflict with others. But just as clearly, the police sometimes abuse this power; hence, we encounter cases such as those I just described. These three cases attracted a huge volume of public and media attention. Consider the sheer number of websites on Google devoted to each: Rodney King (70,000), Abner Louima (10,000), Amadou Diallo (20,000). Many of these sites express outrage against police abuse; they argue that these three Black men were the victims of police brutality.

When one sector of the society is authorized to use force under certain circumstances, this inevitably raises the question of *at what point* police force is acceptable, and when does it become too much force—unacceptable, inappropriate, or deviant. However, this begs an even thornier issue: *Who decides* what's too much force? To put the matter another way: What are the "understandings and standards" of the police about the use of force (Hunt, 1985, p. 316)? And what is *the public's* understanding of what constitutes excessive force? And *which sectors* of the public hold what understandings on this issue? Does this vary by race? Political orientation? How does *the court system* render its judgments? Clearly, these questions are directly relevant to the construction-ist approach to deviance. They address the matter of what different observers, located in different sectors or institutions in the society, consider the illegitimate or deviant use of force.

According to Jennifer Hunt (1985), the police themselves "classify and evaluate" acts of force into three categories—legal, normal, and excessive. Legal force is "going by the book." It is that degree of force that is necessary to subdue a modal (or most common) suspect and take him or her into custody. *Normal* force is made up of those coercive acts that the police consider "necessary, appropriate, reasonable, or understandable" (p. 317). The important thing to note about normal force is that it may or may not be legal, but it is considered a "natural response to normal police to particular situational exigencies" (p. 317). This means that under certain extraordinary circumstances, the police may have to bend or break the law to do their job. In contrast, the third type of force, *excessive* force—popularly known as "police

brutality"—is not deemed by the police as normal, necessary, or justified. This type of force is considered *by the police* illegitimate, immoral, unacceptable—and deviant. The police learn to make these distinctions not in the academy, but on the street, as rookies, in their working inter-action with more experienced officers. The police phrase, "It's not done on the street the way it's taught in the academy," expresses "the perceived contradiction between the formal world of the police academy and the informal world of the street" (p. 318).

The three cases of police violence discussed above illustrate the distinction the police make between "normal" and "excessive" force, and the fact that *their* understanding of what constitutes normal force varies substantially from what the public's understanding is. Let's look at two of these cases—the beating and torture of Abner Louima and the shooting of Amadou Diallo.

No police officers or representatives of the police force or defenders of the police defended the treatment of Louima. (Some observers felt that Swarz was wrongfully convicted, not because they thought that what he did was acceptable but because, they believe he was not the second man in the men's room. And some felt that the original—life—sentences were excessive for aggravated assault, since murder often draws a lesser penalty.) If one were to look through the 10,000 websites called up by a Google search for the entry "Abner Louima," one would search in vain for a single one defending the actions of the police in the Louima case, at least what happened in the station house. In other words, the beating and torture of Abner Louima were regarded by the police, by the public, and by the courts as a case of police brutality, that is, excessive, over-the-top coercive force—illegitimate, illegal, and deviant. The police and the public agree completely on this point; it was completely noncontroversial. The fact that the principal actor was convicted and sentenced to a 30-year term indicates that the court agreed with this view.

While the beating and torture of Louima found no supporters on the part of either the police or the public, on the matter of the shooting of Amadou Diallo there was a much more complicated reaction. African Americans overwhelmingly opposed the action of the police; most in fact regarded it as a crime. The fact that the young man was shot 19 times, and that officers on the scene fired a total of 41 rounds, indicated to many observers that the police displayed a "reckless and depraved indifference to human life." And the fact that Diallo was Black underscored the fact, many argued, that the police resort to violence more readily, and more brutally, when suspects are members of a racial minority.

Still, a division did exist. A *New York Times*/CBS poll taken of New York State residents just after the decision found that half of respondents (50 percent) felt that the jury decision to acquit the officers was wrong, 30 percent said that it was right, and 20 percent said they weren't sure. The fact that Diallo refused to obey orders, did not raise his hands, seemed to be reaching for something in his pocket, and was standing in a dimly lit doorway led some members of the public to believe that his killing was a tragic mistake, not a brutal crime, and hence, that the officers who killed him should have been acquitted of murder. However, this opinion was sharply divided by race. Only 8 percent of Blacks said that the acquittal was the "right" verdict; 77 percent said it was "wrong," and the remainder weren't sure. Whites were more nearly evenly split: 37 percent "right," 40 percent "wrong." Residents of New York City were more likely to think the decision was wrong than those living elsewhere, and women were more likely to think it was wrong than men (www.cbsnews.com/stories/2000/02/28/opinion/mail165965.shtml).

While the public was divided but more opposed to the action of the officers than accepting, among the police, the view that the officers who shot Diallo made a mistake but did not commit a crime was practically universal. In fact, it was as a result of the testimony of the police that an acquittal was rendered. Probably the most compelling testimony at the trial was given by James Fyfe, a former police officer, criminologist, and coauthor of a book on police brutality (Skolnick and Fyfe, 1993). In point of fact, Fyfe usually testifies *against* police officers in cases of police brutality. He is keenly aware of the distinction between justified and unjustified police force. In all likelihood, his views on the shooting reflect those of urban police generally. Fyfe told jurors that Diallo had refused to stop when he was commanded to do

so. "It is the job of the officers to protect life," Fyfe said. Diallo, he continued, "ran from the officers into a building with innocent citizens. It is the job of the officers to prevent him from entering the building and putting its occupants in danger. . . . Things can only get worse if he gets out of sight" (www.courttv.com/archive/national/diallo/021600_ctv.html).

Patrick Lynch, president of the NYPD's Patrolmen's Benevolent Association—which paid a portion of the officers' legal bills—was quoted as saying: "The fear for your life you have. . . , your adrenaline is pumping. You have an obligation to save yourself, save the other officers, the citizens that might be behind you. [All] this comes into play. When we're in the quiet of the courtroom where you can hear a pin drop, it's easy to second-guess. But when you're standing on that stoop and everything is breaking loose, that's what the police officer is dealing with." When asked whether, if Diallo had been a white man, he'd be alive today, Lynch emphatically disagreed. "If it was a white person who ran into a dark alley and turned like they had a weapon, I'm going to save my life, I'm going to save my partner's life—regardless of who's trying to kill me" (www.pbs.org/newshour/bb/law/jan-june00/diallo_3-3.html).

At the end of January 2001, the Justice Department issued a statement to the effect that after an investigation, its Civil Rights Division and U.S. Attorney Mary Jo White concluded that federal charges against the officers "were not warranted." Federal officials determined that they "could not prove beyond a reasonable doubt that the officers willfully deprived Mr. Diallo of his constitutional right to be free from the use of unreasonable force." Acting U.S. Attorney General Eric Holder agreed. This decision indicates that the courts agreed with the police that a tragic mistake had taken place—not a crime (www.cbsnews.com/stories/2000/03/02/national/main167178.shtml). And in this respect, they drew a sharp distinction between this case and those involving the beatings of Rodney King (which resulted in no conviction in state court but two in federal court) and Abner Louima (two convictions at the state level). And clearly, in this respect, the judgments of the police and the courts are the same (the killing of Diallo was not a crime, and was not a deviant act), while both differ sharply with the judgments of the vast majority of the African-American community and roughly half of the white community (who believed the killing of Diallo *was* a crime, and a deviant act as well). Once again, judgments of deviance depend on where one stands.

Let's return to the distinctions I made at the beginning of this section. The beating and torture of Abner Louima was considered totally contrary to the mandates of the police, and had no supporters within the force. In contrast, the shooting of Amadou Diallo was regarded as a tragic accident that grew out of acceptable police mandates, namely, to enforce the law and protect the public. *To the police*, it was a mistake only in retrospect—that is, the policy that caused it was considered good, but in this case, the outcome was bad. The beating of Rodney King was even more complicated. Here, the police were split on the issue. When the unabridged version of the tape was shown to them, many police officers agreed that King was probably intoxicated, that he had "advanced" several times on the officers, that he had refused to obey a command to lie on the ground, and that the two charges from the Taser gun and successive blows from police truncheons had failed to subdue him. Not all officers agreed, and some believed that King should have been subdued by other means. Again, what we are addressing here is not the *reality* of these cases but the *perceived* or *constructed* reality. And in this respect, the officers who attacked Abner Louima committed a deviant act, the ones who shot Amadou Diallo did not, while those who beat Rodney King engaged in an action that was not clear-cut either way.

THE SEXUAL ABUSE OF CHILDREN BY ROMAN CATHOLIC PRIESTS

Sexual contact between an adult and a child is both deviant and criminal. The child molester is considered "the lowest of the low," beyond the pale—the deviant *par excellence*. Even in prison, he or she is despised and persecuted by other prisoners. And since, below a certain age—and the age depends on the jurisdiction—a person is not legally capable of granting sexual consent, any

adult who has sexual contact with a child has committed a crime, even if the child initiated the contact.

The sexual abuse of children by priests is both deviant and criminal, but it poses special issues that make it worth exploring in a discussion on the sociology of deviance. Reports of priestly molestation indicate that the abuse of boys outnumbers that of girls by a factor of 10 to 1. This makes it a form of homosexuality, and hence, doubly deviant. And sexual abuse by a Roman Catholic priest is regarded as an especially heinous act because of the priest's prestige and aura of holiness, as well as the trust parishioners place in their clerics. Catholics consider the priest God's representative on earth—in a sense, a reflection of divinity. As a result, when a Catholic cleric molests a child in his pastoral care, he is corrupting the Church, soiling the cloth of the priesthood, defiling God, and betraying the trust believers have in him. And while the abusive priest tends to act alone, he holds a position in a very large organization. More important for our purposes, the *reactions* of the Catholic hierarchy to charges of sexual abuse of children by priests reveal that *enacting* deviance is not the same thing as *being permitted to engage in* deviant acts. In many social circles, tolerating and covering up priestly abuse is regarded as even more deviant than the abuse itself. In this respect, we have a perfect example of organizational deviance on our hands.

Imagine a spectrum or continuum of organizational deviance that stretches from those that are *completely acceptable* within the organization to those that are *completely unacceptable*. "Completely acceptable" organizational deviance would be those acts that *members of the organization* deem acceptable, but that are judged *un*acceptable outside the organization—say, to the general public, to sectors of the public, to law enforcement, or to the media. Many forms of corporate crime fit this characterization. At the other end of this spectrum, we find acts committed by individuals in an organizational structure that are *discouraged* by the norms of the organization, *contrary* to the mandates of the organization, negatively *sanctioned* by the organization (although they may be concealed from the general public), and that may in fact *undermine* the interests and goals of the organization. In between, we find acts supported by organizational mandates but whose specific execution may hurt the organization. Clearly, some instances of police violence—the Amadou Diallo case included—qualify for the last of these types.

The sexual abuse of children by priests is one of the most extreme cases we could find of a deviant act that is committed *within* an organizational context, *by* individuals who are representatives of the organization, that *corrupts* organizational mandates. (Yet, as we'll find out, it is an act whose perpetrators have not, until very recently, been appropriately punished.) The sexually abusive priest, like the police officer who engages in excessive force, acts *under the cloak of the organization*. Priestly abuse is similar to the case of the police torture of Abner Louima—but very different from the shooting of Amadou Diallo—in that the former was totally contrary to organizational norms, guidelines, and mandates, while the latter was not. As we saw, members of the organization regarded the Diallou shooting as a tragic mistake rather than deviant and criminal behavior *in its totality*. As with the Louima case, there are virtually *no* justifications that are likely to work in the case of abusive priests. Claiming mental disorder is likely to be regarded as a self-serving rationalization, at least to the general public. However, while at all stages in Louima's beating, at least one other officer acted in concert with Volpe's actions, abusive priests nearly always act alone. In fact, so extreme is the case of abusive priests that the act itself is only marginally an instance of organizational deviance. What makes it most interesting as a case of organizational deviance is how Catholic authorities have tolerated it over the years.

To truly launch our discussion, we need to clear away the conceptual and empirical underbrush. The issue has become so tangled and confused that we need to clarify what's being said and what is implied. For starters, as Philip Jenkins points out (1996), the Catholic clergy does not have a monopoly on sexually abusing youthful parishioners. Sexual scandals have rocked Orthodox Judaism (Cooperman, 2002), Jehovah's Witnesses (Goodstein, 2002), and, indeed, all religious faiths. There is no evidence that priests are any more likely to molest children in their care than are non-Catholic clergy. Second, a corollary of this point is that the

vast majority of Catholic priests do *not* molest the children in their flocks. As a result of the recent revelations of abuse, the sins of the few have tainted all Catholic clergy. Third, Jenkins continues, the *stereotype* of sexual molestation by priests is that, typically, very young prepubescent children—six or seven years of age—are being molested. In fact, Jenkins asserts, the *reality* is that priests are most likely to sexually approach minors in their adolescent years—15, 16, and 17 years old—rather than small children. On top of this, we have to add the fact that not every accusation is valid. False accusations have been, and continue to be, made, harming the accused and tainting the Church.

There are many interesting and distinctive features of organizational deviance. Among them, none is so crucially tied in to the importance of social reactions as *how the authorities within the organization react to and deal with the wrongdoing*. In other words, we should not be surprised by the fact that *some* cops use excessive violence on citizens, or that *some* priests sexually molest children in their pastoral care. Deviant behavior has been, is, and will continue to be a fixture in all societies, everywhere, and at all times. *Some* members of *every* society and social collectivity on earth will violate *some* of that society's, and that collectivity's, rules. *No* social grouping on earth is immune from deviance. Incidents of police use of excessive force against citizens and priestly molestation of children can be substantially reduced, but they will never be totally eliminated. In contrast, organizational tolerance by the hierarchy of wrongdoing by the rank-and-file is far more amenable to change.

Organizational tolerance of wrongdoing gets to the heart of the subject matter of the study of deviance. And it is directly relevant to the molestation of children by Roman Catholic priests. Are priests punished for this act? Have they been punished in the past?

Reactions by the Catholic Church in the United States to allegations of child molestation by priests can be divided very roughly into three eras—pre-1985, 1985–2002, and post-2002.

The pre-1985 era can be summed up quite simply. The Catholic Church did very little to punish priests who sexually abused the children in their care. Complaining families were told to keep the matter quiet, authorities in the Church did not contact law enforcement, and priests were typically sent to a program of psychological or spiritual counseling, then transferred to another parish.

This radically changed in 1985.

In 1983, six families in Henry, Louisiana, sued their local diocese and Gilbert Gauthe, the priest of their church, claiming that their boys had been sodomized by the priest. The diocese transferred Gauthe to a treatment center in Massachussetts and made a monetary settlement with the families. The judge who officiated in the case sealed the papers that dealt with the case. But in 1984, another boy stepped forward, and his lawyer filed a suit with the same Lafayette court. The boy, Scott Gaskell, refused to accept the "hush money" settlement. His lawyer, Minos Simon, said, "The whole damn thing was wrapped in a cocoon of secrecy. The church knew damn well this dude had gone ape-wild down in Henry" (Powell, 2002, p. F4).

The civil lawsuit that followed caused the Lafayette district attorney to initiate a criminal investigation. During the investigation, it became clear to Ray Mouton, Gauthe's attorney, that Gauthe was not the only Louisiana priest who had molested children. Mouton, along with Michael Peterson, a psychologist specializing in treating priests, and The Reverend Tom Doyle, a representative of the Church, prepared a report on priestly abuse. In it, they warned of the problem and the impending blizzard of lawsuits the Church would have to deal with, and they suggested some solutions. In 1985, the Church announced that it would form a committee and launch its own probe, and recommended that Mouton, Peterson, and Doyle shut down their investigation. In point of fact, the Church appointed no committee and conducted no inquiry. Meanwhile, in 1985, Gauthe pled guilty to molesting children and was sentenced to a 20-year term and psychiatric treatment. He was released after serving nine years, was arrested in Texas after fondling a three-year-old boy, and was sentenced to a seven-year term of probation. For a time, he counseled sex offenders in a Texas prison. Then, in 1998, a woman accused Gauthe of having raped her 17 years previously; he got off on a legal technicality. Most recently, he worked as a groundskeeper in Houston (Powell, 2002).

The 1985 Gauthe case touched off a firestorm of anger toward the Catholic Church and encouraged dozens of boys, and men who had been molested much earlier, to step forward and lodge accusations against their abusers. Charges were made, investigations—civil, criminal, and ecclesiastical—were launched, offenders were formally charged and punished. Suddenly, the media were ablaze with stories about the sexual abuse of children by priests. Hundreds, indeed thousands, of stories were broadcast about the subject. For the first time, the Roman Catholic Church was forced to acknowledge that this was a major problem and that steps had to be taken to deal with it. Lawsuits mounted. Unlike the stereotype many non-Catholics hold, the Vatican cannot simply write a check every time a local diocese needs cash. Officials had to scramble to compensate the litigants. They sold property, held fundraisers. Many believers began questioning the integrity of their church—even their faith.

As if that had not been enough, in February 2002, John Geoghan, a defrocked priest, was sentenced to a 10-year prison term for fondling a 10-year-old boy. Between 1995 and 2002, more than 130 boys and men charged that Geoghan fondled or raped them. He was named by more than 80 persons who have brought civil suits against the Boston diocese. Geoghan's career of molesting boys stretched back for 40 years. Each time an incident was reported to authorities in the Church, the Church hushed it up, sent Geoghan for counseling, and transferred him to another parish. Nearly all of Geoghan's sexual abuse took place under the auspices of dioceses in Massachusetts.

Here are a few highlights of Geoghan's career as a priestly pedophile:

• In 1966, Geoghan's superior in Blessed Sacrament, the parish church at Saugus, reports that the priest had brought boys into his bedroom—a report his superior later denied having made. Geoghan spends an extended stay in a rectory at Concord. No explanation is given by the Church as to the nature of that stay.
• In 1967, Geoghan is transferred to St. Paul's Church in Hingham. In 1968, a father complains to Church authorities that his son was molested by Geoghan; several members of the same church lodge the same accusation. Geoghan is sent to a therapeutic institute in Baltimore.

• Geoghan is sent to St. Mary's Church in Melrose. There, in the early 1970s, a mother complains to authorities that her four boys had been molested by Geoghan. She is told to keep quiet; a financial settlement is reached.

• In 1974, Geoghan is sent to St. Andrew's in Jamaica Plain. There, Geoghan is accused of molesting seven boys in the same family; the lawsuit is later settled. Geoghan admits the abuse but says he "does not feel it a serious or a pastoral matter." In 1980, Geoghan is placed on sick leave and undergoes psychotherapy.

• In 1981, he is sent to St. Brendan's in Dorchester. There, parents lodge numerous complaints of molestation against Geoghan to authorities. In March 1984, Bernard Law is installed as archbishop of Boston. He is elevated to cardinal in 1985.

• In September 1984, Law removes Geoghan from St. Brendan's, transferring him to St. Julia's parish in Weston. There, he is put in charge of three youth groups, including altar boys. An auxiliary bishop complains to Law about Geoghan's "history of homosexual involvement with young boys." In December, the therapist who had been working with Geoghan declares the priest "fully recovered."

• Between 1986 and 1989, several fresh allegations of molestation involving Geoghan are lodged with the Church. In 1989, Geoghan is placed on sick leave and undergoes therapy in institutes in Maryland and Connecticut. In November, he is released; his evaluation states that he is "moderately improved" and that the likelihood that he will "act out again" is "quite low," though there was no guarantee he wouldn't offend again. However, one psychiatrist who treated Geoghan tells the priest's bishop: "You'd better clip his wings before there is an explosion. . . . You can't afford to have him in a parish." Cardinal Law tells Geoghan: "I am confident that you will again render fine priestly service to the people of God in Saint Julia's Parish."

• In 1990, Geoghan is OK'd for return to priestly duties at St. Julia's. During the early 1990s, more than half a dozen parents make complaints about Geoghan molesting their boys. In 1995, the Church receives a psychiatric evaluation of the priest that recommends that "Father Geoghan should have no interpersonal contact with male minors that is unsupervised." In the same year, Geoghan is accused of molesting a boy during the boy's sister's confirmation ceremony. In 1996, he spends six months in therapy at a psychiatric institute in Ontario.

• In 1996, after approving his retirement status, Cardinal Law says to Geoghan: "Yours has been an effective life of ministry, sadly impaired by illness. . . . God bless you, Jack." He is recommended for retirement.

• In 1997, Church officials review Geoghan's history of sexual abuse.

• In 1998, after suing the Boston diocese, a small portion of Geoghan's accusers are awarded $30 million (later reduced to $10 million). The accusations and lawsuits against Geoghan—and the Boston diocese—mount. Cardinal Law flies to Rome and formally requests the Vatican to relieve Geoghan of his collar. Geoghan is defrocked (www.kenanderson.net/bible/johngeoghan.html; Miller et al., 2002).

Geoghan's 2002 criminal conviction ignited a firestorm of commentary from the media and soul-searching by the Catholic Church. In August 2003, Geoghan, then 68, an inmate in a maximum security penitentiary, was murdered by fellow convict Joseph Druse, a neo-Nazi racist homophobe. Some observers, including Geoghan's victims, said it was a fitting end for a man who caused a great deal of harm to a great many people who trusted him. However, the case of the infamous Father Geoghan produced two seismic changes in how the Roman Catholic Church and its parishioners handled instances of child abuse by priests. The first was the decision by the Catholic hierarchy 2002 to dismiss abusive clerics from the priesthood. And the second was that lay Catholics were no longer willing to keep silent when a priest abused their children. Geoghan's case especially unleashed a torrent of revelations of abuse stretching back decades.

The New York Times undertook its own investigation and found that the sexual abuse crisis that "engulfed" the Roman Catholic Church in the year after the conviction of John Geoghan "has spread to nearly every American diocese" (Goodstein, 2003, p. 1). As of the last day of 2002, the *Times* documented more than 1,200 cases of abusive priests nationwide involving over 4,200 people "who have claimed publicly or in lawsuits to have been abused by priests," although experts believe the number who have remained silent is certainly much larger (p. 1). The fact is, after 2002, the Roman Catholic Church will never be the same again.

Interestingly, in 1993, before the Geoghan case broke open, Cardinal Law had to deal with another abusive priest, Father James Porter of Fall River, who was criminally convicted of abusing 28 children and sentenced to 20 years in prison. In response, Law formed a panel of experts to lay down policy for such cases; a copy of the panel's report was given to every priest in Law's diocese. But the report did *not* recommend that cases be turned over to the police; they were expected to be handled within the Church. Moreover, media attention to the Porter case, as well as to Geoghan, "sent the cardinal around the bend." He especially attacked *The Boston Globe*, whose writers later produced a series of articles that was eventually collected into a volume entitled *Betrayal: The Crisis in the Catholic Church*. Law's response to the attention the media devoted to priestly abuse? "By all means," he intoned, "we call down God's power on the media, particularly *The Globe*" (Miller et al., 2002, p. 49).

Geoghan is extremely atypical, perhaps the very worst offender of a type of offense that is itself statistically atypical. The two sides of the Geoghan case are laid out by the two "missions" I spelled out in Chapter 2—the positivist's mission and the constructionist's mission. The positivist asks the "Why do they do it?" question. What causes child molestation by priests? Are the priests who molest different from those who don't? Is there something in their personalities and background that leads them to abuse the minors in their care? Or is it perhaps the distinctive qualities of the Roman Catholic Church that leads to molestation by the clergy, as some have argued (Wills, 2002)? The constructionist asks a very different question: How do different audiences *define* child abuse by clerics, and *react to* and *deal with* accused offenders? And here, the relevant audiences include the Catholic hierarchy, the offending priests themselves, the Catholic laity, the families of molested boys, the public at large, the media, and law enforcement.

As I said earlier, by itself, priestly sexual abuse is an imperfect case of organizational deviance, since it is committed by individuals (albeit those who occupy an institutional position), and their actions subvert the intentions of the organization. In contrast, the cover-up by Church authorities is a *perfect* case of organizational deviance, since it is usually done by a collectivity—one or more authorities who consult with one another and reach a decision together—and it is done with the (misguided) intention of protecting the organization. And here, it is the cover-up that has been the primary focus of criticism by the media and the public. The cover-up has two aspects. The first aspect relates to civil sanction, and the second, ecclesiastical.

First, unless a case independently came to the attention of secular authorities, prior to 2002, the Church *rarely*—and prior to 1985, *practically never*—reported a case of priestly abuse to the police. The sexual molestation of a child is a crime. Says media pundit Charles Krauthammer (2002): "Why didn't the Church call the cops?" Priests, and the bishops who preside over their conduct, are citizens of nations with laws that apply to everyone living within their jurisdiction. The surprise, says Krauthammer, is not that a tiny minority of priests abused the cloth and their charges. "The surprise is that when it happened—when the first child was abused by a priest—his superiors could see only the need for therapy and ministry." How the Church treats sin, he continues, is not a concern for non-Catholics. How the Church treats crime, "whether it reports criminality occurring within its gates for adjudication and punishment by secular authorities," is of "absolute concern." The fact that such cries of outrage have sounded throughout the country from Catholics and non-Catholics alike is a sure-fire indication that the cover-ups of these crimes by Church authorities are regarded as a serious form of deviance by a substantial portion of the American public.

The ecclesiastical side of the cover-up is this: In the past, when Church authorities received reports of priestly abuse, they almost never "defrocked" the priest, that is, removed him from the priesthood. In 2002, *The Washington Post* requested from the nation's 178 Roman Catholic dioceses complete records of cases of accusations of sexual abuse by priests going back to the 1960s. Ninety-six dioceses supplied the records; 82 refused to do so. In these records, there were a total of 855 priests against whom accusations were made, 218 of which were lodged specifically between January and June, 2002. Of the 355 priests who were removed from office prior to 2002, only 20 were "defrocked." The remainder were asked to retire or were kept on as priests but not allowed to say Mass or engage in the ministry. As of June, all of the 2002 cases were still pending (Cooperman and Sun, 2002). Indeed, anecdotally, prior to 1985, *nearly every* priest against whom parishioners lodged sexual abuse charges was ordered to undergo psychological counseling or therapy, then simply transferred to another parish. Considering the seriousness of the charges, most observers, whether Catholic or non-Catholic, would consider the penalty so minor as to be a "a slap on the wrist."

The question many observers have about such lenient punishments is: Why? Why the silence, the cover-ups, the shuffling of abusive priests from parish to parish, the inability to punish offenders with a sanction as serious as the offense deserves? Why have abusive priests been tolerated and protected by the Church for so long? Why did it take a series of scandals and criminal convictions for the Church to face and deal with the problem?

All organizations are self-protective; all act, in varying degrees, to cover up revelations that would be harmful to their interests. In this respect, as a religious organization, the Roman Catholic Church is different from other religious organizations only in the *degree* to which it is secretive of its sins. And it is clear that the difference lies in the fact that other denominations are far more decentralized. An accusation against an individual rabbi or Protestant minister is not typically considered an accusation against God. (Two possible exceptions: charismatic Protestant sects and the Jewish haredim, or ultra-Orthodox.) In contrast, the belief that priests are the embodiment of God's holiness is far more ingrained in Catholics, from the humblest layperson on up to the Pope himself. An attack on any aspect of the Church is regarded as an attack against God. Just as God must be defended, if anyone in the Church is venal, corrupt, or sinful, the Church must be protected from being undermined, even if it means covering up the venality, corruption, and sins of the wrongdoer. One of the boys in Boston "was struck in the face by his mother when he told her a priest had molested him" (Wills, 2002, p. 9). "By Vatican lights," says Jason Berry, author of *Lead Us Not Into Temptation*, a book about priestly abuse, "the worst

thing a bishop can do is become publicly associated with a scandal" (Miller et al., 2002, p. 48).

Priests—and that most emphatically includes bishops and cardinals—feel that "the source of their wisdom must be their supernatural powers" (Wills, 2002, p. 8). Says Father Donald Cozzens, who has investigated and counseled pedophile clerics, the priest believes "he is not like other men." When he asked the priests he worked with whether they were sorry for causing harm to their victims, their response lacked conviction or remorse. "I don't remember one priest acknowledging any kind of moral torment for the behavior that got them in trouble" (p. 9). Moreover, "the conviction that they are above the law has much to do with the compliance of their victims" (p. 9). A file kept by the Boston diocese on pedophile priest Paul Shanley and released to the public by Shanley's lawyers for his victims' use in court reminds us of that fact. According to Wills: "The man expresses no feelings of guilt, *and his superiors never suggest that he should*" (my emphasis; p. 9). Throughout his dealings with authorities, Shanley "continues to feel that he is the wronged person." And Cardinal Law aided and abetted him in this view by regarding one of his victims as something of a stalker. Said Law to Shanley: "It must be very discouraging to have someone following you" (p. 9). Law and his bishops "express unfailing support and sympathy for Shanley, and no sympathy—indeed little curiosity—about the minors he had sex with" (p. 9). In a letter to an archdiocesan administrator, Shanley admits to having been abused as a teenager, and later in the seminary by several priests. "His superiors worried little about what he did. Was that because they were more concerned with what he knew?" (p. 9).

SUMMARY

Organizational deviance is behavior that is (a) enabled or made possible by one or more actor's position(s) within an organization and is (b) regarded as nonnormative either within or outside a given organization. As a general rule, actions that are seen as an expression of the mandate of the organization are punished mildly or not at all by the organization, whereas those that are seen as corrupting or subverting the organization are handled more severely. However, organizations tend to be self-protective, and hence, the wrongdoing is often covered up to prevent outsiders from tainting and undermining the goals and integrity of the organization.

What makes organizational deviance interesting sociologically is that, for all other types of deviance, *every single person in the society can be evaluated as acceptable or unacceptable along a given axis.* All of us are fat, less fat, or not at all fat; honest or dishonest, or anything in between; atheists, agnostics, or believers; alcoholics, moderate drinkers, or abstainers; and so on. Only for organizational deviance is the relevant dimension *irrelevant* for most of us. Most of us cannot be placed along the relevant dimension because we are not members of the organization in question. Most of us do not have an executive position and hence, cannot be evaluated with respect to whether we have committed corporate crime or not. Only a small percentage of us are police officers, thus we cannot be evaluated as to whether we have engaged in excessive force with a suspect. Very few of us are Catholic priests; therefore, the overwhelming majority of us cannot be evaluated as to whether or not we committed the sexual abuse of children *as* a Catholic priest. (In principle, all adults could engage in child molestation—but not as Catholic priests.) In other words, the position makes the deviant act possible. Since most of do not occupy the relevant position, we stand outside the dimension of evaluation.

However, even though most of us cannot *be* evaluated as having committed or not committed a given form of organizational deviance, all of us evaluate *others* for having done so. And since organizations are not always successful in shielding wrongdoing in their ranks from the prying eyes of others, the general public often becomes a crucial audience that evaluates organizational behavior. Often, the general public's evaluation of wrongdoing in a given organization is radically at odds with evaluations made by members of the organization. Some acts are judged more harshly by the general public than by organization members; occasionally, it is the reverse. Law enforcement, the courts, and the media are additional relevant audiences that render judgments about organizational behavior.

White-collar and corporate crime constitute an important form of organizational deviance. Most of the time, when the term "white-collar crime" is used, it refers to corporate crime. Not all white-collar criminals are rich and powerful. In fact, in the world of white-collar crime, there are a lot more "small fry" than "big fish." Perhaps the best way of dividing up white-collar crimes is to distinguish those that are *on behalf* of an individual *against* the corporation (embezzlement) from those that are on behalf of the corporation against the general public, consumers, or employees (corporate crime). Other types include governmental crime (receiving bribes, violating international treaties) and professional crime (performing unnecessary surgery, overcharging a client).

As deviance, the public's reaction to corporate crime is ambiguous. Public opinion polls reveal that most people regard corporate crimes that harm people as serious offenses. On the other hand, when corporate criminals are judged by a jury, they tend to receive penalties that do not match the seriousness of the offense. Whether corporate crime is a legitimate form of deviance isn't a cut-and-dried matter. Corporate crime tends to be made up of acts that are complex and not easily detected by non-experts; to be intermingled with legitimate business; to cause diffuse victimization; to entail sums of money that are substantially greater than is true of street crimes; to be only rarely prosecuted; to differ from the public's stereotype of what a "crime" is; to be underplayed by the media (unless the sums are vast); to be relatively unstigmatizing for the perpetrators; to be lacking in the intention to harm victims.

We can distinguish two types of police use of force: first, cases that are seen by the police to *undermine* their law-enforcement mandate, and second, those that are regarded as being *in the service of* law enforcement. In the case of the second, the action is judged only in retrospect to have been wrong—a mistake. Most officers regarded the case of the torture of Abner Louima as a clear-cut case of "excessive" force, both deviant and illegal. In contrast, the shooting of Amadou Diallo was seen by most officers as a case of "normal" force, that is, normative and lawful—although, again, a tragic mistake. The case of Rodney King's beating drew more mixed reactions from the police, though it was more similar to Louima's torture than to Diallo's shooting.

Child molestation by Catholic priests is only marginally a case of organizational deviance. But its cover-up by the Church powers is a form of organizational deviance *par excellence*. For years—indeed, probably for centuries—the Catholic Church implicitly condoned sexual abuse of children by priests. The usual punishment was "a slap on the wrist"—counseling and transfer to another parish. A series of cases of priestly abuse that came to the attention of civil authorities, that resulted in criminal prosecution, and that attracted media glare awakened lay Catholics, the general public, and the Catholic hierarchy to the Church's widespread tolerance of the practice. After 2002, such practices were no longer possible on the same scale. It is conceivable that, as a result of the scandal, the way the Catholic Church handles cases of priestly abuse was changed forever.

PERSONAL ACCOUNT: Cases of Shooting of Citizens by the New York City Police Department

Luis Allende

Luis Allende, an unarmed Latino man suspected of a street robbery, was shot dead by a New York City (NYC) Transit Police officer in the Bronx on 9 August 1990. According to the police report, patrol officers received a report that a woman's necklace had been snatched from her; as they were transmitting a description of the robber over the radio, an officer spotted the suspect and Allende flagged down a cab in an attempt to escape. The officers surrounded the cab and ordered Allende, who was sitting in the back seat, not to move. Allende was shot once in the head, allegedly after turning toward one of the officers who was opening the car door to arrest him.

The shooting was found to be within police guidelines as the officer thought that Allende might have been reaching for a weapon, even though he was found to be unarmed. A civil lawsuit filed by Allende's family was still pending in April 1996, claiming that Allende had posed no immediate threat to life when he was shot as the police had the car surrounded and Allende in full vision at the time.

Frankie Arzuega

Frankie Arzuega, an unarmed 15-year-old Puerto Rican boy, was shot dead by a New York City Police Department (NYPD) police officer on 12 January 1996. According to press reports, Arzuega was a passenger in the back seat of a parked car which was approached by three officers from the 90th Precinct in Brooklyn. According to police statements, the driver tried to drive off as he was being questioned by a police officer who was dragged along with the car; another officer then fired through the back window of the moving vehicle, killing Arzuega. No weapons were found in the car. Two other people in the car were reportedly charged afterwards with grand larceny, assault, and criminal possession of a stolen vehicle. According to an article in the *New York Post*, dated 18 January 1996, the shooting was not recorded in the Police Department's log of major incidents, which is distributed within the department and to reporters. News of the shooting became public only after the family contacted a reporter from *El Diario* (an NYC Spanish language newspaper) three days afterwards. Amnesty International was seeking further information on the case, and on the outcome of official inquiries into the shooting in April 1996.

Jacques Camille

Jacques Camille, a Haitian taxicab driver, was shot and wounded by a police officer on 9 April 1992, after police officers stopped his cab looking for robbery suspects. The robbery victim had reported the cab's number to the police. Camille—in his first week as a cab driver—had unwittingly taken the two robbers on board. The officer said he fired after Camille turned suddenly to the officer to protest at being stopped. Several witnesses said Mr. Camille's hands were raised when the officer fired a

PERSONAL ACCOUNT: Cases of Shooting of Citizens by the New York City Police Department (cont.)

single shot, which destroyed a kidney and part of his liver. The officer was tried in a nonjury court on a charge of recklessly shooting Mr. Camille. He was convicted of a reduced charge of misdemeanor assault and sentenced to three years probation. In May 1994 a civil lawsuit for wrongful shooting was settled by the city for $1,500,000.

Anibal Carasquillo

Anibal Carasquillo, an unarmed 21-year-old Puerto Rican man, was shot dead by a police officer in the Flatbush area of Brooklyn on 22 January 1995. The incident reportedly took place after police officers saw him peering into parked car windows. A police spokesperson initially stated that Carasquillo was shot in the chest after turning to face the police officer in a gun stance. However, the NYC Medical Examiner subsequently reported that the autopsy had shown that he was shot in the back. A grand jury subsequently voted not to indict the officer in the case. On 13 March 1996, relatives of Anibal Carasquillo and Yong Xin Huang (another police shooting victim in Brooklyn: see below) occupied the Brooklyn DA's office to demand that he reconvene a grand jury in both cases. After more than three hours, the demonstrators were arrested, including the mother of Anibal Carasquillo and Yong Xin Huang's two sisters. They were charged with obstructing governmental administration and released on bail.

Amnesty International wrote to the Police Commissioner in February 1995 asking to be informed of the outcome of the police investigation into this case but received no response. Amnesty International subsequently wrote to both the NYPD's Deputy Commissioner for Public Information and the Brooklyn District Attorney for information on this and other cases but received no response. A CCRB (Civilian Complaint Review Board) investigation into the shooting was still pending in April 1996, as was a civil action filed by Anibal Carasquillo's family.

David Cotto

David Cotto, aged 20, was shot dead by Brooklyn police officers in his parents' apartment on 1 March 1990. According to the family, Cotto had been in a fight with a neighbor over a card game and was in the apartment washing blood out of his mouth when the police arrived. Cotto's 19-year-old sister Lisette, who witnessed the whole incident, told Amnesty International that the police were abusive to David Cotto, whom they knew, and pushed him to the ground after which there was a violent struggle. Cotto then ran into the kitchen and picked up two knives, which he allegedly held to his own throat, threatening to kill himself. According to Lisette, Cotto dropped the knives after one of the officers maced him and two other officers fired as he was rubbing his eyes and stumbling forward. Both Lisette and the family's attorney maintain that the officers continued firing after Cotto had fallen and was lying on the floor. He was hit by 11 bullets. Lisette, who was standing nearby, was grazed on the knee by one of the bullets. The description of the gunshot wounds in the autopsy report seen by Amnesty International suggests that David Cotto was hit by two shooters firing eight or nine bullets and then received two further shots in the thigh and scrotum when he was lying on his back on the ground.

A grand jury did not return criminal charges against any of the officers involved. According to the Cotto family's attorney, neither of the two officers who shot Cotto were disciplined. The other officer present, a sergeant, was reportedly mildly reprimanded for failing to follow the required procedure for dealing with an EDP (Emotionally Disturbed Person). (This includes calling for prompt emergency medical services backup and use of nonlethal restraining devices such as Velcro straps.)

Amnesty International wrote to the NYPD and the Brooklyn District Attorney for more information about the case but did not receive a response.

PERSONAL ACCOUNT: Cases of Shooting of Citizens by the New York City Police Department (cont.)

Lydia Ferraro

Lydia Ferraro, a white, unarmed, 32-year-old woman, was shot dead on 27 April 1988, after six NYPD officers fired 16 bullets into her car following a car chase in East Harlem. A grand jury voted not to bring criminal charges against any of the officers for the shooting itself, after the police said that they believed she had been reaching for a gun. A civil lawsuit for wrongful death brought on behalf of Ferraro's son was settled for $300,000 in August 1993. According to a summary of the court-agreed settlement, police officers saw Ferraro make an improper turn against traffic lights and began following her, believing that she had driven to Harlem to buy drugs. They were joined by another police car and Ferraro's car was eventually cut off and stopped. The officers approached her car with their weapons drawn; the City claimed that as one officer opened the car door, Ferraro pulled away from him and an officer shot at her. Other officers then opened fire, killing her with multiple gunshot wounds.

A departmental investigation found that the officers who had fired the fatal shots at the end of the chase had acted within police guidelines. Only one officer was disciplined for firing at her car while it was still moving; he had also reportedly tried initially to cover up his role in the shooting by replacing the three spent cartridges he had fired at the car.

Lebert Folkes

Lebert Folkes, a Jamaican immigrant, was shot in the face and injured by an undercover police officer on 11 February 1996. Folkes had been driving his sister's car which was wrongly listed as stolen on a police computer. As he was parking the car outside his home in Queens, NYC, two police officers blocked the car with their own vehicle and ordered Folkes out of the car at gunpoint. Lebert Folkes said that as he was reaching to unbuckle his seat belt, the officer dragged him out of the car onto the ground and shot him. According to press reports, the police alleged that Folkes had initially refused to get out of the car and that the officer's gun went off accidentally during a struggle. Folkes was reported as saying there was no reason for him to struggle, adding "Why would I resist arrest while they had two guns at my head?" According to press reports, Folkes and at least two witnesses said that the police officers did not identify themselves when ordering Folkes out of the car. Police officials are reported to have apologized to Lebert Folkes for the computer error, which had led to the vehicle being wrongly listed as stolen. (Details of the case as reported in *The New York Times*, 13 February 1996.) Amnesty International was seeking more information on the case and the outcome of the police investigation in April 1996.

Yong Xin Huang

Yong Xin Huang, a 16-year-old Chinese boy, was fatally shot by a white police officer in Sheepshead Bay, Brooklyn, on 24 March 1995. He and two other boys had been playing with an air gun (pellet gun) in the driveway of a friend's house and a neighbor had alerted the police. Yong Xin Huang died after being shot at close range behind his left ear. The officer claimed that his gun—a 9-millimeter Glock semiautomatic—went off accidentally during a struggle with Huang who was holding the pellet gun, and that Huang had been facing him at the time. Huang's friends said there had been no struggle and that Huang had his back to the officer when he was shot. They also said that the officer smashed Huang's face into a glass door at the side of the house, which was shattered during the incident. Both the City Medical Examiner's report and an independent autopsy report show that Huang had blunt impact wounds to the top of his head and his face and forehead, which attorneys for Huang's parents have stated are consistent with the allegation that his face was rammed into the door.

PERSONAL ACCOUNT: Cases of Shooting of Citizens by the New York City Police Department (cont.)

A 911 tape of the call to the police, seen by Amnesty International, reveals that the neighbor had correctly reported the approximate age of the "Asian males" as "14 to 16" and stated that they were "playing" with the gun, which she did not know was real or not. In May 1995 a grand jury concluded that no criminal charges should be filed against the officer involved. The Brooklyn District Attorney (DA) issued a public statement immediately afterwards summarizing the "facts" of the case. (The statement added that the information was developed separately from the grand jury investigation and may therefore be lawfully disclosed.) The statement repeated the officer's account of the incident which, the DA said, was consistent with the forensic evidence on both sides. Attorneys with the Asian American Legal Defense and Education Fund (AALDF) wrote to the DA afterwards to express concern that the statement raised questions about the way the DA had presented the case to the grand jury. The AALDF urged that he take the necessary steps to release the minutes of the grand jury proceedings "to further the public's interest in knowing whether the presentation to the grand jury preserves the integrity of the criminal justice system." However, no such information was released. (The grand jury proceedings may be disclosed on an application to a court under certain narrow circumstances.)

A lawsuit on behalf of Huang's family was filed against the City of New York and the officer involved, alleging that Huang's civil rights had been violated through, among other things, the improper use of force, including battery. The lawsuit claimed that the Glock 9-millimeter automatic did not have a safety device and that the pressure necessary to pull the trigger was too slight; despite being aware of this risk the officer had been "reckless and/or grossly negligent" in placing the gun behind Yong Xin Huang's ear. It also alleged that the City of New York was negligent in failing to train the officer in the proper use of a Glock 9-millimeter weapon in

effecting an arrest, and in allowing the use of this particular type of gun despite its lack of a safety mechanism. It further claimed that the NYPD "is negatively predisposed towards Asian Americans and to the Asian American community" which it believed to be a factor influencing the officer's response to the incident resulting in Huang's death.

In March 1996 the city agreed to pay $400,000 damages to the family in an out-of-court settlement.

No disciplinary action was taken against the officer involved. A federal civil rights investigation into the case by the U.S. Attorney's office was being conducted as of April 1996.

Shuaib Abdul Latif

Shuaib Abdul Latif, a black, unarmed 17-year-old, was shot dead by police on 11 January 1994. The shooting occurred after 12 police officers raided a residential building, apparently in search of drugs. The officers descended to a basement area where Latif was hiding in a cubicle. A tenant who lived in the basement arrived shortly afterwards and approached the police, asking what they were doing. According to her testimony, Latif began to rise from a stooped position on hearing her voice; before he had stood up properly an officer, without warning, shouted "There he goes" and started shooting; Latif was shot twice and fell forward to the ground; she then heard a third shot, then two more shots. This tenant was the only civilian eyewitness to the shooting. It was later established that four officers had discharged their weapons. One officer, Officer Sherman, was shot in the thigh from a police weapon although it was not established how this had occurred.

In March 1995 a grand jury concluded that no criminal charges should be brought against any officers involved in the incident. The Brooklyn District Attorney afterwards issued a statement stating that the grand jury had reached its

PERSONAL ACCOUNT: Cases of Shooting of Citizens by the New York City Police Department (cont.)

conclusion after a full review of all the evidence and careful deliberations. The statement then gave a brief summary of the facts and circumstances of the shooting. (The statement added that the information given was developed separately from the grand jury investigation, so it may be lawfully disclosed.) This stated that Latif was shot after rising up suddenly and grabbing Officer Sherman's arm, and that Sherman's gun went off accidentally as they fell during the struggle. The statement adds that two more shots were fired by other police officers and that after Latif got up and started to run, other shots followed. Latif was struck twice and mortally wounded. (Shuaib Abdul Latif, a 17-year-old unarmed teenager shot dead by police in January 1994, was hiding in the basement of a house raided by police and an eyewitness alleges that the police gave no warning when they fired at him. Although the police allege that he was accidentally shot during a struggle with an armed police officer—and the officers were subsequently cleared of wrongdoing—this appears to be contradicted by other evidence; however, the police forensic reports have not been made available to Latif's family.)

A forensic pathologist has reviewed the Medical Examiner's (ME) report and other information on the case for Amnesty International and has noted that critical information is missing. There is no report of whether gunshot residue was found on Shuaib Latif's clothing, which would have been very likely to have been present if he had been shot at close range while entangled with a police officer (as the police and the DA's statement alleged). The ME's report states that the victim's clothing had been processed by the NYPD laboratory for evidence of gunshot residue, before being turned over to the ME's office, but there is no reference to the findings, which suggests that there may, in fact, have been no positive trace. The ME's own laboratory report states that no residue was observed on the clothing (although it does not state whether they actually tested the clothing

themselves for trace residue). There is also no indication as to whether the police test-fired the weapons to see at what range the gunshot residue would have disappeared. (AI [Amnesty International] was advised that in any close struggle the inference is that there will be gunshot residue, although a simple trace test is necessary to be sure; as the distance at which gunshot residue disappears may vary with the type of weapon it would also be necessary to test-fire the gun and match this to the clothing tests.) Also, although one bullet was recovered from Latif's body, the identity of who fired the shot is not given.

In regard to the latter point, the bullets used in the shooting were reportedly nyclad bullets, with a protective plastic coating to prevent lead contamination. According to information from the Latif family attorney, this type of bullet does not leave engravings which can be matched against individual weapons of the same type. This allegedly makes it difficult, or impossible, to identify which officer fired the fatal bullet. Sources have suggested that this is why the grand jury failed to return an indictment in the case. The results of the police internal inquiry into the shooting, including the police laboratory tests, which may provide the answers to some of these questions, have not been made available to the family or their legal representatives.

Negotiations with the city to settle a civil lawsuit filed on behalf of the family of Shuaib Abdul Latif, whose father is a prominent Muslim cleric, were reported to be in their final stages as of April 1996.

Jose Luis Lebron

Jose Luis Lebron, an unarmed Latino boy, aged 14, was shot dead by a police officer from the 83rd Precinct on 31 January 1990. The shooting took place in the Bushwick area of Brooklyn at around 5.30 p.m. after a man in a police patrol car identified him as being one of two youths who

PERSONAL ACCOUNT: Cases of Shooting of Citizens by the New York City Police Department (cont.)

had robbed him of $10. One of the suspects was captured but Lebron ran away and was cut off by the patrol car. He turned to go back the other way, and was shot in the back of the head by an officer who said he thought he was reaching for something in the front of his jacket. Two eyewitnesses denied that Lebron had reached into his jacket; they said that the officer ordered Lebron to freeze, then immediately fired two shots in quick succession when he kept on walking.

In March 1990 a grand jury voted to charge the officer with second-degree manslaughter. In September 1990 the indictment was dismissed by a judge. The District Attorney (DA) brought the case before a grand jury again in 1992 but this time there was no indictment (Lebron's attorney told Amnesty International that the DA did not call or seek the eyewitnesses in the case during the second time it came before the grand jury).

A civil lawsuit was filed on behalf of Lebron's family, which was still pending in April 1996. Amnesty International wrote to the Police Department to ask if any disciplinary charges had been brought against the officer involved but received no reply.

Louis Liranso

Lebron was the second unarmed teenager to be fatally shot by police within a week in the same area. On 27 January 1990, in Bushwick, Brooklyn, 17-year-old Louis Liranso was shot in the back by a female police officer as she was holding him with his hands raised at gunpoint after a drunken brawl near a Chinese restaurant. A grand jury later cleared the officer of wrongdoing, after she told the jury that the gun went off as Liranso turned and grabbed her arm. This contradicted accounts by witnesses that Liranso simply tripped as the officer was ushering him into the restaurant at gunpoint, as well as earlier police reports that he was shot as he lowered his hands and started to turn toward the officer.

Mary Mitchell

Mary Mitchell, black, aged 41, was shot dead by a white police officer in her Bronx apartment in November 1990. The shooting occurred after police officers were called to investigate a violent fight between Mary Mitchell and her daughter. During the fight an officer apparently tried to barricade Mary Mitchell in a room; however, at some point the door opened and the officer dropped his nightstick. He shot Mitchell once in the chest after she grabbed the nightstick and, according to the officer, started swinging it at him. A grand jury charged the officer with second-degree manslaughter. In a nonjury trial in October 1991 a judge acquitted the officer, ruling that Mary Mitchell had been a deadly threat at the time she was shot. The family maintains that as at least eight police officers were at the scene at the time she was shot, less lethal methods could have been used to restrain her, and that she might have been treated differently had she been white.

Douglas Orfaly

Douglas Orfaly, an unarmed Latino man aged 29, was shot and killed by an NYC Housing Authority police officer as he sat in his car on 3 March 1992. The officer, who had been responding to a burglary report, said he thought Orfaly fit the description of the burglar. As the officer moved toward the car, Douglas Orfaly allegedly made a sudden movement and the officer shot him once through the head through the car window. It was reported afterwards that the officer had twice had accusations of excessive force brought against him in civil lawsuits.

In August 1995 the officer was found guilty by a jury of criminally negligent homicide in the shooting and was sentenced to one to four years in prison. He was the first NYC police officer to be convicted of an on-duty homicide since 1977.

PERSONAL ACCOUNT: Cases of Shooting of Citizens by the New York City Police Department (cont.)

Derwin Pannel

Derwin Pannel, a black undercover transit police officer, was shot and wounded by three white NYC Transit Police Department officers who saw him trying to arrest a female fare-evader in a Brooklyn subway on 20 November 1992. The officers, who said they thought he was an armed mugger, fired a total of 21 shots at Pannel: One officer fired all 15 rounds in his 9-millimeter semiautomatic and another six bullets from a .38 caliber revolver. Pannel was hit three times in the back; he was saved by his bulletproof vest but one bullet lodged in the back of his neck causing severe injury. The chief of the NYC Transit Police was reported afterwards as saying that race was not a factor in the shooting. However, representatives of the Guardians Association, a group representing black police officers, said the shooting highlighted the need for greater sensitivity by white officers to the fact that black and other minority officers working undercover may be police officers rather than criminals. The transit police were reported to have included a section on racial awareness in undercover work in its training sessions following the incident. No officers were criminally charged in the incident.

Gerard J. Papa and James Rampersant Jr.

Gerard Papa, a white attorney, and James Rampersant Jr., who is black, were shot at multiple times and beaten by police in a case of mistaken identity in March 1986. A jury later awarded them substantial damages in a federal civil action filed against the city, the NYPD, and the officers concerned. According to the facts as recorded in the court report, Papa and Rampersant were driving down a deserted Brooklyn street when they were boxed in by two unmarked police cars. Police officers in plain clothes jumped from their cars with their guns drawn and allegedly shouted profanities at the men, ordering them to get out of their car. Papa and Rampersant testified that they refused to get out of their car, fearing that they had been caught up in a drug operation, and that the officers did not identify themselves. The police opened fire at the car, one officer allegedly pulling back to reload. The plaintiffs were then pulled from the car and beaten and kicked. Papa sustained a dislocated shoulder, three fractured ribs, and contusions. Rampersant suffered cuts, bruises, and contusions. Both men were charged with attempted murder, criminal mischief, resisting arrest, and other offenses, and spent two and a half days in jail. The case was dismissed after the grand jury refused to return an indictment.

The officers stated that Papa and Rampersant fit the description of two men who had been involved in a purse snatching in the area six days earlier. They defended their actions on the ground that Papa and Rampersant had been trying to escape from the scene and had then refused to get out of their car.

The court trying the civil lawsuit heard evidence that the police had tried to cover up the incident and had not prepared a firearms report until months later. A PBA [Patrolmen's Benevolent Association] lawyer advised the officers not to make any statement when interrogated after the incident, and a supervising sergeant who appeared at the scene testified that he picked up spent cartridges but could not recall what he did with them. No officers were charged or disciplined in the incident.

Eric Pitt and Donald Taylor

Eric Pitt and Donald Taylor, black, were shot dead by a police officer after a car chase in Jamaica, Queens, in December 1994. According to police reports, the chase started after officers were confronted by three men, one of whom fired at them. Pitt and Taylor fled in a car which was forced to a halt by police. According to press reports, each man was then shot once in the head after police said the officer saw one of them make a "furtive gesture." No weapon was found in the vehicle. Amnesty International wrote to the Police Department in February

PERSONAL ACCOUNT: Cases of Shooting of Citizens by the New York City Police Department (cont.)

1995 and in November 1995 asking for information on the outcome of the police investigation into the shooting. However, no response was received.

Hector Rivera

Hector Rivera, an unarmed man of Puerto Rican origin, was shot dead on 29 December 1991, when two Brooklyn police officers were called to a domestic dispute outside his home. He was shot in the chest by one of the officers after police said he put his hand into a paper bag when told to "freeze"; Rivera was apparently holding onto a can of beer wrapped in the bag. The officer was indicted on a second-degree murder charge but a judge dismissed the indictment on the ground that the prosecutor's instructions to the grand jury regarding self-defense had been in error. A second grand jury concluded there should be no charges.

Desmond Robinson

Desmond Robinson, a black undercover plainclothes officer with the NYC Transit Police Department, was shot four times in the back and seriously wounded by a white off-duty NYPD officer in a New York subway on 22 August 1994.

The incident occurred during the evening rush hour when Robinson and other transit officers were chasing two youths reported to be armed; one of the youths dropped a shotgun near the open doors of a train and the gun went off, wounding a woman and setting off panic. The off-duty NYPD officer was standing on the platform and pulled out his off-duty revolver. When he saw Robinson running down the platform with a gun, he mistook him for a criminal and fired five times, four shots hitting Robinson in the back. Several witnesses, including Robinson's police partner, alleged that the officer continued to fire after Robinson was lying on the ground, something denied by the NYPD officer. An investigation by a forensic specialist hired by Robinson's attorneys noted two "shored"

(obliquely oriented) exit wounds, which he said showed signs consistent with the bullets having come into direct contact with a hard surface after exiting the body. The police report of the shooting has not been made public.

A Manhattan grand jury later charged the NYPD officer with first-degree assault for having recklessly shot Robinson, an offense which carries 5 to 15 years' imprisonment on conviction. The officer was brought to trial in March 1996 and was convicted of assault in the second degree, which carries a sentence ranging from probation to three years in prison. Sentencing was deferred until May 1996.

Antonio Rosario, Hilton Vega, and Freddie Bonilla

Antonio Rosario (aged 18) and Hilton Vega (aged 22) were shot dead by police officers on 22 January 1995 inside a Bronx apartment. Two detectives fired a total of 28 shots, killing Rosario and Vega and wounding 18-year-old Freddie Bonilla, who was shot once in the leg.

The police had been called to the apartment by the occupants, an elderly couple who reported that three men had robbed them the day before and said they would return that night. According to the police, the detectives waited for the men inside the apartment from 8.30 p.m. until 11 p.m. when the suspects arrived; they waited for the couple to let them in and then confronted the men. The police said that they fired at the men when Rosario went for his gun. Two .45 caliber pistols and one 9-millimeter handgun, all loaded but not fired, were recovered from the men. (The robbery story has been disputed by relatives of the men, who say they went to the apartment to collect a debt.)

In March 1995 a grand jury voted not to bring criminal charges against the two detectives. However, in July 1995 the CCRB (Civilian Complaint Review Board) concluded that the officers had used excessive force when firing at the men. Although the details of CCRB findings are not

PERSONAL ACCOUNT: Cases of Shooting of Citizens by the New York City Police Department (cont.)

made public, a source familiar with the investigation told the press that the CCRB had found that the detectives were not in danger when the shots were fired; that all the bullets were fired from behind the victims; that both Rosario and Vega had bullet entry wounds under their arms, indicating that their hands were raised; and that they sustained wounds to the backs of their heads, torso, and back. It was reported in the press in August 1995 that a pathologist hired by the family of one of the victims had concluded that the men were lying on the floor when they were shot.

The CCRB sent its report to the Police Commissioner, who publicly criticized the Board for having carried out an investigation into the case while a federal inquiry into the shooting was pending, and he announced that he would not look at the CCRB report until the federal investigation had been completed. However, the CCRB insisted that it had completed its investigation before the federal investigation was announced. (There was also a dispute about the type of bullets used in the shooting. CCRB investigators said that some of the bullets were Teflon-coated, armor-piercing bullets which are not authorized

by the NYPD. IAB (Internal Affairs Bureau) officials told Amnesty International that the CCRB had mistaken Nyclad bullets [wrapped in a nylon coating to avoid lead contamination] for Teflon.)

Amnesty International has reviewed the autopsy report in the case of Hilton Vega, which indicates that he was shot in the back from two sides with different bullets, both coming from behind. There are four bullet holes in the floor, which suggests that he may have been shot while face down on the floor and therefore already disabled. Amnesty International did not have further evidence about the scene—for example, whether there were bullet holes in the floor or wall—to establish more firmly whether he was lying on the floor or standing when shot.

In July 1995 the U.S. Attorney's office began an investigation to determine whether the police had violated the suspects' federal civil rights.

Source: Amnesty International, "Police Brutality and Excessive Force in the New York City Police Department." AI Index: AMR 51/036/1996. July 27, 1996. © Amnesty International. http://web.amnesty.org/library/print/ENGAMR510361996

QUESTIONS

How do you think a member of the NYPD (New York City Police Department) would explain, justify, or rationalize these shootings? Following what's been said in this chapter, which ones, in your opinion, would most officers endorse as consistent with the Police Department's mandate? Which ones would be criticized as not merely mistakes but instances of excessive force—unacceptable, unprofessional, and deviant? Does the approach spelled out in this chapter help us to understand incidents such as these? If so, in what ways? Does a more moralistic approach—"It's wrong and we should do something about it!"—yield more understanding and analytic insight on police shootings? Is the subject even amenable to the deviance paradigm?

Concluding Thought: Is the Sociology of Deviance "Dead"?

Conservatives (Hendershott, 2002) regard the sociology of deviance as an unacceptable approach to wrongdoing. In their view, the field relies on the concept of relativity and hence is incapable of coming right out and indicating which behaviors are evil. In fact, they claim, it is the acceptance of relativity that killed off the sociological study of deviance. It's time, they argue, to call a spade a spade and refer to deviant behavior as the evil that it is. And what's evil is what our traditional values, including the Ten Commandments, *tell* us is evil.

Radicals (Liazos, 1972; Sumner, 1994) also believe that the sociology of deviance is fatally flawed, but for a very different reason. They argue that sociologists who study deviance have—by ignoring it—exonerated the true evil in the world: the harmful actions of the top dogs and fat cats. Real wrongdoing is not the petty crimes and misdemeanors that ordinary people commit, not the scandalous behaviors of street people or the dirty little secrets we keep in the closet. No, they say; we should be pointing fingers at the actions that are *really* harmful: racial discrimination, exploiting the poor and the weak, starting wars, preventing people from reaching their true potential, using power to grab a bigger slice of society's resources. The field of the sociology of deviance is "dead," these critics argue, because it has failed to address the essence of deviance: inflicting harm on the powerless members of the society.

What's wrong with both of these criticisms is that they do not address the field's central mission. The sociology of deviance is not about designating what's "really, truly" evil—that is, *deviant*. Deviance is what's *regarded* or *designated* as wrong, not what's "really" wrong. If someone wishes to moralize, pontificate, preach, or make proclamations about what they consider wrong, well, that's their business. But sociologists of deviance do not study what's wrong in the abstract, what's essentially, fundamentally wrong; they study *designations* of wrongdoing, which is a separate and altogether different enterprise.

As I've said throughout this book, deviance is a universal, trans-cultural, trans-historical concept. Throughout human history, societies have instituted rules for proper behavior, indicated what constitutes wrongdoing, and penalized persons who have violated the rules. There is no society without rules or sanctions, and there is no society in which all members conform to the rules all the time. Both rules and their violation are found everywhere and, as far as we know, throughout recorded time.

Some critics have objected that, in the sense that sociologists now understand it, the actual term *deviance* did not exist until the second half of the twentieth century. Hence, they argue, it does not indicate a universal phenomenon (Best, 2004b). But many terms did not exist until sociologists dreamed them up: *norm, anomie, status hierarchy, social disorganization, differential association, anticipatory socialization, unanticipated consequences,* and so on. Indeed, the same can be said of most terms in a wide range of fields. All of these terms refer to concepts that tell us what is happening in the material world. They predict, explain, analyze, and interpret real-world phenomena. Simply because societies do not have a *term* for deviance processes does not mean that they do not take place. Indeed, they do, they have crucial and fundamental consequences, and it is the sociologist's job to understand them.

Other critics have argued that deviance adopts the "hegemonic" or dominant definition of deviance, that which furthers the interests of the most powerful segments of the society. But the fact is—as Karl Marx pointed out a century and a half ago—definitions applied by the powerful tend to have a powerful impact on everyone else in the society. Moreover, sociological conceptions of deviance allow for definitions contrary to those promulgated by the powerful that are dominant *within designated contexts.* Is atheism deviant? Not among atheists. Is growing marijuana wrong? Check out the pages of *High Times* and find out how one social circle feels. Should homosexuals be legally permitted to get married? Ask homosexuals and find out how they feel. Sociologists do not seize on one definition and proclaim it the only valid definition. Deviance is that which is condemned in a specified group or social setting. If we specify the society as a whole, we'll get one answer; if we specify particular segments of the society, chances are, we'll get a very different answer. It's not the sociologist who defines deviance in a certain way, it's the groups, categories, social circles, or societies we point to.

For at least a decade (Sumner, 1994), pundits have proclaimed the sociology of deviance "dead." For far longer than that, others have *called for* the death of the field (Liazos, 1972). I have argued that a mixed bag of motives is behind these proclamations. As I just said, some of the field's critics object to the fact that it takes an agnostic stand on what's "really, truly" evil. Others imagine that the field really designates as bad that which is regarded as deviant. Still others fantasize that the very *term* "deviance" is pejorative, downputting, demeaning to persons to whom it applies. Regardless of what the motives are, the field is alive and well. Is the sociology of deviance as creative and as innovative as it was in the field's infancy? Probably not. But far from being dead, the subject is taught nearly everywhere, and enrollments remain as high—indeed, even higher—than they were in the field's supposed salad days.

Since I regard robust course offerings and enrollments as considerably more important for a field than mere "minimal signs of life" (Best, 2004a), and acknowledging that a number of "death" advocates base their claim on an assumption of the field's disappearance in catalogues and semester-by-semester offerings, I examined the question of whether and to what extent a deviance course is offered in 25 of the nation's most prestigious institutions of higher learning. (I did not consult distinguished institutions with no graduate program in sociology, such as Tufts, Dartmouth, and Georgetown.) If such information does not address the innovativeness issue, it does confront Hendershott's contentions and those of her colleagues. Reports Hendershott, quoting a colleague: "No one wants to teach about a discipline that died a generation ago."

If this statement is indeed true, then that discipline will not be taught and it will not appear in a college's or university's course listings and catalogues, and it most especially will not be taught in the nation's most prestigious universities. Hence, a perusal of the course offerings at such institutions should indeed verify that this assertion is the case. I checked the websites of these institutions, including all the Ivy League universities, 10 of the highest-ranking state institutions, and eight highly prestigious, non-Ivy private universities, for their recent or current course offerings and/or catalogue course listings.

The fact that a department at an institution of higher learning offers a particular course during a particular semester is in large measure a hit-or-miss affair, depending on a variety of factors—most notably the presence of a specific faculty member, the size and general thrust or orientation of the department, the attitudes of the administration toward a given subject, and the vagaries of scheduling. A small number of subjects in sociology—methods, theory, gender, stratification/inequality, the family—are taught at nearly every four-year institution offering a sociology major. On the other hand, most topics in sociology are offered at some institutions but not others. Even subjects considered important to the field, such as the sociology of education, medicine, work, organizations, and politics, may be missing from a specific institution's undergraduate curriculum.

Contrarily, a particular institution may offer one or more courses in an extremely unusual, even esoteric, subject—courses that are in fact listed practically nowhere else. For instance, at the University of Texas during the fall of 2001, a course on "Women in Hip Hop Culture" and one entitled "Gandhi" were offered. At UCLA, during the fall 2002 semester, "The Sociology of Time" and "Comparative American Indian Societies" were offered. The University of Chicago sociology department offers a course in its 2002–2004 listings entitled "Social Conflict and Aikido." All of these courses sound fascinating, and no doubt their instructors link them to sociology's most foundational missions, but not one of them is standard fare in the sociology curriculum anywhere. Several of them, my guess is, are offered nowhere else.

Of the 25 distinguished sociology departments whose course offerings I consulted, just under two-thirds, 16 out of the 25, listed a course on deviance in their catalogue and/or their current or recent listings. Harvard, Columbia, the University of Pennsylvania, the University of California at Berkeley, UCLA, the University of Michigan, the University of Wisconsin, the University of Virginia, Indiana University, the University of Washington, Northwestern, Duke, Emory, Vanderbilt, Tulane, and the University of Texas recently offered or currently offer a course with "deviance" in its title. (Brown, Cornell, Princeton, Yale, Illinois, the University of North Carolina, Johns Hopkins,

Chicago, and Stanford did not.) Pennsylvania's course description of its deviance offering stated: "The study of deviance and social control is a major topic of sociology." Harvard's "Deviance and Social Control" is the department's most popular course, with the greatest number of students enrolled—and by a wide margin.

The fact that deviance remains a popular course in the curriculum of these prominent sociology departments forces the observer to consider Hendershott's claim that today "few sociologists teach about deviance" (p. 2) with amazement. It is clearly misinformed. If "no one" wants to teach a deviance course, then who's teaching the ones that are actually being offered? It's not clear what her statement that courses on deviance have been "gradually deleted from the curriculum" (p. 5) could possibly mean. She has not bothered to check the content of curricula she so grandly pontificates about.

I also sent requests for data on enrollments in the deviance course to instructors of 34 sociology departments around the country whom I knew to teach the deviance course. (They were among the instructors who responded to a survey I conducted for the previous edition of this book, which entailed a request for syllabi from instructors of the deviance course.) I asked them to supply me with the exact number of students who had taken a deviance course, semester by semester, as far back as their records permitted. Supplying this information usually entailed them contacting their chair, the director of undergraduate studies, or a department secretary, inducing them to search through the records, tabulate the figures, and send this information to me—a fairly substantial commitment of time and effort. Representatives from 19 departments complied with my request, which is a remarkably good response rate, given how time-consuming the commitment was.

In Table 1 I present a summary of that information. Each year that the deviance course was taught or the department was able to supply records in five or more institutions, I combined and tabulated the total number of students enrolled in all of these institutions and the mean and median for all these courses. Records are missing and/or the course was not taught more often for the earlier years than for the later ones. (These figures do not represent the mean and

Table 1   Enrollment in Deviance Courses, 17 Departments, 1977–2002*

Year	Median	Mean	Total Enrollments	Number of Departments
1977	122	202.6	1,013	5
1978	76	125.6	754	6
1979	69	165.0	825	5
1980	53	124.8	998	8
1981	45.5	99.5	796	8
1982	51	95.1	856	9
1983	64	92.8	742	8
1984	97.5	117.1	1,171	10
1985	87.5	121.3	1,213	10
1986	109	138.0	1,242	9
1987	72	128.6	1,029	8
1988	115	160.9	1,448	9
1989	112	159.3	1,434	9
1990	105	139.7	1,537	11
1991	105	163.8	2,130	13
1992	100.5	130.0	1,560	12
1993	83	169.9	2,374	14
1994	65	158.7	2,063	13
1995	102	190.8	2,480	13
1996	85	206.8	2,688	13
1997	90	205.5	3,083	15
1998	60.5	210.0	3,360	16
1999	99	237.0	3,318	14
2000	69.5	177.0	2,832	16
2001	104.3	247.4	3,463	14
2002	89	260.6	3,127	12

*Years during which the course was taught for which five or more departments supplied enrollment records. Two departments that supplied only academic year figures, which overlap calendar years, are not included.

median *per course*, since, in a given year, the course may have been offered more than once at a given institution; they are the mean and median *per institution*, although for the smaller institutions, they are per course.) I rely on the calendar year rather than the academic year, and I did not include figures from the two departments that sent me only academic year figures.

As can be seen from Table 1, enrollments in deviance courses remain robust. In fact, for 2002, the *mean* enrollment figure is higher than it has ever been. With respect to the *median* figure, it is true that the late 1980s to early 1990s were the course's glory days. (Between 1980 and 2002, total undergraduate enrollments for the country as a whole increased somewhat, from 10.5 million to 13.4 million, not enough to substantially influence these figures.) Still, the 2001 median figure was as substantial as it was per annum in the 1988–1992 era. It should be kept in mind that the number of departments supplying these figures is small. Moreover, the departments I received information from were those known to me to offer ongoing courses in deviance. Hence, the number of students enrolled in deviance courses at the institutions I asked to supply me with enrollment figures is influenced by a variety of contingent factors, such as whether or not, during a given year, the course is offered, or a popular instructor teaches the deviance course, or a specific department decides to open more than the usual number of sections or close sections at a specific enrollment figure, or classroom space is available, and so on. Nonetheless, we must be impressed by the continuing vitality of enrollment figures for the deviance course. Once again, instructors are teaching this course, and students are taking it. And once again, the "death" claim—especially as it pertains to the "no one wants to teach about a discipline that died a generation ago" red herring—must be regarded with a certain measure of dubiousness and distrust.

The puzzle is why such a clearly and demonstrably false belief continues to be held. Perhaps, one day, someone will come up with a plausible explanation of this contemporary legend. In any case, one of the lessons we learn from this mistaken belief is that the sociology of deviance, born and nurtured in conflict, remains a "deviant" subfield within sociology.

Appendix:
Student Research Projects

I have taught deviance courses at the undergraduate level at several universities for more than three decades. During some semesters, I've offered my students an optional paper as a substitute for one exam grade, and during other semesters, I've required papers as a major portion of the student's grade. Below, I present several of the better papers students have handed in as requirements for some of these research projects.

BINGE DRINKING
ON THE COLLEGE CAMPUS

The Assignment Ask 10 students—five males and five females—whether or not they consider heavy and/or "binge" drinking wrong or deviant. Include some fraternity/sorority members and some nonmembers. Ask detailed questions. If they do feel it's wrong, ask why; ask them *in what way* they believe it is wrong or deviant. If they do not believe there's anything wrong with it, ask why not. Ask them to be detailed and specific. What do they feel are harmful consequences of binge drinking? (Or why they think there are none, or few such consequences.) What do they believe are some positive consequences? Be natural and creative in your interview, not artificial and mechanical. Read the Thomas Workman article (2001) and construct a set of 10 or so questions based on that discussion. Write a paper consisting of an interesting, meaningful analysis, on the responses to your questions. Draw conclusions. What do your findings tell us about binge drinking as deviance, as well as about deviance as a sociological phenomenon?

BINGE DRINKING

Cara Delguidice

I am a 22-year-old, fifth-year college student. . . . During the past three years, I have worked as a bartender at a bar across the street from the campus. It is one of the four bars that is frequented by the college crowds here. As a bartender, I have an inside view of student drinking. When I am at work, I serve customers; during that time, I remain sober.

Some people might think that my insider's position would compromise the truth of my research conclusions. I believe the opposite to be true: As a bartender, I can be both objective, by gathering information about student drinking in statistical form, and also encourage students to give me their personal drinking stories. By being a bartender,

I can address the conclusions that other researchers have reached.

The Research I monitored the behavior of 40 individuals (20 males and 20 females) over the span of four nights—a Tuesday, a Thursday, a Friday, and a Saturday. Each night that I made my observations, I chose five women and five men. These individuals were either customers of mine, so I could record the alcohol they consumed by checking their cumulated tabs, or, if they were not my customers, I placed myself strategically at the bar so that I could observe them each time they returned to get a drink. When a customer ordered more than one drink at one time, I assumed that he/she was not drinking them all, but was buying for companions. In that case, I counted a round of drinks as one drink. For the purposes of this study, a drink was counted as one drink if it was beer, a mixed drink, a "shooter" (a mixture of alcohol with juice and/or soda), or a straight shot of distilled spirits. Of the four, shots contain the most alcohol.

At the end of their stay at the bar, I approached them and asked them to fill out a brief survey about binge drinking in college. I told them that their answers would be held in the strictest confidence, that they would remain completely anonymous. Because I was acquainted with all the people I approached, they all complied with my request. My questions put into perspective the drinkers' consumption rate, weekly visits to the bar, and perceptions of binge drinking.

Results The average age of the men was 21, which means that, in all likelihood, roughly half of them were, strictly speaking, underage. Half of the 20 men were members of a fraternity and a third were on an athletic team. When I asked how many nights a week, on average, they consume an alcoholic beverage, 15 percent said once a week, 10 percent said twice a week, 45 percent said three times a week, and 30 percent said that they drank four times a week. When I asked how many drinks they usually consume in one sitting, 15 percent said four, 10 percent said five, 20 percent said six, 25 percent said seven, and 30 percent said eight or more. I asked the men in this survey how many drinks in one sitting they considered "binge" drinking. Their average estimate was 10 drinks.

The average age of the women I surveyed was 20.5, which probably means that the majority were underage. When I asked how many times a week the females consume an alcoholic beverage, 10 percent said once a week, 35 percent said twice a week, 50 percent said three times a week, and 5 percent said four times a week. When asked how many drinks on average they consume in a sitting, 5 percent replied four, 15 percent said five, 40 percent six, 25 percent seven, and 15 percent said eight or more. In other words, females were somewhat less likely than males to drink at the higher end of the consumption scale. Finally, when asked how many drinks it takes to "binge" drink, the women's average response was eight.

My observations of these drinkers' behavior were even more interesting than the responses to my survey questions. The actual number of drinks that were consumed, according to my observations, was as follows. For males, 5 percent had four drinks; 5 percent had five drinks; 5 percent had six drinks; 25 percent had seven drinks; 15 percent had eight drinks; 20 percent had nine drinks; 10 percent had 10 drinks; 10 percent had 12 drinks; and 5 percent had 15 or more. For females, 5 percent had three drinks; 15 percent had five drinks; 15 percent had six drinks; 10 percent had seven drinks; 15 percent had eight drinks; 15 percent had nine drinks; and 25 percent had 10 or more.

My observations also indicated that men were more likely to order an unmixed shot of distilled spirits than was true of women. I also found that the athletes and fraternity members drank more shots than the other men. Moreover, the athletes were more likely to drink shots than fraternity members. Overall, the men ordered a higher number of drinks than the women.

When we compare the estimates that customers make about how many drinks they consume, on average, with the average number of drinks I observed that they *actually* consume in a single sitting, for both sexes, their answers underestimated the upper range of actual use. In other words, for a substantial proportion of my interviews, customers thought they drank less in one sitting than they actually did. Only 15 percent of the men estimated that they usually had more than eight drinks; in fact, 60 percent drank more than this amount. In other words, nine out of 20 of the men I interviewed drank more than they thought they usually would.

For the women, a similar pattern appeared. Only 15 percent of the women estimated that they drank eight or more drinks in a typical sitting. In fact, according to my observations, 55 percent of these women actually drank this much. Perhaps even more remarkable, *none* of the women estimated that they drank *more than* eight alcoholic beverages in one sitting, while 40 percent actually did so. In other words, four out of 10 women (40 percent) were inaccurate about the level of their alcohol consumption. Like the males, the females perceived themselves consuming less than they really did. These numbers are very compelling when one realizes that many drinkers are not aware of how much alcohol they consume. It really forces one to think about the difference between perception and reality when it comes to alcohol.

Here's another interesting statistic. The men estimated 10 or more drinks as constituting binge drinking, while the women estimated eight or more drinks as qualifying as binge drinking. During the night I observed their drinking, 45 percent of the men and 40 percent of the women were binge drinkers, as defined by their own standards.

TABLE 1   NUMBER OF DRINKS CONSUMED IN ONE SITTING

	ESTIMATED		OBSERVED	
	Male	*Female*	*Male*	*Female*
3	0	0	0	5
4	15	5	5	0
5	10	15	5	15
6	20	40	5	15
7	25	25	25	10
8	30	15	15	15
9	0	0	20	15
10	0	0	10	25
12	0	0	10	0
15+	0	0	5	0
N	20	20	20	20

How many drinks at one sitting do you think defines "binge drinking"?
Average for Males: 10
Average for Females: 8

Analysis   If we were to consider these students' parents' attitudes toward drinking, it is almost certain that they would condemn the level of drinking indulged in by their children. The attitudes of these parents toward drinking, and their estimates as to what defines binge drinking, would be much stricter than those of their children. Most adults feel that more than a couple of beers is bad or wrong for young adults—and certainly for underage drinkers. My statistics lead me to the conclusion that it is likely that, as a generation of young adults, we probably do consume too much alcohol. As my figures indicate, at least for this bar, on this night, for the people I interviewed, *by their own standards*, they drink too much. Of course, let's keep in mind that I only interviewed and observed 40 people. Obviously, they cannot speak for college students as a whole. And let's also keep in mind that all the people I observed were in a bar. They were customers of mine who agreed to comply with the conditions of this study. Therefore, they may not be typical of the students on this campus. In defense of college students across the country, not all of them go to bars, and it's likely that most of them do not drink as much as my customers do. Still, the figures I found should make all of us think about binge drinking as a possible problem. It certainly raises some issues about underage drinking. And when parents and their children have different notions of acceptable behavior, we have to think about deviance, norm violations, and the university as a not-very-adequate substitute parent.

I took away several important points from Thomas Workman's article on binge drinking in college. The author makes a clear distinction between adult and adolescent drinkers. He argues that men drink more like adolescents—that is, more uncontrolled, in excess—while women drink more like adults, that is to say, in a more controlled fashion, and less excessively. In contrast to Workman, I found that women drank on almost as many days during the week as men did, and were only slightly more likely to drink excessively. But when you consider the women's average weight, and the fact that women's bodies are less capable of metabolizing alcohol, the fact is, pound for pound, the women I observed probably drank more than the men. Unless they had built up a tolerance for alcohol, these women probably consumed more than these men, considering what they should have been drinking. So it's not clear from my findings that Workman's analysis is completely valid.

Workman also puts forth five reasons why men drink like adolescents. For males, drinking alcohol provides a sense of risk, entertainment, opportunity for physical discovery, a lowering of sexual inhibitions, as well being part of the college experience. I agree that these are reasons why males drink in college. But what Workman leaves out of the picture is that women also engage in risky behavior, seek entertainment and self-discovery, wish to lower their sexual inhibitions, and want to take part in the college experience. Many women use alcohol to approach men and say and do things they would not ordinarily say or do. I know many women who leave the bar with someone they did not arrive with. When I asked my respondents whether their inhibitions were lowered after drinking, 95 percent said that they were. However, none of them thought that this was a bad thing.

Drinking is a relief from stress for college students. As long as it is done responsibly, and assuming the drinker has reached the age of 21, there is no reason why a college student should not drink. There are drawbacks to too much drinking, of course. Getting sick and throwing up is one. Driving while intoxicated is another. And as a bartender, I've also witnessed physical violence as a result of too much alcohol far too many times.

My generation probably does drink too much. Still, I do not see a problem with going out and getting drunk and having a good time. This is not because I am a bartender. It is because I am also a social drinker as well. The people in my survey are my friends, my acquaintances, my peers. It is true that adults, including the parents of the people I interviewed and observed, probably consider college drinking excessive. Chances are, they would regard much of the behavior I observed as deviant—in other words, it violates *their* norms, *their* sense of what's right and what's wrong. But my peers do not feel that the behavior I've described in this paper is wrong or deviant. It fits in with contemporary college norms.

It is true that many of the people I talked to do not have a clear idea of what "binge" drinking is.

I think this has a great deal to do with the social stigma that is attached to the term "binge drinker." Most people do not consider themselves binge drinkers. I know I don't. However, if you asked my mom about this, she would have one of two replies. She would either say I drink too much or she would tell you that she does not want me to tell her how much I drink because she doesn't want to know it.

Like most of the people I surveyed, I do not consider myself a binge drinker. Most of my friends wouldn't consider me one, either. At the same time, most adults would consider what we do "binge drinking." In other words, they could consider the number of drinks we consume in one sitting as *deviant*. But we consider it not only normative and acceptable within our own group and age category, but we also don't feel that there's anything wrong with it. Drinking—like deviance—is all about perception. As long as you can keep your life in college in perspective and accomplish what you came here to do, then no one should criticize drinking among college students. After all, isn't college about growing up and finding your place in life, and not just a seat at the bar? Or is it?

PHYSICAL TRAITS OR CHARACTERISTICS AS DEVIANT

The Assignment   Locate one article in a magazine, newspaper, or on the Internet, that discusses or is about a physical trait or characteristic, whether it is the violation of an aesthetic norm (such as extreme ugliness, disfigurement, being an albino, possessing multiple and obvious tattoos, etc.) or a physical disability (blindness, being confined to a wheelchair, etc.). The trait can be involuntary (such as being an albino) or voluntary (being visibly tattooed). Discuss the trait from the point of view of the course—that is, as a form of deviance. Use any concept discussed in this course to illuminate the trait or elucidate what's interesting and sociologically important about it. Examples of such concepts: deviance, stigma, subculture, social constructionism, social conflict, labeling, audiences, etc. Your discussion should be about one page, more or less.

OBESITY

Rhonda Hurston

In our society, physical attractiveness is very highly rated. Preschoolers to adults recognize and respond positively to physical attractiveness. "Physical attractiveness may be the single most important factor in determining popularity among college-age adults" (Berscheid and Walster, 1972). Our society sends out constant messages about physically beautiful people who are thin and perceived to be perfect. Involuntarily acquired deviant characteristics, like being blind or physically handicapped, are perceived to be imperfections; these conditions remind us of our vulnerability.

Voluntary physical characteristics such as tattooing or body piercing are stigmatized more harshly than involuntary characteristics by the majority of the members of the society. People who possess voluntarily-acquired physical characteristics come under strong criticism; they are held responsible for their physical condition because they are considered as having a choice in their behavior (Goode, 1996).

One form of voluntary deviance is obesity. Obesity generates negative social responses that can cut to the core of a person's self-image and sense of worth. Some obese conditions are caused by medical reasons; if society is aware of the medical reason, there is less condemnation. If people are obese because they are lazy and eat too much, there is strong condemnation.

We live in an anti-obese society that values being thin: the smaller the better. Society sends clear signals about what is considered to be normal size. We have created an average-size world that excludes people who are obese. Society perceives obesity as being disgusting and repulsive, which leads to the obese being rejected, condemned, isolated, and humiliated. "The obese, unlike the physically disabled, are held responsible for their physical condition. Fatness, in the eyes of the majority member of society, is viewed as both a physical deformity and as a behavioral aberration" (Cahnman, 1968).

Our society values thinness so much that the thin ideal is unrealistic. It can be reached only with compulsive dieting. This has caused many girls to act out in the form of deviant eating practices associated with anorexia, bulimia, and binge-eating disorders, which are caused by being afraid of becoming obese. In a recent study, 90 percent of white junior-high and high school girls voiced dissatisfaction with their weight (Ingrassia, 1995).

Obese people get little support from the society and even little or no support from members of their family. Family members ridicule them with the intent of motivating the obese person to lose weight. But this ridicule has just the opposite effect and tends to further decrease the self-esteem and self-worth of the obese member.

In our society, the media, celebrities, and advertisements reinforce the thin image. Obesity is a form of physical deviance that can't be masked. Obese women are especially scrutinized about being overweight. Obese people are a segment of the society that is bombarded daily about their physical appearance, making them feel unattractive and worthless. Our society equates weight and physical attractiveness with success and perfection.

Our everyday lives are flooded with information about how unhealthy obesity is. Members of society perceive obesity as a self-inflicted trait. Society attributes obesity to individuals who lack the willpower to control their weight. Obesity is a physical trait thought to have resulted from behavior that elicits negative responses from members of the society, such as disgust and repulsion. The obese suffer from condemnation, rejection, and ridicule. They come to feel responsible for their condition and they accept the condemnation, rejection, and negative treatment with little or no protest (Cahnman, 1968).

REFERENCES

Berscheid, Ellen, and Elaine Walster. 1972. "Beauty and the Best." *Psychology Today*, March, pp. 45–47, 74.

Cahnman, Werner J. 1968. "The Stigma of Obesity." *Sociological Quarterly*, 9 (Summer): 283–299.

Goode, Erich. 1996. "The Stigma of Obesity." In Erich Goode (ed.), *Social Deviance*. Boston: Allyn & Bacon, pp. 332–340.

Ingrassia, Michelle. 1995. "The Body of the Beholder." *Newsweek*, April 24, pp. 66–67.

BODY PIERCING AND TATTOOING

Jennifer Webb

Last year, I was a server at a semi-fine restaurant in Baltimore. Unless I took my tongue ring out, management would reprimand me. After work, I had to make sure I put my ring back in because the tongue heals rather quickly; without a ring, within 16 hours, the hole in the tongue will close up. During the last year, I have had a job as a research assistant at a research institute in Washington. In this job, I do not deal with the public on a day-to-day basis. I purchased an invisible tongue ring to wear, knowing the stigma surrounding body piercing. But once, recently, I forgot to switch to the invisible barbell and was called into my boss's office for a "talk."

I got the article for this assignment from the Internet. It is in two parts and is entitled "Body Art and Employment," by Karen Hudson. Attached to the article, there's a comment, a section called "Point/Counterpoint," by Caille Millner, an 18-year-old from California, who's in favor of body piercing, and one from Annalise Laurent, who's 14, who is against it. Hudson defends the right of people to modify their bodies. In response to the statement by someone she interviews, "you're not gonna get very good jobs with a face full of metal and tats [tattoos] that show," Hudson says "My question is why the hell not? Why should tattoos and piercings have any effects on determining if we are capable of handling a job? Why does a person wearing jewelry and art scare people? Ignorance." Referring to her own "body art," she says it's "a part of me—take me as I am or leave me the hell alone."

Due to the reactions I have had and that Karen Hudson has had regarding body piercing, it is quite obvious that it is considered deviant in the sense that it is likely to evoke negative reactions. The reason that management at the restaurant I worked for gave me for the policy against body piercing is that it is to comply with safety regulations. The fact is, my tongue ring is much less likely to fall into someone's dinner than someone's earring because tongue rings are screw-on. My boss at the research institute provided me with reasoning that I could understand when she said: "This is a conservative establishment and

we must maintain a professional appearance. It's not any different from saying that you can't wear ripped jeans." I am not naïve. I know that, to some people, body piercing seems unprofessional. But this is only because mainstream society has stigmatized it to be so in the same sense that ripped jeans are. Neither is unprofessional in itself, but society has set arbitrary norms that say they are.

After all, I did get my tongue pierced when I was 18 just to be "different." And I have continued to keep my tongue pierced for personal reasons that are not appropriate to discuss in this assignment. On the micro (face-to-face) level, I do not challenge the policies of the restaurant or the institute because they are absolutely right: Clients, subjects, guests, customers will find my body piercing as a negative reflection on my employers. . . . On the larger, macro (or societal) level, Karen Hudson is completely right: It is outrageous that job potential can be held back on the basis of the number of piercings or tattoos that an individual has. The policies and beliefs against body piercing and tattoos . . . have their roots in pure ignorance and closed-mindedness. It is sad that society can evolve to embody a physical characteristic to be a negative reflection of the person inside.

To those who argue that body piercing is unnecessary I would like to ask, is it absolutely necessary for people to drive a Lexus when a Honda gets you from point A to point B reliably? Is it necessary to eat lobster when rice is more filling? Is it necessary to pay professional ballplayers millions when our society is facing an economic scarcity? Is it necessary to delegate employees to make policies against body piercing when some people are losing their jobs? My point is that many things in life are not necessary, but most of us are guilty of seeking happiness in unnecessary things. So why can't those of us who want to pierce our bodies do so?

As opposed as I am to the fact that individuals are pressured to conform to society's norms, I have to admit that after I graduate, I will reluctantly remove my tongue ring which I have grown to love, knowing that employers have been conditioned by society to regard tongue rings as deviant. I would love to fight for the right to be different, to fight until there is a point reached where anything goes—as long as it isn't harmful to individuals and to society—and everyone is free from arbitrary judgments and stereotypes. . . . I suppose I am weak. Or maybe I just realize that the conforming segment of the society is where the jobs are. I certainly do not want to starve to death just to be different or to give myself some pleasure.

Albinism

Andrea Kearns

An article I got from the Internet by James Romenesko, entitled "The White Minority," discusses albinos. The author takes five case studies of albinos and details the lives they live and the struggles they have with the stigma their condition attracts from the majority. One of them describes himself appearing in public as a "one man walking freak show" because of the reactions he receives from others. When he's with other albinos, he says, it "turns into a three-ring circus. . . . Everybody's got to make a comment or something." One of them got into a lot of fights. "It's the whole idea of being a freak in a freak show. It's like, no way." Another of Romenesko's cases reacted by "becoming master of the sharp retort." Becoming more accepting since he got married, he finds that his wife and friends are less tolerant. His wife, he says, has "wanted to punch some people out just for staring. . . . It bothers her more than it does me. It bothers my friends, who are essentially normal. Normal-appearing, anyway."

In elementary school, I took piano lessons in the same class as an albino girl. Because I was so young and had never been exposed to an albino, I would often stare at her pale appearance and gawk at the unusual way she stared at the sheet music. She was nearly blind and had to bring her face inches from the music resting on the piano. I thought she was weird, but my mother calmly explained that she had a genetic disorder called albinism and I should treat her as I would any other classmate (thank goodness I have a mother in the medical profession). I was nice to her, but in a reserved kind of way, continuing to keep my distance. The only real friend she had was her younger brother, who was also an albino.

Albinos are part of a segment of society that is considered deviant. People who glance at an albino will often react negatively. They may back off, stare, or even make an unkind comment, such as call the albino Snow White, Whitey, or Florescent Face. . . . Albinos are born with a reduced amount of pigment in their eyes, skin, and hair that creates a ghost-like appearance. Nearly all are also legally blind and suffer from a condition, called nystagmus, that causes their eyes to dart around involuntarily. Because the condition is so rare—as Romenesko's article says, only one in 17,000 persons suffer from albinism—most people, when confronted by an albino, are taken aback or even frightened by their appearance.

There is no real subculture that is associated with albinism. Since the condition is so rare, there is no large network of albinos to support each other. As the attached article states, albinos must attempt to integrate into conventional, mainstream society. Albinism is an essentialistic trait. There is no question about who is and who is not an albino. Therefore, the constructionist sociologist would not be interested in studying its cause. But there is a stigma associated with an albino's appearance; it is their appearance that makes the person a deviant. This type of deviance can be attributed to something concrete: the albino's looks. In other words, it is a type of physical deviance.

Reading "The White Minority" by James Romenesko was an eye-opening experience for me. It made me see the stigma that albinos face. The girl in my piano class is the only albino I have come into close contact with. Therefore, their struggle was never something I thought about. It is sad, however, that these people, who have no control over the lack of pigment in their eyes, skin, and hair, are considered deviant simply because of how they look.

THE REBEL AS HERO

The Assignment Deviance is behavior, or beliefs, or conditions that, when discovered, tend to attract negative reactions and whose enactors, believers, or possessors tend to be regarded in a negative light by substantial numbers of the members of the society. At the same time, for a variety of reasons, some people who engage in behavior that is normally disvalued are regarded in some social circles as rebels and become heroes to a minority of the society. Locate one article from any source describing a "rebel as hero" and, in one page or so, discuss the relevance of your case for the basic ideas, concepts, and theories we deal with in this course.

The papers I received discussed some of the following "rebels" who, some members of the society believe, are heroes: John Gotti (gangster); Margaret Sanger (early feminist and birth control advocate); Rosa Parks (early civil rights advocate); Tupac Shakur (hip-hop artist and "gangsta rapper" who was killed by members of a rival faction); Marion Barry (former mayor of Washington, D.C., who defied the white power structure and was arrested for smoking crack with a prostitute); Kurt Cobain (rock 'n roll performer, who committed suicide); Louis Farrakhan (leader of the Nation of Islam, a Black separatist religious group that advocates the view that persons of African descent are inherently superior to persons of European descent); Huey Newton (early Black Panther and ex-convict, who was killed in the 1990s by a drug dealer); Charles Manson (mass murderer, leader of an apocalyptic cult); Sun Myung Moon (leader of the Unification Church, who advocates that he is the new Messiah); Eminem (white rapper); Dennis Rodman (controversial, eccentric former NBA basketball player); Britney Spears (pop singer who has had emotional and substance abuse problems); Osama bin Laden (Islamic militant, organizer of the September 11 attack on the United States); Jim Morrison (flamboyant rock 'n roll star in the 1960s who died of a drug overdose); Mike Tyson (heavyweight boxer, convicted and imprisoned for rape); and Jack Kevorkian (advocate of assisted suicides for the terminally ill, now serving a prison sentence). Here are three of the papers I received.

ROBERT DOWNEY, JR.: REBEL AS HERO

Krista Gawkowski

Today, individuals who are part of the sports and entertainment industries are seen as pop cultural icons; they are idols whom society holds in high esteem. We watch them act on our favorite television shows, listen to their songs on the radio, and watch them play for our favorite sports teams. Virtually every aspect of a celebrity's life is plastered in the many cultural media. Their fans number in the many millions, and celebrities become idealized heroes. How quick we are to forget that members of the entertainment and sports industries are human beings just like their fans. Many of them have quirks and idiosyncrasies similar to those of ordinary people. Some celebrities can even be considered deviants. However, . . . fans tend to ignore these shortcomings. They still praise them in spite of their objectionable behavior—sometimes because of it. This "rebel as hero" theme can be applied especially to a substantial proportion of the entertainment industry. In fact, the entertainment industry could be a source of many a sociologist looking into the behavior of social deviants because of the lifestyle that many celebrities lead. It is a fast-paced, "money is no object, no one ever says no, if you don't take it seriously, you don't get hurt" type of lifestyle, one that is often conducive to deviant behavior such as excessive drinking, drug abuse, unconventional sexual behavior, wearing strange or inappropriate clothing, and strange or inappropriate ways of handling oneself in public and in front of the media.

When I think of a rebel as a hero, Robert Downey, Jr., the actor, comes to mind. Constant battles with drug use, periods of incarceration, participation in treatment programs, and other encounters with the criminal justice system have plagued Downey's life. However, he is also considered a talented actor with a large fan base. Downey's most recent television role was that of Ally McBeal's love interest in a program of the same name on Fox. He was nominated for an Emmy for the part and won both a Golden Globe and Screen Actor's Guild Award for it. It is obvious from these nominations that his colleagues consider Downey to be an asset to the entertainment business. Downey is currently looking into movie deals, all the while battling his substance problems. . . .

Perhaps the most important issue at hand is what message society is sending to itself. Why is it acceptable for Downey to be held in such high regard by such a large proportion of the society? Why is he not labeled as a deviant and ostracized by the majority, the way that someone who is not famous or part of the entertainment industry would be if he or she did the same things? These issues seem to suggest that the "rebel as hero" contradicts the very validity of the concept of deviance. If there is no social condemnation of an act by a majority of the population, then is the

person who committed the act really a deviant? The answer to these questions is that it depends on the relevant audience. There is a range of opinions on the matter. Some may consider Robert Downey, Jr., a deviant; as a result they ignore his pop icon status. Others may say that Downey is a deviant, but we should accept his behavior because of what he contributes to society. Still others regard his deviant behavior as something positive and admire him for it. . . .

Downey's case makes us realize that perhaps some of today's rebellions will turn into tomorrow's conventionality. Will all deviant behaviors of persons in the public eye become acceptable simply because of the public following of the celebrities who commit such behavior? Is this fair to ordinary people who are not part of the entertainment and sports worlds, who, unlike our celebrities, are labeled as deviants and suffer the consequences of their actions? Only a close eye kept on the developments and breakthroughs on this matter will answer such questions.

Muhammad Ali: The Rebel as Hero

Alexis M. R. Mitchell

At a time when Blacks in the South were expected to "know their place" and observe the rules of the white man, the "deviant" behavior of the man who later became Muhammad Ali, Cassius Clay, made him a very controversial figure. By violating the mores of American society during the 1960s, Cassius Clay became a hero to many members of the society. He grew to question society's values, laws, leadership, and government. Clay began to reflect on his identity and, as a result of his exposure to the Black Muslim movement, he came to discover himself as Muhammad Ali.

Ali's largest boxing audience—conventional, traditional whites—began to question his behavior. The undisputed heavyweight champion of the world, presumably a respected, establishment figure in American society, was now a member of a radical, militaristic group.

In 1967, Ali was sentenced to five years in prison (though his conviction was reversed in 1971) and his title as heavyweight champion was revoked (and regained in 1974, in a title fight against George Foreman) as a result of his refusal,

based on his Muslim faith, to be drafted into the war in Vietnam. Such beliefs and actions led many Americans to see Ali, and the Muslim faith, as anti-American.

As a prizefighter, Clay's unprecedented flamboyant behavior violated the humble good sportsmanship expected of a great boxer. He made the language of ridicule into an art form. According to the encyclopedia entry on Muhammad Ali I located on the Internet by John Gennari: "A brilliant showman and provocateur, Ali enlisted the media—especially television—as an integral part of his competitive strategy." His "flamboyance and self-promotion challenged a traditional unwritten code under which black athletes were expected to be dutiful, modest, and respectful of white authority." He referred to himself as "the greatest."

Mainstream American society finally succumbed to Ali's influence. They came to believe that Ali was a man of integrity and principle, and respected him for standing up to the less attractive norms of the society by taking his name as a Muslim and refusing to be drafted into the military on the grounds of his faith at a time when such actions were looked down upon and regarded as deviant.

Ali became a role model for African Americans, Muslims, and athletes in general, especially for children, whom he gave hope, pride, and faith in their potential to become more than what society tells them they can be.

According to social constructionists, Ali is a good example of a person who has exhibited deviant characteristics. He was a radical. He questioned the ways of the society he lived in at a time when that was unacceptable. Through his defiance of society's norms and values, he became one of the greatest figures in American history. He was a true "rebel as a hero."

CHE GUEVARA: REBEL AS DEITY

Mary Doherty

Ernesto "Che" Guevara is a global icon. The image of the intense, bearded revolutionary can be found on t-shirts, posters, stickers, and many other forms of media as a symbol of alternative thought and action. He gained notoriety in the 1960s as a leading guerrilla rebel in Latin America calling for an end to the capitalist/imperialist exploitation of the people. Upon his death in 1967, Che became a martyr.

Che, schooled in medicine in Buenos Aires, was an educated man who was familiar with the works of Marx, Engels, and Freud. Having witnessed the political crises in Argentina (once referred to as the most "European" country in Latin America), it makes sense that he would have formed a negative opinion of the military and the politicians it produced—such as Juan Peron and his left-fascist regime. Although he did not participate or show interest in student demonstrations, it is clear that Che was thinking outside the box at an early age. It was the political corruption he observed that caused him to pursue an alternative to the conventional career paths available to him.

Instead of becoming a middle-class general practitioner, Che joined Fidel Castro and his followers in Cuba. There, he and others received training in guerrilla warfare, which was very much influenced by the teachings of Mao Tse-tung. Che flourished under Fidel's leadership, developing an absolutist perspective, and soon became known for his ruthlessness and cruelty toward defectors and dissidents. After the success of the Cuban revolution on New Year's Day, 1960, he became Castro's right-hand man. He was very much responsible for pushing the Cuban leader toward a

type of communism unlike the orthodox Soviet model. As an active participant in the new Cuban government as well as an observer in several developing countries in South America, Asia, and Africa, Che was always trying to incite revolution. He actively organized the attempt at revolution in Bolivia in 1967, and he failed. He and his comrades were captured and executed by the Bolivian army, photographed, and buried in unmarked graves near a town called Vallegrande, the location of a Bolivian army base. His death marks the beginning of the cult of Che.

Although he is now an idol, public opinion did not always favor Che's Marxist ideology or its methods. Guerrilla warfare has been the hallmark of the fighting that has occurred in Latin America since the conquest by the Spanish in the sixteenth century. These tactics involve groups of irregular troops who employ deception and ambush versus the more traditional battlefield combat. For those methods to be effective, however, a sympathetic populace must figure into the equation. This is most likely why Che did not succeed. He stressed propaganda and terrorism, which usually result in a fearful populace rather than a sympathetic or supportive one.

Once Che was killed, the threat factor associated with him was diminished, thus leaving room for his deeds to become legend. . . . Che Guevara is so well known because, though there are many deviants in many societies, very few are real rebels who actively challenge or attempt to undermine the status quo, and even fewer who show any measurable degree of success. Che Guevara met with much hostility in his life and he was punished by execution—two good indicators of his deviant status. Many feared the power that his name and image held with the masses, and his death, which made him into a martyr, resulted in his current status as the patron saint of Vallegrande and the universal icon of revolutionary thinking and action.

What's Deviant? Does It Depend on the Relevant Audience?

The Assignment Think about one act you have engaged in, belief you have expressed, or physical trait you possess that is likely to be regarded as offensive or deviant to the society as a whole, that the majority of the population is likely to have negative feelings about and, if they were to discover that you engage or engaged in it, believe it, or possess it, are likely to have negative feelings about you and react negatively to you as a consequence. In other words, describe an example of personal "societal" deviance." Then picture a social circle, group, category, or idiosyncratic individuals in the population who are likely to tolerate or accept that act, belief, or physical trait. Using the concepts and distinctions made in this course, discuss the act, the belief, or the trait and how it is likely to be judged societally, that is, in the society as a whole, and then how it is likely to be judged situationally, that is, in a smaller, unconventional social collectivity. If you can think of examples of actual negative reactions that have taken place in response to your engaging in this behavior, expressing the belief, or possessing the characteristic, please describe, discuss, and analyze them.

Now do the reverse: Choose an example of an act, a belief, or a physical trait that you engaged in or held or hold, or possessed or possess that is *unacceptable* or deviant in a nonmajority circle, group, category, or among certain individuals, that would be regarded as *acceptable* among the majority. Again, discuss what it is in as much detail as you can and how it would be regarded in these two collectivities, using the concepts and definitions we've discussed so far.

Because of the personal nature of the behavior discussed below, the authors of these papers are anonymous.

Tongue Piercing/Kissing

A "deviant" trait that I possess—voluntarily acquired—is tongue piercing. I had my piercing done about two years ago because I wanted to try something crazy, something that would be shocking to people who saw me as an innocent girl. After I had my tongue pierced, I immediately went home and yelled, "Hey, Mom!" Then I stuck out my tongue. Her reaction was not anger but shock. Despite my mother's eventual acceptance of my piercing, however, in my experience, I have found that in mainstream society, tongue piercing is viewed very negatively. I have been denounced by some family members, told that I have self-mutilated my body. Some people assume that my tongue piercing is for the purpose of heightening the pleasure of oral sex, giving me the stigma of being an "easy" girl. At one job, I was given an ultimatum that if I did not take out my tongue ring, I would not be hired. I was discredited on the assumption that my tongue ring would affect my job performance. These negative reactions have come from a wide variety of people, in several different social locations, including family members, friends, acquaintances, employers, and even strangers.

On the other hand, there are some small circles of individuals who are very accepting of my piercing. Mostly these individuals are in the subculture of people who have body piercing on some part of their anatomy in addition to the ears. We noticed each other, we have a topic of conversation, and we can share experiences. My tongue piercing is accepted and tolerated in any situation with these people. Then there are some people who do not have their body pierced, but who find my piercing fascinating and cool, and want to know about it. . . . This example of "horizontal" judgments of deviance, that is, negative reactions among the majority and accepting reactions among certain minorities, means that what's deviant has a situational reality. It depends on the person and the situation. If I am with friends at a party and someone notices it, it's not a big deal. If I am the maid of honor at a wedding and giving a speech during the wedding reception among family and friends, and someone notices it, they are likely to regard it as unacceptable and inappropriate. I may even be discredited. As a whole, the reactions I receive from my piercing stem from many different ideologies, mostly negative, some positive, and are dependent on the situation and the people who make up the evaluating audiences.

It came to my attention about a year ago that an activity I engage in, that in my eyes, and in most of society's eyes, is completely acceptable, is actually considered deviant to some individuals. A fundamentalist Christian friend of mine told me that I was committing a sin by kissing my boyfriend. Kissing, he said, is only acceptable within the context of marriage. The nonmajority circle of my friend and his fellow Christian Bible school students believe that kissing, holding hands, as well as the very *thought* of such activities, are sins in the eyes of God. As he explained it to me, "It's like walking all over the cross Jesus died on." While it is apparent that the majority of society would disagree and be completely tolerant and accepting of kissing, holding hands, and thinking lustfully about your partner, fundamentalist Christians see things otherwise.

This type of deviance as seen from a fundamentalist Christian standpoint is an absolutist judgment. It is a "vertical" way of thinking about rules. Bible Christians believe that God made the rules, the Ten Commandments, and everyone is subject to those rules. It doesn't matter what different human collectivities believe—it is God's law alone that counts. If a rule is broken—although forgiveness is possible—the act is considered "deviant." This absolutist perspective is that kissing is wrong everywhere because of God's law. It is consistent with the idea that deviant acts are the work of the Devil—a form of demonological thinking. That "deviant" behavior is the work of the Devil is a nonscientific, nonevidentiary perspective, a point of view that is not interested in the facts, only the absolute righteousness of the rule. Although I, along with the majority, see no harm in kissing, at least at an acceptable age, such rigid, strict, absolutist beliefs still exist in today's society. Bible schools and fundamentalist Christian families reinforce the idea that whether you kiss or kill, you are sinning and, hence, engaging in deviant behavior.

It is apparent from these two examples from my own life that what is considered deviant is at bottom subjective. Different individuals react in different ways to behaviors, beliefs, and conditions. It is important to understand that with the exception of very extreme cases, such as murder and rape, an act that is viewed by the majority as deviant will most likely be accepted by some social circle, group, or idiosyncratic individuals. And conversely, a perceived normal and acceptable behavior for most of the society may be considered deviant in some nonmajority circles. What is deviant is most definitely relative to the audience making judgments about the behavior.

STRIPPING/LEADING A CONVENTIONAL LIFESTYLE

According to the sociological definition, my current occupation is considered deviant. Most people in our society would not consider taking their clothes off in public for money an acceptable form of behavior, let alone a decent way of making a living. I am a 26-year-old exotic dancer—or as some people like to say, a "*stripper*." I am comfortable with what I do. Stripping for money is what I do; however, it does not define who I am. I feel no shame in what I do nor do I believe that I am doing harm to anyone, including myself. It is perfectly legal. I pay taxes just like most people do. However, this behavior, which I believe to be acceptable, is offensive to the majority of the society. Stripping has negative connotations in mainstream culture. In my experience, the majority of Americans believe that strippers are whores, addicted to drugs, stupid, and grew up in broken, dysfunctional homes. I grew up in a happy, loving, lower-middle-class Catholic family. I was never abused, and I maintain close ties with my immediate as well as extended families. I am happily married to a loving, sensitive, and supportive husband, and have a 6-year-old stepson. I graduated from a female-only, private Catholic high school with a 3.0 grade point average. I have an Associate in Applied Sciences degree in criminal justice from a community college and am currently pursuing my Bachelor of Science from a major state university.

Nonetheless, I am hesitant to tell people where I work and what I do, not because I am ashamed but because I am afraid I will not be taken seriously or will be judged according to what that person's attitude or experience is with the strip club scene. For instance, I became friendly with a young woman in one of my classes. Because of my relationship with her, I came to feel comfortable telling her where I worked. When I did, she thought I was joking. I insisted that I was being perfectly honest. She then asked me a series of questions about my job, such as "Aren't you embarrassed to do that?" And "Don't you find it degrading to do that?" Because of her absolutistic, judgmental view, she stopped sitting next to me and rarely spoke to me again.

On the other hand, my regular customers, both male and female, feel that there is nothing wrong with receiving money for entertaining people with one's naked body. If someone finds stripping offensive, they don't have to go to strip clubs. All the participants are there of their own free will, there is no physical or sexual contact between strippers and clients, the dancing performed is tasteful; in our club, women do not spread their legs wide open, bend over, or do "floor work."

Ironically, among my coworkers, I am considered deviant in that I am in a monogamous, healthy relationship, have had no plastic surgery to enhance my appearance, and will soon be graduating from college. Most of the dancers I have worked with refer to themselves as "lifers." This means that they have been dancers and nothing else for most of their lives and invest in themselves to preserve and enhance their appearance to continue dancing for as long as they can. A majority of the women I work with enjoy the strip club life and do not wish to work at any other occupation. They live for the excitement and the lavish lifestyle. Their occupation as stripper is how they identify themselves; it is part of their identity. Many have invested their savings in a way that will permit them to retire comfortably, although some have not. Either way, they do not see any reason to waste their time and money on an education. In this sense, I am a "situational" deviant because I violate the beliefs of the majority of strippers (the "lifers").

At the same time, they are "societal" deviants in that they are exotic dancers. To the majority of the society, having a monogamous, healthy relationship, no kind of physical augmentation, and graduating from college are positive and praiseworthy, not deviant, and so mainstream values support me and not them. Therefore, I may display situational deviance in the smaller social circle but I am accepted by the majority of the society on the very same terms that deemed me deviant in the smaller circle.

PREMARITAL PREGNANCY/CONVENTIONAL MARRIAGE AND MOTHERHOOD

Some five years ago, after a series of disappointments, I found myself thinking about the life choices that led to the self-destructive and drug-induced stage of my rebellious youth. After several failed attempts to reclaim stability and peace of mind, I sought the company of a man who seemed to have the ambition I once claimed to have. After a brief romance—two months to be exact—I discovered that I was pregnant. Following a sweep of mixed emotions, our decision to make a go of marriage, parenthood, and just plain adulthood turned out to be for the best. For the most part, our families were supportive, but I was as conscious of the stigma of my condition as I was of my increasingly protruding belly. I'm

sure a rush of whispers followed me down the aisle in my off-white wedding "tent."

To the society at large, I had fallen into the ranks of many of my friends, who were young mothers themselves. I was treated as a statistic when I pulled out my WIC (Women Infant Care) checks at the supermarket or my Medicaid card at the doctor's office. The situation was compounded by the fact that we were quickly running out of money. Being pregnant is one thing, being pregnant and *poor* played tricks on my mind, making me feel I deserved my status. Getting pregnant was just what lower-class girls did. Other people didn't see that I was determined to go to college, even graduate school. Conventional society had no idea at first glance that my fiancé was an honors student pursuing graduate school. We felt embarrassed that we had put ourselves in such a situation when we knew we were so much smarter than that.

Religious principles entered the picture on my mother's side. While she was overwhelmingly supportive, I felt more shame as a result of the premarital pregnancy when I was in her social network than I did in my own. After we told her that we were going to get married, the minister who agreed to perform the ceremony asked me and my fiancé to live separately during the months prior to the wedding in order to acknowledge our sins and begin afresh with our marital vows. Our decision to marry just one month prior to the birth of our daughter was prompted by this "sin." It was an effort to "make things right."

Although there was this feeling of disgrace when I was in the company of people my parents' age, I was welcomed into the "pregnancy club" by a network of friends who had had much the same experience and had felt similar emotions and physical discomforts. I was encouraged to embrace their company and was helped whenever possible. What made me different, however, was my commitment to a marriage. Not one of my friends who had children was successful at maintaining a relationship with her boyfriend/father. In fact, the constant disputes, financial struggles, and otherwise "Jerry Springer" moments of my friends were essential to my decision not to become a permanent fixture in that little social network.

On the other hand, my decision to keep my child, get married, and live a more-or-less conventional lifestyle also led to the failure of several relationships, which remain severed to this day. One good friend in particular, who had no children, was distressed not only by the news of my marriage but also by my decision to go through with the pregnancy. She had a difficult time understanding the change in my priorities that made me unable to party with her any more. The close bond we had as best friends and "smoking buddies" was sacrificed for the new role I took on. Her resentment manifested in verbal attacks, snide remarks, and comments questioning my "integrity" and "loyalty" as a friend. I felt that loyalty to my child should be much greater than my loyalty to her. As a free spirit, determined never to be chained to the conventions of family life, she argued that I was a

"sell-out." There were times when her views forced me to question my choices.

I think people who take a stance against the conventions of mainstream society feel betrayed when one of their own strays from the pack and adopts a more conservative lifestyle. It is an example of "situational" deviance—by becoming more conservative, in her eyes, I was violating her norms of partying, doing drugs, drinking, and devoting my life to pleasure seeking. But in my case, I had no choice. I have not taken the easy way out. I can no longer escape anxiety with drugs or abdicate personal responsibility with antiestablishment views. . . .

When people ask how long I've been married, the response in years will always match my daughter's age. Judgments of my character can easily be made in the course of polite conversation. . . . Though statistically it may no longer be abnormal to be pregnant and unmarried, the continued success of my marital relationship is nothing short of an anomaly.

DATE RAPE

The Assignment The following is an "action project" proposed by B. Keith Crew (1999). I have adapted it only slightly.

Have six friends (three males, three females) read the story below, then ask them the follow-up questions. Indicate the gender and age of each person. In as much detail as you can supply, record the answers of each of your respondents. Analyze their responses in light of the basic concepts, ideas, and theories we've covered so far in this course. Your analysis is as important as the responses you receive.

Discussion Guidelines Compare the answers of yourself and your friends, and your classmates and their friends. What proportion of respondents do not define these events as rape? Does the fact that Jennifer was so drunk affect the perception of her as a victim? Do men and women respond differently to the questions? In what ways? Do any of the responses illustrate the rape myths discussed in class? After discussing the issue in your group, what advice would you give Jennifer? What consequences should occur to Bruce (Crew, 1999)?

Action Project: Date Rape

Berenice Juarez

The following is an action project on date rape. Specifically, the goals of this assignment are to (1) show variation in attitudes toward date rape, particularly along gender lines, and (2) assess the impact of rape myths on perceptions of date rape. To achieve these goals, a short story on date rape was read to six college students, three of them females, ages 19, 20, and 21, and three of them males, ages 18, 20, and 21. After reading the story to these participants, I asked them some follow-up questions about the story. This project's findings indicate that there is some variation along gender lines when it comes to perceptions about date rape. However, for both sexes, the belief that date rape is less serious and less terrifying than stranger rape prevails to some degree.

This is the story that I read to my six respondents:

Bruce and Jennifer are college students who know each other casually. One night about a month ago, they had sex. They didn't see much of each other after that until a few nights ago. They met at a beer party. Jennifer got extremely drunk, and Bruce escorted her to her apartment. At Jennifer's apartment, they "made out" for a while, but then she passed out, dead drunk. At this point, Bruce partially removed her clothes and had sexual intercourse with her. He left without waking her up. The next day, Jennifer woke up with only vague, addled memories of the night's events. She calls Bruce and asks him if they had had sex the previous night. He laughs and says, "Of course, don't you remember how great it was?" At this point, Jennifer becomes very upset and calls you to tell you what happened.

After reading this story to my six respondents, I asked them the following five follow-up questions:

a. Did Bruce rape Jennifer?
b. Why do you think this was (or was not) rape?
c. Should Jennifer report the incident to the police?
d. What should Jennifer do?
e. Who shares more of the responsibility for what happened, Bruce or Jennifer? Why?

During the course of the interviews with my six participants, other questions were asked and other points for discussion were raised. These will be analyzed in the following pages. At the end of this paper, I will also add a note regarding my own personal answers to this story.

Let us begin by examining the respondents' answers to the first question: "Did Bruce rape Jennifer?" All three female respondents answered affirmatively to the question. One female respondent emphasized her answer to the question in the following manner: "Yes. My answer to this question is yes. And that is an *emphatic* yes."

Among the males, no one answered negatively to the first question. However, their answers were not as emphatic. The breakdown in their answers to the question of whether or not Bruce had raped Jennifer was as follows. One male said that Bruce had indeed raped Jennifer. The other two males answered by saying, "It depends." (All of the names I give my participants are fictional to protect their anonymity.) When I asked one respondent, John, age 18, to elaborate his answer, he said that "technically" it had been rape, but "a simple answer cannot be given to this question. You have to take into consideration the whole context of the story and then figure out whether it had indeed been rape." Well, I said, I have read the whole story to you, so taking into consideration the whole story, or the overall context of the story, as you have stated, what is your answer to the question of whether or not Bruce raped Jennifer? "Once again," he responded, "my answer is that it depends. It depends from what angle you want to look at it. From a technical perspective, yes, it was rape. But from a 'normal' perspective so to speak, I don't think it was rape."

This response led me to the next question: "Why do you think this was (or was not) rape?" I asked John to clarify for me what he meant by rape under a "technical" versus a "normal" perspective.

Well, okay, let me explain myself. Technically, what happened to Jennifer was rape because Bruce had sex with her without her consent. She was drunk, right? So she couldn't say yes or no to Bruce. Under this "technical" definition what happened is rape. But under my normal defini-tion, it's not rape because it just doesn't follow. Jennifer was making out with Bruce, right? So who's to say that she wouldn't have said yes? Maybe she did want to do it with him. . . . I mean, she was making out with him. She just didn't get a chance to say yes.

But you cannot be sure, I said. What if all she wanted to do was to make out but not have sex? "See, that's the point," John answered. "You don't have enough evidence so how can you call it rape?"

When I asked the other male respondent, Andy, 20, what he meant by "it depends," he did not offer such an elaborate answer as John did. In fact, after a long pause, he said he guessed it was rape. "So you're not sure?" I asked. "Yeah," Andy said, "I guess technically it was rape. It was nonconsen-sual. So yes, it was rape." What is important to note here, however, is the fact that out of the six partici-pants, only two of the males were hesitant to qual-ify the act as rape, whereas all three of the women had no doubt in their minds that what happened was rape. As one female, Gloria, 21, put it: "Rape means doing something to someone without their conscious permission. Bruce plainly took advan-tage of Jennifer because she was drunk. It's no puzzle. It was rape." My other female respondent, Stephanie, 20, took an even stronger approach to the question of why she thought Bruce had raped Jennifer. "Umm, she was not conscious. *Hel-LO?*" With the tone of her voice, Stephanie wonders how someone could *not* consider the event as a rape.

Interestingly enough, the answer to the third question, "Should Jennifer report the incident to the police?" produced the most interesting answers. It was also the question whose answers followed gen-der lines most closely. For instance, although their explanations varied, all of the males said that Jen-nifer should not report the incident to the police. In contrast, two of the females said that Jennifer should report the incident to the police and one said she shouldn't. Indeed, the answers given to this question strongly illuminate date rape percep-tions. . . . When asked if Jennifer should report the incident to the police, John answered as follows.

> Absolutely not. My God, she's not gonna get any-thing accomplished. [Laughs out loud.] I mean, can you imagine what a police station would be

like if all the girls who go through what Jennifer went through reported it to the police? Please! Girls know better than to do that. Nothing will get done. And if somebody at the police station told Jennifer that maybe something could get done, it's not like they're gonna gather enough evidence to arrest Bruce. No, I don't think Jennifer should report the incident to the police.

On the other hand, Andy was more ambivalent in his answer to this question:

> Ummm. . . . It depends, I guess. I guess if she [Jennifer] feels greatly morally injured, then she should go to the police. But I think she should try to resolve this issue without police interven-tion. Like, maybe she could confront Bruce or something. Yeah, I don't really know what would be best for her to do.

Max, 21, my third male participant, went even further than John or Andy in discouraging police intervention.

> No [she should not report the incident to the police]. She should realize that this was 50 per-cent her fault. She has no right to use the law against the guy. I mean, what happened was not completely Bruce's fault because they had had a previous relationship. So I think there should be a common perception that since they were mak-ing out, then they probably would have had consensual sex if she had not passed out. Plus, Bruce had also been drinking. So he was under the influence, and maybe he didn't know what the hell he was doing either. So how can Jennifer blame him for everything? They're both at fault, in my opinion.

Among the females, only Gloria thought that Jennifer should not report the incident to the police because this kind of incident "does not proceed with the law. The police can't do anything about it because there was no violence or anything so it's not really rape under the law." In contrast, the two other females *did* think that Jennifer should report the incident to the police. Stephanie, for example, voiced an extremely strong view about the use of the law against this kind of incident:

> Hell, yes! [Jennifer should report the incident to the police.] If Jennifer's got the balls to do it, she should go to the police and raise hell for what

this bastard did. She should turn him in. And if for some reason there's not enough evidence or something, she should frame him. She should make up stuff and frame him. He deserves it. All men who get away with this shit deserve it!

Virginia, 19, my third female respondent, also thought that Jennifer should report the incident to the police:

> Yes, Jennifer has to do it. She has to understand that her rights as a woman..., no, no, no, as a human being, any human, were violated. Her body was taken against her conscious consent. If that's not a violation of your rights then I don't know what is. Women shouldn't allow this. Jennifer *has* to report this to the police.

The variation along gender lines is quite clear when we examine the answers to the question of whether Jennifer should report the incident to the police. In general, it seems that women are much more likely than men to see merit in reporting an incident like the one in the story to the police.

When asked the fourth question, "What should Jennifer do?" the answers varied among all respondents, with no variation along gender lines. Both Andy and Gloria said the best thing for Jennifer to do would be to talk to Bruce about what happened. Gloria thought that this would be the best solution because "Jennifer can't go to the police." According to Gloria, what happened to Jennifer does not "proceed with the law." Andy seemed more confused about the situation. He admitted that he did not know what would be the best course of action for Jennifer to take. Thus, he reasoned that maybe by talking to Bruce about what happened, there could be some sort of "mental and emotional reconciliation."

Max and John, on the other hand, thought that the best course of action for Jennifer would be to do something that would insulate her against future incidents such as the one in the story. Thus, according to Max:

> I would tell Jennifer that she should use her head and not get drunk at keggers. Damn it, doesn't she know what a stupid thing that is? I would tell her that under the influence, it is easy to make stupid mistakes like the one she made. So I think the best thing for her to do is to obtain some sense of

responsibility over her actions. Of course, I would tell her all this in a polite way.

Similarly, John echoed Max's point of view by pointing out that Jennifer should be more responsible about the things she does so that "bad things won't happen to her." Interestingly enough, only Stephanie mentioned getting medical attention:

> What I think Jennifer should do is to go to the hospital and get checked up. Personally, I would think that this is a priority. There will always be time to get back at this guy. But more than anything, she's gotta go to the hospital and get checked out and make sure she's okay physically.

Hence, answers about what Jennifer should do vary according to what each respondent sees as the most important issue to address—the present or the future. The males seemed to be more concerned about Jennifer's future and placed a great deal of emphasis on devising future strategies of prevention, developing a sense of responsibility about her actions, and so on. On the other hand, the females tended to see the current situation as more urgent and requiring immediate attention. For example, Virginia insisted that Jennifer go to the police. Gloria said that it was "vital" that Jennifer talk to Bruce about what happened. Finally, Stephanie placed a great deal of attention on getting medical attention.

Finally, with the last question, "Who shared more responsibility for what happened?" once again, I found variance along gender lines. Not one of the females placed any responsibility on Jennifer for what happened. As Stephanie eloquently put it:

> Bruce shares *all* responsibility for what happened. Women's vaginas have the right not to be touched if the women do not express consent. The whole thing about women "asking for it" is bullshit. Women have the right to get drunk and party without having to worry about being taken advantage of by a guy. I mean, our bodies have rights!

On the other hand, although none of the males placed full responsibility on Jennifer, two of the males did ascribe some responsibility to her. Both Max and John said that Jennifer should have to share half the responsibility for what happened because she did not "take care of herself." By this they said they meant that Jennifer did not drink responsibly and did not make sure that she had a group of friends with her to take care of her in case she got drunk.

The findings in this project are very consistent with the date rape literature. Susan Estrich points out differences in perception between "aggravated" and "simple" rape. Aggravated rape, according to Estrich, entails cases with "extreme violence, multiple assailants, no prior relationship between victim and offender" (1987, p. 20). Simple rape, in contrast, "includes cases in which none of these 'aggravated circumstances' is present" (p. 20). As Estrich points out, what is interesting about perceptions of aggravated versus simple rape is that it appears that most women "forced to have sex by men they know see themselves as victims, but not as legitimate crime victims" (p. 12). This perception is illustrated by Gloria's perception that Jennifer was for all intents and purposes raped, but she does not think that Jennifer's situation "proceeds with the law." In other words, Gloria does not think that Jennifer is a legitimate rape victim because there was no violence. This view is clearly consistent with general perceptions of what constitutes aggravated versus simple rape.

Perhaps what is reassuring is that Gloria was the only female in this study who held the perception of Jennifer being an illegitimate rape victim. The other two females clearly saw Jennifer as a legitimate rape victim. Nevertheless, what is interesting about the views of these two females is that they were skeptical about the system's response to rape. Both Stephanie and Virginia thought that Jennifer should report the incident to the police, but both expressed fears that the system would be unable to help Jennifer. As we recall, Stephanie—anticipating a negative or indifferent response from the criminal justice system—said that if Jennifer could not come up with convincing proof of rape then she should just "frame" Bruce. Indeed, some victims of date rape feel that they will not be believed or taken seriously as victims of crime when they report a date rape to the police, and often, realistically speaking, this is in fact the case (Schwartz, 2001). "In New York, for example, researchers studying police files found than 24 percent of the rape complaints in nonstranger rapes were judged by the police to be without merit, compared with less than 5 percent in the stranger cases" (Estrich, 1987, p. 16).

Another rape myth or stereotypical, preconceived assumption about rape that this project illustrated was the idea that if rape occurs between nonstrangers that had a previous relationship, then the rape incident should be considered less serious and less deserving of the system's attention than is true of cases of stranger rapes. This view is based on the assumptions that, first, prior relationships are truly private disputes that are not the business of the public prosecution system. Second, the assumption is that prior relationship cases are less serious and defendants less blameworthy because such cases involve a claim of certain rights on the part of the accused that attacks by strangers do not involve. And third, an attack by a nonstranger is somehow less terrifying and therefore less deserving of punishment.

This project illustrated these generalizations. Two out of the three males interviewed for this project said that Jennifer was partly blameworthy for what happened to her. According to John and Max, Jennifer's fault was that she got drunk without assessing the risk of possible consequences. Gloria and Andy's answers illustrate the belief that an attack by an acquaintance is somehow less terrifying than by a stranger. . . . Gloria and Andy figure that since the incident occurred between two former lovers, it is possible that if Jennifer talks to Bruce, some sort of emotional reconciliation can take place. . . . Most males seem to base their conclusion that Jennifer shared a contributory fault for what happened because she did not drink responsibly or assess appropriately the risks associated with drinking. None of the females felt that way.

As a final note, I believe that Bruce raped Jennifer. I believe this because Bruce took advantage of Jennifer while she was unconscious. Thus, she was unable to voice her explicit consent of whether she wanted to have sex or not. It does not matter that they were "making out" prior to sexual intercourse. The fact is, Jennifer did not give her conscious consent. Thus, Bruce taking sexual advantage of Jennifer while she was unconscious qualifies as rape. Personally, I believe that Jennifer should contact the police. She is a crime victim and she deserves justice. Finally, I believe that Bruce is totally responsible for what happened. He took advantage of a woman without her consent. That is a crime—period. Thus, Bruce and Bruce alone is responsible for this crime.

Comparing Victim with Non-Victim Crimes

The Assignment Select and read two articles on two separate crimes from newspapers, magazines, and/or the Internet. It must entail a story involving the enactment of a specific crime committed by a specific person—not a discussion of crime in general. One of the two crimes that is described must be one in which there is direct, clear-cut, personal victimization, while the other one should entail no direct, clear-cut personal victimization.

In three or four sentences, describe each crime. Is it an "Index" crime? (Index crimes are the seven that the FBI tabulates each year as "crimes reported to the police"; they are rape, murder, robbery, assault, burglary, motor vehicle theft, and larceny-theft.

In the case of a crime with a victim, explain who the victim is (or who the victims are)—not the name of the victim but the category of persons who are at the receiving end of the act—for instance, "the storeowner who was robbed," "the child who was assaulted," "the woman who was raped." In the case of the non-victim or victimless crime, speculate who might be the indirect "victims" of the crime—for instance, "society," "women," "the poor," and so on.

Sachin Vaidya

In "Teen Killed in Apparent Liquor Store Robbery," a news item I took from the Internet, a 17-year-old high school student attempted to rob a liquor store and was shot dead by the store clerk. . . . In this story, two events took place—the attempted robbery and the homicide or killing of the attempted robber. The victim of the attempted robbery is, first, the store clerk, whose life was in danger, and second, the owner of the store, who stood to lose money. Robbery is an FBI Index Crime. The store clerk defended himself from harm and possible death by shooting the robber. Since he was a clerk in a liquor store that has experienced problems with robbery in the past, he was probably justified in using force to ensure his safety. Thus, his killing the robber was not a crime.

In the second article I chose, "U.S. Park Police Commander Accused of Indecent Exposure," an article that appeared in *The Washington Post*, a park police officer is accused of exposing himself to a woman in a park near Washington. The woman was able to get the license plate number of the vehicle driven by the fleeing officer. Indecent exposure is not among the FBI's Index Crimes and it does not have a direct victim, that is, someone who was overtly physically or monetarily harmed by the act. However, there may be a number of indirect victims, aside from the possible psychological harm the witness may have suffered as a result of the act. These other victims include: the park police department, which might have suffered embarrassment; and the family of the officer, since he will probably lose his job, and his wife and children, if he has them, will suffer embarrassment. The community may not respect the park police, or police in general, as much as before or hold them in such high regard.

Ariel Prager

In an edition of *The New York Times Online*, I located a story about a man, Vincent Serrano, now 37, who named a Roman Catholic priest as having abused him between 1974 and 1981. The priest, named James T. Hanley, forced Serrano to have sex with him; the acts included groping, sodomy, oral sex, and masturbation. Since Rev. Hanley allegedly forced a minor to have sex, his actions are legally regarded as sexual assault, abuse, molestation, and/or corruption of the morals of an underage minor. Mr. Serrano was a clear-cut victim of the abuse. . . . This crime has a clear-cut victim—Mr. Serrano. If he can prove that the priest forced him to engage in sodomy, then such an act could be classified as an instance of rape, an Index Crime.

Another article in *The Washington Post Online* tells the story of the U.S. government's indictment of three Colombian rebels on cocaine charges.

These rebels, all members of FARC (the Revolutionary Armed Forces of Colombia), allegedly had conspired to "deliver planeloads of cocaine into the United States since 1994." Authorities believe that the amount of cocaine that they planned to deliver exceeded five kilograms. This act involved no clear-cut victim because there was no individual person who was directly harmed by the crime. However, one can imagine the implications that such a drug shipment could have on the American population. Thus, it is safe to assume that American society as a whole would be the victim of this crime. This is because the influx of drugs into our society would make the drugs more readily available to vulnerable subgroups, such as children. Cocaine is an extremely harmful drug and, therefore, a large shipment to this country could result in devastating health problems, and, clearly, the most vulnerable category of this crime would definitely be the nation's children.

Megan Scribner

I found an article in *The Washington Times* about Andrea Yates, a 37-year-old housewife who drowned all of her five children. This is an example of an Index Crime—murder. After killing her children, she called the police; after they arrived, she showed them the bodies of her children, whose ages ranged from six months to seven years. During her trial, her attorneys and her husband argued that she suffered from severe postpartum depression and that she believed that she had no choice but to kill her children to save them from Satan. The jury did not grant her the insanity plea, and Ms. Yates was convicted of murdering her children and sentenced to 40 years imprisonment before she can be eligible for parole. In this case, there are several clear-cut, direct victims. The five children she murdered are obviously the main victims of the crime. They were very important and special to many people, who will suffer an enormous loss because of their deaths. These people include the father, first of all, as well as grandparents, cousins, aunts, and uncles, all of whom will clearly be affected by the loss of these five young family members. Victimization may also extend out into the children's neighborhood, the schools the children attended, and the children's playmates. As a result of this crime, their mother's murder of these five children has inflicted clear-cut, direct victimization on all the people who had contact with the children on a regular basis; they are going to be victims of this crime until their deaths.

I found the article on a victimless crime in *SF Gate News Online*. It seems that an *MTV Real World* cast member named Jaime Murray bungee-jumped 150 feet off the Golden Gate Bridge. An officer with the California Highway Patrol arrested Murray for trespassing, stating that the stunt was "ill advised and dangerous." Added the patrol officer, "He could have died." Murray, uninjured in the jump, said that he was trying to send a message to young people to "spread love." Said Murray: "This jump is my way of drawing attention to the need for a positive movement of personal growth and social healing." He was cited and later bailed out of jail. The bungee jump is an example of a victimless and non–Index Crime. Although there is no clear-cut, direct victim in this crime, it is considered an issue of public safety, a crime by virtue of the fact that the government places restrictions on behavior for the good of the people. Restrictions were placed by the California state legislature, I would guess, to prevent death and injury that could occur as a result of such a stunt—for instance, in case the cord snapped or to prevent any high bridge from becoming a location of daredevil acts of this type. In addition, when someone pulls a stunt like that, others can be harmed—for instance, when cars stop on congested roadways to watch it.

While it is apparent that Murray caused no harm to anyone except, potentially, himself, one may speculate that there may have been some indirect victims. By Murray stopping his car on the bridge to unload bungee equipment and perform the act itself, he could have held up traffic, distracted drivers, or caused an accident. It's possible that people in boats on the water or on land who saw a man jumping from a bridge not knowing at first if he had been attached to a bungee cord would have been shocked and worried that someone was committing suicide. Any future copycats, who would be taking their lives in their hands, may be considered indirect victims as well. And those who follow in his footsteps will be risking the penalties breaking the law entails.

COMPARE AND CONTRAST MENTAL ILLNESS WITH PHYSICAL DEVIANCE

The Assignment Compare and contrast mental illness with any form of physical deviance. How do they differ; how are they similar? Be specific; be detailed. Use concepts from this course. Demonstrate that you have learned something.

Is mental illness and/or disorder a form of deviance? Are undesirable physical characteris-

tics a form of deviance? If so, in what way? If not, why not?

From a constructionist perspective, what are the most interesting and significant features of mental illness/disorder as a form of deviance? That is, why should a sociologist of deviance with a constructionist orientation be interested in mental illness or disorder? Answer the same questions for physical characteristics.

As deviance, how do mental illness/disorder and physical characteristics differ from some of the other forms of deviance we've looked at so far, such as crime, drug use/abuse, and heterosexual deviance and homosexuality?

Marie Quigley

According to my online encyclopedia, mental illness can be defined as a "mental disorder of such severity as to render its victim incapable of managing his affairs or of conforming to social standards." The key phrase I noticed in this definition is "conforming to social standards." It suggests that society creates and lives by certain standards that people must meet in order to be viewed as normal. Constructionists say that society defines deviance, and different societies define deviance in different ways. For instance, in some societies it is not only acceptable to be overweight, it is preferred. However, in the United States, obese people are stigmatized because the way they look does not fit our society's norms or ideals.

A physical disorder like obesity has one important similar characteristic with mental illness. The similarity is that both of the conditions are stigmatized in our society. At the mention of mental illness, most people envision a murderer who kills in cold blood because he has no feelings; he is not right "up there." Although it is not uncommon for people to go to see a psychologist and/or psychiatrist, most people hide the fact that they are or have been going to one. People are afraid that others will think they have mental problems. Having mental problems is not the accepted norm in our society. Likewise, obesity is stigmatized in our society for many reasons. People assume that they are lazy and cannot take control over their lives; they feel that the person's

obesity is their own fault. Obese people are also stigmatized because they are often found to be unattractive and disgusting by many people. There are many images of ideal people that can be seen everywhere, from magazines to movies. These images show us how our society defines beauty; being obese is the exact opposite of the ideal, which is an extremely thin body type.

The major discrepancy between mental illness and obesity is that people with mental illness most likely do not have any physical traits that indicate their deviant quality. At first, they can look like an average or normal person. People who know about their illness are the ones who stigmatize them. . . . However, the deviant trait of obese people is an outward physical feature that everyone can see. They are automatically stigmatized by people who see them. However, they would not be viewed in this negative way if they were talking on the phone or computer and the person speaking to them had never seen them before. Usually, obese people are more readily accepted when people get to know them and do not judge them by their looks but their personality. The opposite may be true for people with mental illness.

Constructionists are interested in mental illness and undesirable physical characteristics because they want to know how they are defined by the people in their society, how people treat them, and what provisions the society makes for them. Even though these conditions are not usually the person's fault, society stigmatizes them because they are so different from the rest of us and what we expect. People might treat the mentally ill with special care, trying not to upset them. Normal people often act as if the mentally ill cannot control themselves. People treat the obese as if they are lazy gluttons who have allowed their bodies to become severely overweight. Overweight people even have specialty clothing stores where they can shop for clothes that fit them. These stores are part of the stigmatizing process which separates obese people from normal people because of their weight.

Mental illness and unattractive physical characteristics differ from some other forms of deviance [that are behavioral in nature], such as crime, heterosexual deviance, and homosexuality, because the traits they have are not usually their fault. They cannot control their mental illness or weight. Also, physical characteristics are visible to everyone; they are not something that those people can easily hide; that is why people with unattractive physical characteristics are stigmatized more.

Matthew Slade

Mental disorders and physical forms of deviance are quite different when compared to other forms of deviance, but when compared with one another, they are somewhat similar. For both mental illness and physical deviance, an individual usually will not have a choice as to whether or not to acquire them. Thus, for both, an individual with them does not choose to become deviant. A person does not choose to have a mental illness, and most people who possess negatively valued physical characteristics do not choose their condition—in extreme cases, the loss of a limb, paralysis, and blindness. These conditions are usually caused by genetics or accidents, but nonetheless, they can be regarded as a form of deviance. If you compare schizophrenia with a physical form of deviance, such as having only one arm, there are many similarities. Both are involuntary, but the person who has these conditions will still receive negative reactions from mainstream society.

This is interesting because if you think of voluntary forms of deviance such as crime and drug abuse, voluntary deviants are sometimes stigmatized *less* than involuntary deviants. The reasons are not that hard to come by. For instance, a criminal may have an easier time fitting into mainstream society than a person with one leg because the condition of the disabled is more visible than is true of the behavior of most voluntary deviants. A person with a mental disorder may not have enough understanding to interact with normal people in the society, something that makes them immediate outcasts. Both of these conditions are deviant purely because they draw stigma from the rest of the society and not necessarily because they cause the society harm. . . . Why should it be so bad that a person only has one arm or 20 tattoos or has no pigmentation in his or her skin? These conditions simply don't appeal to the majority of the society and this is the main cause of their being deviant. Negative reactions from the general public are the measuring rod for deviant attributes, behavior, and beliefs.

Both mental illness and undesirable physical characteristics are considered forms of deviance, defined by the reaction they cause when their possessors are confronted with the general public. An individual with either of these two defects will attract negative feelings and reactions, and will be isolated by the members of mainstream society. Teenagers with Down syndrome will be isolated from other children because their peers will feel uncomfortable in their presence and not know how to handle interaction with them. Likewise, a teenager with only one arm might be isolated for the same reason as the child with mental illness. The inability of most individuals to deal with the unintentional faults of others defines deviance in a nutshell. People with either mental or physical disabilities are constantly set apart as members of "different" groups in the general society. These individuals face discrimination at all levels of society, including school, the workplace, in public among strangers, and so on. Laws have been put in place to prevent such discrimination, but these laws only help to reinforce the belief that these people are different, and sometimes increase stigma instead of deter it.

Constructionists view forms of deviance based on what makes the trait deviant, meaning what causes members of society to view it as deviant. It is easy to understand why crime and drug abuse are seen as deviant. It is mainly due to the harm that these activities cause to the overall well-being of the society, their victims, and their participants. The stigma associated with crime and drugs comes mainly from the negative value placed on the harm that they cause. In contrast, when a constructionist looks at why a mental disorder or an undesirable physical trait is considered deviant, it is a different question. According to a constructionist, once mainstream society no longer views it as deviant, the stigma disappears. For example, if a society decides to make marijuana legal, then those individuals who were once stigmatized for smoking weed would no longer draw negative feelings, and therefore it would not be deviant.

However, if the stigma associated with not having two legs were to vanish, the individual would still have only one leg. The label does not create the condition, rather it just makes the condition deviant. What is considered undesirable about the condition will remain. Being able to see is a positive value, and if the blind can't see, they can't perform in a valued activity, regardless of the deviant status of being blind. The same cannot be said for all physical characteristics because some forms are self-inflicted and can be removed if necessary—for instance, body piercing. Most people have a hard time understanding the constructionist approach because the way they look at deviance is not part of the way we look at things. To a social constructionist, a person can be labeled as insane even if they are not really insane. Their view is that stigma is something that is attached onto someone by the mainstream members of the society for no reason at all. But what they don't consider is the fact that if you take the deviant label away from a person with a mental or physical characteristic that is defective, the individual will still have the condition.

The main difference between mental/physical disabilities and other forms of deviance is that there is no choice on the part of the individual to have them, aside from a few chosen physical characteristics such as tattoos and possibly obesity. An individual does not choose to be mentally retarded or have one leg, but they do choose to use drugs or have sex with a member of the same gender. This lack of choice leads to a different kind of stigma for involuntary deviants, and it tends to be more sympathetic. Although society does isolate members of such categories, they are treated less harshly, in most cases, than those deviants who are believed to have control over their acts. (Before, I said that voluntary deviants can fake being conventional members of mainstream society because they can hide their normative violations. But once other people know about their behavior, this is different.) This is because the individual is not a deviant by choice and is therefore deviant only because their trait draws stigma. A person who cannot walk may be socially isolated and shunned, but he is not condemned in the same way because everyone knows he did not choose to be the way he is. Compare this to homosexuality and to homosexuals. The behavior is condemned and the people who engage in the behavior are condemned and stigmatized because not only are they considered bad and undesirable, the people who engage in the behavior choose to do it, it is not "given" to a person like mental and physical deviance. This produces a different kind of stigma.

References

Abanes, Richard. 1996. *Rebellion, Racism, and Religion: American Militias*. Downers Grove, IL: InterVarsity Press.

Adler, Freda, and William S. Laufer (eds.). 1995. *The Legacy of Anomie Theory*. New Brunswick, NJ: Transaction.

Adler, Freda, William S. Laufer, and Gerhard O. W. Mueller. 2004. *Criminology* (5th ed.). New York: McGraw-Hill.

Adler, Jerry. 1996. "Adultery: A New Furor Over an Old Sin." *Newsweek*, September 30, pp. 54–60.

Adler, Patricia A. 1985, 1994. *Wheeling and Dealing: An Ethnography of an Upper-Level Drug Dealing and Smuggling Community* (1st & 2nd eds.). New York: Columbia University Press.

Adler, Patricia A., and Peter Adler. 1998. "Foreword" to Jeff Ferrell and Mark S. Hamm (eds.), *Ethnography at the Edge: Crime, Deviance, and Field Research*. Boston: Northeastern University Press, pp. xii–xvi.

Adler, Patricia, and Peter Adler. 1994. "Observational Techniques." In Norman K. Denzin and Yvonna S. Lincoln (eds.), *Handbook of Qualitative Research*. Thousand Oaks, CA: Sage, pp. 377–392.

Adler, Patricia A., and Peter Adler (eds.). 2003. *Constructions of Deviance: Social Power, Context, and Interaction* (4th ed.). Belmont, CA: Wadsworth.

Adler, Patricia A., Peter Adler, and E. B. Rochford, Jr. 1986. "The Politics of Participation in Field Research." *Urban Life*, 14: 363–376.

Agnew, Robert 1992. "Foundations for a General Strain Theory of Crime and Delinquency." *Criminology*, 30 (February): 47–87.

Agnew, Robert 1995. "The Contribution of Social-Psychological Strain Theory to the Explanation of Crime and Delinquency." In Freda Adler and William S. Laufer (eds.), *The Legacy of Anomie Theory*. New Brunswick, NJ: Transaction, pp. 113–137.

Aho, James A. 1994. *This Thing of Darkness: A Sociology of the Enemy*. Seattle: University of Washington Press.

Akers, Ronald L. 1985. *Deviant Behavior: A Social Learning Approach* (3rd ed.). Belmont, CA: Wadsworth.

Akers, Ronald L. 1991. "Self-Control as a General Theory of Crime." *Journal of Quantitative Criminology*, 7 (2): 201–211.

Akers, Ronald L. 1998. *Social Learning and Social Structure: A General Theory of Crime and Deviance*. Boston: Northeastern University Press.

Alexander, Jeffery (ed.). 1985. *Neofunctionalism*. Thousand Oaks, CA: Sage.

Allon, Natalie. 1973. "The Stigma of Overweight in Everyday Life." In G. A. Bray (ed.), *Obesity in Perspective*. Washington, DC: U.S. Government Printing Office, pp. 83–102.

Allon, Natalie. 1976. *Urban Life Styles*. Dubuque, IA: W. C. Brown.

Allon, Natalie. 1982. "The Stigma of Overweight in Everyday Life." In Benjamin B. Wolman (ed.), *Psychological Aspects of Obesity: A Handbook*. New York: Van Nostrand Reinhold, pp. 130–174.

American Psychiatric Association (APA). 1994. *Diagnostic and Statistical Manual of Mental Disorders* (4th ed.). Washington, DC: APA.

Andrews, George, and David Solomon (eds.). 1975. *The Cocoa Leaf and Cocaine Papers*. New York: Harcourt Brace Jovanovich.

Anonymous. 2000. "He's Shedding His Human Skin." *The Chronicle of Higher Education*, January 28, p. A12.

AP (Associated Press). 2001. "Most Gays, Bisexuals Feel More Accepted, Poll Finds." November 13.

APA (see American Psychiatric Association)

Armor, David J., J. Michael Polich, and Harriet B. Stambul. 1976. *Alcoholism and Treatment*. Santa Monica, CA: Rand Corporation.

Arriaga, Ximena B., and Stuard Oskamp (eds.). 1999. *Violence in Intimate Relationships*. Thousand Oaks, CA: Sage.

Aseltine, Robert H., Jr., Susan Gore, and Jennifer Gordon. 2000. "Life Stress, Anger and Anxiety, and Delinquency: An Empirical Test of General Strain Theory." *Journal of Health and Social Behavior*, 41 (September): 256–275.

Ashley, Richard. 1975. *Cocaine: Its History, Uses, and Effects*. New York: St. Martin's Press.

Atwater, Lynn. 1982. *The Extramarital Connection: Sex, Intimacy, and Identity*. New York: Irvington.

Bader, Chris, Paul J. Becker, and Scott Desmond. 1996. "Reclaiming Deviance as a Unique Course from Criminology." *Teaching Sociology*, 24 (July): 316–320.

Baker, Al. 2001. "With Pride and Corsages, Gay Proms Reach Suburbs." *The New York Times*, April 23, pp. A1, A18.

Barnett, Gene, Vojtech Licko, and Travis Thompson. 1985. "Behavioral Pharmacokinetics of Marijuana." *Psychopharmacology*, 85 (1): 51–56.

Barnett, Ola W., Cindy L. Miller-Perrin, and Robin D. Perrin. 1997. *Family Violence Across the Lifespan*. Thousand Oaks, CA: Sage.

Barret, Robert L., and Bryan E. Robinson. 2000. *Gay Fatherhood: Encouraging the Hearts of Gay Dads and Their Families*. San Francisco: Jossey Bass.

Barry, Kathleen. 1984. *Female Sexual Slavery*. New York: New York University Press.

Barry, Kathleen. 1995. *Prostitution of Sexuality*. New York: New York University Press.

Bartell, Gilbert. 1971. *Group Sex: An Eyewitness Report on the American Way of Swinging*. New York: New American Library/Signet.

Becker, Gary S. 1968. "Crime and Punishment: An Economic Approach." *Journal of Political Economy*, 76 (April): 169–217.

Becker, Howard S. 1953. "Becoming a Marijuana User." *American Journal of Sociology*, 59 (November): 235–252.

Becker, Howard S. 1955. "Marijuana Use and Social Control." *Social Problems*, 3 (July): 35–44.

Becker, Howard S. 1963. *Outsiders: Studies in the Sociology of Deviance*. New York: Free Press.

Becker, Howard S. (ed.). 1964. *The Other Side: Perspectives on Deviance*. New York: Free Press.

Becker, Howard S. 1970. *Sociological Work: Method and Substance*. Chicago: Aldine.

Becker, Howard S. 1973. "Labelling Theory Reconsidered." In Howard S. Becker (ed.), *Outsiders: Studies in the Sociology of Deviance* (expanded ed.). New York: Free Press, pp. 177–212.

Beeghley, Leonard. 2003. *Homicide: A Sociological Explanation*. Lanham, ND: Rowman & Littlefield.

Begley, Sharon. 1996/1997. "Infidelity and the Science of Cheating." *Newsweek*, December 30, 1996/January 6, 1997, pp. 57–59.

Belkin, Aaron. 2003. "Don't Ask, Don't Tell: Is the Gay Ban Based on Military Necessity?" *Parameters*, Summer, pp. 108–119.

Bell, Daniel. 1961. "Crime as an American Way of Life: A Queer Ladder of Social Mobility." In *The End of Ideology: On the Exhaustion of the Political Ideas in the Fifties* (rev. ed.). New York: Collier Books, pp. 127–150.

Bell, Robert. 1976. *Social Deviance* (2nd ed.). Homewood, IL: Dorsey Press.

Beloff, John. 1980. "Seven Evidential Experiments." *Zetetic Scholar*, no. 6 (July): 91–94.

Benson, Michael L. 1985. "Denying the Guilty Mind: Accounting for an Involvement in a White-Collar Crime." *Criminology*, 23 (November): 589–599.

Ben-Yehuda, Nachman. 1980. "The European Witch Craze of the 14th to 17th Centuries: A Sociologist's Perspective." *American Journal of Sociology*, 86 (July): 1–31.

Ben-Yehuda, Nachman. 1985. *Deviance and Moral Boundaries*. Chicago: University of Chicago Press.

Ben-Yehuda, Nachman. 1986. "The Sociology of Moral Panics: Toward a New Synthesis." *The Sociological Quarterly*, 27 (4): 495–513.

Berger, Joseph, with Jane Gross. 1998. "From Mental Illness to Yale to Murder Charge." *The New York Times*, June 19, pp. B1, B4.

Berger, Peter L. 1963. *Invitation to Sociology*. Garden City, NY: Doubleday-Anchor.

Berger, Peter L. 1967. *The Sacred Canopy: Elements of a Sociological Theory of Religion*. Garden City, NY: Doubleday.

Berger, Peter L., and Thomas Luckmann. 1966. *The Social Construction of Reality: A Treatise in the Sociology of Knowledge*. Garden City, NY: Doubleday.

Berger, Philip B., Beatrix Hamburg, and David Hamburg. 1977. "Mental Health: Progress and Problems." In John H. Knowles (ed.), *Doing Better and Feeling Worse: Health in the United States*. New York: W. W. Norton., pp. 261–276.

Bernard, Jesse. 1982. *The Future of Marriage* (2nd ed.). New Haven, CT: Yale University Press.

Bernstein, Nina. 1999. "Back on the Streets Without a Safety Net." *The New York Times*, September 13, pp. B1, B6.

Berscheid, Ellen, and Elaine Walster. 1972. "Beauty and the Best." *Psychology Today*, March 1972, pp. 43–46, 74.

Best, Joel. 2004a. *Deviance: Career of a Concept*. Belmont, CA: Wadsworth.

Best, Joel. 2004b. "Deviance May Be Alive, But Is It Intellectually Lively? A Reaction to Goode." *Deviant Behavior*, 25, forthcoming.

Beuf, Ann Hill. 1990. *Beauty Is the Beast*. Philadelphia: University of Pennsylvania Press.

Bittner, Egon. 1970. *The Functions of the Police in Modern Society*. Rockville, MD: Center for Studies of Crime and Delinquency, National Institute of Mental Health.

Black, Donald J. (ed.). 1984. *Toward a General Theory of Social Control*. Orlando, FL: Academic Press.

Black, Donald W. 1999. *Bad Boys, Bad Men: Confronting Antisocial Personality Disorder*. New York: Oxford University Press.

Blumer, Herbert. 1969. *Symbolic Interactionism*. Englewood Cliffs, NJ: Prentice Hall.

Bogdan, Robert. 1988. *Freak Show: Presenting Human Oddities for Amusement and Profit*. Chicago: University of Chicago Press.

Bogdan, Robert. 1992. "A 'Simple' Farmer Accused of Murder: Community Acceptance and the Meaning of Deviance." *Disability, Handicap and Society*, 7 (4): 303–320.

Bolton, Ralph. 1995. "Tricks, Friends, and Lovers: Erotic Encounters in the Field." In Don Kulick and Margaret Willson (eds.), *Taboo: Sex, Identity and Erotic Subjectivity in Anthropological Fieldwork*. London & New York: Routledge, pp. 140–167.

Bolton, Ralph. 1996. "Coming Home: The Journey of a Gay Ethnographer in the Years of the Plague." In Ellen Lewin and William L. Leap (eds.), *Out in the Field: Reflections of Lesbian and Gay Anthropologists*. Urbana: University of Illinois Press, pp. 147–168.

Bourgeois, Philippe. 1995. *In Search of Respect: Selling Crack in El Barrio*. Cambridge, UK: Cambridge University Press.

Bourque, Linda Brookover. 1989. *Defining Rape*. Durham, NC: Duke University Press.

Box, Steven. 1983. *Power, Crime, and Mystification*. London & New York: Tavistock.

Brackman, Harold. 1996. "Farrakhanspiracy: Louis Farrakhan and the Paranoid Style in African-American Politics." *Skeptic*, 4 (3): 36–43.

Braithwaite, John. 1985. "White Collar Crime." *Annual Review of Sociology*, 11: 1–21.

Braithwaite, John. 1989. *Crime, Shame, and Reintegration*. Cambridge, UK: Cambridge University Press.

Brecher, Edward M., et al. 1972. *Licit and Illicit Drugs*. Boston: Little, Brown.

Broad, William J. 1994. "Wreckage in the Desert Was Odd but Not Alien." *The New York Times*, September 18, pp. 1, 40.

Broad, William J. 1997. "Air Force Details a New Theory in U.F.O. Case." *The New York Times*, July 25, p. B7.

Broadway, Bill. 2003. "Homosexuality in the Biblical Sense." *The Washington Post*, August 9, pp. B9, B8.

Brody, Jane E. 2003. "Gay Families Flourish as Acceptance Grows." *The New York Times*, July 1, p. D7.

Bromley, David G. 1991. "Satanism: The New Cult Scare." In James T. Richardson, Joel Best, and David G. Bromley (eds.), *The Satanism Scare*. New York: Aldine de Gruyter, pp. 49–72.

Broude, Gwen J., and Sarah J. Greene. 1976. "Cross-Cultural Codes on Twenty Sexual Attitudes and Practices." *Ethnology*, 15 (October): 409–429.

Brown, Chip. 1996. "They Laughed at Galileo Too." *The New York Times Magazine*, August 11, pp. 41–45.

Brown, David. 2002. "Report Holds Key to Longer Life Expectancy." *The Washington Post*, November 4, p. A9.

Brown, DeNeen L. 2003. "Canada's Parliament Endorses Gay Marriage." *The Washington Post*, September 17, p. A23.

Brownmiller, Susan. 1975. *Against Our Will: Women, Men, and Rape*. New York: Simon & Schuster.

Brulliard, Karin. 2003. "In Texas, a Darwinian Debate." *The Washington Post*, February 16, p. A7.

Bruner, Jerome. 1993. "The Autobiographical Process." In Robert Folkenflik (ed.), *The Culture of Autobiography: Constructions of Self-Representation*. Stanford, CA: Stanford University Press, pp. 242–245.

Bruni, Frank. 1998. "Behind the Jokes, a Life of Pain and Delusion." *The New York Times*, November 22, pp. 45, 50.

Burgess, Robert L., and Ronald L. Akers. 1966. "A Differential Reinforcement Theory of Criminal Behavior." *Social Problems*, 14 (Fall): 128–147.

Bursik, Robert J., and Harold G. Grasmick, 1993. *Neighborhoods and Crime: The Dimensions of Effective Community Control*. New York: Lexington Books.

Buss, David M. 1994. *The Evolution of Desire: Strategies of Human Mating*. New York: Basic Books.

Byck, Robert (ed.). 1974. *Cocaine Papers by Sigmund Freud*. New York: Stonehill.

Byron, Christopher. 1992. "Drug Problems." *New York*, June 15, pp. 18–19.

Cahnman, Werner J. 1968. "The Stigma of Obesity." *Sociological Quarterly*, 9 (Summer): 283–299.

Calhoun, Thomas C. 1992. "Male Street Hustling: Introduction Processes and Stigma Containment." *Sociological Spectrum*, 12 (1): 35–52.

Califia, Pat. 1988. *Macho Sluts*. Boston: Alyson Publications.

Callaway, Enoch, III. 1958. "Institutional Use of Antarctic Drugs." *Modern Medicine, 1958 Annual*, Part I (January 1–June 15): 26–29.

Carlson, Peter. 2003. "*Bride* Discovers Gay Weddings, but Plays It a Little Too Straight." *The Washington Post*, August 26, p. C2.

Carnes, Patrick. 1983. *Out of the Shadows: Understanding Sexual Addiction*. Minneapolis: CompCare.

Carnwath, Tom, and Ian Smith. 2002. *Heroin Century*. London & New York: Routledge.

Cassidy, John. 1995. "Who Killed the Middle Class?" *New Yorker*, October 16, pp. 113–124.

Chambliss, William J. 1964. "A Sociological Analysis of the Law of Vagrancy." *Social Problems*, 12 (Summer): 67–77.

Chambliss, William J. 1973. "The Saints and the Roughnecks." *Society*, 11 (December): 24–31.

Chambliss, William J. 1976. "Functional and Conflict Theories of Crime." In William J. Chambliss and Milton Mankoff (eds.), *Whose Law? What Order? A Conflict Approach to Criminology*. New York: John Wiley, pp. 1–28.

Chapkis, Wendy. 1997. *Live Sex Acts: Women Performing Erotic Labor*. New York: Routledge.

Charlton, James I. 1999. *Nothing About Us Without Us: Disability, Oppression, and Empowerment*. Berkeley: University of California Press.

Charon, Joel M. 1995. *Ten Questions: A Sociological Perspective* (2nd ed.). Belmont, CA: Wadsworth.

Chasnoff, Ira J., et al. 1989. "Temporary Patterns of Cocaine Use in Pregnancy." *Journal of the American Medical Association*, 261 (March 24–31): 1741–1744.

Clarke, Ronald V., and Marcus Felson (eds.). 1993. *Routine Activity and Rational Choice*. New Brunswick, NJ: Transaction.

Clausen, John A. 1981. "Stigma and Mental Disorder: Phenomena and Terminology." *Psychiatry*, 44 (November): 287–296.

Clinard, Marshall B. 1952. *The Black Market: A Study of White Collar Crime*. New York: Rinehart.

Clinard, Marshall B. 1964. "The Theoretical Implications of Anomie and Deviant Behavior." In Marshall B. Clinard (ed.), *Anomie and Deviant Behavior: A Discussion and Critique*. New York: Free Press, pp. 1–56.

Clinard, Marshall B., and Robert F. Meier. 2004. *Sociology of Deviant Behavior* (12th ed.). Belmont, CA: Wadsworth.

Cloward, Richard, and Lloyd E. Ohlin. 1960. *Delinquency and Opportunity: A Theory of Juvenile Gangs*. New York: Free Press.

Cockerham, William C. 2003. *Sociology of Mental Disorder* (6th ed.). Upper Saddle River, NJ: Prentice Hall.

Cohen, Albert K. 1955. *Delinquent Boys: The Subculture of the Gang*. Glencoe, IL: Free Press.

Cohen, Albert K. 1959. "The Study of Social Disorganization and Deviant Behavior." In Robert K. Merton, Leonard Broom, and Leonard S. Cottrell, Jr. (eds.), *Sociology Today: Problems and Prospects*. New York: Basic Books, pp. 461–484.

Cohen, Lawrence E., and Marcus Felson. 1979. "Social Change and Crime Rate Trends: A Routine Activity Approach." *American Sociological Review*, 44 (August): 588–608.

Cohen, Lawrence E., Marcus Felson, and Kenneth C. Land. 1980. "Property Crime Rates in the United States: A Macrodynamic Analysis, 1947–1977." *American Journal of Sociology*, 86 (July): 90–118.

Cohen, Maimon M., Michelle J. Marinello, and Nathan Back. 1967. "Chromosomal Damage in Human Leukocytes Induced by Lysergic Acid Diethylamide," *Science*, 155 (17 March): 1417–1419.

Cohen, Stanley. 1972. *Folk Devils and Moral Panics*. London: MacGibbon & Kee.

Cohen, Stanley. 1985a. *Visions of Social Control*. Cambridge, UK: Polity Press.

Cohen, Stanley. 1985b. Review of Donald J. Black (ed.), *Toward a General Theory of Social Control*. (Orlando, FL: Academic Press, 1984), in *American Journal of Sociology*, 91 (November): 714–717.

Cohen, Stanley. 2002. *Folk Devils and Moral Panics* (3rd ed.). London & New York: Routledge.

Colapinto, John. 2000. *As Nature Made Him: The Boy Who Was Raised as a Girl*. New York: HarperCollins.

Cole, Stephen. 1975. "The Growth of Scientific Knowledge: Theories of Deviance as a Case Study." In Lewis A. Coser (ed.), *The Idea of Social Structure: Papers in Honor of Robert K. Merton*. New York: Harcourt Brace Jovanovich, pp. 175–220.

Cole, Stephen, and Harriet Zuckerman. 1964. "Inventory of Empirical and Theoretical Studies of Anomie." In Marshall B. Clinard (ed.), *Anomie and Deviant Behavior: A Discussion and Critique*. New York: Free Press, pp. 243–311.

Coles, Claire D. 1992. "Effects of Cocaine and Alcohol Use in Pregnancy on Neonatal Growth and Neurobehavioral Status." *Neurotoxicology and Teratology*, 14 (January–February): 1–11.

Conklin, John E. 1972. *Robbery and the Criminal Justice System*. New York: Lippincott.

Conklin, John E. 1998. *Criminology* (6th ed.). Boston: Allyn & Bacon.

Cook, Philip J., and Daniel Nagin. 1979. *Does the Weapon Matter?* Washington, DC: Institute for Law and Society.

Cooperman, Alan. 2002. "Sexual Abuse Scandal Hits Orthodox Jews." *The Washington Post*, June 29, p. A2.

Cooperman, Alan, and Lena H. Sun. 2002. "Hundreds of Priests Removed Since '60s." *The Washington Post*, June 9, pp. A1, A18.

Coser, Lewis A. 1956. *The Functions of Social Conflict*. New York: Free Press.

Covington, Jeanette. 1995. "Racial Classification in Criminology: The Reproduction of Radicalized Crime." *Sociological Forum*, 10 (4): 547–568.

Cowell, Alan. 1994. "Israeli's Death: Atrocity or Act of War?" *The New York Times*, October 17, p. A11.

Cowley, Geoffrey. 1994. "The Culture of Prozac." *Newsweek*, February 7, pp. 41–42.

Cowley, Geoffrey. 1996. "The Biology of Beauty." *Newsweek*, June 3, pp. 61–66.

Cowley, Geoffrey. 1998. "Is AIDS Forever?" *Newsweek*, July 6, pp. 46–47.

Cowley, Geoffrey, et al. 1990. "The Promise of Prozac." *Newsweek*, March 26, pp. 28–41.

Cowley, Geoffrey, et al. 1991. "A Prozac Backlash." *Newsweek*, April 1, pp. 64–67.

Cressey, Donald R. 1953. *Other People's Money*. New York: Free Press.

Cressey, Donald R. 1960. "Epidemiology and Individual Conduct: A Case from Criminology." *Pacific Sociological Review*, 3 (Fall): 47–58.

Cressey, Donald R. 1988. "Poverty of Theory in Corporate Crime Research." *Advances in Criminological Theory*, 1 (1): 31–56.

Crew, R. Keith. 1999. "Action Project: Date Rape." In Martin D. Schwartz and Michael O. Maume (eds.), *Teaching the Sociology of Deviance* (4th ed.). Washington, DC: American Sociological Association, pp. 69–70.

Crews, Frederick. 1995. *The Memory Wars: Freud's Legacy in Dispute*. New York: New York Review of Books.

Curra, John. 2000. *The Relativity of Deviance*. Thousand Oaks, CA: Sage.

Currie, Elliott P. 1968. "Crimes without Criminals: Witchcraft and Its Control in Renaissance Europe." *Law and Society Review*, 3 (August): 7–32.

Currie, Elliott P. 1993. *Reckoning: Drugs, the Cities, and the American Future*. New York: Hill & Wang.

Dabney, Dean. 1995. "Neutralization and Deviance in the Workplace: Theft of Supplies and Medicines by Hospital Nurses." *Deviant Behavior*, 16 (3): 313–331.

Daly, Kathleen, and Meda Chesney-Lind. 1988. "Feminism and Criminology." *Justice Quarterly*, 5 (December): 497–538.

Davis, Fred. 1964. "Deviance Disavowal: The Management of Strained Interaction by the Visibly Handicapped." In Howard S. Becker (ed.), *The Other Side: Perspectives on Deviance*. New York: Free Press, pp. 119–137.

Davis, Kingsley. 1937. "The Sociology of Prostitution." *American Sociological Review*, 2 (October): 744–755.

Davis, Kingsley. 1949. *Human Society*. New York: Macmillan.

Davis, Kingsley. 1971. "Prostitution." In Robert K. Merton and Robert Nisbet (eds.), *Contemporary Social Problems*. New York: Harcourt Brace Jovanovich, pp. 341–351.

Davis, Kingsley. 1976. "Sexual Behavior." In Robert K. Merton and Robert Nisbet (eds.), *Contemporary Social Problems*. New York: Harcourt Brace Jovanovich, pp. 219–261.

Davis, Kingsley, and Wilbert E. Moore. 1945. "Some Principles of Stratification." *American Sociological Review*, 10 (April): 242–249.

Davis, Lennard J. (ed.). 1997. *The Disability Studies Reader*. New York: Routledge.

Davis, Nanette J. 1980. *Sociological Constructions of Deviance: Perspectives and Issues in the Field* (2nd ed.). Dubuque, IA: William C. Brown.

Davis, Nanette J. 2000. "From Victims to Survivors: Working with Recovering Street Prostitutes." In Ronald Weitzer (ed.), *Sex for Sale: Prostitution, Pornography and the Sex Industry*. New York & London: Routledge, pp. 139–155.

Davison, Bill. 1967. "The Hidden Evils of LSD." *The Saturday Evening Post*, August 12, pp. 19–23.

Davison, Gerald C., John M. Neale, and Ann Kring. 2004. *Abnormal Psychology* (12th ed.). New York: John Wiley.

DeBeauvoir, Simone. 1953. *The Second Sex* (trans. & ed. H. M. Parshley). New York: Alfred Knopf.

DeFleur, Melvin L., and Richard Quinney. 1966. "A Reformulation of Sutherland's Differential Association Theory and a Strategy for Empirical Verification." *Journal of Research in Crime and Delinquency*, 3 (January): 1–11.

DeJong, William. 1980. "The Stigma of Obesity: The Consequences of Naive Assumptions Concerning the Causes of Physical Deviance." *Journal of Health and Social Behavior*, 21 (March): 75–87.

Delacoste, Frederique, and Priscilla Alexander (eds.). 1998. *Sex Work: Writings by Women in the Sex Industry* (2nd ed.). San Francisco: Cleis Press.

Denzin, Norman K. 1989. *Interpretive Biography*. Newbury Park, CA: Sage.

Diamond, Milton, and H. Keith Sigmundson. 1997. "Sex Reassignment at Birth: Long-term Review and Clinical Implications." *Archives of Pediatrics and Adolescent Medicine*, 151 (March): 298–304.

DiFranza, Joseph R., and Robert A. Lew. 1995. "Effects of Maternal Cigarette Smoking on Pregnancy Complications and Sudden Death Syndrome." *Journal of Family Practice*, 40 (April): 385–394.

Dion, Karen K. 1972. "Physical Attractiveness and Evaluation of Children's Transgressions." *Journal of Personal and Social Psychology*, 24: 207–213.

Dishotsky, Norman, William D. Loughman, Robert F. Mogar, and Wendell R. Lipscomb. 1971. "LSD and Genetic Damage," *Science*, 172 (April 30): 431–440.

Doherty, Edmund G. 1978. "Are Different Discharge Criteria Used for Men and Women Psychiatric Inpatients?" *Journal of Health and Social Behavior*, 19 (March): 107–116.

Dohrenwend, Bruce P., and Barbara Snell Dohrenwend. 1976. "Sex Differences and Psychiatric Disorder." *American Journal of Sociology*, 81 (May): 1447–1454.

Donnerstein, Edward, Daniel Linz, and Steven Penrod. 1987. *The Question of Pornography: Research Findings and Policy Implications*. New York: Free Press.

Donovan, John E. 1996. "Problem Behavior Theory and the Explanation of Adolescent Marijuana Use." *Journal of Drug Issues*, 26 (3): 379–404.

Douglas, Jack D. 1976. *Investigative Social Research: Individual and Team Field Research*. Thousand Oaks, CA: Sage.

Douglas, Jack D., and Frances C. Waksler. 1982. *The Sociology of Deviance: An Introduction*. Boston: Little, Brown.

Downes, David, and Paul Rock. 2003. *Understanding Deviance: A Guide to the Sociology of Crime and Rule Breaking* (4th ed.). Oxford, UK: Oxford University Press.

Drummer, O. H. 1994. *Drugs in Drivers Killed in Australian Road Traffic Accidents*. Melbourne: Victorian Institute of Forensic Pathology, Monash University.

Duneier, Mitchell. 1999. *Sidewalk*. New York: Farrar, Straus, and Giroux.

Dunham, H. Warren. 1964. "Anomie and Mental Disorder." In Marshall B Clinard (ed.), *Anomie and Deviant Behavior: A Discussion and Critique*. New York: Free Press, pp. 128–157.

Dunham, H. Warren. 1965. *Community and Schizophrenia: An Epidemiological Analysis*. Detroit: Wayne State University Press.

Dunne, Brenda J., and John P. Bisaha. 1979. "Precognitive Remote Viewing in the Chicago Area: A Replication of the Stanford Experiment." *Journal of Parapsychology*, 43 (March): 17–30.

Durkheim, Emile. 1933. *The Division of Labor in Society* (trans. George Simpson). New York: Macmillan (orig. pub. 1893).

Durkheim, Emile. 1938. *The Rules of the Sociological Method* (trans. Sarah A. Solway and John H. Meuller, ed. George E. G. Catlin). Chicago: University of Chicago Press (orig. pub. 1895).

Durkheim, Emile. 1951. *Suicide: A Study in Sociology* (trans. John A. Spaulding and George Simpson; ed. George Simpson). New York: Free Press (orig. pub. 1897).

Dworkin, Andrea. 1981. *Pornography: Men Possessing Women.* New York: Perigee.

Dworkin, Andrea. 1987. *Intercourse.* New York: Free Press.

Earleywine, Mitch. 2002. *Understanding Marijuana: A New Look at the Scientific Evidence.* Oxford, UK & New York: Oxford University Press.

Edgerton, Robert B. 1969. "On the Recognition of Mental Illness." In Robert B. Edgerton (ed.), *Perspectives in Mental Illness.* New York: Holt, Rinehart & Winston, pp. 49–72.

Edgerton, Robert B. 1976. *Deviance: A Cross-Cultural Perspective.* Menlo Park, CA: Cummings.

Egan, Timothy. 1989. "Putting a Face on Corporate Crime." *The New York Times,* July 14, p. B8.

Eitle, D. J. 2002. "Exploring a Source of Deviance-Producing Strain for Females—Perceived Discrimination and General Strain Theory." *Journal of Criminal Justice,* 30 (September–October): 429–442.

Elias, Norbert. 1994. *The Civilizing Process* (trans. Edmund Jephcott). Oxford, UK & Cambridge, MA: Blackwell Publishers (orig. pub. 1939).

Elliott, Delbert S., and Suzanne S. Ageton. 1980. "Reconciling Race and Class Differences in Self-Reported and Official Estimates of Delinquency." *American Sociological Review,* 45 (February): 95–110.

Ellis, Kate, et al. (eds.). 1988. *Caught Looking: Feminism, Pornography, and Censorship.* Seattle: Real Comet Press.

Ericson, Richard V., Patricia M. Baranek, and Janet B. L. Chan. 1991. *Representing Order: Crime, Law, and Justice in the News Media.* Toronto: University of Toronto Press.

Erikson, Kai T. 1962. "Notes on the Sociology of Deviance." *Social Problems,* 9 (Spring): 9–21.

Erikson, Kai T. 1964. "Notes on the Sociology of Deviance." In Howard S. Becker (ed.), *The Other Side: Perspectives on Deviance.* New York: Free Press, pp. 307–314.

Erikson, Kai T. 1966. *Wayward Puritans: A Study in the Sociology of Deviance.* New York: John Wiley.

Erikson, Kai T. 1967. "A Comment on Disguised Observation in Sociology." *Social Problems,* 14 (Spring): 366–373.

Erikson, Kai T. 1990. "Toxic Reckoning: Business Faces a New Kind of Fear." *Harvard Business Review,* 68 (January–February): 118–126.

Esterson, Allen. 1993. *Seductive Mirage: An Exploration of the Work of Sigmund Freud.* Chicago: Open Court Press.

Estrich, Susan. 1987. *Real Rape.* Cambridge, MA: Harvard University Press.

Etcoff, Nancy L. 1999. *Survival of the Prettiest: The Science of Beauty.* Garden City, NY: Doubleday.

Evans, Rhonda. 2003. *A History of the Service of Ethnic Minorities in the U.S. Armed Forces.* Santa Barbara, CA: Center for the Study of Sexual Minorities in the Military.

Falwell, Jerry, Ed Dobson, and Ed Hindson. 1996. "Wrongdoing as an Offense in the Eyes of God." In Erich Goode (ed.), *Social Deviance.* Boston: Allyn & Bacon, pp. 12–14.

Faris, Robert E., and H. Warren Dunham. 1939. *Mental Disorders in Urban Areas.* Chicago: University of Chicago Press.

Feagin, Joe R., and Robert Parker. 1990. *Building American Cities: The Urban Real Estate Game* (2nd ed.). Englewood Cliffs, NJ: Prentice Hall.

Fears, Darryl. 2002. "Hate Crimes Against Arabs Surge, FBI Finds." *The Washington Post,* November 26, p. A2.

Feder, Barnaby J. 1997a. "Multitude of Tobacco Lawsuits Provides Bargaining Chips for Negotiators." *The New York Times,* April 17, p. D23.

Feder, Barnaby J. 1997b. "Surge in Teen-Age Smoking Left an Industry Vulnerable." *The New York Times,* April 20, pp. 1, 28.

Felson, Marcus. 1987. "Routine Activities and Crime Prevention in the Developing Metropolis." *Criminology,* 25 (November): 911–931.

Felson, Richard B. 1991. "Blame Analysis: Accounting for the Behavior of Protected Groups." *The American Sociologist,* 22 (Spring): 5–23.

Fenster, Mark. 1999. *Conspiracy Theories: Secrecy and Power in American Culture.* Minneapolis: University of Minnesota Press.

Ferrell, Jeff. 1998. "Criminological *Verstehen*: Inside the Immediacy of Crime." In Jeff Ferrell and Mark S. Hamm (eds.), *Ethnography at the Edge: Crime, Deviance, and Field Research.* Boston: Northeastern University Press, pp. 20–42.

Ferrell, Jeff, and Mark S. Hamm (eds.). 1998. *Ethnography at the Edge: Crime, Deviance, and Field Research.* Boston: Northeastern University Press.

Fiedler, Leslie. 1978. *Freaks: Myths and Images of the Secret Self.* New York: Simon & Schuster.

Fiffer, Steve. 1999. *Three Quarters, Two Dimes, and a Nickel: A Memoir of Becoming Whole.* New York: Free Press.

Finestone, Harold. 1964. "Cats, Kicks, and Color." In Howard S. Becker (ed.), *The Other Side: Perspectives on Deviance.* New York: Free Press, pp. 281–297.

Fischer, Anita, Janos Marton, E. Joel Millman, and Leo Srole. 1979. "Long-Range Influences on Mental Health: The Midtown Longitudinal Study, 1954–1974." In Roberta Simmons (ed.), *Research in Community Health,* vol. 1. Greenwich, CT: JAI Press, pp. 305–333.

Foderaro, Lisa W. 1995. "A Voyage to Bedlam and Part Way Back." *The New York Times,* November 9, pp. B1, B4.

Ford, Clellan S., and Frank A. Beach. 1951. *Patterns of Sexual Behavior.* New York: HarperCollins.

Foucault, Michel. 1967. *Madness and Civilization: A History of Insanity in the Age of Reason* (trans. Richard Howard). New York: New American Library/Mentor.

Foucault, Michel. 1979. *Discipline and Punish* (trans. Alan Sheridan). New York: Vintage Books.

Fox, John. 1990. "Social Class, Mental Illness, and Social Mobility: The Social Selection-Drift Hypothesis for

Serious Mental Illness." *Journal of Health and Social Behavior*, 21 (September): 260–267.

France, David. 2001. "Scouts Divided." *Newsweek*, August 6, pp. 45–51.

Frank, Nathaniel. 2002. "Real Evidence on Gays in the Military." *The Washington Post*, December 3, p. A25.

Freedman, Rita. 1986. *Beauty Bound*. Lexington, MA: Lexington Books.

Freidson, Eliot. 1966. "Disability as Deviance." In Marvin B. Sussman (ed.), *Sociology and Rehabilitation*. Washington, DC: American Sociological Association, pp. 71–99.

Freidson, Eliot. 1970. *Profession of Medicine: A Study of the Sociology of Applied Knowledge*. New York: Dodd, Mead.

Friedman, Wolfgang. 1964. *Law in a Changing Society*. Harmondsworth, UK: Penguin Books.

Friedrichs, David O. 2004. *White Collar Crime: Trusted Criminals in Contemporary Society* (2nd ed.). Belmont, CA: Wadsworth.

Gabriel, Trip. 1994. "Heroin Finds a New Market Along Cutting Edge of Style." *The New York Times*, May 8, pp. 1, 22.

Gagnon, John H., and William Simon. 1973. *Sexual Conduct: The Social Sources of Human Sexuality*. Chicago: Aldine.

Gallagher, Bernard J., III. 2002. *The Sociology of Mental Illness* (4th ed.). Upper Saddle River, NJ: Prentice Hall.

Gardner, Martin. 1957. *Fads and Fallacies in the Name of Science* (2nd ed.). New York: Dover.

Garfinkel, Harold. 1967. *Studies in Ethnomethodology*. Englewood Cliffs, NJ: Prentice Hall.

Garland, David. 1990. *Punishment and Modern Society: A Study in Social Theory*. Chicago: University of Chicago Press.

Garner, David M., et al. 1980. "Cultural Expectations of Thinness in Women." *Psychological Reports*, 47: 483–491.

Gelsthorpe, Loraine, and Alison Morris. 1988. "Feminism and Criminology in Britain." *British Journal of Criminology*, 28 (Spring): 223–240.

Gibbons, Don C. 1992. *Society, Crime, and Criminal Behavior* (6th ed.). Englewood Cliffs, NJ: Prentice Hall.

Gieringer, Dale. 1990. "How Many Crack Babies?" *The Drug Policy Letter*, 11 (March/April): 4–6.

Gildenberg, Bernard D., and David E. Thomas. 1998. "Case Closed: Reflections on the 1997 Air Force Roswell Report." *Skeptical Inquirer*, 22 (May/June): 31–36.

Gilmin, Debra L. 2002. *Body Work: Beauty and Self-Image in American Culture*. Berkeley: University of California Press.

Givens, James B. 1977. *Society and Homicide in Thirteenth-Century England*. Stanford, CA: Stanford University Press.

Glassner, Barry. 1982. "Labeling Theory." In M. Michael Rosenberg, Robert A. Stebbins, and Allan Turowitz (eds.), *The Sociology of Deviance*. New York: St. Martin's Press, pp. 71–89.

Glassner, Barry. 1999. *The Culture of Fear: Why Americans Are Afraid of the Wrong Things*. New York: Basic Books.

Glazer, Myron. 1972. *The Research Adventure: Promise and Problems of Field Work*. New York: Random House.

Goffman, Erving. 1961. *Asylums*. Garden City, NY: Doubleday-Anchor.

Goffman, Erving. 1963. *Stigma: Notes on the Management of a Spoiled Identity*. Englewood Cliffs, NJ: Prentice Hall/Spectrum.

Goldberg, Carey. 1997. "On Adultery Issue, Many Aren't Ready to Cast the First Stone." *The New York Times*, June 9, pp. A1, A18.

Goldman, Douglas. 1955. "Treatment of Psychotic States with Chlorpromazine." *Journal of the American Medical Asssociation*, 157 (April 19): 1274–1278.

Goldstein, Avram. 2001. *Addiction: From Biology to Drug Policy* (2nd ed.). New York: Oxford University Press.

Goleman, Daniel. 1986. "To Expert Eyes, Streets Are Open Mental Wards." *The New York Times*, November 4, pp. C1, C3.

Goode, Erich. 1972. "Marijuana and Crime." In *Marihuana: A Signal of Misunderstanding*, The Technical Papers of the First Report of the National Commission on Marihuana and Drug Abuse, Appendix, vol. I. Washington, DC: U.S. Government Printing Office, pp. 447–469.

Goode, Erich. 1975. "On Behalf of Labeling Theory." *Social Problems*, 22 (June): 570–583.

Goode, Erich. 1992. *Collective Behavior*. Fort Worth, TX: Harcourt Brace.

Goode, Erich. 1996a. "The Ethics of Deception in Social Research: A Case Study." *Qualitative Sociology*, 19 (1): 11–33.

Goode, Erich. 1996b. "The Stigma of Obesity." In Erich Goode (ed.), *Social Deviance*. Boston: Allyn & Bacon, pp. 332–340.

Goode, Erich. 2000. *Paranormal Beliefs: A Sociological Introduction*. Prospect Heights, IL: Waveland Press.

Goode, Erich. 2002. *Deviance in Everyday Life: Accounts of Unconventional Lives*. Prospect Heights, IL: Waveland Press.

Goode, Erich. 2003. "The MacGuffin That Refuses to Die: An Investigation into the Condition of the Sociology of Deviance." *Deviant Behavior*, 24 (November–December): 507–533.

Goode, Erich. 2005. *Drugs in American Society* (6th ed.). New York: McGraw-Hill.

Goode, Erich, and Nachman Ben-Yehuda. 1994a. "Moral Panics: Culture, Politics, and Social Construction." *Annual Review of Sociology*, 20: 149–171.

Goode, Erich, and Nachman Ben-Yehuda. 1994b. *Moral Panics: The Social Construction of Deviance*. Oxford, UK & Cambridge, MA: Blackwell.

Goodstein, Laurie. 2002. "Ousted Members Say Jehovah's Witnesses' Policy on Abuse Hides Offenses." *The New York Times*, August 11, p. 20.

Goodstein, Laurie. 2003. "Trail of Pain in Church Crisis Leads to Nearly Every Diocese." *The New York Times*, January 12, pp. 1, 20–21.

Gorer, Geoffrey. 1967. *Himalayan Village: An Account of the Lepcha of Sikkim* (2nd ed.). New York: Basic Books.

Gottfredson, Michael R., and Travis Hirschi. 1990. *A General Theory of Crime*. Stanford, CA: Stanford University Press.

Gouldner, Alvin W. 1968. "The Sociologist as Partisan: Sociology and the Welfare State." *The American Sociologist*, 3 (May): 103–116.

Gouldner, Alvin W. 1970. *The Coming Crisis of Western Sociology*. New York: Basic Books.

Gove, Walter R. 1972. "The Relationship Between Sex Roles, Marital Status, and Mental Illness." *Social Forces*, 51 (September): 34–44.

Gove, Walter R. 1975a. "The Labelling Theory of Mental Illness: A Reply to Scheff." *American Sociological Review*, 40 (April): 242–248.

Gove, Walter R. 1975b. "The Labelling Perspective: An Overview." In Walter R. Gove (ed.), *The Labelling of Deviance*. New York: John Wiley/Halstead/Sage, pp. 35–81.

Gove, Walter R. 1979a. "The Labelling Versus the Psychiatric Explanation of Mental Illness: A Debate That Has Become Substantially Irrelevant (Reply to Horwitz)," *Journal of Health and Social Behavior*, 20 (September): 89–93.

Gove, Walter R. 1979b. "Sex, Marital Status, and Psychiatric Treatment: A Research Note." *Social Forces*, 58 (September): 89–93.

Gove, Walter R. (ed.). 1980a. *The Labelling of Deviance: Evaluating a Perspective*. Thousand Oaks, CA: Sage.

Gove, Walter R. 1980b. "Labeling and Mental Illness: A Critique." In Walter R. Gove (ed.), *The Labelling of Deviance: Evaluating a Perspective*. Thousand Oaks, CA: Sage, pp. 35–81.

Gove, Walter R. (ed.). 1982. *Deviance and Mental Illness*. Thousand Oaks, CA: Sage.

Gove, Walter R. 1989. "On Understanding Mental Illness and Some Insights to be Gained from the Labelling Theory of Mental illness" (unpublished paper).

Gove, Walter R., and Terry R. Herb. 1974. "Stress and Mental Illness Among the Young: A Comparison of the Sexes." *Social Forces*, 53 (December): 256–265.

Gravelle, Jane, and Dennis Zimmerman. 1994. "The Marlboro Math." *Outlook (The Washington Post)*, June 5, pp. C1, C4.

Grealy, Lucy. 1995. *Autobiography of a Face*. New York: HarperCollins.

Green, Jesse. 2001. "The New Gay Movement." *New York*, March 5, pp. 27–28, 82.

Greenberg, Joel. 1995. "Shared Hate: Jews and Arabs Mark Mosque Slayings." *The New York Times*, February 17, p. A3.

Greenwald, John. 1997. "Smoking Gun." *Time*, March 31, pp. 32–35.

Grinspoon, Lester, and James B. Bakalar. 1976. *Cocaine: A Drug and Its Social Evolution*. New York: Basic Books.

Gronfein, William. 1985. "Psychotropic Drugs and the Origins of Institutionalization," *Social Problems*, 32 (June): 437–454.

Gross, Edward. 1978. "Organizational Crime: A Theoretical Perspective." In Norman Denzin (ed.), *Studies in Symbolic Interaction*. Greenwich, CT: JAI Press, pp. 55–88.

Groth, Nicholas, with H. Jean Burnham. 1979. *Men Who Rape: The Psychology of the Offender*. New York: Plenum Press.

Gruenbaum, Adolph. 1993. *Validation in the Clinical Theory of Psychoanalysis: A Study in the Philosophy of Psychoanalysis*. Madison, CT: International Universities Press.

Gurr, Ted Robert. 1989. "Historical Trends in Violent Crime: Europe and the United States." In Ted Robert Gurr (ed.), *Violence in America*, vol. I. Newbury Park, CA: Sage, pp. 21–54.

Hall, Jerome. 1952. *Theft, Law, and Society* (2nd ed.). Indianapolis: Bobbs-Merrill.

Hamm, Mark S. 1998. "The Ethnography of Terror: Timothy McVeigh and the Blue Centerlight of Evil." In Jeff Ferrell and Mark S. Hamm (eds.), *Ethnography at the Edge: Crime, Deviance, and Field Research*. Boston: Northeastern University Press, pp. 111–130.

Handy, Bruce. 1997. "Roswell or Bust." *Time*, June 23, pp. 62–67.

Harkey, John, David L. Miles, and William Rushing. 1976. "The Relationship between Social Class and Functional Status: A New Look at the Drift Hypothesis." *Journal of Health and Social Behavior*, 17 (September): 194–204.

Harlow, Caroline Wolf. 1987. "Robbery Victims." *Bureau of Justice Special Report*, April, pp. 1–10.

Harries, Keith D. 1997. *Serious Violence: Patterns of Homicide and Assault in America* (2nd ed.). Springfield, IL: Charles C Thomas.

Hart, Timothy C., and Callie Rennison. 2003. "Reporting Crime to the Police, 1992–2000." *Bureau of Justice Statistics Special Report*, March, pp. 1–7.

Hawkins, E. R., and Willard Waller. 1936. "Critical Notes on the Cost of Crime." *Journal of Criminal Law, Criminology, and Police Science*, 26 (January): 679–694.

Hawkins, Richard, and Gary Tiedeman. 1975. *The Creation of Deviance: Interpersonal and Organization Determinants*. Columbus, OH: Charles E. Merrill.

Heidensohn, Frances. 1968. "The Deviance of Women: A Critique and an Enquiry." *British Journal of Sociology*, 12 (2): 160–175.

Hendershott, Anne. 2002. *The Politics of Deviance*. San Francisco: Encounter Books.

Hendrix, Melissa. 1993. "Is It a Boy or a Girl?" *Johns Hopkins Magazine*, November, pp. 10–16.

Henshel, Richard L. 1990. *Thinking About Social Problems*. San Diego: Harcourt Brace Jovanovich.

Hevey, David. 1992. *The Creatures Time Forgot: Photography and Disability Imagery*. London: Routledge.

Hicks, Robert D. 1991. *In Pursuit of Satan: The Police and the Occult*. Buffalo: Prometheus Books.

Hiller, Dana V. 1981. "The Salience of Overweight in Personality Characterization." *Journal of Psychology*, 108: 233–240.

Hiller, Dana V. 1982. "Overweight as a Master Status: A Replication." *Journal of Psychology*, 110: 107–113.

Hines, Terence. 1988. *Pseudoscience and the Paranormal: A Critical Examination of the Evidence*. Buffalo: Prometheus Books.

Hirschi, Travis. 1969. *Causes of Delinquency*. Berkeley: University of California Press.

Hirschi, Travis. 1973. "Procedural Rules and the Explanation of Crime." *Social Problems*, 21 (Fall): 159–173.

Hitt, Jack. 2000. "The Second Sexual Revolution." *The New York Times Magazine*, February 20, pp. 34–41ff.

Hockenberry, John. 1995. *Moving Violations: War Zones, Wheelchairs, and Declarations of Independence*. New York: Hyperion.

Hollingshead, August B., and Frederick C. Redlich. 1958. *Social Class and Mental Illness*. New York: John Wiley.

Holmes, Ronald M., and Stephen T. Holmes. 2001. *Murder in America* (2nd ed.). Thousand Oaks, CA: Sage.

Hoover, Eric. 2002. "Binge Thinking." *The Chronicle of Higher Education*, November 8, pp. A34–A37.

Honorton, Charles. 1985. "Meta-analysis of Psi Ganzfeld Research." *Journal of Parapsychology*, 40 (March): 51–91.

Honorton, Charles, and Diane C. Ferrari. 1989. "Fortune Telling: A Meta-Analysis of Forced-Choice Precognition Experiments." *Journal of Parapsychology*, 53 (December): 281–308.

Horgan, Constance, Kathleen Carley Skwara, and Gail Strickler. 2001. *Substance Abuse: The Nation's Number One Health Problem*. Princeton, NJ: Robert Wood Johnson Foundation.

Horwitz, Allan V. 1990. *The Logic of Social Control*. New York: Plenum Press.

Hough, Michael. 1987. "Offenders' Choice of Target: Findings from Victim Surveys." *Journal of Qualitative Criminology*, 3 (3): 355–369.

Humphreys, Laud. 1970. *Tearoom Trade: Impersonal Sex in Public Places*. Chicago: Aldine.

Humphreys, Laud. 1975. *Tearoom Trade: Impersonal Sex in Public Places* (2nd ed.). New York: Aldine.

Hunt, Jennifer. 1985. "Police Accounts of Normal Force." *Urban Life*, 13 (January): 315–341.

Hunt, Morton. 1971. *The Affair: A Portrait of Extra-Marital Love in Contemporary America*. New York: New American Library/Signet.

Inciardi, James A. 1987. "Beyond Cocaine: Basuco, Crack, and Other Coca Products." *Contemporary Drug Problems*, 14 (Fall): 461–492.

Ingrassia, Michelle. 1995. "The Body of the Beholder." *Newsweek*, April 24, pp. 66–67.

Irwin, H. J. 1994. *An Introduction to Parapsychology* (2nd ed.). Jefferson, NC: McFarland.

Jacobs, Bruce A. 1998. "Researching Crack Dealers: Dilemmas and Contradictions." In Jeff Ferrell and Mark S. Hamm (eds.), *Ethnography at the Edge: Crime, Deviance, and Field Research*. Boston: Northeastern University Press, pp. 160–177.

Jang, Sung Joon, and Byron Johnson. 2003. "Strain, Negative Emotions, and Coping Among African Americans: A Test of General Strain Theory." *Journal of Quantitative Criminology*, 19 (March): 79–105.

Jaroff, Leon. 1997. "Did Aliens Land?" *Time*, June 23, pp. 68–71.

Jenkins, Philip. 1996. *Pedophiles and Priests: Anatomy of a Contemporary Crisis*. New York & Oxford, UK: Oxford University Press.

Jenkins, Philip. 1998. *Moral Panic: Changing Concepts of the Child Molester in Modern America*. New Haven, CT: Yale University Press.

Jenkins, Philip. 2002. "The Myth of the Pedophile Priest." *Pittsburgh Post-Gazette*, March 3.

Jensen, Eric L., Jurg Gerber, and Ginna M. Babcock. 1991. "The New War on Drugs: Grass Roots Movement or Political Construction?" *Journal of Drug Issues*, 21 (3): 651–667.

Johnson, Anne, et al. 1994. *Sexual Attitudes and Lifestyles*. Oxford, UK: Blackwell Scientific Publications.

Johnson, Eric A., and Eric H. Monkkonen (eds.). 1996. *The Civilization of Crime: Violence in Town and Country since the Middle Ages*. Urbana: University of Illinois Press.

Johnson, Ida M. 2002. "Rape, Date and Marital." In David Levinson (ed.), *Encyclopedia of Crime and Punishment*. Thousand Oaks: Sage, pp. 1346–1352.

Johnston, Lloyd D., Patrick M. O'Malley, and Jerald G. Bachman. 2002a. *National Survey Results on Drug Use, 1975–2001*, vol. I: Secondary School Students. Bethesda, MD: National Institute on Drug Abuse.

Johnston, Lloyd D., Patrick M. O'Malley, and Jerald G. Bachman. 2002b. *National Survey Results on Drug Use, 1975–2001*, vol. II: College Students & Adults Ages 19–40. Bethesda, MD: National Institute on Drug Abuse.

Johnston, Lloyd D., Patrick M. O'Malley, and Jerald G. Bachman. 2003a. *National Survey Results on Drug Use, 1975–2002*. vol. I: Secondary School Students. Bethesda, MD: National Institute on Drug Abuse.

Johnston, Lloyd D., Patrick M. O'Malley, and Jerald G. Bachman. 2003b. *National Survey Results on Drug Use, 1975–2002*. vol. II: College Students & Adults Ages 19–40. Bethesda, MD: National Institute on Drug Abuse.

Jones, Edward E. 1986. "Interpreting Interpersonal Behavior: The Effects of Expectancies." *Science*, 234 (October): 41–46.

Jones, Edward E., et al. 1984. *Social Stigma: The Psychology of Marked Relationships*. New York: W. H. Freeman.

Jones, Helen C., and Paul W. Lovinger. 1985. *The Marijuana Question and Science's Search for an Answer*. New York: Dodd, Mead.

Jones, James H. 1997. *Alfred C. Kinsey: A Public/Private Life*. New York: W. W. Norton.

Jones, Russell A. 1977. *Self-Fulfilling Prophecies: Social, Psychological, and Physiological Effects of Expectancies.* Hillsdale, NJ: Lawrence Erlbaum.

Jones, Trevor, Brian MacLean, and Jock Young. 1986. *The Islington Crime Survey: Crime, Victimization, and Policing in Inner City London.* Aldershot, UK: Gower.

Kagay, Michael R. 1990. "Deficit Raises as Much Alarm as Illegal Drugs, Poll Finds." *The New York Times,* July 25, p. A9.

Kandel, Denise M., and Mark Davies. 1996. "High School Students Who Use Crack and Other Drugs." *Archives of General Psychiatry,* 53 (1): 71–80.

Katz, Irwin. 1981. *Stigma: A Social Psychological Analysis.* Hillsdale, NJ: Lawrence Erlbaum.

Katz, Jack. 1988. *Seductions of Crime: Moral and Sensual Attractions of Doing Evil.* New York: Basic Books.

Kelly, Delos H. (ed.). 1996. *Deviant Behavior: A Text-Reader in the Sociology of Deviance.* New York: St. Martin's Press.

Kendall, R. E., et al. 1971. "Diagnostic Criteria of American and British Psychiatrists." *Archives of General Psychiatry,* 25 (August): 123–130.

Kerr, Peter. 1986. "Anatomy of an Issue: Drugs, the Evidence, the Reaction." *The New York Times,* May 15, pp. 1, 15.

Kessler, Ronald C. 1979. "Stress, Social Status, and Psychological Distress." *Journal of Health and Social Behavior,* 20 (September): 259–272.

Kessler, Ronald C., et al. 1994. "Lifetime and 12-Month Prevalence of DSM-III Psychiatric Disorders in the United States." *Archives of General Psychiatry,* 51 (1): 8–19.

Kessler, Suzanne J. 1990. "The Medical Construction of Gender: Case Management of Intersexed Infants." *Signs: Journal of Women in Culture and Society,* 16 (1): 3–26.

Kety, Seymour S. 1974. "From Rationalization to Reason." *American Journal of Psychiatry,* 131 (September): 957–963.

Kinsey, Alfred C., Wardell B. Pomeroy, and Clyde E. Martin. 1948. *Sexual Behavior in the Human Male.* Philadelphia: W. B. Saunders.

Kinsey, Alfred C., Wardell B. Pomeroy, Clyde E. Martin, and Paul H. Gebhard. 1953. *Sexual Behavior in the Human Female.* Philadelphia: W. B. Saunders.

Kipnis, Laura. 1996. *Bound and Gagged: Pornography and the Politics of Fantasy in America.* New York: Grove Press.

Kirk, Stuart A., and Herb Kutchins. 1994. "Is Bad Writing a Mental Disorder?" *The New York Times,* June 20, p. A17.

Kirshenbaum, Gayle. 1991. "A Potential Landmark for Female Human Rights." *Ms.,* September–October, p. 13.

Kitsuse, John I. 1962. "Societal Reactions to Deviant Behavior: Some Conceptual Problems." *Social Problems,* 9 (Winter): 247–257.

Kitsuse, John I. 1972. "Deviance, Deviant Behavior, and Deviants: Some Conceptual Problems." In William J. Filstead (ed.), *An Introduction to Deviance: Readings in the Process of Making Deviants.* Chicago: Markham, pp. 233–243.

Kitsuse, John I. 1975. "The New Conception of Deviance and Its Critics." In Walter R. Gove (ed.), *The Labelling of Deviance: Evaluating a Perspective.* New York: John Wiley/Halstead/Sage, pp. 273–284.

Kitsuse, John I. 1980. "The New Conception of Deviance and Its Critics." In Walter R. Gove (ed.), *The Labelling of Deviance: Evaluating a Perspective.* Thousand Oaks, CA: Sage, pp. 381–392.

Klass, Phillip J. 1997. *The Real Roswell Crashed Saucer Cover-Up.* Buffalo: Prometheus Books.

Klockars, Carl B. 1974. *The Professional Fence.* New York: Free Press.

Kolata, Gina. 1992a. "Maker of Sleeping Pill Hid Data on Side Effects, Researchers Say." *The New York Times,* January 20, pp. A1, B7.

Kolata, Gina. 1992b. "Finding a Bad Night's Sleep with Halcion." *The New York Times,* January 20, p. B7.

Konigsberg, Eric. 1998. "The Cheating Kind." *The New York Times Magazine,* March 8, p. 65.

Kornhauser, Ruth. 1978. *Social Sources of Delinquency: An Appraisal of Analytic Models.* Chicago: University of Chicago Press.

Kramer, Peter D. 1993. *Listening to Prozac.* New York: Penguin Books.

Krauthammer, Charles. 1993. "Defining Deviancy Up." *The New Republic,* November 22, pp. 20–25.

Krauthammer, Charles. 2002. "Why Didn't the Church Call the Cops?" *The Washington Post,* June 7, p. A27.

Kreisman, Dolores, and Virginia D. Joy. 1974. "Family Response to Mental Illness of a Relative: A Review of the Literature." *Schizophrenia Bulletin,* 10 (Fall): 34–57.

Kristof, Nicholas D. 2003. "Believe It, or Not." *The New York Times,* August 15, p. A29.

Krohn, Marvin D., and Ronald L. Akers. 1977. "An Alternative View of the Labeling Versus Psychiatric Perspectives on Societal Reaction to Mental Illness." *Social Forces,* 56 (December): 341–361.

Krug, Etienne G., Linda L. Dahlberg, James A. Mercy, Anthony B. Zwi, and Rafael Lozano (eds.). 2002. *World Report on Violence and Health.* Geneva: World Health Organization.

Krugman, Paul. 2003. *The Great Unraveling: Losing Our Way in the New Century.* New York: W. W. Norton.

Kunkel, Karl R. 1999. "Reclaiming Deviance as a Unique Course from Criminology: Revisited." *Teaching Sociology,* 27 (January): 38–43.

Kurtz, Paul. 1978. "Is Parapsychology a Science?" *Skeptical Inquirer,* 3 (Winter): 14–32.

LaFree, Gary. 1989. *Rape and Criminal Justice: The Social Construction of Sexual Assault.* Belmont, CA: Wadsworth.

Lakshmi, Rama. 2002a. "Mob Attacks Indian Train; 57 Killed." *The Washington Post,* February 28, p. A13.

Lakshmi, Rama. 2002b. "Avenging Hindu Mobs Attack Muslims in India." *The Washington Post,* March 1, p. A14.

Lamy, Philip. 1996. *Millennium Rage: Survivalists, White Supremacists, and the Doomsday Prophecy*. New York: Plenum Press.

Landman, Janet T., and Robyn Dawes. 1982. "Psychotherapy Outcome: Smith and Glass' Conclusions Stand Up Under Scrutiny." *Psychological Bulletin*, 57: 504–516.

Lane, Charles. 2003a. "Sodomy Ruling Spurs Challenges to Military's Policy on Gays." *The Washington Post*, August 4, pp. A1, A5.

Lane, Charles. 2003b. "Justices Overturn Texas Sodomy Ban." *The Washington Post*, June 27, pp. A1, A16.

Langlois, Judith H., et al. 2000. "Maxims or Myths of Beauty: A Meta-Analytic and Theoretical Review," *Psychological Bulletin*, 126 (May): 390–423.

Laumann, Edward O., John H. Gagnon, Robert T. Michael, and Stuart Michaels. 1994. *The Social Organization of Human Sexuality: Sexual Practices in the United States*. Chicago: University of Chicago Press.

Lawson, Anette. 1988. *Adultery: An Analysis of Love and Betrayal*. New York: Basic Books.

Leighton, D. C., et al. 1963. *The Character of Danger: Psychiatric Symptoms in Selected Communities*. New York: Basic Books.

Lemert, Edwin M. 1951. *Social Pathology: A Systematic Approach to the Study of Sociopathic Behavior*. New York: McGraw-Hill.

Lemert, Edwin M. 1953. "An Isolation and Closure Theory of Naive Check Forgery." *Journal of Criminal Law, Criminology, and Police Science*, 44 (September–October): 296–307.

Lemert, Edwin M. 1958. "The Behavior of the Systematic Check Forger." *Social Problems*, 6 (Fall): 141–149.

Lemert, Edwin M. 1964a. "Social Structure, Social Control, and Deviation." In Marshall B. Clinard (ed.), *Anomie and Deviant Behavior: A Discussion and Critique*. New York: Free Press, pp. 57–97.

Lemert, Edwin M. 1964b. "The Behavior of the Systematic Check Forger." In Howard S. Becker (ed.), *The Other Side: Perspectives on Deviance*. New York: Free Press, pp. 211–224.

Lemert, Edwin M. 1972. *Human Deviance, Social Problems, and Social Control* (2nd ed.). Englewood Cliffs, NJ: Prentice Hall.

Lemley, Brad. 2000. "Isn't She Lovely?" *Discover*, January, pp. 43–49.

Leonard, Eileen B. 1982. *Women, Crime, and Society: A Critique of Theoretical Criminology*. New York: Longman.

Lerner, Melvin J. 1980. *The Belief in a Just World: A Fundamental Delusion*. New York: Plenum Press.

Levine, Martin P., and Richard R. Troiden. 1988. "The Myth of Sexual Compulsivity." *Journal of Sex Research*, 25 (August): 347–363.

Liazos, Alexander. 1972. "The Poverty of the Sociology of Deviance: Nuts, Sluts, and Preverts." *Social Problems*, 20 (Summer): 103–120.

Liem, Ramsay, and Joan Liem. 1978. "Social Class and Mental Health Reconsidered: The Role of Economic Stress and Economic Support." *Journal of Health and Social Behavior*, 19 (June): 139–156.

Lindesmith, Alfred R., and John H. Gagnon. 1964. "Anomie and Drug Addiction." In Marshall B. Clinard (ed.), *Anomie and Deviant Behavior: A Discussion and Critique*. New York: Free Press, pp. 158–188.

Lingeman, Richard R. 1974. *Drugs from A to Z* (2nd ed.). New York: McGraw-Hill.

Link, Bruce G. 1987. "Understanding Labeling Effects in the Area of Mental Disorders: An Assessment of the Effects of Expectations of Rejection." *American Sociological Review*, 52 (February): 96–112.

Link, Bruce G., and Frances T. Cullen. 1989. "The Labeling Theory of Mental Disorder: A Review of the Evidence." In James Greenly (ed.), *Mental Illness in Social Context*. Detroit: Wayne State University Press.

Link, Bruce G., Frances T. Cullen, Elmer Struening, Patrick Shrout, and Bruce P. Dohrenwend. 1989. "A Modified Labeling Theory Approach to Mental Disorders: An Empirical Assessment." *American Sociological Review*, 54 (June): 400–423.

Link, Bruce G., Bruce P. Dohrenwend, and Andrew E. Skodol. 1986. "Socioeconomic Status and Schizophrenia: Noisome Occupational Characteristics as a Risk Factor." *American Sociological Association*, 51 (April): 242–258.

Linton, Simi. 1998. *Claiming Disability: Knowledge and Identity*. New York: New York University Press.

Linz, Daniel, and Neil Malamuth. 1993. *Pornography*. Thousand Oaks, CA: Sage.

Lipton, Eric. 2001. "A Challenge to Gay Boy Scouts." *The New York Times*, February 27, p. A21.

Lofland, John. 1966. *Doomsday Cult: A Study of Conversion, Proselytization, and Maintenance of Faith*. Englewood Cliffs, NJ: Prentice Hall.

Lofland, John. 1969. *Deviance and Identity*. Englewood Cliffs, NJ: Prentice Hall.

Lofland, John, and Rodney Stark. 1965. "Becoming a World Saver: A Theory of Conversion to a Deviant Perspective." *American Sociological Review*, 30 (December): 862–875.

Loftus, T. A. 1960. *Meaning and Methods of Diagnosis in Clinical Psychiatry*. Philadelphia: Lea & Febinger.

Lombroso, Cesare, and William Ferro. 1916. *The Female Offender*. New York: Appleton.

Long, Gary L., and D. S. Dorn. 1983. "Sociologists' Attitudes Toward Ethical Issues: The Management of an Impression." *Sociological and Social Research*, 67: 288–300.

Louderback, Llewellyn. 1970. *Fat Power: Whatever You Weigh Is Right*. New York: Hawthorn Books.

Lowman, John, Robert J. Menzies, and T. S. Palys (eds.). 1987. *Transcarceration: Essays in the Sociology of Social Control*. Gower, UK: Aldershot.

Lyman, Stanford M., and Marvin B. Scott. 1970. *A Sociology of the Absurd*. New York: Appleton-Century-Crofts.

Lynch, Michael J., and W. Byron Groves. 1995. "In Defense of Comparative Criminology: A Critique of General Theory and the Rational Man." In Freda Adler and William S. Laufer (eds.), *The Legacy of Anomie Theory*. New Brunswick, NJ: Transaction, pp. 367–392.

Lyng, Stephen. 1998. "Dangerous Methods: Risk Taking and the Research Process." In Steven Ferrell and Mark S. Hamm (eds.), *Ethnography at the Edge: Crime, Deviance, and Field Research*. Boston: Northeastern University Press, pp. 221–251.

MacAndrew, James. 1997. *The Roswell Report: Case Closed*. Washington, DC: U.S. Government Printing Office.

Mack, John. 1995. *Abductions: Human Encounters with Aliens* (rev. ed.). New York: Bantam Books.

MacKinnon, Catherine A. 1979. *Sexual Harassment of Working Women*. New Haven, CT: Yale University Press.

MacKinnon, Catherine A., and Andrea Dworkin (eds.). 1998. *In Harm's Way: The Pornography Civil Rights Hearing*. Cambridge, MA: Harvard University Press.

Maddox, George L., Kurt W. Back, and Veronica Liederman. 1968. "Overweight as Social Deviance and Disability." *Journal of Health and Social Behavior*, 9 (December): 287–298.

Madigan, Nick. 2003. "Professor's Snub of Creationists Prompts U.S. Inquiry." *The New York Times*, February 3, p. A11.

Mairs, Nancy. 1997. *Waist-High in the World: A Life among the Disabled*. Boston: Beacon.

Malamuth, Neil M. 1981. "Rape Proclivity among Males." *Journal of Social Issues*, 37 (4): 138–157.

Malamuth, Neil M., Christopher L. Heavey, and Daniel Linz. 1992. "Predicting Men's Antisocial Behavior Against Women: The Interaction Model of Sexual Aggression." In Gordon C. Nagayama Hall (ed.), *Sexual Aggression: Issues in Etiology and Assessment, Treatment, and Policy*. New York: Hemisphere, pp. 63–97.

Mann, Peggy. 1985. *Marijuana Alert*. New York: McGraw-Hill.

Marquis, Christopher. 2002. "Military Discharges of Gays Rise, and So Do Bias Incidents." *The New York Times*, March 14, p. A24.

Martin, Dell. 1976. *Battered Wives*. San Francisco: Glide Foundation.

Marx, Karl, and Friedrich Engels. 1947. *The German Ideology*, Parts I & III. New York: International Publishers (orig. written 1846).

Matthews, Roger, and Jock Young (eds.). 1986. *Confronting Crime*. Thousand Oaks, CA: Sage.

Matza, David. 1969. *Becoming Deviant*. Englewood Cliffs, NJ: Prentice-Hall.

Maxwell, Sheila Royo. 2001. "A Focus on Familial Strain: Antisocial Behavior and Delinquency in Filipino Society." *Sociological Inquiry*, 71 (Summer): 265–292.

Mazerolle, Paul, and Jeff Maahs. 2000. "General Strain and Delinquency: An Alternative Examination of Conditioning Influences." *Justice Quarterly*, 17 (December): 753–778.

Mazerolle, Paul, and Alex R. Piquero. 2001. "General Strain Theory, Situational Anger, and Social Networks—An Assessment of Conditioning Influences." *Journal of Criminal Justice*, 29 (September–October): 445–461.

McCabe, Donald L. 1995. "The Influence of Situational Ethics on Cheating Among College Students." *Sociological Inquiry*, 63 (3): 362–374.

McCaghy, Charles H. 1967. "Child Molesters: A Study of Their Career as Deviants." In Marshall B. Clinard and Richard Quinney (eds.), *Criminal Behavior Systems: A Typology*. New York: Holt, Rinehart & Winston, pp. 75–88.

McCaghy, Charles H. 1968. "Drinking and Disavowal: The Case of Child Molesters." *Social Problems*, 16 (Summer): 43–49.

McCaghy, Charles H., Timothy A. Capron, and J. D. Jamieson. 2003. *Deviant Behavior: Crime, Conflict, and Interest Groups* (6th ed.). Boston: Allyn & Bacon.

McClenon, James. 1984. *Deviant Science: The Case of Parapsychology*. Philadelphia: University of Pennsylvania Press.

McGarry, Kevin. 2003. *Fatherhood for Gay Men: An Emotional and Practical Guide to Becoming a Gay Dad*. Binghamton, NY: Haworth Press.

McIntosh, Mary. 1968. "The Homosexual Role." *Social Problems*, 16 (Fall): 182–192.

Mechanic, David. 1989. *Mental Health and Social Policy* (3rd ed.). Englewood Cliffs, NJ: Prentice Hall.

Meier, Robert F. 1982. "Perspectives on the Concept of Social Control." *Annual Review of Sociology*, 8: 35–55.

Mendelsohn, Daniel. 1996. "We're Here! We're Queer! Let's Get Coffee!" *New York*, September 30, pp. 25–31.

Mendelsohn, Daniel. 2000. *The Elusive Embrace: Desire and the Riddle of Identity*. New York: Alfred Knopf.

Mercer, Jane R. 1965. "Social System Perspective and Clinical Perspective: Frames of Reference for Understanding Career Patterns of People Labeled as Mentally Retarded." *Social Problems*, 13 (Summer): 18–34.

Merton, Robert K. 1938. "Social Structure and Anomie." *American Sociological Review*, 3 (October): 672–682.

Merton, Robert K. 1948. "The Self-Fulfilling Prophecy." *Antioch Review*, 7 (Summer): 193–210.

Merton, Robert K. 1949. *Social Theory and Social Structure*. New York: Free Press.

Merton, Robert K. 1957. *Social Theory and Social Structure*. (rev. & expanded ed.). Glencoe, IL: Free Press.

Merton, Robert K. 1968. *Social Theory and Social Structure*. New York: Free Press (enlarged ed.). New York: Free Press.

Merton, Robert K. 1971. "Social Problems and Sociological Theory." In Robert K. Merton and Robert Nisbet (eds.), *Contemporary Social Problems* (3rd ed.). New York: Harcourt Brace Jovanovich, pp. 793–845.

Messner, Steven F., and Richard Rosenfeld. 1997. *Crime and the American Dream* (2nd ed.). Belmont, CA: Wadsworth.

Miall, Charlene E. 1986. "The Stigma of Involuntary Childlessness." *Social Problems*, 33 (April): 268–282.

Michael, Robert T., John H. Gagnon, Edward O. Laumann, and Gina Kolata. 1994. *Sex in America: A Definitive Survey*. Boston: Little, Brown.

Miller, J. Mitchell, and Richard Tewksbury (eds.). 2001. *Extreme Methods: Innovative Approaches to Social Science Research*. Boston: Allyn & Bacon.

Miller, Judith Droitcour, and Ira H. Cisin. 1980. *Highlights from the National Survey on Drug Abuse: 1979*. Rockville, MD: National Institute on Drug Abuse.

Miller, Lisa, et al. 2002. "Sins of the Fathers." *Newsweek*, March 4, pp. 43–52.

Miller, Walter B. 1958. "Lower Class Culture as a Generating Milieu of Gang Delinquency." *Journal of Social Issues*, 14 (3): 5–19.

Millman, Marcia. 1975. "She Did It All for Love: A Feminist View of the Sociology of Deviance." In Marcia Millman and Rosabeth Moss Kantor (eds.), *Another Voice: Feminist Perspectives on Social Life and Social Science*. Garden City, NY: Doubleday-Anchor, pp. 251–279.

Millman, Marcia. 1980. *Such a Pretty Face: Being Fat in America*. New York: W. W. Norton.

Mills, C. Wright. 1940. "Situated Actions and Vocabularies of Motive." *American Sociological Review*, 5 (December): 316–330.

Milner, Christina, and Richard Milner. 1972. *Black Players: The Secret World of Black Pimps*. Boston: Little, Brown.

Minai, Naila. 1981. *Women in Islam: Tradition and Transition in the Middle East*. New York: Seaview Press.

Minton, Henry L. 2002. *Departing from Deviance: A History of Homosexual Rights and Emancipatory Science in America*. Chicago: University of Chicago Press.

Mitchell, David T., and Sharon L. Snyder (eds.). 1997. *The Body and Physical Differences: Discourses of Disability*. Ann Arbor: University of Michigan Press.

Monestier, Martin. 1987. *Human Oddities* (trans. Robert Campbell). Secaucus, NJ: Citadel Press.

Money, John, and Anke A. Erhardt. 1972. *Man & Woman, Boy & Girl: Differentiation and Dimorphism of Sexual Identity from Conception to Maturity*. Baltimore: Johns Hopkins University Press.

Money, John, and Patricia Tucker. 1975. *Sexual Signatures: On Being a Man or a Woman*. Boston: Little, Brown.

Monto, Martin A. 2000. "Why Men Seek Out Prostitutes." In Ronald Weitzer (ed.), *Sex for Sale: Prostitution, Pornography, and the Sex Industry*. New York & London: Routledge, pp. 67–83.

Mooney, Linda A., Robert Grambling, and Craig Forsyth. 1992. "Legal Drinking Age and Alcohol Consumption." *Deviant Behavior*, 13 (1): 59–71.

Morgan, Robin. 1977. *Going Too Far*. New York: Random House.

Morin, Richard, and Alan Cooperman. 2003. "Majority Against Blessing Gay Unions." *The Washington Post*, August 14, pp. A1, A10.

Morral, Andrew R., Daniel F. McCaffrey, and Susan M. Paddock. 2002. "Reassessing the Marijuana Gateway Effect." *Addictions*, 97 (December): 1493–1504.

Murphy, Jane M. 1976. "Psychiatric Labeling in Cross-Cultural Perspective," *Science*, 191 (12 March): 1019–1028.

Musto, David F. 1987. *The American Disease: Origins of Narcotic Control* (expanded ed.). New York: Oxford University Press.

Nahas, Gabriel G. 1973. *Marihuana—Deceptive Weed*. New York: Raven Press.

National Institute on Alcoholism and Alcohol Abuse (NIAAA). 1987, 1997, 2000. *Alcohol and Health*, Sixth, Ninth, and Tenth Special Reports to the U.S. Congress from the Secretary of Health and Human Services. Rockville, MD: NIAAA.

National Institute on Drug Abuse (NIDA). 1991. *National Household Survey on Drug Abuse: Population Estimates, 1991*. Rockville, MD: NIDA.

Nettler, Gwynn. 1974. "On Telling Who's Crazy." *American Sociological Review*, 39 (December): 893–894.

Nettler, Gwynn. 1984. *Explaining Crime* (3rd ed.). New York: McGraw-Hill.

Neuspiel, D. R., et al. 1991. "Maternal Cocaine Use and Infant Behavior." *Neurotoxicology and Teratology*, 13 (March–April): 229–233.

Newman, Graeme. 1976. *Comparative Deviance: Perception and Law in Six Cultures*. New York: Elsevier.

NIAAA (see National Institute on Alcoholism and Alcohol Abuse).

NIDA (see National Institute on Drug Abuse).

Nussbaum, Emily. 2000. "A Question of Gender." *Discover*, January, pp. 93–99.

O'Brien, Robert, and Sidney Cohen. 1984. *The Encyclopedia of Drug Abuse*. New York: Facts on File.

O'Brien, Robert E. 1985. *Crime and Victimization Data*. Thousand Oaks, CA: Sage.

O'Donnell, John A., and Richard R. Clayton. 1982. "The Stepping-Stone Hypothesis—Marijuana, Heroin, and Causality." *Chemical Dependencies: Behavioral and Biomedical Issues*, 4 (3): 229–241.

Orcutt, James D. 1983. *Analyzing Deviance*. Homewood, IL: Dorsey Press.

Oreskes, Michael. 1990. "Drug War Underlines Fickleness of Public." *The New York Times*, September 6, p. A22.

Ousey, Graham C., and Michelle Campbell Ausustine. 2001. "Young Guns: Examining Alternative Explanations of Juvenile Firearm Homicide Rates." *Criminology*, 39 (November): 933–967.

Paige, Karen Ericksen. 1977. "Sexual Pollution: Reproductive Sex Taboos in American Society." *Journal of Social Issues*, 33 (2): 144–165.

Palmer, Stuart, and Arnold S. Linsky (eds.). 1972. *Rebellion and Retreat: Readings in the Forms and Processes of Deviance*. Columbus, OH: Charles E. Merrill.

Park, Robert E. 1926. "The Urban Community as a Spatial Pattern and a Moral Order." In Ernest W. Burgess (ed.), *The Urban Community*. Chicago: University of Chicago Press, pp. 3–18.

Parker, Robert Nash. 1995. *Alcohol and Violence: A Deadly Combination of Two American Traditions*. Albany: State University of New York Press.

Parker, Sheila, et al. 1995. "Body Image and Weight Concerns among African American and White Adolescent Females: Differences that Make a Difference." *Human Organization*, 54 (2): 103–114.

Parrot, Andrea, and Steven Allen. 1984. "Acquaintance Rape: Seduction or Crime? When Sex Becomes a Crime." Paper presented at the Eastern Regional Society for the Scientific Study of Sex. April 6–8.

Parsons, Talcott. 1951. *The Social System*. New York: Free Press.

Pearlin, Leonard I., and Joyce S. Johnson. 1977. "Marital Status, Life Strains, and Depression." *American Sociological Review*, 42 (October): 704–715.

Pearson, Geoffrey. 1987. *The New Heroin Users*. London: Basil Blackwell.

Peebles, Curtis. 1994. *Watch the Skies! A Chronicle of the Flying Saucer Myth*. Washington, DC: Smithsonian Institution Press.

Pernanen, Kai. 1991. *Alcohol in Human Violence*. New York: Guilford Press.

Perrow, Charles. 1984. *Normal Accidents: Living with High-Risk Technologies*. New York: Basic Books.

Petrunik, Michael. 1980. "The Rise and Fall of 'Labeling Theory': The Construction and Deconstruction of a Sociological Strawman." *Canadian Journal of Sociology*, 5 (3): 213–233.

Pfohl, Stephen J. 1977. "The 'Discovery' of Child Abuse." *Social Problems*, 24 (February): 310–323.

Pfohl, Stephen J. 1994. *Images of Deviance and Social Control: A Sociological History* (2nd ed.). New York: McGraw-Hill.

Phillips, Derek L. 1964. "Rejection of the Mentally Ill: The Influence of Behavior and Sex." *American Sociological Review*, 29 (October): 755–763.

Piquero, Nicole Leeper, and Mariam D. Sealock. 2000. "Generalizing General Strain Theory: An Examination of an Offending Population." *Justice Quarterly*, 36 (September): 449–484.

Plummer, Kenneth. 1975. *Sexual Stigma: An Interactionist Account*. London: Routledge & Kegan Paul.

Plummer, Kenneth. 1979. "Misunderstanding Labelling Perspectives." In David Downes and Paul Rock (eds.), *Deviant Interpretations*. London: Martin Robinson, pp. 85–121.

Plummer, Kenneth. 1982. Symbolic Interactionism and Sexual Conduct: An Emergent Perspective." In

Mike Brake (ed.), *Human Sexual Relations: Toward a Redefinition of Politics*. New York: Pantheon Books, pp. 223–241.

Polk, Kenneth. 1991. Review of Michael R. Gottfredson and Travis Hirschi, *A General Theory of Crime*. Stanford, CA: Stanford University Press, 1990, in *Crime and Delinquency*, 37 (2): 275–279.

Pollack, Earl, and Carol A. Taube. 1975. "Trends and Projections in State Hospital Use." In Jack Zussman and Elmer Bertsch (eds.), *The Future Role of the State Hospital*. Lexington, MA: D.C. Heath, pp. 31–55.

Pollak, Otto. 1950. *The Criminality of Women*. Philadelphia: University of Pennsylvania Press.

Polsky, Ned. 1998. *Hustlers, Beats, and Others* (expanded ed.). New York: Lyons Press.

Potter, R. H. 1999. "Deviance 'Down Under' or How a Deviance Assignment Became a 'Folk Devil.' " In Martin D. Schwartz and Michael O. Maume (eds.), *Teaching the Sociology of Deviance* (4th ed.). Washington: American Sociological Association, pp. 52–60.

Powdermaker, Hortense. 1960. "An Anthropological Approach to the Problem of Obesity." *Bulletin of the New York Academy of Medicine*, 36: 286–295.

Powell, Michael. 2002. "A Fall from Grace." *The Washington Post*, August 4, pp. F1, F4–F5.

Priest, G. L. 1990. "The New Legal Structure of Risk Control." *Daedalus*, 119: 207–228.

Pryor, Douglas W. 1996. *Unspeakable Acts: Why Men Sexually Abuse Children*. New York: New York University Press.

Quindlen, Anna. 1990. "Hearing the Cries of Crack." *The New York Times*, October 7, p. E19.

Quinney, Richard. 1965. "Is Criminal Behaviour Deviant Behaviour?" *British Journal of Criminology*, 5 (April): 132–142.

Quinney, Richard. 1979. *Criminology* (2nd ed.) Boston: Little, Brown.

Radin, Dean. 1997. *The Conscious Universe: The Scientific Truth of Psychic Phenomena*. New York: HarperEdge.

Radin, Dean, and Diane C. Ferrari. 1991. "Effects of Consciousness on the Fall of Dice." *Journal of Scientific Exploration*, 5 (1): 61–83.

Ravenholt, R. T. 1984. "Addiction Mortality in the United States: Tobacco, Alcohol, and Other Substances." *Population and Developmental Review*, 10 (December): 697–724.

Ravo, Nick. 1987. "Drinking Age Is Said to Fail for Students." *The New York Times*, December 21, pp. A1, B15.

Ray, Marsh B. 1964. "The Cycle of Abstinence and Relapse Among Heroin Addicts." In Howard S. Becker (ed.), *The Other Side: Perspectives on Deviance*. New York: Free Press, pp. 163–177.

Ray, Oakley, and Charles Ksir. 2002. *Drugs, Society, and Human Behavior* (8th ed.). New York: McGraw-Hill.

Reckless, Walter C. 1950. *The Crime Problem*. New York: Appleton-Century-Crofts.

Reiger, Darrel A., et al. 1988. "One-Month Prevalence of Mental Disorders in the United States Based on Five Epidemiological Catchment Areas Sites." *Archives of General Psychiatry*, 45 (November): 977–986.

Reinarman, Craig. 2000. "The Social Construction of Drug Scares." In Patricia A. Adler and Peter Adler (eds.), *Constructions of Deviance: Social Power, Context, and Interaction*. Belmont, CA: Wadsworth, pp. 147–158.

Reiss, Albert J., Jr. 1964. "The Social Organization of Queers and Peers." In Howard S. Becker (ed.), *The Other Side: Perspectives on Deviance*. New York: Free Press, pp. 181–210.

Rennison, Callie Marie. 2001. "Criminal Victimization 2000, Changes 1999–2000 with Trends 1993–2000." *Bureau of Justice Statistics, National Crime Victimization Survey*, June, pp. 1–15.

Rennison, Callie Marie, and Michael R. Rand. 2003. "Criminal Victimization, 2002." *Bureau of Justice Statistics, National Crime Victimization Survey*, August, pp. 1–12.

Rhodes, William, Patrick Johnston, and Ryan Kling. 2001. *The Price of Illicit Drugs: 1981 through the Second Quarter of 2000*. Washington, DC: Executive Office of the President, Office of National Drug Control Policy.

Rhodes, William, Mary Layne, Anne-Marie Bruen, Patrick Johnston, and Lisa Becchetti. 2001. *What America's Users Spend on Illegal Drugs*. Washington, DC: Executive Office of the President, Office of National Drug Control Policy.

Richardson, Diane. 1996. "Heterosexuality and Social Theory." In Diane Richardson (ed.), *Theorising Heterosexuality*. Buckingham, UK: Open University Press, pp. 1–20.

Richardson, Gale A., and Nancy L. Day. 1994. "Detrimental Effects of Prenatal Cocaine Exposure: Illusion or Reality?" *Journal of the American Academy of Child and Adolescent Psychiatry*, 33 (January): 28–34.

Richardson, James T., Joel Best, and David G. Bromley (eds.). 1991. *The Satanism Scare*. New York: Aldine de Gruyter.

Riley-Smith, Jonathan. 1987. *The Crusades: A Short History*. New Haven, CT: Yale University Press.

Rimer, Sara. 2003. "Boy Scouts Under Fire; Ban on Gays Is at Issue." *The New York Times*, July 3, p. A16.

Rimland, Bernard. 1969. "Psychogenesis versus Biogenesis: The Issue and the Evidence." In Stanley C. Plog and Robert B. Edgerton (eds.), *Changing Perspectives in Mental Health*. New York: Holt, Rinehart & Winston, pp. 702–735.

Roberts, Cathy. 1989. *Women and Rape*. New York: New York University Press.

Robertson, Roland, and Laurie Taylor. 1973. *Deviance, Crime, and Socio-Legal Control*. London: Martin Robertson.

Robins, Lee N. 1975. "Alcoholism and Labeling Theory." In Walter R. Gove (ed.), *The Labeling of Deviance*. New York: John Wiley/Halstead/Sage, pp. 21–33.

Rodmell, Sue. 1981. "Men, Women, and Sexuality: A Feminist Critique of the Sociology of Deviance." *Women's Studies International Quarterly*, 4 (2): 145–155.

Roiphe, Katie. 1997. "Adultery's Double Standard." *The New York Times Magazine*, October 7, pp. 54–55.

Ronai, Carol Rambo. 1995. "Multiple Reflections of Child Sex Abuse: An Argument for a Layered Account." *Journal of Contemporary Ethnography*, 23 (January): 395–426.

Ronai, Carol Rambo, and Carolyn Ellis. 1989. "Turn-Ons for Money: Interactional Strategies of the Table Dancer." *Journal of Contemporary Ethnography*, 18 (October): 271–298.

Rosenhan, David L. 1973. "On Being Sane in Insane Places." *Science*, 179 (January 19): 250–258.

Rosenthal, Jack. 1981. "The Pornography of Fat." *The New York Times*, May 29, p. A26.

Rotenberg, Mordechai. 1974. "Self-Labeling: A Missing Link in the 'Societal Reaction Theory of Deviance.'" *Sociological Quarterly*, 15 (April): 335–355.

Rubington, Earl, and Martin S. Weinberg (eds.). 2002. *Deviance: The Interactionist Perspective* (8th ed.). Boston: Allyn & Bacon.

Rumbarger, John J. 1989. *Profits, Power, and Prohibition: Alcohol Reform and the Industrializing of America, 1800–1930*. Albany, NY: State University of New York Press.

Rushing, William. 1979a. "The Functional Importance of Sex Roles and Sex-Related Behavior in Societal Reactions to Residual Deviants." *Journal of Health and Social Behavior*, 20 (September): 208–217.

Rushing, William. 1979b. "Marital Status and Mental Disorder: Evidence in Favor of a Behavioral Model." *Social Forces*, 58 (December): 540–556.

Russell, Diana E. H. 1975. *The Politics of Rape: The Victim's Perspective*. New York: Stein & Day.

Russell, Diana E. H. 1998. *Dangerous Relationships: Pornography, Misogyny, and Rape*. Thousand Oaks, CA: Sage.

Russell, Katheryn. 1992. "Development of a Black Criminology and the Role of the Black Criminologist." *Justice Quarterly* 9 (December): 667–683.

Ryan, William. 1976. *Blaming the Victim* (2nd ed.). New York: Vintage Books.

Sagarin, Edward. 1969. *Odd Man In: Societies of Deviants in America*. Chicago: Quadrangle Books.

SAMHSA (see Substance Abuse and Mental Health Services Administration).

Sampson, Harold, et al. 1964. "The Mental Hospital and Family Ties." In Howard S. Becker (ed.), *The Other Side: Perspectives on Deviance*. New York: Free Press, pp. 139–162.

Sanday, Peggy Reeves. 1981. "The Socio-cultural Context of Rape: A Cross-Cultural Study." *Journal of Social Issues*, 37 (1): 5–27.

Sanday, Peggy Reeves. 1990. *Fraternity Gang Rape: Sex, Brotherhood and Privilege on Campus*. New York: New York University Press.

Sanday, Peggy Reeves. 1996. "Rape-Prone versus Rape-Free Campus Cultures." *Violence Against Women*, 2 (June): 191–208.

Sanders, Clinton R. 1989. *Customizing the Body: The Art and Culture of Tattooing*. Philadelphia: Temple University Press.

Sanders, Stephanie A., and June Machover Reinisch. 1999. "Would You Say You 'Had Sex' If. . . ?" *Journal of the American Medical Association*, 281 (January 20): 275–277.

Sandwijk, P. P., P. D. A. Cohen, and S. Musterd. 1991. *Licit and Illicit Drug Use in Amsterdam*. Amsterdam: Institute for Social Geography.

Scarce, Rik. 1995. "Scholarly Ethics and Courtroom Antics: Where Researchers Stand in the Eyes of the Law." *The American Sociologist*, 26 (Spring): 87–112.

Scheff, Thomas J. 1966. *Being Mentally Ill: A Sociological Theory*. Chicago: Aldine.

Scheff, Thomas J. 1974a. "The Labeling Theory of Mental Illness." *American Sociological Review*, 39 (June): 444–452.

Scheff, Thomas J. 1974b. "Reply to Nettler." *American Sociological Review*, 39 (December): 894–895.

Scheff, Thomas J. 1984. *Being Mentally Ill: A Sociological Theory* (rev. ed.). New York: Aldine de Gruyter.

Schlitz, Marilyn, and Elmer Gruber. 1980. "Transcontinental Remote Viewing." *Journal of Parapsychology*, 44 (December): 305–318.

Schmalleger, Frank. 1996. *Criminology Today*. Upper Saddle River, NJ: Prentice Hall.

Schneider, Allison. 1999. "The Academic Path to Pariah Status." *The Chronicle of Higher Education*, July 2, pp. A12–A24.

Schoenfielder, Lisa, and Barb Wieser (eds.). 1983. *Shadow on a Tightrope: Writings by Women on Fat Oppression*. Iowa City, IA: Aunt Lute.

Schultes, Richard Evans, and Albert Hofmann. 1979. *Plants of the Gods: Origins of Hallucinogenic Use*. New York: Alfred van der Mark Editions.

Schur, Edwin M. 1971. *Labeling Deviant Behavior: Its Sociological Implications*. New York: Harper & Row.

Schur, Edwin M. 1980. *The Politics of Deviance: Stigma Contests and the Uses of Power*. Upper Saddle River, NJ: Prentice Hall/Spectrum.

Schur, Edwin M. 1984. *Labeling Women Deviant: Gender, Stigma, and Social Control*. New York: Random House.

Schwartz, Martin. 2001. "Date Rape on College Campuses." In Alex Thio and Thomas C. Calhoun (eds.), *Readings in Deviant Behavior* (2nd ed.). Boston: Allyn & Bacon, pp. 94–98.

Schwartz, Richard D., and Jerome H. Skolnick. 1964. "Two Studies of Legal Stigma." In Howard S. Becker (ed.), *The Other Side: Perspectives on Deviance*. New York: Free Press, pp. 103–117.

Scott, James C. 1985. *Weapons of the Weak: Everyday Forms of Peasant Resistance*. New Haven, CT: Yale University Press.

Scott, Marvin B., and Stanford M. Lyman. 1968. "Accounts." *American Sociological Review*, 33 (February): 46–62.

Scull, Andrew. 1984. *Decarceration: Community Treatment and the Deviant—A Radical View* (2nd ed.). Cambridge, UK: Polity Press.

Scull, Andrew. 1988. "Deviance and Social Control." In Neil J. Smelser (ed.), *Handbook of Sociology*. Thousand Oaks, CA: Sage, pp. 667–693.

Scully, Diana. 1990. *Understanding Sexual Violence: A Study of Convicted Rapists*. Boston: Unwin Hyman.

Scully, Diana, and Joseph Marolla. 1984. "Convicted Rapists' Vocabulary of Motive: Excuses and Justifications." *Social Problems*, 31 (June): 530–544.

Scully, Diana, and Joseph Marolla. 1985. "Riding the Bull at Gilley's: Convicted Rapists Describe the Rewards of Rape." *Social Problems*, 32 (February): 251–262.

Seelye, Katharine Q. 1995. "Helms Puts the Brakes to a Bill Financing AIDS Treatment." *The New York Times*, July 5, p. A12.

Sharp, Susan F., et al. 2001. "Purging Behavior in a Sample of College Females: A Research Note on General Strain Theory and Female Deviance." *Deviant Behavior*, 22 (March-April): 171–188.

Sheley, Joseph F. 1995. *Criminology: A Contemporary Handbook* (2nd ed.). Belmont, CA: Wadsworth.

Shenon, Philip. 1990. "War on Drugs Remains Top Priority, Bush Says." *The New York Times*, September 6, p. A22.

Short, James F., Jr. 1964. "Gang Delinquency and Anomie." In Marshall B. Clinard (ed.), *Anomie and Deviant Behavior: A Discussion and Critique*. New York: Free Press, pp. 98–127.

Short, James F., Jr. 1990. "Hazards, Risk, and Enterprise: Approaches to Law, Science, and Social Policy." *Law and Society Review*, 24 (1): 179–198.

Siegel, Larry. 2003. *Criminology* (8th ed.). Belmont, CA: Wadsworth.

Simon, Jesse, and Jack Zussman. 1983. "The Effect of Contextual Factors on Psychiatrists' Perception of Illness: A Case Study." *Journal of Health and Social Behavior*, 24 (2): 186–198.

Skogan, Wesley G. 1986. "Fear of Crime and Neighborhood Change." In Albert J. Reiss, Jr., and Michael Tonry (eds.), *Communities and Crime*. Chicago: University of Chicago Press, pp. 203–229.

Skogan, Wesley G. 1990. *Disorder and Decline: Crime and the Spiral of Decay in American Neighborhoods*. New York: Free Press.

Skolnick, Jerome H., and James J. Fyfe. 1993. *Above the Law: Police and the Excessive Use of Force*. New York: Free Press.

Slovic, Paul, Baruch Fischoff, and Sarah Lichtenstein. 1980. "Risky Assumptions." *Psychology Today*, June, pp. 44–48.

Slovic, Paul, Mark Layman, and James H. Flynn. 1991. "Risk, Perception, Trust, and Nuclear Waste: Lessons from Yucca Mountain." *Environment*, 33 (April): 28–30.

Smart, Carol. 1976. *Women, Crime, and Criminology: A Feminist Critique*. London: Routledge & Kegan Paul.

Smith, Mary Lee, Gene Glass, and Thomas Miller. 1980. *The Benefits of Psychotherapy*. Baltimore: Johns Hopkins University Press.

Snyder, Charles R. 1964. "Inebriety, Alcoholism, and Anomie." In Marshall B. Clinard (ed.), *Anomie and Deviant Behavior: A Discussion and Critique*. New York: Free Press, pp. 189–212.

Sobal, Jeffery, and Donna Maurer (eds.). 1999a. *Interpreting Weight: The Social Management of Fatness and Thinness*. New York: Aldine de Gruyter.

Sobal, Jeffery, and Donna Maurer (eds.). 1999b. *Weighty Issues: Fatness and Thinness as Social Problems*. New York: Aldine de Gruyter.

Solzhenitsyn, Aleksander I. 1974. *The Gulag Archipelago, 1918–1956: An Experiment in Literary Investigation, I–II* (trans. Thomas Whitney). New York: Harper & Row.

Spence, Jonathan D. 1988. *The Question of Hu*. New York: Alfred Knopf.

Spillane, Joseph F. 2000. *Cocaine: From Medical Marvel to Modern Menace in the United States, 1884–1920*. Baltimore: Johns Hopkins University Press.

Spira, Alfred, et al. 1992. "AIDS and Sexual Behavior in France." *Nature*, 360 (3 December): 407–409.

Spira, Alfred, et al. 1993. *Les Comportments Sexuels en France*. Paris: La Documentation Francais.

Spitzer, Robert L. 1975. "On Pseudoscience in Science, Logic in Remission, and Psychiatric Diagnosis: A Critique of Rosenhan's 'On Being Sane in Insane Places.'" *Journal of Abnormal Psychology*, 84 (5): 442–452.

Spitzer, Robert L. 1976. "More on Pseudoscience in Science and the Case for Psychiatric Diagnosis: A Critique of D. L. Rosenhan's 'On Being Sane in Insane Places' and 'The Contextual Nature of Psychiatric Diagnosis.'" *Archives of General Psychiatry*, 33 (April): 459–470.

Srole, Leo, et al. 1962. *Mental Health in the Metropolis: The Midtown Manhattan Study*. New York: McGraw-Hill.

Stein, Rob. 2004. "Obesity Passing Smoking as Top Avoidable Cause of Death." *The Washington Post*, March 10, pp. A1, A16.

Steinem, Gloria. 1982. "Erotica and Pornography: A Clear and Present Difference." In Laura Lederer (ed.), *Take Back the Night: Women on Pornography*. New York: Bantam Books, pp. 21–25.

Stoller, Robert J., and R. H. Geertsma. 1963. "The Consistency of Psychiatrists' Clinical Judgments." *Journal of Nervous and Mental Disease*, 137 (January): 58–66.

Strah, David, et al. 2003. *Gay Dads: A Celebration of Fatherhood*. New York: Jeremy Tarcher/Putnam.

Stunkard, Albert J. 1976. *The Pain of Obesity*. Palo Alto, CA: Bull Publishing.

Styles, Joseph. 1979. "Outsider/Insider: Researching Gay Baths." *Urban Life*, 8 (July): 135–152.

Substance Abuse and Mental Health Services Administration (SAMHSA), 2001. *Summary of Findings from the 2000 National Household Survey on Drug Abuse*. Rockville, MD: Department of Health and Human Services.

Substance Abuse and Mental Health Services Adminstration (SAMHSA). 2002. *Results from the 2001 National Household Survey on Drug Abuse*: Volume I, *Summary of National Findings*. Rockville, MD: Department of Health and Human Services.

Substance Abuse and Mental Health Services Administration (SAMHSA). 2003. *Results from the 2002 National Survey on Drug Use and Health: National Findings*. Rockville, MD: Department of Health and Human Services.

Suchar, Charles S. 1978. *Social Deviance: Perspectives and Prospects*. New York: Holt, Rinehart & Winston.

Summers, Anne. 1981. "Hidden from History: Women Victims of Crime." Satyanshu K. Mukherjee and Jocelynne A. Scutt (eds.), *Women and Crime*. North Sydney: George Allen & Unwin Australia, pp. 22–30.

Sumner, Colin. 1994. *The Sociology of Deviance: An Obituary*. London: Open University Press.

Sutherland, Edwin H. 1939. *Principles of Criminology* (3rd ed.). Philadelphia: Lippincott.

Sutherland, Edwin H. 1940. "The White Collar Criminal." *American Sociological Review*, 5 (February): 1–12.

Sutherland, Edwin H. 1949. *White Collar Crime*. New York: Dryden.

Sutherland, Edwin H., and Donald R. Cressey. 1978. *Criminology* (10th ed.). Philadelphia: Lippincott.

Swarns, Rachel L. 2003. "Daughter Spurs Shift in Gephardt's View on Gays." *The New York Times*, November 1, pp. A1, A11.

Tannenbaum, Frank. 1938. *Crime and the Community*. New York: Ginn.

Targ, Harold, and Russell E. Puthoff. 1974. "Information Transmission Under Conditions of Sensory Shielding." *Nature*, 251 (October 18): 602–607.

Tausig, Mark, Janet Michello, and Sree Subedi. 2004. *A Sociology of Mental Illness* (2nd ed.). Upper Saddle River, NJ: Prentice Hall.

Taylor, Ian, Paul Walton, and Jock Young. 1973. *The New Criminology: For a Social Theory of Deviance*. London: Routledge & Kegan Paul.

Tedeschi, James T., and Richard B. Felson. 1994. *Violence, Aggression, and Coercive Actions*. Washington, DC: American Psychological Association.

Terhune, K. W., C. W. Ippolito, and D. J. Crouch. 1992. *The Incidence and Role of Drugs in Fatally Injured Drivers*. Washington, DC: U.S. Department of Transportation, National Highway Traffic Safety Administration.

Thio, Alex. 1995. *Deviant Behavior* (4th ed.). New York: HarperCollins.

Thio, Alex. 2004. *Deviant Behavior* (7th ed.). Boston: Allyn & Bacon.

Thoits, Peggy. 1985. "Self-Labeling Processes in Mental Illnesses: The Role of Emotional Distance." *American Journal of Sociology*, 91 (September): 221–249.

Thomas, W. I., and Florian Znanieki. 1918–1920. *The Polish Peasant in Europe and America*. Chicago: University of Chicago Press.

Thomas, W. I, and Dorothy Swaine Thomas. 1928. *The Child in America: Behavior Problems and Programs*. New York: Alfred Knopf.

Thompson, Rosemarie Garland (ed.). 1996. *Freakery: Cultural Spectacles of the Extraordinary Body*. New York: New York University Press.

Thompson, Rosemarie Garland. 1997. *Extraordinary Bodies*. New York: Columbia University Press.

Tittle, Charles R. 1995. *Control Balance: Toward a General Theory of Deviance*. Boulder, CO: Westview Press.

Tittle, Charles R., and Robert F. Meier. 1990. "Specifying the SES/Delinquency Relationship." *Criminology*, 28 (May): 271–299.

Tittle, Charles R., Wayne J. Villmez, and Douglas A. Smith. 1978. "The Myth of Social Class and Criminality: An Empirical Assessment of the Empirical Evidence," *American Sociological Review*, 43 (August): 643–656.

Tobias, Sheila. 1997. *Faces of Feminism: An Activist's Reflections on the Women's Movement*. Boulder, CO: Westview Press.

Torke, Hans-Joachim. 1997. "From Muscovy towards St. Petersburg, 1598–1689." In Gregory L. Freeze (ed.), *Russia: A History*. New York: Oxford University Press, pp. 55–86.

Torregrossa, Luisita Lopez. 1996. "Up in Smoke." *The New York Times Magazine*, August 25, pp. 40–46.

Torrey, E. Fuller, with Anne E. Bowler, Edward H. Taylor, and Irving I. Gottesman. 1994. *Schizophrenia and Manic Depressive Disorder: The Biological Roots of Mental Illness as Revealed by the Landmark Study of Identical Twins*. New York: Basic Books.

Toufexis, Anastasia. 1991. "Innocent Victims." *Time*, May 13, pp. 56–60.

Townsend, John Marshall. 1978. *Cultural Conceptions of Mental Illness*. Chicago: University of Chicago Press.

Townsend, John Marshall. 1980. "Psychiatry versus Societal Reaction: A Critical Analysis." *Journal of Health and Social Behavior*, 21 (September): 268–278.

Traub, Stuart H., and Craig B. Little (eds.). 1999. *Theories of Deviance* (5th ed.). Itasca, IL: Peacock.

Troyer, Ronald J., and Gerald E. Markle. 1983. *Cigarettes*. New Brunswick, NJ: Rutgers University Press.

Truzzi, Marcello. 1980. "A Skeptical Look at Paul Kurz's Analysis of the Scientific Status of Parapsychology." *Journal of Parapsychology*, 44 (March): 35–55.

Truzzi, Marcello. 1982. "J. B. Rhine and Pseudoscience: Some Zetetic Reflections on Parapsychology." In K. Ramakrishna Rao (ed.), *J. B. Rhine: On the Frontiers of Science*. Jefferson, NC: McFarland, pp. 177–191.

Truzzi, Marcello. 1987. "Introduction." In Stanley Kripper (ed.), *Advances in Parapsychological Research*, 8: 221–271.

Turk, Austin T. 1980. "Analyzing Official Deviance: For Non-partisan Conflict Analyses in Criminology." In James A. Inciardi (ed.), *Radical Criminology: The Coming Crisis*. Thousand Oaks, CA: Sage, pp. 249–264.

Turner, Ronny E., and Charles Edgley. 1983. "From Witchcraft to Drugcraft: Biochemistry as Mythology." *Social Science Journal*, 20 (October): 1–12.

Turner, R. Jay, and John W. Gartrell. 1978. "Social Factors in Psychiatric Outcome: Toward a Resolution of Interpretive Controversies." *American Sociological Review*, 43 (June): 368–382.

Unnever, James D. 1987. Review of James M. Byrne and Robert J. Sampson (eds.), *The Social Ecology of Crime*. New York: Springer-Verlag, 1986, in *Contemporary Sociology*, 16 (November): 845–846.

Usborne, David. 2003. "Gay with Children." *New York*, November 3, pp. 28–33, 44.

Valentine, Charles A. 1968. *Culture and Poverty: Critique and Counter-Proposals*. Chicago: University of Chicago Press.

Victor, Jeffrey S. 1993. *Satanic Panic: The Creation of a Contemporary Legend*. Chicago: Open Court.

Viscusi, W. Kip, 2002. *Smoke-Filled Rooms: A Postmortem on the Tobacco Deal*. Chicago: University of Chicago Press.

Vold, George B., Thomas J. Bernard, and Jeffrey B. Snipes. 2002. *Theoretical Criminology* (5th ed.). New York: Oxford University Press.

von Drehle, David. 2003. "Gay Marriage Is a Right, Massachusetts Court Rules." *The Washington Post*, November 19, pp. A1, A8.

von Hentig, Hans. 1948. *The Criminal and His Victim*. New Haven, CT: Yale University Press.

von Hoffman, Nicholas. 1975. "The Sociological Snoopers." In Laud Humphreys, *Tearoom Trade* (2nd ed.). New York: Aldine, pp. 177–181.

Vowell, Paul R., and David C. May. 2000. "Another Look at Classic Strain Theory: Poverty Status, Perceived Blocked Opportunity, and Gang Membership as Predictors of Adolescent Violent Behavior." *Sociological Inquiry*, 70 (Winter): 42–60.

Walker, Alice, and Pratibha Parmar. 1993. *Warrior Marks: Female Genital Mutilation and the Sexual Blinding of Women*. New York: Harcourt Brace.

Warheit, George J., Charles E. Holzer, III, Roger A. Bell, and Sandra A. Avery. 1976. "Sex, Marital Status, and Mental Health: A Reappraisal." *Social Forces*, 55 (December): 459–470.

Waring, Elin, David Weisburd, and Ellen Chayet. 1995. "White-Collar Crime and Anomie." In Freda Adler and William S. Laufer (eds.), *The Legacy of Anomie Theory*. New Brunswick, NJ: Transaction Publishers, pp. 207–225.

Warren, Carol A. B., and John M. Johnson. 1972. "A Critique of Labeling Theory from the Phenomenological Perspective." In Robert A. Scott and Jack D. Douglas (eds.), *Theoretical Perspectives on Deviance*. New York: Basic Books, pp. 69–92.

Warwick, Donald P. 1973. "Tearoom Trade: Means and Ends in Social Research." *The Hastings Center Studies*, 1 (1): 27–38.

Weaver, Richard, and James MacAndrew. 1995. *The Roswell Report: Fact vs. Fiction in the New Mexico Desert*. Washington, DC: HQ United States Air Force.

Weber, Max. 1946. *From Max Weber: Essays in Sociology* (trans. & ed. Hans H. Gerth and C. Wright Mills). New York: Oxford University Press.

Weber, Max. 1963. *The Sociology of Religion* (trans. Ephraim Fischoff). Boston: Beacon Press (originally published in 1922).

Webster, Richard. 1995. *Why Freud Was Wrong: Sin, Science, and Psychoanalysis*. New York: Basic Books.

Weil, Andrew. 1972. *The Natural Mind: A New Way of Looking at Drugs and the Higher Consciousness*. Boston: Houghton Mifflin.

Weinberg, Martin S., Colin J. Williams, and Bo Laurent. 1999. "Medicalizing and Demedicalizing Hermaphroditism." In Earl Rubington and Martin S. Weinberg (eds.), *Deviance: The Interactionist Perspective*. Boston: Allyn & Bacon, pp. 433–448.

Weintraub, Bernard, and Jim Rutenberg. 2003. "Gay-Themed TV Gains a Wider Audience." *The New York Times*, July 29, pp. A1, C5.

Weisburd, David, and Elin Waring, with Ellen F. Chayet. 2001. *White-Collar Crime and Criminal Careers*. Cambridge, UK: Cambridge University Press.

Weisburd, David, Stanton Wheeler, Elin Waring, and Nancy Bode. 1991. *Crimes of the Middle Classes: White-Collar Offenders in the Federal Courts*. New Haven, CT: Yale University Press.

Weitzer, Ronald (ed.). 2000. *Sex for Sale: Prostitution, Pornography, and the Sex Industry*. New York & London: Routledge.

Wellings, Kaye, Julia Field, Anne Johnson, and Jane Wadsworth. 1994. *Sexual Behavior in Britain: The National Survey of Sexual Attitudes and Lifestyles*. New York: Penguin.

Wheeler, Stanton. 1960. "Sex Offenses: A Sociological Critique." *Law and Contemporary Society*, 25 (Spring): 258–278.

Whitam, Frederick L. 1977. "The Homosexual Role: A Reconsideration." *The Journal of Sex Research*, 13 (February): 1–13.

Whitam, Frederick L., and Ronin M. Mathy. 1986. *Male Homosexuality in Four Societies: Brazil, Guatemala, the Philippines and the United States*. New York: Praeger.

Wilkinson, Gregg S. 1975. "Patient-Audience Social Status and the Social Construction of Psychiatric Disorder: Toward a Differential Frame of Referential Hypothesis." *Journal of Health and Social Behavior*, 16 (March): 28–38.

Williams, A. F., M. A. Peat, and D. S. Crouch. 1985. "Drugs in Fatally Injured Young Male Drivers." *PharmChem Newsletter*, 14 (1): 1–11.

Williams, Joyce E., and Willard A. Nielson, Jr. 1979. "The Rapist Looks at His Crime." *Free Inquiry into Creative Sociology*, 7 (November): 128–132.

Williams, Linda. 1989. *Hard Core: Power, Pleasure, and the "Frenzy of the Visible."* Berkeley, CA: University of California Press.

Williams, Linda. 1993. "A Provoking Agent: The Pornography and Performance Art of Annie Sprinke." In Pamela Church Gibson and Roma Gibson (eds.), *Dirty Looks: Women, Pornography, Power*. London: British Film Institute Publishing.

Williams, Terry. 1996. "Exploring the Cocaine Culture." In Carolyn D. Smith and William Kornblum (eds.), *In the Field: Readings in the Field Research Experience* (2nd ed.). Westport, CT: Praeger, pp. 27–32.

Williams, Terry, Eloise Dunlap, Bruce D. Johnson, and Ansley Hamid. 1992. "Personal Safety in Dangerous Places." *Journal of Contemporary Ethnography*, 21 (October): 343–374.

Wills, Garry. 2002. "Scandal." *The New York Review of Books*, May 23, pp. 6–9.

Wilson, William Julius. 1996. *When Work Disappears: The World of the New Urban Poor*. New York: Random House.

Winick, Charles. 1964. "Physician Narcotic Addicts." In Howard S. Becker (ed.), *The Other Side: Perspectives on Deviance*. New York: Free Press, pp. 261–279.

Wish, Eric D. 1995. "The Drug Use Forecasting (DUF) Program." In Jerome H. Jaffe (ed.). *Encyclopedia of Drugs and Alcohol*. New York: Simon & Schuster/Macmillan, pp. 432–434.

Wolfe, Linda. 1976. *Playing Around: Women and Extra-Marital Sex*. New York: New American Library/Signet.

Workman, Thomas. 2001. "Pleasure versus Public Health: Controlling Collegiate Binge Drinking." In Alex Thio and Thomas Calhoun (eds.), *Readings in Deviant Behavior* (2nd ed.). Boston: Allyn & Bacon, pp. 137–144.

Wright, James D., Peter H. Rossi, and Kathleen Daly. 1983. *Under the Gun: Weapons, Crime, and Violence in America*. New York: Aldine de Gruyter.

Wright, John Paul, et al. 2001. " 'The Root of All Evil'? An Exploratory Study of Money and Delinquent Involvement." *Justice Quarterly*, 18 (June): 239–268.

Yacoubian, George S., Jr. 2000. "Assessing ADAM's Domain: Past Problems and Future Prospects." *Contemporary Drug Problems*, 2 (Spring): 121–135.

Yarrow, Marian Radke, et al. 1955. "The Psychological Meaning of Mental Illness in the Family." *Journal of Social Issues*, 11 (December): 12–24.

Young, Jock. 2003. "Merton with Energy, Katz with Structure: The Sociology of Vindictiveness and the Criminology of Transgression." *Theoretical Criminology*, 7 (August): 389–414.

Zador, Paul L. 1991. "Alcohol-Related Risk of Fatal Driver Injuries in Relation to Age and Sex. *Journal of Studies on Alcohol*, 52 (4): 302–310.

Ziegler, Charles A. 1997. "Mythogenesis: Historical Development of the Roswell Narratives." In Benson Saler, Charles A. Zieger, and Charles B. Moore, *UFO Crash at Roswell: The Genesis of a Modern Myth.* Washington, DC: Smithsonian Institution Press, pp. 1–29.

Zola, Irving Kenneth. 1964. "Observations on Gambling in a Lower Class Culture." In Howard S. Becker (ed.), *The Other Side: Perspectives on Deviance*. New York: Free Press, pp. 247–260.

Zuger, Abigail. 2002. "The Case for Drinking (All Together Now: In Moderation!)." *The New York Times*, December 31, p. D1, D6.

Photo Credits

Name Index

Subject Index